PUBLIC BUDGETING
IN AMERICA

Fifth Edition

PUBLIC BUDGETING
IN AMERICA

Robert W. Smith, Ph.D.
Clemson University

Thomas D. Lynch, Ph.D.
Louisiana State University

PEARSON
Prentice
Hall

Upper Saddle River, New Jersey 07458

Library of Congress Cataloging-in-Publication Data

Smith, Robert W.
   Public budgeting in America / Robert W. Smith and Thomas D. Lynch.—5th ed.
     p. cm.
   Lynch's name appears first on the earlier ed.
   Includes bibliographical references and index.
   ISBN 0-13-097993-7
    1. Budget—United States. I. Lynch, Thomas Dexter II. Title.

HJ2051.L93 2004
352.4'8'0973—dc22

                                          2003055448

Editorial Director: Charlyce Jones-Owen
Editorial Assistant: Maureen Diana
Production Liaison: Joanne Hakim
Executive Marketing Manager: Heather Shelstad
Senior Marketing Assistant: Jennifer Bryant
Manufacturing Buyer: Sherry Lewis
Cover Art Director: Jayne Conte
Cover Design: Karen Salzbach
Composition/Full-Service Project Management: Melissa Scott/Carlisle Communications
Printer/Binder: Courier Westford

Credits and acknowledgments borrowed from other sources and reproduced, with permission, in this
textbook appear on appropriate page within text.

Pearson Education LTD., London
Pearson Education Singapore, Pte. Ltd
Pearson Education, Canada, Ltd
Pearson Education—Japan
Pearson Education Australia PTY, Limited

Pearson Education North Asia Ltd
Pearson Educación de Mexico, S.A. de C.V.
Pearson Education Malaysia, Pte. Ltd
Pearson Education, Upper Saddle River, New Jersey

10 9 8 7 6 5 4 3 2 1
ISBN 0-13-097993-7

CONTENTS

6   ANALYTICAL PROCESSES   192

PREFACE

This fifth edition makes improvements to previous editions by drawing upon the strength of a collaborative effort. Specifically, this edition adds a co-author—Robert Smith, who comes to this task with considerable state government budget experience. We believe this edition continues and enhances the blend of practical application, theory, and empirical rigor necessary for understanding public budgeting in the United States. Our collaboration in this edition focuses on balancing the strength of a winning approach with timely additions and updated tables, charts, and graphs. This revised material complements the successful approach of the earlier editions, which explained budgetary practice and process as they developed in the twentieth century. It was our task in this fifth edition to develop an explanation of public budgeting in a twenty-first century context.

Indeed, public budgeting is an evolving endeavor, and the past twenty years have witnessed legislation and practices that have tried to cope with budget crises at the federal, state, and local levels. Unfortunately, many of these efforts have not adequately addressed the complex structural, governance, and process issues fundamental to public budgeting. Our approach was to address recent budget developments and related phenomena with a focus on the problem itself. We are optimistic that the level of academic inquiry and professional expertise in the field of public budgeting is up to the task. However, the real challenge is to bring these energies to bear on the fundamentals of the budgetary process for meaningful long-term reform.

To this end, this text blends the experiences of a former state budget practitioner and the insights of an accomplished budget scholar. Of particular note is the chapter on the use of analysis in the budget process. The result is a text that is reorganized, relevant, and timely for students and teachers of public budgeting. At the same time, it is difficult to separate budgeting from issues of financial management, and so we address both subjects in a manner that stresses the interrelationships between the two. Finally, because there are few texts that focus on the details of budget practice and process, we believe that this book is an essential read for students and practitioners interested in a full understanding of budgeting in America.

We acknowledge our appreciation to everyone who has contributed to this revised edition. We wish to especially thank the Prentice Hall editorial staff including Heather Shelstad, John Ragozzine, and Suzanne Remore. Also, a special thanks goes to Jessica Drew, Jennifer Bryant, and the anonymous reviewers from Prentice Hall who worked on this project. The authors would also like to thank Melissa Scott of Carlisle Publishers Services for her patience, fine editing, and other suggestions to improve this fifth edition. We also gratefully acknowledge the technical and support services provided by Rob Carey, a Ph.D. student and researcher in the Policy

Studies program, and Stacey Davenport and Courtenay Ryals of the Department of Political Science at Clemson University.

Finally, this text would not be possible without the unwavering support and commitment of our wives and families. A loving thanks goes to Kathleen C. Gallagher-Smith and Keegan and Nolan Smith. Another loving thanks goes to Cynthia E. Lynch for her tolerance and patience as this edition was prepared.

Robert W. Smith, Ph.D.
Thomas D. Lynch, Ph.D.

1

BUDGET FORMATS

AND PREPARATION

This chapter addresses the topics of budget formats, building the budget, budget reviews, and legislative adoption. It covers the following:

- why budget formats are significant;
- the various budget formats and how they apply to general policy, budget balancing, and the improvement of government management; the role and work of the central budget office in initiating the process of building the budget;
- the central role and tasks of the agency in preparing the budget;
- the importance of the steps associated with executive and legislative reviews of the budget;
- the use of executive budget hearings in the review process;
- the ingredients and preparation of the executive budget document; the congressional budget timetable;
- the legislature's deliberative process on the budget; and
- the formats used in legislative adoptions of budgets.

BUDGET FORMAT

The Important Means

In 1997, Pettijohn and Grizzle demonstrated that budget format and process do influence the outcome of the process. Budget formats define the readers' reality and channel the readers' attention and thought processes. In 1982, Edward Lehan said, "People tend to think in terms of what is put in front of them. This axiom of human behavior plays a heavy role in the budgetary process." For example, line-item budgeting (see Exhibit 1–1) tends to take decision makers' attention away from policy issues and forces them to consider expenditure items. At the local level of government in the United States, about 51 percent of the cities use a line-item budget format. Thus, most people think about the correctness of the size of the various expenditure items rather than the larger issues of the correctness of the programs and policies associated with those items. For exercising control, line-item budgeting is very useful—especially for controlling employees tightly in an agency. The line-item format stresses accountability in terms of what organizations spend their money on, but it does not address the larger question of what the government should accomplish with its money. By

EXHIBIT 1–1   Line-Item Budget Format: Code Enforcement

	PAST YEAR	CURRENT YEAR	BUDGET YEAR	BY-CY
Personal Services	$49,000	$52,000	$60,000	$8,000
Contractual Services	6,000	5,900	6,590	690
Supplies	576	1,200	1,606	406
Total	55,576	59,100	68,196	9,096

Source: Thomas D. Lynch and Cynthia E. Lynch. "The Road to Entrepreneurial Budgeting." *Journal of Public Budgeting, Accounting, and Financial Management,* 9, 1 (Spring 1997), 161–180.

assuring the government agency spends money on only acceptable expenditures, line-item budgeting achieves a type of accountability, but it shows little faith in the manager's ability to direct and ultimately to achieve program objectives. By adding the auditing process to line-item budgeting, government management focuses on expenditures, thus creating a type of accountability that confronts corruption, helps discourage public employees deviating from strict instructions, and enhances tighter control over the employees' behavior. For these reasons, most governments utilize some form of line-item budgeting at some level within their organization.

INFORMATION TO NOTE

The analysts can make each line item represent a large category or a very detailed one such as a particular person's salary and fringe benefits. Thus, the list of line items can be very short or very long, but usually the list is very long. This type of budgeting is almost always used during the current year and often used in making budget year decisions. The analysts intend the columns to represent the years that are important for the decision makers to know. Usually, the analysts show the format for each organizational unit or subunit. Thus, there are at least as many tables as there are units in the whole organization. In this case, the subunit is code enforcement in a housing department. Notice that the analyst can add the numbers from other subunits to give a total for the unit and then the analyst can add the units together to give total line-item expenditures for larger groups such as a department or the government as a whole.

Notice the format is essentially a spreadsheet that an analyst can link to other spreadsheets, thus easily aggregating the information to higher levels in a pyramid organization. The years shown can vary, but those in Exhibit 1–1 are a common listing. Other columns can include agency budget year (BY) recommendation, city manager recommendation, BY + 1, BY + 2, and so on. For budget year decisions, the BY-current year (BY-CY) column becomes important for the dominant incremental approach to budgeting, and the justifications following the table in a normal budget format would explain the increases and sometimes the decreases. Usually, the budget justifications are very short, such as one or two sentences.

In the twentieth century, policy makers considered rational decision making good management, and policy making and the line-item approach frustrated them. Planning-programming budgeting, zero-base budgeting, and target-base budgeting (TBB) are variations of rational budget making that use variations of performance budgeting. Chapter 3 explains each of them. The line-item budget was good in terms of accountability but did not help make better rational decisions. Exhibit 1–2 illustrates program budgeting where the format focuses decision makers on planning and rational analysis. At the local level, about 10 percent of the jurisdictions use program budgeting. At the state level, forty-seven states use some form of program budgeting. With that focus, executive management, with its strong top-down direction and stress on efficiency and economy in administration, apparently becomes possible. With program budgeting, the budget became a tool to achieve effective operational direction and direct optimal efficiency. Incrementalists can easily accommodate to program budgeting because they can use the same columns as used in line-item budgeting, but with this approach their mental focus shifts from line-item or object expenditures to major unit activities. This approach is more properly associated with rational budgeting because the use of programs is almost absolutely necessary to achieve rational analysis.

Analysts can identify many programs in a given unit, but they are wiser to identify only a few that reflect the activities of the unit. The analyst is usually wiser to fold staff and support activities of the unit into the unit's major activity programs. Budget analysts use this budgeting approach primarily in the budget year for larger policy decisions. In larger organizations, this approach is useful also in the current year because of the need to delegate responsibility significantly. The analyst should always crosswalk (explained in Chapter 5) this format with the line-item budget format for at least current year purposes because the accounting department must use line-item categories as the state law requires it. This crosswalk, which is a simple matrix table for a given year with the rows representing line items and the columns representing programs, permits the analyst to see the interrelationship of the two budget formats. Analysts use this format for units and subunits, but the programs selected need to reflect the larger whole government program structure decided by the central budget office or legislature. One is wise to avoid using a program (for example, Plan Examination) across unit and subunit lines so that higher policy makers can always fix responsibility for performance or lack of performance on a specific unit and its managers. Notice again that the analysts can vary the columns depending on policy maker decision-making needs and that interlocking spreadsheets

EXHIBIT 1–2   Program Budget Format: Code Enforcement

	PAST YEAR	CURRENT YEAR	BUDGET YEAR	BY-CY
Plan Examination	$10,000	$11,333	$12,331	$998
Inspection	34,576	34,888	40,339	5,451
Education	11,000	12,879	15,526	2,647
Total	55,576	59,100	68,196	9,096

are very useful, especially to sum up the subunit data to higher levels in the government. Again, the policy makers can use the BY-CY column to more easily make their incremental decisions. In such an approach, analysts write the budget justifications in the budget itself near the table and addresses in the justification the BY-CY amount for each program. If the policy makers prefer a rational approach to decision making, then the analyst does not use this column and she or he can write the justifications de nova in an approach called zero-base budgeting by only addressing the BY column. If the analyst uses rational analysis, then she or he can use benefit cost ratios, marginal rates of return, or some other reasoning to justify the amount selected in the BY column for each program. However, the latter rational justifications are possible only if budget analysts add some type of performance information addressed to program outcomes or outputs to the justification material.

Program budgeting and performance budgeting (see Exhibit 1–3) assume the modernist approach of philosophers like Jeremy Bentham (see Chapters 2 and 3) that rationality is not only possible in human decision making but also desirable. This approach allows decision makers to focus their policy debates among themselves on their policy differences and choices among alternative selections of programs and program levels of spending. Program budgeting is therefore a useful tool for strategic planning as it focuses the human mind on policy issues, and professional program analysts can bring added value to the policy makers by helping them make more informed policy decisions. Built on the program budgeting tradition of desiring greater rationality in public policy making, the performance budgeting takes the programs in program budgeting and adds the use of specific performance measures reflecting program outputs, program outcomes, or both. Chapter 5 defines the former as the products and services produced by the programs and the latter as the impacts of those products or those outputs on individuals or the larger society served by the programs. Today, professionals call the latter type performance budgeting and sometimes outcome budgeting. With performance budgeting, analysts and decision makers focus on questions of efficiency and effectiveness with the use of outputs focusing on efficiency and outcomes focusing on effectiveness. The arguments about the impossibility of using rationality in budgeting particularly apply to the various forms of performance budgeting.

Which budget format (line-item, program, or performance) is the best? Given that the format does influence the decision-making focus, then the selection depends on the analyst's desired decision-making environment. What mind-set does the analyst wish to create? The three major concerns of a budget officer are (1) to raise the level of debate among policy makers and to observe the reactions of various stakeholders in the budget process for future cues, (2) to ensure that the budget office maintains policy control for the policy makers, and (3) to improve the quality of management in the government. Given these objectives, the choice of format can still vary substantially, depending on what the analyst wishes to stress in a given political and managerial context. However, the budget analyst may not be in a position to determine the format because it is often set by statute or by senior budget officials in the government.

The example in Exhibit 1–3 shows the CY and BY, but an analyst can add other super columns. For example, she could show a CY-BY column, prior year (PY) column, and so on. In this exhibit, the critical added information is performance data that reflect the outputs of the program. For example, the output of the education program

EXHIBIT 1–3   Performance Budget Format: Code Enforcement

	Current Year			Budget Year		
	OUTPUT	INPUT	OUTPUT (Unit Costs)	INPUT	OUTPUT	OUTPUT (Unit Costs)
Plan Exams	$658	$11,333	$17.22	$744	$12,331	$16.57
Inspections	$18,765	$34,888	$1.86	$19,370	$40,339	$2.08
Education (graduates)	$11,300	$12,879	$1.14	$12,335	$15,526	$1.26
Total	$59,100			$68,196		

Note the categories are the same as in the program format.

Source: Thomas D. Lynch and Cynthia E. Lynch. "The Road to Entrepreneurial Budgeting." *Journal of Public Budgeting, Accounting, and Financial Management,* 9, 1 (Spring 1997), 161–180.

is the number of graduates. Ideally, the performance indicator selected will have a quantitative and qualitative aspect. For example, in this case, the analyst assumes the graduates matriculate with a certain level of expertise.

An analyst could also add to the table outcome performance data to reflect the impact of the program upon the society or individuals in society. An example of benefit to society would be the number of jobs currently being filled by master's level graduates instead of lower educational level graduates. An example of benefits to individuals would be the increased income of persons after attaining their graduate education. Analysts find such information difficult to obtain and debatable in terms of correctness. Nonetheless, analysts must appreciate that program outcomes are very powerful analytical information for policy makers. Program output performance measures are usually easier to define and obtain.

A common mistake in selecting performance measures is to use not output or even outcome data but instead process data. Such data tell managers the daily functions that employees accomplish such as the number of clients seen, calls answered, and forms processed. If policy makers and analysts confuse process, output, and outcome data, then they can misuse the information and arrive at inappropriate management and policy decisions. As with program budgeting, analysts should crosswalk this format with the line-item format. With the new Government Accounting Standards Board policy on the use of performance measures, crosswalks become essential.

Fortunately, the budget officer need not select only one budget format because he or she also works with an operating budget, a capital budget, and various other documents in the budget process. For example, the submitted budget from the chief executive could be an outcome budget; the current year operating budget given to agencies could be a line-item budget; and the capital budget for the budget year could be a zero-based budget. In addition, the budget officer could present supporting materials based on a rational analysis such as cost-benefit analysis. Thus, some flexibility exists in the means to accomplish the objectives. This chapter addresses only the format of the chief executive's budget in order to simplify the explanation of budget formats.

In an excellent book entitled *Effective Budgetary Presentations: The Cutting Edge,* compiled by Girard Miller, the Government Finance Officers Association presents examples of the common components of local government budgets. These components are the budget cover, table of contents, organization charts, transmittal letter, financial summaries, goals and objectives, revenues, departmental and activity budgets, program budget summaries, performance measurements, enterprise and internal service funds, capital outlay, special analyses, accompanying documents, readers' guides, budgetary procedures, budget preparation instructions, and legislative adoption. Students should review this unique collection of samples to understand some of the format possibilities available to a budget office.

In summary, each format developed in the twentieth century channels thought differently. Line-item budgeting tends to take decision makers away from policy issues and to focus attention on expenditure savings. Program budgeting tends to focus attention on policy differences and on choices among policy options. Performance budgeting places the focus on questions of efficiency, effectiveness, or both. Analysts can use all three formats in incremental budgeting, but rational budgeting needs either the program or performance formats.

Two surveys (one in 1986 and the other in 1996) examine local government budget practitioners drawn from the active membership roster of the Government Finance Officers Association (GFOA). They asked what type of budget format each jurisdiction uses, used five years ago, and expected to use five years from the survey. The formats cited were line item, performance, program, zero-base/target-base, and hybrid. In 1986 and 1996, the line-item format predominated with 83 and 86 percent, respectively, either using it exclusively (58 and 51 percent) or in a hybrid arrangement (25 and 35 percent). Both surveys showed a trend away from the exclusive reliance on the line-item format toward a hybrid format. In the late 1990s, agency managers, legislators, stakeholders, and citizens use the products of performance-based systems. At the state level, Texas, Oregon, Virginia, and Florida led the way. Phoenix, Arizona, and Charlotte, North Carolina, were early pioneers at the local level of government.

Cheryle A. Broome identified the following lessons and factors after examining performance-based budgeting in those key reform states:

- Government must see performance budgeting as a solution to their decision-making needs and craft the system to address those needs.
- Reformers need to spend time visualizing how they will use the performance-based budgeting system.
- Reformers must recognize that they must approach a performance-based system with a desire to learn about their organizations.
- Reformers need to realize the performance-based budget can only add value to public policy decision making but it cannot transform the essential political and human nature of budget decision making.
- Performance-based budgeting only works when key political leaders and stakeholders use the performance information to make their decisions.
- The process of developing measures is difficult but reformers can make clear progress.
- Implementing the performance-based budget reform requires time and deliberate progress building on succeeding successes.
- There is no "off-the-shelf" plan that reformers can import, as each reformer must tailor the performance-based system to their government.

Distinguished Budgets

In 1994, the Government Finance Officers Association (GFOA) established an annual award program for Distinguished Budget Presentations. The procedures followed in the awards program are similar to those in the GFOA Certificate of Conformance in Financial Reporting program. Interested local governments send their last annual budget, supporting material, and an entry fee to the GFOA. At least three GFOA member reviewers examine each, using evaluation criteria that stress the budget as a policy document, an operations guide, a financial plan, and a communication device. GFOA recognizes the budget as a policy-setting instrument and wishes to make sure that officials explicitly make policy. The criteria call for general government and specific unit statements of policy, which can be in the form of goals and objectives, mission statements, or strategies. The budget document must explain any change in policy since the last annual budget document. Thus, the GFOA awards programs adopt an incremental approach to budgeting. Ideally, the budget documents should explain the rationale for the policy as well as the policy implementation and monitoring process. In addition, the criteria demand that the budget document or supporting material explains the budget development process, including its amendment process.

GFOA realizes that the budget is also an important operational guide during the current year to all the units in government. Thus, clarity of purpose in terms useful to bureaucratic units is imperative. The budget document must tie budget programs and line items to specific government organizational units. The criteria call for stating the workforce of each unit in terms of the organization chart and for presenting the information for both the current and budget years. The budget document should explain the criteria used in capital spending decisions, including the effects on daily operations and operating expenditures. In addition, the budget document should include specific objectives, performance targets, and important deadlines for department heads. The budget must provide a means to measure and permit accountability for performance or lack of performance in government.

GFOA recognizes that the budget document must define the technical relationship of financial structure to the operations of government. Thus, the document must explain the following technical topics in a manner understandable to the lay reader: the major revenue sources; the bases for forecasting, including predictions of events or factors that will influence forecasts; the organization of funds used by the government; the end-of-the-year projections of financial conditions; a capital financing element (a separate capital budget is possible for larger governments); a consolidated picture of operations and financial activity; the debt management issues; and the accountability basis used by the government.

To GFOA, communication to the public is extremely important. The image of government is often not positive, in part because the public does not understand what government does for it. Given that the budget is usually the single best comprehensive presentation of a government plan to use its tax resources, the budget officer must communicate those policies in a manner in which the general public can understand government's programs, policies, and financial needs. To accomplish the goal of better communication, the GFOA criteria call for the following: a draft version of the budget prior to government adoption; clear summary information on the budget, covering topics of interest so that the media and the public can understand key points such as the size of programs, the revenue sources, and the policy changes of concern to the public; and communication devices that aid in understanding large complex sets of information. These devices include a budget message, a table of contents, a glossary of terms, an identification of the basic units in the budget, charts and graphs with narrative explanations, key assumptions used in preparing the budget, a cross-index, and supplemental information, including statistical tables.

The evaluation criteria define "a good budget document" and largely imply what is a good budget process. The criteria do not call for a particular approach to budgeting such as ZBB (explained in Chapter 3), but they do require data presentations that allow incremental decision making and also encourage the use of program categories and performance measures. Thus, the criteria do reflect some definite normative guidance on what GFOA considers important in a budget document.

GFOA and local governments take the award program for Distinguished Budget Presentations quite seriously, but as time goes on local governments are more easily meeting once demanding standards. Of the first eighty-one governments submitting their budgets for review, fifty-one (63 percent) received the award. Given that GFOA does not require governments to participate and few truly unprofessional governments would participate, this early rate of failure was significant. The first city to receive an "especially notable" award was Dayton, Ohio, and Dayton remains among the best budget offices in the world. Since Dayton got the award, many more cities have joined the ranks of the best. The governments that received a budget award from GFOA are justifiably proud of their professional achievement. Not only does the budget award program define "good budgeting," it also serves as an important stimulant for improving the quality of local government budgeting in general.

Robert C. Rickards examined Texas cities and counties using the GFOA budget criteria. He used two reviewers who looked at sixty-nine cities and eighty-six counties in Texas. They applied the GFOA criteria, concluding that Texas cities on average had "acceptable" budget documents but Texas counties had "very weak" presentations. This is a common pattern, as cities tend to have better management practices than do counties or special districts. Improvements in budgeting are not likely to come from longer budget presentations but from more professional efforts. Providing a glossary of terms, specifying the presentation's accounting basis, explaining the budget process and amendment procedure, discussing capital spending impacts and debt management issues, and providing draft budgets to the public are some of the common budget improvements that cities can easily accomplish. The biggest common shortcoming was the readability of the budget presentations—with many of them resembling accounting tables unintelligible to anyone except the persons preparing them. Beyond such common sense recommendations, the author noted that governments could improve budget presentations by emulating good budget presentations of other governments and by following the professional recommendations that exist in the literature.

Ends Defining Means

From a format design perspective, the desired ends should influence what format or formats an analyst uses. A tendency of budget presenters is to apply a standard approach for similar budget situations, and this is desirable because it permits comparisons. Nevertheless, various programs do deserve individual presentations in order to highlight the most useful information for decision-making purposes. Format designers should decide first on the general format and then on extra information useful for specific programs.

Analysts should weigh three common concerns when deciding on a format:

- How can the budget help decision makers deal with general policy matters?
- How should the budget be balanced?
- How can decisions of policy makers be used to improve the quality of government management?

Four common difficult situations associated with helping elected decision makers formulate policy are as follows:

- Situation one: trying to get elected officials to focus on the major policy issues rather than on insignificant and time-consuming issues that make relatively little difference to the future of the community
- Situation two: fostering a decision-making environment in which budget analysts reduce counterproductive political tensions so that policy makers can make important and timely policy
- Situation three: sensitizing decision makers to the future-year implications of their decisions
- Situation four: achieving awareness that budget decisions do relate to specific government actions that affect individuals and society

Analysts handle the first situation with program budgeting and formalized budget approaches like PPB and ZBB (explained in Chapter 3). The latter is especially useful as a means to inform novice political executives of the policy implications of budget decisions. In addition, the narrative accompanying the budget document, usually in the form of a formal budget message by the executive, also highlights policies that decision makers should focus on. Aaron Wildavsky argued line-item budgeting—which permits more face-saving because it focuses attention on relatively unemotional subjects such as salaries, travel, and supplies—best handles the second situation. Requiring revenue and expenditure forecasts possibly five or more years beyond the BY or requiring a financial program schedule addresses the third situation. Using outcome budgeting handles the fourth situation. Dealing with the challenge of balanced budgets commonly requires the following: getting both policy makers and government agencies to accept the existence resource constraints, helping policy makers justify to the public the need for more government resources (for example, higher property taxes), and shifting political pressure from the more controversial revenue sources to the more acceptable revenue sources.

The TBB approach (explained in Chapter 3) best suits the first situation, which assumes a given revenue level and works from that assumption. Ideally, with TBB, agencies will not consider budget decisions beyond the arbitrarily established limit. The limitation of such an approach is that policy makers arbitrarily establish amounts of money that do not eliminate government problems.

The second situation occurs when policy makers decide that government needs more taxes, but the public is not yet supportive of that policy position. Budget officers can prepare budgets to stress the need, to show how government action can resolve that need, and to demonstrate the necessity for more money if government is to resolve that need. Program budgeting is particularly useful if the format combines with appropriate measures of program services and social needs. The third situation is more complex. Governments receive their revenues from various sources, of which some are more politically sensitive at various times than others. One way to help deal with that political reality is to minimize pressure on the politically sensitive revenue sources by shifting as much cost as possible to less sensitive revenue sources. For example, if property tax is a hot political issue, then budgets can increase user fee revenues as much as possible to cover expenses. The budget format can show, for each expense item, the source of revenue. This would permit the probing inquiries, which would seek to shift the burden to the least politically sensitive revenue source.

Striving to improve government management usually includes the following:

- Stressing efficiency and productivity measures in government management
- Establishing top level control procedures in order to ensure that employees carry out policy and the organization minimizes any fraud
- Establishing proper review practices to minimize overhead costs
- Stopping unnecessary end-of-the-year purchases
- Improving management through better use of new technology and development of professionals and other employees

Performance budgeting or, more commonly, separate ad hoc productivity studies, internal audits, and the hiring of program evaluators address the first concern. Edward A. Lehan advocates a budget format (see Chapter 5) that includes marginal analysis and allows decision makers to consider the optimum funding level, which will result in the greatest productivity. Using a line-item format, which assigns dollars to specific units, can address the second concern. Another strategy a budget analyst can often employ is to increase the audit and inspector general staffs. Greater organizational sophistication addresses the third concern. Formats, which include overhead comparative and longitudinal cost data, focus attention on that concern and are helpful. Good accounting practices address the fourth concern. An analyst can include in the budget and accounting data illustrations of the problem or present the data in a special analysis accompanying the budget document. A narrative, which discusses plans for the use of new technology and how the organization will develop staff, addresses the fifth concern. To upgrade technology, which should result in productivity improvements, the budget can single out new funds as a first-priority concern. Budget officers can include professional development (for example, training) as one of the fringe benefits of employment and thus make training less vulnerable to normal line-item budget cuts.

EXHIBIT 1–4 A New Process Matrix: Brokering, Monitoring, Steering

Progressive/Liberal versus Information Era Purposes of Budgeting		
PURPOSE OF BUDGETING	**PROGRESSIVE/LIBERAL ERA**	**INFORMATION ERA**
Source of Direction	Planning	Strategic Brokering
Method of Direction	Management	Steering
Purpose of Direction	Control	Monitoring

Source: Thomas D. Lynch and Cynthia E. Lynch. "The Road to Entrepreneurial Budgeting." *Journal of Public Budgeting, Accounting, and Financial Management*, 9, 1 (Spring 1997), 161–180.

In summary, one can choose among budget formats in order to better highlight particular concerns. Such highlighting will not necessarily guarantee specific decisions, but it will channel the thought of policy makers.

In the information era, entrepreneurial budgeting is only beginning to appear, but this chapter makes some observations to explain this innovation. As the twenty-first century begins, Exhibit 1–4 points out the information age has shifted the very purpose of budgeting as organizations move away from a command and control to a more decentralized approach to policy making and management. In the information era, budgeting takes its direction not from planning but from strategic brokering. It is a process of continuously scanning the entire environment for options and possibilities that better fit the organization's objectives. This holistic approach means that decision makers always search for better partnerships and relationships to service the objectives of the whole. This approach brings the problem identifiers and problem solvers together with a continuing concern for mutual learning and discovery as they share insights, experiences, puzzles, and solutions.

The method of giving direction also shifts from management in the progressive/liberal (discussed in Chapter 3) era to steering in the information era. Now organizations increasingly are not vertical but horizontal, using much greater decentralization. To be successful, organizations must be more agile, adapting to the swift changes in direction so common in the information age. Policy makers use steering to set output and outcome objectives and parameters for managers and other employees so that they know what decision makers expect of them even if decision makers do not tell them or do not provide explicit guidance to what task the lower level employees must accomplish.

With entrepreneurial budgeting, the steering comes from four directions. First, it comes from the direct language of the appropriation acts and other legislation that policy makers tie to specific measurable performance indicators of desired program outputs and outcomes. Second, it is from the direct orders of the elected and properly appointed leaders of the government, but those orders must be consistent with the laws of the nation. Third, it is in the deep roots of the nation's culture. For example, in the United States, democracy is important and accountability runs ultimately to the people. There is a desired and actual linkage of accountability between elected and appointed officials and the public. According to the Government Accounting Standards Board (discussed in Chapter 7), government agencies entrusted with resources and authority for applying them have a responsibility to render a full accounting of their activities. This accountability should identify not only the objects for which policy makers devote the public resources but also the manner and effect of their application. A fourth direction for steering can be found in absolute values and ethics. One place to look for these ethical standards is in the code of ethics of such groups as the National Association of State Budget Officers (NASBO), the Government Finance Officers Association, the American Society for Public Administration, and other professional organizations. Another place to look is in the field of philosophy. Still another is the teachings of the religious community. A final place to look for ethical standards is our families. Given the stress placed on individual initiative and the empowerment given professionals in the information age, entrepreneurial government will have its greatest difficulty facing up to the challenge of values and ethics. It is hoped that extensive and continuing training in the use of conformance and virtue ethics can significantly help individuals meet those challenges.

In the information age, the direction in budgeting shifts from control to monitoring. Accurate feedback is essential in the information age, and given the advances in both hardware and software, remarkable feedback arrangements are now possible. The information age requires workers to self-adjust; and throughout the organization, policy makers and managers can use information to see if the parts and the whole organization adjust correctly to changing circumstances, including policy and management direction. Policy makers need not base the information they select on the rational model of decision making as the decision makers can request information based on the concerns of the major program stakeholders. Analysts can use such concerns to help define program outcomes and output information needs.

In the information age, monitoring is the process of providing accurate, reliable, and timely feedback to all appropriate parties. Exhibit 5–1 in Chapter 5 is the Holistic Systems Approach, which provides an explanation of the feedback monitoring system. The model conceptualizes budgeting as a system with a cause and effect relationship running from input, to process, to output, and finally to outcome. Analysts select performance measures for each element of the government program and define input as the resources used to fuel the program including workforce time, money, and leadership direction. Process is the daily work activities of the program. Outputs are the products and services of the program. Outcomes are the impacts of the program output on individuals and society.

Monitoring embraces all of the functions that Allen Schick describes as essential to all budgets. In addition, monitoring helps encourage self-accountability and provides the whole system with information necessary for readjusting strategic brokering decisions. The monitoring system ensures that all interested parties know what actually occurs in each program in terms of inputs, process, outputs, and outcomes. The public can hold policy makers and program managers accountable for the results of their decisions and performance through the democratic process. This approach to feedback can use the best practices of the program based on historical information to establish a standard for current best practices, which is called benchmarking. Hence program teams will have the data needed to strive toward organizational excellence.

A Different Age—A Different Mindset

About 1800, the French economist J. B. Say coined the term "entrepreneur." He said, "The entrepreneur shifts economic resources out of an area of lower and into an area of higher productivity and greater yield." In other words, the entrepreneur uses resources in new ways to maximize productivity and effectiveness. Increasingly, public leaders ask civil servants to operate governmental programs as entrepreneurs, including generating reasonable revenue for their programs. Public administrators can no longer fixate themselves on spending only. They are now being asked to think about the revenue side of the budget also. With entrepreneurial budgeting, public managers must develop new revenue sources for their activities. An entrepreneurial spirit in budgeting means changing the management and policy approach used in the public sector to get those institutions to think in entrepreneurial ways. In other words, public institutions must use their resources in new ways to heighten both their efficiency and their effectiveness. This is not saying the public sector should be run like a business, as there are fundamental differences between the public and the private sector. Rather, the focus should be on governing and delivering public services in a significantly more entrepreneurial manner.

The practice of entrepreneurial budgeting is in its early development stage, but this chapter describes its elements. It is a method of budgeting whereby policy and chief executives establish the total spending limits and policy priorities. They provide program managers with the flexibility and private sectorlike incentives to determine how best to spend their budgets and the means to accomplish the priorities. In exchange for the increased spending authority, policy makers hold managers accountable for results. Ideally, the approach seeks to create an organizational environment that is lean, decentralized, innovative, flexible, adaptive, efficient, and effective.

In traditional twentieth-century command and control budgeting, policy makers wait for department heads and program managers to submit requests to them. In entrepreneurial budgeting (EB), much greater delegation occurs. Expenditure limits and performance measures are often benchmarked against the previous or current year, thus providing a point of departure for steering decisions. Policy makers sometimes express their budgets in a formula that holds overall spending to a percent increase or decrease of the current year budget. The EB budgets are quite brief—sometimes only a few pages long and in sharp contrast to the progressive era control-oriented line-item budget that was commonly quite long. Like program and performance budgeting, this approach focuses policy making on the big policy issues instead of on the line items where there is a tendency on the part of policy makers to use those items to micromanage agencies.

Entrepreneurial budgeting is a fundamental, radical departure from the older command and control approach to budgeting. Entrepreneurial budgeting is part of a larger mind-set change that requires focused attention on transforming the bureaucratic behavior of agency heads or program directors into thinking about revenue generation and efficiency-oriented management. This new approach to budgeting requires administrators to focus on the program's bottom line performance rather than just spending the appropriated moneys before the end of the fiscal year. See Exhibit 1–5 for a demonstration of the entrepreneurial budget format.

EXHIBIT 1–5 Performance, Entrepreneurial, and Competitive Budgeting Format: Code Enforcement

Performance, Entrepreneurial, and Competitive Budgeting Format: Code Enforcement

REVENUE SUMMARY	PAST YEAR	CURRENT YEAR (CY)	BUDGET YEAR (BY)	BY-CY
Total Revenue Needed	$55,576	$59,100	$68,196	$9,096
Less:				
Plan Examination Fees	10,000	11,888	12,331	998
Inspection Fees	30,000	30,000	40,000	10,000
Tuition	11,000	2,879	15,526	2,647
TOTAL	51,000	54,767	67,857	13,645
Subsidy from the General Fund	4,576	4,333	339	(4,549)

	Past Year			Current Year		
PROGRAM STUDY	OUTPUT	INPUT	UNIT COST	OUTPUT	INPUT	UNIT COST
Plan Exams (Average)	111	$2,000	$18.02	132	$2,377.60	$15.01
Contractor One	110	2,000	18.18	134	2,377.60	17.74
Contractor Two	109	2,000	18.35	129	2,377.60	18.43
Contractor Three	107	2,000	18.59	132	2,377.60	18.01
Contractor Four	114	2,000	17.54	131	2,377.60	18.15
Contractor Five	115	2,000	17.39	134	2,377.60	17.74
Total Plan Exams	555	10,000	18.02	660	11,888.00	17.17
Inspections (Average)	2,000	6,915.2	3.46	3,753	6,866.60	1.83
Contractor One	2,050	6,915.2	3.37	3,750	6,866.60	1.83
Contractor Two	2,140	6,915.2	3.23	3,690	6,866.60	1.86
Contractor Three	1,930	6,615.2	3.49	3,860	6,866.60	1.78
Contractor Four	1,830	6,915.2	3.49	3,770	6,866.60	1.82
Contractor Five	2,000	6,915.2	3.78	3,695	6,866.60	1.86
Total Inspections	10,000	34,576.0	3.46	18,765	34,933.00	1.86
Education (Average)	1,176	2,200	1.89	2,260	2,575.80	1.14
Contractor One	1,100	2,200	2.00	2,250	2,575.80	1.14
Contractor Two	1,180	2,200	1.86	2,210	2,575.80	1.12
Contractor Three	1,200	2,200	1.83	2,100	2,575.80	1.23
Contractor Four	1,400	2,200	1.57	2,235	2,575.80	1.10
Contractor Five	1,000	2,200	2.20	2,290	2,575.80	1.12
Total Education	5,880	11,000	1.89	11,300	12,879.00	1.14
Total Code Enforcement	16,435	55,576	3.38	30,725	59,100.00	1.92

EXHIBIT 1–5 *(continued)*

PROGRAM STUDY	Budget Year			BY-CY		
	OUTPUT	INPUT	UNIT COST	OUTPUT	INPUT	UNIT COST
Plan Examinations (Average)	149	$2,466.2	16.55	17	$199.60	$11.74
Contractor One	147	2,466.2	16.78	18	199.60	11.09
Contractor Two	150	2,466.2	16.44	16	199.60	12.47
Contractor Three	149	2,466.2	16.55	17	199.60	11.74
Contractor Four	151	2,466.2	16.33	18	199.60	11.09
Contractor Five	148	2,466.2	16.66	16	199.60	12.47
Total Plan Exams	**745**	**12,331.0**	**16.55**	**85**	**998.00**	**11.74**
Inspections (Average)	3,874	8,067.8	2.08	121	1,090.2	9.01
Contractor One	3,870	8,067.8	2.08	121	1,090.2	9.01
Contractor Two	3,850	8,067.8	2.09	123	1,090.2	8.86
Contractor Three	3,900	8,067.8	2.07	125	1,090.2	8.72
Contractor Four	3,810	8,067.8	2.12	119	1,090.2	9.16
Contractor Five	3,990	8,067.8	2.06	117	1,090.2	9.32
Total Inspections	**19,370**	**40,339.0**	**2.08**	**605**	**5,451.0**	**9.01**
Education (Average)	2,465	3,105.2	1.26	343	529.4	1.54
Contractor One	2,465	3,105.2	1.26	345	529.4	1.58
Contractor Two	2,520	3,105.2	1.23	347	529.4	1.52
Contractor Three	2,410	3,105.2	1.29	338	529.4	1.57
Contractor Four	2,400	3,105.2	1.29	340	529.4	1.56
Contractor Five	2,530	3,105.2	1.23	345	529.4	1.53
Total Education	**12,325**	**15,526.0**	**1.26**	**1,715**	**2,647.0**	**1.54**
Total Code Enforcement	**32,440**	**68,196.0**	**2.10**	**2,405**	**9,096.0**	**3.78**

Source: Thomas D. Lynch and Cynthia E. Lynch. "The Road to Entrepreneurial Budgeting." *Journal of Public Budgeting, Accounting, and Financial Management,* 9, 1 (Spring 1997), 161–180.

This approach asks them, "How can one insert competitiveness into an essentially monopolistic activity we call government service?" The agency heads and program managers are at liberty to allocate and expend their money in the best possible way to achieve the policy mission mandates. In exchange for this liberty, however, each program must have clear mission statements and measurable goals using specific performance measures in order to hold agency heads and program managers accountable to policy makers. Given the pluralistic form of government in the United States, that may be impossible for some programs. One of the most distinguishing features of the entrepreneurial budget is the ability of the agency and, in some cases, even the program to keep a portion of both their unspent money and earned income.

Government can use market mechanisms and competition successfully. In the progressive/liberal era, budgeting used monopolistic public agencies to manage public functions. In contrast, entrepreneurial government adopts a competitive approach and, to the extent possible, it abandons the monopolistic approach. Government can apply a true competitive process or arrangement to almost all its services and functions. Phoenix, Arizona, provides an often-cited example of this kind of competition. The city decided to privatize its solid waste collection. Greater Phoenix divided itself into five zones. Over a five-year period, the city offered publicly a multiple year contract for each zone. The city of Phoenix safeguarded a true competitive process by ensuring that at least a minimum of three contractors provided service. The result was better service at a lower cost to the public.

Other budget offices can use this same entrepreneurial approach used by the city of Phoenix and can apply it to almost all government services and functions. As noted by Lawrence Martin, there are many public services that lend themselves easily to privatization or contracting out, including garbage collection, snow removal, food services, and vehicle towing. Joining the ranks of the newly privatized services are prisons, school systems, and homeless shelters. Policy makers usually use the concept of privatization to select and contract with a single provider, thus merely switching from a public to a private monopoly. If this situation occurs, the disadvantages of having a monopoly continue. Therefore, policy makers should use competition in selecting the service provider in order to create a competitive situation. An alternative to privatization that still achieves competition is to divide the function into competitive teams of government employees.

Ideally, the key to the successful competitive process is to always have at least three service providers for the same service. Policy makers can apply such competition to most services or functions that they can divide into reasonable areas, time periods, or activities. For example, they can contract out auditing on a functional basis to accounting firms and data collection companies. They can also contract out the work of the city prosecutor's office to law firms on a geographical or functional basis. Thus, the number of high-cost public employees can diminish radically or stay constant, depending on the entrepreneurial approach taken to incur savings and avoid high costs such as personnel benefits, office space, office supplies, equipment, and support services. By maintaining a minimum of three service providers for every service, the competitive market force ensures the best service for the best price. Where service areas are too small to divide, policy makers can partner service coalitions among several governments or agencies (for example, city, county, state, and federal) to create the necessary economy of scale.

Thinking Differently

The most difficult hurdle to overcome in implementing entrepreneurial budgeting is organizational resistance. For example, the bureaucratic cultural mind-set must accept the notion that government can and, in some cases, should make money. Creating a willingness to embrace such new ideas is a serious obstacle to this reform. In addition, these reforms may involve larger amounts of data, higher levels of computer skills, and greater analytical talent. Realistically, such talent and data are sometimes not available.

However, the real hurdle to entrepreneurial budgeting is the willingness to reinvent the analyst's approach to budgeting because the analyst must redefine the government's budget process. Entrepreneurial budgeting calls for deep, broad thinking including the probing into the comparative worth of goals and the relative benefits of programs. It also requires an accurate financial and performance information system in an environment in which the agency asking for money is often the one that supplies the unaudited performance information to the policy makers. Thus, the environment encourages potentially inaccurate and biased performance reporting, creating an unfortunate impediment to the success of entrepreneurial budgeting.

Entrepreneurial Attitudes

The critical points to remember with cultivating an entrepreneurial climate are the same as the ten points that define the principles of entrepreneurial thinking:

- Competition between service providers
- Using market mechanisms
- Energizing earning potential
- Empowering citizens
- Customer-driven satisfaction
- Mission-driven organizations
- Decentralized authority
- Proactive and preventative actions
- Measured performance
- Acting as a catalyst to other sectors

Together, these ten characteristics create a stream of thinking that encourages government to deliver high-quality public services. They also define the major obstacles in handicapping and even preventing successful reform. Empowering citizens by giving them input in the determination of services is part of being customer-driven and helps distinguish entrepreneurial from command and control government.

Empowering citizens helps define the quality of service parameters and equity issues within which the entrepreneurial spirit can work. Citizens help define the possibilities of strategic brokering. Citizens are a familiar part of the budget process as they propose and pass measures that affect the collection and disbursement of public funds. A good example is California's Proposition 13, which was a citizen-led initiative. Citizens can petition, demonstrate, agitate, sue, advertise, speak, write, publish, and vote.

However, longtime observers of citizen action and interest groups note that key to their success is access to information and knowledge. For proper strategic brokering to occur, all parties must access accurate and unbiased information. Therefore, in entrepreneurial budgeting, citizens have as great a stake, if not greater, than other de-cision makers in the quality and accuracy of budget-related documentation and data.

Energizing earning potential, creating competition between and among service providers, and allowing market mechanisms to work to determine unit costs liberate the program managers and agency heads to discover endless possibilities. However, such strategies also create potential public interest problems. Radical changes in or-ganizations and management patterns may be necessary to achieve the organizational mission. Managers may decide to turn a profit in one program to fund a "lost leader" in another as an entrepreneurial strategy. Using user fees in new forms like franchis-ing, licensing, and increasing investment return are but a few ways information age managers can become entrepreneurs.

However, each of these situations can raise ethical questions, which are likely to be the most serious problems of the information age. Answers to ethical questions about the distribution of services will not be easy in entrepreneurial budgeting as pro-cedural responses to disparities in this approach to budgeting are often difficult to identify and manage. Empowered agencies can become nonresponsive to the overall public good in their quest to satisfy their customers rather than the larger public in-terest. The whole must be the orientation, but pressures to serve the parts over the whole will make servicing the whole quite difficult and could easily doom entrepre-neurial budgeting to ultimate failure.

An underlying concern for entrepreneurial innovations is that analysts must de-termine the true cost of the service in order to know the break-even point. Analysis must answer: "How can the analyst determine the rate of return on an investment if the true cost of the investment is unknown? How can managers seek profits if they cannot determine true spending? How can an analyst determine an appropriate sub-sidy if the true cost of the service is a mystery, including the hard-to-calculate sup-port services and leadership costs?" Decision makers must use analyses to answer the above questions but adequate answers may not be forthcoming. In Exhibit 1–5, the entrepreneurial budget format (1) exposes the amounts the general fund subsidizes the various programs, (2) relies on public pressure to do away with those subsidies where feasible, and thus (3) encourages agencies to search for new ways to make money from profitable services. With entrepreneurial budgeting, decision makers would greatly expand the use of enterprise and internal service funds in government accounting as discussed in more depth in Chapter 5.

Whether the budget format adopted for the jurisdiction is line-item, program, or entrepreneurial, the actual construction of the budget follows an established cal-endar and incorporates distinctive features that are part of the formal budget presen-tation.

BUILDING THE BUDGET

Budget Coordination

Exhibit 1–6 presents a slightly modified budget calendar once used by the city of Los Angeles. The calendar is important to the building of the budget because it establishes

EXHIBIT 1–6   Budget Calendar, Los Angeles

Date and Action to be completed

January 2 Mayor's Budget Policy letter requesting department heads to submit proposed work programs and budget estimates for ensuing fiscal year.
The budget office transmits with a letter the necessary forms and revisions to budget manual.

February 1 City Administrative Officer approves staff budget assignments, which are thereafter distributed to the staff.

February 15 Current level work programs and budget estimates received from department heads.

March 1 Service betterment budget estimates, if any, received from department heads.

April 10 City Administrative Officer reviews tentative Capital Improvement Expenditure Program and, upon approval, transmits it to the Public Works Priority Committee by April 10.

April 10 City Administrative Officer submits annual salary recommendations to City Council by April 10.

April 10–30 Hearings conducted by the Public Works Priority Committee to determine final priority of capital projects to be included in Capital Improvement Expenditure Program for ensuing year.

April 10–17 Preliminary budget hearings held by City Administrative Officer and Budget Coordinator with the Assistant Budget Coordinator and staff analyst for each department.

April 18–28 City Administrative Officer assisted by Budget Coordinator conducts departmental budget hearings with each department head. The staff analysts present their recommendations for that department budget and the City Administrative Officer gives each department head an opportunity to express his or her viewpoint.

May 1 Final date for submission by City Controller of the official estimates of revenue from all sources (other than general property taxes).

May 1 City Administrative Officer submits his or her official estimate of revenue from general property taxes.

May 1–5 Mayor, assisted by City Administrative Officer, conducts budget conferences with each department head. Attended by Council members, press, and taxpayer groups.

May 5–12 Final budget decisions made by Mayor assisted by City Administrative Officer.

May 12–31 Budget printed under supervision of City Administrative Officer.

June 11 Mayor submits proposed budget to City Council.

June 1–20 Council considers Mayor's veto of any item and may override Mayor's veto by two-thirds vote.

June 20–25 Mayor considers any modifications made by City Council and may veto such changes.

June 25–28 Council considers Mayor's veto of any item and may override Mayor's veto by two-thirds vote.

July 11 Beginning of fiscal year—budget takes effect.

Source: City of Los Angeles, 2002.

essential deadlines. Preparing a budget is a complex undertaking involving the whole government. The budget office achieves coordination by first deciding who must do what and when in the budget calendar. Its milestones include the following:

- distribution of instructions and forms;
- preparation of revenue estimates;
- return of completed budget request forms;
- completion of review and preliminary preparation work assigned to the central budget agency;
- completion of executive review and executive determination of final budget content;
- submission of the budget to the legislative body;
- completion of budget hearings;
- preliminary legislative determination of the content of the appropriation ordinance or budget;
- final action by the legislative body;
- executive approval or veto of the adopted budget and legislative action;
- completion of administrative actions, if any, needed to finalize budget appropriations; and
- the beginning of the fiscal year.

Program Financial Schedule

On a quarterly basis, the government's central budget office (OMB at the federal level) can require each department and agency to transmit a program financial schedule to it. This now fairly common budget requirement provides useful information allowing the central budget office to forecast expenditures better. The schedule categorizes the program by activity, method of finance, and fiscal year. Schedules commonly forecast five years beyond the budget year and sometimes include measures associated with the desirable application levels. OMB divides the projections into obligations and expenditures, thus providing useful information to economists and analysts concerned with the government's cash flow.

Analysts of the central budget office can use the data to estimate likely expenditure demands in preparing their budget call and in issuing executive guidance on budget preparation. Analysts should not view these forecasts as extremely accurate, but merely as an indication of likely financial patterns given existing policy. In each quarter, policy can change and other factors can evolve, making periodic updating essential.

The Budget Call

Once the central budget office prepares the preliminary estimates of expenditures and budget calendar, it proceeds preparing the budget call, which gives guidance to all the departments and agencies on how to go about preparing the budget. In many governments, including the federal government, the central budget office standardizes and provides guidance with official bulletins and circulars such as OMB Circular A-11. Agency budget officials need only refer to the established procedures and report forms. In addition to the standard operating procedures (SOP), each year the central budget office issues special guidance in the form of a "policy" letter, "allowance" letter, an executive policy message, or a statement on the budget. The federal government uses the "policy" letter to convey executive guidance and budget ceilings. The "allowance" letter comes later to inform federal agencies and departments of presidential or OMB decisions after the executive review process.

Budget Guidance

At the state and local level, the executive policy message or statement on the budget requests budget information from the agencies and establishes government-wide guidance on budget preparation. For example, the policy may be one of "hold-the-line," retrenchment, or expansion. Also, budget guidance announces programs and activities the agencies are to emphasize or de-emphasize.

Common subjects discussed in municipal statements include mandated increases, such as pension payments, salary increments, and debt service; raises or changes in taxes; requests to hold the line or identify inadequate services requiring expanded effort; plea for economy; explanation of local economic trends influencing the budget; and explanation of who must provide what information and when it is due (the budget calendar).

The detailed explanation call may be in the form of a budget instruction booklet, which provides guidance to the agencies and departments. The booklet contains the preliminary statement of executive budget policy; the table of contents, including listing of forms; the budget calendar; general instructions; and specific instructions for each form, including a sample form.

Budget office follow-through is essential, as the office must send instructions to the chief departmental officials. Each level of government will repackage the instructions and reissue them to lower levels. Eventually, the program managers receive the information requests. Meetings are useful at all levels to clarify and avoid possible confusion. The budget office should take special care to explain any changes in the procedures. Every official involved should understand the current financial status and likely trends, including personnel pay trends. The budget office always must emphasize the need for accurate, prompt, uniform replies. The Municipal Finance Officers Association publications, which this chapter cites in its references, explains the types of forms required.

The budget call always asks for a statement of government functions, activities, and work programs, or some narrative explaining what services citizens receive for their tax dollars. The general instructions asking for this budget explanation normally stress the desirability of brevity, clarity, and comprehensiveness. The explanation should reflect any program changes and even emphasize those changes. Each level in the executive branch uses the information, with the central budget and department levels focusing upon having a complete inventory of government activities keyed to specific units assigned to functions and activities. The descriptive detail is greater at the unit and agency level.

Agency call

Exhibit 1–7 is a sample agency call for estimates used in past federal budget training manuals. The call draws attention to the executive policy and the required forms the agency is to use. This call points out that the agency is still operating under a continuing resolution

EXHIBIT 1–7   Agency Call for Estimates (Sample)

August 1, 20PY

MEMORANDUM TO ASSIST DIRECTORS AND DIVISION HEADS

Subject: Instructions for Preparation of the Budget Estimates for FY 20BY

The 20BY budget submission to the Office of Management and Budget (OMB) will conform generally to the program and activity structure used for the 20CY budget estimate. The overall budget estimate will be prepared to reflect policy and program decisions which resulted from budget meetings held by the Director on the 20BY budget.

For purposes of the presentation to OMB, descriptive materials for the various programs should be brief statements covering the points outlined in the following format. It is expected that the submission to the Congress will be a more detailed budget.

Since no appropriation has been approved for the Agency for 20CY, the program estimates for that fiscal year will be the same as in the 20CY Budget to the Congress. Under item "C." of the instructions, supplementary data is being requested for the preparation of staff salary estimates and travel and other administrative expenses that are spread among the activities shown in the Salaries and Expenses appropriation.

Estimates and drafts of the justification material must be received by the Budget Office by August 20.

Comptroller

Source: Resource Conservation Agency, Washington, DC 20550.

for the current year, and it makes reference to instructions, which are particularly sensitive. The call states who should prepare the information (for example, assistant directors and division heads) and when the information is due (for example, August 20). Note the call only allows the agency twenty days to compile the information. Tight deadlines do occur in budgeting. If the budget office used zero-base budgeting, the instructions would require alternative decision packages and priority rankings as discussed in Chapter 3.

Preparing a budget at the agency level is a difficult task. The agency must assemble the material from the units, and the budget figures in particular must conform to agency policy set down by the agency head. The budget office normally calculates personnel statistics and cost information to compute the salaries and expense portion of the budget. If the agency has field units, then those units make the process more complex. Extreme accuracy and consistency are important because their absence denotes sloppy preparation and poor management.

The format of the agency budget requests varies greatly depending upon which budget reform happens to be in vogue. Examples of the possible formats are a detailed line-item presentation that permits greater control over the bureaucracy, a program budget that stresses policy issues and their budget implications, a performance budget that relates input to program accomplishments, a zero-base budget that focuses on marginal value and prioritization, or an incremental budget that stresses changes from past policy decisions.

The format selected is important, but a more important factor is the quality of professionalism devoted to preparing and reviewing the budget. Good professionalism calls for in-depth understanding of the agency and the related budget implications as explained in Chapter 6. Too often the budget office establishes the format due to some politically inspired budget reform movement instead of the central budget office or legislature tailoring the reforms to the need of the whole government and the agency budget office to the type of programs it administers.

BUDGET REVIEWS

Once the agency prepares the budget, the review process begins in the executive and legislative branches. The agency first meets with the department officials. They conduct a complete examination of the budget request, often including budget hearings. Departmental budget offices make decisions, and the agency budget office revises its requests based on department level decisions. Usually, the department recommends cuts, but it is a friendlier reviewer than the government's central budget office. The latter unit next reviews the agency or compiled departmental budget. The central budget office makes its recommendations to the chief executive, and sometimes departmental officials make direct last-minute appeals to the chief executive. Finally, after the final approval of the chief executive, the central budget office releases the chief executive's budget.

Budget Hearings

Usually, the agency submits its budget to the reviewing party, who carefully analyzes the submission. Chapter 5 describes how analysts conduct program and budget analyses. After the initial analysis of the submission and any other available material, the reviewing party, such as the department budget office, seeks additional information. Often, the budget office does this using formal written questions to the agency on specific inquiries, and sometimes the office makes more informal inquiries. The reviewers—budget examiners—prepare an analysis of the material and background material for a hearing. Departments need hearings because they enable the budget officer and the department executive to obtain a better understanding of an agency's request and reasons supporting that request.

Agencies also prepare for hearings. The depth of preparation varies, but the agency is wise to prepare carefully. Agency analysts can develop questions that the reviewers can ask and write responses to those questions so that the agency's leaders can become prepared for the hearing. The analyst can prepare a plan of action or strategy for the hearing, keeping in mind the factors discussed in the chapter on budget behavior (explained in Chapter 4).

The hearing itself is semiformal, with testimony rarely transcribed at the department or OMB level. The chief executive of the department often chairs the meeting to ask questions and gain an understanding of the agency budget requests. The principal department budget officer is present and plays an active role. Often, analysts prepare the department questions for the department chief executive in order to facilitate the process. Usually, the department hearing begins with the agency head presenting a statement and follows with department questions and agency answers. Regardless of the style used, the agency should explain its program, especially any program changes. The questioners should probe for elaboration on vague points in the presentation as well as potential political or management problems that surface from the department inquires. The hearing is only for information purposes, and this forum is inappropriate for tentative or final department decisions because more deliberation is necessary.

After the department completes the hearing, the department and agency budget analysts carefully review their notes and reconsider the submission and other material. Department analysts also review the guidance from the departmental chief executive. Often, the reviewers ask some additional questions by phone or in writing. The departmental budget office then prepares the final analysis and recommendations. The department budget officer then briefs the departmental chief executive on the budget. The style of briefing and of department budget decision making depends upon the chief executives as some delegate the entire responsibility to the budget office and others review the requests in detail. Usually, the pressure of time on the chief executive prevents long, detailed reviews of requests. A set of briefing information usually includes the following:

- summary of agency requests;
- recommendations of budget office;
- summary of the past year's chief executive's ideas relative to the budget;
- added suggestions by the budget office;
- preliminary budget (balanced for state and local government);
- and summary of policy issues.

A similar process is in place for hearings that take place between the department and a central budget office at the federal, state, and local levels. These budget hearings are the opportunity for the departments to defend their overall budget requests to the central budget office. These hearings take place after the departmental reviews and departmental hearings. In fact, the departments have another set of hearings to navigate when they must defend their budgets before members of the legislature. These legislative hearings are discussed later in this chapter.

Just as the budget calendar, program financial schedule, call letter, and hearings are generic features in the formative stages of the budget process, the actual preparation of the budget document has common components and accompanying reports.

Executive Budget Document

Budget Message

Budgets sent to legislatures and city councils are almost always accompanied by a budget message. The contents vary depending upon the political situation. Usually, the message includes a discussion of the financial condition of the government and a commentary on the current year operating budget, such as "the current budget is and will continue to be balanced." Messages mention revenue highlights, including revenue estimates, new revenue sources, and prospects on increased or new taxes. The message usually puts the government budget situation into perspective by citing major trends in finance, population changes, income level shifts, and so on. The message explains the principal elements of the proposed expenditures, including the rationale for any major program changes. The message mentions sensitive topics like mandatory increases as well as pay and fringe benefit policy and cites problem areas not addressed by the proposed budget, often with an explanation for that omission. At the local level, the message could also explain the relationship between the operating and capital budgeting. The message summarizes the highlights of the budget and blunts political criticism if possible.

The Budget Summary and Details

Budget Summary

A summary of the budget is essential. It should present consolidated summaries of revenues and appropriations. At the federal level, the budget summary presents various economics-related information. At the local level, the comparative statement of resources includes the following:

- cash surplus at the end of the first prior year,
- estimated receipts for the current year,
- anticipated expenditures during the current year,
- estimated cash surplus at the end of the current year,
- anticipated income during the budget year,
- proposed expenditures during the budget year, and
- projected cash surplus at the end of the budget year.

Analysts can include additional information in the local budget summary. They often include a statement on the tax rate and the assessed valuation of the property, including amount of land, improvements, and exemptions. A statement on other revenue sources is useful. They sometimes include the statement of appropriations by organization unit. Finally, they mention a summary of appropriation to various activities.

Budget Detail

After the summary material, the budget presents the detailed revenue and expenditure estimates. The budget officer groups the revenue estimates and presents them by comparing the budget year estimates with the prior year and current year. The budget officer adds appropriate footnotes to explain tax rates, tax base, and nonrecurring humps or valleys in the estimates. He or she explains all the assumptions used in preparing the revenue estimates. The detailed expenditure estimates often include the following:

- a narrative explanation of the functions of each department, suborganization unit, and activity, as well as a separate section for comments on the major changes proposed in each activity;
- a listing by department and suborganization unit of the objects of expenditure and by activity with an identification of proposed resource changes;
- a listing by position title for each unit and activity as well as any proposed changes; and
- an identification of the workload volume being undertaken in conjunction with each activity.

The public usually considers the executive budget document the budget, even though the legislature may make significant changes and in fact ultimately approves the document that the government agencies must follow (consistent with the legislature wielding its power of the purse). In some jurisdictions, the legislature passes and approves what is called the budget. Regardless of the stress given the executive budget document, it is extremely influential in the decision-making process. The document is the chief executive's plan. The legislature must make any modification to the executive budget with the awareness that any changes it makes are simply additions or deletions. Even in the federal government where legislators sometimes say the president's budget is dead on arrival, legislators still raise the questions of either "Where is the extra money going to come from?" or "What programs are going to be cut?" If one legislator suggests deletions to the executive budget, the easier but still difficult question raised is either "Where is the extra money going to be spent?" or "What taxes should be cut?" These are not simple questions, and the executive budget becomes the point of departure for legislative consideration of the budget.

The Federal Timetable: The Congressional Budget

Budget Milestones

In the earlier discussion of the budget calendar, it was noted that target dates were set for legislative action on the budget. For many governments, legislatures may consider the executive presumptuous to state target dates for the legislatures because of the separation of powers concept. In spite of that attitude, most budget people can estimate fairly accurately what the target dates are in the legislative budget process. Often the legislative body will state its own targets in its rules. The one forcing deadline is the beginning of the new fiscal year, by which, everyone agrees, the legislature should adopt the budget. The other deadlines fall between the time when the legislature receives the chief executive's budget and the beginning of the fiscal year.

In the federal government, the 1974 Budget Act as amended sets the congressional deadlines. These critical targets, coupled with serious prodding by the budget committees, encourage the congress to pass timely appropriation legislation, avoiding the pre-1974 practice of passing appropriation legislation three to six months into the current year. Unfortunately, Congress rarely meets its own targets, but both the targets and the active pushing of the budget committees are essential because they set a standard. Budget committees use social and political pressure to achieve responsible congressional action.

Congress often overlooks the seriousness of not passing timely appropriations. If Congress or any legislature does not pass appropriation legislation before the beginning of the current year, then the government cannot pay its employees or anyone else. Government operations cease to exist because no one has the authority to spend money. If Congress cannot reach a decision on appropriations prior to the beginning of the new fiscal year, then the legislative body passes a continuing resolution, which usually says that the government can continue to obligate and spend at last year's budget levels. The wording of the continuing resolution could also say the government can proceed at the lower levels of either last year's budget or the approved version of the House or Senate bill. The legislature usually frames the wording to set spending at the lowest amount the legislature is likely to pass. Managing a program under a continuing resolution is not an overwhelming problem for an agency unless the final legislation provides the manager with significantly less or more money than the amount in the continuing resolution. If Congress provides less money, the entire program may have to stop sometime in the middle of the current year. If Congress provides more money than the amount in the continuing resolution, the agency may have to obligate money recklessly in order to use it during the remainder of the current year. Either situation creates bad public management, which Congress can compound significantly by repeatedly using the continuing resolution year after year, as Congress usually does.

Congressional Budget Timetable

The congressional budget deliberative process starts with the presidential submission of the Current Services Budget. This budget alerts the Congress, especially the Congressional Budget Office (CBO), the budget committees, and the appropriation committees, that they should anticipate specific revenue, expenditure, and debt levels unless they change current policy. The Current Services Budget also provides a baseline of comparison against the later presidential budget.

The president of the United States sends the presidential budget, with the Current Services Budget, to the Congress fifteen days after Congress convenes in the new calendar year (for example, January 20). The budget customarily follows the State of the Union address to Congress. Presidents usually address Congress with a specific budget message, which the president makes with more details and specifics than those provided in the earlier State of the Union speech. The budget messages vary in content with a president's style, but the earlier discussion follows a common pattern, with the exception that the president places more emphasis on the national economy.

By February 1, the Congressional Budget Office must send its annual report to the budget committees. This report analyzes the economy, the Current Services Budget, and the president's budget. It suggests alternative levels of spending. Interestingly, the original legislation called for an April 1 submission, but the CBO realized this did not give the budget committees sufficient time to digest the CBO report, so mutual consent changed the date.

By March 15, the various committees, like appropriation, must submit their respective reports to the budget committees. This is a tentative financial guess by the committees on revenue, expenditure, and debt. The committees use the CBO report, the president's budget, and the detailed backup information supplied by the agencies to help them arrive at reasonable budget estimates.

One month later, on April 15, each budget committee reports its recommended budget resolution. This resolution represents the difficult compromise on the entire budget: the revenues, expenditures, and debt, as well as targets for each committee important to the budget process. One month later, on May 15, each chamber votes on its own resolution. An inability to reach a decision would destroy the process, and this sometimes occurs. Opposition can come from the conservatives for wanting to cut taxes more and from the liberals for spending too little money. The resolutions need not be the same in each chamber. May 15 is also the deadline for reporting all authorization bills. Congress doesn't want unanticipated expenses resulting from authorization legislation, so this deadline is essential.

The law requires within seven days after Labor Day in September that Congress concludes its final action on appropriation bills. This gives the appropriation committees several months to hold their hearings and make their difficult decisions. Next, the law requires by September 15 that Congress performs its final action on the second budget resolution. This permits last-minute changes due to any intervening circumstances since Congress passed the first resolution. Often, there may be no difference between the first and second resolution, but the law provides an opportunity for flexibility. By September 25, Congress should pass all final actions on budget reconciliation, thus providing a uniform consolidated congressional budget in each chamber.

Congress uses the remaining days in September to resolve differences between chambers, pass the legislation, accommodate a presidential veto, and reconcile or override the veto. Congress can do all of this if there is good cooperation among the chambers and the president. However, such cooperation is rare, the result being that delays occur and Congress must pass one or more continuing resolutions if the federal agencies are to have any funds to operate their programs. The federal fiscal year begins on October 1.

Legislative Considerations: Federal, State, and Local

At all levels of government, legislative bodies consider budgets and budget supporting material. This information is the key to proper legislative understanding of government operations. The considerations and the subsequent legislation permit the legislative oversight activity to exist. The purse strings are important. If legislators identify weaknesses, they often can reshape policy with their redrafted budget. The budget consideration in legislatures is a much more open process than is the executive review. Thus, legislative budget hearings serve as a forum for better community understanding of government as well as a device to permit citizens to express their views on budget matters. The time needed for legislative consideration of the budget varies with the size of government. Committees must have time to study the budget and related information, conduct hearings with public officials and possibly with interested citizens, discuss policy internally, and finally enact the legislation. Usually, sixty days is a reasonable time for smaller local governments.

Legislatures organizationally decide budgets based mostly on the size of their government. Larger governments have standing committees with highly competent professional staff support. Legislatures organize their committees and staffs on a partisan or a nonpartisan basis. Given the complexity of government and budgeting, most states and local governments hire professionally trained and experienced analysts. Exhibit 1–8 presents an illustrative page from a legislative analyst's review of a budget request. The reader will notice how a good analyst can focus attention upon the items, which should concern the legislator.

The legislative hearing is the standard method used to gather information and focus on potential problems of concern to the legislature. Careful analyses often isolate these problems for legislators. Legislatures conduct their hearings differently from executive budget hearings. With legislative hearings, staffs often create a transcript, and there are usually more friendly and sometimes hostile questions of the agency personnel, reflecting the fact that some legislators are friendly and others are hostile. Just as in the executive hearings, the agency is wise to prepare for the hearings with briefing books, to plan strategies and tactics, and to have rehearsals. The hearings are usually scheduled more at the convenience of the legislative committee than of the agency. Follow-up questions are common, as in executive hearings. Legislative committees do not make decisions at hearings, but rather at their closed-door "mark-up" sessions that follow the hearing.

If public participation is part of the hearing as is likely in most governments, then the committee normally takes care to give due notice of the time and place. Failure to give due notice or to notify all the likely interested "publics" can result in heated public criticism and the need to hold the hearing again, especially at the local level.

The legislatures usually have the power to modify the executive's budget, but that is not always the case in local government. Even if the power exists, modifications are difficult because all components of the budget are interdependent. If the legislature adjusts one figure upward, another figure must be cut if the budget is to balance. Exhibit 1–9 illustrates one city council's modifications.

The adoption of the budget can vary in terms of detail. Analysts should itemize the appropriations by department in order to fix responsibility. Some argue that analysts should itemize them by major object classification and others by program or activity. There is no one correct way. Object classification is good for greater control, especially when there is a low threshold of trust afforded the government's middle- and lower-level managers. Program classifications are good for situations that need management flexibility to operate effectively and efficiently. Detailed line-item budgets are extremely inflexible. The legislature should accompany the budget with—or make part of the budget—a formal resolution on the final official revenue estimate used by the legislature at the time of the budget's adoption.

EXHIBIT 1–8   Legislative Analyst's Review Sheet, Department of Hospitals and Institutions, BY Budget Request

NEWARK CITY HOSPITAL

The BY Budget request of $6,469,185.00 for the Newark City Hospital shows an increase of $229,131.67 over CY Operations as follows:

BY Budget

Appropriations	$6,453,424.00	CY Request	$6,469,185.00
CY Emergencies	115,149.96		
	$6,568,573.96		
Less Cancellations	328,520.63		
Net CY Operations	$6,240,053.33	CY Operations	$6,240,053.33
		Increase	$ 229,131.67

The request for 1,270 employees is 25 less than the 1,295 in CY.

PAGE and LINE

4		There were 29,669 less patient days in CY than in CY-1 resulting from a drop in admissions from 18,760 in CY-1 to 15,460 in CY, a net drop of 3,300.
5		The average day's stay per patient dropped from 9.5 to 9.1.
		The average daily admissions dropped from 60.9 in CY-1 to 56.4 in CY, a net drop of 4.5 admissions. The average daily census of patients in the hospital dropped from 575.6 in CY-1 to 549.9 in CY, a drop of 25.7 in CY.
6	1 & 2	What is the status of the Medical Director and the Assistant Medical Director?
6	3	Will the Comptroller's position be filled? Is the present incumbent Joseph Rubino to remain on the hospital payroll?
10	12A	Has the hospital filled this position?
19	37	Is this position going to remain in the hospital?
25		New employee, Director of Surgery. In accordance with policy followed in similar cases the appropriation for this employee will be deleted because there is no valid ordinance supporting it. The legislature will make appropriation after adoption of the ordinance and before final adoption of the budget by amending the approved budget.
41	103A	Bernice Lippe replaced the Director of Nurses on January 14, BY, at the minimum salary of $47,500.00. Her salary as Assistant Director of Nursing Education on Page 112 was $46,460. The legislature should delete one pay from the Director of Nurses' appropriation and one pay remaining in the Assistant Director of Nursing Education's line on Page 112.

Source: Modified New Jersey Budget.

Legislative Adoption

The ultimate budget is the legislative adoption version, which a legislature can make as several appropriation laws (the federal government's approach), one massive, complex appropriation law (used by many states), or a relatively brief text (used by some

EXHIBIT 1–9   Schedule Setting Forth Changes Made by City Council in City Manager's Original Estimate of BY Budget

	MANAGER'S ESTIMATE	REVISED AMOUNT
Office of City Manager	$146,135	$138,246
Reason for Change—Reduced cost of annual report, reduction of .5 man year administrative analyst. Add cost of salary increase.		
Secretary-Treasurer	166,844	169,484
Reason for change—Add cost of salary increase.		
Accounting	77,686	74,751
Reason for change—Delete one accountant position. Add cost of salary increase.		
Data Processing	179,470	181,303
Reason for change—Add cost of salary increase.		
Purchasing	30,867	31,539
Reason for change—Add cost of salary increase.		
Tax	400,390	408,861
Reason for change—Add cost of salary increase.		
Legal	99,472	101,636
Reason for change—Add cost of salary increase.		
Retirement Administrator	22,731	23,043
Reason for change—Add cost of salary increase.		
Personnel and Civil Service	29,703	50,349
Reason for change—Add cost of salary increase. Add cost of salary and wage survey.		

local governments). Sometimes the budget submitted to the legislative body includes the recommended act or ordinance. Often budget ordinances are complex because of state legal requirements. In some jurisdictions, the resolution includes tax rates, purchasing authority, personnel action authorizations, and transfer procedures. Some use broad legislative grants of authority, and others have extensive line-item detail for each government unit.

What is clear in this legislative phase is that the budget is indeed a political document. Politics pervades the budget process throughout its formulation, presentation, analysis, legislative review, and execution. Oftentimes during legislative enactment, interest groups or the general public criticizes lawmakers for pursuing pork-barrel projects or adding "member-items" in the budget. Yet, because the legislature may be prone to seek cuts in the executive budget for the purposes of funding its legislative projects, this doesn't necessarily mean the rigor or the review and analysis is any less important than that of the executive and central budget office. What this means is that politics influences spending decisions as reflected in the budget. Moreover, this is the essence of both public budgeting in America and democracy in action.

At the local level, the budget ordinance often acknowledges receipt of an executive budget from the county manager, recounts earlier publication and a public hearing, summarizes appropriation by fund and category, estimates revenue, levels property taxes, authorizes administrative transfers of appropriations within a fund, and approves and reapproves funds for ongoing capital improvements.

REVIEW QUESTIONS

1. Explain how budget formats channel thought. Explain how formats can direct thought to and highlight general policy matters, budget balancing issues, and improvement of the quality of government management.
2. Compare and contrast twentieth-century budgeting with twenty-first-century budgeting.
3. Why are the program financial schedules and budget calendar important preliminary steps to the budget call?
4. What budget instructions are important in building a budget? Why?
5. Contrast executive and legislative hearings.
6. Why is the central budget office "powerful"?
7. What information should be in an executive budget? Why?
8. Explain the significance of the congressional budget timetable. What procedures or legal changes can Congress establish that would get it to pass a budget before the beginning of the fiscal year?
9. Contrast the virtues of a simple versus a comprehensive budget ordinance or law.
10. In the final analysis, who dominates the budget process, the legislature or the executive?

REFERENCES

ARONSON, J. RICHARD, and ELI SCHWARTZ (eds.). *Management Policies in Local Government Finance.* Washington, DC: International City Management Association, 1975.

BROOME, CHERYLE A. "Performance-Based Budgeting Government Models: Building A Track Record." *Public Budgeting and Finance,* 15, 4 (Winter 1995), 3–17.

BURKHEAD, JESSE. *Government Budgeting.* New York: Wiley, 1956.

COTHAN, DAN A. "Entrepreneurial Budgeting: An Emerging Form." *Public Administration Review,* 53, 5 (September/October 1993), 445–454.

DRUCKER, PETER F. *Innovation and Entrepreneurship.* New York: Harper, 1985.

———. *Managing for the Future, the 1990s and Beyond.* New York: Truman Taley Books/Plume, 1989.

———. *The New Realities.* New York: Harper & Row, 1989.

FISHER, LOUIS. *Presidential Spending Power.* Princeton, NJ: Princeton University Press, 1975.

GABLER, T., and A. OSBORNE. "Entrepreneurial Government Makes Good Sense." *The Public Manager,* 21, 3 (Fall 1992), 4–6.

Government Accounting Standards Board. "Government Accounting Series Concept Statement Number 2 on Concepts Related to Service Efforts and Accomplishments Reporting." Norwalk, CT., 1995.

GRIZZLE, GLORIA A. "Does Budget Format Really Govern the Actions of Budgetmakers?" *Public Budgeting and Finance,* 6, 1 (Spring 1986), 60–70.

HAMMER, MICHAEL, and JAMES CHAMPY. *Reengineering the Corporation: A Manifesto for Business Revolution.* New York: Harper Business, 1992.

HAQUE, AKHLAQUE. "Edmund Burke: The Role of Public Administration in a Constitutional Order." In Thomas D. Lynch and Todd Dicker (eds.), *The Handbook of Organization Theory and Management.* New York: Marcel Dekker, 1998.

JASPER, HERBERT N. "A Congressional Budget: Will It Work This Time?" *The Bureaucrat,* 3, 4 (January 1975), 429–443.

JONES, L. R. "Aaron Wildavsky: A Man and Scholar for All Seasons." *Public Administration Review,* 55, 1 (January/February 1995), 3–16.

KING, MERRILL S. "The Entrepreneurial Budgeting System of Texas Parks and Wildlife Department." Paper presented at the American Society for Public Administration, San Antonio, Texas, 1995.

LEHAN, EDWARD A. *Simplified Governmental Budgeting.* Chicago: Municipal Finance Officers Association, 1982.

LYNCH, THOMAS D. "Budget System Approach." *Public Administration Quarterly,* 13, 3 (Fall 1989), 321–341.

———. *Policy Analysis in Public Policymaking.* Lexington, MA: Lexington Books, 1975.

———. *Public Budgeting in America.* 5th ed. Englewood Cliffs, NJ: Prentice Hall, 1995.

LYNCH, THOMAS D., and CYNTHIA E. LYNCH. "The Road to Entrepreneurial Budgeting." *Journal of Public Budgeting, Accounting, and Financial Management,* 9, 1 (Spring 1997), 161–180.

MARTIN, LAWRENCE. "Contracting Out: A Comparative Analysis of Local Government Practices." In Thomas D. Lynch and Lawrence Martin (eds.), *Handbook of Comparative Public Budgeting and Financial Management.* New York: Marcel Dekker, 1993, 225–239.

———. "Jeremy Bentham: Utilitarianism, Public Policy and the Adminsitrative State." In Thomas D. Lynch and Todd Dicker (eds.), *The Handbook of Organization Theory and Management.* New York: Marcel Dekker, 1998.

MILLER, GIRARD (compiler). *Effective Budgetary Presentations: The Cutting Edge.* Chicago: Municipal Finance Officers Association, 1982.

MOAK, LENNOX L., and KATHRYN W. KILLIAN. *Operating Budget Manual.* Chicago: Municipal Finance Officers Association, 1963.

Municipal Performance Report, 1, 4 (August 1974).

NAISBITT, JOHN. *Global Paradox.* New York: Avon Books, 1994.

OSBORNE, DAVID, and TED GABLER. *Reinventing Government.* New York: Plume, 1993.

O'TOOLE, DANIEL E., and BRIAN STIPAK. "Patterns and Trends in Budget Format Innovation Among Local Governments." *Public Budgeting and Financial Management,* 4, 2 (1992), 287–310.

O'TOOLE, DANIEL E., JAMES MARSHALL, and TIMOTHY GREWE. "Current Local Government Budgeting Practices." *Government Finance Review,* 12, 6 (December 1996), 25–28.

PETTIJOHN, C. D., and G. A. GRIZZLE. "Structural Budget Reform: Does it Affect Budget Deliberations?" *Journal of Public Budgeting, Accounting, and Financial Management,* 9, 1 (Spring 1997), 26–45.

REICH, ROBERT. *The Work of Nations.* New York: Vintage Books, 1992.

RICKARDS, ROBERT C. "City and County Budget Presentations in Texas: The Current State of the Art." *Public Budgeting and Finance,* 10, 2 (Summer 1990), 72–87.

SAY, JEAN BAPTISTE. *A Treatise on Political Economy: or the Production, Distribution, and Consumption of Wealth,* C. R. Prinsep and Clement C. Biddle, trans. New York: Augustus M. Kelley, [1880] 1971, p. 111.

SCHICK, ALLEN. "The Road to PPB: The Stages of Budget Reform." *Public Administration Review,* 26 (December 1966), 243–258. Reprinted in Jay M. Shafritz and Albert C. Hyde, *Classics of Public Administration.* Oak Park, IL: Moore Publishing Company, Inc., 1978, 249–267.

SMITH, LINDA L. "The Congressional Budget Process—Why It Worked This Time." *The Bureaucrat,* 6, 1 (1977), 88–111.

U.S. CIVIL SERVICE COMMISSION, Bureau of Training, The Management Science Training Center. *Budget Formulation.* 1976.

WILDAVSKY, AARON. *The Politics of the Budgetary Process.* Boston: Little, Brown, 1964.

2

PUBLIC BUDGETING IN CONTEXT

Public budgeting is a mystery to most people—even to many professionals working in the government. People know that chief executives, such as the president of the United States, propose budgets to legislative bodies and that these groups, such as the Congress, in turn make decisions on taxes and what programs will receive financial support. If they work in government, they know that agencies prepare budget requests as a means to justify "the budget" and that detailed procedural controls exist, which often limit their managerial discretion. In the personal lives of most people, the family budget is a source of tension because of the need to live within one's income. Thus, most people assume that public budgeting must deal with similar matters but that it must involve much more complex accounting techniques.

This chapter examines what public budgeting is and the contextual factors necessary to understand public budgeting in the American context. Public budgeting is an activity that many people view from their own perspectives and, thus, they do not comprehend the full complexity of budgeting. In other words, the meaning of "public budgeting" is very much dependent upon perspective. The primary contextual factor in America—and all budgeting in every country—is ideology. In America, that ideology is a mixture of views on democracy, capitalism, federalism, decision-making theory, accounting, and economics. Each helps define how we approach and understand the purpose of public budgeting. This chapter should help the reader understand the following:

- the various significant perspectives on budgeting, including that of the public manager;
- important budgetary and political realities;
- the nature of the budget cycle (that is, phases, cycle variations, overlapping of cycles) and the activities associated with each budget phase;
- the influence of technology on society including government;
- the significance of ideology in influencing how we approach public budgeting;
- the role of federalism as a factor in budgeting;
- the significance of normative decision-making theory to public budgeting;
- the major tools of monetary policy, what aspects of the economy they primarily affect, and their significance to public budgeting;
- the variety of ways in which the federal government can act to stimulate or depress the economy and the theory behind such actions; and
- an explanation of how economic policy has and has not worked since the 1960s.

WHAT IS PUBLIC BUDGETING?

Perspectives on Budgeting

One can define a term by seeking out the common usage or one can create a definition for one's own intellectual and conceptual purposes. The former approach helps us understand the various perspectives that people bring to a given activity. The latter approach is useful when an author wants a reasonably uniform body of thought. This chapter uses both approaches.

We can view public budgeting from many perspectives, as illustrated by Professor Sydney Duncombe in Exhibit 2–1. Reading the variety of statements helps one to appreciate the various academic and practical perspectives found in the practice of public budgeting. There are many such perspectives, of which none is exclusively "correct." The parable of the three blind men and the elephant helps us understand the significance of perspective. One of the blind men examined the tail and pronounced his description of the animal. Another felt a large foot and leg and then argued that the first man's description was inaccurate. The third man, after examining the beast's trunk, said that the other two were quite wrong in their descriptions. The storyteller was said to laugh at the foolish arguing among the blind men because the storyteller could see all of the elephant. The point of the parable is not the importance of "better" perspective but rather the foolishness of the storyteller for not recognizing that his arrogance blinded himself ironically because of his sight. Each person was correct and each was wrong because our individual perspectives always prevent us from easily understanding another's "truth."

When one works in the world of public budgeting, various key actors in the budget process come from each perspective. The person trained as a lawyer sees the phenomenon called budgeting as a sort of legal process. The economist and politician describe the phenomenon differently based upon their perspectives. The public manager sees budgeting differently from the others. None is incorrect, because all of them define the phenomenon based upon their educational or professional perspectives. They become incorrect, like the storyteller, when their arrogance blinds them to the significance of perspective when defining and understanding the phenomenon of public budgeting.

For the purposes of this textbook, the more important perspectives are those of the politician, the economist, the accountant, and especially the public manager. Given a democratic society, budgets are the tool used to frame much public policy; thus the politician's perspective is important. Both economists and accountants have professional perspectives, which greatly influence how we understand budgeting and how we believe we should practice it. Economists give us theories and techniques that help us define how we should budget, what factors to weigh, and how to weigh those factors in making budget policy decisions. Accountants give us conceptual frameworks in which to execute and evaluate budgets. Public managers must understand each of the previous perspectives when managing the affairs of government through the budget process.

Politicians

Political leaders are often painfully aware that they make many of their most important policy decisions during the budget process. Former New York City Mayor

EXHIBIT 2–1   What are the Main Purposes of Budgeting?

I view the budget system as *a means of balancing revenues and expenditures*. Our constitution requires a balanced budget and in preparing our budget we first make careful estimates of revenues for the next year. We then reduce agency budget requests to our revenue estimates for the next year.

I look on the budget process as a *semi-judicial process* in which state agencies come to the legislature to plead their case just as I plead the case of my clients in court. Our job as a legislative committee is to distribute the *available* funds equitably among state agencies.

The main purpose of the budget system is *accountability*. The people hold the legislature accountable through the electoral process. The legislature holds state agencies accountable by reviewing their budgets, setting the appropriation levels the people want, and letting state agencies know how the people want their money spent through statements of legislative intent.

The most important single reason for a budget system is *control*. State agencies would spend the state bankrupt in two years if there weren't an adequate means of controlling their spending. The appropriations are the first line of defense against overspending. Important second lines of defense lie in allotment systems, position controls, and controls over purchasing.

The executive budget document should be *an instrument of gubernatorial policy*. When a Governor comes into office there are certain programs and policies he [or she] would like to see accomplished during the term of office. Many of these program and policy changes cost money and the Governor will have to either raise taxes or cut expenses to pay for these changes. The people expect the Governor to show accomplishments and the budget is a major means of showing these accomplishments.

Budgeting is *public relations*. I write my budget justifications in the way I think will best gain the appropriations I need. If the budget examiner likes workload statistics, we'll snow the examiner with statistics. If a key legislator would be influenced by how the budget will affect constituents, we put that in the request.

A budget is *an instrument of good management*. Careful use of workload statistics, performance accounting, and standards of performance will tend to ensure that personnel are effectively utilized.

A budget is really *a work plan with a dollar sign attached*. As an agency official, I am committing myself to certain levels of program that I promise to attain if I receive my full budget request. When the Governor and the legislature discuss cutting my budget, I describe as accurately as I can the reduction in program level that will result.

The budget is *an instrument for planning*. A good budget system requires agency officials to project costs and program levels at least several years ahead. Such a system requires agency officials to examine the costs and benefits of alternatives to present programs in order to plan changes in programs where necessary. In short, budgeting should be an annual means for agency heads to reexamine the objectives of their programs and the effectiveness of the means used to accomplish these objectives.

Budgeting is *the art of cutting* the most fat from an agency request with the least squawking.

Source: Unpublished previously and prepared by Sydney Duncombe, 1977.

Abraham Beame said, "the budget is everything" when his city underwent its fiscal crisis during the 1970s. Mayor Beame was quite sensitive to the financial crisis of his city and the resulting policy dilemmas confronting him. Henry Maier, the former mayor of Milwaukee, once said, "The budget is the World Series of Government." This mayor in the early 1980s had to support a 20 percent increase in property taxes. Both mayors were aware that they made many—if not most—of the major political decisions when they proposed the government's budget and a legislative body (for example, the city council) adopted it.

An observer can view the budgetary process as a political event conducted in the political arena for political advantage. Politics—being a reflection of human nature—has its best and worst sides. In some instances, politicians or individuals who influence politicians merely seek money or, more often, power for themselves. In other instances, politicians seek political advantage to further some larger purpose, including aiding others selflessly. Motivations differ, but politicians seek political advantage, and that is a constant. Thus, one significant perspective on budgeting is political.

Economists

Economists view budgetary decisions with the assumptions that politicians make budget decisions within restricted financial conditions and that economic analysis can therefore help identify the best decision. Every budget decision involves potential benefits, which society or a group in society may or may not obtain; it also involves "opportunity cost" for those same people. If the government spends its available money for one program, then it does not fund another program or it funds it at a lower level. In other words, governments lose opportunities in every budget decision and there never seems to be enough money for every program. When policy makers have to make choices, economic analysis can help them evaluate the comparative benefits and costs, including opportunity cost. This view of budgeting focuses upon decision making and places a high premium upon the contribution of analysis to helping decision makers make "better" decisions.

Accountants

Accountants stress the importance of capturing accurate financial information. To accountants, the budget is the statement of desired policy, and they wish to compare information on actual expenditures with the budget to judge whether public managers followed public policy, as well as to question the wisdom of the original policy. The accountant's view largely defines how public managers understand how they should execute the budget and how some of their evaluators will judge their actions.

None of these views—the politician's, the economist's, and the accountant's—is incorrect by itself. Each perspective is valuable in getting a more comprehensive understanding of public budgeting. Interestingly, the perspective of the public manager most closely approximates that of the storyteller in the parable. Public managers must try to achieve a more comprehensive view, but they cannot fall into the trap of arrogantly believing that their view is anything more than one valid perspective among others.

A Public Manager's Perspective

Viewed from a public manager's perspective, the budget is often the principal vehicle for developing government plans and policies. There can be a separate planning process, but often such a process develops vague statements without stressing relative priorities. The budget states specific dollar amounts relative to proposed government activities in a particular time period, and these decisions reflect the government's plans and policies much more accurately than most planning documents.

The budget also represents the chief executive's legislative program. It states which programs the public managers will address, emphasize, or ignore given the limited resources available to the government. Mayors' or governors' legislative programs may be in other public statements, but their budget request to the legislative body is the comprehensive and detailed presentation of their position on what government should do for society.

There are several different ways to categorize the request for funds to finance a government, but they all outline planned functions, programs, and activities. Program and performance budgets more clearly explain the relationship of money requested and government activities. However, even line-item budgets, which focus upon what specific items the government is to purchase, provide the knowledgeable reader with detailed planned government activities.

Most budgets present the planned program for the year against a background of past experiences and future needs. A type that does not is zero-base budgeting (ZBB), but even ZBB usually cites past experience to demonstrate the type of activities government will likely fund in the planned next year. In some instances, budgets project future needs beyond the planned budget year in order to suggest the future-year implications of the budget-year decisions. In budgeting, decision makers find past and future information highly useful: the past gives them an impression of what the program can accomplish and the future gives them warning of the long-run implications of current budget-year decisions.

Strictly speaking, the budget is considered a request for funds to run the government, but some think of it as the actual policy decision of the legislature. The chief executive normally makes the request to his or her city council, legislature, or Congress. The budget also states the revenue and other sources of resources (for example, debt financing) needed to balance the suggested expenditures. Once the legislative body modifies or approves the budget, the executive branch develops the operating budget for the current year. Traditionally, actors in the budget process call the chief executive's document, which the chief executive sends to the legislature, *the budget.* In the federal government, Congress receives the budget but passes several appropriation bills that constitute the modified approved federal budget.

An Operational Definition

As the reader notices from the previous discussions, various actors in the policy-making process use the term "budget" in a variety of ways. Each may be quite correct, given the perspective of the user of the word. In public administration, the following definition is quite functional:

> A "budget" is a *plan* for the accomplishment of *programs* related to *objectives* and *goals* within a definite *time* period, including an estimate of *resources required,* together with an estimate of the *resources available,* usually compared with one or more *past periods* and *showing future requirements.*

The budget always represents what someone wishes to do or have someone else do. It is a tool to help us control our affairs. Once the government spends the money, an analyst can contrast the budget plan to the actual money spent, but at that point it no longer represents something called a budget; rather, it represents actual obligations or expenditures. Prior to that time, the budget may change its composition many times. The persons who prepare the chief executive's document that they send to the legislature usually call their document "the budget," whereas the bureaucrats who implement the legislatively approved appropriations usually call their approved current-year plan the "operating budget."

People writing budgets have programs and program accomplishments in mind. Often, those people have rather vague notions of the exact nature of each program and their desired goals and objectives. Dealing with and avoiding vagueness are two of the major challenges of public budgeting. This is particularly complicated when certain decision makers want budgets to be purposely vague to mask sensitive information in the budget or seek to advance certain political agendas through the budget. But in spite of vagueness, people preparing budgets do believe that the government will use the requested funds for some set of activities and that those activities will result in accomplishments that are worthwhile.

Budgets focus upon a specific time future period called the budget year (BY). In some instances, the year used corresponds to the calendar year, but usually a government selects an arbitrary year called the fiscal year (for example, October 1 to September 30). Policy makers plan for bureaucrats to obligate and usually to spend the budgeted money in the current year (CY). Analysts call prior years to the budget year (BY) prior or past years (PY) and call the current time period in which the government operates the current year (CY) or base year. They refer to future fiscal years beyond the budget year as budget year plus one (BY + 1), budget year plus two (BY + 2), and so on. These future fiscal years are sometimes referred to as out years. For example, let us say we are preparing the budget for the fiscal year (FY) 2010 but we are actually in FY 2009. The BY is 2010. The CY is 2009. The PY is 2008. The BY + 1 is 2011.

Analysts plan budgets for a specific future time period, and therefore they always need an estimate for the resources required during that future time period. The estimates include the revenue as well as the expenditures. Estimating is another challenge of budgeting. For the purposes of the present discussion, estimating and forecasting are used synonymously. However, estimating implies making educated guesses about future revenues or expenditures, whereas forecasting suggests a more formal and rigorous approach in the estimating process. Budget managers can never be certain that government will raise a specific dollar sum or that the government can live within its proposed expenditures. Managers can more easily control for the latter, but unexpected emergencies or problems do occur.

In order to facilitate a better understanding of the requested resources, the budget analysts usually compare the BY requests against the PY and CY actual obligations or expenditures. This provides a basis for comparing and permits the decision maker to focus on the difference or increment between the CY and the BY. This approach to budgeting is called *incremental budgeting.* In ZBB, one ignores the differences and demands that budget advocates justify the whole BY amount without consideration to previous year budget amounts. However, as this chapter will explain later in more depth, proponents of ZBB overstate this distinction between incremental and ZBB.

Increasingly, budget analysts show numbers beyond the BY, including columns in a spreadsheet for the BY + 1, BY + 2, BY + 3, BY + 4, and BY + 5. This showing of future requirements helps the decision maker realize that BY decisions have impacts beyond one budget year. A good illustration of this technique is budgeting for long-term capital projects like buildings or bridges. Typically, construction of such infrastructure will take place over a number of years, and the annual budget for BY +1 and beyond must reflect yearly budgeted costs for each phase of the construction process. Thus, a policy maker may decide that government can afford a given set of decisions for the budget year, but such a decision would not be wise because of the likely requests that agencies will make on the future budget. Unfortunately, policy makers often ignore future budget implications, which decision makers call *precedents,* causing yet another unnecessary problem in public budgeting decision making.

Budget Realities

When you examine a budget, there are many tables and charts. If you work in government, you will find that you must complete many forms in the preparation, execution, and evaluation of a budget. Although the details in the forms and tables are an essential part of budgeting, you will never completely understand a budget by examining forms and tables per se. The numbers and the formats used represent merely the means and not the ends of public budgeting.

Budgeting is a good, and usually the best, reflection of actual government public policy. Budgeting certainly is a better reflection of public policy than formal speeches or written statements made by policy makers. Politicians realize that they must get elected to hold office; thus, clarity of expression may be dysfunctional to them because clarity might make unnecessary political enemies. Also, politicians find that verbalizing policy in law is often difficult and they do so poorly. In contrast, the budget document presents the planned priorities and the programs in a meaningful way to the bureaucrats who must carry out the policy. This chapter is not saying that the budget reflects all policy, because some important policy matters have no fiscal implications. Nor is it saying that all budgets clearly present policy. But an expert can read the policy message in a budget that a bureaucracy will put into operation.

A budget focuses upon a given year (the budget year), but its preparation, execution, and evaluation take place over a period of several years (the budget cycle). Going back to the FY 2010 example, the legislature should finish the preparation and approval of the 2010 budget year just prior to the beginning of the fiscal year (October 1, 2009). In order to have an approved budget on time, the preparation and approval process must begin much earlier. Sometimes the preparation begins a full year or more before the beginning of the budgeted fiscal year. During FY 2010, the bureaucracy uses the operating budget to guide current-year obligation and expenditure decisions, but after FY 2010 the legislature cannot appropriate any more money for the year that has passed, though it can appropriate additional money for FY 2011. For some governments, the law permits open-ended expenditures to fulfill past obligations, but almost always sound practices place a zero to one year limit on when accountants can pay expenditures to fulfill obligations. The rules of accounting permit suspending the date requirement in order for accountants to close the accounts formally. The final stage in the budget cycle is auditing and evaluating the program resources obligated in the earlier current year. This can take place one to several years after the completion of the fiscal year. In other words, the FY 2010 budget cycle can start as early as 2009 and end as late as 2013.

Budgeting is highly emotional, detailed, and labor-intensive work. When policy makers decide to fund or not to fund programs, these budgets profoundly affect people, even changing their lives. Not surprisingly, budget decisions evoke strong emotions because the stakes are high and the consequences are important. Budgets are also detailed. The one cardinal sin for a budget officer is an arithmetic error because that is one mistake everyone can catch and criticize. Budgeting is persuasion; and the existence of criticism makes persuasion much more difficult for advocates to accomplish. Each number is usually important to someone. Thus, budget analysts cannot treat any mistake, especially arithmetic mistakes, lightly. However, another reality of budgets is that they are often hundreds and thousands of pages long, filled with tables. For example, the New York State Budget (Appendix) for 2001 is 550 pages long and the Budget of the United States (Agency Appendix) for 2002 totals 1,296 pages. Moreover, these appendices do *not* even constitute the entire budget documents of their respective governments. Each budget actually consists of these appendices plus hundreds of pages of other narrative as well as financial and statistical information, which in total constitute the "budget."

The preparation of this mass of information requires much work. Deadlines drive the process and require intensive 50- to 60-hour-plus workweeks, especially prior to a major deadline such as submission of material to a legislative committee. Budget analysts and policy makers find the work consuming because it requires from them almost complete devotion to the process. Participants usually find the work extremely interesting because of the interrelationship of budgeting and politics.

Students of public budgeting must use concepts developed in political science, economics, accounting, the behavioral sciences, finance, and other disciplines. Political science helps the budget person understand the political nature of government and the public policy-making process. Economics provides useful analytical tools and highly influential theories. Accounting provides the means to keep track properly of the complex array of dollars. The behavioral sciences help the budget person understand the human as a part of the budget process. Finance gives the practitioner some conceptual tools to use, especially relative to the revenue and debt aspects of budgeting. Public administration helps bring this information together and adds some concepts of its own. Students of public budgeting should draw upon a broad interdisciplinary background so that they can more easily deal with their challenging problems.

Public budgeting does require highly specialized knowledge, critical behavioral patterns, and important skills. Budget analysts can learn these lessons through experience, but an analyst can greatly facilitate the learning process through formal education. This textbook sets out the primary knowledge useful to those involved in public budgeting as well as to those wishing to better comprehend government by understanding public budgeting. However, public budgeting requires more than knowledge. To be effective, analysts should master certain important behavioral patterns that they can acquire through experience or a carefully designed learning laboratory. Also, they should develop certain skills, such as being able to translate possible policy positions into dollars and cents almost instantly in order to deal effectively in active political bargaining situations. Public budgeting is one of the most professionally challenging and often most emotionally rewarding activities in public administration.

An important public budgeting reality is that public budgeting is very big money. The 2002 federal budget outlay was over $2.2 trillion. All the levels of government expenditures in the United States make up about 35 percent of the gross national product. State and local government is also huge today. In 1929, the combined federal, state, and local expenditure was $10.4 billion. Today, even small states have budgets in that range and California's expenditures rank it—if it were a separate country—among the highest national budgets of the world. Many cities, counties, and school districts have budgets over $1 billion.

Political Realities

Policy makers decide budgets through politics, with analysis being only ammunition in the decision-making process. Sometimes the politics are crude and unethical; sometimes reason and ethical views prevail. Often the decisions involve complex, conflicting values supported by minimal analysis, but they are decisions that policy makers must make. The analyses used in public budgeting are only significant to the political actors if those actors use the analyses in their deliberations. Even when used and not ignored, the analyses are merely some of the ammunition to persuade other political actors. In some cases, an appeal, such as to the nation's pride or to an ideology, may be more significant than an elaborate technical analysis. In other situations, an analysis persuades other political actors but only if the analyst does the analysis in a timely manner.

Budgets are proposed plans. The budget presentations sometimes can make the difference for a program, but in some instances the presentation will make no difference because the program is politically weak. In other instances, the program may be so politically strong that even a bad budget presentation will not defeat the program. Often, the proposed plan or budget of the executive is a significant factor in the public decision making because the quality of the presentation communicates the likely managerial competency of the program's managers.

Political sacred cows do exist. An influential member of Congress or political executive can successfully demand a specific project or program. The appropriateness of the project or program (sometimes referred to as "pork barrel projects") is irrelevant, but the power of the political actor is very relevant. The nature of the American political system almost ensures the existence of sacred cows. Campaign promises and less desirable motivations sometimes create sacred cows, but usually the percentage of sacred cow programs and projects are relatively few in number. If sacred cows dominate the budget, then public management suffers because only highly political and time-consuming debate can stop the foolish programs or projects, and usually such action is not likely to occur in a highly political environment. In public budgeting, the professional must learn to accept the political nature of budget decision making unless the professional feels that the budget decision violates a moral principle or law.

Political causes of the day strongly influence public budgeting. The causes vary over time, but some contemporary ones include national security, energy, environment, poverty, recession, and inflation. Policy makers who decide on budgets understand the importance of political causes because their positions on those causes influence people to vote for or against them. Therefore, politicians wish to know how budgets relate to those causes so that they can appeal to the voters in the next election. Not surprisingly, agencies and chief executives often cast their budget justifications in terms of those causes. At a minimum, the agency should always prepare answers to questions involving the causes of the day, including any politically sensitive topics. For example, in a time of recession, with large numbers of people unemployed, analysts will justify a major defense project first on the basis of providing jobs and second on the basis of national security.

THE BUDGET CYCLE

The Nature of the Cycle

The **budget cycle** takes place in four phases, which can extend over several years. The first phase is *planning and analysis at the agency, bureau, or department level.* Here, analysts explore the issues and prepare the agency budget. The second phase is *policy formulation,* which involves extensive executive and legislative reviews and decisions. The third phase is *policy execution* and *reinterpretation* when the budget becomes operational. The final stage involves *audit and evaluation of the implementation.* At the beginning of the third phase, the current-year operating budget goes into effect. Prior to that date, analysts need enough time to consider the issues, conduct analyses, prepare the budget, and permit various executive and legislative groups to modify the evolving budget. After the end of the current year, accountants need time to close accounts and evaluators need to audit and evaluate the programs. This latter phase can take place in a few months, but often involves several years.

Cycles vary from one government to another and from one agency to another. If the government or agency is small, then the smaller numbers of people usually require a briefer budget cycle. In a large agency with many field units, coordination is difficult and analysts need more time to prepare the budget document. The federal budget process is particularly important because state and local governments sometimes use the federal government as a model and—more importantly—local and state governments depend on federal transfer payments, such as revenue sharing and grant programs. If the federal government delays making its budget decision, many other groups are affected.

One confusing reality of public budgeting is that the budget person and agency must operate with overlapping budget cycles. On the same day, a federal budget person may have to review the evaluations covering last year's program, prepare readjustments covering the current year's operating budget, and answer congressional questions on the budget year covering the next fiscal year. The agency decision makers and budget analysts find this situation confusing. Not surprisingly, people working in budgeting learn to refer to their work by specific fiscal years to minimize their confusion.

Budget Phases

Planning and Analysis.   Planning-programming-budgeting (PPB) popularized an expanded planning and analysis phase in the 1960s, but the phase was not original to PPB reforms. The New York Bureau of Municipal Research encouraged planning and analysis at the beginning of the twentieth century. Almost all budget preparation involves some analysis, but budget reformers greatly expanded the amount and sophistication of analysis in this phase during the PPB reform era and the current phase that stresses budget accountability. Planning and analysis can take many forms, but the disciplines of economics, operations research, and systems analysis developed most of the techniques. They include modeling, sensitivity analysis, and survey research, but this text does not discuss them because they are not commonly associated with budgeting. This textbook does introduce other techniques, such as forecasting and cost-benefit, cost-effectiveness, and marginal utility analyses (see Chapter 5).

The planning and analysis phase takes place at the beginning of the budget cycle, but analysis does occur at other periods in the cycle. In the policy formulation stage, time is a key factor so there is not the luxury of being able to prepare elaborate analyses. Analysts only have time for quick original analysis or reapplication of earlier analyses during this phase. There is little analysis, except for forecasting, done in the policy execution phase. However, governments do a great deal of analysis in the audit and evaluation phase. The techniques, analytical problems, and focus of analysis change somewhat as each budget phase occurs.

Policy Formulation.   In the policy formulation process, analysts develop the budget, and policy makers adapt and change it. The budget defines who gets what moneys, thus providing meaningful guidance to government agencies. Based on the chief executive's budget office guidance, the agency budget office prepares its recommended budget, which it sends to the department budget office for its review. The department head makes his or her decision on the entire department budget, and then the agency budget office adjusts its requests in terms of the department head's decisions. Next, both the department and agency budget office advocate their budget to the government's chief executive and eventually to the legislative policy makers. The agency's clientele group, elements in the legislative branch, and the highest levels of the executive branch may support the agency's budget or aspects of that budget. But regardless, the agency is the advocate of its budget through the whole process. The reviewers and modifiers of the budget include the department, the chief executive and his or her staff, and the legislature. As noted in Chapter 4, a variety of conflicting influences converge and shape the budget from various levels in the executive branch, the legislature, clientele groups, the media, and even sometimes the judiciary branch.

The federal process especially is elaborate, but it does illustrate the steps in the policy formulation process. Prior to this phase, the agency must submit a quarterly program financial plan, which gives budget reviewers initial indications of likely fund requests five years beyond the budget year. At the beginning of the phase, the central executive branch budget office (for example, the U.S. Office of Management and Budget) issues guidelines to the federal departments and agencies for the development of the new budget. Then the various agencies issue their budget calls to agency personnel in order to compile the necessary information for the budget. The agency uses this information to prepare its budget.

The remaining portion of the policy formulation phase involves budget reviews and eventually decisions on the budget. The agency submits the budget to the department budget office. The format can vary in style from a line-item to a program budget to decision packages. The department budget office and the highest officials review the budget and decide upon the department's recommended budget. The agency makes the necessary changes, and the agency submits through the department the revised budget to the Office of Management and Budget. Acting for the president, the OMB recommends revised and final budget decisions. The president makes his or her decisions, resulting eventually in an approved budget. Some presidents permit a department to appeal an OMB recommendation, but usually the OMB recommendation is very influential. Under federal law, the president submits a *current services budget,* which is a version of incremental budgeting, to Congress with the president's budget. According to law, Congress should review the submission and pass appropriate bills prior to the beginning of the new fiscal year.

Policy Execution. In the policy execution phase, the budget—in the form of an appropriation bill—gives policy guidance to bureaucrats. This phase takes place during the current year, and government managers must make all of their obligations in this year in order for accountants to correctly attribute them to that year. The executive branch can sometimes change earlier decided budget policy during this phase by not spending the planned resources or by shifting funds from one activity to another. As a general practice, the latter does not occur on significant policy matters. If it did occur without legislative approval, then the legislature would consider those government units not acting accountably, meaning the agency would be inconsistent with legislative policy. At the worst, such behavior is illegal and can result in the legislature punishing the agency through its appropriations or other decisions. An *impoundment* is the executive decision not to spend appropriated funds. The nonspending can take the form of a delay in spending in the intended budget year or of a recession from the budget. On the state level, some executives have the power of line-item vetoes or impoundment, depending on the state constitution.

At the agency and department level, managers use the allotment to control the rate of obligation and disbursement of resources. An *allotment* is a control mechanism in the budget process used at the department and agency level to meter the rate of obligation or spending, especially on programs or budget line items that lower-level administrators within the agency can easily exhaust in an untimely manner before the end of the current year. This power assures that the agency should control the rate of obligation and spending of its funds for proper economic and managerial purposes. With the greater emphasis upon macroeconomics, the federal government carefully controls the rates of both obligation and disbursement. Sometimes, presidents use the allotment power for political purposes, such as ensuring maximum and timely obligations on key programs at the correct moment in a political campaign. Agency political appointees can abuse the allotment power by treating it like an illegal impoundment, but no one has raised it publicly as an abuse of power yet. Usually, agency leadership uses allotments entirely for economic and managerial purposes.

Legislatures phrase *authorizations* and *appropriations* in technical budget language, which agencies often find significant. The normal appropriation is for the budget year only, but the language need not be so limiting. For example, the appropriations may be *open ended*, thus permitting the agency to obligate the funds in subsequent fiscal years if an agency does not obligate the money entirely in the current year. Other technical devices are *contract* and *bond authority*. The Congress can also place special conditions on appropriations. For example, the appropriation can read, "$150 million is appropriated under section 204 of XYZ legislation but none of this money can be used to build a flag pole in front of the Bureau of Standards building nor can any money be spent on the ABC project." Often the legislature does not include such detailed conditions in its appropriation language, but instead legislative leaders include such conditions in nonlegally binding reports, which accompany the appropriation bill. Agencies are very sensitive to such requests, and usually they will comply with those directions unless some very unusual circumstance exists. In order to negate yearly contract authority permitted under law, appropriations committees sometimes say that an agency can obligate no more than a specific amount during a given fiscal year.

Federal and state policy makers find the use of the authorization and appropriation distinction extremely useful, given the complex budget decisions that they make. Often local governments do not make the authorization and appropriation distinction because a two-stage process is not as useful to them. There are normally fewer city councilors or county supervisors, so they do not need a more elaborate two-stage process to coordinate their decision making and assure accountability.

Once the department makes the allotment, the agency prepares its current-year operating budget. Normally, the operating budget is not the desired sophisticated managerial tool, which has proper linkages to accounting, management-by-objectives (MBO), progress reporting, and program evaluation. Ideally, the agency's operating budget should inform the agency's units how much and at what rate they can obligate and disburse moneys for resources. If tied to MBO, the operating budget reflects the decisions made in the MBO process. Agency management should use a classification scheme to record unit management progress and account for actual obligations and disbursement. This practice permits upper agency management to verify that the lower-level units executed the budget and MBO policy decisions of the agency. Also, program evaluators can do their work only if the agency leadership clearly states the desired program outcomes and outputs (as noted in Chapters 5 and 6) and necessary cooperation exists among the evaluators, managers, and budget persons.

Audit and Evaluation.   The final phase takes place after the current year is complete. Auditors and program evaluators should start some of their audit and evaluation work much earlier than this phase of the cycle, but the focus of their work is the preparation of their final reports, which takes place in this final phase. Groups including the agency, the department, the central audit office of government, and the legislature (using its oversight function) should conduct the audit and evaluation activities. Audits often check if the agency records its transactions properly and obligates its resources legally. Increasingly, auditors, especially at GAO and state audit offices, expand audits to include program and performance evaluation. However, separate audit units at the agency and department level often do such evaluations in order to avoid later problems with auditors and evaluators. Legislative bodies conduct oversight hearings and investigations, which can be program and performance evaluations but usually are merely a process to collect opinions on a topic.

Laws are sometimes quite specific in requiring audits and performance evaluations. States have audit agencies, and states require auditing in and of local governments. States often require a local government to conduct audits, and then the local government must submit its annual audit to the state. The state audit office then examines the local audit and conducts further investigations as needed, which sometimes results in criminal prosecutions. States sometimes have legislative review commissions, which conduct performance evaluations. Often, accountants, who lack training in program and performance evaluation, staff audit agencies. However, audit agencies increasingly hire students with masters in public administration to do evaluation, and they are starting to train their accounting staff to evaluate public programs. In the federal government, the requirement of many programs to have set aside money for program evaluation causes a great use of program evaluation.

Local Government Budget Cycles

There are some differences among federal, state, and local government budget cycles. For example, revenue estimation is very important in local and state government, particularly in the planning and analysis phase because elected leaders must balance their budgets. At the state and city level, finance or central budget offices usually do the estimating of the major revenues. Budget formulation practices vary in local government, but often there is a small central budget staff. In small governments, procedures can be more informal, but sometimes state law or local charters require very formal practices such as elaborate public hearings. After receiving input from the city agencies and guidance from the city manager or mayor, a central budget office prepares the city budget. The chief city executive sometimes serves as the person who resolves outstanding issues, acting like an appeals court. The exact budget procedure used depends upon each local government, with some having the agency heads reporting directly to the city council or county elected board of supervisors.

Local governments vary greatly in how they review and decide their budget. Usually, budgets are detailed line-item documents that part-time nonexpert board members review and approve in a short time. Not surprisingly, elected local board and council members find budgets confusing and frustrating. When reviewing budgets, elected board members usually focus their attention upon small items in the budget that they can easily understand or they look for their pet projects that are politically important to them. They rarely conduct a comprehensive review of the submitted budget. Because state law requires them, local governments conduct public hearings in connection with the legislative deliberations on their budgets.

Once the local legislative body approves the budget, the focus of the central budget office turns to control. In some local governments, the city council or county board of supervisors must approve almost any change in the approved line item. In other local governments, the city manager and sometimes even department heads, especially if the people also elect them, can make large changes without local legislative prior approval.

CONTEXT OF AMERICAN BUDGETING

Ideology

Ideas are powerful, especially when shared by many people, because they guide behavior. We predicate the very notion of what is a "good" or "bad" activity or action on our shared ideas. Thus, ideas place **value** on people, things, activities, and even on other ideas. Sometimes ideas are logically consistent or nearly consistent, forming complete belief systems that many people share. This sharing guides entire civilizations. We call these belief systems *ideologies,* and every culture has them.

In the United States, two important ideologies—democracy and capitalism—influence the conduct of public budgeting. Other belief systems and subsystems are important, but are not central to this simplified sketch. "Democracy" is a term that can have many meanings, as illustrated by the use of the word in American and many communist societies. In the United States, democracy evolved largely from English roots in the context of a colonial reaction against the economic mercantilism policies of England. The result was a democracy at the beginning of the republic that stressed limited representational government that respected the rights of political minorities. In the premachine age and agriculture-oriented colonies, the culture considered certain rights, such as freedom of the press, so essential they built them into the new nation's Constitution. The founding fathers viewed those rights as means to prevent tyranny and permit the peaceful evolution of a government. In over two hundred years, the definition of *voter,* a key concept of democracy, extended from almost all white male adult landholders to any eighteen-year-old and older citizen of either sex and of any racial background.

James Madison's Federalist Paper Number 10 of the 1780s largely explains the American democratic system of government. Whether individuals and groups acted out their political wishes for altruistic or selfish motivations, they soon learned that acting in groups and directing their political efforts at partisans in the political process maximized their influence on government. Partisans interact and adjust policy based on relative strengths of lobbying forces and the appeal of the varying influential but shifting ideologies. The success of policy for any given moment may be due to economic interests but often even that interest rests on the strength of shared and effectively argued belief systems.

In America, the meaning of *democracy* rested on the notions of partisan bargaining, minority and fundamental human rights, diffusion of power, and the influence of partisans through collective action over time. Public budgeting is a means and thus it reflects the ideological culture of which it is a part. For example, in the United States, a system of diffused political power makes budget decisions through an often-difficult partisan bargaining process, especially when the partisans only consider their perspective rather than that of the nation as a whole. Partisans make decisions and then attempt to influence each other by a process called *lobbying.* An illustration is a public agency clientele group (that is, those affected directly by the agency's activities) that can and does lobby the legislature and the executive. Thus, a complex mixture of influences from the executive, legislature, and clientele guide and largely determine an agency's actions. Usually, the most significant means to achieve influence on an agency is the policy document called the *budget*.

In America, one can see the influence of the concept called *democracy* in the budget process. Examples include public hearings, freedom of information, and "sunshine" laws and regulations, as they are manifestations of minority and fundamental human rights acquired from an earlier time. These seriously taken requirements open discussion of budget details to the media and the interested public. The American system of government, which political scientists call a *presidential system* to contrast it with *parliamentary* democracy, requires some degree of cooperation between executive and legislative leadership in order to achieve the necessary policy mandates as prescribed in fundamental documents like the *Constitution*. In other words, the leadership of the country needs to act with some degree of oneness of the country in mind if it is to make policy for the country. The belief system called *democracy* does greatly influence the way Americans and many other peoples go about making their public budget decisions.

The second major American ideology is *capitalism,* which has complementary roots to nineteenth-century democracy. Just as the American Revolution was a reaction against mercantilist policies, capitalism arose in opposition to the same early economic policy. Interestingly, in 1776, the Second Continental Congress published the U.S. Declaration of Independence and Adam Smith wrote *The Wealth of Nations*. Most economists consider the latter the best explanation of capitalism. Americans warmly embraced both views and they still greatly influence America today, including how it goes about making budget decisions.

Extreme capitalism reached its zenith in the late nineteenth century when Social Darwinism of the late 1880s reinforced it. Capitalism seeks to limit the role of government in the economic activities of society. Under capitalist ideology, there is a role for government in society, but capitalism limits the role to "public goods" like national defense. However, under capitalism the policy makers can extend the role of government to include the following:

- coping with public allocations for the general good, like public education and pollution control; and
- avoiding inconvenient private monopolies on such things as highways, bridges, and water systems.

When twentieth-century liberals and socialists argued for the redistribution of wealth, advocates of capitalism raised severe protest to the use of government control to achieve those ends. More extreme capitalists even argued against government being used to achieve economic stabilization and growth.

From the 1890s to the present, contrary economic (and related political) belief systems arose. One advocated a predominantly guiding role for government over society. Another argued for total governmental control over society. The *progressive* political movement, which argued for a guiding role, felt that government should intervene in the social and economic conditions in society in order to ensure that society met its national concerns. Progressives, who were quite successful politically, had many accomplishments, including child labor laws, the income tax, the Federal Reserve System, social security, a national park system, and other landmark legislation that defines the current American public policy.

Communists and some *Socialists* advocated a total role for government in society. They felt that government, which the working class rather than the capitalist elite should control, should run the society and curb economic abuses on the working class. The most visionary advocates of this belief system expected that a classless society would eventually evolve and eliminate the need for government to act as the people's trustee. In over one-third of the world's population, that belief system dominates today. In the United States, the socialist belief system challenged the social conscience of the nation.

However, that belief system only influenced but did not direct the passage of many progressive reforms such as the reduced workweek and worker safety requirements. After 1932, the Progressives and many of the less radical American Socialists merged politically into the twentieth-century liberal movement, which stressed economic as well as political equality. They played an active and successful role in advocacy of consumerism, the protection of the environment, the fight for equal opportunity, and the implementation of workplace and product safety.

In the United States, the current internal major political battles focusing on the correct mix of the public and private sectors continues to be the major issue dividing partisans. For purposes of public budgeting, the important point to understand is that partisans take this ongoing ideological debate very seriously and the partisan nature of the dispute affects the budgeting process itself. The very size and scope of government is at issue; thus, the question of "what the government should budget" is also at issue. Attitudes about how government can and should influence the overall national or regional economy are critical to how government conducts its budgeting process. For example, stressing economy, efficiency, and productivity arises out of capitalism and its economic doctrines. The use of enterprise funds and government corporations also evolved from the ideological debate. A later unit in this chapter will discuss current economic thinking and its influence on budgeting.

Federalism

The United States is a federated government and budgeting differs on each level. The scope, size, and different nature of programs lead to the differences in budgeting. However, in public budgeting, the similarities are more striking than the dissimilarities. At the national level, especially when liberals control the government, budget decision makers focus greater effort on expenditure as opposed to revenue decisions. They see taxes as important, but stress control, management, and planning expenditures. They actively debate the state of the economy and the role of the budget in stimulating the economy as they see their role as very significant in shaping both presidential and congressional budgets. They consider the revenue side of the budget in terms of its influence on the economy. Until recently, the typical agency budget officer did not consider the revenue aspects of the budget. The highest levels in OMB and Congress addressed macroeconomic concerns such as the impact of proposed expenditures. Some of them have a strong desire to improve the analysis associated with public budgeting, including enhancing government productivity.

The national government manages many of its programs in cooperation with state and local governments, but the nature of that cooperation varies sometimes because of ideology. The political center and right tend to favor less federal control over shared programs than does the political left. Sometimes, federal government interacts directly with citizens, as in the case with veteran programs. Traditionally, state and local governments wish minimum federal guidance in managing their programs and oppose categorical and block grants that have many federal controls on them. Revenue-sharing programs have few federal control strings attached to them. In any event, state and local governments must still budget for federal funds they receive. The sharing of revenue between levels of government results to some extent with intergovernmental government programs, with local governments providing the actual day-to-day service to the public.

State governments have a great deal of power over local governments. For example, unlike the federal government, state governments mandate that local governments balance their budgets. Although local governments sometimes do not meet legal requirements, these requirements are influential to local governments. States commonly focus their efforts upon highways and education, with increasing interest being addressed to health, environmental control, and welfare. Like the federal government, state governments often provide direct assistance to local governments and often act as pass-through agents for the federal government. Unlike the federal government, state governments can directly control local governments. For example, state laws often mandate many local budgeting requirements such as public hearings.

The form of local government varies from large cities to small villages and townships. Each unit of government has a budget process, which concerns balancing revenue and expenditure. Local governments provide direct services, including public safety, education, and sanitation. Many local government activities·require large expenditures for capital items like schools and roads; thus, debt administration is an important aspect of local government. Transfer payments, in the form of grants and revenue sharing, are an important source of revenue for many local governments.

The complex overlapping jurisdictions, economies of scale, and the growth of suburban areas and decline of cities are important to local government budgeting. The overlapping of jurisdictions means that tax collection is more complex and coordination of services is difficult. The advantage of *economy of scale* is limited when we prefer smaller governments unless they can join together with other governments in cooperative arrangements. The increased population of suburban areas strains the expertise and capability of the suburban governments to cope with their challenge. For example, they must develop budgeting expertise, while dealing with massive program growth. The declining tax base for larger central cities places extreme pressure on their budgets. Each problem is significant and helps explain the challenge of local budgeting.

Decision-Making Models

Public budgeting is a government decision-making process. Not surprisingly, several models, which originated from political philosophy theories, explain how we *should* make public policy decisions. Reformers of the budget process take these theories or conceptual models seriously. Therefore, we must understand these theories and models in order to comprehend contemporary budgeting and public budgeting reforms. A *conceptual model* is a tool that enables the user to understand and deal with complex phenomena. We judge a tool as "good" or "bad" in terms of the user's purpose. A hammer, for example, may be a good tool for building a shed, but it is a bad tool for chopping wood. Professionals should judge conceptual tools or theories in terms of the model's usefulness in helping them accomplish their tasks. Ideologies, which dominate a culture, induce a logical paradigm within which decision makers must accomplish their tasks and thus help define what is "good" and "bad."

Ideology, the moral and spiritual approach we collectively take in making life's decisions, and the workability of ideas, largely define the environment of decision makers. The American democratic and economic ideology helps define the environment decision makers use. For example, consensus and partisan adjustment are part of the democratic ideology and that in turn explains the political context in which public budgeting operates. Our approach to morals and spirituality also influences the manner in which we make budget decisions. Thus, if decision makers allow their own ego, emotional drama, and pride to dominate their character, then they debase the human context in which policy makers decide budgets. The timely workability of ideas in an analysis of a policy problem is often a significant factor. Policy makers and managers often find themselves in situations where they must make decisions because even a so-called nondecision is an *authoritative allocation of resources* in budgeting. If the data or analyses are not available, then the decision maker must make do with conventional wisdom, personal biased judgment, or contemporary political ideology. Thus the "doable" or practical—even in terms of performing policy analysis—is significant in terms of what policy makers select as their decisions.

Professionals can judge decision-making models in terms of their applicability to their decision-making environment. If the model is not in harmony with their environment, then the model is "bad," meaning the model is not appropriate to that particular user's situation or purposes. However, that same model might be quite appropriate to another person in his or her time and circumstances. Thus, what might be good budgeting practice in America might be bad budgeting in another country or be bad budgeting at a different time in America.

Although several models exist, this chapter cites only two decision-making models because the incremental change model and the ideal-rational model are the two commonly used in budgeting. We should associate the incremental model with the democratic theory that heavily influenced the creation of the American republic. With firm roots in nineteenth-century conservative thought such as that of Edmund Burke in England, the incremental model accepts that major public policy change should be slow and done in incremental steps. It asserts that no decision maker or set of decision makers can understand the full extent of the implications of major policy changes. According to the incremental model, political forces mutually should adjust their positions and, over time, change public policy. This inherently conservative approach means that the political system bias is against radical, innovative change. The incremental model was embraced and defended by Aaron Wildavsky, who argued that budgets are the cumulative product of past political decisions as reflected in the current year budgets of governments.

An example of this approach follows. At the national level, an agency develops a budget, advocates it to its department, the president's Office of Management and

Budget, and Congress. In the budget approval process, the agency takes the role of advocate; the reviewer (for example, the Office of Management and Budget) questions the wisdom of the proposal. After the reviewer decides, the process continues with other subsequent actors in the review process sometimes calling into question the earlier reviewer's decisions. This process is consistent with the incremental change model in that policies usually mutually and slowly adjust over years because someone advocates and someone accommodates.

The incremental change model helps the professional understand the political environment of public policy making, but it is not useful in understanding technical and analytical decision-making tools that are commonly and currently employed in more sophisticated budget environments. In the political environment that this textbook discusses in more depth in Chapter 4, strategies and conflicts arise among the participants (clientele groups, agencies, departments, the central executive budget office, and the legislature). Definable strategies exist that require such ploys as cultivating an active clientele group, the development of confidence in the professional competency of the agency, and skill in tactics that exploit temporary opportunities. Technical policy analyses are not central to the incremental approach except to the extent that they might strengthen a political argument in the partisan accommodation process. From the perspective of the incremental change model, program and budget analyses must be timely, accommodate the seizing of political opportunities, and be comprehensible to those who must use the analysis in partisan bargaining situations.

In the twentieth century, reformers of the budget process usually predicate their arguments using the rational model, which reformers often base on the utilitarian thinkers such as Jeremy Bentham, John Mills, and John Stuart Mills. This modernistic model systematically breaks decision making down into six phases:

- establish a complete set of operational goals, with decision makers allocating relative weights to different goals that they wish to achieve;
- establish a complete inventory of other values and resources using those relative weights;
- prepare a complete set of alternative policies open to the policy makers;
- prepare a complete set of valid predictions of the cost and benefits of each alternative, including the extent to which each alternative will achieve the various operational goals, consume resources, and realize or impair other values;
- calculate the net expectations for each alternative by multiplying the probability of each benefit and cost for each alternative by the utility of each, and calculate the net benefit (or cost) in utility units; and
- compare the net expectations and identify the alternative (or alternatives, if two or more are equally good) with the highest net expectations.

In fewer words, using the rational model calls for decision makers to define their goals, analyzing their alternatives and selecting the alternative that best meets their goals. This approach shifted the very understanding of the concept of *value* to mean worth defined only in terms of satisfying individual or group interests. Thus, the Greek concept of *value* in terms of character or worth to the community disappeared.

The rational model helps us understand the heart of most twentieth-century budget reform and the technical difficulties of analyses. Much of the history of budget reform involves various alphabetical reform efforts such as PPB and ZZB, which

Chapter 3 discusses. In all cases, the desire was to improve the policy decision-making situation because the reformers assumed key leaders such as the president or city manager could implement the rational model of decision making. They disagreed with the nineteenth-century conservative belief in *incrementalism* and thought that rational decision making would achieve better public policy. As a result of this belief, social scientists developed many analytical techniques, and Chapter 5 discusses many of the ones especially important to budgeting.

The problems with the ideal-rational model are that it (1) requires you to assume the infinite is finite, (2) does not use feedback information and evaluation techniques, and (3) often improperly lets you assume that you can use ratio scales in analysis. The model asks us to think that the task of making endless calculations, defining endless alternatives, and performing endless analyses can exist and a policy maker can do each of those tasks in a timely manner. Thus, those working with the model often try to amend their model by using parameters such as adopting the best solution within a given time frame. Herbert Simon's so-called *satisficing model,* which this chapter explains later, is a good illustration of that. Another problem is the model does not recognize the usefulness of feedback and evaluation. Thus, another common variation to the rational model is to add to the rational model evaluation including research design as noted in Chapter 6. A third problem, which involves mathematics, is using the wrong quantifiable value because of the improper technical use of a ratio scale in calculations.

Herbert Simon's *satisficing model* calls on a decision maker to use the rational model of decision making with key changes. First, the decision maker defines his or her set of alternatives in terms of established limitations such as time and money. Second, the first acceptable alternative that the decision maker finds within the established limits is the one selected. We commonly make hiring decisions using this method of decision making. This model has much to do with the Nobel committee's decision to award Simon the *Nobel Prize in economics* as his model is a major alternative to the traditional economic assumption of the rational actor. In addition, his model has had significant influence on the development of computer software especially in terms of so-called *artificial intelligence* (AI).

Although there may not always be analytical solutions to problems, policy makers find analytical techniques helpful in many situations, and sometimes even a weak analysis can be better than doing nothing analytically. However, in spite of the attempts to improve rational analyses, there are barriers to its usefulness. For example, the technical skill levels in organizations are often low, and decision makers are either not able to use the analytical techniques, or worse they use those techniques incorrectly, thus lowering the quality of public policy making.

Neither the incremental nor the rational decision-making model is adequate for all situations. The incremental change model is powerful because it helps the professional understand the role of program and budget analysis in the budget-making process. Although significant, the incremental model often cannot help policy makers when a technical analysis can point the decision makers toward better decisions. The rational model gives the professional a remarkable set of tools that can help policy makers in important situations. However, it can also lead to false and naïve expectations because the model ignores the political context and even demands the impossible in terms of analysis. This model encourages some individuals in the budget process to neglect timeliness, seek needlessly expensive data, search endlessly for alternatives, and quest for clarity in objectives that will not be forthcoming. The rational model can be useful, and the professional should learn its related analytical techniques but not without a full understanding of its limitations.

The Influence of Technology

Reformers of twentieth-century public budgeting created a budget process that maximized executive command and control. Policy makers made those reforms when

- society evolved slower than now,
- manufacturing was the engine that created most new jobs,
- large corporations and large governments used hierarchy to control and direct their organizations,
- mass markets were the key to economic success, and
- strong family units were the dominant groups in the population.

In the early years of the twenty-first century, society feels almost the polar opposite conditions. We live in a time of:

- breathtaking change,
- service and knowledge industries that create the new jobs,
- organizations using networks and webs to define their structures,
- markets that are global but also with market niches often being critically important to making profit in the private sector, and
- socially more isolated communities with fragmented family units.

Information technology changed society. As late as 1970, Alvin Toffler said in *Future Shock* that the computer was the driving force for change in our new society. John Naisbitt, who wrote *Megatrends* in 1982, called attention to the remarkable shifts occurring in society due to the rapid evolution of the computer and related software, which made using information in daily work activities radically different. The very nature of how we can and do accomplish our work tasks shifted dramatically. Information dependence means that organizations now work better if webs rather than hierarchies connect their units together. In 1983, Robert B. Reich, who wrote *The Next American Frontier,* stressed that we needed to alter the older outdated management methods to suit our new realities. In the 1992 *Work of Nations,* Reich argued that the new information made those skilled in resolving problems, problem-identification, and strategic brokering critical to society. Organizations, especially large ones, have little choice but to become information based if they are to find themselves competitive or reasonably productive.

Rapidly evolving information technology combined with competition on a world scale made the shift possible and even forced the shift to occur. We simply must evolve rapidly to information-based organizations with the consequence of not only flatter organizational structures but also fundamental changes in the way we do work in organizations. To be successful, the evolution cannot involve small changes but rather must involve radical redesigns of all processes, including public budgeting. As the complexities of society grow, the need for a flexible, adaptive, and responsible government increases. Words from Thomas Jefferson on his monument in Washington, DC, tell us, "As new discoveries are made, new truths discovered, and manner and opinions change, institutions must advance also to keep pace with the times." Now, we must reengineer our systems, controls, and general mentality, which were the products of the reforms of one hundred years ago.

Over time, fundamental factors such as technologies shape our ideas. For example, the industrial revolution, with its mass production made possible by the machine age, shaped the twentieth century with its drive for political centralization. The machine age made mass production possible and oriented the entire economy and political system away from the earlier agricultural society.

In contrast, the information age has shaped the twenty-first century toward a globally interdependent and decentralized political and managerial system. The information age—with its impact on the storage, movement, and analysis of data—means that humans share vast amounts of information, and this sharing encourages us to adopt remarkably faster technologically induced changes into society. The machine age encouraged command and control centralized societies with public budget systems designed to work rationally. The information age encourages entrepreneurial decentralized but globally interdependent societies with public budget systems designed to achieve coordination and with program productivity that stresses effectiveness.

ECONOMIC INFLUENCES ON BUDGETING

Twin Evils

As noted earlier in this chapter, capitalism, with progressive and socialist modifications, provides the ideological economic climate for the United States. The dispute between capitalism and socialism centers on the role of government in society and thus on the appropriateness of what policy makers should include in their public budget. Today, there is a belief that government can make a difference in the overall economy, but disagreement exists on the question of what government should and should not do to help the economy achieve the desired condition of minimum unemployment with minimum inflation.

The agreed-upon twin economic evils are *severe unemployment* (mild unemployment is called a **recession** and a severe recession is called a **depression**) and a *sustained increase in price without an equal increase in value* (a mild increase is called **inflation** and a radical increase is called **hyperinflation**). Both result in significant hardships for the people of the world. Unemployment means that many people who want jobs cannot find them. Usually, during a recession, the economy does not grow or grows very slowly; as a result, families do not receive adequate money for a decent existence. Inflation often means that people can buy fewer goods and services with the same amount of money. Inflation especially hurts people on fixed incomes or slow-rising incomes.

The principal macroeconomic goals are as follows:

- *Full employment:* Practically, this means about a 4 percent unemployment rate in the United States. At this rate, there are about as many people looking for jobs as there are jobs available.
- *Maintenance of price stability:* Inflation increases prices. This brings a shift in the distribution of real income from those whose dollar incomes are relatively inflexible to those whose dollar incomes are relatively flexible. Thus, inflation hurts those on fixed incomes, such as the elderly.
- *Steady constant economic growth:* As the population increases, maintaining or improving the past standard of living is only possible with economic growth.
- *An adequate supply of collectively consumed goods:* Some activities are public in nature and involve services for the good of the society. These include police protection, national defense, highways, schools, and so on.

Exhibit 2–2 shows the U.S. employment rates from 1929 to 2001. The reader can easily understand why historians call the 1930s "the Great Depression" since economists consider more than 4 to 5 percent unemployment as unacceptable and the unemployment rate in that era reached a high of 24.9 percent.

EXHIBIT 2–2   Unemployment Rates for Selected Years 1929–2001 (% of Civilian Workforce)

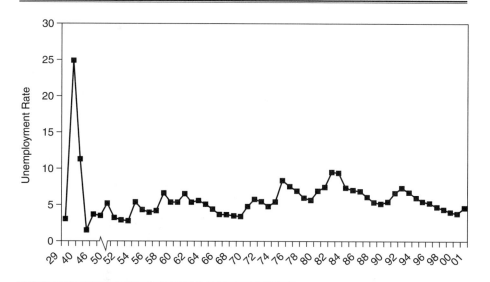

Source: U.S. Department of Labor, *Economic Report of the President,* U.S. Department of Commerce, *Statistical Abstract of the United States.* Washington, DC: Bureau of the Census 2001. Bureau of Labor Statistics, U.S. Department of Labor, *Selected Unemployment Indicators.* Washington, DC, 2002.

Some inflation is common, but the rate of inflation can rise to hyperinflation levels. Prices can rise so fast that no one can receive or hold money. In Germany in 1923, the rate of hyperinflation was so high that paper currency became almost worthless and the people used it as wallpaper; barter reasserted itself as the principal method of trade. However, in a higher civilization, people cannot sustain themselves under a barter economy and their standard of living falls. Hyperinflation occurs when a government enormously expands the money supply to finance large-scale expenditures. Mild inflation exists for reasons that this chapter will discuss later.

Throughout modern society, recession and inflation have occurred in a fairly well-defined cycle except for the late 1990s. Contemporary economic theory addresses these twin problems by asking how they occur and what we can do to avoid them. In the last half of the twentieth century, the economic theories that address those evils are monetary and fiscal policy, with supply side economics being added in the last quarter of the century. All involve public budgeting.

Exhibit 2–3 is a Phillips curve, which helps describe the relationship between the unemployment rate and the rate of inflation. Note that there is an inverse relationship. In the exhibit, as unemployment goes down, inflation goes up. Also note the odd locations of the points for 1970 and 1971, which reflect a different pattern than those for the 1960s.

EXHIBIT 2–3   The Phillips Curve

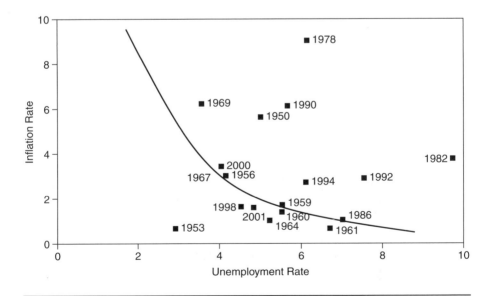

Source: Lloyd G. Reynolds. *Economics,* 4th ed. Homewood, IL: Richard D. Irwin, 1973, p.174. With updated unemployment rates. Used by permission.

Influence of Economics

When Franklin D. Roosevelt became president of the United States, the country was in the Great Depression. He advocated and the Congress strongly agreed that action was necessary and that policy leaders needed to create jobs. Economic theory did not motivate or influence FDR, but the large number of unemployed people, as cited in Exhibit 2–2, did influence him. The Great Depression was a political turning point for the United States. Before that time, social and economic thinking called for minimum or *laissez faire* government. Prior to 1929, Adam Smith, Herbert Spencer, and Charles Darwin highly influenced policy makers. They felt that the least government was the best government. Nature and business should define its own course without government interference because an invisible force guided and enabled society to evolve into a higher, improved state. In 1933, the unemployment rate was 24.9 percent of the potentially working population. This was not an improved state. Thus, the Great Depression challenged the core belief of capitalism, and the political process experienced a harsh awakening. Voters and many intellectual leaders decided the capitalist economic theory was wrong.

The idea that policy makers could and should use government to address the Depression gained widespread approval, and government became the accepted positive instrument to guide society. No longer was *the least government the best government*. FDR launched massive "New Deal" public works programs; and ironically, today, most economists agree that although his programs were very bold for his times, they were not bold enough. The government spending for World War II is what got the United States and the world out of the Depression. The New Deal programs convinced many Americans that a strong, active federal government was "a good thing" and shifted the economic ideology of the nation. In addition, World War II and the subsequent Cold War convinced even more Americans that the United States must remain a strong military power. Thus, since 1929, these economic and international realities altered the public's view of the role of government in American society.

In the mid-1960s and 1970s, fiscal economic theory (also called Keynesian economics) directed some of our most significant government decisions. A new and somewhat revised set of government units arose as the institutional means to consider and implement fiscal policy. Especially at the national level, fiscal theory became the context in which policy makers made their major decisions. Those units included the Council of Economic Advisors, the Office of Management and Budget (OMB), and the Department of the Treasury. Each helps consider economic policy, but under fiscal policy once the Congress and the president decide on the budget, the OMB is the major institution of fiscal policy in the executive branch. In the legislative branch, the Congressional Budget Office (CBO), the Joint Economic Committee, the House and Senate Budget and Appropriations Committees, the House Ways and Means Committee, and the Senate Finance Committee all play important roles. The CBO and the budget committees are particularly important in setting overall fiscal policy. Partly independent of both Congress and the president, the Federal Reserve System largely establishes the nation's monetary policy. The detailed workings of each group are beyond the scope of this text, and readers are encouraged to take economics courses to pursue those subjects.

MONETARY POLICY

Central Bank

The Federal Reserve System (FED), which is the central bank for the United States, controls the economy's supply of money and credit. This supply in turn affects unemployment and inflation. The Federal Reserve tries to expand money and credit to foster greater employment and to contract money and credit to combat inflation. The FED influences member banks, and they in turn influence business and the public. Because banks must maintain a reserve-to-loan ratio established by the FED and borrow money from the Federal Reserve System banks, they can influence the nation's money supply. The three main Federal Reserve tools are as follows:

1. open-market operations,
2. discount-rate policy, and
3. changes in the legal reserve requirement of the member banks.

Two other less significant tools are (4) moral suasion and (5) selective controls over margin requirements for loans made to buy stocks.

The Federal Reserve's most frequently used tool is *open-market operations.* The Federal Reserve's Open Market Committee frequently meets to decide to buy or sell government bonds or bills. Selling results in tightening the *money supply,* and buying results in expanding it. For example, selling $10 million in government bonds depresses the overall money supply. The buyers of the bonds will draw checks at a member bank, and the Federal Reserve will present the checks to the member bank for payment. That bank will then lose an equivalent amount of its reserve balance. This will contract the money supply, often by $50 million. This anti-inflationary tactic results in decreasing the total money supply.

Another FED tool is the *discount rate,* which is the interest the Federal Reserve charges member banks for short-term loans. An increase in the discount rate increases interest rates, which makes money more expensive, thus discouraging people from borrowing. This contracts the economy. The reverse FED action stimulates the economy.

The third tool, changing the FED *reserve requirement,* is the most powerful but most clumsy tool. The previous example assumed a 20 percent reserve requirement. The Federal Reserve Board can raise or lower that required legal ratio within congressionally established limits. The FED can also tighten the money supply by requiring member banks to maintain a greater reserve, thus shrinking the loan amount available. The converse increases the money supply. Changing reserve requirements is the most powerful FED tool, but the FED uses it infrequently because of its clumsy nature.

The minor tools are also useful. *Moral suasion* (for example, "jawboning," which means threatening key private groups with government action unless they cooperate with government policy) might involve merely appealing directly to key banks or other groups in society. Sometimes the appeal alone is sufficient. *Selective credit controls* are another important tool, as they involve stock margin requirements.

The Federal Reserve establishes how much credit a stockbroker can provide a person in the buying of common and preferred stocks. This selective control acts in the same manner as the reserve requirement.

Effectiveness

The major advantages of monetary policy are as follows:

- The FED can reach and apply these decisions rapidly due to the less political nature of the Federal Reserve.
- This macroeconomic theory works if the FED takes proper vigorous action, especially in combating inflation, but it can and often does create a recession as it combats inflation.

The advantages are significant, but policy makers should understand the use of monetary policy in terms of its effect on society. Federal Reserve policy severely affects companies in industries such as housing, which depend heavily upon external credit. When banks restrict loans, the groups having higher credit ratings have preference on getting loan money; thus, smaller and newer businesses suffer. Therefore, tight monetary policy affects certain sectors of our economy more than others and affects certain groups (for example, the young and the minorities) more than others do. The events of fall 1966 illustrate the dangers of restrictive monetary policy. At that time, the policy

- brought the capital market to the brink of crisis,
- caused a radical decline in home construction,
- threatened the solvency of intermediaries (for example, banks), and
- left banks reluctant to make long-term loans, which caused harm in the long run to the productivity of the country.

Monetary Policy and Public Budgeting

Monetary policy is significant to public budgeting in at least two important ways. First, all levels of government borrow and invest. Monetary policy affects their available credit and especially the interest rates they pay. The interest paid and earned by government is important as this policy can increase or lower the price of their capital projects, which are normally paid for with borrowed funds. This fact shall become more apparent in subsequent chapters. Second, monetary policies heavily influence government programs (for example, housing, environment protection) that use borrowed money. Analysts could not perform budget justifications and satisfactory budget reviews without a thorough understanding of the effects of monetary policy on those programs. With respect to the impact of monetary policy on public budgets, Eric Patashink (2000) argues that the 1990s were "the period of the monetarist" when the Federal Reserve Board had more to do with setting budgetary policy than the allocation of resources and revenue decisions proposed in the budget.

FISCAL POLICY

In fiscal policy, there is an assumed relationship between the total spending level in the economy and the existence of either unemployment or inflation. Economists can think of total spending in terms of the gross domestic production of the society. The *gross domestic product* (GDP) equals personal consumption plus gross private domestic investment plus government purchases of goods and services plus net exports of goods and services. The GDP is the total productive activity in a country during a certain period of time. If GDP is at the proper level, then the unemployment rate and the inflation rate are at acceptable levels. In Exhibit 2–3, the reader will notice the inverse relationship between the unemployment rate and inflation. Economists usually believe that the ideal rates are about 4 to 5 percent unemployment and about 3 percent inflation—rates that happened in 1966, 1967, and the late 1990s.

Role of Government

How does a society reach these goals each year? This is the challenge of fiscal policy. Examine again the definition of GDP. Notice the key ingredients are both private and public. Exhibit 2–4 defines the ingredients of the GDP in billions of current dollars. Today, the GDP is much larger, but the key relationships are the same. The private sector is the most significant (about 86 percent), but the public sector is large (about 17 percent). Notice that state and local government represents about 57 percent of the public sector, and social security and defense are major programs of the federal government. The national economy ideally should achieve the correct total GDP. If the private sector is spending too low, then the government can act positively by raising its level of spending or influencing the private sector to raise its level of spending to the correct level. If the level is too

EXHIBIT 2–4   2000 Gross Domestic Product (in Billions of Dollars)

Personal consumption expenditure	$6,757.3
Gross private domestic investment	1,832.9
Net exports of goods and services	−371.0
Government purchases	1,743.4
Federal	595.1
National defense	376.9
Non-defense	218.2
State and local	1,148.3
Gross Domestic Product	$9,962.7

Source: U.S. Department of Commerce. *Survey of Current Business.* 2000. Table 1.1 Gross Domestic Product (http://www.bca.doc.gov./bea/articles/national/nipa/2001/0301dpga.pdf)

high, the economy will probably suffer inflation; and if the level is too low, the economy may suffer unemployment. Policy makers view fiscal powers operating in terms of fighting inflation or unemployment.

According to fiscal policy theory (see Exhibit 2–5), government action can influence the economy by (1) buying and selling, (2) taking and giving, and (3) lending and borrowing. By buying as a consumer, it stimulates the economy. By selling, it depresses prices. By increasing taxes, it depresses the income because consumers and corporations have less to spend. By giving tax rebates, it stimulates the economy. By having a budget surplus, it depresses the economy; and by deficit spending, it stimulates it. Fiscal powers exist through government action because the federal government is a major actor in the economy.

There is no one fiscal policy solution to an economic problem. An examination of the preceding paired powers of government implies that policy makers reasoning from fiscal policy can disagree on the appropriate fiscal solution. This does not imply that all methods or techniques will give the same results. For example, if policy makers desire faster consumer stimulation, then rebates are probably better than deficit spending because the latter takes much longer to be felt in the economy. On the other hand, if the problem is chronic, then deficit spending for public works may be the best solution. Possibly, the economic problem is temporary and isolated, thus, concentrated spending in one major product such as steel may be the best solution. To stimulate job creation, the solution may be to buy and stockpile, or to depress inflationary price increases, the solution may be to sell the stockpile.

Fiscal policy does not necessarily condemn the existence of a public debt or a national budget deficit. If the government can easily service its debt by making timely interest and principal payments and the large government borrowing does not significantly raise the market price for national or international borrowed money, then there is no difficulty in having a public debt (as pointed out in a later chapter). However, a chronic national deficit that policy makers allow to build up a larger national debt may lead to serious difficulties. For example, the debt payments may interfere with the government's ability to finance other useful projects or drive up interest costs on all public and private debt. Large interest payments can also help create a nonprogressive redistribution of income. Note that these problems are manageable and do not

EXHIBIT 2–5   Fiscal Policy Powers

GOVERNMENT POWERS	EXAMPLES
1. Buy or sell	1. Purchase of goods or sale of stockpiles
2. Take or give	2. Taxes or rebates
3. Lend or borrow	3. Surplus or deficits in the budget

Source: Based on Rodger L. E. Miller. *Economics Today,* 4th ed. New York: Harper & Row, 1982.

speak against a deficit in one or more particular years. Also, there are beneficial aspects of a large national public debt:

- The public debt provides the means for the Federal Reserve to increase or decrease the money supply in connection with reserve requirements.
- It provides needed liquidity for all the financial and nonfinancial businesses.
- It provides a safe investment for the unsophisticated and unwary investor.

There are built-in fiscal stabilizers in the U.S. economy. Several fall outside the scope of this text, but one that economists call *transfer payments* is important to public budgeting. They tend to automatically rise substantially during periods of recession and fall during prosperity. For example, when unemployment is high, more people receive unemployment compensation and eventually they may also receive welfare and food stamps. Another example is farm price supports, which increase automatically when agriculture prices need supports. Today, emergency public works programs also begin automatically. Transfer payments constitute a large share of the national budget. During prosperity, these transfer payments tend to automatically shrink.

Using Macroeconomic Theories

In the early 1960s, there was excessive unemployment in the nation. In fiscal terms, the actual GDP was less than the desirable GDP level but prices were stable. The fiscal policy adopted was a tax cut. Congress passed the Investment Tax Credit of 1962 and later the Revenue Act of 1964. The former stimulated the private sector to increase investment, thus stimulating income, employment, and the economic growth rate. The latter reduced tax liabilities, thus stimulating consumption. The policy was successful. In 1965, Congress enacted further tax reductions and the fiscal policy seemed sound.

By early 1966, unemployment fell below 4 percent, and predictably (see Exhibit 2–3), the price level (inflation) rose. Congress took only modest steps to increase taxes, but government purchases changed sharply. This was a period of guns and butter—a war in Vietnam and a war on poverty. In 1967, President Johnson did ask for a temporary tax surcharge, but Congress took no action. The FED acted as noted earlier. The strong use of monetary policy tools caused a credit crunch with high interest rates and induced a recession in the home building industry. In early 1968, the situation got worse. President Johnson requested another "war tax," but Congress refused to enact this politically unpopular tax. Finally, in June 1968, Congress passed a compromise tax surcharge, but it proved ineffective.

President Nixon inherited a serious economic problem. Tight monetary policy continued. The U.S. role in the Vietnam War began to diminish and government cut its purchases. The Vietnam War boom ended by late 1969, and a recession started by 1970. The 1960s experience with using fiscal policy indicates that it is not a tool that politically sensitive policy makers can easily apply. Although economists might say that they wish quick action from our political leaders, Congress is going to act slowly because tax increases are unpopular. Thus, a significant lag occurs and the economic problem typically gets worse.

Look again at Exhibit 2–3 and notice 1970 and 1971. Unlike the other years, they are not on the Phillips curve, meaning that in those years Americans experienced both relatively high unemployment and inflation. Apparently, in those years the Phillips curve shifted to the right. In other words, Americans experienced a time in which both unemployment and inflation were at unacceptable levels at the same time. Economists call this *stagflation*—economic stagnation accompanied by price inflation. This phenomenon perplexed economists and political leaders. In August 1977, a Treasury Department official was quoted referring to President Carter's knowledge of stagflation as saying, "I don't think that he understands why there's high inflation and high unemployment at the same time. But, then neither does anyone else."[1]

Although confusion on this subject remains, some facts can help us understand the phenomenon. The recession fell disproportionately on narrow groups—particularly the young and blacks. Monetary policy curbed economic activity in the sectors of the economy dependent on borrowing, but the nation evolved into a service economy, which is not as sensitive to monetary policy tools. Inflation, which originated mostly in food and oil price increases, rippled throughout the economy. The then-new labor and industry custom of applying automatic cost-of-living increases prevented the traditional groups from absorbing the inflation loss; thus, the effects of inflation were lengthened. In other words, the American economy after 1975 was more complex than before, and the aggregate monetary and fiscal policy actions of the 1960s were not as effective as they once were because key factors changed.

President Reagan approached the stagflation economy with a new macroeconomic theory, which Professor Arthur B. Laffer of the University of Southern California largely developed. One aspect of this supply-side theory is the relationship between tax rates and tax revenues as shown in the Laffer curve in Exhibit 2–6. In this exhibit, the vertical line represents the tax rates and the horizontal line represents tax revenues. The two extremes of zero tax rate and 100 percent tax rate produce no tax revenue. In between, the curve demonstrates that at some point an increase in tax rates actually reduces tax revenue. At the higher rates, individuals reduce their taxable work effort, spend more time seeking ways to reduce tax liabilities, and engage in more nontaxed activities. In other words, the economic policies encouraged a diminished supply of goods and services in the national economy. The implication for budgeting is that if marginal tax rates exceed that key point, then, ironically, a reduction in tax rates will actually lead to an increase in tax revenues and stimulate a greater supply of goods and services in the economy.

President Reagan and his economic advisors felt that the way to get the American economy out of stagflation was to cut the tax rates, but they also applied other policy changes to stimulate the production of greater supplies of goods and services in the economy. Because tax cuts would result in higher budget deficits, they also advocated cutting government expenditures (with the exception of military expenditures, which they

---

[1] Robert J. Samuelson, "The Enemy Among Us," *National Journal*, 9, 42 (October 15, 1977), 1619.

EXHIBIT 2–6   Laffer Curve

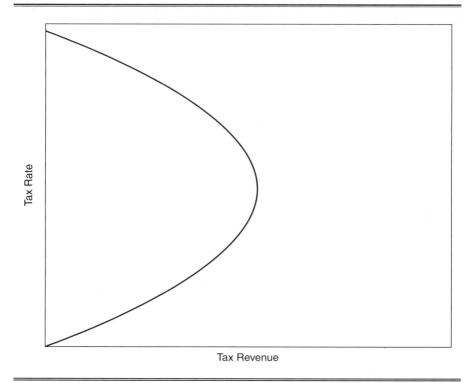

Tax Rate

Tax Revenue

Source: Dom Bonafede. "Reagan's Supply-Side Policies Push Economics Writers into the Spotlight." *National Journal,* 1337 (September 26, 1981), p. 1723.

increased). The immediate result was lower inflation, higher unemployment, and a much higher yearly federal deficit. Given the automatic fiscal stabilizers built into the government programs, the federal budget expenditures grew to offset rising unemployment, and revenues fell because there were fewer taxpayers. The larger federal debt—coupled with a monetary policy of high interest rates and other factors—resulted in high interest rates, which retarded economic growth and recovery. However, the FED policy and, possibly, the Reagan economic policy did solve the inflation problem.

President Clinton inherited an economy with high unemployment and large yearly federal deficits. He also inherited a Congress that was controlled by his political party. He felt that the national fiscal policy needed to bring the federal budget closer to a yearly balance because lowering federal borrowing would cause a lower market interest rate, and that would stimulate job production and economic growth. With a great deal of political effort, the democratically controlled Congress barely passed a budget that both increased taxes and held expenditure increases down significantly. In the next election, the voters reacted to the increase in taxes, and Congress was now under the control of the Republican Party. Nevertheless, the fiscal policies of the Clinton administration worked: both inflation and unemployment moved to ideal levels, and the economy continued to grow steadily. Before the end of the Clinton administration, the budget was in balance (actually showing a surplus), and plans existed to retire the national debt. In their analysis of budgeting during the Clinton administration, Larry Joyce and Roy Meyers (2001) conclude that despite more partisan and combative relations with Congress, the administration improved the capacity of the federal government in terms of budget process and fiscal management.

George W. Bush also left his mark on the federal budget process. In a sharp contrast with the previous administration, in June of 2001 President Bush signed into law a massive tax cut totaling some $1.3 trillion. This tax package, along with a rising deficit, renewed recessionary pressures, costs associated with a war with Iraq and Homeland Security, and a desire to increase military spending to reverse Clinton administration budget policies (which saw defense spending decline as a percentage of the budget while mandatory and nondefense discretionary spending increased) defined the Bush administration's fiscal policy agenda.

Macroeconomic Policy and Public Budgeting

At the national level, macroeconomic policy largely influences federal budgets. Once policy leaders determine their macroeconomic policy, it provides guidance for budget-year decisions especially concerning the following:

- the overall size of the budget, including revenue and expenditure totals;
- the types of spending, such as capital investment versus direct payments;
- the timing of spending programs;
- the balance of activities—federal programs do work at cross purposes, and policy leaders must decide which programs to emphasize and which to de-emphasize;
- the size of entitlement programs, and the amount available for the controlled programs;
- the building or selling of stockpiles;
- jawboning big labor or big corporations; and especially
- tax policy.

A federal budget professional and most state and local budget officers must understand macroeconomic theories. Political leaders use the various macroeconomic theories to make their many key budget decisions. Budget analysts justify and review budgets using macroeconomic theories. With expertise in the CBO and budget committees' staffs, Congress is likely to be more effective in using fiscal policy than it was in the late 1960s, but political survival of members of Congress still discourages congressional action that can hurt the likelihood of being reelected. Thus, raising taxes is not wise for them even if it is good fiscal policy for the nation.

OTHER ECONOMIC TOPICS

A text of this nature cannot cover all aspects of economics important to public budgeting in a single chapter. Subsequent chapters present various microeconomic concepts, but this chapter, which addressed macroeconomics, must limit its scope. To learn more about macroeconomics, students should read additional economics texts, especially public finance books. The following subjects are worth investigating at greater length:

- multiplier effect;
- economic growth;
- balance of payments;
- regional economics;
- public interest, including Rawl's "justice is fairness" implication to economics;
- pareto-optimality;
- welfare economics;
- labor economics;
- public goods theory; and
- public choice theory.

REVIEW QUESTIONS

1. Explain the various perspectives one can have on public budgeting and how each perspective can affect the definition of public budgeting. What should this mean to you as a person putting together a government budget?
2. Assuming someone defines policy as "a guide to action," explain how budgeting is really a statement of government policy. In what way is this understandably significant to policy makers, public managers, and clientele groups of public agencies? Given this fact, what should each group do? What are the implications in terms of achieving policy for the whole nation?
3. What is the budget cycle? In what way is this important to someone who wishes to influence public policy? What implications does the cycle have to the use of analysis? How does the local budget cycle differ from the federal one? Again, how is this important to someone who wishes to shape public policy?
4. Technologies shape society. In what ways can we see this in terms of public budgeting?
5. How do the American ideologies significantly shape the public budgeting process?
6. Explain the federal context of American budgeting and the significance of that context on managing public programs.
7. What are the major normative decision-making theories and how do they affect public budgeting as a practice?
8. Explain why inflation and unemployment rates act in inverse relationship. What happened in 1970 and 1971 that cast doubt upon macroeconomic theories?
9. Why does the shift in the American economy from an industrial to a service economy make any difference to the effectiveness of monetary policy?
10. How can liberals and conservatives disagree on fiscal policy but still base their thinking on fiscal policy?

11. In fiscal policy, why is public debt not bad *ipso facto?* Explain why entitlement programs are consistent with fiscal policy.
12. Explain the economic theories that Reagan relied upon in making his economic recommendations. Contrast them to the fiscal policy and monetary policy theories.
13. Compare and contrast the fiscal and monetary policies used by the current president with the former three presidents.

REFERENCES

BAKKER, OEGE. *The Budget Cycle in Public Finance in the United States.* The Hague: W. P. Van Stockum, 1953.

BARTIZAL, JOHN R. *Budget Principles and Procedures.* Englewood Cliffs, NJ: Prentice Hall, 1942.

BRUNDAGE, PERCIVAL FLACK. *The Bureau of the Budget.* New York: Holt, Rinehart & Winston, 1970.

BUCHANAN, JAMES M. *The Demand and Supply of Public Goods.* Chicago: Rand McNally, 1968.

BUCK, A. E. *Public Budgeting.* New York: Harper & Row, 1929.

BURKHEAD, JESSE. *Government Budgeting.* New York: Wiley, 1965.

BURKHEAD, JESSE, and JERRY MINER. *Public Expenditure.* Chicago: Aldine, 1971.

CENTER FOR THE STUDY OF AMERICAN BUSINESS. *The Supply-Side Effects of Economic Policy.* St. Louis, MO: Washington University, 1981.

DAHL, ROBERT A. *A Preface to Democratic Theory.* Chicago: University of Chicago Press, 1956.

DAVID, JAMES E., JR. (ed.). *Politics, Programs and Budgets.* Englewood Cliffs, NJ: Prentice Hall, 1969.

DORFMAN, ROBERT. *Measuring the Benefits of Government Expenditures.* Washington, DC: Brookings Institution, 1965.

DRUCKER, PETER F. *Innovation and Entrepreneurship.* New York: Harper, 1985.

———. *Managing for the Future, the 1990s and Beyond.* New York: Truman Taley Books/Plume, 1989.

———. *The New Realities.* New York: Harper & Row, 1989.

DUE, JOHN F., and ANN F. FRIEDLAENDER. *Government Finance.* 5th ed. Homewood, IL: Richard D. Irwin, 1973.

GABLER, T., and A. OSBORNE. "Entrepreneurial Government Makes Good Sense." *The Public Manager,* 21, 3 (Fall 1992), 4–6.

HAMMER, MICHAEL, and JAMES CHAMPY. *Reengineering the Corporation: A Manifesto for Business Revolution.* New York: Harper Business, 1992.

HAQUE, AKHLAQUE. "Edmund Burke: The Role of Public Administration in a Constitutional Order." In Thomas D. Lynch and Todd Dicker (eds.), *The Handbook of Organization Theory and Management.* New York: Marcel Dekker, 1998.

HAVENMAN, ROBERT H., and JULIUS MARGOLIS. *Public Expenditure and Public Analysis.* 2d ed. Chicago: Rand McNally, 1977.

JOYCE, LARRY G., and ROY T. MEYERS. "Budgeting during the Clinton Presidency." *Public Budgeting and Finance,* 21, 3 (Spring 2001), 1–21.

LEE, ROBERT D., and RONALD W. JOHNSON. *Public Budgeting Systems.* Baltimore, MD: University Park Press, 1973.

LYNCH, THOMAS D. "Budget System Approach." *Public Administration Quarterly,* 13, 3 (Fall 1989), 321–341.

MARTIN, LAWRENCE. "Jeremy Bentham: Utilitarianism, Public Policy and the Administrative State." In Thomas D. Lynch and Todd Dicker (eds.), *The Handbook of Organization Theory and Management.* New York: Marcel Dekker, 1993.

MILLER, RODGER L. E. *Economics Today.* 4th ed. New York: Harper & Row, 1982.

MOAK, LENNOX L., and ALBERT M. HILLHOUSE. *Local Government Finance.* Chicago: Municipal Finance Officers Association, 1975.

Municipal Performance Report, 1, 4 (August 1974).

MUSGRAVES, RICHARD A., and PEGGY B. MUSGRAVES. *Public Finance in Theory, and Practice.* New York: McGraw-Hill, 1973.

NAISBITT, JOHN. *Global Paradox.* New York: Avon Books, 1994.

NAISBITT, JOHN. *Megatrends.* New York: Warner Books, 1982.

NICHOLS, DOROTHY M. *Modern Money Mechanics.* Chicago: Federal Reserve Bank of Chicago, 1975.

OSBORNE, DAVID, and TED GABLER. *Reinventing Government.* New York: Plume, 1993.

PATASHINK, ERIC. "Budgeting More, Deciding Less." *The Public Interest* (Winter 2000), 65–76.

RABIN, JACK, and THOMAS D. LYNCH. *Handbook on Public Budgeting and Financial Management.* New York: Marcel Dekker, 1983.

REICH, ROBERT. *The Next American Frontier.* New York: Times Books, 1983.

REICH, ROBERT. *The Work of Nations.* New York: Vintage Books, 1992.

REYNOLDS, LLOYD G. *Economics.* 4th ed. Homewood, IL: Richard D. Irwin, 1973.

SAMUELSON, PAUL A. *Economics.* 10th ed. New York: McGraw-Hill, 1976.

SIMON, HERBERT. *Administrative Behavior.* 3rd ed. New York: Free Press, 1976.

SWAN, WALLACE K. "Theoretical Debates Applicable to Budgeting." In Jack Rabin and Thomas D. Lynch (eds.), *Handbook on Public Budgeting and Financial Management.* New York: Marcel Dekker, 1983.

TOFFLER, ALVIN. *Future Shock.* New York: Random House, 1970.

TRUMAN, DAVID. *The Governmental Process.* New York: Knopf, 1951.

WILDAVSKY, AARON. *The Politics of the Budgetary Process.* Boston: Little Brown, 1964.

3

TOWARD MODERN

BUDGETING

This chapter explains how American public budgeting evolved into its present condition and identifies critical issues that shaped the evolution of public budgeting. This chapter helps the reader understand the following:

- the major historical reforms that shaped public budgeting in America;
- how those issues implicitly influence what we perceive as the "proper" role of budgeting in government;
- the executive focus on contemporary budget reforms;
- the legislative focus on contemporary budget reforms;
- what shapes budget reform;
- the role of government in society and of budgeting in government; and
- the state of modern budgeting in America.

PRELUDE

Parliament versus the King

Early English history influenced public budgeting in the United States. For example even the word "budget" originated in the Middle English *bouget,* meaning bag or wallet. Using a great leather bag, the king's treasurer—later called the exchequer—carried on his horse the documents that explained the king's fiscal needs to the Parliament. The Normans called a bag *bouget.* Over time, the vocabulary changed so that the people called the document *budget,* and they called the process to prepare and execute the document *budgeting.*

English history is largely a story of struggle between the king and the Parliament over who politically controlled the nation. To a greater extent than other feudal realms, the newly established Norman kingdom of England in 1066 stressed the power and authority of the king over all others, including the important nobles. In England, the elite barons, who controlled large landed estates, held their estates as tenants-in-chief of the king rather than being actual property owners, as we understand the concept today. By 1215, King John, who was a descendant of William the Conqueror of 1066, ruled the Norman kingdom but had already lost the continental portion of his kingdom, including Normandy, that he inherited from his brother—King Richard. While engaging in a civil war with many of his English barons and other nobles, he attempted to achieve peace by signing a treaty, called the **Magna Carta,** with the rebelling barons. The twelfth article of that document stated that the king could not impose taxes "unless by the common council of the realm." Within a generation, the people called the "council of the realm" a new name—*Parliament.*

In the important Reformation period a few hundred years later, another civil war tested the power of the king versus Parliament to its utmost. By 1649, not only had the parliamentary forces prevailed over King Charles I in battle, but also the parliamentary forces had beheaded the king. Oliver Cromwell, who was a parliamentary leader, emerged first as a military leader and then became the first dictator of England, Scotland, and Ireland. A few years after his death, key elements of the army rebelled against the only other English dictator, who was Cromwell's son, and the army successfully supported the restoration of King Charles II in 1660. The tension between the Crown and Parliament continued. Charles II and the other Stuart kings favored a divine-right-of-kings interpretation of their power, and some of them considered adopting Catholicism as the kingdom's religion. In 1688, the Parliament forced the Stuart King James II from the throne, asking King William and Queen Mary (the sister of James II) to share the throne. A key historical result of the Reformation era was the English Bill of Rights of 1688, which established that the government could not compel any person to pay a gift, loan, or tax "without common consent by Act of Parliament." For a long period, this law established the concept of shared legislative and executive power, which in England over time evolved into the present parliamentary government with its dominant legislative branch. In the period in which America was forming its basic institutions, the English branches of government became closer to coequal when the king agreed to an annual specified grant of funds that Parliament controlled.

This struggle, or tension, between the legislative (the Parliament) and the executive (the king) is also one of the most important characteristics of public budgeting in the United States—a struggle that continues in various forms to this day. However, at the time of the American Revolution in 1776, the stress was upon legislative supremacy. The political leaders greatly suspected the use of executive power, given that the new nation's leaders fought their Revolution against the "tyranny" of the king. From the end of the American Revolution to 1789, the founders of the republic ran the country under a weak executive system defined by the Articles of Confederation.

With the adoption of the *Constitution* in 1789, the accepted principles of proper government shifted away from a weak central government, with a weak executive. It moved toward a much stronger executive authority and a national government, with the founders wanting a balance or *separation of powers* between the legislative and executive branches of government. James Madison was particularly influential in arguing for continued legislative-executive tension because he believed that such tension was not only functional but also necessary. In *The Federalist Papers,* which was a series of New York City newspaper articles that explained the rationale for the 1789 constitution, Madison argued that the fundamental law of the nation should separate the exercise of power in government, especially between the legislative and executive branches. The Madison version of *separation of powers* prevents an executive abuse of power, yet still permits strong executive leadership to exist. Since the beginning of the republic, almost every budget reform addresses or affects this intended tension and balance of power between the legislative and executive branches of government.

Colonial America

England viewed its colonies differently than did other colonial powers such as Spain. All colonies served the greater glory and economic well-being of the mother country. However, English colonialism saw great wealth being built not with conquest or the mining of silver and gold found in the colonies as seen by Spain. Instead, England adopted *mercantilism,* which was an economic policy focused on a complex trading relationship that required the colonies to provide one or more cash crops of extreme value such as sugar, indigo, tobacco, or cotton to the mother country in Europe. Colonists sold their crops to the mother country and bought finished goods prepared in the mother country as well as buying other key "goods" such as slaves from Africa to service the American plantations. Mercantilism, which crystallized as policy during the middle 1600s, required a government to enforce the closed trading relationship and a strong navy to protect that relationship.

Back in the American colonies, colonists generated the money through taxation to govern themselves. The king's representatives administered the government, but because of English culture the colonial legislatures were miniature parliaments in which leading colonists actually decided policy for the colonial governments. The separation from England, which the primitive means of transoceanic transportation abetted, fostered greater independence and led to even greater colonial self-reliance.

In the early 1700s, England and France fought yet another war in Europe, but this time the war included North America where the colonists called it the French-Indian War. To help pay for this expensive war in the English colonies, England needed more revenues and imposed additional taxes (for example, the Stamp Act) on the colonies. This unilateral English decision seemed unfair to the colonists because their representatives were not a part of the English Parliament and their legislatures did not vote on the war taxes. Reasoning from the Magna Carta of 1215 and the more recent English Bill of Rights of 1688, the colonies felt that the English decision was "taxation without representation" and therefore wrong. The English Parliament and the king saw the money as both necessary and beneficial to the king's subjects in America. The English felt the issue of taxation without representation seemed rather silly and pretentious for economic satellites of the mother country. Thus, early American public budgeting issues were among the most important in the emotionally charged circumstances that created the American Revolution.

Not surprisingly, those strong feelings helped shape the U.S. Constitution. For example, Article I, Section 9 of the Constitution requires that all matters dealing with revenue must originate in the House of Representatives. The founders of the United States were not content to say that Congress had to act on revenue matters, as the English Bill of Rights had said of Parliament a century earlier. Rather they stated that this particular policy issue had to start with the chamber of Congress that was the most representative of the people. Today, the president presents his budget somewhat as the king's treasurer did. The House passes the appropriation bills first. The Senate often acts as an appealing body and eventually the two chambers agree upon the appropriations. However, Americans still consider the House as the leading chamber in matters concerning revenues and appropriations.

Budgeting in the 1800s

For the first few years of the U. S. federal government, Alexander Hamilton, who was the influential first Treasury secretary, thought the new government should follow a mercantilist policy with a strong national government led by a strong active president. He viewed his role as being much like that of the English exchequer, and in reality his department was the most significant nonmilitary department in the new federal nation. The national government's major revenue source was custom duties, which arose from trade, and the Treasury Department's Coast Guard was an important naval force in ensuring their proper collection. To Hamilton, paying the very large Revolutionary War debt was important and his policies prevailed.

Hamilton was a leader of the early Federalist faction, which became the Federalist Party. Federalists, who were primarily in the northern cities, saw trade and the creation of finished goods within the new nation as important to the development of the country. To them, a strong president should lead a strong national government responsible for the welfare and defense of the country. The nation's leaders were trustees of the people. The government's budget and financial policies were their primary tools for exercising strong executive leadership.

Thomas Jefferson was the leader of the anti-Federalist faction, which first became the Republican-Democratic Party and later the Democratic Party. Jefferson, who was against the centralizing power that Hamilton advocated, not only supported a weaker central government but also a more extreme separation of powers within the government where Congress was the dominant partner. He felt that on all policy matters, including budgetary decisions, the new Congress should dominate. For about a century, most presidents following Jefferson felt strong executive leadership on comprehensive budget matters was improper. Interestingly, Jefferson's own administration showed strong executive leadership not only on his part but also on the part of his Treasury Secretary Albert Gallatin. Nevertheless, Jefferson's ideological views became the policy and his famous phrase—*the best government is the least government*—largely defined government policy during the 1800s. The emerging capitalists, who came into existence rapidly in western Europe and in the new American republic, found this policy ideally suited for them.

As the nineteenth century evolved, Congress eroded its original unified approach to deciding budgets. By 1865, Congress established a separate House Appropriations Committee so that Congress could consider revenue and expenditures separately. By 1885, there were eight separate committees that recommended appropriations. This disunity lessened the congressional budgetary focus of power; but, except for periods of war or depression, large budgets were not a concern of the federal government. In this era, there was a constrained view of what government should do in society, so budgets were small. Also the major revenue source—the customs—provided more revenue than was thought necessary for expenditure needs, so Congress had the unusual problem of dealing with large surpluses. In addition, congressional land grants (for example, for the building of the continental railroad), rather than money, financed many important government programs.

Progressive Reform Movement

The beginning of the twentieth century provided an apt milieu for the *Progressive* political movement to create modern budgeting. The end of the nineteenth century was radically different from its beginning. When Jefferson was president, America was an agricultural country with a vast frontier that allowed continuous opportunities for new immigrants and for those seeking new possibilities. At the end of the nineteenth century, America was a manufacturing country and the nation had a closed frontier. These changes, which *machine age* technology helped induce, required an active government that used modern budgeting techniques to set policies for society. During the machine age, technology forced centralized urban employment, created a large economic middle class, and generated massive production of goods. With capitalist policies, huge private concentrations of wealth came into existence, often at the expense of workers' circumstances for working and living. In addition, there were serious harmful impacts on the environment, and political corruption on a huge scale became common, especially in the cities.

Like the socialists, the progressives demanded political change that would address the negative implications of the new capitalist society; but unlike the socialists, the progressives did not favor government ownership of manufacturing, mining, and other industries. However, they did favor strong government leadership in society, especially by a strong government executive in the tradition of Alexander Hamilton. The Progressive political movement existed in both major political parties and until 1912 was strongest in the Republican Party. The Progressive political movement gained popular support, which included demands for municipal reforms to curtail corruption. The modernist political philosophers—such as Jeremy Bentham, Edmund Burke, and, later, Georg Wilhelm Friedrich Hegel—influenced their views. In the spirit of centralizing and rational decision making, the modern budgeting reform of the era successfully called for legislative bodies to decide their revenues and expenditures as a whole just prior to the beginning of the government's new fiscal year. The most effective municipal reformers were the National Municipal League (founded in 1899) and the New York Bureau of Municipal Research (1906).

The latter is one of the most remarkable in the history of American reform groups. One of the leaders was Charles Beard, a noted historian and founder of the academic discipline of political science. Luther Gulick and other members of that bureau were also instrumental in founding *public administration* as a study and practice so that the government would accomplish its policies in an economical and efficient manner. The research arm of the bureau moved to Washington, DC, and evolved into today's Brookings Institution. The bureau moved its training arm to Syracuse University in 1925, becoming the Maxwell School of Syracuse University. The bureau served as a model and "motherhouse" for many other bureaus throughout the country. The members of the bureau led and staffed almost every major governmental reform committee between 1910 and 1950.

Not surprisingly, the New York Bureau of Municipal Research was highly influential in budget reforms. One year after its creation, it prepared the first detailed report demonstrating the need for adopting a municipal budget system. In that same year, the bureau produced an object classification budget for the New York City Department of Health. By 1912, observers of government change could see the bureau's recommended reforms in the federal Taft Commission report, which called for object (line-item) classification budgeting in all federal departments and agencies. By the 1920s, most of the major American cities reformed their budget practices. In 1929, A. E. Buck, a staff person of the bureau, wrote the first text on public budgeting, which set a pattern that students of public administration can continue to observe in textbooks, including this one.

The desire to strengthen the executive authority stimulated budget reform. Political leaders such as Woodrow Wilson believed that reforms could strengthen executive authority if citizens also could vote for candidates who had the power to carry out their promises. Unlike Jefferson, Wilson argued against a congressionally dominated government. He felt the government's chief executive should be strong and that budget reform was one of the best ways to strengthen the executive. Wilson, like other progressives, argued for the professionalization of the career administrators (that is the creation of a civil service) who would report and be responsive to elected decision makers.

EVOLUTION

Prior to 1921

In the early 1900s, the federal government started to experience large federal expenditures and yearly budget deficits. The customs revenue was not adequate as a national government revenue source, thus, Congress passed the federal income tax. This new tax solved the fundamental revenue problem, since Congress could increase the tax rate to provide the necessary government revenue. However, this tax also attracted the keen attention of members of the business community, as they now had a vested interest in minimizing the money that the government took from them as corporations and wealthy individuals. Business interests, which dominated the times, stressed the importance of economy, efficiency, and government retrenchment. Many people felt like Jefferson that the least government was the best government.

President Taft issued a report prepared by the Commission on Economy and Efficiency Goals titled "Need for a National Budget." The report stressed that preparing a unified executive budget was the responsibility of the president. Two themes—economy and efficiency, and strengthening democracy—motivated the reform. The report reasoned that a budget would better enable the president to plan activities so that government could maximize economy and efficiency. The report also reasoned that a president's budget would strengthen the president's power—thus citizens could vote for or against a person who had the power to fulfill campaign promises. President Taft was not immediately successful in having his reforms enacted, and Woodrow Wilson's income tax temporarily took the pressure off the budget reform measure. However, by 1921, Congress accepted those reforms.

Prior to 1921, agencies still followed the Jefferson tradition of preparing their estimates and transmitting them to the Treasury Department, which passed them on to Congress. Treasury conducted no analyses. The various congressional committees considered the estimates with minimum coordination among themselves. The agencies did sometimes overspend the appropriations, and Congress felt obligated to appropriate the overspent amount. Presidents did not participate in the budget process and no overall executive branch budget plan existed.

Budgeting and Accounting Act of 1921

Until 1921, pressures for budget reform continued, especially with the expense of World War I. The Budget and Accounting Act of 1921 made two important changes. It had the president create a national budget, and it established an independent audit agency (the General Accounting Office) of government accounts as a congressional agency. The law specifically required the president to submit a budget, including estimates of expenditures, appropriations, and receipts for the ensuing fiscal year. The new legislation created the Bureau of the Budget (BOB) in the Treasury Department. Section 909 of the legislation states:

> The Bureau, when directed by the President, shall make a detailed study of the departments and establishments for the purpose of enabling the President to determine what changes (with a view of securing greater economy and efficiency in the conduct of the public service) should be made in (1) the existing organization, activities, and methods of business of such departments or establishments, (2) the appropriations, (3) the assignment of particular activities to particular services, or (4) the regrouping of services. The results of such study shall be embodied in a report or reports to the President, who may transmit to Congress such report or reports or any part thereof with his [or her] recommendation on the matter covered thereby.

This landmark legislation greatly strengthened the president and created the powerful BOB as a strong arm of the president. The new law required the agencies to submit their estimates and supporting information to the BOB. The bureau could and did prepare the president's budget, which was the executive branch (president's) proposal to the Congress. Essentially, the law required the agencies and departments in the executive branch to support the president's budget. The law prohibited agencies from initiating direct and uncoordinated contacts with Congress. Specifically, the amended 1921 law established that all agencies had to send their developed and recommended legislation to the BOB for the BOB's review and clearance. This clearance function greatly increased presidential power because it allowed the president to ensure the executive branch was in step with presidential policy.

As noted earlier, the Budget and Accounting Act of 1921 also created a congressional agency called the General Accounting Office (GAO) to audit independently the government accounts. The comptroller general, who is appointed to a fifteen-year term by the president, heads this agency. The purpose of the audits is to verify that the agencies use government funds for legal purposes, but increasingly GAO audits also examine program performance and conduct special studies of interest to Congress. The placement of the agency prevents improper pressure being exerted upon it by members of the executive branch.

The president's 1937 Committee on Administration Management (Brownlow Committee) recommended the strengthening of BOB's management activities. The 1921 legislation gave the bureau certain managerial responsibilities, but BOB had not exerted them. The Brownlow Committee's report eventually led to the Reorganization Act of 1939. This in turn led to establishment of the Executive Office of the President and the transfer of the BOB to that new office. President Roosevelt defined the duties of the bureau as follows:

- to assist the president in the preparation of the budget and the formulation of the fiscal program of the government;
- to supervise and control the administration of the budget;
- to conduct research in the development of improved plans of administrative management, and to advise the executive departments and agencies of the government with respect to improved administrative organizations and practice;
- to aid the president in bringing about more efficient and economical conduct of the government services;
- to assist the president by elevating and coordinating departmental advice on proposed legislation and by making recommendations as to presidential action on legislative enactment, in accordance with past practices;
- to assist in the consideration and clearance and, where necessary, in the preparations of proposed executive orders and proclamations;
- to plan and promote the improvement, development, and coordination of federal and other statistical services; and
- to keep the president informed of the progress of activities by agencies of the government with respect to work proposed, work actually initiated, and work completed, together with the relative timing of work between the several agencies of the government, all to the end that the work programs of the several agencies of the executive branch of the government may be coordinated and that the moneys appropriated by the Congress may be expended in the most economical manner possible with the least possible overlapping and duplication of effort.

The Bureau became the strong right arm of a strong president.

1940s and 1950s Reforms

During World War II, the bureau became even more important with all activities directed toward the war effort and the need to increase taxes and incur record deficits. The bureau assumed added duties, including supervision of government financial reports and establishing personnel ceilings. In 1945, Congress extended the bureau's budget function to include the government corporations and required the corporations to maintain their accounts on a program basis with full cost information. The Government Corporations Act of 1945 also directed the GAO to appraise the corporations in terms of their performance rather than merely in terms of the legality and propriety of their expenditures. Congress eventually extended this provision to all GAO reviews.

The Full Employment Act of 1946 called for economic planning and a budget policy directed toward achieving maximum national employment and production. The late 1940s saw the addition of more duties to the BOB. The Classification Act of 1949 required the director to issue and administer relations involving reviews of agency operations. The Travel Expense Act of 1949 assigned the director regulatory functions on travel allowances.

The Hoover Commission, appointed by President Truman in 1947, submitted its report in 1949, recommending that the president do the following:

- adopt a "performance budget" based on functions, activities, and projects;
- survey, recommend, and improve the appropriation structure;
- separate the budget estimates of all departments and agencies between current operating and capital outlays; and
- establish clearly the president's authority to reduce expenditures under appropriations "if the purposes intended by the Congress are still carried out."

Several reforms resulted from the Hoover Commission, but the Budget and Accounting and Procedures Act of 1950 was particularly important. It recognized the need for reliable accounting systems, and Congress gave the president the authority to prescribe the contents and arrangements of the budget, simplify the presentations, broaden the appropriations, and make further progress toward performance budgeting.

The Second Hoover Commission (1955) led to more technical but equally important budget reforms. It called agencies to maintain their accounts on an accrual basis and encouraged cost-based budgets. In addition, it encouraged synchronization between agency structure and budget classifications. The President's Commission on Budget Concepts in 1967 did not address any fundamental budget reforms but concerned itself with smaller technical issues. In summary, the post-1940 period saw many reforms that continued to strengthen the executive budget process.

By the 1950s, there were three accepted formats for budgeting—*line-item, program,* and *performance*—with two underlying and often conflicting philosophic perspectives on budgeting—*incremental* and *rational.* In *line-item budgeting* (Exhibit 3–1), budget analysts identify the items (for example, salaries, supplies) necessary to operate each government unit for the next fiscal year. As noted in Chapter 1, *program* and *performance* budgeting are more sophisticated approaches. In the former, analysts define a logical grouping of government activities, and decision makers allocate money to those activities. Performance budgeting goes one step further by identifying specific program outputs, which decision makers associate with specific program money requests. Exhibit 3–2 illustrates performance budgeting.

Incremental Versus Rational Debate

In the 1950s and later, those working in budgeting tended to follow either the *incremental* or the *rational philosophic* approaches to budgeting or employed some combination of the two. The former stressed that policy makers should view budget

EXHIBIT 3–1   Anderson County Line-Item Budget

ECONOMIC DEVELOPMENT

MAJOR AND MINOR OBJECT CLASSIFICATION	BUDGET FY 1998–99	DEPARTMENT REQUESTED	BUDGET FY 1999–00
Personnel Services:			
000-101 Salaries-Full Time	155,385	166,080	166,080
000-102 Salaries-Part Time	0	0	0
000-120 State Retirement	10,645	11,380	11,380
000-130 F I C A (County Contribution)	9,635	10,300	10,300
000-135 Medicare (County Contribution)	2,255	2,410	2,400
000-160 Health Insurance (County Contribution)	12,280	14,240	14,240
000-199 Requested Position(s)	0	49,245	49,245
TOTAL PERSONAL SERVICES	**$109,200**	**$253,655**	**$253,655**
Operating Expenses:			
000-201 Advertising	10,000	10,000	10,000
000-204 Books and Publications	2,065	2,065	2,065
000-206 Credit Card Charges	50	50	50
000-211 Dues and Membership Fees	595	595	595
000-215 Food	2,500	2,500	2,500
000-216 Fuel and Oil	500	500	500
000-217 Awards and Recognition	75	75	75
000-228 Insurance—Vehicles	850	850	850
000-236 Meals (Subsistence)	1,500	1,500	1,500
000-243 Postage	2,000	2,000	2,000
000-245 Printing	16,500	16,500	16,500
000-247 Rent—Equipment	3,400	3,400	3,400
000-251 Repairs to Equipment	500	500	500
000-252 Repairs to Vehicles	135	135	135
000-256 Registration and Tag Fee	30	30	30
000-269 Supplies—Office	5,350	5,350	5,350
000-275 Telephone	7,000	7,000	7,000
000-277 Training for Employees	1,000	1,000	1,000
000-279 Travel	3,500	3,500	3,500
000-293 Lodging	2,500	2,500	2,500
000-294 Registration Fees	1,395	1,395	1,395
TOTAL OPERATING EXPENSES	**$61,445**	**$61,445**	**$61,445**
Contractual:			
000-308 Catering	500	500	500
000-314 Development Construction	100,000	100,000	100,000
000-347 Photocopy Equipment Maintenance	1,500	1,500	1,500
000-348 Aerial Photography	2,000	2,000	2,000
TOTAL CONTRACTUAL	**$104,000**	**$104,000**	**$104,000**
DEPARTMENT TOTAL	**$355,645**	**$419,100**	**$419,100**

Source: Anderson County, SC 1999–2000 Budget.

EXHIBIT 3–2   Hoover Commission Performance Budget Model

MEDICAL CARE

Summary: This appropriation request in the amount of $43,648,008 is to provide for the care of a daily average of 28,696 sick and injured, maintenance and operation of 34 hospitals, 2 medical supply depots, 2 medical storehouses, 6 medical department schools, 11 research facilities, operation of 432 other medical activities ashore, instruction of personnel in non-naval institutions, and care of an estimated 1,859 dead; and for Island Government—6 hospitals, 80 dispensary beds, and instruction of native practitioners. Specific programs are as follows:

1. Medical and Dental Care Afloat—to provide technical medical and dental equipment, supplies, and services for an average of 232,485 personnel at sea,and initial outfits for 4 new naval vessels to be commissioned in 1948 .... $ 2,822,923
2. Medical and Dental Care Ashore 48,419,168
3. Care of the Dead—to provide services, supplies, and transportation for an estimated 1,859 deaths in 1948 502,700
4. Instruction of Medical Department Personnel 2,645,347
5. Medical and Dental Research—to provide civilian employment of 328 and supplies and equipment to operate and maintain 6 research facilities and 5 field research units in 1948 2,519,742
6. Medical and Dental Supply System 2,936,396
7. Island Government 1,910,463
8. Departmental Administration—to provide civilian employment of 550, travel, telephone, telegraph, supplies, and equipment for the departmental administration of the responsibilities of the Bureau of Medicine and Surgery in 1948 1,432,100

    Appropriation Request, 1948 .... $43,648,008

Source: Hoover Commission, 1949.

decisions as essentially incremental, with the current fiscal year serving as the base upon which decision makers judge the new budget year requests. This is why budget formats often show the PY, CY, BY, BY-CY—so that decision makers can examine the totals and the incremental difference between the budget year and current year. The rational perspective, which economists popularized, stresses that rational decision making requires examining budget decisions using a set of objectives and analytical techniques to help discern the best decision possible.

    The incremental versus rational debate has its roots in philosophy. Modernist philosophers, like Jeremy Bentham, believed that rationality is not only possible in human decision making but also desirable. Although program and performance budgeting can be incremental, they tend to reflect modernist philosophy. A counter position of nineteenth-century conservatives, like Edmund Burke, maintained that such an assumption was foolish; rather, they believed, reasoning from existing precedent was the best that human decision making could achieve. In the late twentieth century, Aaron Wildavsky best articulated that position in the public budgeting literature.

Critics of incremental decision making stress that the CY numbers may remain the same in the BY, but that significant policy shifts can occur even if the numbers remain constant. They argue that agencies may focus their budget arguments on the BY-CY difference, but the presentation hides the real policy change from the policy makers. Incremental advocates, like Wildavsky, agreed that this is a true distortion, but insisted that a simple analytical reform called *current services* solved the distortion problem. With a new budget column for current services in the budget year, policy makers can compare the CY numbers against the BY current services column. The new BY current services column maintains the current year policies but allows the BY numbers to go up or down as long as the CY policies remain into the BY. Thus, policy makers can see that budget numbers change even though policies remain the same.

Those with an incremental philosophic perspective in budgeting argued that the rational budget approaches are logically absurd and inconsistent with our pluralist political system, which accepts a multiple-value culture. Rationalists counter that the analytical techniques associated with their perspective help executive branch decision makers make more intelligent decisions and the techniques can be equally helpful to legislative policy makers.

Twentieth-Century Purposes of Budget

In the twentieth century, the accepted three common purposes behind the budget activity were **control, management,** and **planning,** as noted in Chapter 1. If *control* is the main purpose, the analyst designs budget formats to ensure that agencies spend money according to established policy and that agencies use no resources for illegal purposes. If *management* is the purpose, the analyst designs the budget process to stress managing people in the bureaucracy in order to achieve maximum efficiency and economy in government programs. If *planning* is the purpose, the analyst designs the process to emphasize improvements in the political decision-making process. These three stresses are not mutually exclusive. All of them exist in most budget processes, but the three-purpose distinction is conceptually useful. Reformers in various decades tended to emphasize one budget purpose over the others, but the other purposes did not cease to exist.

If reformers stress control, they wish to guarantee fiscal accountability. They are fearful of corruption and of leaving the decisions of public employees unchecked. An argument to increase the strength of the chief executive, which may also achieve greater economy and efficiency in government, seeks greater executive budget control. Thus, strong chief executives can enhance their strength through improved budget control mechanisms. Strong, rigid control over bureaucracy can also mean greater red tape that fosters inefficient and uneconomical activities because there is not enough management flexibility to permit lower-level units to deal with their changing situations. Budget control is a high administrative cost activity. Recording all transactions for every line item requires many people even in this era of the computer. Another cost of budget control is subtler in its effect upon government. By stressing control, the analytical emphasis is upon detail. Therefore, policy makers tend to ignore the big policy decisions and government becomes less responsive to the problems of society.

The early public budget literature stressed the control function. Given the well-publicized political corruption of the era, the reformer stress on control is certainly understandable. The reforms included such well-known budget features as the following:

- *Annual budget:* revenues and expenditures presented for one fiscal year period;
- *Comprehensive budget:* all revenues and expenditures included in the budget;
- *Detailed line items:* presenting the exact amount government planned to spend for every separate thing or service that government would purchase;
- *Identification of all transactions:* recording every obligation and transfer of money and liquidation of obligation; and
- *Apportionment and allotment:* an executive branch mechanism to regulate the rate and actual spending of authorized funds.

If reformers stress management, they view the budget as an executive tool to achieve effective operational direction with greatest efficiency. If that is the goal, managers want to use performance budgeting (that is, categorizing the planned activities to stress the relationship of money to achievement) and to implement productivity improvements (that is, getting greater results for the same or relatively fewer resources). One strategy to improve productivity is to decentralize the details of running the agency to lower levels while stressing overall accountability of lower units to accomplish specific program outcomes. Typically, more conservative and business-oriented reformers wish to enhance management, and, not surprisingly, conservative Republican presidents stressed such reforms in the 1920s, early 1930s, 1970s, and 1980s. However, under the leadership of Vice President Al Gore, the Democratic Clinton administration stressed management improvement in the 1990s.

If reformers wish greater planning in decision making, they see the budget as a way to bring greater rationality and analysis into the public policy-making process. The poor decision-making situation of top policy makers and the noncoordinated nature of many decision-making processes appall these reformers. They believe that coordinated and rational decision making is important and that more planning and greater use of analysis will improve the decision-making process. This type of reformer stresses the importance of analysis, data, and categorizing the budget to facilitate analysis. In the 1960s, these reformers implemented PPB (planning-programming-budgeting) and thus the greater use of analysis in public budgeting. In the 1970s, this same type of reformer implemented ZBB (zero-base budgeting) to bring another kind of rational analysis to the budget decision-making process.

AN EXECUTIVE FOCUS

Planning and Analysis

Reformers created *planning-programming-budgeting* (PPB) in the federal government—continuing today in some state and local governments—to institutionalize analysis in the executive branch decision-making process. The advocates of PPB believed that public budgeting was the key to most of the important decisions made in government and that public policy making lacked adequate analysis for top-level decision makers. They believed that procedural reforms could insert essential analysis into the public budgeting process, thus improving public policy making.

PPB had its beginning in 1907 when the New York Bureau of Municipal Research developed the first Program Memorandum. In the 1930s, welfare economics developed many of the same techniques later associated with PPB. Later, the Hoover Commission advocated performance budgeting, and federal executive staff organized budgets into programs in the 1940s. In the 1950s, operations research and systems analysts developed techniques later associated with PPB.

Secretary of Defense Robert McNamara popularized PPB in the 1960s. Secretary McNamara, who had a strong analytical background, asked Charles Hitch to apply the concepts developed at Rand Corporation to the Defense Department. The McNamara management of the Department of Defense impressed many people, especially President Johnson. In 1965, President Johnson ordered every federal department and agency to use PPB. In time, PPB also spread to many state and local governments as well as to governments around the world.

Many critics, especially Republicans and the peace movement activists, considered the guns and butter era, in which PPB existed, as a time of major policy failure in the country. Interestingly, the critics disagreed on the reasons for the failure but not on there being a failure. The United States was fighting an internal expensive "war on poverty" and a more expensive external war in Vietnam. Johnson recruited strong, intelligent people (called the "best and the brightest") to run the country, but their goals outmatched the available talent and resources of the nation. PPB, which was an attempt to use the rational model of decision making within the executive branch policy-making process, also failed.

Upon winning office, the Nixon administration declared PPB dead, but the verdict was too harsh. Although the Nixon administration officially deleted PPB from the U.S. Office of Management and Budget (the renamed Bureau of the Budget) official guidelines, a few federal agencies continued its use, and most agencies continued a much greater use of analysis in their budgeting processes. PPB did upgrade the decision-making process in some federal agencies, but in many others it was never really tried or it just was not effective.

A common misunderstanding of PPB is to equate it with analysis. Although PPB calls for greater use of analysis, especially in the early part of the budget cycle, it is not a form of analysis but rather an attempt to institutionalize analysis into the public budgeting process. PPB does encourage the application of marginal utility analysis, cost-benefit studies, cost-effectiveness analysis, sensitivity analysis, pay-off matrix, present values, and other techniques in early budget cycle decision making.

Some say analysis is an art form, whereas others say it is a science that examines alternatives, views them in terms of basic assumptions and objectives, and tests as well as compares alternatives. All this is done with a purpose of finding "useful" information or recommendations to help resolve policy questions. Although developed by various disciplines, the varying techniques share the same goal of bringing rationality to the policy-making process.

Policy makers modified the traditional budget process with PPB. First, they stressed the use of analysis, particularly in the early stages of the budget cycle. Second, they called for the categorization of government programs into a "program structure" in order to facilitate analytical comparisons making a greater use of data. Third, they made key actors in budgeting believe that the use of output measures, five-year projections beyond the budget year, and mandated special studies, which analysts addressed to specific major program issues, were essential. What are the lessons that we can learn from the PPB experience? This chapter summarizes them in Exhibit 3–3.

Management by Objectives

At the beginning of the second Nixon administration, the White House and the Office of Management and Budget strongly encouraged the federal departments and agencies to use *management-by-objectives (MBO)*. This technique sets out specific objectives for agencies and requires regular high-level periodic reports on the progress toward achieving those objectives. The Nixon administration's use of MBO varied from the conventional MBO, especially by not stressing lower-level participation in the formulation of objectives. Also OMB did not use regulations to implement MBO within the executive branch as it had done with PPB and other major management reforms. Instead, informal memorandum from OMB mandated the various departments and agencies to use MBO forms when answering OMB requests for information. Serious government-wide presidential use of MBO was short-lived and died with the end of the Nixon administration. However, the reform did have a lasting influence because many federal departments and agencies did integrate the technique into their standard operating procedures.

In a few agencies, there was an attempt to link MBO and public budgeting. Such a linkage is theoretically possible, but reformers rarely do it. Analysts accomplish the linkage by using a matrix table with MBO objectives and budget activities. The matrix table squares contain the amount of money needed to carry out the objective during the budget year. If a given program had multiple objectives, the budget analyst would either apportion the money or, more likely, not place the sums in mutually exclusive categories. Also, the analysts might not be able to associate all program activities with the objectives used in MBO. The advantage of linking objectives and money is to ensure that policy makers have resources available to meet their high-priority objectives.

Zero–Base Budgeting

Zero-base budgeting (ZBB) is an approach to public budgeting in which policy makers judge each budget year's activities in a self-contained fashion, with little or no reference given to the policy precedents of the current or past years. In contrast, policy makers in incremental budgeting focus on the difference between the current year (CY) and the budget year (BY). In making the distinction between ZBB and incremental budgeting, the reformers advocating ZBB give the false impression that practical policy results are different because of the two types of budgeting. In ZBB as practiced, the analysts typically will want and need information on the past funding

EXHIBIT 3–3   Lessons Learned from the PPB Reform Experience

THEORETICAL AND CONCEPTUAL ISSUES

- Budget reformers did not explain program budgeting, policy analysis, and other related concepts clearly to the bureaucrats involved in government budgeting. Thus, the reforms were a difficult challenge for the practitioner who had to apply them in varying and often complex situations. This approach to budgeting requires a great deal of effort and creative talent to tailor and personalize the reforms to the various agency situations.
- The rational model, as an ideal for practitioners, did result in serious political or technical mistakes.
- The use of a program structure did sometimes limit policy analyses because the subjects of analyses vary and the use of only one categorization greatly limits the necessary range of analyses.
- Some government programs often did not have and are likely never to have logical, consistent operational objectives. Policy makers use vagueness as a tool in achieving their necessary political consensus. Therefore clarity of program purpose from a clear set of output and outcome objectives does not and even cannot exist because openly stating conflicting views might harm a delicate political compromise among policy makers. Public administrators inherit this confusion and must deal with it even though mostly rational based analytical techniques cannot work with such ambiguity.
- Some types of analysis are helpful only for relatively narrow but often important policy questions. The ability of the analysts and the nature of the subject they examine constrain the use of analysis in practical circumstances. Analysis is often most useful on technical questions.

IMPLEMENTATION

- Reformers must devote a significantly large amount of money and many talented people to make PPB and reforms like PPB work. Realistically, those sums of money and especially those talented people may not exist.
- Government needs to adopt a phased implementation plan for reforms of this kind to have any chance of success. Reformers should introduce the changes first to the agencies and portions of agencies most likely to accept the change. Then, reformers should introduce the innovations to resisting agencies last. As a matter of realism, reformers must understand that they will find great resistance from some managers that will effectively prevent successful implementation in their areas of the organization. Reformers can use training and hiring policies to minimize the problem, but reformers cannot avoid entirely such resistance. Thus, reformers need to win over management slowly to the reform concept and in some cases the reformers will have to replace some managers who remain uncooperative.
- The key person for ensuring the effective use of policy analysis is the agency head. One criterion for hiring a person for this position needs to be his or her desire and ability to use policy analysis effectively. Another useful technique in successful implementation of a reform of this type is a tailor-made orientation course designed for the new agency head which includes the use of policy analysis in public policy making.
- Achieving coordination of policy among the policy analysts and planners, the budget officer, the accountants, the lawyers, the public affairs officer, the analysts preparing the agency's progress reports, and the program managers within an agency is a particularly difficult and continuing problem.

EXHIBIT 3–3 *(continued)*

POLITICAL FACTORS

- The use of plans, covering a five-year period, does not limit the political options available to policy makers.
- Policy analysis rarely addresses the political costs and benefits of a program to specific key individuals such as legislators, but good analyses do address analytical questions that set out political costs and benefits in general.
- Major political actors may find that not using analysis with explicit objectives is critical to their ability to reach some compromise decisions in their specific political situations. However, there is no reason to believe that policy makers cannot achieve greater clarity of objectives in most policy-making circumstances in spite of the need for political compromise.

HUMAN FACTORS

- People in an agency must believe that the reform is a significant and legitimate undertaking. The real test for them will be how seriously key people (like the agency head) and key agencies (such as the Office of Management and Budget) treat the reform. If these people and groups continually demand and use the products of this reform, then the agency will believe the reform is significant and worth its attention.
- Positive and politically practical recommendations must be the products of the reform. If analysts using the new techniques do not generate positive and politically practical policy recommendations, then the people who are directly responsible for implementing the reform in the agency will lose critical creditability among their organizational peers and also among the key decision makers who use the products.

MANAGEMENT

- Systematic attempts to institutionalize policy analysis do tend to centralize governmental decision making.
- Reforms like PPB rarely reduce the size of government organizations.

Source: Thomas D. Lynch. *Policy Analysis in Public Policymaking.* Lexington: MA: Lexington Books, 1975.

levels and accomplishments, especially for forecasting purposes as used in incremental budgeting. Certainly in incremental budgeting, the analysts typically will want information on all activities being planned for the budget year; however, their focus will be upon the program changes from the current year to the budget year. In both situations, unless the analyst is new to the job, the reality is that he or she is already aware of much of the program information from reviewing last year's budget. An analyst would use that information in preparing the budget regardless of what the budget office called the budgeting process.

ZBB requires more effort than other versions of budgeting. Although associated with the Carter administration, the U.S. Department of Agriculture in 1964 used a ZBB approach to prepare its budget. It was an additional exercise on top of the usual budget process. Typically, ZBB requires voluminous documentation and a great deal of high-level official departmental time and energy. Critics of ZBB note that, except for a few small decisions, departments usually reach the same conclusions as they would with the less expensive incremental approach. However, new higher-level officials typically do feel that they gain a much fuller understanding of their organization because of the ZBB experience. Like previous administrations, the Reagan administration upon assuming office abandoned the budget reform process of its predecessor.

ZBB came to the federal government because of Peter A. Pyhrr and President Jimmy Carter. Pyhrr used ZBB successfully in Texas Instruments, wrote a book titled *Zero-Base Budgeting,* and authored an extremely influential 1973 article in *Harvard Business Review.* The then-governor of Georgia—Jimmy Carter—read about ZBB and invited Mr. Pyhrr to help him apply the approach to the state of Georgia. Presidential candidate Carter talked a great deal about the virtues of ZBB, and President Carter required its adoption by the federal government. A few cities and several states (including Georgia, New Jersey, Idaho, Montana, and Illinois) adopted ZBB. Although its initial advocates were enthusiastic, the assessment of its success and failure is unclear, but the few empirical studies done on ZBB reached negative conclusions.

There are several different ZBB approaches. Typically, ZBB consists of preparing budget proposals and alternative levels of spending grouped into "decision packages." Program and higher-level managers then rank those decision packages in the order of priority. The lowest levels don't get funded. Decision packages are self-contained units for budget choice containing input and output data (that is, resources needed to operate the program and the products of the program) as well as the expected levels of performance for each defined level of expenditure. The manager, who is responsible for each discrete activity at the lowest level of an organization capable of formulating a budget, prepares alternative decision packages. Each level of management, including the original manager who prepared the decision package, ranks the packages; thus, each level focuses on marginal utility and comparative analyses. Often the ZBB guidelines stipulate a package should include one decision reflecting the minimum cost essential to carry out the activity effectively. Some states select arbitrary percentages (for example, 50 or 80 or 90 percent of last year's request) to ensure that higher-level decision makers do consider an amount smaller than last year's request. Managers and executives then rank the decision packages by priority. A chief executive can and does establish a cutoff point for the government as a whole, as well as for each agency. The executive branch budget office submits the budget to the legislature reflecting only the packages above the cutoff.

There are some serious problems in using ZBB. The most obvious is that it can be a paper monster that buries executives in an avalanche of documents. ZBB necessarily means thousands of decision packages. For example, in Georgia there were 10,000 decision packages, and no chief executive can review each one. Budget analysts must create mechanisms to manage the paperwork, limiting it to only the critical decisions. Another problem is that ZBB asks decision makers to use this technique on programs that budget appropriations essentially do not control, such as veterans' benefits, social security, interest payments on the national debt, retirement payments to federal workers, and food stamps. Thus, ZBB asks some agencies to do that which is logically impossible. Policy makers cannot intelligently apply ZBB to these programs, yet this set of programs represents over 75 percent of the federal budget and is significant in many state and local budgets as well. Thus, ZBB is worthless for much of the budget, but it does have use in capital budgeting decisions. In addition, the technique neither helps judge priorities between budget activities such as defense, welfare, and environment nor lends itself to grant-in-aid programs where policy makers intended communities to define their own objectives and priorities. Analysts cannot use marginal analysis on grant-in-aid programs because the federal granting agency cannot accurately forecast benefits of projects that local governments have not yet decided or submitted to the federal government. The federal agency does not even know who qualifies or what benefits the grantees will forecast from the federal money.

There are some apparent advantages to ZBB. In programs involving clear operational missions, such as highways, recreation, and public works, program analysts and decision makers find the technique analytically relevant. The approach shifts budget attention away from adding to the current-year program and focuses consideration upon increases to the minimum level of operational support. The approach is successful in educating newly appointed higher-level executives and their staffs on the nature of government programs. In some few cases, the approach may also stimulate redirection of resources within budgets and programs into more productive activities.

TBB and Envelope Budgeting

There is a semirational approach to budgeting that rejects PPB and its foundations but does require extensive budget expertise, including analytical capacity. Several U.S. cities call it *target-base budgeting* (TBB), and Canada labels it "envelope budgeting." In contrast to PPB, TBB is a top-down rationing process, which establishes priorities and defines limits at the top to force choice among alternatives at the bottom. Top officials check their revenue forecasts, establish targets for the various ministries based on their political choice, and create a discretionary or policy reserve used for very few programs and projects. Target-base budgeting uses a qualified rational decision-making model but only for those extra few programs and projects the government funds from the discretionary or policy reserve. Under TTB, budget guidelines require government units to submit their budget amounts within centrally decided targets. However, the units can also request added funding from the discretionary or policy reserve (for example, 5 percent of the total budget), but the unit must use rational analyses to justify the use of that money.

TBB does not require an enormous amount of analysis as found in ZBB, but the analysis that is done is often similar to that found in zero-base budgeting. In deciding policy reserve projects and programs, analysts would use cost accounting, productivity studies, performance measurement, strategic planning, and MBO. TBB is top-down centrally controlled in that central government policy makers set department target allocations, but TBB decentralizes policy by encouraging department heads to prioritize programs and projects as well as to be innovative within their lump sum target allocations.

Generally, departments have more autonomy under TBB than under other forms of twentieth-century budgeting, and in some important ways TBB anticipates twenty-first-century budgeting. With TBB, policy makers can fund the political priority projects and programs in either the target amounts or the policy reserve. How this is done depends on the policy makers within the jurisdiction. Within the target amounts, central policy makers permit department heads to make their management trade-off among line items, among programs, and sometimes among capital and operating budgets. With TBB, department staff persons can propose revenue enhancements, suggest actions designed to achieve productivity increases, and recommend alternative means to avoid service and personnel losses when central targets cut into the base budgets of their departments.

As reported by Irene S. Rubin, TBB does have its problems. The political decision to include a new program in the budget base may encourage department heads to obscure service level reductions in other areas that have resulted from funding the new initiatives. Thus, the dubious methods induced by the TBB budget process obscure the implicit policy trade-off, and the resulting inaccurate budget policy document would not enlighten the elected policy makers properly. TBB permits nonrational reallocation decisions such as across-the-board cuts and making political trade-off decisions among departments.

Prior to, but certainly since the 1921 Budget and Accounting Act, presidents have exerted their influence in the budget process primarily as budget proposers. Presidents submit the federal budget to Congress and thereby establish spending priorities as well as the overall fiscal parameters that will guide the presidents' legislative and policy agendas for the year. Some presidents, more so than others, have used the budget and embraced budget reforms or initiatives to exert varying degrees of influence to advance their agendas. Sometimes presidents exert more of a symbolic influence over the budget process. There is no better example of this symbolic dimension than budgeting during the Reagan administration.

President Reagan stormed into office determined to reduce the size of the federal government and to devolve government decision making down to the state and local levels. One of the vehicles to achieve this end was the budget. During his term, downsizing of the federal government (although federal spending for defense actually rose) and massive tax reductions were implemented through or in conjunction with his budget proposals. And although President Reagan is not associated with any budget reform or innovation, he did advance and strengthen OMB by adding a third important executive power. The first OMB power was that this staff agency of the president pulled together the executive branch agency budget requests and developed the president's budget recommendation. The second power was the legislative clearance process (see Exhibit 3–4), which covers agency legislative proposals, agency reports and testimony on pending legislation, and enrolled bills. OMB ensures that proposals, reports, and testimony conform to presidential policy and coordinates agency recommendations on presidential vetoing. The third power, which Executive Order 12291 added in 1981, requires all federal agencies that propose regulatory

EXHIBIT 3–4   Executive Legislative Clearance Process

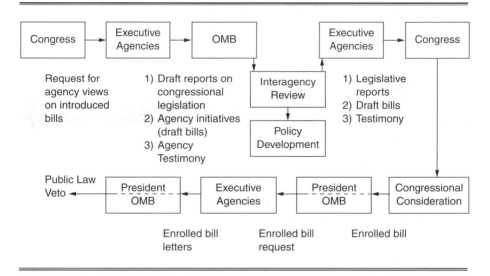

changes to send them to OMB for its clearance on regulatory budget and economic implications of the changes. This third power greatly strengthens OMB's influence, especially over entitlement programs.

The Bush administration also did not create any new budget innovation but did involve itself with financial management reforms. For example, the Chief Financial Officer's Act of 1990 reaffirmed fiscal accountability and the primacy of sound financial management practices.

Reinventing Government

Heavily influenced by David Osborne and Ted Gaebler, the Clinton administration reform or innovation was *reinventing government.* While meaningful reforms emerged from all of the efforts identified under the rubric of "reinvention," there was clearly a symbolic dimension to these efforts. President Clinton came into office with a mandate for rebuilding the capacity of government to solve many of the problems critics argued were beyond the ability of government to address. One of the ways to restore faith in government was to make government more accountable, more citizen focused, more performance oriented, and more cost effective. President Clinton's vehicle for achieving performance-driven government was the annual budget. Yet it was clear the budget was only one tool to implement these changes as evidenced by a package of legislation including the Government Performance and Results Act of 1993 (requiring that performance data be submitted with budget requests), the Government Management Reform Act of 1994 (agency filing of detailed financial audit reports), and the Federal Acquisition Streamlining Act of 1994 (new guidelines to improve all aspects of a cumbersome federal procurement process). Vice President Al Gore led this entrepreneurial effort that sought to decentralize, increase management flexibility and adaptability, establish competition within government, create a learning managerial style, be customer oriented, stimulate creativity in management, use minimal resources, and streamline government activities. This reform seeks to create alternative service delivery using techniques such as contracting out, privatization, public / private partnerships, load shedding, vouchers, and volunteers.

Scholars of public administration associated the Clinton reforms with total quality management (TQM), reengineering, and virtual organizations. Emerging from the private sector, TQM stresses achieving greater performance and higher productivity by creating a quality culture, having a customer focus, seeking constant improvement, striving to better communicate, defining performance with measures, and empowering employees. Reengineering radically changes organizations; some of its key concepts are as follows:

- fit management needs with government purposes;
- eliminate the old and redesign or reengineer the new;
- link the engineering effort to the organization;
- ground the effort in information technology;
- design it to permit constant changing;
- emphasize work through empowerment, teams, and participatory decision making;
- project workers to be laid off;
- have a clear and workable understanding of the problem;
- value and recognize visionary leaders;
- understand that timing is critical;
- provide opportunities for retraining and early retirement; and
- reconsider and then determine the organization's mission and goals.

Virtual organizations, which are a key element of the reform, have little structural definition, and decision makers often design these temporary organizations to stimulate continuous change. They are often teams or task forces that executives bring together to meet a particular mission, and then the executives dissolve the teams or task forces when they complete their mission. Virtual organizations are often flat networks that are highly dependent on modern communication and employ self-management. Their customers and suppliers commonly design the products of these organizations. Commonly in virtual organizations, members are well educated, highly trainable, and flexible to new tasks and skill requirements.

At the national, state, and local levels of government in the United States and other countries at the beginning of the new century, the major development is *performance* or what some call *outcome budgeting*. At the U.S. federal level, Congress enacted the Government Performance and Results Act of 1993 (GPRA) and embarked on a massive experiment leading to the full use of performance budgeting. The experiment proved that federal agencies can prepare strategic and performance plans that include measurable indicators of performance. The agencies reported that the reforms enabled them to review and reformulate their mission statements, achieve greater clarity of objectives, and create a better logical relationship between mission statement and outcome measures. Congress, the ultimate judge of the utility of performance data under the 1993 law, has made few negative comments, which is the most praise to be expected from Congress on this type of reform. Although the 1993 act established the year 2000 as the targeted year for inclusion of performance data, and indeed most federal agencies link their budgets to performance data and measures, the verdict is still out on the overall effectiveness of the performance experiment as a lasting "federal budget reform."

With the election of George W. Bush in 2000, the federal government seems committed to continue the performance orientation in its agencies and programs. Nonetheless, performance budgeting has dominated the budget process at the federal and state levels in the United States, and many outstanding variations of performance budgeting exist in several countries, including Australia, New Zealand, and the United Kingdom. The local level of government increasingly uses performance budgeting.

A LEGISLATIVE FOCUS

The 1974 Budget Reform Motivations

The Congressional Budget and Impoundment Control Act of 1974, a landmark piece of budget reform legislation, represented the first significant shift of budget power back to the legislative branch in the twentieth century. The law's passage dramatically relates to the events surrounding President Nixon's resignation from the highest office in the country. The 1974 legislation created a unified congressional budget reform, making Congress a coequal branch with the executive on budgetary matters.

President Nixon and the Democrat-controlled Congress constantly battled because Nixon sought to decrease the role of government in society, and Congress moved in the opposite direction by passing legislation to redress various societal problems using a larger government. In this struggle, Nixon had the political advantage because defeating programs is much easier than initiating them. One Nixon tactic was to use the highly questionable presidential impoundment power on a wide range of programs, including those programs on which Congress had overridden his presidential veto. Another tactic used was to say that Congress was acting in an irresponsible manner because of its piecemeal and uncoordinated approach to appropriations. As Herbert Jasper—an important actor in developing the 1974 legislation—pointed out, Congress was most upset at Nixon's charge of reckless congressional spending.

The illegal breaking into Democratic Party headquarters by White House employees (called the Watergate crisis) politically weakened President Nixon and strengthened Congress. The 1974 act, which was one of several reforms directed toward strengthening the legislative branch, expanded the Congressional Research Service and the General Accounting Office and strengthened congressional oversight activities. Besides creating a unified congressional budget approach, this important legislation neutralized the previous *de facto* presidential impoundment powers.

Students of budgeting should view the 1974 legislation in the context of the historical tension between the executive and legislative branches, which the nation's founders built intentionally into the American system of government. After the Jefferson administration, Congress clearly controlled the purse strings, but Congress itself split the power of appropriation over the years. With the passage of the 1921 legislation and a series of strong presidents at the beginning of the twentieth century, the power of the executive greatly increased against a fractionalized Congress. With the 1974 legislation, Congress once again focused its purse string powers in an attempt to deal more effectively with a strong executive.

Unified Congressional Budget Reforms

The 1974 legislation made several changes. It created the new Senate and House Budget Committees, created a new Congressional Budget Office, required *current services* estimates, and required various reforms addressed to the presidential budget. The new committees' duties included drafting overall budget targets, preparing reconciliation bills between budget resolutions and appropriation bills, and putting pressure on the entire Congress to meet established budget deadlines. Linda Smith, a former House Budget Committee staff person, pointed out in *The Bureaucrat* (a professional journal based in Washington and now called *The Public Manager*) that the political opposition challenged the concept of a unified budget approach in congressional budgeting, but the process worked, at first.

The 1974 unrealized reformer hope was that Congress would pass its annual appropriation bills prior to the beginning of the new fiscal year. Unfortunately, Congress fell quickly into its old habit of not passing a budget on time in spite of its unified approach to passing a yearly federal budget. In fact, later Republican congresses had an even worse record of untimely budgets than their earlier Democratic counterparts. The 1974 reform gives the appearance of a comprehensive examination of the budget, but the reforms strengthened political interest groups who sought to have Congress fund their programs, thus providing single issue oriented groups an easy means to threaten the whole budget to further their policy aims. Instead of being a step forward, the reform was a step backward into even worse partisanship and special interest group politics that hurt the larger public interest even more.

One good aspect of the reform is the Congressional Budget Office (CBO). It is a source of nonpartisan budget expertise for both chambers of Congress. The 1974 act charges CBO to present the Congress with respectable and viable alternatives on aggregate levels of spending and revenue. The office must also make cost estimates for proposed legislation reported to the floor and provide cost projections for all existing legislation. The act requires CBO to prepare an annual report covering "national budget priorities" and "alternative ways of allocating budget authority and budget outlays." One last important duty is to keep score on administration and congressional actions related to the budget. See Exhibit 3–5 for a complete list of responsibilities.

Although partisan congressional leaders sometimes publicly denounce the CBO, the agency does provide useful reports and reasonably accurate forecasts to Congress. For example, its economic forecasts are typically more accurate than those produced by executive branch agencies and the scorekeeping reports are particularly useful in congressional committees. CBO is not the congressional counterpart to the executive

EXHIBIT 3–5   CBO Responsibilities

BUDGETARY ESTIMATES

Scorekeeping.   Each spring, the Congress formulates and adopts a concurrent resolution on the budget, setting expenditure and revenue targets for the fiscal year to begin on the coming October 1. In September, the Congress reviews the detailed spending and taxing decisions it had made during the summer in the form of individual bills. It then arrives at and adopts a second concurrent resolution, reconfirming or changing the totals in the spring resolution. While the first resolution sets targets, the second establishes an actual ceiling for spending and a floor for revenues. CBO keeps score of congressional action on individual bills, comparing them against targets or ceilings in the concurrent resolutions. The Balanced Budget and Emergency Deficit Control Act of 1985, the Balanced Budget and Emergency Deficit Control Reaffirmation Act of 1987, and the Budget Enforcement Act of 1990 assign further duties that require CBO to prepare various sequestration reports to the Congress and the Office of Management and Budget. The office issues periodic reports showing the status of congressional action.

Cost Estimates.   Four types of cost estimates are required of CBO by the budget act:

CBO prepares, to the extent practicable, a five-year estimate for what it would cost to carry out any public bill or resolution reported by congressional committees (except the two appropriating committees).

CBO furnishes to a reporting committee a report on each committee bill providing new budget authority. Each report shows (a) a comparison of the bill with the most recent concurrent resolution, (b) a five-year projection of outlays associated with the bill, and the amount of new budget authority and resulting outlays provided for state and local governments.

CBO also furnishes to a reporting committee an analysis of each bill providing new or increased tax expenditures. The reports cover (a) an assessment of how the bill will affect levels of tax expenditures most recently detailed in a concurrent resolution, and (b) a five-year projection of the tax expenditures resulting from the bill.

As soon as practicable after the beginning of each fiscal year, CBO prepares a report that analyzes the five-year costs of continuing current federal spending and taxing policies as set forth in the second concurrent resolution. The purpose of these projections is to provide a neutral baseline against which the Congress can consider potential changes as it examines the budget for the upcoming fiscal years.

FISCAL AND PROGRAMMATIC ANALYSIS

Fiscal Analysis.   The federal budget both affects and is affected by the national economy. The Congress thus must consider the federal budget in the context of the current and projected state of the economy. To provide a framework for such considerations, CBO prepares periodic analyses and forecasts of economic trends. It also prepares analyses of alternative fiscal policies.

Inflation Analysis.   Beginning in 1979, CBO prepared estimates of the inflationary effect of major legislative proposals and, more generally, identifies and analyzes the causes of inflation. These estimates are intended to provide the Congress with guidelines, as it undertakes new programs, of the cost in terms of inflation that these programs might entail.

Mandate Analysis.   The Unfunded Mandates Reform Act of 1995 requires CBO to prepare estimates of the direct costs of all federal mandates that are contained in legislation reported by any authorizing committee that affect state, local, and tribal governments or the private sector.

(continued)

EXHIBIT 3–5   CBO Responsibilities, *continued*

Program and Policy Analysis

CBO undertakes analyses of programmatic or policy issues that affect the federal budget. These reports include an examination of alternative approaches to current policy; all reports are non-partisan in nature. These reports are undertaken at the request of (1) the chairman of the committee or subcommittee of jurisdiction of either the House or the Senate; (2) the ranking minority member of a committee of jurisdiction of either the House or the Senate; or (3) the chairman of a Task Force of the House Budget Committee.

Annual Report on Budget Options

By April 1 of each year, CBO furnishes to the House and Senate Committees on the Budget a report that combines many aspects of the functions outlined above. The annual report presents a discussion of alternative spending and revenue levels, levels of tax expenditures under existing law, and alternative allocations among major programs and functional categories.

Note: CBO's analyses usually take the form of published studies comparing present policies and programs with alternative approaches. The responsibilities of CBO are (1) budgetary estimates, and (2) fiscal and programmatic analysis.

Source: 21.S. Congressional Budget Office, 2002.

branch OMB. That type of power rests with the budget and appropriation committees. Instead, CBO provides essential information so that Congress knows the fiscal implications of various proposals and can act in a deliberate manner on fiscal policy matters.

Other 1974 innovations are the OMB "current services estimates" and the CBO "baseline budget projections." Scholars of budgeting give a neutral rating to the usefulness of those reforms. The OMB submits its *current services* budget authority and outlay estimates covering the next and future fiscal years as Congress begins its budget deliberations. These estimates assume that the existing services shall continue following current program policy, but OMB does adjust them to reflect inflation and other factors that may raise costs but do not change program policy. A parallel concept is the CBO baseline budget projections. Typically, they are an extrapolation of budget trends for the next five years. The estimates also assume that current policies remain the same and the projections only reflect inflation, workload changes mandated by law, and other nonpolicy factors. For most programs, baseline projections are higher than current funding levels.

The president submits his or her budget no later than early February for the fiscal year that begins next October 1. Congressional budget actions are (1) adoption of budget resolutions, (2) passage of appropriations bills, and (3) passage of other budget-related legislation such as authorization legislation, reconciliation bills, tax changes, modifications of entitlement programs, and adjustments to the debt limit. The president's recommendations do not bind Congress in preparing its budget decisions.

Within six weeks after the president's budget submission, each House and Senate committee must submit its "views and estimates" report on budget matters relevant to its committee. The House and Senate Budget Committees use these reports and the CBO analyses including the baseline projections to prepare their budget resolutions. The budget resolution, which Congress should adopt by April 15, contains revenues and spending levels for five years but Congress is only bound by the first year. Being a concurrent rather than a joint resolution, the budget resolution does not receive the president's signature and the resolution does not have statutory effect.

The budget resolution has three main sections: *aggregates, functional allocations* of spending, and (optionally) *reconciliation instructions*. The aggregates include total revenues and any desired changes in those levels, total new budget authority, total outlays, the budget surplus or deficit, the debt limit, and the total new direct loan obligations and new primary loan guarantee commitments. For the House only, the budget resolution includes total entitlement authority that the budget resolution allocates to each committee. Each budget committee allocates the new budget authority, outlay, direct loan, and loan guarantee levels among twenty functional categories such as national defense, international affairs, energy, and agriculture. The budget act divides the allocations between mandatory and discretionary totals. The appropriation subcommittees may not build their appropriation bills in excess of the so-called 602b (referring to a section of the budget law) allocations given to them. Reconciliation instructions direct specific House and Senate committees to report legislation conforming spending, revenue, or debt-limit levels under existing law to current budget policies.

Budget resolutions are not always effective, but Congress has passed many reforms designed to strengthen the follow-through on its budget resolutions. To ensure a greater chance that the resolutions are effective, the House and Senate budget committees act as scorekeepers by issuing reports that estimate the cost for legislation reported out of committee for floor action and that compare it to the 602 allocations. Since 1990, Congress allows individual members to call parliamentary "points of order" to declare a proposed legislation not eligible for floor consideration because it violates the 602 allocations as defined in the scorekeeping report. In addition since 1990, added mechanisms exist including spending caps for discretionary appropriations and a pay-as-you-go provision for mandatory expenditures. The latter requires the makers of the new legislation to identify what trade-off they are making against the programs in the existing budget.

In summary, Congress decides the annual appropriations in thirteen regular appropriations bills under the jurisdiction of parallel House and Senate appropriations subcommittees that recommend spending levels to the full committees. The appropriation committees subdivide their spending amounts among their subcommittees. When the entire House or Senate considers appropriations legislation, the members of Congress can compare the recommendation with the amount decided by the respective appropriation committee. In some circumstances, the congressional budget process such as the parliamentary point of order does bar consideration of an appropriation measure if the measure breaches the assigned limit. Thus, the various congressional budget reforms have increased the internal discipline within Congress on budget matters.

If the unified approach to legislative appropriations started in 1974 had been successful, Congress should meet its own deadlines. Unfortunately, it does not. Typically, Congress does not pass the appropriation bills by the start of the fiscal year as required by the 1974 law. An interim device is the "continuing resolution," which provides appropriations for a few months while Congress continues to deliberate. Congress should use the "continuing resolution" infrequently when it cannot make a timely decision, but the reality is that the "continuing resolution" has become the norm in congressional appropriation making. In some years, Congress substitutes continuing resolutions for appropriation bills, causing needless management difficult in the federal departments. Unfortunately, in the 1990s the Republican congresses refused to pass even continuing resolutions. They brought the government to a halt in an attempt to force the president to agree with their policy position. This brinkmanship ploy did not work in that they had to yield by passing necessary legislation and the people reacted negatively against them at the next election. Congress can and does also enact supplemental appropriations to provide additional funding not covered in regular appropriations bills. In complex and questionable strategies, either the executive or legislative branch can also abuse this need to be flexible to force the other branch to accept its policies.

Backdoor or Nondiscretionary Spending

One of the concerns of the 1974 reform advocates was the use of nondiscretionary or *backdoor spending* (the commitment of federal funds outside the effective control of the appropriation process). Reformers argued that backdoor spending is contrary to the concept of a unified consolidated congressional budget because policy makers cannot balance some activities against the competing claims of other activities. The 1974 legislation outlawed or tried to control backdoor spending, with some major exceptions. Without those major exceptions, Congress would not have passed the legislation.

There are various forms of *nondiscretionary spending.* One is a *permanent appropriation,* by which Congress allows the program to spend whatever is necessary following congressional guidelines. This near blank check is theoretically possible, but in practice Congress usually does place some limits on its use. Another is *contract authority,* by which government officials *can* obligate the government through legal contracts, and subsequently Congress must pass appropriations to fulfill the obligation. *Borrowing authority* is similar except the government official can borrow money, and subsequently Congress must pass appropriations to liquidate the debt. Yet another method is *mandatory spending* for congressionally established *entitlements,* such as unemployment compensation, food stamps, payments on the national debt, veterans' benefits, and so on. Congress sets or allows payment levels through programmatic rules set down in legislation and administrative regulation. If there is a recession, many of these programs require government *automatically* to pay more in unemployment compensation, welfare, and food stamps. Later, Congress must pass appropriations to cover the obligations. Economists consider *earmarked revenue* to be a *backdoor spending method* because government can only spend funds from a specific source (for example, gasoline tax) for a specific activity (for example, highways). Thus, they argue earmarking prevents a unified consolidated consideration of the budget. The use of the *unexpended balance* (that is, money appropriated but not spent in the last fiscal year) by carrying it over to the next year

is also contrary to the unified approach, but the law allows it in
various nondiscretionary spending exceptions add up to abo
year's federal budget.

Impoundment

As noted earlier, the extensive use of impoundment by Republican President Nixon,
who impounded large sums of money because he did not favor the programs that
Congress enacted and funded, upset the Democratic Congress. Nixon used the impoundment because it was a *de facto* veto, which Congress could not override. Not
surprisingly, Congress felt that Nixon violated the spirit, if not the letter, of the
Constitution. The judicial branch concurred with the majority in Congress. In every
instance that someone took the expense and time to battle the Nixon administration
on impoundment in the courts, the president lost and the administration had to
spend the money. The delays caused by the court challenges, however, tended to
create a *de facto* veto that served the president's aims and frustrated Congress. Unfortunately, there is a cost to such political perfidy. This combination of the executive illegal holding of funds and of the judicial decision-making process (1)
crippled the administration of government programs due to the uncertainty over
funding, and (2) practically did lower government program funding levels, not
withstanding the Constitution.

The 1974 legislation addressed the problem by redefining the impoundment
powers. The Congress and the courts pointed out that neither the Constitution nor the
law granted the president the impoundment power. The executive branch argued that
ample precedent existed over the many years of the nation's history. Congress recognized the best solution was to redefine the impoundment powers so that the president
could not cripple programs regardless of the contested validity of the impoundment
powers. Congress, wishing to prevent a president from overruling the will of Congress
on government spending issues, created a pragmatic solution. In 1974, Congress created two versions of an impoundment. If the presidential impoundment is to defer the
spending appropriated by Congress, then *either* the House *or* the Senate can force the
release of funds by passing a resolution calling for their expenditure. If the impoundment is to cut or rescind the appropriations, then *both* House *and* Senate must pass
rescission resolutions within forty-five days of the rescission or it is not valid.

In *Immigration and Naturalization Service v. Chadha,* the Supreme Court
struck down the one-house legislative veto as unconstitutional. Thus, the implication
is that there was no way to overturn presidential deferrals except by passing a law,
which the president could then veto. This left the president with a *de facto* line-item
veto. At first the Republican Reagan administration did not attempt to use this apparent advantage over the Democratic Congress, but eventually the administration
did employ it. Not surprisingly, the reaction was a legal suit. The plaintiffs argued that
Congress never intended to give the president the deferral power that resulted from
the *Chadha* case. The federal courts agreed and found in favor of the plaintiffs.

One technical problem in writing the 1974 law was how to deal with a president
who might not inform Congress of an impoundment. The threshold of trust between

gress and the president was very low in 1974. The legislative solution required the president to send a message to Congress requesting an impoundment, including setting forth the rationale for it. The legislation then stated that if the president did not comply with the law, then the comptroller general (a congressional branch employee) would report the impoundment to Congress. If the president did not comply, the law directed the comptroller general to go to the courts to get a court order forcing compliance.

The ultimate strategy behind the law was complex. The Constitution provides for a means to impeach the president and requires the president to execute faithfully the laws of the nation. If the courts rule that the president did not follow the law faithfully, then the president has an extremely weak defense during an impeachment. At that point, both the legislative and judicial branches declared that the president needed to comply with the law and he was not doing so in spite of his constitutional requirement. In other words, the 1974 act set up President Nixon for a possible impeachment. However, other grounds for impeachment (the Watergate crisis) existed and rather than face the disgrace of impeachment and being removed from office, Nixon became the first and only president to resign.

Vice President Ford, who became President Ford after Nixon's resignation, almost got trapped in the 1974 legislation. The near trap began with a minor test of the impoundment process by the Ford administration. Ford did send the required impoundment messages to Congress and did comply with the will of Congress except in one situation. On October 4, 1974, President Ford transmitted his impoundment messages, including the deferment of approximately $264 million in contract authority for the section 235 housing program, but the legislation was due to lapse on August 22, 1975. The comptroller general, acting under the 1974 law, reasoned that this would permit only fifty-two days to obligate the money, thus it was a *de facto* rescission, and under the law the comptroller general reported the error in a formal message to Congress. This meant that Congress had forty-five days to act, and without congressional action the executive branch had to spend the money; Congress did not act, nor did the president release the funds so that the department could spend the money. The comptroller general then notified Congress of his intention to bring a lawsuit and the Senate passed a resolution in support of the comptroller general. Therefore, on April 15, 1975, the comptroller general of the United States filed the required lawsuit in U.S. District Court for the District of Columbia.

The suit named Gerald Ford, president of the United States; James T. Lynn, director of the Office of Management and Budget; and Carla A. Hills, secretary of Housing and Urban Development as defendants. The Ford administration challenged the 1974 legislation on the grounds that (1) by instituting the lawsuit the comptroller general was improperly carrying out an executive function, and (2) the Constitution provided means other than the courts for resolving disputes between the branches of government. The legal arguments continued, but the case came to an abrupt end without a court resolution. On October 17, 1975, Carla Hills announced she would reactivate the section 235 program and there was no longer a need for a legal suit. The game playing in Washington continued and this time Congress won a round.

Exhibit 3–6 presents the early history of post-1974 impoundment. Ford won cancellation of only 7 percent of the funds he proposed for rescission. Carter was more successful. However, we need to judge Reagan's success rate during two periods of time. In his first two years, he had a 69 percent success rate but it dropped to 2 percent in his last years in office. The difference reflects the change in the makeup of the Congress. The impoundment power can be a useful presidential tool only when a president has greater influence in the Congress. The impoundment power certainly does not equal that of a governor's line-item veto but under the correct conditions it is significant.

In the Clinton administration, the Republican Congress passed the line-item veto (Line Item Veto Act of 1996), which almost every modern president sought. Technically, the new law merely amended the 1974 impoundment provision and various disgruntled legislators immediately tested the constitutionality of the law. In time, the U.S. Supreme Court ruled the new law was unconstitutional because it violated the separation of powers concept established in the Constitution. During the brief period the law existed, President Clinton used the line-item veto sparingly, thus preventing his opponents from arguing that he significantly lessened congressional power with his use of it. The line-item veto reform did not appear in the form of an amendment to the Constitution because of the political difficulty of achieving a two-thirds vote for it in both the House and Senate. Thus, the likelihood of this reform becoming national policy in the near future is very unlikely.

Reconciliation

The ploy, which the congressional Republicans and the conservative Democrats (called "Boll Weevils") tried in the Congress soon after President Reagan took office, surprised the major architect of the 1974 budget act, Richard Boiling. Although the 1974 act reconciliation provision clearly says that a concurrent resolution on the budget may "determine and recommend changes in laws, bills, and resolutions . . . ," the Democratic congressional leadership carefully avoided serious confrontation with its own powerful committee chairpersons. With Ronald Reagan's election in 1980, the Republicans not only captured control of the White House and the Senate, but also gained a working majority in the House of Representatives when they joined forces with Democratic conservatives. Working with his congressional allies, President Reagan effectively employed the previously unused reconciliation power.

The confrontation and its success were a surprise to the House leadership, as illustrated in Exhibit 3–7. The Republican-controlled Senate concurred with President Reagan's budget suggestions (for example, increased national defense, reduced taxes, and a huge cut in domestic spending). It passed the necessary instructions to other committees in its first concurrent budget resolution. The real confrontation occurred in the House, where a Republican/Boll Weevil coalition, which supported the president's views, dramatically overturned on the House floor the Democratic budget resolution. This monumental budget resolution, called Gramm-Latta I, contained instructions for budget reductions in fifteen House committees and fourteen Senate committees, required very large outlay reductions (that is, of $56 billion), and provided reconciliation savings from discretionary and entitlement programs.

As called for by the 1974 act, the congressional committees responded. The Republicans quickly fashioned another ploy, which was a massive reconciliation bill

EXHIBIT 3–6   1975–95 Rescissions and Deferrals (dollars in millions)

TYPES OF IMPOUNDMENTS	PROPOSED	ACCEPTED	PERCENTAGE ACCEPTED
Rescissions			
Ford (1975–77)	$7,405	$ 530	7.2
Carter (1977–81)	6,946	2,580	37.1
Reagan (1981–82)	23,269	16,080	69.1
Reagan (1983–88)	20,011	400	2.0
*Bush (1989–92)	13,436	2,150	16.0
*Clinton (1993–95)	4,725	2,345	50.0
Total Rescissions	75,792	24,085	32.0
Policy Deferrals			
Ford (1975–77)	22,904	14,145	59.2
Carter (1977–81)	12,905	7,314	56.7
Reagan (1981–82)	6,788	6,174	91.0
Reagan (1983–88)	22,333	7,736	34.6
*Bush (1989–92)	NA		
*Clinton	NA		
Routine Deferrals			
Ford (1975–77)	16,623	16,610	99.9
Carter (1977–81)	17,943	17,928	99.9
Reagan (1981–88)	66,817	66,284	99.2
Total Routine Deferrals	101,383	100,822	99.4

TYPES	PROPOSED	ACCEPTED	PERCENT OF ACCEPTED
Anti-deficiency Act Deferrals*			
Bush (1989–92)	36,367	36,367	100
Clinton (1993–95)	21,482	21,482	100
Total Anti-deficiency Act Deferrals	57,849	57,849	100

Beginning with Fiscal Year 1998 all deferrals were under the Anti-deficiency Act. The Balanced Budget Reaffirmation Act of 1987 (P.L. 100–119) eliminated policy deferrals and OMB now categorizes deferrals as anti-deficiency and other.

Source: U.S. Office of Management and Budget. Cited in Allen Schick, *The Capacity to Budget.* Washington, DC: The Urban Institute Press, 1990, p.112. *Data for Bush and Clinton: General Accounting Office, "Impoundments: Historical Data or Proposed and Enacted Revisions for Fiscal Years 1974–1995, GAO/OCG-96-3, January 18, 1996.

EXHIBIT 3–7   House Speaker Thomas P. O'Neill, June 25, 1981

I have never seen anything like this in my life, to be perfectly truthful. What is the authority for this? Does this mean that any time the President of the United States is interested in a piece of legislation, he merely sends it over? You do not have any regard for the process, for open hearings, discussions as to who it affects, or what it does to the economy? But because a man, who does not understand or know how our process works, sends it over, are we to take it in bulk?

. . . Do we have the right to legislate? Do we have the right to meet our target or can he in one package deregulate, delegislate, the things that have taken years to do?

Source: Congressional Record, June 25, 1981, #3383–85.

called Gramm-Latta II. This extraordinary law changed eligibility rules for entitlement programs (for example, food stamps), limited programs earlier authorized, and rewrote major parts of substantive law. No committee held hearings on the law; rules strictly limited amendment possibilities; the debate lasted only two days; and the House passed the law in a single vote rather than a section-by-section vote. Speaker O'Neill was in shock. The Republican ploy clearly demonstrated that reconciliation was a powerful budget tool, but the Republicans altered the reconciliation instructions from the first budget resolution. Although reconciliation remains important, the use by the Republicans significantly changed its importance and they diminished its potential effectiveness as a tool of legislation.

Sunset Legislation

In many states and in the federal government, legislators use sunset legislation. The sunset concept is that government programs should automatically expire unless a legislature takes positive action to renew the programs every few years. The form of the sunset legislation varies; in most instances, the sunset provisions permit the program to remain on the law books, but the authorization for its funds expire with the sunset. In other words, the program technically exists, but no money can be spent on the program unless the legislature reenacts the authorization section of the law. The cycle for renewal varies, but often the sunset provision uses a staggered five-year cycle.

Both the federal and state levels of government use sunset legislation, with Colorado and Florida being the leading states. Colorado was the first state to enact major sunset legislation, but the law limits it to the state's regulatory agencies. In June 1976, Florida also passed sunset legislation directed toward regulatory agencies, but it also set termination dates for both the agencies and substantive laws. Congress enacts sunset legislation by placing sunset provisions in its many authorization bills, but it has not passed comprehensive sunset legislation. With sunset legislation, the legislature staggers the termination schedule of government programs so that the legislature reviews all targeted programs over a period of time. It exempts some government programs, such as interest payments on the national debt, retirement, health care, and disability programs. Congress controls the review process so that it can decide the form, scope, and time allotted for each review it thinks is appropriate for the program.

The term "sunset legislation" is misleading because the phrase gives the impression that there will be wholesale termination of government programs. A legislature would not be wise to have such a policy because if there is a strong enough reason to create and fund a program in the first place, then there is strong enough reason to believe the legislature will reenact the program. Reenacting every piece of legislation is an unnecessary workload for any legislature. Therefore, some programs may expire under sunset, but not on a wholesale basis. Legislatures that use sunset are wise to allow for termination of only the authorization section of the law rather than the whole law. This avoids a great deal of needless legislative paperwork and still means that the agencies must justify their programs' existence to the legislature.

Federal Budget Madness Years

Not withstanding the entire set of budget reforms, the current federal budget process is inadequate, especially during economic lean years. Naomi Caiden described the process as "preventing consistent policy making, and encouraging deadlocks, blackmail, and symbolic voting."[1] Typically, the Congress passes not timely appropriation measures but make-shift continuing resolutions after the beginning of each fiscal year. Federal agencies brace for payless days during the yearly budget crises, members of Congress are weary of endless rounds of budget decisions, and brinkmanship politics best describes budget decisions between the president and Congress and the Republicans and the Democrats.

Carl Grafton and Anne Permaloff characterized the failed federal budget process as follows:

- the many special political interests concern congressional leaders more than the larger public interest,
- the little connection between programs and money fragments the budget process,
- key officials do not take the necessary time to familiarize themselves with budgets,
- key officials willingly accept less than their best from the process, and
- key decision making takes place in unreasonable and unrealistically short time frames.

During the economic lean years of the 1980s and spilling over into the 1990s, Congress passed three major laws to cure the federal budget crisis. These laws were (1) the Gramm-Rudman-Hollings Act (also called the Balanced Budget and Emergency Deficit Control Act of 1985), (2) a revised Gramm-Rudman-Hollings Act in 1987 (called the Balanced Budget and Emergency Deficit Control Reaffirmation Act), and (3) a Budget Enforcement Act (BEA) of 1990. The provisions of each law were complex and ineffective. The first two established deficit reduction targets for specific fiscal years. The third law sets targets within categories. However, each law left major loopholes, such as ignoring the required funding of the savings and loan financial disaster, which required major federal funding to remedy the problem. As

---

[1] Naomi Caiden, "The Myth of the Annual Budget," *Public Administration Review* 42, 6 (November/December 1982), 516–523.

noted earlier in this chapter, another failed reform was the Republican attempt to create a presidential line-item veto by amending the 1974 act's impoundment provisions.
The combined failure in federal budgeting means the following:

- the collapse of budget regularity,
- the encouragement of deceitful accounting practices, a premium on gimmicks that produce short-term improvement but that do not ease the structural problem,
- strained relationships between the president and Congress,
- lessening the effective leadership of the president,
- congressional congestion and frustration,
- overloading the ability of the political leaders to reach an effective solution,
- crowding out other important national concerns, and
- insufficient time to respond to emerging issues and priorities.

The failure of the federal budget process reached its worst situation in 1995 with
a series of partial government shutdowns. For example, the national parks closed and
the State Department stopped issuing passports to U.S. citizens. How did the situation
get this bad that elected officials would deliberately hold the American people hostage
because Congress and the president could not reach an agreement on the budget?

In earlier years, the problem was bad and then the situation got worse. In 1985,
Congress did not pass one appropriation bill by the beginning of the fiscal year, and
it missed its own May 15 budget resolution deadline by seventy-five days. Congress
reacted against its own inaction, which the economic lean times made worse, by passing the already discussed 1985 budget act. Immediately, disgruntled congresspersons
brought a court case, and eventually the Supreme Court ruled that one key provision
of the 1985 law violated the Constitution. A fallback provision in the law proved insufficient to force Congress to have the necessary self-discipline to act responsibly.
Again after many debates, Congress passed the 1987 law, which set new congressional target dates reducing the yearly deficit. This new legislation defined a baseline
that was to force discipline because available spending became a function of the projected caps on mandatory and discretionary spending. The legislation created a complex process of sequestration, which Congress thought was so unpalatable politically
to itself that both it and the president would work together to avoid triggering the
process. The dramatic stock market crash of 1987 did not produce the dreaded depression as had the earlier 1929 crash, but it did act as a catalyst to force a budget
deficit reduction agreement for the next two years.

The budget crisis continued into the 1990s. A huge sequestration, with a radically negative impact on government programs, seemed likely as the 1992 presidential
year came into sight. Thus, Congress passed the Budget Enforcement Act of 1990 that
included expenditure cuts and revenue increases in spite of President Bush's pledge of
"Read my lips, no new taxes." The law also set new baseline limits with three so-called
"firewalls" for defense, international aid, and domestic spending. The firewall rules
prevented budget cuts in some areas in response to budget increases in other areas. The
1990 law created a pay-as-you-go (PAYGO) mechanism to enforce adherence to
spending caps. When supporters of a program wished to increase its funding, then rules

called for corresponding decreases in funding in other programs or the advocate needed to specify how Congress would raise the additional revenues. The BEA and the companion Omnibus Budget Reconciliation Act of 1990 did not affect the budget deficit immediately, but over time they did limit the growth of government programs.

President Clinton, with a Democratic Congress, assumed office in January 1993. In August 1993 with strong White House support, the Democratic Congress, by the closest margin with a party vote, approved the Omnibus Budget Reconciliation Act. The law essentially cut even popular programs, raised taxes in some areas, and raised the targets for budget deficit reductions. This set the stage for 1995. In a bi-election year, the Republicans gained control of Congress. Almost immediately a budget collision occurred when the Republican Congress sent to the president two unacceptable bills, including a stopgap continuing appropriation and another measure allowing for short-term treasury borrowing to prevent the federal government from missing its debt payments. Clinton vetoed the measures, forcing a partial government shutdown. The administration solved the debt service problem by temporarily raiding the civil service employees pension fund. Again the Republicans passed legislation cutting popular programs, and again the Democratic president vetoed the legislation. After weeks passed, the Republican Congress and the Democratic president reached a series of minor compromises that put the bureaucracy back in business. In the next election, the people reelected Clinton by a wide margin and the Republicans barely maintained their majority in Congress.

By 1997, politics changed. The continuous growth of the national economy and the hard-fought budget cuts plus revenue increases combined to produce the hoped for balanced budget. The Balanced Budget Act and Taxpayer Relief Act of 1997 passed with presidential approval. The law made permanent the requirement that budget resolutions cover a five-year period, and Congress extended its highly successful PAYGO sequestration requirements through fiscal year 2002. By 1999, forecasters presented Congress with a new problem: a half-trillion dollar budget surplus within the next ten years. The decades-long deficit crisis had officially ended.

As long as one party controls the executive branch and the other party controls the legislative branch, the federal budget is likely to continue to be a source of major political disagreement and embarrassment for advocates of democracy. The chronic high budget deficit years of the 1980s stopped when the Clinton administration and the Democratic Congress, with a dramatic one-vote margin, voted to increase taxes and cut various government programs. At the next election, the Democrats paid the political price by losing control of Congress, largely because they had increased taxes. Nevertheless, the yearly deficit problem disappeared over a few short years because the national economy grew and the increased revenues made a balanced, and even a surplus, budget eventually possible. However, partisan budget politics and various ploys worsened in the late 1990s until the Republicans in Congress suffered election losses due primarily to their confrontational political approach to the budget process. But the directions of political winds constantly change, and with these changes come the corresponding impact on budgets and the budget process.

In 2000, Republican George W. Bush defeated Vice President Al Gore, and at least until May of 2001, the Republicans controlled the White House and both houses of Congress. During this time, the Bush administration successfully orchestrated a massive $1.3 trillion tax cut, but simply didn't have time to leave a more lasting Republican imprint on the budget. With the defection of Republican Senator James Jeffords of Vermont, who became an independent, the Senate went Democratic, thus, the delicate and partisan balancing act between a politically divided Congress and a Republican president continued. The 2002 elections saw both houses return to Republican control. Recessionary pressures foretell a problematic and stalled economy through the early 2000's.

In the 1990s, with surplus budgets, reformers argued the older and more comfortable themes of the 1950s—improving government programs through the use of performance measures and improving public financial management. This older budget reform theme started in 1990 when the Chief Financial Officers Act required the development and reporting of systematic measures of performance for twenty-three of the larger federal agencies. In 1993, the Government Performance and Results Act (GPRA) focused on a phased implementation of performance budgeting by requiring federal agencies to prepare strategic plans, prepare annual performance plans, and have the president submit an annual program performance report comparing actual performance with those plans.

Of course, the revisited older themes did not mean that happiness settled on capital hill. In 1993, both the General Accounting Office and the Congressional Budget Office prepared preliminary studies on the Clinton budget and financial reform suggestions. These respective studies observed that the prospects for long-term reforms were problematic due to the difficulty of measuring government performance itself. They concluded the biggest obstacle to the effective use of performance measures was the identification of the measures themselves. Somehow, returning to budget cynicism was almost civil by budget-gaming standards typically employed in Washington politics.

Reformers continue to argue for budget change, but few reforms have much chance of success. One dramatic reform was the Balanced Budget Amendment to the Constitution. Although the amendment was part of the Republicans' *Contract with America,* getting the necessary two-thirds vote in both House and Senate proved impossible in spite of the federal budget madness in Washington. Given the fact that the budget deficit crisis is over, the political likelihood of the amendment passing is very low. A second reform advocated by Vice President Gore was a biennial budget, but this idea is not popular in Congress. A third reform often discussed would create a federal capital budget, but again Congress is not interested. A fourth reform would be to advance a constitutional amendment creating an automatic continuing resolution if Congress fails to act in a timely manner on appropriations. Again the two-thirds requirement makes this reform unlikely. A fifth reform would establish a joint resolution setting the budget targets as a matter of law rather than the present current budget resolution. The now common *omnibus budget reconciliation law* essentially does this, except much later in the budget process. A sixth reform often mentioned would require Congress to strengthen its leadership by reducing the number of its committees involved in money matters. The fifth and sixth reforms are possible and are likely to be the focus of debate over the next few years.

New Public Management

In 1993, Osborne and Gaebler in *Reinventing Government* called for revolutionary change in conventional wisdom using the words "reengineering," "entrepreneurial management," "empowerment," and "privatization." The policy makers accepted many of the reform prescriptions. For example, between 1992 and 1996, President Clinton cut a total of 244,000 positions from the federal government. Vice President Al Gore prepared the concurrent publication of the *Report of the National Performance Review* (1993), which pushed the reinvention legacy. Both of these publications received wide national and international press and attention. Local, state, and national governments around the world quickly adopted many of the reform principles, especially privatization of government services. Services that had been thought of as government-only shifted either to the private sector or to new public-private partnerships.

In the 1970 and 1980s, an antibig government movement swept the nation and the world. The movement started in the late 1970s with the Proposition 13 antitax initiative and picked up steam in the 1980s with President Ronald Reagan and Margaret Thatcher, prime minister in Great Britain. To many influenced by this movement, the old Jefferson adage that "the best government was the least government" meant something new; now "least" meant less taxes but also fewer government programs. The bombing of a federal building in Oklahoma by American-grown radicals helped curb the antigovernment mood in the late 1990s. The Clinton administration's popular policies demonstrated that government could solve its deficit problems, run an economy, and address the important problems in the country. Yet, the economic success of the 1990s did not have enough coattails to propel Vice President Al Gore into the White House in the 2000 elections. Despite losing the popular vote, George W. Bush was elected president in the electoral college. Faced with a surprising downturn of the economy in 2001 and determined to make good on a massive tax cut during the election, President Bush slowly put his imprint on the budgetary and fiscal priorities of the federal government. Less government but better government is the theme that has characterized the Bush administration. How this theme manifests itself in distinctive or innovative proposals for budgetary reform have yet to be seen. President Bush, as governor of Texas, did embrace performance measurement and budgeting for government agencies and is continuing the performance and quality reforms introduced during the Clinton administration. The terrorist attacks of September 11, 2001 also helped shift the American mood away from antigovernment policies toward a "semisupportive" attitude of government. Another reality of the George W. Bush administration is a return to annual budget deficits.

The State and Local Challenges

State and local governments are almost always passing balanced budgets. When recessions exist, they place serious strain on state and local budget processes, but they meet the fundamental challenge of making resource allocation decisions within the context of balancing revenues and expenditures. As the United States enters the twenty-first century, the potential for a recession or at least a prolonged economic slowdown are real. This downturn is now being evidenced in a number of states that are struggling to close budget deficits (for example, South Carolina facing a $500 million shortfall, while North Carolina faces a $900 million gap). In view of the slowing economy and lower revenue estimates, states and some local governments are facing some difficult decisions in the short term. This provides the impetus at all levels of government for greater professional expertise to improve forecasting, capital financing, financial management, and the use of performance measures. However, most local governments are not beyond line-item budgeting and most do not use performance budgeting to judge the efficiency and effectiveness of their programs. Despite decade-long efforts to improve budget analysis and provide professional training for budget officials, many state and local budget processes do not reflect the use of sophisticated analysis due to either limited professionalism or, more likely, the meager demand for its use by elected officials.

Reformers cannot meet the challenges of budgeting merely with limited changes in bookkeeping because the challenges require very complex analytical policy improvements and often radical management innovations. In the twentieth century, state and local governments "got by" if they achieved yearly balanced budgets and accurately kept the accounting records. The result was an increasingly bad public image for government, as services seemed to worsen as tax revenues went up. Good budgeting and financial management are not the cure for the ills of society, but they can be the means of achieving higher performance for reasonable taxpayer dollars. For example, governments can usually improve forecasting, can produce greater revenues with their idle cash, can find better ways to do the job of government, and can improve the analyses used in budget allocation decisions. The National Conference of State Legislatures found at the state level that performance measures were not yet creditable to influence budget allocation decisions significantly, but nevertheless state leaders viewed performance measures as useful. Analysis using performance measures can be much more useful, but only if states and local governments require a high level of budget professionalism.

In the last few decades, the local and state level experienced a growth in the use of performance measures. Robert Lee compared state budget development between 1970 and 1995 and found much greater use of program effectiveness and productivity information in the 1990s. The most cited local government example is Sunnyvale, California, due to the very popular Osborne and Gaebler *Reinventing Government* book. That city uses a performance budget with specific service objectives and productivity measures linked to a larger plan. The Government Finance Officers Association (GFOA) developed a local government budget awards program, which is having an impact on the quality of budgeting in local government and does strongly encourage the use of performance measures. Under this program, governments voluntarily submit their annual budget documents to GFOA, which, in turn, sends them to GFOA member peer reviewers. If the government's budget document gets a passing grade, then the local budget office gets a passing grade and a GFOA award. Sunnyvale and many other cities have received that award.

With the onset of the twenty-first century, more sophisticated budgeting that uses performance measures is becoming the normal expectation of the budget professional. Since 1992, the Governmental Accounting Standards Board (GASB) has encouraged governments to report not just traditional financial and accounting data in their budgets and financial reports but also information about service efforts and accomplishments (SEA). In addition, bond-rating companies look for the use of performance measures in local government budgeting processes as a criterion to rate local government bonds. Increasingly, state audit agencies use performance measures in their auditing, and states employ outcome performance measures in their budget practices.

REVIEW QUESTIONS

1. The roots of the executive/legislative struggle go back as far as 1215, but the struggle greatly influences how budgeting is done in the United States today. Explain those roots and how that struggle helps us understand modern budgeting. In what ways do we see that struggle taking place in modern budgeting?
2. Compare and contrast the rationalist approaches to budgeting (for example, PPB, MBO, and ZBB) with the incremental approaches. Explain how the role of analysis varies—if it does—in each approach.
3. Compare and contrast line-item budgeting, program budgeting, and performance budgeting.
4. Compare and contrast budgeting in the industrial age versus the information age.
5. Explain the 1974 congressional budget reforms. What did Congress wish to accomplish with the 1974 act and what means did Congress devise to accomplish those ends? To what extent was Congress successful and not successful?
6. How has politics shaped the federal budget process? In your opinion, for better or worse?
7. The current federal budget process is said to be inadequate. Why? What ideas have reformers developed to solve that inadequacy? What reforms could help resolve the identified problems? Why do you think they would work?
8. Some budget scholars describe the 1980s and 1990s as a period of "automatic budgeting" or "budgeting on automatic pilot." What do you think they mean by this? Provide some specific examples.
9. The professional challenges of state and local budgeting are significant. What are those challenges? What should professionals do to meet those challenges?

REFERENCES

ADVISORY COMMISSION ON INTERGOVERNMENTAL RELATIONS. *ACIR State Legislative Program.* Vol. 4, *Fiscal and Personnel Management.* Washington, DC: Government Printing Office, November 1975.

ALYANISDARY-ALEXANDER, MAND. (ed.). *Analysis for Planning, Programming and Budgeting: Proceedings of the Social Cost-Effectiveness Symposium.* Washington, DC: Washington Operation Research Council, 1968.

ASPIN, LES. "The Defense Budget and Foreign Policy: The Role of Congress." *Daedalus* (Summer 1975), 155–74.

BAKKER, OEGE. *The Budget Cycle in Public Finance in the United States.* The Hague: W. P. Van Stockum, 1953.

BARTIZAL, JOHN R. *Budget Principle and Procedure.* Englewood Cliffs, NJ: Prentice Hall, 1942.

BEAUMONT, ENID. "The New York Case from a Public Administration Perspective." *The Bureaucrats*, 5, 1 (April 1976), 101–12.

BEKER, JEROME. "Measuring Cost Effectiveness in Human Services." *Canadian Welfare*, 51, 1 (January/February 1975), 5–6.

BENSON, GEORGE, et al. (eds.). *The American Property Tax: Its History, Administration and Economic Impact*. Claremont, CA: Institute for Studies in Federalism, Clairmont Men's College, 1965.

BLACK, GUY. "Externalities and Structure in PPB." *Public Administration Review*, 31, 6 (November/December 1971), 637–43.

BREAK, GEORGE F. *Agenda for Local Tax Reform*. Berkeley: Institute of Government Studies, University of California, 1970.

BRUNDAGE, PERCIVAL HACK. *The Bureau of the Budget*. New York: Holt, Rinehart & Winston, 1970.

BUCK, A. E. "Performance Budgeting for the Federal Government." *Tax Review* (July 1949).

CAIDEN, NAOMI. "The Myth of the Annual Budget." *Public Administration Review*, 42, 6 (November/December 1982), 516–23.

COTHAN, D. A. "Entrepreneurial Budgeting: An Emerging Reform?" *Public Administration Review*, 53 (1993), 445–54.

CURRO, MICHAEL J., and CAROLYN L. YOCOM. "Federal Budget Practices in the 1990s." In Fred Thompson and Mark T. Green (eds.), *Handbook of Public Finance*. New York: Marcel Dekker, 1998.

FISHER, LOUIS. "Annual Authorizations: Durable Roadblocks to Biennial Budgeting." *Public Budgeting and Finance*, 3, 1 (Spring 1983), 23–40.

FLEISCHMAN, RICHARD K., and R. PENNY MARQUETTE. "The Origins of Public Budgeting: Municipal Reformers During the Progressive Era." *Public Budgeting and Finance*, 6, 1 (Spring 1986), 71–77.

GOOD, DAVID. "Envelope Budgeting: The Canadian Experience." Paper prepared for the 1983 Annual American Society for Public Administration National Conference, New York, April 17, 1983.

GORE, ALBERT A. "From Red Tape to Results: Creating a Government That Works Better and Costs Less." *Report of the National Performance Review*. Washington, DC: U.S. Government Printing Office, 1993.

GOVERNMENTAL ACCOUNTING STANDARDS BOARD. *Concepts Statement No.2 of the Governmental Accounting Standards Board on Concepts Related to Service Efforts and Accomplishments Reporting*. Norwalk, CT: Governmental Accounting Standards Board, 1994.

GRAFTON, CARL, and ANNE PERMALOFF. "Budgeting Reform in Perspective," *Handbook on Public Budgeting and Financial Management*. New York: Marcel Dekker, 1983, 89–124.

HARTMAN, ROBERT W. "Congress and Budget-Making." *Political Science Quarterly*, 97, 3 (Fall 1982), 381–402.

HOWARD, JAMES A. "Government Economic Projections: A Comparison Between CBO and OMB Forecasts." *Public Budgeting and Finance*, 7, 3 (Autumn 1987), 14–25.

JOHNSON, VAN R. "Optimizing Productivity Through Privatization and Entrepreneurial Management." *Policy Studies Journal*, 24, 3 (1996), 444–63.

LEE, ROBERT D. "A Quarter Century of State Budgeting Practices." *Public Administration Review*, 57, 2 (March-April 1997), 133–140.

LELOUP, LANCE T. "After the Blitz: Reagan and the Congressional Budget Process." Paper presented at the Southern Political Science Association Meeting, Memphis, TN, November 5–7, 1981.

LEWIS, C. W. "History of Federal Budgeting and Financial Management from the Constitution to the Beginning of the Modern Era." *Public Budgeting and Financial Management*, 1, 2 (1989), 193–214.

LYNCH, THOMAS D. "The Budget System Approach." *Public Administration Quarterly*, 13, 3 (Fall 1989), 327.

———. *Federal Budget and Financial Management Reform*. Westport, CT: Quorum Books, 1991.

———. *Policy Analysis in Public Policymaking*. Lexington: MA: Lexington Books, 1975.

McCAFFERY, JERRY. "Features of the Budgetary Process." In Roy T. Meyers (ed.), *Handbook of Government Budgeting*. San Francisco: Jossey-Boss 1999.

OSBORNE, D., and T. GAEBLER. *Reinventing Government: How the Entrepreneurial Spirit Is Transforming the Public Sector, From Schoolhouse to Statehouse, City Hall to the Pentagon*. Reading, MA: Addison-Wesley, 1992.

RABIN, JACK, and THOMAS D. LYNCH (eds.). *Handbook on Budgeting and Financial Management*. New York: Marcel Dekker, 1983.

RUBIN, IRENE S. "Budgeting For Our Times: Target Base Budgeting." *Public Budgeting and Finance,* 11, 3 (Spring 1991), 5–14.

SCHICK, ALLEN. *The Capacity to Budget.* Washington, DC: The Urban Institute Press, 1990.

———. "Manual on the Federal Budget Process." Washington, DC: U.S. Congressional Research Service, December 24, 1991.

THURBER, JAMES A. "Congressional Budget Reform: Impact on the Appropriations Committees." *Public Budgeting and Finance,* 17, 3 (Fall 1997), 62–73.

TYER, CHARLIE, and JENNIFER WILLAND. "Public Budgeting in America: A Twentieth Century Retrospective." *Journal of Public Budgeting, Accounting and Financial Management,* 9, 2 (Summer 1997), 189–219.

WENZ, THOMAS W., and ANN P. NOLAN. "Budgeting for the Future: Target Base Budgeting." *Public Budgeting and Finance,* 2, 2 (Summer 1982), 88–91.

4

BUDGET BEHAVIOR

Human beings do public budgeting; thus, we can understand a great deal about budgeting by examining the factors that influence human behavior. This chapter first examines how the key political roles in the budget process interact. The next major topic is an in-depth examination of the agency budget office and the perspectives associated with the office. The final major topic is a careful examination of the strategies associated with the game of budgeting. This chapter examines the following:

- political influence patterns among the key actors in the budget process;
- means commonly used to cultivate an active clientele;
- duties of an agency budget office;
- perspective of a budget officer and typical behavioral patterns;
- four common philosophic attitudes of budget officers toward the budget process;
- approaches budget officers develop to build the confidence of other stakeholders in the variety of analysis, information, and reports produced by the agency budget office;
- significance of program results in budgeting;
- preparation process for hearings;
- review setting;
- "spenders'" strategies;
- "cutters'" strategies;
- strategies used to support new programs;
- important cautions in public budgeting; and
- myth of the budget-maximizing bureaucrat.

POLITICS AND PERSPECTIVE

Four Institutional Roles

Students can understand American public budgeting in terms of four institutional roles that the Constitution defines indirectly. Each role has a definable behavior. Exhibit 4–1 shows the interrelationships among four of the groups that interact continually in the budget process. Two additional roles are very important, but, as this chapter will explain later, they become involved only if key trigger events transpire.

The four institutional roles present the ongoing influential actors in the American budget game with its unique role of independent executive leadership. In parliamentary systems, the chief executive and the legislature are the same, and thus the major political actors play their roles differently. The four institutional roles are the

EXHIBIT 4–1   Interrelationships of Institutional Roles in Public Budgeting

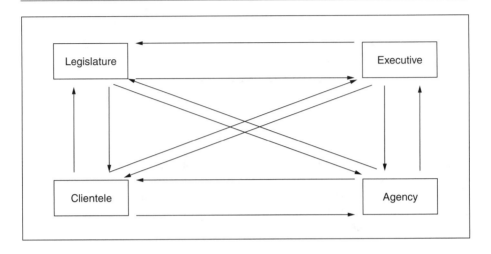

agency, the *executive,* the *legislature,* and the *clientele.* Two other groups, the *courts* and the *media,* are significant, but Exhibit 4–1 does not explain them because their influence patterns are not constant. The *agency,* the institution responsibile for managing the programs, prepares the initial budget submission and subsequent detailed budget submissions. It is responsible for budget execution throughout the fiscal year, and, in this sense, it can be said that the process begins and ends in the agency. This is one of two institutional roles not defined by the Constitution, but it is the most important because it is the group that provides the services to the public. It is the group all others try to influence in terms of policy and guidance. This chapter defines *executive* to mean the chief executive, his or her staff, and the central budget office. The executive department, of which the agency is a part, plays an odd role. In the early stages of the budget cycle, it acts as an extension of the executive, but as the budget cycle progresses its role shifts to that of a superagency and ally of the agency in the budget process. The *legislature* is the legislative branch of government, such as Congress in the federal government. The *clientele* is an interest group, which the agency's programs affect (for example, senior citizens affected by the Social Security Administration). It is a segment of the public that is most interested in the operations of the agency because it is directly helped or harmed by the agency. Thus, it takes an active interest in the agency's policies. Although not referenced in the Constitution, in a pluralistic political system it is the group that the writers of the Constitution had in mind.

The double lines in Exhibit 4–1 represent several two-way influence patterns. The agency influences the executive through its budget request, and the executive's budget decision is one form of executive influence on the agency. The executive influences the legislature through its executive budget requests, and the passage of laws is one form of influence upon the executive. The agency's programs, by definition, affect its clientele. Clientele groups are well-known for their lobbying (influencing) activity on legislators, but they also lobby and influence the chief executive and the agency. It is less well-known that legislatures and executives can influence clientele groups directly. To make matters more complex, an influence pattern may involve more than two groups. For example, a clientele group influences Congress on appropriation legislation that ultimately becomes law, and then the language of that appropriation legislation influences the agency.

A case study involving the U.S. Maritime Administration illustrates the influence patterns. In the Nixon administration, there was a strong desire at the highest levels in the U.S. Office of Management and Budget to phase out operating and ship-building subsidies at an accelerated rate. OMB required the Maritime Administration to launch an analytical study of exactly how it was to accomplish this. Somehow, Representative Sullivan, who headed the House Appropriations subcommittee, discovered the OMB study. She was extremely upset that OMB wished to change policy clearly established in the law and phoned OMB Director Mayo. No one recorded the substance of that conversation, but we know the director withdrew his request for the study. This series of events illustrates the influence of the central budget office on an agency as well as the strength of a single legislator on a central budget office.

Students of budgeting sometimes do not fully appreciate the strong influence of a clientele group on politicians and a government agency. Because active clientele groups contribute to the very expensive political campaigns of politicians, they are very significant in the political process. In *Policy Analysis in Public Policymaking,* Thomas Lynch presented several case studies involving the budget process in the U.S. Department of Transportation (DOT). In February 1970, the Office of Management and Budget called for a special analytical study by the Urban Mass Transportation Administration (UMTA) of that agency's policy guidance for capital grants reflected in the published *Information to Applicants.* In time, UMTA prepared the study and a revised *Information to Applicants.* Before it became official, UMTA formally sent a letter (as required by OMB Circular A-85) to inform state and local government associations of the proposed new guidelines. The Circular A-85 requires an informal agency-to-clientele interrelationship prior to the time that the agency issues its final policy so that the clientele can voice its concern about a proposed policy directly to the agency.

In this instance, surprise was the reaction of the representatives of the transit industry and the cities. They took strong exception to the "unrealistic data demands and planning analyses" that the new requirements imposed on them. They felt that DOT committed a breach of faith because there was no informal consultation prior to sending the official notification of a change in agency policy as required by the OMB circular. The clientele reacted by developing a counterstrategy—as soon as they knew about the proposed change through less than proper channels, they met with agency officials and tried to define the most undesirable aspects of the new selection criteria. The agency officials felt that they came closer to accommodating the clientele's wishes while keeping within the strict OMB policy prescriptive given the agency. This case illustrates the infrequently documented influence of a clientele group directly on an agency.

Legislative groups and chief executives can and do directly influence clientele groups, sometimes in very public meetings. Such influence is most noticeable at the large conventions of these groups when high-ranking legislators or executives address the members and argue for their particular policy. Less publicized meetings occur when legislative and executive officials request cooperation or seek lobbying support for key legislation.

"End runs" and finesses do occur in this complex four-way relationship (sometimes called a policy network). For example, an agency can influence its clientele group by pointing out the implications of existing proposed policy of the legislature or the executive. The clientele group can then go either to the legislature or the executive and note the importance of its support in the next election. Usually, the politicians pay attention. A more complex situation would be when the agency such as the highway department proceeds with some policy (for example, conserving fuel by requiring a fifty-five-mile-an-hour speed limit on the highways) that its clientele group (for example, the trucking industry) may find distasteful. The agency might be able to counter likely clientele pressure by having the president lobby the clientele group (for example, address the trucking industry members at their national conventions) and Congress. This would strengthen the chances of success for the agency, but it would cost the president important political capital, which he or she might consider not worth the price. Additionally, the political influence might not sufficiently curb clientele resistance to the policy change, and the president might have used his or her political capital with no positive result being accomplished.

In the budget process, the agency-to-clientele-to-legislature triangular relationship—called the iron triangle—is a common and important pattern. The more sophisticated clientele groups, recognizing that the size of the budget and the individual programs are significant to them, realize that they must interact with the legislature and the agency but not necessarily with the executive if that person is not skilled in political persuasion. Often, an informal communication network exists between the agency and the clientele group. The clientele formally monitors and analyzes all the important policy developments. It then communicates its understandings on those policy developments to its clientele members and often asks its members to contact key politicians directly. Sometimes clientele groups launch active campaigns to build strong lobbying pressure on a particular budget issue of importance to them.

Courts and the media are influential political players. Article 3 of the U.S. Constitution and the very important *Marbury v. Madison* case give courts legitimacy to decide if an action of the executive or a law passed by the legislature is constitutional, meaning enforceable by the courts. Courts become involved in public policy when someone brings a legitimate case to the court system and the courts decide they want to hear the case. Courts create public policy because of a legal doctrine called *stare decisis,* meaning let the decision stand. Once a higher court decides a legal precedent, then other lower courts must apply that precedent when they find themselves in similar situations. Thus, higher courts can and do establish public policy. In a particular case, the court can rule that even a prison warden must obey the court or become a client of the prison system. That threat is influential.

The trigger mechanism involving the media in public policy is the newsworthiness of a media story. The news editors must decide if their readership or viewers would find a story that involves public policy interesting. The first amendment of the Constitution establishes freedom of the press; thus, it gives a set of private corporations called the media unique constitutional protection against censorship by the government. Being private corporations, they wish to make money and they do so primarily by selling advertising, which the public views because the public finds the news stories between the advertising copy interesting. These stories influence the politicians because the people who watch and read the news are the same people who vote the politicians into office. To get elected, politicians need to have a lot of people know them personally or about them generally. Being in a news story costs politicians little, but paying for advertising costs them a great deal of money. Therefore, politicians are very sensitive to reporters' and editors' needs, especially if the media might include them in their stories. By printing or airing stories, the media set the policy agenda for the politicians and thus influence public policy.

State and local influence patterns normally are not as complex as those found on the federal level. However, large state and local governments have patterns more similar to the federal level. Not surprisingly, the seriousness of lobbying and clientele groups relates to the money or potential money involved; thus, large governments with large programs tend to have the most active clientele groups. In medium and small governments, clientele groups can and do act less formally. Often, clientele groups express their interests through nonpaid part-time volunteers who use simple phone calls, faxes, and e-mail. However, the home district meetings of clientele group members from the legislator's district tend to carry the most weight with politicians. Often, these clientele members express their on-the-record views in public hearings, possibly even in a demonstration, or in a media event they organize. Highly emotional confrontations are rare on budget issues, but they do occur.

The agency, executive, legislature, and clientele have separate institutional roles. Each perceives itself as a separate group, although individual exceptions exist—for example, an agency political appointee may identify solely with the chief executive rather than with the agency. Also, each group (for example, the clientele) can see itself as several groups, and those subdivisions may come into conflict and neutralize the influence of the whole clientele group. For example, the Maritime Administration clientele is the maritime unions and maritime companies. When they work together, they are surprisingly powerful for their respective sizes. However, their alliance can and does break down on specific issues. In Congress, sometimes the substantive and appropriation committees come into conflict, thus lessening the influence of Congress. In the executive, two staff agencies such as the White House staff and the Office of Management and Budget can be in conflict over policy issues. However, in the executive branch, the chief executive can more easily arbitrate internal disputes than can the legislative branch and the clientele groups.

Role Objectives and Enemies

The agency and its leadership almost always have pride or a sense that the agency's programs are worthwhile. The career employee recognizes that his or her job and income rely on the agency's objectives. In some instances, an almost missionary zeal and self-identification with the agency can exist among the top agency leadership. In other instances, the zeal may be only a belief that what the agency does is a worthwhile function. Rarely do top agency leaders disagree with the mission or the fundamental value of the agency and its programs.

Another factor to consider is the budget process itself. The law itself places the agency always in the position of requesting and defending. Reviewers always doubt the agency and demand facts and better arguments from it. Not surprisingly, when the agency comes under attack from clientele, the legislature, chief executive, or media, the agency executives often find themselves defending the agency policy position or management accomplishments. Presidents, governors, and mayors sometimes act surprised when their agency appointees argue the agency position because they assume their appointee will support the chief executive position automatically, but the role itself is a powerful force in defining behavior. Moreover, even though these appointees may "tow the line" on agency policy objectives consistent with the chief executive mandate, running the agency on a day-to-day basis tends to align appointees with their agency's viewpoints and operating needs.

Given the dual elements of self-worth and role demands, if chief executive agency appointees do not speak for their agencies, then that odd behavior should surprise and possibly even upset the chief executives. Agency heads view issues from the perspective of the agency's mission and the people in the organization that they lead. Does a change further or detract from the agency's mission? Will the people in the organization benefit or lose from a change? Agency leaders naturally think in those terms and justify their budgets with those questions well in mind. However, after conducting a careful empirical study of agency leadership behavior, Lee Sigelman concluded that leaders' support for truly major agency expansion is not as extremely widespread as many public choice theorists claim. He noted that a substantial number of agency leaders actually call for little or no agency expansion. In other words, agency administrators do request and defend their budgets, but that does not mean that they necessarily pursue a budget-maximizing strategy. Some may act out of self-interest defined in terms of salary, perquisites, reputation, power, and patronage. However, the facts show that motivations are much more complex than a deliberate, single-minded pursuit of bureaucratic self-interest.

The chief executive plays a different role. The executive wishes to economize, cut requests, and coordinate programs. There is an arm's length relationship between the executive and the agency leadership in spite of the fact that agency political appointees serve at the pleasure of the executive. The executive must maintain the option of saying "no" to an agency request. Staff for the chief executive must review agency requests carefully as executive cuts are necessary for purposes of economy and better allocation of resources around the executive branch. When the chief executive makes his or her budget decisions, there is the expectation that the agency will formally support the executive decision, even though the agency may not perceive the decision to be in its own best interest. The chief executive maintains discipline in several ways:

- The executive's staff must clear agency formal statements before the agency provides information to the public.
- Budget requests must follow the executive's budget and allowance letter.

- The political influence of the chief executive is significant and can be important to an agency in subsequent political battles.
- The chief executive can fire the agency head.

Another factor for state and local government agency heads to consider is that their chief executives can sometimes veto or reallocate items in line-item budgets. These powers vary greatly from one government to the next, but some chief executives can unilaterally reconstruct the council-approved budget using the line-item veto. The only limit on the executive power is the likely political resistance the chief executive would receive from the legislature or city council. When chief executives wield this type of power, agency officials hesitate to challenge or to try to circumvent them.

The legislature (sometimes called council, board, or commission) plays an entirely different role. It is the elected deliberative body of the people, typically composed of well-intended, intelligent individuals, who often have their individual or group policy agenda. However, when dealing with budget matters, legislatures often confront both confusing information and little time to make decisions. At the federal level and in some large state and local governments, the legislatures may dominate the policy-making process at the exclusion of the agencies and chief executive, but this is not often the situation. Typically, legislatures do not initiate most policy issues, but rather play a more reactive role compared with the chief executive or clientele groups. They tend to give their attention to their pet projects and the issues of local popular concern in their districts rather than to have a unified comprehensive vision of the government's budget. Some legislatures face pressures to cut the executive budget in order to free resources that can be redirected to fund legislative priorities, pet projects, or member items.

The clientele members' interests focus on how government programs affect them. They meet and discuss in conferences the significance of existing legislation, the chief executive's attitudes toward programs, and the policies of the agency. Sometimes the clientele works as a team, but often various subclient groups pursue their own agenda, with some coordination among some groups. Sometimes they even work at cross-purposes with other groups. Clientele groups vary in political skill and levels of activity, with success often depending on clientele leadership, the stakes involved, the organizational network, the dedication of the members to the issue, and the strategies and tactics employed by the groups.

The paths of clientele influence vary. Often a special agency-clientele relationship occurs because an unofficial policy of job rotation exists. For example, a chief executive appoints a former lobbyist or key member of a clientele group to a high-level government position that is important to the clientele group. In addition, sometimes clientele groups influence policy because they supported the winning president or influential congressperson. At a minimum, supporting the winner tends to create a useful cordial climate when policy makers decide issues of interest to the lobbyist. However, either traditional (that is one-on-one frequent interaction with the politician) or grassroots (that is having individuals in the home district confront the politician) lobbying is the standard path of influence.

In addition, formal and informal relationships can exist between the agency and the clientele, as illustrated in the UMTA and Maritime case examples cited earlier.

Agencies and clientele groups can have anticlientele groups. For example, consumer groups can oppose manufacturing interests and government regulating bodies. In recent years, more lobbying groups from both the right and left of the political spectrum as well as business groups have actively engaged in influencing policy so that lobbying is a major industry in government centers like Washington.

Defining the "good and bad guys" depends on each participant's values, issues, and perspectives. For some agencies, there is a pattern in which various actors tend to be allies on most issues. This need not be the situation. From the agency's point of view, the executive may be the stumbling block on one issue and the essential ally on another. From the clientele's viewpoint, the agency may be an enemy causing red tape or a vital agency necessary for the survival of the clientele members. In order to define the "good and bad guys," each participant in the process must reconsider each situation separately. Rarely does a uniform and consistent pattern exist over time where one set of actors are always friends and another set are always enemies. The patterns evolve and change; thus, the actors must adapt to a dynamic environment.

Cultivation of an Active Clientele

For most government agencies, there is no problem identifying a clientele group. Highway departments are well aware of their clientele. The Veterans Administration hears from its clientele. However, some agencies cannot easily identify clientele groups. For example, the United States Information Agency does not serve people in this country. What group is its clientele? The U.S. Bureau of Prisons does not have an active clientele group. In such cases, the nature of the organization or its mission may even preclude a clientele group; thus, the pluralist style of American government handicaps such agencies in the political process.

The most obvious way for an agency to cultivate a politically supportive clientele is for the agency merely to carry out its programs consistently. However, an agency can use some strategy to build a supportive clientele. In the first place, the clientele members should understand and appreciate the full extent of the benefits they receive from the agency's programs. Mute clientele members, especially, are not useful in the politically charged environment of budgeting, so the agency must encourage them to be active. Thus, the first part of the agency strategy is to educate its clientele on the benefits of the agency's program to the client. In the second place, most legislatures represent the whole population, so a breadth of clientele members across the nation, state, or city is best if the clientele wishes to lobby the legislature more successfully. Thus, the second part of the strategy is to broaden the agency programs so that they benefit clientele in all districts of the legislature. Third, some clientele members may be in a better position to aid the agency, such as a group in the House Appropriations Committee chairperson's home district. Thus, the third part of the agency strategy is to target its information and clientele relations so that key clientele members exist in the home district of key legislature members for the agency.

Agencies can use strategies to both expand and concentrate their clientele. For example, an agency can take care to provide grants or assistance across the country or to build a balanced set of programs that appeals to several specific sectors of society. Agencies can have their public information officers explain their programs to the public, and active attendance at clientele conferences is very important. Agencies can add some clientele members by changing or adding attractive services for clientele or potential supportive groups. For example, in an area where senior citizens are well organized, the parks department is wise to have programs for the elderly. Often the intensity of clientele support is important, so the agency can alter its programs in such a way as to benefit a particularly influential political group.

The legislature and the executive must hear the clientele if they are to be effective. In some instances, the clientele members organize themselves poorly or cannot comprehend the complex pluralistic American democratic institutions. Congresspersons, senators, and legislators often assume that if they do not hear from supporters, no one cares. They only tend to pay attention to the squeaky wheels. Given the need to cut most budgets, the tendency is to cut where no one cares enough to complain. Legislators do consider themselves to be guardians of the Treasury, but they do not like the uncomfortable feeling they get when cuts return to haunt them at the next election. They find saying "no" to an impassioned plea is very unpleasant regardless of their party label. An agency usually does not—and should not—advocate to its clientele members that they should lobby the legislature. Agency officials, however, can honestly explain that a small budget will not permit them to address the needs of the clientele and the budget size is a problem that the legislature can correct. Most savvy clientele leaders usually reach the obvious conclusion that they should lobby, and they do so.

Sometimes the agency's program structure attracts or discourages clientele. If the agency is broad-based but only narrow focus groups do the effective lobbying, then the agency might find poor support for its programs in the legislature. Agencies can broaden their appeal by the way they structure their programs. For example, the National Institute of Health uses its subunits to focus upon specific diseases that correspond to the active health clientele groups. As a result, very active and strong lobbying supports its programs. Sometimes this strategy can backfire: a strong clientele group can dominate the agency's funding, thus preventing the agency from serving the broader public interest because the glamorous subunit takes what resources the legislature considers available. Thus, the subunit does well, but the whole agency actually suffers in total funding. Another agency strategy is to create an advisory committee. Even the most conservative group of advisors tends to advocate the desirability of the agency's program to the legislature. This strategy can lead to increased and more effective clientele support.

Agency Budget Office

The agency budget office develops and orchestrates the budget process for the agency; but the duties of each office vary, as they sometimes include the accounting function and an analytical/planning unit. There are some common duties that describe what an agency budget office does. The following is a list of duties from one former agency budget office—the Budget Division of ACTION in the federal government:

- In conjunction with the appropriate operating officials, develops budget estimates for programs and offices, conducts budget reviews, and recommends budget allocations
- In conjunction with appropriate operating officials, develops, presents, and justifies ACTION's budget submission to the Office of Management and Budget and to the Congress, including financial and personnel exhibits, budget narrative material, and budget back-up data
- Prepares Agency witnesses for hearings before the Office of Management and Budget and the Congress
- Recommends budget office priorities as the result of Office of Management and Budget and Congressional budget guidance for use within the Agency
- Prepares apportionments, allotments, and maintains overall control of Agency financial resources and position allocations
- Issues operating budgets, including staffing levels (position and average grade allocations), to all offices, regions, and posts and ensures budget execution with legislative authority and limitations
- Conducts budget reviews and analyses during the fiscal year and recommends reprogramming actions and other funding adjustments
- Recommends and implements budgetary procedures, budget controls, and reporting systems and makes recommendations regarding the financial aspects of the management information system to improve financial management within the Agency
- Works with appropriate operating officials to help manage programs and coordinate the budget with Agency plans and objectives
- Acts as the Agency's primary point of contact with other governmental agencies on budget matters

Source: Budget Execution Responsibilities, ACTION, 1975.

Perspective of the Budget Officer

The budget officer sees the world in terms of dollars, accuracy, and legality. The agency must always translate its activities into money. While discussing new or old policy ideas, budget officers eventually will ask, "What does this mean in terms of money?" To them, accuracy of what they present is essential. As presented later in this chapter, budget officers place great importance on acquiring the confidence of others. Not making mistakes, especially in simple math, increases the confidence of others in the professionalism of the budget office. Budget officers must take care to establish procedures that double-check tables, ensure final typing is error free, and verify the accuracy of stated facts.

Legality is also a concern. If money is spent for reasons not permitted by law, then the budget officer may go to jail. There are few agency-level decisions that the budget officer does not know about, and often the law fixes responsibility for agency action on the agency head and budget officer. Thus, knowing key decisions may become a matter of not going to jail or receiving other serious sanctions. Wisdom dictates that the budget officer must be sure of the legality of questionable matters in order to avoid later problems. Much of the work of the budget officer is repetitive. The budget process has an established pattern, and after a few years the substantive issues of the agency also take on a familiar pattern. Budgeting is largely repetitive and the filling out of reports tends to make the work mechanical.

Deadlines are the guiding force for a budget officer. Sometimes they seem impossible, and often they are crucial because untimely budget presentations may miss rare and critical political windows of opportunity for policy makers. A common situation is to see a budget officer working late at night or on the weekends in order to meet some deadline. If the budget officer misses a deadline, then someone—usually the agency head or worse—is upset. More significantly, the agency may have lost an important opportunity or may have handicapped itself in a decision-making situation.

Timeliness can mean the survival itself of the agency's program. On the other hand, higher-level decision makers sometimes impose a foolish deadline. The wiser budget person misses the deadline and takes the extra time to prepare a better submission because he or she knows the quality of the submission will make a difference and being late will not be significant. The knowledge of how and when the policy makers will use the information should be the basis for the budget person's decision to ignore a deadline.

The budget officer can use the budget submission to minimize or surface policy disagreements. As an organizational artist, the budget officer realizes that he or she can present a budget in many ways in spite of the requirements of format. For political or internal management reasons, budget officers can hide or minimize specific policy or management issues often by placing the issue within a larger, more dominant subject. In many situations, surfacing disagreement is a much better strategy. The budget officer can surface an issue by presenting it with some prominence in the budget document. This forces decision makers to deal with the problem and try to resolve it. In many instances, outside political forces, such as a major media story on the subject, mandate the budget officer surface a disagreement because ignoring it would be unwise politically. In many instances, budget officers make important political and management decisions; thus, his or her political and management judgment is important. In this regard, budget officials may become *de facto* politicians themselves.

Deadlines and other pressures force the budget officer to use the satificing or incremental approach to most decision-making situations as opposed to the pure rational method, which is often impossible in the political environment of government decision making. Hence, budget officials often find themselves in the position of negotiator, where trade-offs and bargains are part and parcel of the budget process. When someone of importance demands a budget submission and the timeliness of that submission is important, then even a satisfactory answer rather than an ideal answer pleases the budget officer. Budget officers prepare budgets under extreme pressure, and they must do the best that they can in the time available. Searching endlessly for the ideal answers on all occasions is not compatible with the realities of budgeting.

Agency Budget Behavior

As explained earlier in this chapter, loyalty to an agency is a common behavioral phenomenon. Budget officers believe in their agency's mission and feel that their role is important for the well-being of the agency. Blind loyalty does not exist because program weaknesses are known. A more balanced loyalty prevails, which recognizes faults but believes the program is or can be essentially sound. Individuals working in a public agency take pride in their work. This can lead to the desire to expand the projects and programs. The desire of agencies to expand their programs often frustrates budget reviewers, but modest expansion tendencies are positive indicators of the health of program management. Policy makers should not criticize agencies for being enthusiastic program supporters. While recognizing that the central budget office role may call for them to disapprove of agency expansion, budget reviewers should applaud positive attitudes in agencies.

The political context of budgeting often forces analysts to realize that politics supersedes rationality. What might appear to be the best analytical solution to a policy problem is not necessarily the best position for the agency to take. Recall that agencies exist in a context of powerful interacting forces. When a person sails, the best sailing course may not be directly toward the ultimate objective. Sometimes tacking left and right into the wind is necessary to overcome the direct force of the opposing wind. In public administration, the best budget game strategy may not be to advocate or oppose a position but rather to wait for the clientele or legislature to react to circumstances that develop with time. Judgment is essential.

There often is some flexibility in budgeting as a result of what some call *gimmicks*. How to employ those gimmicks is another important budget officer talent. For example, the timing of when to make obligations and disbursements can be significant, and usually the budget officer is in a position to control that timing. The fact that a budget officer can sometimes assign a given expense item to one of two programs is another "gimmick" or "trick." This choice permits the budget officer some often-needed flexibility. Even the standard tools of transferring funds between programs or journal vouchering can be used strategically to give budget officers flexibility. "Gimmicks" exist because policy makers give discretion, and a budget officer can use that discretion to ease the burden of managing the program.

Public budgeting requires decision making. Even decisions not to act also represent a policy choice. If a budget reviewer delays a program or project for another year, that is a decision that often has important implications. Budget officers may base their decisions on sound reasoning, and those decisions do affect people, who do react. Therefore, budget officers must live with criticism from clientele, the media, and others because budget decisions often generate strong feelings, even if not sound reasoning. Also, budget officers often must make their decisions on meager information; thus, this contributes to the possibility of their self-doubt. If the budget officer cannot emotionally deal with criticism and doubt, then he or she should consider a different type of work because doubt and criticism are a part of the job.

Public budgeting requires the highest professional characteristics. Later, this chapter explains more about the importance of confidence, which the budget officer establishes through his or her professionalism. Honesty and integrity are essential professional characteristics. This means that the budget officer does prepare the *strongest case possible* budget justification for a program, and it does mean that "possible" includes avoiding lies and misrepresentations. No one faults a budget officer for being sensitive to shifting political causes (for example, new environment, energy, inflation, or unemployment policy concerns) and framing budget justifications to take advantage of those shifting but temporarily persuasive rationales. This political sensitivity comes together with accuracy, legality, honesty, integrity, and other factors to constitute a professional demure. Yet there is often a fine line that budget officers must walk between professionalism and game playing, particularly when strategic misrepresentation (for example, not fully elaborating on a budget proposal or its implications) can border on the unethical.

One unfortunate characteristic of some budget officers is arrogance. This trait exists more in budget reviewers found in units like the department budget offices and the U.S. Office of Management and Budget (OMB). Lord Acton once stated that power corrupts and absolute power corrupts absolutely. Even budget officers and budget analysts possess some power because of the nature of their job; this power corrupts a few but many more become a little or significantly intoxicated by it. They know they have power and they let others know it with their arrogance. For example, young examiners, who were mild-mannered before they started working for the governor's budget office, visit the "field" and realize that they have power over an agency because their recommendations are influential. Thus, they start acting cavalier, flippant, or even bossy to agency persons who have much higher civil service ranks and longer government experience then they do. Such behavior is not professional because it often leads to a needless lack of cooperation from the agency and makes the examiner's job that much more difficult. In addition, budget officers who wish to cultivate long-term positive relationships with their agencies may burn some bridges that will affect subsequent budget negotiations in the future. Another concern stemming from this arrogant attitude is that many times the agency budget officer is looking for a career move that might involve working for the agency for which he or she has budgeted. In this event, it would be more beneficial to have friends in the agency rather than enemies.

Budget officers are almost always career civil servants who work quite closely with politically appointed agency or department heads. The position of an agency head, which is responsible politically to the chief executive, can disturb the close rapport to the budget officer, who tends to be more sensitive to the agency perspective. Occasionally, the expected exclusive allegiance to the chief executive conflicts with loyalty to the agency, causing an extremely difficult emotional dilemma. When such situations arise, the budget officer will become quite aware of the dilemma because the agency head's handling of that dilemma will influence directly the budget process. Understanding the dilemma is helpful, but there are no easy answers to this type of situation that tests the moral character of the agency head and budget officer.

Public budgeting is an activity that requires responsible people. In the federal government, the law dramatizes this responsibility. Under the Anti-deficiency Act a budget officer cannot legally overobligate or permit his agency to spend an amount in excess of the OMB apportionment. If he or she does so, then the attorney general can bring a legal case against the budget officer, and higher-level management or the courts can fire, fine, or sentence the budget officer to jail. Exhibit 4–2 quotes the passage from the Anti-deficiency Act that details the action required when violations occur. A fine or jail sentence results from willful violations. Although such violations are rare, budget officers know this law.

Good professionals love the budget game, but they may not enjoy the intensity of budget game playing, especially in Washington, DC. Although they find the game both challenging and exciting, they may also find the game playing morally questionable. Professional codes of conduct and ethics rules in government help guard against such dilemmas. For example, both the National Association of State Budget Officers (NASBO) and the Government Finance Officers Association (GFOA) have strong ethics codes and provide guidance in situations where budget officers find their ethics challenged. Budget officers usually get a sense of their importance and appreciate the responsibility associated with budgeting. Often, they enjoy the need to work under pressure and yet deliver quality work. They love knowing all the complexities of budgeting and being able to use their skills to make a difference in government and the larger society. They love the intrigue and excitement of both politics and public management.

What the Research Says

Katherine Willoughby surveyed ten southern state budget offices to understand what guides budget officer behavior. She focused on state government budget analysts and discovered that they took their decision-making clues primarily from gubernatorial direction, agency efficiency, and changes in workload data when policy makers reviewed spending plans. Less important were the influence of the agency head and the legislative agenda. Of least importance were the acquisitiveness of the agency head and public support for the program. She noted that the fiscal stability of the state and the age of the analysts were also factors in influencing their decisions.

Sydney Duncombe and Richard Kinney, who examined how five states budget officials defined agency budget success, concluded that agency budget success is a complex, multidimensional concept that goes beyond maximizing state appropria-

---

EXHIBIT 4–2   Anti-Deficiency Act (Section 3527 of Revised Statutes, as amended)

Actions required when violations occur.

1. *Administrative discipline; fines; or imprisonment.* In addition to any penalty of liability under other law, any officer or employee of the United States who shall violate subsections (a), (b), or (h) of this section shall be subjected to appropriate administrative discipline, including, when circumstances warrant, suspension from duty without pay or removal from office; and any officer or employee of the United States who shall knowingly and willfully violate subsections (a), (b), or (h) of this section shall, upon conviction, be fined not more than $5,000 or imprisoned for not more than two years, or both.

2. *Reports to President or Congress.* In the case of a violation of subsections (a), (b), or (h) of this section by an officer or employee of an agency, or of the District of Columbia, the head of the agency concerned or the Commissioner of the District of Columbia, shall immediately report to the President, through the Director of the Office of Management and Budget, and to the Congress all pertinent facts together with a statement of the action taken thereon.

---

tions. They found most budget professionals were "satisfiers" and not "maximizers." Aaron Wildavsky correctly concluded that budget strategies and objectives were contingent upon climate and circumstance. In Exhibit 4–3, note that perceptions vary significantly among agency officials, executive budget staff, and legislative budget staff. Budget reviewers believe agencies define success in terms of protecting programs and "winning the budget influence game." Agencies view good relations as significantly higher measures of their budget success than do their executive and legislative opponents.

Current research on agency budget success has identified optimal strategies but more in the context of revenue cutbacks or revenue growth. Alternatively, a 1999 study by James W. Douglas examined agency budget success through the lens of reallocation decisions provided to state agencies under an innovative budget reform (redirection) in the state of Georgia. Other recent studies have focused more on central budget office and executive branch budget success under performance-based budgeting (PPB) in the states. See Katherine Willoughby and Julia Melkers' study on effectiveness of PPB in the states. Duncombe and Kinney's work represents an important contribution to understanding success from an agency, legislative, and budget official perspective.

Four Views

Chapter 2 explained decision-making models and their importance. Normative theories influence people working in budgeting, and this section discusses four ideal types that describe typical reactions to normative theories. The four ideal types are *the true rational believer, the pure reactive person, the budget-wise person* (the cynic), and *the wise budget person.*

The True Rational Believer.   Under the influence of the rational model, there are people working in public budgeting who strongly believe decision making should use *only* the pure rational approach. If any decision does not follow that approach, then they consider the decision highly questionable and in error due to lack of professionalism or the unfortunate intrusion of politics into proper decision making. They try to ensure that at least significant decisions follow the rational model by (1) setting goals and objectives, (2) defining alternatives, (3) analyzing alternatives, and (4) selecting the best decision when making their recommendation to policy makers.

Such faith in the rational decision-making theory leads to unfortunate consequences in public budgeting. Many public organizations have vague, multiple, and sometimes mutually inconsistent goals and objectives. Therefore, articulating specific goals and objectives, as required in most rational analyses, sometimes is logically impossible. In addition, many types of nonrational analyses add value to the decision-making process. If the rational approach limits the range of thinking that an analyst applies to a problem, then rational analytical techniques may not help, and in fact can be dysfunctional to the decision-making challenge facing the analysts and policy makers. This constraint limits the usefulness of analysis and thus handicaps policy makers unnecessarily.

EXHIBIT 4–3 Importance of Selected Budget Success Measures as Seen by Budget Officials (% reporting "Very Important")

Measures of Budget Success	AGENCY OFFICIALS (N=50) RANK %	EXECUTIVE BUDGET STAFF (N=25) RANK %	LEGISLATIVE BUDGET STAFF (N=25) RANK %
1. Whether good relationships were maintained with the legislative budget staff	1 60	5 28	7 24
2. Whether good relationships were maintained with the governor and budget staff	2 58	5 28	5 28
3. Whether the agency was able to protect existing programs from being cut below the amount needed to continue at the existing level	3 54	2 48	1 44
4. Whether the agency had to lay off staff this year	4 53	4 36	2 32
5. Percent of agency budget request funded by the legislature.	5 35	3 40	7 24
6. Percent of agency budget request funded by the government.	6 34	1 52	9 20
7. Whether the agency was able to fund new programs this year	7 24	10 16	2 32
8. Percent increase in approp. above current year	8 14	7 20	2 32
9. Percent increase in approp. over a 4–year period	9 12	8 8	5 28
10. Whether the agency was able to spend its entire appropriations.	9 12	8 8	10 0

Source: Sydney Duncombe and Richard Kinney. "Agency Budget Success: How It Is Defined by Budget Officials In Five Western States." Public Budgeting and Finance, 7, 1 (Spring 1987), pp. 24–37.

Another problem with the rational model is that it implies no limits exist to the defining of alternatives and the analysis of alternatives. As Thomas D. Lynch points out in *Policy Analysis in Public Policymaking,* some individuals will proceed to spend large sums of money on analysis when the end results will be as useful as a much more limited analytical effort. The rational model motivates those individuals to pursue the possible alternatives and exhaustively examine those alternatives. Another related problem with the rational model is that true believers sometimes don't appreciate the importance of feedback in analysis; thus, policy makers ignore helpful feedback.

A subtler problem of the rational model is the inherent assumption that only one omnipresent perspective exists for all persons. Recall from Chapter 2 the fable involving several blind men and an elephant. The storyteller stresses how each blind man examines a different segment of the elephant and proceeds to argue with the other blind men over the nature of the beast. Ironically, the storyteller assumes that there is only the one perspective of the sighted person. All parties, including the storyteller, make their assumptions from their relational perspective. Therefore, their unique perspectives limit all parties in understanding the elephant—a limitation they can transcend only through a larger perspective of the whole. The rational model leads us to make the mistake of taking only one perspective. Similarly, budget officers are wiser to recognize that there are many perspectives, some shared perceptions, and one perspective of the whole commonly called the public interest. Unfortunately, the common use made of the rational model in public budgeting does not encourage such a sophisticated understanding.

The Pure Reactive Person.   In contrast to the rational believers are the pure reactive budget persons. These people act in a stimulus-response pattern limited to their immediate reaction to events that affect them. The budget calendar and the requests from higher authority govern these people. They give little thought to shaping events or somehow making a difference for the whole society through their own efforts. Instead, they define their job as merely a task that they need to do as defined in their job description or the demands placed on them by others. Decision-making models, such as the rational model, mean little to these persons. They typically justify their mechanical responses using the mantra of "I am only following the directions of my bosses." Such people believe that the politically elected and appointed officials alone should make policy decisions and that civil servants should merely respond to the wishes of the political officials.

The hazard of this approach is that civil servants become subjects of the mindless and potentially foolish mistakes of government decision making by not recognizing the uniqueness and importance of their own position or analysis. From their vantage point, the budget person can often comprehend both the political actor's viewpoint and the viewpoint of those working at the lower-management level in government. By having the budget person merely reacting to a political operative, the government as a whole loses the important insight of the budget expert. Thus, more errors are likely to occur that harm the larger public interest. An aggressive, outspoken budget staff that expresses its opinions can greatly improve policy making and government management, but a staff that only reacts to policy makers permits them to make unnecessary—often significant—errors. Better policy makers recognize the value of an aggressive and outspoken budget staff as opposed to a reactive one.

The Budget-Wise Person.   These people are aware of all the forms and tables in budgeting practice, but discount them almost completely because they consider the government's decisions are only political. They are often cynical about life in general and stress the political nature of "public administration." They can cite dramatic examples from their personal experiences of gross politically inspired decision making, sometimes involving corruption and often involving vote trading. While such decision making does typically preclude effective public management, budget-wise people stress that such decision making is inevitable. To them, all that a budget staff can do is react and watch events unfold. Unfortunately, in some government settings, the cynic is correct; but in many others, the well-prepared budget justifications can influence the political actors who can think in terms of the larger public interest when reminded of that responsibility. Professional budgeting can and often does mean effective public management. At minimum, professionalism will attune policy makers to the consequences of their budgetary actions. If a cynical view dominates the mindset of budget staff, then that staff has lost a valuable opportunity for creating a more effective government for all citizens.

The Wise Budget Person.   People of this type recognize that politics is sometimes of overriding importance in the budget decision-making process. They also understand that analysis has its limitations but can often greatly help in decision-making situations. Professional public budgeting can significantly help policy making and government management. It is hoped that this text will help more people be wise budget persons.

Develop Confidence

Having the confidence of the budget reviewers, especially the appropriations committees, is extremely important to the budget officer. If confidence doesn't exist, any reviewer or set of reviewers can ask hard questions and force the agency to justify every detail in a time-consuming activity that only keeps good agency managers from managing their programs correctly. If the appropriations committees lack confidence, they can write into the appropriation bill or committee report very specific special conditions, thus tying the hands of the agency and making program administration a nightmare even for good managers. However, if the budget officer can create confidence in the agency budget request in the minds of the reviewers, the reviews are less difficult and policy makers give the agency greater administrative discretion. This, in turn, makes management easier for the skilled public official.

Often, there is a natural tendency on the part of the reviewers to place confidence in agency budget officers if they do their job correctly because policy makers tend to accept the facts and management judgments as truthful. The sheer complexity of the budget plus the lack of time to review budgets mean that policy makers or their analysts cannot review every budget in depth. Typically, reviewers must place priority on and give greater attention to examining the more questionable requests or the politically sensitive subjects. On most subjects, budget reviewers tend to trust the expertise of the budget officers who have gained a strong professional reputation. Such trust, on the part of the budget reviewers, saves them valuable time in meeting a tight budget time schedule. Thus, an agency budget officer is wise to create a reputation of being highly professional and responsive to legislative reviewers.

The following criteria capture the key elements of the ideal professional budget officer. In order to gain the needed trust, such a person should be

- a master of detail;
- hard working;
- concise;
- frank, yet strategic;
- self-effacing and devoted to the work;
- tight with the taxpayer's money;
- capable of recognizing a political necessity when it is present; and
- conscientious about keeping key reviewers (for example, congresspersons) informed of sensitive changes in policy or important developments.

Budget officers find that a reputation of playing it straight is wise. Lying, covering up, and being tricky are highly undesirable characteristics for the career civil servant. But budget officers must be thoughtful negotiators with a strategic view of dealings with potentially adversarial legislative members and their staffs. Memories can be long among top reviewing staffs. If reviewers, especially appropriations committees, feel that a budget officer misled them, then they can take strong punitive actions, such as tying the agency into administrative knots with special appropriation language. On the other hand, a positive reputation can even mean securing emergency or supplemental funds on the basis of skimpy hearings, that is, getting funds almost entirely on the integrity of the budget officer.

Professional friendships enhance reputations. A close personal relationship with budget reviewers, such as the agency's congressional subcommittee staff, can ease tensions. Years of outstanding service are even more significant than friendships because such experience often builds a sense of integrity and trust, which constitutes "professional friendships." In many cases, shared work experiences and service together in professional associations build these professional friendships.

Career budget officers recognize that political "necessity" is one of the intangible characteristics associated with building the confidence of political leaders in the budget staff. However, judgment can differ on the question of what is a "necessity." Some accommodation to favors and pet projects do and should occur in a democracy, but such practices can move from the unusual to the expected. When this occurs, public managers cannot carry out effective public management. Ironically, turning political leaders down when their requests are not reasonable in terms of the larger public interest is another dimension of how a budget officer builds the confidence of political leaders in the professionalism of the budget officer. Techniques for pleasant turndowns include the following:

- "My hands are tied"—other factors may exist, such as an executive mandate that precludes the favor.
- "Maybe in the future"—the administrator may grant the favor, but the timing is simply not wise.
- "But look at the other positive actions we took"—stress that other decisions were in their favor or to their liking and appeal to the notion that one should only expect to win a "fair share" of the time.
- "It cannot be done"—administrators can cite economic, technical, or other reasons why the request is either impossible or extremely unwise to fulfill.

Administrators can use other strategies to minimize granting favors, which might not be in the public interest. For example, they can delay action on the favor. If they are truly serious, the political actors will pursue their requests until they get action. Administrators can delay action; thus, they use time to filter the true "necessities." A parallel strategy is to submit on the most intensely sought favors and pet projects. Administrators can also measure intensity by examining the means used to bring pressure upon the agency. Regardless of how political leaders show intensity of their requested "favors," the strategy is to submit on the more intense favors and resist on the less intense favors.

Strategies and techniques can help budget officers, but in a few cases they must face the negative consequences if they are to remain ethical and moral persons. Sometimes budget officers must face a no-win situation due to their professional or personal ethics or the need to support persons in the bureaucracy such as the agency head. In some instances, allowing one political actor (for example, a congressperson) to do battle with another political actor (for example, a political appointee or the media) is a ploy that can mitigate the situation. However, such a ploy can result in making two enemies and losing rather than gaining their confidence. In other situations, the budget officer may merely have to use time to heal relationships or hope that key actors don't blame the budget officer but blame the deed. The negative consequences to a budget officer may be severe, but sometimes one's professional integrity requires action, which ironically can harm one's professional reputation.

There is no developed method for establishing confidence. All that a budget officer can do is be aware of the techniques and strategies available, observe others that are successful, and use careful judgment. No one approach is useful for all budget reviewers for all situations. A budget officer must consider each set of circumstances separately before she or he takes action.

Results

Confidence in a government program often rests with an agency demonstrating that it achieves positive results. Demonstrated results are a significant means to build policy makers' and clientele groups' confidence in budget officials because they see the benefits of the government programs.

There is an important distinction between an agency accomplishing its purpose and clientele or political leaders feeling that the agency serves them. Politically, the latter is more significant, especially if the clientele and the political leaders feel the agency has served the larger public interest. Often the distinction between achieving agency objectives and serving the public interest is only theoretical because accomplishing objectives should translate to serving the public interest. Unfortunately, sometimes the assumed theoretical linkage does not exist. Also, the people—the agency's potential clientele—may be unaware of the importance of the government program to them, may have come to take it for granted, or may not feel that the program is important. As noted earlier in this chapter, agency clientele members are important in the political context in which an agency operates. If the potential clientele members are not active supporters of the program, then the agency may fail in the budget process, given the usual political competition for funding support.

For an agency, serving a large, appreciative, and strategically placed clientele is ideal. The best type of clientele brings its satisfaction to the attention of decision makers, such as the appropriations committees and the chief executive. Such a happy harmony of circumstances does not always exist, so agencies must make attempts to develop alternative means to build and maintain the essential support.

If an agency doesn't enjoy overwhelming public support, it can make a persuasive case to policy makers by citing its tangible accomplishments. In the budget justification process, it can place emphasis on its program accomplishments. The criteria used to claim success are sometimes the subject of debate, and sometimes policy makers or budget officers use semantic confusion to rationalize criteria that define success. In such circumstances, the merits of the accomplishments are less persuasive, and other policy makers usually consider the budget justification as weak. Nevertheless, almost any citation of accomplishment is usually highly desirable in a budget justification.

If the listing of results is not sufficiently impressive, the agency can extend an invitation to the decision makers or anyone likely to influence the policy makers (the legislature or the media) to visit the agency. An agency can make a case for a budget by showing the need (for example, poor people suffering), the activity (for example, the production of a missile), or the heroic efforts by an overworked staff (for example, emergency room care at a hospital) to budget reviewers and other influential people. Often this technique is extremely useful. The U.S. space program used this approach quite successfully to maintain high public interest in its efforts. However, there are significant risks. This demonstration may not impress the reviewers, and this can translate into lower budgets rather than increased or sustained budget support.

Visits and other attempts to explain highly complex programs can be problematic. Most political decision makers are not experts, so sometimes budget officers must explain the program using nontechnical words that may oversimplify the essential message. If the explanations are too simple, then the budget reviewers do not understand the complex nature of the challenge, and the level of funding might seem unwarranted to them. If the explanations are too complex, then the reviewers might question the clarity of the management direction, and again the reviewers might lower the level of funding or cut the program entirely. Selecting the exact visit format and the precise substance of the message to be conveyed can indeed be a challenge, depending upon the complexity of the program. A hazard of demonstrating tangible accomplishment is that reviewers may praise the program and then cut it because the agency has met its program objectives. Policy makers design government programs to meet a problem, and success may mean the problem ceases to exist. If that occurs, the program should cease to exist. The irony is that losing one's job seems like a punishment rather than a reward.

Not having tangible accomplishments that agencies can demonstrate is a disadvantage to some government programs. For example, unless there is a catastrophe to demonstrate emergency preparedness, that agency cannot point to any tangible accomplishment. Another example is the International Communications Agency, which broadcasts propaganda overseas. How does one deal with such programs when the agency cannot easily demonstrate tangible results? Budget officers are constantly on the lookout for agencies using the following ploys:

- "Our program is priceless"—they argue that results are not evident but if the program did not exist, what cost would there be in human lives if disaster occurred?
- "Results of our program cannot be measured"—they argue that no one can present data showing results given the nature of the program. This might be a truthful argument, but it will not persuade policy makers.
- "Results will be evident in the future"—they argue that they cannot present evidence of results now because the program is new or the program's results are only evident when an emergency occurs. This is a more appealing argument, but skeptics can say that an emergency is the wrong time to find out that the program does not work.
- "Figures show"—they argue facts and figures show results, even though decision makers do not find the figures relevant. This is a foolish ploy, given the potential loss of confidence that could result.
- "In this complex situation, the figures confirm"—they argue by ignoring the questionable cause-effect relationships within a multiple causal situation. This is a reasonable ploy for a weak situation, but budget officers must take care in the wording so that the statements are positive and not false. The agency should avoid extreme claims that the agency cannot justify.
- "Please notice that we reviewed more than a thousand applicants"—they argue by focusing not on results but on the procedures and process measures of the organization. The critical observant reviewer can always ask, "So what?" However, making a display of facts and figures is better than saying nothing because the information does demonstrate some agency activity did take place.
- "You must appreciate that we cannot prove the relationship of this to later achievement, but we know such a relationship exists"—they argue that faith alone establishes the relationship between the program and the desired benefit to society. If the subject of the program is something that policy makers take for granted, then the budget officer might be successful with such an argument, but the *if* becomes critical.

Preparing for Hearings

Hearings often are important in building confidence of a legislature in an agency and its leadership. In some situations, hearings only provide a public record that agency policy makers consider the concerns of legislators or clientele. However, hearings can and often do affect executive and legislative decision makers, given the competing pressures on their time and the inadequate preparation they give to reviewing the budget material supplied them by the agency. Hearings are particularly important in establishing confidence of the policy makers in the agency management. Program officials who cannot answer or who poorly answer questions create an impression that those running the organization don't really understand what they do.

Rehearsals for budget hearings are essential. The numbers of hearings vary by agency and government, but four hearings on the agency budget alone are the minimum number in the federal government. As noted in an earlier chapter, rehearsing or holding mock hearings is a standard practice. Agency administrators play the role of key reviewers such as the appropriations committee chairperson. Agency heads learn to anticipate and answer tough questions before the hearing in order to avoid later difficulties. Mock hearings are an excellent device to expose weak justifications, to build effective agency coordination in handling questions, and to appreciate the perspective of the reviewer. Mock hearings also help budget officers decide what subjects they should discuss and stress in the traditional opening statement.

The key to preparing for budgeting hearings is to do sufficient research to avoid or minimize surprises. A surprise usually makes the administrator appear to be ignorant and can rattle him or her to the point of answering all the remaining questions poorly. A diligent search of past hearings and statements often indicates what the reviewers consider important. Also a review of the program itself and public reactions to the program are essential in framing the tough questions. Often the rapport of the budget officer with others, such as people in the central budget office, can be a vital resource for anticipating potential problem areas in future hearings.

Briefing books for hearings are useful and highly recommended. Typically, they include only the tough or standard questions and answers that the agency budget officer anticipates. They might include a brief discussion on the perspectives of each reviewer, but such information is often common knowledge. Also such descriptions can fall into the wrong hands, leading to unnecessary embarrassment.

Questions in hearings come from a variety of sources, including the reviewer (for example, a senator), staff, clientele, and even the agency itself. Agency budget officers sometimes plant questions, including the agency supplying entire lists of questions for the committee to ask the agency in the committee hearings. Sometimes the planted questions are the most difficult so that the agency can go on record on a subject in the best possible manner. Planted questions rarely occur at the department and OMB hearings, but they are common in Congress, where friendly legislators wish to help an agency. In some instances, the relationship between agency and legislative committee staffs is so close that the effect is the same as having planted questions.

Formal presentations at hearings create a "portrait" of the agency leadership in the minds of reviewers. Thus, hearings are an agency opportunity to paint a self-portrait of credibility and generate a favorable mood toward the agency leadership. With the portrait, the agency can take on such mantles as protector-of-the-public-safety, scientist, statesman or stateswoman, guardian-of-the-environment, and so on. As explained earlier, effective hearing presentations tend to ward off unpleasant and time-consuming probes of an agency.

The best way to make a positive impression at a hearing is to know the budget. There is no adequate substitute for being knowledgeable, but budget officers should couple knowledge with a good, organized presentation. Usually, succinct presentations and answers offer the reviewer a later opportunity to go deeper into a subject using follow-up questions effectively. Presenters and reviewers need to be careful in leaving the impression that they are not slighting an important subject. Reviewers usually forgive an administrator for not knowing a program detail; in fact, presenters often supply such data for the record after the hearing. However, reviewers are less forgiving of administrators who do not know answers to questions involving management direction. Presenters can often anticipate reviewers' questions—even on details—and answer them at the time of the hearing with the result of an impressive performance that builds the confidence of the reviewers in the ability of the agency. It is also important to make sure that the appropriate agency staff members are in attendance to answer specific program questions or to provide detailed information that can bolster an agency presentation.

Hearings are a game with certain taboos. Agency officials recognize that they have two masters—the legislature and the executive—but agency officials cannot challenge the chief executive's budget, even though they may wish for more support. Nevertheless, everyone present can tell if the officials mean otherwise. Agency heads and budget officers achieve this communication by

- exhibiting a marked lack of enthusiasm when answering questions;
- being too enthusiastic for credibility;
- refusing to answer legislators' questions by protesting loyalty to the chief executive; and
- yielding only after sharp, pointed questioning from the legislators at the hearing.

These taboos are significant. If the agency is not adhering to the established executive branch policy set by the central budget office or the department, then the chief executive or department head can fire the agency head and other political appointees. Top administrative leaders take "speaking against the administration" extremely seriously. In a few instances, the central budget office or department game strategy might be to have the agency not resist legislative desires to increase the budget over executive branch requests. Such a ploy allows the executive to blame budget increases on the other branch of government. How the agency should respond requires the agency heads to judge each situation separately.

Another taboo is that the agencies should not publicly admit yielding to clientele pressure. The agencies are accountable to all the people; thus, yielding to one client is an admission of favoritism rather than serving the public interest. Agency heads are also saying that they do buckle to interest group pressure. Instead, agency heads should carefully phrase their language to say the agency always wishes to receive advice from citizens and does act upon suggestions that have intrinsic value to the public. Thus, the agency hopes to leave the impression that it responds to sound advice but makes decisions only on the merits of the situation. Diplomatically, the agency conveys the message that "interest group pressure" does not unduly influence it.

STRATEGIES

Reviewers versus Reviewed

The budget game requires advocates and reviewers. The agency is the advocate or presenter, but clientele groups and sometimes even legislators are advocates. The reviewers are the department officials, the central budget office (for example, OMB), the House appropriations subcommittee, and the Senate appropriations subcommittee. As the budget moves through the budget cycle, reviewers change roles and become advocates. For example, after the central budget office reviews the budget requests and the executive branch makes its final decisions, then that former reviewer is an advocate to the legislative appropriations subcommittees. The primary advocate, however, is always the agency. If the advocates and reviewers play the game well, there always exists an arm's length relationship between them. Both play the role with caution, care, and an awareness of the natural tendencies associated with each role. A requirement for a good game is that each party knows the rules and strategy. Ideally, all the game players should be highly skilled professionals. An uneven game sometimes means unreasonable cuts or unreasonably high budgets. Both results are undesirable.

One risk in this budget game can be the failure of the agency to make a professional and convincing budget justification. For example, occasionally, an agency will resubmit the previous year's budget with the only change being the fiscal years mentioned in the text. When this occurs, the reviewers naturally should question the budget request. At a minimum, intervening variables since the last year budget request would cause some program changes not mentioned in the last budget justification. The possibility of an *identical* budget request approaches zero because administrative environments always change. A distinct likelihood exists that someone ordered the agency to use the same budget level as the previous year's budget, but to use the *identical* budget request implies no agency ability to adapt to changing conditions. Part of the budget game is to at least give the appearance of managing the program; when budget officers use last year's numbers, the agency does not give that appearance.

Reviewers often do not approve the agency budget request intact; they usually reduce (cut) the request in some area. There are several common rationales given for cutting budgets:

- a climate of opinion exists that was against spending;
- strong views by influential decision makers necessitated the cut;
- spending on your program became a political football; and
- there was an overriding need to balance the budget.

The reason cited may address the management capability or fundamental objectives of the agency's program. However, such statements are more difficult to rationalize against the superior expertise of the agency on those topics. The preceding reasons are less subject to dispute and appeal; thus, reviewers are more likely to cite them.

Some ironies can exist with budget cutting. An agency might wish to have a certain program cut or might even cut its own program. For example, maybe the agency leadership lost faith in a program; internal discipline called for cuts; or higher priorities in some programs meant cuts in other programs. Interestingly, cuts can sometimes stimulate the political mobilization of the agency's clientele; thus, without those earlier cuts, the agency would not eventually get subsequent year higher budget numbers due to political backlash.

Another phenomenon, which can occur, is interlegislative conflict. One obvious area of conflict is between the two legislative chambers (House and Senate). Legislative procedures intend conference committees to resolve House-Senate disputes, but one chamber can use budget strategies to dominate the conference committee deliberations. For example, the Senate might raise the amount it passes in order to achieve its desired amount through compromise in the conference committee with the House. Another tactic is to have a chamber pass a resolution supporting its conferees, thus, permitting the conferees to cite the solidarity and intensity of feelings of their chamber in their conference committee arguments. Conference committees are often unpredictable, and most agencies would prefer to avoid this uncertainty unless one chamber cuts its requests significantly. A less obvious area of conflict is between the substantive committee and the appropriations committee. In some instances, the agency can be the innocent victim of such disputes.

Spenders' Strategies

There are game strategies that an agency can apply in seeking to get its budget requests approved. This section explains the various strategies that spenders commonly use, but does not attempt to comment in-depth upon how, when, and in what way the spenders should apply these strategies to maximize their effectiveness. Such matters require judgment based upon each separate budget situation.

There are some fairly common safe strategies that spenders employ. For example, they often pad their budget requests because they wish to meet unanticipated contingencies and compensate for the fact that reviewers often cut requests almost automatically. Obvious or nondefensible "padding" leads to an important loss of confidence, thus resulting in very hostile hearings, but usually advocates can easily defend "extras." In practice oftentimes, padding of budgets does occur as a deliberative strategy, especially for advancing crucial programs that are unlikely to be opposed. In this context, padding is often advanced as a defensible technique (see discussion of budget boosting on pages 146–147). A related advocate strategy is always to ask for more. This demonstrates an aggressive agency that has a strong belief in its mission. The reviewer might not consider the increase request merited, but addressing the increase might force the reviewers to forget to argue the possibility of a program level decrease. In connection with this strategy, the agency carefully spends or obligates all of its current year's funds. If there is any surplus, the reviewer may argue that the agency's current funding is more than adequate and there is no need for additional money in the budget year. Another safe strategy is to alter the written or oral budget presentations as much as possible to highlight the best aspects of the agency's program and minimize the worst aspects.

Budgeting is a complex activity. "Sleight-of-hand" tricks do exist and they can be part of a budget strategy. For example, advocates round their numbers in budgets often to the nearest hundred thousand or even million. For some small but politically important budget items, the practice of rounding *can be* an advantage because the small numbers might establish an important precedent. Recasting the budget into different categories than those used in the previous year is another "trick." The advocates use the redone categories to focus attention upon or away from programs, depending upon the budget's strategic purposes. Also, redone categories inhibit longitudinal analysis, and this could be an advantage to the agency. In addition, there are a variety of backdoor spending devices: one of them is a no-year fund. Using unobligated appropriations or disobligated appropriations (that is, the agency previously obligated funds but then subsequently withdrew the obligation, often because of nonuse by grantees) to finance projects beyond the apparent level of budget-year appropriations is another sleight-of-hand trick. For example, let us say that an agency has $15 million left over from last year's budget and also has $20 million disobligated from previous years. Technically, the agency budget office should deduct the $35 million from the next year budget request, but typically the advocates do not cite or poorly cite the subtraction in their budget submission.

Another sleight-of-hand trick is the fund transfer. An agency can often transfer money from one account to another. By using several transfers among several funds, the advocate can create the illusion that the agency obligated the money. Advocates can use this unprofessional trick even to defraud the government or mislead reviewing groups such as prospective bond buyers. Careful accounting and auditing can uncover such abuses, but such work is detailed and time-consuming.

Most spenders' strategies are direct and simple. The agency merely points out that the tasks it performs have expanded and they need more money to fund the program. Another common strategy is to point out the backlog of requests or tasks. The argument is then made that the agency needs an increase in funding to eliminate the backlog and that any budget cut would increase the size of the backlog. Appealing to a national standard by showing that the agency can meet the standard with a given higher level of budget support is a third advocate strategy or argument. Advocates who are highly professional groups (for example, medical and educational) often use this strategy.

Sometimes the strategy is to argue with rational economic concepts. A program activity might involve a fee, such as an entrance fee or license. The agency argues that a given budget expenditure level would attract more people to the activity, thus increasing the revenue from the activity that goes to the agency. The increased revenue might be larger than the expenses in the budget, thus allowing the agency to expand its budget even more. A more complex argument is that an increased budget for a program like a subsidy would increase the operation and payroll size. The agency argues the multiplier effect of the subsidy means that the government would recover more in additional taxes (for example, income tax) than it paid for the subsidy. Another argument is that an increased budget would permit greater agency productivity owing to an enhanced cost average per unit or the use of the extra money to purchase laborsaving devices.

Sometimes advocates predicate their arguments on emotion. The agency argues that the revenue of the government has grown and that the agency should receive a fair share of the growth. Arguing that a high-level commitment exists on the project and there is no option but to fund the program is a bolder strategy as it is mere assertion. A less bold but equally emotional strategy is to plead that the program is "squeezed to the bone" and a certain funding level is essential for meaningful program operation.

In many situations, the agency wishes to start a new program but the advocates realize they must mask the newness or precedent using a "foot-in-the-door wedge" or "camel's nose under the tent." Advocates know that reviewers have a much higher standard for new programs than they have for existing programs. The agency will often argue that the money does not represent a new initiative but rather a continuation of old programs. This might be quite true literally, but the change might constitute an entirely new major emphasis that, logically, reviewers should consider as a new program. Treating programs in this manner may bias reviewers against the initiative. This often happens when the agency's advocates try to mask the newness by claiming it really is the old program with such a small change that it is insignificant.

Spenders' strategies can constitute a high political risk for the agency and agency officials. One strategy is to react to a request for cuts by suggesting reviewers cut projects first that enjoy strong political support. By cutting the "sacred cows" or popular programs, the cutters place themselves in a politically difficult position, and the political process may force them to withdraw the cut. The risk to the agency head is that the use of the strategy might offend the chief executive and result in the firing of the agency head. A second strategy is to shift the blame. The agency points out that if the reviewer does not fund the full requested amount, then the agency will not undertake certain essential activities. The agency makes it clear to the reviewer that the agency will place the responsibility for not funding the activity on the reviewer. In some situations, such responsibility and the related political implications sober reviewers; thus, they act favorably on the budget request.

A third strategy is to argue that a cut is irresponsible and that the reviewers must fund the project at the requested level or not fund it at all. This is a sound argument for many projects because there is a lower limit at which management cannot sustain a project as viable. The risk in such an argument is that the reviewer might indeed decide to cut the whole project. A fourth high-risk strategy is to spend fast to be short. The agency deliberately spends the money at a fast rate and then goes back to the reviewers for supplemental appropriations. Advocates employ this strategy infrequently, but it does occur, especially when the executive or legislature asks the agency to absorb large cuts. This is an extremely high-risk strategy because of the likelihood that the reviewers will consider top agency officials irresponsible and poor managers. Firing of top officials is often a result of the use of such strategies.

Cutters' Strategies

Just as there are game strategies for an agency, there are strategies that reviewing groups use. Some strategies are safe and are fairly standard. Other strategies are essentially counterstrategies used against spenders' arguments and ploys. The discussion here, like the previous spenders' section, addresses the strategies and not an in-depth treatment of their application in a variety of contingencies.

The safe approaches include reducing increases, questioning hidden "revenues," cutting less visible items, and employing delay. The political support for existing programs can be quite strong and the pressure for increases might be strong also. However, the exact size of the increase is almost always open to discussion, and cuts to the increases are easier to sustain. Thus, cutting increases is almost always a safe cutter strategy. Another safe approach is to investigate and try to isolate "hidden" revenue, such as the use of the previous fiscal year's appropriations or the use of existing government property rather than the purchase of new property. Usually, a cutter can find some savings within the agency and few can fault the results. Another approach is to cut the less visible or less politically supported items. A cutter should employ this approach with some discretion because such "savings" may be a false economy. For example, the city water department can defer the replacement program for a city water pipe system but the wiser policy is probably a yearly systematic program. Delay is a particularly easily applied strategy. Whenever a cutter conducts another study or causes delays for other reasons, the result is that the cutter does not include the item in the budget. This is one of the most successful cutter's strategies because the cutter justifies a delaying by merely raising a question and the spender carries the burden to answer the question.

Several fairly standard cutter arguments and ploys exist. One is always to cut something. If reviewers make no cuts, advocates question reviewers' credible power over them. Also, reviewers know that the spenders have a natural tendency to include items that they could do without. Thus, their cuts eliminate those "frills." A second approach is to argue that initial allocations are unnecessary. If nothing starts, then cutters diminish budget expansion. A third approach is to defer or reject projects on the grounds that spenders cannot spend the initial dollars correctly by the end of the fiscal year. New programs often experience difficulty in staffing themselves; thus, they rarely can do a decent job in the first year. By arguing that a program will not do a decent job in the first year, each year the cutter prevents the program from coming into existence. A fourth approach is never to allow the advocate to establish a precedent because precedents lead to continued budget expansion.

An effective cutter ploy is to argue that there is only so much money and that a finite amount only is available for program increases. This is the basis for TBB as explained in Chapter 3. The cutter then asks the question: whose turn is it? This focuses the policy debate away from the amount and gets the various units in government to argue against each other. A contrasting but sophisticated ploy that a cutter uses in some circumstances is to eliminate interagency competition on some common area because the interagency competition drives up agency budgets due to the expansive nature of competition itself in the public sector.

The cutter need not accept or live with strategies employed by the spender. Counterstrategies do exist. If the agency says the increase is "so small," the counter is to argue that no item is too small to eliminate or to suggest that the spenders can absorb such small items without a budget increase. If the agency argues that it should have a fair share of the growth, the cutter can ask what is "fair" and never accept any definition provided by the spender. Another counterstrategy is to challenge the workload data provided by the spender. Often spenders collect such data poorly, and cutters can easily challenge the spenders on methodological grounds. In addition, the cutter can usually argue that the agency productivity increases should result in the agency's absorbing any so-called needed budget increases. Cutters can even argue that spenders should decrease their program due to their productivity improvements.

One spender's strategy is to place the blame on the cutter for the cuts, but the cutter need not accept that blame. The cutter can force the agency officials to declare what they believe should be cut first. If the spender is likely to put forth political "sacred cows" to cut, knowing that cutting them is politically impossible, the cutter can anticipate and neutralize the strategy by insisting that the agency not submit certain items on the "to-be-cut" list. Cutters usually have the advantage because they need only question, and the spender carries the burden of proof in the budget justification process.

The strongest spender asset in budget game playing is expertise, and spenders must take care to maintain the expert's credibility. Spenders can employ the various strategies cited here, but they must execute them without losing their aura of being truthful experts on their programs. Thus, a cutter's raising doubt about the agency's expertise is always an excellent ploy, and the spender must seriously confront the use of such a ploy firmly and directly.

In the 1980s and most of the 1990s, an important phenomenon in state and local governments was cutback management, sometimes due to financial crisis and sometimes due to reengineering. Those experiencing the need to cut programs rarely appreciate it. If recession motivates the experience, then the cutback steps taken are usually about the same in all situations. First, the government must accept the need to make cutbacks. However, denial usually occurs before there is acceptance. At the state and local level, when revenues prove inadequate and their constitutions require balanced budgets, governments make the needed cuts. Second, although some high-level officials might wish to use selective cuts of programs, political pressure usually results in first cutting the least painful aspects of programs such as unfilled positions, deferrable capital items, and maintenance projects. Third, the government halts raises, budget offices put on hiring freezes, and political leaders consider across-the-board reductions with selective exemptions from those reductions. Although it is wise to protect reserves, especially to compensate for forecasting error possibilities, typically reserves go very quickly in periods of recession. Politically and psychologically, an across-the-board approach provides an egalitarian appeal that politicians find easier to accept than targeted reductions. From a management point of view, targeted cuts are often wiser as they provide an excellent way to enhance productivity, but political and psychological reasons often outweigh more rational approaches.

In the 1980s and the early 1990s, fiscal crises in state and local governments were widespread. For example, in 1991 over thirty-eight states had major budget shortfalls. The 1990–1991 economic recession had a more significant effect on state and local government than the previous 1970s and 1980s recessions. Governments responded with a combination of largely ad-hoc tax and user fee increases, program cuts,

EXHIBIT 4–4   Cutback Strategies

Strategies	Number of States
Reducing the Number of Workers	
Freeze on filling vacancies	34
Early retirement	18
Voluntary (temporary) leave	15
Mandatory furloughs	12
Reduced hours	10
Job sharing	5
Increasing workweek	1
Layoffs	13
Reducing the Costs of Employees	
Deferred pay increase	18
Reducing costs of benefits	6
Shutdown of state operations	3
Pay cuts	2
Lag payrolls	2
Reorganizing State Workforce	**7**

Source: Marvin Druker and Betty Robinson. "State's Responses to Budget Shortfalls: Cutback Management Techniques." In Thomas D. Lynch and Lawrence Martin (eds.), *Handbook of Comparative Public Budgeting and Financial Management.* New York: Marcel Dekker, 1993, p. 195.

government restructuring, "passing the buck" to other governments, and reducing their employment. Again in the 2000 and 2001 fiscal years, many state and local governments experienced another wave of downsizing and cuts resulting from a nationwide economic slowdown. According to the National Association of State Budget Officers, sixteen states were experiencing declining revenues, and executive budget proposals reflected cuts and restructuring of programs. Exhibit 4–4 presents the cutback strategies employed according to a 1991 survey done by Marvin Druker and Betty Robinson. They reported that constraints on the implementing of those strategies were

- concern for service level,
- need to comply with mandates,
- legislative restriction,
- union contracts,
- civil service rules, and
- court-ordered restrictions.

Gary Mattson grouped the municipal fiscal stress strategies into cutback adoption, privatization, and revenue enhancing. Cutback strategies include wage freezes, hiring freezes, layoffs, capital budget deferrals, and across-the-board cuts. Layoffs are the least popular strategy. Privatization strategies include contract out, load shedding, and use of coproduction with volunteers. Load shedding is the least popular strategy. Revenue enhancing includes greater use of user fees and local tax options. The latter is the least popular.

New Programs

The previous strategies are for typical day-to-day budget situations. New programs require extraordinary efforts on the part of the spenders. Often policy makers establish new programs in reaction to a crisis or what some consider a crisis. Policy makers rarely manufacture crises, but groups do take advantage of crises to establish new programs or radically increase existing programs. The political climate in a crisis is such that political forces concur that the need is obvious and the debate centers on the "solutions." But even that debate is different in that the political climate calls for a solution, and agency delay is an unacceptable condition. Policy makers lower budget justification standards and what key policy makers want from an agency, which is for them to propose a solution. Although not unimportant, efficiency becomes a less significant topic under these conditions. In such an environment, agencies have a much greater opportunity to get viable ideas accepted, and new or radical increases in programs do occur at these times.

Agency or clientele advertising and effective selling can sometimes result in the creation of new programs. Dramatic names or labels such as *Mission 66* or *Headstart* can capture enough popular attention if there is also a good presentation of the new program. A well-organized budget justification effort can start new programs, but not if there is the presence of anticlientele groups (even small groups) as they are almost always fatal to new programs. Budget justifications are rarely successful due to advertising and effective selling by themselves. Typically, advocates link their budget justifications to a popular cause of the day (for example, environment, pollution, national defense, inflation, unemployment) to gain needed extra support. Ironically, agency overselling sometimes is dysfunctional because the new program can become so popular that the agency's other programs suffer. As a strategy, advocates should not underrate advertising and effective selling, but the times and circumstances are more significant in the beginning of most new programs.

Cautions

Unlike a parlor game, the budget game has serious consequences. Spenders and cutters use strategies, and sometimes one side or the other plays the game poorly. If both sides play the game well, society is better served in the budget process. One particularly serious game fault is when the agency leadership forgets that the agency is a *public* agency designed to serve *all* the people. True, its clientele is only part of the public, and most of the agency's dealings need only concern its clientele. However, circumstances do exist when the public nature of an agency prohibits continuous harmonious relations with its clientele group (for example, a coal company dealing with the Interior Department on a strip-mining question). Clientele groups can capture public agencies.

The mood of the times often is much more important than given strategies of spenders or cutters. Such moods change, creating a significant climate that favors, disfavors, or is neutral to specific programs. Government officials are sensitive to current events and recognize that those events are much like the weather for the farmer. The weather is very important and the farmer can do some things to mitigate the bad effects of weather, but it is still a largely uncontrolled governing force. Agencies must accept some political storms as either a favorable or unfavorable reality that simply occurs.

This chapter notes one last caution. If the mood of the times becomes favorable to a program and the reviewers become converts to the mission of an agency, the agency will discover a new budget game role expectation exists. Under the new rules, reviewers expect the agency to think and act very big when they request its budgets. The meaning of "big" depends on the size of the government and the dimensions of the problem. If the agency doesn't think in expansive terms, then criticisms, such as being overly concerned about "petty economies," are likely to occur. Such different role expectations are sometimes difficult for the agency to comprehend and adapt to quickly, given the usual budget game rules, but the agency must accommodate to the role expectation change or be subject to remarkably unpleasant political pressure.

THE MYTH OF THE BUDGET-MAXIMIZING BUREAUCRAT

In 1971, William A. Niskanen wrote *Bureaucracy and Representative Government,* in which he argued that bureaucrats always attempt to maximize government budgets and are successful in the attempt. In 1974, William C. Mitchell said that the Niskanen book was the most significant work yet produced by an economist on the role of bureaucracy and that the book should attain the status of a classic in the study of bureaucracy. Indeed, Niskanen's book is the most cited study on this subject. The impact of the Niskanen book was remarkable, especially in politically conservative circles. He intellectualized bashing the bureaucrat, and such bashing became the proper, intellectually elite "thing to do." In turn, the media, politicians, and others scapegoated government employees for society's problems, and radical fringe groups in particular, chanted their hatred of bureaucrats. This society-induced animosity toward government workers continued to rage until two or three radicals bombed the federal building in Oklahoma City and killed many career public servants in the late 1990s.

In 1991, André Blais and Stephane Dion edited *The Budget-Maximizing Bureaucrat: Appraisals and Evidence.* Their book used empirical information to test the Niskanen model that he based on public choice theory. Using empirical research done independently by several researchers on this subject, Blais and Dion found Niskanen's theoretical model and his assumptions problematic. According to Blais and Dion, Niskanen made two crucial assumptions in his theory. The first is that bureaucrats attempt to maximize their budgets. A bureau, which is a government organization, seeks an appropriation or grant from a "sponsor," meaning a legislature in the case of government. In Niskanen's theory, a bureaucrat is a senior career official in a bureau. Niskanen argues that bureaucrats maximize bureau budgets because their actions benefit themselves. They do this ultimately to get higher salaries, perquisites, reputations, power, patronage, output, ease of making changes, and ease of managing "their" bureau. Niskanen argues that a type of social contract exists between the top level bureaucrat and the bureau employees. The employees support the bureaucrat and the bureaucrat seeks higher bureau budgets, which increases the employee's opportunities for promotion and enhanced job security.

The second assumption is that bureaucrats largely succeed in maximizing their budgets. Why are bureaucrats so successful? Niskanen argues that relative incentives and available information, under most conditions, give the bureau overwhelmingly dominant monopoly power. Politicians who are interested in reelection do not view savings from bureau operations as their personal income and thus are largely indifferent to savings in bureau operations. Even if politicians want savings and increases to bureau productivity, the lack of performance information from the bureaucrats handicaps the politicians' decision making. In 1974, Jean-Luc Migue and Gerard Belanger amended the Niskanen model by asserting that bureaucrats are foremost concerned with managerial discretion and that it is the discretionary budget that they seek to maximize. Niskanen (1975) conceded that Migue and Belanger might also be correct. However, just as in the first version, the revised version of the Niskanen model says that the bureaucrats still direct their efforts toward getting larger bureau budgets.

The empirical findings cited in the Blais and Dion book tell us that bureaucrats do often systematically request larger budgets but few seek extremely large increases in their budgets. Commonly, bureaucrats seek only moderate annual increases over the long haul, but this action does tend to increase bureau budgets significantly over time. The evidence points to a stronger desire by bureaucrats to avert budgetary cuts than to obtain the largest possible increases. Thus, the evidence more properly supports a **budget-boosting** rather than a budget-maximizing strategy. Julie Dolan has noted in her survey of the Senior Executive Service (SES) that there is data suggesting SES personnel actually preferred less spending than the public did on large spending categories. This confirms that Niskanen's theory of the budget-maximizing bureaucrat might not adequately predict budget behavior. However, it is difficult to suggest from Dolan's findings alone that, alternatively, all bureaucrats seek to minimize public spending. What this may suggest is that bureaucrats are in fact concerned about their programs and concerned about the efficiency and cost-effectiveness in government. Sometimes, this might require minimizing public spending, and other times it may mandate modest increases. Hence, **budget boosting** remains a powerful tool for explaining budgetary behavior by bureaucrats.

Bureaucrats do not benefit much financially from budget increases because there is little relationship between the growth of bureaus and of bureaucrats' salaries. Then why do bureaucrats seek higher bureau budgets? According to Blais and Dion, there are three possible answers. One possibility is that bureaucrats seek larger bureau budgets because they define their interest in terms of power, instead of increasing their financial worth. They equate larger bureau budgets with more power for them as directors of bureaus. Unfortunately for the ideologues, direct empirical evidence on this explanation does not exist and thus does not support their reasoning. A second possibility is that bureaucrats are rather stupid and mistakenly believe that budget increases are in their personal or power interest. Blais and Dion discount this explanation as unlikely. Although ideological conservatives might not accept this explanation, Blais and Dion state a third possible reason: maybe bureaucrats are mission oriented and actually believe in the mission of their organization. In fact, the empirical evidence does support this explanation. We are left with the very strong possibility that bureaucrats actually believe in their work and are altruistic. For some that are willing to let available evidence shape their opinions, this is not much of a surprise.

The empirical evidence does support that bureaucrats have a substantial impact on budgets and that impact does tend to mean larger budgets. Again, this is not surprising as bureaucrats are high-level managers and their recommendations should carry significant weight with elected policy makers. In addition, some politicians do support higher budgets for bureaus, so bureaucrats' asking for more money will receive a positive support from their "sponsors," meaning friendly legislators in many situations. Of course, some politicians are not supportive, as that is the nature of politics and the representative system of government called democracy. Niskanen assumes that bureaucrats have an advantage in the budget process due to their control of key information. However, according to Blais and Dion, adequate empirical information on this subject does not confirm this key assumption in the Niskanen model. In addition, the passive sponsor assumption of the Niskanen model is clearly false because politicians are far from being powerless in budgetary decisions, as this book clearly states.

REVIEW QUESTIONS

1. What political influence patterns exist in the federal government in terms of budgeting? Why are they important to understand?
2. Why is it important for an agency to cultivate a clientele? How is that done? What problems and cautions are important to understand?
3. What are the typical duties of an agency budget officer? What views and behaviors should he or she anticipate?
4. What is the agency budget officer's perspective? Contrast that to the executive and legislative perspective.
5. Why are confidence, results, and hearings important? Explain how an agency can enhance the confidence of reviewers and clientele in agency program management. How can a budget officer prepare his or her agency for hearings?
6. What strategies can advocates of spending and critical reviewers use in the budget process?
7. What is the Niskanen model? Is it correct? In what ways is it significant in our society?

REFERENCES

ANTHONY, ROBERT. "Closing the Loop Between Planning and Performance." *Public Administration Review* (May/June 1971).

ANTON, THOMAS J. *The Politics of State Expenditure in Illinois.* Urbana: University of Illinois Press, 1966.

AXELROD, DONALD. "Post-Burkhead: The State of the Art or Science of Budgeting." *Public Administration Review* (November/December 1973).

BENDOR, JONATHAN. "Review Article: Formal Models of Bureaucracy." *British Journal of Political Science,* 18 (1988), 353–95.

BLAIS, ANDRÉ, and STEPHANE DION (eds.). *The Budget-Maximizing Bureaucrat: Appraisals and Evidence.* Pittsburgh, PA: University of Pittsburgh Press, 1991.

DOLAN, JULIE. "The Budget Minimizing Bureaucrat? Empirical Evidence From the Senior Executive Service." *Public Administration Review,* 62, 1 (January 2002), 42–50.

DOUGLAS, JAMES W. "Agency Strategies and Determinants of Agency Success Under Redirection in Georgia." *State and Local Government Review,* 31, 1 (Winter 1999), 31–42.

DRUKER, MARVIN, and BETTY ROBINSON. "State's Responses to Budget Shortfalls: Cutback Management Techniques." In Thomas D. Lynch and Lawrence Martin (eds.), *Handbook of Comparative Public Budgeting and Financial Management.* New York: Marcel Dekker, 1993.

DUNCOMBE, SYDNEY, and RICHARD KINNEY. "Cutbacks—Idaho Style." *Public Budgeting and Finance,* 4, 2 (Summer 1984), 87–98.

————. "Agency Budget Success: How It Is Defined By Budget Officials In Five Western States." *Public Budgeting and Finance,* 7, 1 (Spring 1987), 24–37.

LYNCH, THOMAS D. *Policy Analysis in Public Policymaking.* Lexington, MA: Lexington Books, 1975.

MATTSON, GARY A. "How Iowa's Small Towns Cope with Financial Retrenchment." *Small Town* (March–April 1989), 18–24.

MIGUE, JEAN-LUC, and GERARD BELANGER. "Towards a General Theory of Managerial Discretion." *Public Choice,* 17, 1 (1974), 24–43.

MITCHELL, WILLIAM C. "Book Review." *American Political Science Review,* 68, 4 (1974), 1775–77.

NATIONAL ASSOCIATION OF STATE BUDGET OFFICERS. *Fiscal Survey of the States.* Washington, DC: NASBO, 2001.

NISKANEN, WILLIAM A. *Bureaucracy and Representative Government.* Chicago: Aldine Atherton, 1971.

————. "Bureaucrats and Politicians." *Journal of Law and Economics,* 18, 3 (1975), 617.

SIGELMAN, LEE. "The Bureaucrat as Budget Maximizer: An Assumption Examined." *Public Budgeting and Finance,* 6, 1 (Spring 1986), 50–59.

WILDAVSKY, AARON. *The Politics of the Budgeting Process.* Boston: Little, Brown, 1964.

WILLOUGHBY, KATHERINE G. "Patterns of Behavior: Factors Influencing the Spending Judgments of Public Budgeters." In Thomas D. Lynch and Lawrence Martin (eds.), *Handbook of Comparative Public Budgeting and Financial Management.* New York: Marcel Dekker, 1993.

WILLOUGHBY, KATHERINE G., and JULIA E. MELKERS. "Implementing PBB: Conflicting Views of Success." *Public Budgeting and Finance,* 20, 1 (Spring 2000), 85–120.

5

ANALYSIS APPLIED TO

BUDGETING

Although budgeting can exist with very little analysis, analysis can significantly add value to the budget decision-making process and certainly justifies the hiring of higher caliber budget analysts. This chapter introduces a wide variety of analytical techniques useful in public budgeting, but the chapter is not a presentation on how to do the various analytical techniques as that subject is beyond the scope of this book. Rather, the chapter shows how significant types of analysis can relate to budgeting and improve the quality of budgeting if budget offices use the techniques. The first section focuses on the theory of analysis, which is central to its usefulness in budgeting. The following sections describe the difficulties associated with applying the theory, describe useful elementary analyses, explain the important analytical tool called *crosswalk*, focus on revenue and expenditure forecasting, explain productivity analysis, and explain benefit-cost analysis. At the completion of this chapter, the reader should know the following:

- a theoretically useful model that is consistent with the context of a democratic society;
- application difficulties associated with the model;
- simple analytical techniques that help us understand key relationships;
- the three common approaches to revenue forecasting as well as the basics of econometrics;
- expenditure forecasting approaches including bargaining, unit cost, and time series methods;
- how an analyst can use an econometric model in expenditure forecasting and simulation;
- the basics of productivity analysis, underlying productivity through regression analysis, and how to strengthen budget requests;
- the difference between benefit-cost and cost-effectiveness analysis;
- the fundamental concepts associated with benefit-cost analysis; and
- the analytical limitations to the benefit-cost technique.

THEORETICAL FOUNDATION

The Holistic System Theory

The assumed desirability of accountability in the public sector as well as an assumed chain of cause and effect within the system serve as the basis for the Holistic System Theory (HST) (Exhibit 5–1), which Thomas Lynch developed from the work of Jesse

EXHIBIT 5–1   Holistic System Theory

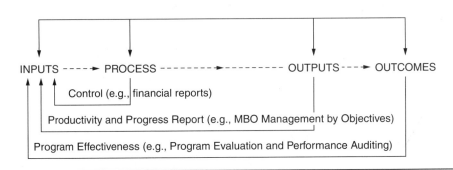

INTERVENING VARIABLES

INPUTS - - - - ► PROCESS - - - - - - - - ► - - - - - - - - - OUTPUTS - - - ► OUTCOMES

Control (e.g., financial reports)

Productivity and Progress Report (e.g., MBO Management by Objectives)

Program Effectiveness (e.g., Program Evaluation and Performance Auditing)

Burkhead. However, this model is similar in important elements to the one developed by Herbert Simon much earlier.

In the HST, the cause and effect chain runs from input, to process, to outputs, and finally to outcomes. *Inputs* are the ingredients needed to run the system, and they include money, expertise, and policy direction. *Process* is the performance of administrative activities such as answering the phone, typing on the computer, and talking on the phone. *Outputs* are the products and services produced by the unit such as roads completed and students graduated. Finally, *outcomes* are the impacts of the government program on individuals and society such as the greater movement of commerce and people and the higher creative capability of the population. Between the beginning of the chain and the end—and especially between outputs and outcomes—*intervening variables* from the political, economic, and social environment exist and influence the chain of causality. Significantly, this theory assumes that the input eventually and necessarily causes the outcomes, even though that cause may not be sufficient to produce the effect itself.

The HST chain of cause and effect means that policy makers and managers can monitor accountability theoretically using three feedback mechanisms. Analysts can monitor *process* by examining conventional accounting reports. They can monitor *outputs* using productivity and progress reporting. And they can monitor *outcome* using program effectiveness analysis such as program evaluations. In all cases, they need to adjust for intervening variables such as lobbying from clientele groups, media news stories about the impact of the program on the public, and technological change.

The use of these more formal feedback mechanisms permits policy makers and management to know what process as well as program outputs and outcomes actually exist, so they can compare them to their intended process, outputs, and outcomes. Alternatively, they can compare the actual process, outputs, and outcomes to benchmarks, their previous accomplishments, or what stakeholders think the organization should accomplish. Thus, the public can hold policy makers and managers accountable for the results of their decisions and their performance. According to J. D. Stewart, accountability consists of the following five distinct levels or steps on a ladder: policy, program, performance, process, and legality. According to the Government Accounting Standards Board (GASB), accountability is the paramount objective of government financial reporting. HST lends itself to these views of accountability.

Analysts can use the HST in both democratic and authoritarian society. In a democratic society, policy differences among various leaders and peoples are a primary and institutionally accepted aspect of policy making. Social values compete in an ongoing (and, one hopes, nonviolent) decision-making process over what should be the nation's policy. The theory does not assume there is one correct government solution or best set of values. It *does* assume that the conflict in political values does not necessarily give consistent and clear guidance to government program managers and that policy makers will not necessarily select logically consistent government policy. The theory assumes that usually the persons supplying information will communicate salient data that permits policy makers to confront and deal intelligently with their multiple-valued electorate. Therefore, analysts must understand and define program output measures, in particular, in the political context of the government and the larger society it serves.

Public budgeting is a phenomenon that exists at the nexus of policy making and management. The chain of cause and effect within the system links policy and management. The theory assumes that government programs do, and even should, influence individuals and society. In addition, it assumes increases and decreases in government programs will make an important impact on individuals and society. Budgeting, in part, is the allocation of resources based upon decisions, but implicit in each such decision is a process to carry out that allocation. No one can separate management totally from policy because the means to carry out the policy do influence eventual outcomes. This theory assumes that there is a chain of cause and effect, or at least policy makers believe such a chain exists.

The HST helps decision makers and budget analysts who prepare information in support of decision makers. Two important concerns of budget analysis are program *effectiveness* and *efficiency*. Analysts achieve insight on the first by looking at program outcomes and the *ratio of input to outcome*. Notice that between input and outcome is process. This is typically where managers can enhance both program effectiveness and efficiency. By examining process and the ratio of input to output, managers need to creatively seek ways to improve their process and thus possibly even lessen the amount of input while increasing output and outcome. The role of the budget analyst in the budget office is not to make policy but to raise the level of debate among the decision makers. They do this by using the HST to help political leaders and managers focus on the truly significant policy and related management questions. Thus, the budget office should facilitate accountability and encourage more intelligent decision making about the allocation of government resources.

As noted in Exhibit 5–2, there is growth in the use of program information associated with analysis in the budgetary process. According to unique survey research done by Robert D. Lee, Jr., growth in performance measures particularly took place in state governments in the early 1970s, and they maintained the growth.

EXHIBIT 5–2   Program Information in State Budget Documents (percent)

	1970	1975	1980	1985	1990
Effectiveness measures included					
Most agencies	2	24	28	26	24
Some agencies	27	40	43	49	41
None	71	36	30	26	35
Productivity measures included					
Most agencies	8	26	28	24	33
Some agencies	37	48	49	52	44
None	55	26	23	24	24
Future-year effectiveness measures included					
Yes	2	18	19	13	26
No	98	82	81	88	74
Future-year productivity measures included					
Yes	8	20	19	18	37
No	92	80	81	83	63

Source: Robert D. Lee, Jr. "The Use of Program Information and Analysis in State Budgeting: Trends of Two Decades." In Thomas D. Lynch and Lawrence Martin (eds.), *Handbook of Comparative Public Budgeting and Financial Management.* New York: Marcel Dekker, 1993, p. 173.

In a 1997 article, Professor Lee noted that from 1990 to 1995 a noticeable decline occurred in the conduct and use of program analysis by the states, but other information reported later in this chapter showed an increase from 1995. At the local level, a 1996 survey showed performance measures were a part of the budget process of most cities. Nevertheless, research on the state of Georgia indicates developing valid and reliable evaluation measures might occur, but using them in actual budget decision making on a systematic basis does not yet exist in that state. At both the agency and central budget office levels in Georgia, Thomas Lauth reported top officials did not use performance measures during budget preparation and review.

As noted earlier in Chapter 3, people in an agency must believe that key decision makers in government use performance measures seriously before that reform influences organizational behavior beyond meeting requirements. To the extent it occurs, performance measures are significant in government management and decision making as indicated by Professor Lee's research. Exhibit 5–3 shows that top state executive and legislative decision makers do use effectiveness and productivity analyses.

Program Impact

The focus in budget examination is on understanding existing and planned management strategy as well as upon program effectiveness. Regardless of the approach (for

EXHIBIT 5–3   Use of Analysis in State Budgeting (percent)

	1970	1975	1980	1985	1990
Central budget office assists depts. regarding program analyses					
Substantial	4	21	10	7	9
Some	38	50	56	68	75
Practically none	58	29	33	24	17
Executive budget decisions based on effectiveness analysis					
Substantial	15	20	11	21	26
Some	23	59	70	64	64
Rarely	62	20	20	14	11
Executive budget decisions based on productivity analysis					
Substantial	19	27	21	29	45
Some	32	54	64	67	55
Rarely	49	19	15	5	0
Legislative decisions based on effectiveness analysis					
Substantial	25	20	12	12	9
Some	19	48	66	73	74
Rarely	56	32	22	15	17
Legislative decisions based on productivity analysis					
Substantial	19	20	10	15	13
Some	25	32	56	76	81
Rarely	56	48	34	10	6

Source: Robert D. Lee, Jr. "The Use of Program Information and Analysis in State Budgeting: Trends of Two Decades." In Thomas D. Lynch and Lawrence Martin (eds.), *Handbook of Comparative Public Budgeting and Financial Management.* New York: Marcel Dekker, 1993, pp. 175 and 178.

example, PPB, ZBB, or TBB) to budget preparation, a common theoretical framework exists that assumes a cause-and-effect interrelation between the program's inputs and its ultimate impacts on the society or environment. The examiner (also called the budget analyst in this book) assumes that such a relationship can and should exist, and then attempts to discover if the actual or intended approach to managing the program can and is likely to lead to the intended program outputs and outcomes. Also, the examiner wants those results accomplished with the greatest program effectiveness consistent with the political values of the policy makers.

Policy makers intend almost all government programs to impact society or individuals in some way, or they would not have passed the legislation. Often, the policy makers wish to impact society, but they do not have a clear vision of the desired impact, and often, as a group, they do not have internally consistent vision of that policy among themselves; regardless, there almost always is some purpose behind each law and government program. That purpose includes an assumed cause-and-effect relationship: that is, the intended government program output is to make the desired impact (outcome) on society. This sometimes poorly articulated assumption behind the policy is central to much of the analysis useful in budgeting. For example, the budget analysts can determine if a budget resource request and even the program itself is "worthwhile" given the results of that program.

According to the "rules" of budget game playing discussed in Chapter 3, the agency has the burden of proving the worth of a program and a specific budget year resource request. The agency must justify the budget to the department, the executive, and the legislative body. Often those involved act as if absolute proof exists that a given program is worthwhile. Unfortunately, those holding such a view are not aware of the philosopher Descartes, who is the father of modernism and what we consider to be the scientific method. With the Latin expression *"Cogito, ergo sum,"* Descartes explained that **absolute** proof for any subject other than one's own existence is impossible. Thus, we are left with the need to use other criteria less than absolute in justifying programs in the budget process.

In public administration, the criterion of "necessary but not sufficient" is normally the best. For example, if the ultimate desired effect is to reduce the crime rate, holding the police force responsible for that effect may seem reasonable until one realizes that poor police work is not the only reason for the existence of crime. Good police work may be necessary, but it alone is not sufficient to reach a low crime rate. Too often analysts and decision makers apply the harsher "necessary and sufficient" criterion in judging the worth of government programs. This unfortunate conceptual mistake merely leads to false expectations and frustrated administrators and citizens.

Conceptually, an analyst should develop a program impact theory that applies to each program. Given a set of resources and the conditions in society, a government program can produce outputs that in turn will lead to outcomes. The budget request reflects in part the program inputs, but other inputs include leadership direction and human energy. If the government successfully manages a program, then management achieves outputs objectives. If articulated correctly, those objectives guide lower officials and administrators in the bureaucracy. The outcomes are the achieved objectives one cites in program evaluations. Those impacts or outcomes are what higher-level decision makers should view in judging the success or failure of government programs.

Theory is the heart of any good budget justification. The person justifying the budget should argue that the agency would achieve the desired impacts on society or individuals if the policy makers give the agency the requested resources. The theory should be the conceptual means to explain the causal relationship between the requested resources and the desired impact. If the desired end results do not occur, then two types of failure are possible: (1) the agency did not do its job correctly, or (2) the program impact theory was incorrect. Alternatively, intervening variables could have altered the situation to have also prevented the desired impact.

If the agency conceptually separated outputs and outcomes correctly and gathered the necessary data and rules on intervening variables, then analysts can determine the type of failure. If management met its output objectives, then analysts can eliminate "the agency did not do its job correctly" failure. This permits proper focus upon "the theory was incorrect" failure, which is the responsibility of the highest-level decision makers for using the wrong theory or the academic community for not developing adequate theories. Once analysts identify the failure, then they can focus their attention on discarding faulty theories and developing more useful theoretical understandings. This identification of failure is particularly significant and helps us understand the relationship of social science research and the needs of higher-level administrators.

Data measures are critical because the theory makes the assumption that the analyst can accurately describe each key portion of the model (for example, input, process, output, and outcome). Data measures for input are easy to define because line-item budget detail or aggregate numbers representing money and positions almost always exist. Data measures for process usually are not difficult to acquire and not critically needed for most budget analyses. Analysts can obtain output data measures by asking what the unit produces in terms of products or services. For most units and programs, analysts can isolate data measures without difficulty, but analysts might not collect such information on a routine basis. Outcome and outcome data measures are often very difficult to obtain, as government units often do not routinely record the individual and societal impacts of their programs.

Deciding what data measures to use is not an easy task. Typically, the best process is for the analyst to reason backward from the desired outcomes to inputs while focusing upon a specific unit and program. The analyst should ask the question "What impact does this particular program have upon the organization (if a service unit in an organization administers the program) or upon society (if the program directly affects society)?" Then, the analyst should seek specific means to measure that impact. Next, the analyst should identify the program outputs by seeking to understand exactly what the unit does or produces that causes those previously identified program outcomes. Data measures of output should give an accurate picture of what takes place. Analysts should define outputs by determining if they are relevant in the context of program outcomes. Analysts can omit the process stage, but this stage of analysis does permit a more in-depth appreciation of what management can do to increase organizational efficiency and effectiveness. In reasoning backwards, the last stage is input. What input contributes to and affects the process, output, and outcome? Policy makers need to know what input does not contribute to output and outcome because then they do not need to appropriate those resources, thus saving taxpayer dollars.

Since at least the turn of the nineteenth to twentieth century, reform groups, such as the Hoover Commission, recommended the use of performance measures and even performance budgeting. In the 1990s, there was an increasing interest in performance measures in the United States. This was due to the stress on performance measures by the Government Finance Officers Association and the increased use of measures by the better-managed governments in the United States and the world, and its stress by the chief financial officers and the General Accounting Office at the federal level. This stress was in turn made possible by the research on performance measures by the Urban Institute and others.

The Governmental Accounting Standards Board (GASB), which accounting professional organizations established to improve state and local government accounting standards, studied the possibility of requiring the use of performance measures as part

of the typical accounting process in state and local government. Such GASB requirements mean future governments wishing to say that they practice generally accepted accounting practices must collect performance measures on their programs as part of their
accounting process. GASB defines three broad categories of performance measures or
Service Effort and Accomplishment (SEA) that roughly correspond to the HST: service effort, service accomplishment, and effort related to accomplishment. The SEA categories are as follows:

1. Measurement of effort (called input in this chapter)
    a. Measures of financial resources
    b. Measures of nonfinancial resources
        (1) personnel
        (2) other
2. Measurement of accomplishment
    a. Output measures
        (1) service or product quantity
        (2) quantity of a service or product that meets a certain quality requirement
    b. Outcome measures
3. Measurement that relates effort to accomplishment
    a. Effort to output—efficiency
    b. Effort to outcome—effectiveness

At the local level of government in America, measures do influence budget allocation
decisions. One study found that workload measures have a 3.57 of 5 degrees of influence. Effectiveness measures have a 3.48 of 5 degrees of influence. Efficiency
measures have a 3.16 of 5 degrees of influence. A 1999 survey found governments
satisfied with their performance measurement systems in terms of measuring input
and outputs. However, they were less satisfied with measurements of outcome and efficiency. Seventy-one percent of the cities and 67 percent of the states used performance measures. More than half of the cities and states used benchmarking as a means
of determining how well they do.

APPLICATION DIFFICULTIES

In public administration, analysts can find the application of HST difficult, but they
can anticipate the difficulties. Common mistakes that analysts will make when using
the HST are

- conceptually mixing outputs, outcomes, process, and data measures;
- confusing the types of appropriate output measures;
- not understanding how to vary the application of the concept to staff and service units;
- not perceiving that staff inability to determine outcome and output measures might reflect a poor professional education; and
- not fully appreciating that an inability to determine outcome and output measures might
  indicate an inability of the program to manage itself.

Mix-Up

An analyst using the wrong measures in the wrong place is a common mistake in applying the HST. For example, an agency might insist on using descriptive measures that explain its administrative process. Those measures often indicate work effort (for example, working ten hours to write the report) or ratio of staff to clients (for example, student/teacher ratio of 30 to 1). There is nothing wrong with such measures per se, but analysts must also determine program output and outcome measures separately. For example, a student/teacher ratio of 30 to 1 may be an efficient use of teacher resources; however, teaching 30 students might not be an effective form of program delivery depending on the curriculum being taught. Analysts need to define each measure correctly for each element in the model. If they do not, they might believe—erroneously—that they are addressing program effectiveness questions with the use of process data alone.

Analysts can also confuse outcomes and outputs. In fact, many analysts improperly use the two interchangeably. This unfortunate mistake leads to improper analysis because only with proper identification of model components is it possible to determine program effectiveness and efficiency. An analysts can consider a state transportation program that paves 4,000 lane miles of road per year as an output. Yet, issues of which 4,000 lane miles (location) and how they were paved (four-inch depth versus seven-inch depth) influence how one understands the outcome measures. Again, the best approach to avoid such confusion is to address program outcome first and reason backward to program outputs. In addition, the analysts must define the exact way an agency determines the measure and make sure there is consistency in the use of the indicators over time.

Types of Output Measures

Public administrators are sometimes unaware that program outputs, especially services, consist of two types that they should treat differently. The first type is the result of a project with a defined end product or service. Constructing a building or writing a report are examples of that output type. The second type reflects a desire to provide ongoing services or products within some defined limits of acceptability. As long as the managers perform the service correctly within those limits, then evaluators judge the output as satisfactory. Analysts define failure or "less than satisfactory service" by the number of occasions that the level of service falls outside the ideal limits.

Commonly, analysts are unaware of how best to define the second type of output. Administrators will judge a license bureau by the number of licenses issued rather than the percent of licenses issued within an acceptable waiting time. They do not consider the quality of output and ignore important managerial considerations. They count end products or services but overlook the program output quality.

Staff and Service Units

When first introduced to the model, individuals tend to focus upon units that are the primary service producers within the government. As they start to apply the model, they discover staff units (for example, budget offices) and service units within line departments (for example, bus maintenance). They become confused about how to apply the concept in situations in which staff and service units do not have a direct impact upon citizens and society.

The best approach is to work backward from outcomes. If the analyst or manager focuses on a bus maintenance unit in public transit, the first point to understand is that the overall purpose of public transit is the movement of people. Analysts need to ask, "How does the maintenance unit contribute to that overall transit output?" The answer is the bus maintenance unit's output—for example, how does the unit keep the bus fleet in operation at all times? The answer may be the unit preventatively maintains ten buses each week. That would be one measure of the unit's program output.

In the HST, analysts find how to handle a staff unit like a budget office confusing. The first point to understand is that the role of a staff unit is to service the government so that it can work effectively. For example, a budget unit should do the following:

- help raise the level of debate for policy makers so that policy makers are more likely to make better decisions,
- monitor budget execution so that the units in the organization follow the policy of the duly constituted decision makers, and
- promote and foster better public management within the government.

Analysts can develop specific data measures for each program output and outcome for a staff unit just as they do for line units.

The second point is that analysts should understand outcomes as a function of the program outputs. Let us look at how to create program output measures for the budget office using the three defined program outcomes. First, analysts need to create program output measures for the program outcome of raising the level of debate in the policy process. The obvious output measure is the budget document itself. The analysts must keep in mind that program outputs, such as the annual budget document and various reports, are not sufficient by themselves to create the desired program outcome measures (such as better policy) per se but they are necessary. Therefore, analysts should judge if a given output is a "good one" in terms of its likelihood of helping to create one of the desired program outcomes, such as raising the level of policy debate.

In the next outcome example used, analysts would select a program output measure linked to the program outcome of monitoring budget execution. In that case, the analysts want to know how functional the product or service of the budget unit is in terms of the budget unit's ability to get other government units to follow policy. Analysts selecting program output measures addressed to improving public management program outcome need to consider if the ad hoc reports and studies are likely to improve public management. Thus, analysts selecting program output measures must understand them in terms of their likely positive contribution to the office's outcomes.

Nonperformance Option

Sometimes government units do not achieve their program outputs and outcomes. One possible reason for failure may be the professional inadequacy of people like

budget analysts in defining appropriate outputs and outcomes or insufficient cooperation from an agency in defining necessary data measures. Selecting data measures
is a difficult professional challenge because even so-called perfect measures are
sometimes inappropriate because of the time taken to collect those measures or the
high costs associated with collecting the data. Therefore, analysts must use their professional judgment in trading off the quality of the measure against the effort used to
collect the data measure.

When top agency personnel fail to make a reasonable attempt to resolve trade-
off problems, an unacceptable situation occurs. In such cases, analysts in the budget
office need to apprise their budget office leadership of the situation, and then the leadership must decide whether to force the agency to develop the desired output and outcome measures. Agency officials see the central budget office analysts come and go
either through promotions or job attrition. The agency therefore often has better expertise and information than the central budget office does. Moreover, the agency officials are usually defensive. Central budget analysts must balance intermediate and
long-range policy objectives against the value of the budget battle at hand. Budget offices can win many of this type of organizational battle but not all of them; thus,
budget offices must decide which particular battle they wish to fight and when they
wish to fight it. Typically, government executive leadership willingly supports the
budget office leadership on such matters, as it is in the best interest of executive leadership to have such information.

A possible reason why analysts cannot define adequate program outcome and
outputs in a government unit is that the agency performs no useful service. Often
when an agency is particularly uncooperative in defining outcomes and outputs, its
behavior is simply a defensive attempt to cover up their poor management. The
budget office and top management must appreciate that possibility and take care that
the analysts eliminate all other explanations. Typically, charges of agency cover-up
of bad management evoke attacks upon the professional competency of the budget
office by the agency program manager. If challenges of this type are likely, budget office leadership should involve top executive assistance as soon as possible so that the
government leadership can intelligently deal with this type of negative defensive behavior that often is very harmful to government management.

DATA MEASURE CONSTRAINTS

The application of this model depends on the constraints associated with the use of
data measures. To use this HST model properly, the analysts must have an understanding of quantitative techniques and research methods. For example, some data
measures apply only to an ordinal data scale, and uninformed analysts can misapply
an analytical technique by using ratio data scales. For the most sophisticated users
of analyses, the best scale is ratio, but that is often impractical or impossible given
the character of the problem and data. A common mistake made with research methods is that an analyst uses a simple case study rather than a more complex research
design to ensure establishing beyond reasonable doubt that the program input caused
the output and eventual outcome.

The best measures to use are uniform in nature and contain a high number of units of output or outcome from which the analyst can assume the same level of quality exists in each unit of output or outcome. For example, the water and sewer systems measure their output in gallons of water or sewerage processed at an acceptable level of quality. Measures of this type permit the use of the most powerful analytical techniques. Unfortunately, many program outputs are not susceptible to this ideal type of measure. For example, a planning unit's output of an updated comprehensive plan is not ideal for budget analytical purposes because this output is one in number, and merely noting that the office completed a plan does not address its quality. This does not mean that the budget analyst does not use the updated plan as an output, but he or she would add some qualitative judgment of quality using an ordinal or even interval scale measure. For example, the fact that the peer group of government planning agencies awarded the planning unit an award for preparing a distinguished plan is an ordinal measure of quality.

A common ploy by agency officials is to use measures that are ratios between ideal and actual performance. For example, animal control agencies might compare the number of strays to actual captured dogs. Usually, the ratio can show they managed the program reasonably well, but agencies can give the impression that more resources (input) would improve the ratio. The problem with such ratios is that the ideal is often a highly questionable figure, and the ratio measure might not reflect true outcomes and outputs. If analysts define the stray dog problem as the existence of stray dogs, then the measure of dogs captured might be quite correct. If the dog problem is more accurately described as strays in inappropriate areas, then analysts should define the outcomes differently. Maybe the dog problem is capturing strays within a given time after a citizen registers a complaint. If so, analysts should restate again the animal control unit outputs to indicate how many dogs animal control captured within acceptable time constraints. Notice that occasionally an analyst can have an identical or almost identical outcome and output for operational purposes.

Although analysts may find perfect program outcomes and outputs, there is still the analytical challenge of selecting one or more data measures. In some circumstances, the data measures the analysts select could be more expensive to acquire than the cost of the programs they measure. Obviously, analysts must make a practical trade-off in deciding if added clarity in the budget decision-making process is worth the added cost of the data measure.

Another problem with data measures is that they can react with and influence negatively the workings of a program they measure. For example, the knowledge that decision makers use data measures can encourage some managers and employees to distort the data or foster defensive behavior, such as not performing their jobs correctly so that the measures "look good." When this occurs, both managers and employees do not face up to and resolve their problems. Analysts must understand that these situations occur and go the next step of anticipating the situations. They can do this by recognizing the measurement process creates negative dysfunctional energy within the organization, and then they can frame the use of measures to minimize the existence of that energy. If analysts do not do this, then organizations will devote significant time and resources to dysfunctional organizational activities. In other words, those managers and employees will waste government resources and not serve the public interest.

Analysts should consider using nonreactive measures rather than measures that people in the organization could consciously manipulate. For example, worn tile in front of a museum exhibit indicates popularity, and popularity indicates an active interest in a museum exhibit, which analysts can say is a program outcome. Usually, nonreactive measures are already available or easily available; thus, they are inexpensive to acquire. Another advantage is that their apparent lack of connection with key program events means that monitoring them will not affect the measurement instrument itself. The major challenge of using nonreactive measures is that the analyst must possess a creative imagination in order to identify them and their relationship to program outcomes and outputs. Additionally, such measures are rarely ideal in terms of measuring outputs or outcomes perfectly. Nevertheless, analysts should use them when possible because of their significant advantages.

ELEMENTARY ANALYSIS

Defining Relationships

Most analysis used in budgeting is not and need not be complex. *Trend charts, scatter diagrams,* and *simple regression analysis, marginal cost analysis, discounting to present value,* and *Kraemer's Chi Square* are relatively simple analytical techniques. Budget requests, final budgets, year-end estimates of current expenses, and actual performance often involve important causal relationships that lend themselves to simple analyses. If analysts can identify those relationships, then the budget analyst's job is easier and more valuable in the decision-making process. Typically, analysts best explain relationships using a conventional scale, but sometimes using a logarithmic scale or index numbers can clarify what the analysts want the data to say. One common relationship is to show a given variable as it changes over time. If a trend apparently exists, then long-term forecasting becomes easier and future events become more predictable.

In many situations the relationship between two variables is more difficult to determine. One approach is to place the two variables on two axes, as illustrated in Exhibit 5–4. The analyst then places dots representing each simultaneous occurrence of the two variables. The result is a *scatter diagram* that might indicate a relationship between the two variables. Exhibit 5–4 shows such a relationship for a car between maintenance cost and miles driven. The line is a *simple regression analysis* defining that relationship.

Marginal Cost and Discounting

Another useful technique is *marginal cost analysis*. The initial cost of a government program is often expensive, whereas further effort leads to lower unit costs. This means that in many circumstances the analyst should understand that marginal costs are lower. This might prove highly significant. For example, if an agency is asking for a proportionate increase in funding, the analyst might question this request because marginal costs should not increase proportionately.

EXHIBIT 5–4   Illustration of Statistical Analysis

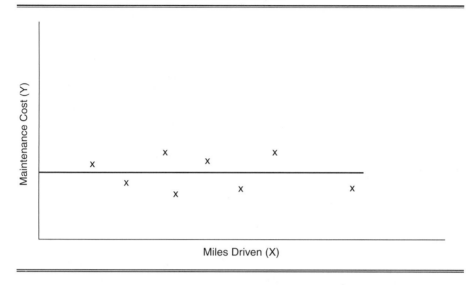

In order to perform marginal cost analysis, analysts must separate the data into one-time *fixed costs* and *recurring costs.* Common one-time fixed costs include research, project planning, engineering, tests, evaluations, land purchases, facility construction, equipment, and initial training. Common recurring costs include personnel expenses, employee benefits, maintenance, direct contributions to people, payments for services, and overall and replacement training. The fixed costs remain the same, but the recurring costs increase with added units. Thus, as the units increase, the unit cost decreases. Analysts can plot these data points on a simple chart or describe them in simple statistical expressions.

Another technique is *discounting to present value.* A dollar received or spent in the future is not equivalent to a dollar received or spent today. Therefore, analysts must make adjustments if they are to make comparisons over time or from one time to another. The technique is similar to the statistical concept used to compute compound interest at the bank. This technique is useful when analysts make comparisons, but the two subjects must not occur during the same time period or involve different financing methods.

Fred A. Kramer cited a simple but common situation to illustrate the use of this analytical technique. A city must choose between (1) contracting with a private garbage collector for $65,000 per year or (2) having city employees collect the garbage. The latter option would require a $40,000 truck and some yearly operating expenses. Without discounting to present value, the best option is apparently to let the city employees collect the garbage. With them, the cost is $315,000 over the five years of the truck's life. With a private contractor, the cost is $325,000. Thus, using city workers would apparently save the city $10,000 over a five-year period. With discounting, the best option changes to the private contractor. The following shows the important arithmetic:

SAVINGS IN THE YEAR	×	8% DISCOUNT FACTOR	=	PRESENT VALUE
1	$10,000	.926		$ 9,260
2	10,000	.857		8,570
3	10,000	.794		7,940
4	10,000	.735		7,350
5	10,000	.681		6,810
Total Present Value of Annual Savings (Years 1–5)	=			$39,930

In the example, the private contract is the best buy because the *total present value* of annual savings is less than the $40,000 capital investment. If policy makers used city employees, the city would pay $40,000 for a truck but save $50,000 over five years. The application of discounting to the yearly savings lets us realize that the true savings are not $50,000, but $39,930 because the analyst should consider the value of money over time. Thus, discounting shows us that the options are nearly equal, but the contracting option saves the city $70.

Caution is important in using the discount technique. Numbers have a way of seeming so final and clear. Realistically, analysts must carefully weigh the ingredients in the question in terms of their sensitive character. An output of a program is sensitive when an analyst can alter the results using a minor change in a variable. If the analysis is highly sensitive, then policy makers can question any recommendations made on the basis of the analysis because the technique does not warrant the implied certitude. For example, analysts can abuse this technique by changing the annual returns or savings, the life of the asset, the amount of the investment, the discount rate, or the annual returns in the earlier years. This does not mean that the decision maker should not use the analysis, but the analysts should use it with a complete understanding of the possible distortions associated with the analysis.

CROSSWALKS

Conceptual Bridge

One of the most useful analytical tools for the budget examiner is the *crosswalk*. It is a simple matrix table relating different categories that serves as a conceptual bridge between two organizational means to describe and control agency activities. By constructing several bridges, the examiner can explore various organizational perspectives on what policy makers should do and what they actually do as well as check important interrelations. Some of the more common categories that analysts can crosswalk are the following:

- programs, projects, activities, tasks;
- uniform object classifications;
- appropriation structure;
- major organizational units;
- objectives used in connection with management-by-objectives or program evaluations; and
- funds (including grants-in-aid) used in government accounting.

A very useful crosswalk is between the program and the uniform object classification (also called line-item or object). In many sophisticated budget offices, analysts employ both program and line-item categories. In order to maintain consistency, the crosswalk is a valuable tool because it shows the interrelationship of the two ways of looking at the budget. In addition, a careful examination of the crosswalk helps to isolate potential problems, such as inadequate resources for some line items in some programs.

Another useful crosswalk is between fund and line item. Often an agency can draw upon several funds in its daily operations. Thus, an analyst can associate a given line-item expense with two or more funds. The crosswalk is a display of information that can help the manager decide which fund to charge a line item against. By looking at a cumulative crosswalk of expenses in an organization, a budget analyst can see if management used the funds together in a meaningful way and more intelligently judge the budget request in a given fund for the next year.

The appropriation-to-unit crosswalk is also useful. Sometimes a legislature provides funds that several organizational units use. A tool to keep track of which unit is responsible for each portion of the money is the crosswalk. Without such a tool, lower-management responsibility is unclear and judging management performance becomes more difficult.

At the federal level, the program-and-authorization crosswalk is very useful at the agency level. In the executive branch, analysts prepare budgets using the concept of program. In the legislative branch, analysts justify budgets and discuss them in terms of legal authorization language. Thus, the agency budget official must use both the concepts of program and legal authorization in justifying and defending requests for funds. As a means to translate more easily and to ensure a consistency between executive and legislative information, the crosswalk is a valuable tool.

An unused but potentially significant crosswalk is between the Management By Objectives (MBO) objectives and the program structure or appropriation structure. MBO can be an extremely useful public management technique, but often management applies it without reference to the budget. This is foolish because how can one reasonably expect managers to meet objectives without also establishing that necessary resources are available to conduct the program? Analysts should not treat the two in isolation, but many agencies do. If agencies treat them separately, then this strongly indicates a lack of coordination of policy and management direction within the agency. Both MBO and the budget are tools to achieve management direction, and management should use them with one voice.

If the agency's activities fulfill more than one objective at a time with the same resources, then the analysts should treat the objectives-and-resources crosswalk differently from the other crosswalks. Typically, each matrix square states dollar amounts representing mutually exclusive activities. This permits the analysts to use the crosswalk to check for internal consistency by merely comparing the horizontal and vertical summary columns and rows to see if they are equal. In the case where resources meet two or more objectives, analysts can count dollar amounts more than once if they fulfill more than one purpose. For example, a given activity may increase safety and reduce energy consumption (for example, enforcing the fifty-five-mile-per-hour speed limit). Thus, the crosswalk matrix squares would show the dollar amount (maybe even the name of the activity) under two different vertical categories. This type of double counting can also exist with a crosswalk using MBO objectives.

Determining Consistency

The budget examiner can ask to see various crosswalks for the reasons suggested previously. Essentially, crosswalks help the examiner determine if the agency has internally consistent management direction and control capability to ensure the integrity of that direction. If the agency does not act with one management direction, the crosswalks expose that problem. If the agency cannot provide crosswalks, this suggests poor management. An agency can manage its affairs well without using crosswalks. But if the agency provides consistent management direction, then it should be able to construct crosswalks on the demand of the budget examiner. If it cannot construct crosswalks or if the ones it provides show inconsistent management policy, then the budget examiner should probe further to isolate the exact nature and reasons for the internal management inconsistency.

Examiners can also use crosswalks to check for external consistency of management direction with past publicly announced positions and orders of higher authorities. A set of crosswalks is among the best evidence of the exact management policies of an agency. Those policies might not be consistent with the past policies or positions articulated to the public or policy directives from agency higher authorities. If the budget examiner happens to have the crosswalks from past budgets, then he or she can compare them with the most recent crosswalks. In this manner, examiners can isolate policy shifts of lower-level management that are not consistent with executive policy. If there is inconsistency, then the examiner would be wise to probe further to determine the reason for the inconsistency.

REVENUE FORECASTING

Three Approaches

Revenue forecasting calls for a separate treatment of each revenue source. The standard approach is, first, to determine the patterns associated with each revenue source. Next, the analyst must determine the base and make the forecast based on assumptions from the determined pattern. Forecasting is merely a sophisticated form of guessing, which depends on good data and good judgment that the analysts refine often through experience. The techniques of forecasting range from the simple to the complex, but the analysts should know and consider using all of the techniques while always applying the principle of conservatism (that is, underestimating revenue and overestimating expenditures). Notwithstanding this accepted advice, governments do not always use that principle. In a study of state government forecasts of sales tax receipts, William Earle Klay and Gloria A. Grizzle discovered a slight tendency on the average to overstate revenue.

Information is important in revenue forecasting, and analysts should retain certain background information. This includes copies of legislation, legal history, administration factors concerning the tax, or any change in charts showing changes in the tax rate over time and the monthly yield, with an explanation of any abnormal change in the trend line. Also, the analysts should collect data on any significant variables that affect the revenue yield.

The three revenue-forecasting approaches are *qualitative, time series,* and *causal analysis. Qualitative* (also called judgmental) approaches are, in essence, based solely or primarily upon human judgment, but analysts can use math with this approach. William Earle Klay of Florida State University surveyed the revenue forecasting practices of all fifty states and found that thirty used panels, interagency work committees, or conferences in their revenue forecasts. Typically, economists constituted these "expert" groups of forecasters, but occasionally states include politicians. Forecasters should use expert judgment when key revenue elements are highly variable, no history exists, or political considerations (for example, intergovernmental transfers) strongly influence revenues. At the local level, judgment ranked 4.36 of 5 in terms of its significance in budgeting forecasting.

Time series (for example, trend analysis) builds on data that analysts collect over time and can show chronologically on graphs. One such approach uses the last completed year as a basis for the revenue estimate (in France, this method is called "rule of penultimate year"), assuming that there is growth in the economy and related revenue sources. Another simple technique—*the method of averages*—is to average the revenue generated over the last three to five years. Again, the analysts make the assumption that there is a growth trend in the tax source, rather than a decline or an uneven tax yield. A more sophisticated method involves using moving averages and attributing greater weight to more recent revenue yields. A still more sophisticated method is the Box-Jenkins method, which this chapter will describe later in the expenditure estimates section. Typically, analysts show the trends on arithmetic graphs, but some analysts prefer semilogarithmic graphs because they reveal rates of change in tax yields more clearly. At the local level, trend projections ranked 4.31 of 5 in terms of their significance in budget forecasting.

When using time series techniques, the forecaster has a special interest in the nature of seasonal fluctuations that occur within a year, the nature of multiyear cycles, and the nature of any possible long-run trends that might underlie the seasonal and cyclical fluctuations. The major weakness of this approach is that analysts cannot easily identify economic turning points. Analysts should use trend analysis to forecast revenue items that are not highly variable and that (1) amount to minor percentages of the budget or (2) are not dependent upon economic or political considerations.

Causal methods deal, not with the history of a single variable, but with the historical interrelationship between two or more variables. One or more predictor variables forecast tax yield directly or indirectly by first forecasting the future tax base. For example, multiplying the estimate of the average tax to be collected per taxpayer by an estimate of the number of taxpayers results in a forecast of income tax revenue. Analysts can use various survey techniques to determine these two predictor variable estimates. Some communities use a payroll tax. To forecast the revenue, they estimate the area payroll and tax rate and multiply them. A variation is to calculate the tax rate by occupational groups. A third method is first to determine the interrelationship between personal income and leading economic indicators and then to use the leading indicators to determine personal income. Analysts determine the tax yield from the personal income. For sales taxes, analysts forecast the state sales, and they calculated tax yield from the level of sales.

For these causal forecasting methods to be accurate, analysts must select the correct predictor variables, define their interrelationship to tax yield correctly, and, finally, collect accurate data. An added advantage to these methods is that they can help policy makers reflect upon various "what if" options for taxes and other policies so that they can better gauge the implications of their policy choices. Drawbacks to these methods include the need to collect extensive accurate data, the cost of developing causal models, and high computer costs. Fortunately, advances in technology decrease computer costs. If changing economic conditions strongly influence revenues, causal models (for example, econometrics) are especially useful.

Accuracy in revenue forecasting is important, especially when the forecast predicts more money than the government actually receives. Because the state and local governments must balance the budget, a revenue shortfall means policy makers must make difficult decisions, and these are less painful when forecasts are accurate. If there are revenue shortfalls in the current year, then policy makers should make unwelcome midyear adjustments, which typically include not hiring replacements, elimination of travel, and other easily cut cost items. If those cuts do not save the needed money during the current year, then decision makers can resort to payless "paydays." If forecasts, embarrassingly, result in unpredicted revenue surpluses, then the government faces the politically difficult task of explaining higher than needed tax receipts to the voting public or forcing politicians to say no unnecessarily to clientele groups.

Econometric Forecasts

Econometric forecasts are complex analyses that have many causal variables and are often computer-dependent. The age of econometrics began in the 1930s with Jan Tinbergen, a Dutch economist. He developed a number of equations to represent the workings of his nation's economy. In America, state governments' use of econometrics has occurred mostly since 1978, with few local governments using the technique today (some exceptions are New Orleans, Dallas, Winston-Salem, and Mobile). At the local level, econometric equations ranked 2.46 of 5 in terms of their significance in budgeting forecasting. The basic equation is $Y = f(X)$, with Y the dependent variable, affected by the independent, explanatory, predictor variable X. The statement merely says that Y is somehow dependent on (is a function of) the value of X. To develop a revenue-forecasting model, the following are essential:

- develop a data history or time series for all variables;
- develop a set of mathematical expressions that best explains the past relationships among the variables; and
- devise a means of identifying the future values that one or more of the explanatory variables will assume.

Causal models may consist of a single regression equation or several regression equations. Exhibit 5–5 presents the revenue forecasting methodologies used for the Ohio general fund in 1984–1987. Semoon Chang used a single regression equation for his econometric model for Mobile's sales tax receipts. At the other extreme, Florida's state estimates make use of 123 regression equations. Many analysts rely upon popular national econometric models such as those provided by Chase Econometrics, Data Resources, Inc., and Wharton Econometric Forecasting Associates. In the past and to a large extent now, practitioners do not use sophisticated models. When they do, consultants have constructed them, and often the models have gathered dust on the shelf of the practitioners. This method involves statistics—sometimes complex ones. Often, unless staff can explain the statistical concepts so that state and local decision makers can understand them, the techniques become unpopular and do not inform official judgment. To use these techniques, analysts should understand the following statistical concepts:

- R squared coefficient of determination, which shows the proportion of variation in the dependent variable attributable to variation in the independent variables;
- the T test of relationship with a particular independent variable;

EXHIBIT 5–5   Revenue Forecasting Methodologies for Selected Ohio General Fund Taxes

Source	% of Total Receipts	Method	Variables
Personal Income Tax	37	Simulation Model	Growth in Personal Income
Non-Auto Sales Tax	27	Regression Analysis	Disposable Income & Industrial Production Index
Corporate Franchise	9	Regression Analysis	US Corporate Profits Before Taxes and Industrial Products Index
Public Utilities	8	Time Series for Each Utility	Various
Auto Sales Tax	7	Regression Analysis	Personal Consumption Expenditures for Motor Vehicles & Ind. Products Index
All Other	12	Time Series/CPI Index	Various

Source: William J. Shkurti. "A User's Guide to State Revenue Forecasting." *Public Budgeting and Finance,* 10, 1 (Spring 1990), p. 84.

- the F test concerning the significance of the equation as a whole;
- the Durbin-Watson statistic, which is an indicator of whether serial correlation exists, thereby suggesting that important information has been omitted;
- the standard error of estimate; and
- the mean absolute percentage of error.

FORECASTING PRACTICES

In 1993, John Forrester examined the use of the various types of revenue-forecasting techniques in American cities. The most common combinations of techniques were expert and other, trend and other, and deterministic and other. Exhibit 5–6 presents his findings. Jane McCollough and Howard Frank reported on a survey of municipal governments in 1992. They found the most used revenue-forecasting techniques were judgmental (75.9 percent), trend-line (48.6 percent), and moving averages (36.2 percent). They reported the less used techniques were Box-Jenkins (97.6 percent), classical decomposition (91.0 percent), exponential smoothing (91.0 percent), and econometric (80 percent).

FORECASTING TECHNIQUES IN BRIEF

Box-Jenkins Model:—One type of Autoregressive Integrated Moving Average (ARIMA) methodology used for the analysis and forecasting of time series data (primarily univariate). The technique involves preparation of data, model selection, establishing coefficients and algorithms, checking of the model, and computation of the forecast. The model selection and checking against the time series data continue until a point that fits is identified.

EXHIBIT 5–6   Use of Revenue Forecasting Techniques (n = 108) (percent)

FORECASTING TECHNIQUES	TAXES			FEES	REVENUES FROM	
	PROPERTY	SALES	UTILITY	CHARGES	STATE	FEDERAL
None	2.8	18.5	25.0	3.7	5.6	18.5
Expert	5.6	2.8	5.0	10.2	15.7	25.9
Trend	12.0	14.8	17.6	11.1	10.2	6.5
Deterministic	9.3	0.9	2.8	4.6	7.4	7.4
Econometric	3.7	11.1	5.6	2.8	3.7	1.9
Expert and Other	42.6	31.5	25.0	43.5	29.6	21.3
Trend and Other	47.2	37.0	30.6	50.9	35.2	20.4
Determ. and Other	34.3	18.5	19.4	32.4	14.8	9.3
Econ. and Other	17.6	24.1	16.7	24.1	12.0	8.3
State Force. & Ot.	6.5	10.2	6.5	4.6	16.7	1.9

Source: John P. Forrester. "Use of Revenue Forecasting Techniques." In Thomas D. Lynch and Lawrence Martin (eds.), *Handbook of Comparative Public Budgeting and Financial Management.* New York: Marcel Dekker, 1993, p. 154.

Classical Decomposition:—A technique that breaks down time series data into seasonal, trend, and irregular components using moving averages.

Econometric Modeling:—An all encompassing approach that utilizes single or multiple regression and other statistical procedures, and incorporates a variety of causal variables to explain past relationships between variables in order to predict future values associated with those variables.

Exponential Smoothing:—A method to reduce irregularities or random fluctuations in time series data by essentially producing a weighed average that, in turn, provides a clearer picture of underlying behavior of the data series.

Judgmental Model:—A technique that adjusts the average of time series data based upon seasonal, cyclical, or other trends (or errors) for the purpose of calculating new forecasts that better represent long-term trends in the data series.

Empirical information indicates that revenue forecasting at the state and local level is not accurate. In a 1985 study, the Public Policy Institute of New York documented revenue-forecasting practices of thirty-two states responding to its survey. It reported the accuracy of state revenue estimates varied between +15 and −25 percent, with a variance of plus or minus 2 to 5 percent most common. William Earle Klay and Gloria A. Grizzle, in their study of state sales tax forecast accuracy, discovered one state underestimated by 31.6 percent and another overestimated by 40.6 percent. Exhibit 5–7 presents Irene S. Rubin's findings on the accuracy of revenue forecasting in Illinois. She surveyed 102 cities and found that accuracy (defined as plus or minus 2 percent) varied from a high of 61.6 percent for property taxes to a low of 16.0 percent for property tax replacement (a small transfer payment from the state). Interestingly, cities overestimated utility taxes 57.8 percent of the time. Rubin asked why the estimates were so poor. She concluded that fiscal stress was the most important predictor of revenue bias and bad forecasting. In other

EXHIBIT 5–7   Accuracy of Revenue Estimates Number

Source	No. of Cities	Percent Under	Percent Accurate	Percent Over
Property	112	18.8	61.6	19.6
Sales	118	47.5	31.4	21.1
Income	118	39.0	26.3	34.7
Utility	45	22.2	20.0	57.8
Prop. Tax Replacem.	100	76.0	16.0	8.0
Motor Veh.	114	54.4	29.8	15.8
Rev. Shar.	108	32.4	34.3	33.3

Source: Based on an Illinois Revenue Survey, 1987 cited in Irene S. Rubin. "Estimated and Actual Urban Revenues: Exploring the Gap." *Public Budgeting and Finance,* 7, 4 (Winter 1987), pp. 83–94.

words, when economic times become difficult, cities tend to balance their budgets by poorly estimating their revenues. She noted the type of local government was not a good predictor of poor estimates.

Measuring historic accuracy of revenue forecasts within a jurisdiction is simply a matter of contrasting forecasts with actual receipts. Once analysts make these comparisons, they can determine where they need to improve their forecasting. Usually, large inaccuracies in small revenue items are not significant because often such inaccuracies tend to cancel each other out in the aggregate. Serious problems occur when there are modest errors in large revenue sources because those errors can mean a city or state has a significant revenue shortfall. Usually, the further away the forecast from the forecasted event, the more likely a forecast error will occur; thus, forecasters prefer late forecasts whenever possible. William J. Shkurti associates good revenue forecasting with reasonable economic assumptions, sound estimating techniques, constructive use of alternative forecasts, a system of monitoring, revision and evaluation, and a clear and complete presentation. At the state level, a variety of revenue-forecasting practices exists, including single executive agency forecasts, council of outside economic advisors, and consensus forecasting.

Sometimes revenue estimates are inaccurate because of political interference. For example, Maine's Republican Governor John R. McKernan, Jr. faced a serious campaign challenge in his second term. As Eileen Shanahan reported in a December 1991 issue of *Governing* magazine, the Maine governor noted that being honest in his state revenue forecast lessened his chances of being reelected. Unfortunately, McKernan intentionally made gargantuan revenue estimating "mistakes" to achieve a balanced budget and then told the voters that the state was all right. After the election, Maine enacted draconian budget cuts hurting the quality of Maine public service. The same article cites another politically inspired poor forecasting by Massachusetts Republican Governor William R. Weld. Unfortunately, some politicians unethically disguise and lie about unpleasant forecasting realities in the hope that the expert forecasts will be wrong. Some forecasting errors are of a technical nature. Often, analysts can improve their forecasting with more detailed data, more timely information, more sophisticated use of computers, and sometimes by making it harder for elected officials to politicize the forecasting process.

In order to cushion the negative possibilities of estimating revenue short, governments create contingency reserve funds, which are sometimes called "rainy day funds." Even if the government has good revenue-forecasting practices, statistical error margins make the use of such reserves a good method to ensure a continuous flow of public service without resorting to disruptive schemes such as hiring freezes. No single formula exists to decide the optimum level of such reserves, and in periods of fiscal stress maintaining any reserves becomes politically very difficult. The likely statistical error margin in a great deal of forecasting is 5 percent; therefore, 5 percent of the total revenue is a reasonable reserve fund level.

EXPENDITURE FORECASTING

Bargaining and Unit Cost Approaches

The burden for estimating expenditures usually rests on the agency, but the techniques are often similar to those of revenue forecasting. In some situations, analysts use a bargaining approach, in which the analysts temper an agency's estimate of its optimum program by the economic and political climate, including budget call instructions. Analysts can also use agency estimates based on detailed work plans that involve months to prepare or based on agency judgments that involve only a few minutes to prepare. The central budget office should review the request, refine, cut, and add to the judgment of the agency, sometimes with the participation of political executive and legislative officials. The final adopted expenditures represent the collective judgment of dozens of officials and staff.

Another set of expenditure forecasting techniques uses accounting information that calculates unit cost data. This method is similar to "fiscal impact analysis," which calculates the municipal costs of proposed local real estate developments by using per capita cost multipliers, the average cost of providing a certain level or standard of service, and other simple calculations. The three major steps in the unit cost approach are (1) choosing a level of analysis, (2) analyzing units and unit costs, and (3) making necessary assumptions and calculations.

In selecting the level of analysis, budget analysts will often use the object code level, but analysts can use subcode or functional levels. For example, Arlington County, Virginia, records each employee's anniversary date, wage rate, grade, longevity increase (if any), fringe benefit costs, and other data as a subcode level. Using this information, the computer does an annual projection of the wages and fringe costs for each employee, and aggregates these costs into the desired object codes, divisional units, departments, and funds. In Syracuse, New York, analysts break down expenditures by department into labor, nonlabor, fringe, and miscellaneous expenditures using a function-department code. Analysts aggregate these relatively gross jurisdiction forecasts. Analysts do the second step of analysis by examining past and current units and unit costs. For example, the analyst charges the gallons of heating fuel to Object Code 306 of the Building Management Department. A more sophisticated forecast would be to multiply the unit cost by the price index when the analyst calculates his or her specific future-year forecasts.

The third step is to include assumptions for future years and then simply to multiply. For example, in the heating fuel situation, assume that a heating unit will consume 50,000 gallons in the BY at a cost of $2 per gallon. The calculation is 50,000 multiplied by $2 equals $100,000, and the analysts budget this in an object code such as 306 of the Building Management Department. The result is an annual or multiyear forecast for a particular expenditure that analysts can aggregate to arrive at a total expenditure forecast.

Time Series Methods

Many agencies use an *incremental* or *trend-line* approach in expenditure forecasting. Historical data define the trend line that shows the expenditure pattern over time. The slope of the line is the rate of change. The formula for a line is $Y = a + bX$ where Y

is the dependent variable, X is the independent variable, and b is the slope of the line. The trend line establishes a historical pattern, and the forecaster need only take the next time period (for example, BY) and read up to the trend line and over to the expenditure level. In Exhibit 5–8, this approach shows that the expenditure forecast for the BY is $50,000. Analysts use judgment to determine any appropriate deviation from the trend based upon factors likely to cause unusual change.

Two other time series methods are *moving averages* and *exponential smoothing*. In moving averages, one adds up the expenditures in past time periods and averages them. The assumption is that averaging the values will minimize data randomness and seasonality. Thus, the more data points the analyst uses, the smoother the forecast. One limitation of the method is that it depends on sufficient data observations; thus, it is not useful for new programs. In addition, it is only useful for short-term forecasts involving one to three time periods and is unable to forecast a change in the underlying trend.

In exponential smoothing, one uses the last forecast value and the estimated "alpha factor weight" of any value between 0 to 1 (for example, 0.1, 0.5, 0.9) and takes the difference between the forecast value for the most recent time period and the actual value realized. For example, $5,000 was spent in the CY and $4,500 in the PY. To calculate the BY with a 0.8 alpha factor, the forecaster calculates $5,000 + 0.8 ($4,500 − $5,000), which yields a BY forecast of $4,850. If the forecaster expects little data randomness, then he or she would use a small alpha factor; conversely, much data randomness would make a high alpha appropriate. The major advantages of this technique over moving averages are that the analysts need fewer data points and this technique better reflects recent rapid trend changes. The inherent disadvantage of the technique is the necessity for forecasters to use an arbitrary assignment such as the alpha factor.

EXHIBIT 5–8   Trend-Line Forecast

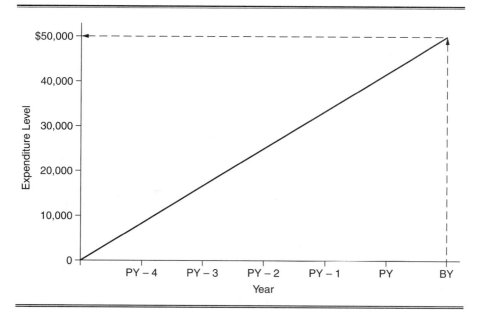

A third time series technique is *adaptive filtering*. The four steps of the technique are as follows:

- develop a forecast by taking a weighted average of the previous observations,
- compare the forecast and actual value realized and calculate errors,
- adjust the weights in the weighted average to minimize calculated error, and
- apply the new set of weights to forecast the subsequent period.

The analyst repeats the process, as new actual data become known. This technique requires many calculations, which the analyst usually does with a computer. The technique is particularly useful when a great deal of historical data is available and when those data exhibit considerable randomness.

A fourth technique is *autoregressive moving averages* (ARMA), of which there are two types: *autoregressive models* and *moving average models*. Autoregressive models (AR) assume that future values are linear combinations of past values. Moving average models (MA) assume that future values are linear combinations of past errors. Autoregressive models use past data on the dependent variable at various time intervals to develop the forecast. Moving average models seek to eliminate the randomness of data by dropping a past observation, as a new one becomes available. Analysts use Box-Jenkins techniques to select and test ARMA models. ARMA techniques tend to produce very good one- to three-year forecasts. The techniques themselves are very complex, but computer software has eliminated most of the time and cost problems associated with the analysis.

The Box-Jenkins method is a systematic elimination procedure to identify the most appropriate ARMA model and determine the appropriate forecasting model. First, the analyst uses various statistical tests and judgmental evaluations to identify the model. Second, the analyst uses a trial-and-error approach via statistical estimation techniques to determine the data array with the smallest mean square error. Third, after an analyst constructs an adequate model, he or she derives a forecasting equation that reflects the data through the current period. A bonus of this technique is that it not only forecasts, but it does so with delineated limits of reliability.

Expenditure Econometric Model

Analysts predicate various expenditures on factors that lend themselves to econometric models. For example, at the state level, analysts directly relate social service expenditures to the state economy, and they relate education and criminal justice expenditures to state demographics and economic factors. They use models not only to predict likely expenditures but also to help policy makers understand the most sensitive factors that influence each functional activity.

One such example is the Massachusetts Welfare Model developed by Data Resources, Inc. That model used short-term forecasts and sensitivity analyses of eligible clients, caseload information, and expenditures in various welfare assistance categories. The model contained the following:

1. earnings distribution of the state and individuals;
2. an estimation routine for calculating Aid to Families with Dependent Children (AFDC) and General Relief (GR) eligibles (after welfare reform the forecast would be of TANF) from a combination of welfare policy standards and state demographic parameters applied to the earnings distributions for families and unrelated individuals;
3. econometric equations explaining eligibles' rate of participation in AFDC and GR, by sex and family status;
4. econometric equations explaining average expenditures per case in AFDC and GR;
5. identities deriving AFDC and GR caseloads by a combination of items 2 and 3; and
6. identities deriving AFDC and GR total expenditures by a combination of items 4 and 5.

The model used 77 variables, including economic, welfare policy, and endogenous variables, as well as welfare eligibles definitions, rates of participation, miscellaneous inputs, and numerous simultaneous econometric equations. Washington State developed a similar multivariate forecast model with a fourteen-month average prediction error of only .42 percent (analysts consider below 2 percent as excellent).

Analysts used the model both for forecasting and *simulation* ("what if" analysis). It forecasts welfare eligibles, caseloads, and expenditures by program. It forecasts the earnings distributions of families and individuals. It simulates the impact on eligibles, caseloads, and expenditures of alternative U.S. and state economic scenarios. It simulates the impact on welfare caseload of changes in the unemployment compensation program. And finally, it simulates the impact on eligibles, caseloads, and expenditures of alternative welfare policies such as

- a cost-of-living increase,
- a change in the income deduction for work-related expenses,
- a change in the assistance tables reflecting new budget levels by family size and living arrangements, and
- a change in federal statutes.

In forecasting, the model works in several steps. First, the analyst uses U.S. and state economic data to derive family earnings distributions and to determine persons eligible for welfare. Next, the analyst calculates the welfare participation rates, using such factors as work availability and wage opportunities (typically, if the economy worsened, welfare benefits and participation are higher). In the example, the analyst calculates welfare caseload and total projected welfare expenditures. Finally, he or she determines administrative costs.

In simulations, the model works with "what if" scenarios. For example, "What if policy makers changed the 5 percent federal eligibility regulations to exclude persons with any income?" The model calculated the changes and predicted the mean monthly caseload and other factors.

Because of the federal transition from "welfare" to "workfare" programs in 1996, and the corresponding budgetary pressures at the state level, reliance on such econometric models to determine caseloads is even more important. Although states like Massachusetts have made the transition and have new service delivery organizations like the Transitional Aid to Families with Dependent Children office, econometric models are important tools for planning and budgeting purposes. Private contractors like Mathematica Policy Research, Inc. have microsimulations that incorporate these techniques and present policy alternatives depending on how variables are introduced into the formula/simulation.

PRODUCTIVITY ANALYSIS

Productivity

Productivity is a measure of efficiency expressed usually as the ratio of the quantity of output to the quantity of input used in the production of that output. Commonly, productivity focuses upon output of labor per hour of change or changes in cost per unit of output. It does not measure the work completed versus the work the agency needs to complete.

The concept of productivity is often misunderstood. It is falsely tied to harder physical work, when it is in fact tied to doing the work with the same or less effort but still increasing output. Management usually achieves productivity gains by initiating better work procedures, like the use of computers, or by creating better worker attitudes toward the job. In quantifying productivity, analysts can confuse the concepts of outcomes and outputs. Reliance on an output like lane miles paved might not adequately address concerns associated with the quality of the road surface being paved. Analysts can use outcomes (benefits to individuals and society) instead of outputs (products of the program). There are often too many intervening variables between outcomes and outputs to permit a meaningful usage of outcomes, thus, intervening outcomes may become necessary to define the direct relationship between measuring outputs, intervening outcomes and final outcomes, and the measures of efficiency or effectiveness. Another conceptual confusion is that an increase in productivity may reflect a cost reduction, but a cost reduction is not always a result of an increase in productivity. Other reasons for cost reduction can exist, such as a simple budget cut. However, too often we do equate productivity with cost reduction.

A federal government study on productivity addressed the reasons for increases in productivity. A commonly cited reason for a productivity increase was an increase in the workload, thus allowing the agency to lower its unit cost. Fixed and variable costs explain how productive advantages can result from increased workloads. In other cases, productivity increases because of improved training, better use of job evaluations, greater upward mobility, or the use of a career ladder to develop the workforce. In some instances, greater productivity is due to automation and the use of new laborsaving equipment.

Although productivity is a simple concept, there are no simple uniform answers for increasing productivity. Analysts must examine each situation separately. The federal study illustrates this point by saying that greater productivity resulted from (1) improved morale derived from job redesign and enrichment, and (2) reorganization and work simplification. The study seems to say that making a job more complex and making a job simpler both result in greater productivity. Understanding the human factor, which the analyst should relate to the job situation, resolves this apparent contradiction. For some people, the job is too complex and beyond their abilities; the answer for them is work simplification. For other people, the job is too simple and their boredom leads to poor work habits; the answer for them is job enrichment, such as rotation or a larger range of responsibilities. To achieve sound increases in productivity, analysts must base their recommendations on knowledge of management science as well as human behavior. Exhibit 5–9 is a useful checklist developed by the National Center for Productivity and Quality of Work Life.

The same federal study also cited some common reasons for declines in productivity. Analysts cannot always factor increased product complexity out of the measurements, and that complexity can mean less productivity. For example, increased environmental, safety, and legal requirements mean added work steps, equipment, or additional features. This may be in the public interest, but one of the disadvantages to government is higher production cost meaning a loss in productivity. Another reason for loss is a steady and sharp decline in workload that management does not match with staff reductions. Either human compassion or labor agreements can mean lower productivity, but again other practical reasons might supersede the desire for efficiency. A third common reason for a decline is, ironically, the installation of a new or automated system. For a period of time during the installation, workers must operate both the automated and old system, thus decreasing productivity until management phases out the old system. These reasons are significant and suggest the complex issues that prevent us from always achieving increased productivity.

Simple Regression Analysis

The basic assumption of *regression analysis* is that analysts relate change in the dependent variable Y to change in the independent variable X, either positively or negatively. In regression analysis, the independent variable need not necessarily cause the dependent variable, but a relationship does exist, which may be causal in nature. Simple regression analysis uses a straight line $Y = a + bX$ that describes the relationship. The slope b is the regression coefficient and measures the change in Y given one unit of change in X. The constant a represents the distance between the points where the regression line intercepts the Y axis and the origin. In order to draw the regression line, the analyst uses the *least-squares method*. This type of analysis assumes a normal probability distribution for the observations and assumes that the error values are independent of each other (that is, no autocorrelation exists).

Exhibit 5–10 and Exhibit 5–11 use a simple linear regression for neighborhood libraries in an urban county. The independent variable X is the full-time-equivalent circulation staff working at each library unit. There is an assumed relationship between circulation staff size and actual books in circulation during the CY. Exhibit 5–11 states the input and output data and shows how an analyst uses the least-squares method to determine the line on Exhibit 5–10. Note that the line fits or explains the various actual data observations, which are coded library values.

EXHIBIT 5–9   What Do You Know About Your Productivity?

The following set of questions can be used as a self-audit to determine what your organization is doing and what your organization may need to do to make programs more productive.

1. IS THE EFFICIENCY OF STAFF PERSONNEL MEASURED?
   - Are critical outputs identified for each program?
   - Are work counts and time-utilization records maintained for these critical outputs? Are unit times developed for the outputs? Are trend data available for the unit times? Is unit cost information available?
   - Are efficiency *data* reported periodically to management?
   - Are unit times compared among regions? Are they compared with other organizations doing similar work in or out of government?

2. ARE PERFORMANCE STANDARDS SET FOR CRITICAL PROGRAM OUTPUTS?
   - Are time standards used?
   - Standards cover what percentage of the work?
   - Are performance reports regularly prepared and distributed to persons responsible for performance?
   - Are standards used by supervisors for day-to-day operations to plan and schedule work? Are the standards used in planning and budgeting?

3. IS PROGRAM EFFECTIVENESS MEASURED?
   - Are performance indicators available that address program effectiveness?
   - Do performance indicators include the target population, the level of service, and the desired impact?
   - Are measurable goals tied to indicators of program effectiveness?

4. IS THE QUALITY OF WORK PROPERLY CONTROLLED?
   - Are error and timeliness *data* maintained and reported on a regular basis? Are quality standards used?
   - Is quality of performance measured and reported on a regular basis?

5. IS OVERALL PRODUCTIVITY PERFORMANCE MEASURED?
   - Do analysts use measures that combine effectiveness and efficiency related to achieving results? Do analysts use cost-effectiveness measures?
   - Do analysts identify major cost elements for each program and do they determine costs?

6. ARE METHODS AND PROCEDURES ANALYZED FREQUENTLY?
   - Are your *managers* currently aware of what others do in operations similar to yours? Do managers review mechanization and new technology continually for possible application to your operation?
   - Are staff specialists asked to make improvement studies?
   - Do supervisors and employees make suggestions on improving operational details?

7. ARE EMPLOYEES MOTIVATED TO PERFORM AT A SATISFACTORY LEVEL?
   - Are employees told how well they perform?
   - Are merit increases and awards tied to performance?
   - Are "quality of working life" motivational techniques used?

Source: Based upon National Center for Productivity and Quality of Work Life. *Improving Productivity: A Self Audit and Guide.* Washington, DC: National Center for Productivity and Quality of Work Life, 1978, pp. 10–11, 13.

EXHIBIT 5–10   Book Circulation

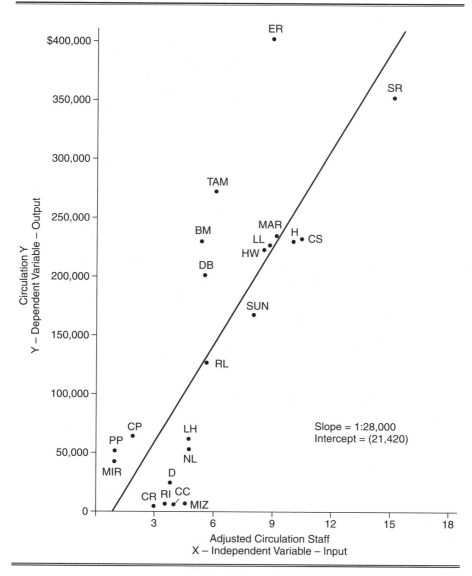

How does this type of analysis assist in the budget process? Essentially, the regression line is the CY average productivity curve for the library system. Libraries to the left and above the line are more productive; hence, management can examine them to see what they are doing right. Of course, management also can exam the least productive units. Another useful feature of this analysis is that any requested additional FTE circulation staff for a unit should generate, ideally, the normal productivity output. Budget analysts can query, "Will the library indeed generate the desired circulation, or will management lower productivity if it adds

EXHIBIT 5–11   Productivity for Libraries—Circulation Staff (Input): Circulation (Output)

Library Outlets	Input	Output	$(x-\bar{x})$	$(y-\bar{y})$	$(x-\bar{x})(y-\bar{y})$	$(x-\bar{x})^2$
BM	4.5	233170	−1.54	85750.68	−132134.01	2.37
CP	2.0	62222	−4.04	−85197.32	344274.62	16.33
CR	3.0	2939	−3.04	−144480.32	439351.51	9.25
CC	4.0	4929	−2.04	−142490.32	290809.79	4.17
CS	10.7	238127	4.66	90707.68	422615.34	21.71
D	3.6	25615	−2.44	−121804.32	297313.27	5.96
D/CC	0.0	0	0.00	0.00	0.00	0.00
DR	5.6	203404	−0.44	55984.68	−24684.16	0.19
ER	8.3	406135	2.26	258715.68	584462.24	5.10
H	9.7	236389	3.66	88969.68	325548.15	13.39
HW	8.6	2048727	2.56	57307.68	146655.57	6.55
LL	8.7	227368	2.66	79948.68	212590.81	7.07
LH	4.8	63214	−1.24	−84205.32	104491.14	1.54
M	8.8	234892	2.76	87472.68	241345.08	7.61
MR	1.0	45184	−5.04	−102235.32	515358.94	25.41
MZ	4.5	7449	−1.54	−139970.32	215681.54	2.37
NL	4.7	55722	−1.34	−91697.32	122957.77	1.80
PP	1.0	50406	−5.04	−97013.32	489035.32	25.41
RL	5.7	137722	−0.34	−9697.32	3305.90	0.12
RI	5.5	5129	−0.54	−142290.32	76966.13	0.29
SR	14.7	355862	8.66	208442.68	1804924.13	74.98
SI	7.8	165386	1.76	17966.68	31605.03	3.09
TM	5.7	277234	−0.34	129814.68	−44255.01	0.12
Total	132.9	3243225	0.00	0.00	6468219.11	234.83
Averages	6.04	147419.32				
Slope	27543.89					
Intercept	−18970.81					

$$b = \frac{\Sigma(x - \bar{x})(y - \bar{y})}{\Sigma(x - \bar{x})^2}$$

$$b = \frac{6468219.11}{234.83} = 27{,}544.26 \text{ slope}$$

$y = bx + c$

$c = y - bx$

$c = 147419.32 - ((27543.89)(6.04))$

$c = -18970.81 \text{ intercept at y}$

NOTE: Due to computer rounding, this number is 25.04 higher than these summary numbers.

the staff?" Regression analysis is useful in determining and fostering greater productivity in public organizations.

Analysts consider multiple regression analysis more useful than simple regression analysis because multiple regression uses more independent variables. Thus, it should yield a more accurate fit when compared to actual data. Usually, however, analysts should keep the number of variables to a minimum (for example, four). Typically, analysts use multiple regression analysis to sort down the likely variables of causality.

Productivity and Budgeting

Agencies can strengthen their budget requests by citing productivity measures. Usually reviewing authorities more readily accept cost estimates based on data involving productivity. In addition, the inclusion of performance data in budget documents can bolster justification for increases of fend-off possible cuts. See Exhibit 5–12 for useful guidance

EXHIBIT 5–12 Government Finance Officers Association Statement on Performance Measurement in Budgets and Finance

A key responsibility of state and local governments is to develop and manage programs, services, and their related resources as efficiently and effectively as possible and to communicate the results of these efforts to the stakeholders. Performance measurement when linked to the budget and strategic planning process can assess accomplishments on an organization-wide basis. When used in the long-term planning and goal setting process and linked to the entity's mission, goals, and objectives, meaningful performance measurements assist government officials and citizens in identifying financial and program results, evaluating past resource decisions, and facilitating qualitative improvements in future decisions.

The Government Finance Officers Association (GFOA) recommends that program and service performance measures be developed and used as an important component of long-term strategic planning and decision making that should be linked to governmental budgeting. Performance should

- be based on program goals and objectives that tie to a statement of program mission or purpose;
- measure program outcomes;
- provide for resource allocation comparisons over time;
- measure efficiency and effectiveness for continuous improvement;
- be verifiable, understandable, and timely;
- be consistent throughout the strategic plan, budget, accounting, and reporting systems;
- to the extent practical, be consistent over time;
- be reported internally and externally;
- be monitored and used in managerial decision-making processes;
- be limited to a number and degree of complexity that can provide an efficient and meaningful way to assess the effectiveness and efficiency of key programs; and
- be designed in such a way to motivate staff at levels to contribute toward organizational improvement.

GFOA encourages all governments to utilize performance measures as an integral part of the budget process.

Over time, performance measures should be used to report on the outputs and outcomes of each program and should be related to the mission, goals, and objectives of each department.

(continued)

EXHIBIT 5–12 *(continued)*

Governments in early stages of incorporating performance measures into their budget process should strive to

- develop a mission statement for government and its service delivery units by evaluating the needs of the community;
- develop its service delivery units in terms of programs;
- identify goals, short- and long-term, that contribute to the attainment of the mission;
- identify program goals and objectives that are specific in time frame and measurable to accomplish goals;
- identify and track performance measures for a manageable number of services within programs;
- identify program inputs in the budgeting process that addresses the amount of service units produced;
- identify program efficiencies in the budgeting process that addresses the cost of providing a unit of service;
- identify the program outcomes in the budgeting process that address the extent to which the goals of the program have been accomplished;
- take steps to ensure that the entire organization is receptive to evaluation of performance;
- integrate performance measurements into the budget, which at a minimum contains by program the goals, input, output, efficiency, and outcome measures; and
- calculate costs and document changes that occur as a direct result of the performance management program in order to review the effectiveness of the performance management program.

As governments gain experience, they are encouraged to develop more detailed information and use a variety of performance measures to report on program outcomes. These measures should be linked to the goals of the programs and the missions and priorities of the organization. Governments should

- ensure that the benefits of establishing and using performance measures exceed the resources required to establish performance measures;
- develop multiyear series of efficiency indicators to measure the effectiveness of service delivery (are accomplishments being met?) within programs;
- develop a mechanism to cost government services;
- analyze the implications of using particular measures for decision making and accountability;
- use customer or resident satisfaction surveys;
- adopt common definitions of key efficiency and effectiveness performance measures to allow intergovernmental comparisons;
- develop, measure, and monitor more detailed information within programs; non-financial performance measures in making and evaluating decisions;
- use community condition measures to assess resident needs that may not be addressed by current programs;
- develop and periodically review supportable targets for each performance measure;
- evaluate the data to use long-term resource allocation and budget decisions for continuous improvement; and
- utilize performance information in resource allocation decisions and report the efficiency and effectiveness and the extent to which the program goals have been accomplished.

In the final analysis, GFOA recognizes that the value of any performance measurement program is derived through positive behavioral change. Stakeholders at all levels must embrace the concept of continuous improvement and be willing to be measured against objective expectations. GFOA urges governments to recognize that establishing a receptive climate for performance measurement is as important as the measurements themselves.

Source: As adapted from the Government Finance Officers Association *Public Policy Statements on Performance Measurements* and *Recommended Budget Practices*. Chicago: GFOA, 1999.

EXHIBIT 5–13   Selected Illustration of a Presentation of Output Data in the 1975 Budget Appendix Federal Mediation and Conciliation Service Salaries and Expenses

The Service, under Title II of the Labor Management Relations Act of 1947, assists labor and management in mediation and prevention of disputes affecting industries engaged in interstate commerce and defense production, other than rail and air transportation, whenever in its judgment such disputes threaten to cause a substantial interruption of commerce. Under the authority of Executive Order 11491 of October 29, 1969, as amended by Executive Order 11616, dated August 26, 1971, the Service also makes its mediation and conciliation facilities available to Federal agencies and organizations representing Federal employees in the resolution of negotiation disputes.

Mediation Service. During 1973, dispute notices and other notifications affecting 117,884 employers were received by the Service. Cases totaling 21,745 were assigned for mediation, and 21,032 mediation assignments were closed during the year. About 89 percent of the mediation assignments closed which required the services of mediators were settled without work stoppages. A total of 26,973 mediation conferences were conducted by mediators during 1973. The workload shown above includes assignments closed in both the private and public sectors. Cases in process at the end of 1973 totaled 5,449; this is the normal carryover of open cases from month to month, with seasonal fluctuations. The following chart shows a 5-year comparison of workload data:

Dispute Workload Data

	1969	1970	1971	1972	1973
Cases in process at the beginning of the year	5,260	5,113	5,020	4,889	4,736
Mediation assignments	21,839	19,769	21,727	19,308	21,745
Mediation assignments closed	21,986	19,862	21,858	19,461	21,032
Cases in process at end of year	5,113	5,020	4,889	4,736	5,449
Mediation conferences conducted	31,605	30,334	32,293	29,223	26,973

Source: Extracted from p. 878 of the 1975 Budget Appendix.

on the application of performance measurement in budgeting and financial management. Those requests are more impressive and help establish agency credibility. Exhibit 5–13 is from the 1975 U.S. Budget Appendix and demonstrates that the use of performance data is not a recent innovation. It illustrates how hard facts strengthen the agency's justification of its budget even in an agency such as the Mediation and Conciliation Service. Exhibit 5–14 illustrates how productivity measures melded into a budget justification document. The most helpful data and measures are the following:

- productivity indices, which relate end products produced to human physical effort or cost measures;
- unit cost ratios, which relate work performed to all or a part of the cost of performing the work;

EXHIBIT 5–14   Illustration of Selected Agency Productivity Trends: The Defense Supply Agency

Since the activation of DSA, constant management attention to the basic goal of maximum efficiency has produced significant operating economies. In the early years of DSA, 1962–1966, increased productivity was realized through manpower reductions as numerous organizational and procedural improvements were effected. However, it was not until FY 1967 that a formal output and productivity evaluation system was installed. Since that time, overall output per man-year [person-year] has increased almost 30 percent.

The chart below depicts the composite productivity trend for the agency from FY 1967 through FY 1973. The index shown was derived from the basic data which constituted DSA's input to the Government-wide productivity project. Improvement has averaged about 5 percent per year for the past six years. DSA currently employs about 52,000 military and civilian personnel in performing its assigned mission. Had the increase in productivity reflected on this chart not been realized, today's job would require about 10,000 more personnel than are currently employed.

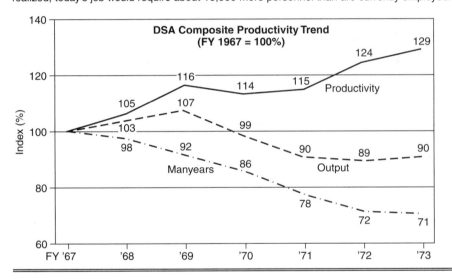

Source: Adapted from pp. 35–36 of the Joint Financial Management Improvement Program, "Report on Federal Productivity, Volume II: Productivity Case Studies," June 1974.

- work measuring ratios, which relate work performed to physical needs of humans in carrying out the work;
- program or workload data, which show trends in the program work; and
- statistical data, such as regression analysis, which relate experience data to human physical effort.

Glen Hahn Cope investigated the relationship of performance or productivity measures to improved productivity. Seventy percent of her respondents reported that management used the information developed for the budget process for other management purposes in their government. Fifty-nine percent reported that management used the management and budget information to increase the jurisdiction's productivity. She also asked if the respondents thought improvements in the budget process could actually improve their organization's productivity. Seventy-seven percent said yes. Cope concluded that budgetary information not only is useful for management purposes but also contributes to improved local government productivity beyond its use in budgetary decision making.

THE BENEFIT-COST CONCEPT

Concept: What and Why

The rather simple belief that policy makers should judge projects on the basis of project cost versus project benefits is the bases for *benefit-cost analysis*. At best, benefit-cost analysis is a guide for investment decision. It can help decision makers decide if they should undertake specific expenditures, if the scale of the project is appropriate, and what the optimum project size should be. Some treat benefit-cost as a framework for a general theory of government investment.

Analysts sometimes confuse cost-effectiveness analysis with benefit-cost analysis, but there are advantages to maintaining the distinction. Cost-effectiveness assumes benefits and does not compare them with cost as in benefit-cost analysis. In cost-effectiveness analysis, the analyst wishes to determine the least costly means to achieve the objective. Because both methods use inputs, alternatives, and outputs, cost-effectiveness analysis may very well include benefit-cost considerations. However, cost-effectiveness can often be the more effective analytical technique, and blurring the distinction between the techniques tends to blind practitioners to the comparative advantages of the techniques. Both have their advantages, but analysts can often use cost-effectiveness where benefit-cost is a meaningless technique.

The sophisticated benefit-cost analysis is useful. It can establish a framework for reasonably consistent and uniform project evaluations at the staff level. This can lead to greater discipline in the political process because weak projects will appear inferior, thus making their funding difficult in an open political setting. The technique is most useful when the choice set is narrow and the decision involves economic alternative investments. The technique draws increasing criticism when intangibles and complex social values are present in the analysis. Benefit-cost analysis does not address well intangible or vague value perspectives such as reallocation of wealth.

Benefit-cost analysis involves defining a *choice set, analytical constraint measurements,* and a *choice model.* Analysts must make their analysis manageable before they can perform their work within a reasonable time frame. Thus, they must establish a range of projects. Analysts must understand, state, and treat them either as side considerations of the analysis or as analytical constraints (for example, legal, political, distributional, financial, and physical). Benefit-cost analysis involves measurements; therefore, all the challenges and analytical limitations of data apply to benefit-cost analysis. Analysts must understand those challenges and limitations. If they do not, then they will make serious analytical mistakes, and they will give decision makers misleading advice. A full treatment of this topic is beyond the scope of this text. The choice model is the means used to relate the estimated costs and benefits. It is the model (formula) analysts use to decide how they will incorporate the measures into the overall analysis.

Procedures

The procedures of benefit-cost analysis involve defining the *objective functions, benefits,* and *costs* as well as calculating present value. The objective functions specify without weighing the ultimate values used in the analysis. Examples include increasing national income, aggregate consumption, supply of foreign exchange, and employment. Analysts must quantify the functions, or they cannot treat them in their analysis. Analysts usually define benefits as present value of the contributions in relationship to the objective function. They sometimes define costs in terms of reducing the objective function, in terms of the present value of the resources that they employ, and in terms of opportunity costs as a consequence of implementing the project.

The calculations in benefit-cost analysis are complex owing to several factors. Analysts must measure both benefits and costs over time in order to permit a broad view of project impacts, especially economic consequences. They measure benefits by the market price of the project outputs or the price consumers willingly pay. They measure costs by the monetary outlays necessary to undertake the investment. Both occur over time. Unlike the private sector, analysts calculate *externalities* (that is, project effects on others, which occur because of the project's existence—such as downstream pollution from a plant) into the public sector benefit-cost analysis because the public sector does concern itself with the public interest rather than with particular private interests. Also, analysts value opportunity costs because they assume that full employment and scarce resources exist. This means that some worthwhile choices are foregone once the policy makers make the decision to undertake the project. Thus, the analysts consider opportunity costs as project costs. If the assumption is incorrect (for example, if full employment does not exist), then analysts should revise costs downward.

Alternative Choice Models

Policy makers often use the ranking of alternative projects as the means to decide what project to fund. The ranking depends on the choice model (formula) used. The various models do not give the analyst the same results. The eight models are the following:

Benefit-cost	Based on discounted present value
Benefit/cost	Ratio of present value of benefits and costs
Rate of return or marginal investment	Discount rate that puts the benefits and efficiency costs at equilibrium
Payout period	Number of years of benefit needed so that the benefit equals the cost

Each model has its inherent bias. The benefit-cost model biases the decision in favor of large projects because of the manner in which the analyst must calculate the figures. Any deductions from benefits rather than adding to costs would affect ratios and thus would affect the benefit/cost model. If benefits or costs do not occur evenly over time, the analyst cannot properly compute this in his or her mathematical models unless special provisions permit this unevenness.

Virtually all practitioners prefer the benefit-cost (discounted present value) model. It focuses on explicit treatment of budgetary and other constraints as well as project indivisibility and interdependencies. This model forces the separate treatment of those matters without confusing them with the determination of the proper discount rate. Also, calculation of present value is not a behind-the-scenes adjustment because the analyst must treat it openly in the analysis.

Benefit–Cost Ingredients

A purpose of this chapter is not to explain how analysts perform benefit-cost analysis but rather to stress the sophisticated analytical nature of the technique as well as its inherent limitations. Too many professionals advocate and even use the technique without understanding its true analytical sophistication. It is a worthwhile technique, and those interested in public budgeting should study it. However, the first step is to recognize the complex nature of this type of analysis and be especially sensitive to its limitations.

The remainder of this section examines key factors associated with benefit-cost analysis. This chapter stresses the limitations and cautions that analysts should associate with this technique. Being sensitive to the analytical problems associated with the technique is important. A full explanation of how to apply the technique is beyond the scope of this text, and readers should learn more about this and other analytical techniques in further study.

Benefits and Estimation

This technique classifies benefits as *primary, secondary,* and *intangible.* Primary benefits are the values of goods or services resulting from project conditions. Analysts include them in their analysis. Common examples are additional crops due to land irrigation and annual savings in flood damages. Analysts subtract associated costs (for example, seed for irrigated land) from primary benefits. A secondary benefit either stems from the project or the project induces it, but it does not directly result from the project. The inclusion of secondary benefits is controversial. Intangibles are nondollar-value benefits (for example, aesthetic quality of the landscape), which, by definition, analysts cannot include in their benefit-cost calculations.

What gets counted as "benefits" is important. Therefore, if the major benefits are intangibles, then the analysis does not include much of the project's worth and the numbers present a false picture. Also, if the major benefits are secondary, the inclusion of them is controversial and the resulting analytical conclusions are subject to a complex debate involving the technique more than the project. The purpose of analysis is to aid decision makers, and the result of using controversial techniques is to confuse further the decision-making process.

Benefit-cost analysis is almost always used prior to the project's existence; therefore, analysts estimate costs and benefits over the projected life of the project.

Cost estimates include construction engineering, relocation of households, erosion, and third-party effects. Benefits are harder to estimate, especially if they do not occur evenly over time. Analysts must make decisions on when to stop counting, what not to count, how to count, and how to aggregate benefits. These decisions may greatly affect the analysis; therefore, controversial decisions may lead to controversial analytical conclusions.

One commonly voiced concern is how to handle costs that already have occurred (that is, *sunk costs*). Sunken costs are the difference between the value of an asset in its current use and its value in an alternative use. This is not a controversial subject because they are almost uniformly treated as irrelevant to the project cost, and analysts do not include them in the analysis. Sunk costs may be of significant political concern, but analysts do not add their value into the project cost.

Discount Rate

The most controversial ingredient of benefit-cost analysis is the *discount rate.* The controversy centers not on its proper role in the analysis, but on how analysts should determine it. It is significant because a higher discount rate means that analysts will justify fewer projects, especially if they have costs accumulating over a long period of time. The rationale for a discount rate is that policy makers could invest those resources used in the target project elsewhere, thus yielding future resources larger than the amount invested; therefore, the analysts should consider that yield in his or her analysis.

Users of this technique advocate several approaches to determining discount rates. One says that a discount rate should have a bias toward present goods over future goods, whereas another argues for giving higher value to future goods. Others argue analysts should base opportunity cost on equivalent private investments, whereas still others say analysts should add and subtract external effects from those private opportunity costs. The debate is endless and most analysts end up by using an arbitrary interest cost of federal funds (such as the Treasury bond rate) in a certain period as the selected rate.

If the projects analyzed are similar in size and duration, then the rate used is not significant as long as the analyst uses the same rate for all projects. If not, then the analytical results become controversial.

Externalities, Risk, and Other Considerations

Benefit-cost analysis includes externalities, but they are difficult to determine. *Technological externalities* involve the physical input-output relationship *of* other producing units. *Pecuniary externalities* involve the influences of the project *on* the prices of other producing units. For example, a public recreation facility may affect demand on, and thus the price of, nearby private facilities. Measurement of externalities is treacherous. Ideally, analysts include only "important externalities" in their analysis. Interestingly, analysts do not include the influence on the local wage rate in their analysis, as they do not consider it "important." Controversy can easily exist on the inclusion of externalities as well as the measurement of them.

Often, benefits and costs involve *risk* and *uncertainty.* *Risk* is a probability function usually based on experience. *Uncertainty,* in its purest meaning, is not subject to probability determination. Thus, an analyst can include risk in the analysis but cannot include uncertainty. Methods of calculating risk and uncertainty vary. Some methods establish a higher permissible rate than 1.0. Some use a higher rate of discount and some rationalize the arbitrary benefit stream cutoff by referring to risk and uncertainty. An analyst can deal with risk by including a probability function in an already complex formula, but he or she must treat uncertainty, by definition, arbitrarily. Such treatment leads to controversy over the analytical results.

Two other considerations illustrate the complexity of this technique. As was pointed out, sometimes analysts use private opportunity costs to determine public project opportunity costs. The danger is that private market costs are higher owing to the different tax statuses and costs of financing. Another consideration is that user charges may not be independent of the benefit measures. User charges restrict use; thus, they reduce the benefits. Benefit-cost analysis requires a great deal of thought and care. If the analyst does not provide professional treatment of these matters in his or her analysis, then embarrassing controversy can develop over the quality of the analysis.

Benefit-cost analysis biases decision making toward values that an analyst can compute with money. It does not work well with projects concerning social equality; thus, the technique tends to discriminate against the poor. For example, an analyst often computes the value of one or more lives in terms of earning power of those lives: an analyst treats an airplane passenger as worth more than a bus rider because the average earnings of a bus passenger are much lower than the average earnings of an airplane passenger. This technique cannot treat well values such as equality of opportunity or beauty. If the project involves such higher values, then the use of the benefit-cost technique itself creates a controversy that does not enhance the decision-making environment.

REVIEW QUESTIONS

1. Explain the budget system model, its consistency with democratic theory, and the importance of data measures.
2. Explain the various application difficulties associated with using the HST model.
3. Scatter diagrams, marginal costs, and discounting are useful *analytical* techniques in budgeting. Explain why.
4. Explain the significance of a crosswalk as an analytical tool. What should an analyst crosswalk and why?
5. Compare and contrast qualitative, time series, and causal analysis approaches to revenue forecasting. Explain why good forecasting is important to government.
6. Compare and contrast the various approaches to expenditure forecasting.
7. Misunderstanding the productivity concept can lead to what types of difficulties? What are some of the most common reasons for government not to increase productivity? Why are there no simple uniform answers to the question of how to increase productivity?
8. Explain how regression analysis can help one achieve greater productivity.
9. Compare and contrast benefit-cost and cost-effectiveness analyses.

10. Explain why benefit-cost is a sophisticated and difficult technique to apply. Explain how an analyst can abuse benefit-cost analysis as a technique. Are there any downsides to benefit-cost analysis for public policy decision making?

REFERENCES

BAHL, ROY, and LARRY SCHROEDER. "The Role of Multi-Year Forecasting in the Annual Budgeting Process for Local Governments." *Public Budgeting and Finance,* 4, 1 (Spring 1984), 3–13.

BURKHEAD, JESSE, and JERRY MINER. *Public Expenditure.* Chicago: Aldine, 1971.

Committee for Economic Development. *Improving Productivity in State and Local Government.* New York: Committee for Economic Development, March 1976.

COPE, G. H. "Walking the Fiscal Tightrope: Local Government Budgeting and Fiscal Stress." *International Journal of Public Administration,* 15, 5 (1992), 1097–1120.

DAVIES, THOMAS R., and JAMES A. ZINGALE. "Advanced Software for Revenue Forecasting: What to Consider Before Investing in Technology." Paper prepared for the 1983 American Society for Public Administration National Conference, New York, April 17, 1983.

FEW, PAULA K., and A. JOHN VOGT. "Measuring the Performance of Local Governments in North Carolina." *Government Finance Review,* 13, 4 (August 1997), 29–34.

FORRESTER, JOHN P. "Use of Revenue Forecasting Techniques." In Thomas D. Lynch and Lawrence Martin (eds.), *Handbook of Comparative Public Budgeting and Financial Management.* New York: Marcel Dekker, 1993.

FOUNTAIN, JAMES R. "Governmental Accounting: Where Is It Heading?" *Public Budgeting and Finance,* 7, 4 (Winter 1987), 95–103.

GARSOMBKE, H. PERRIN, and JERRY SCHRAD. "Performance Measurement Systems: Results from a City and State Survey." *Government Finance Review,* 15, 1 (February 1999), 9–12.

HATRY, HARRY R. "Overview of Modern Program Analysis Characteristics and Techniques: Modern Program Analysis—Hero or Villain?" Washington, DC: Urban Institute, 1969.

HATRY, HARRY R., LOUIS BLAIR, DONALD FISK, and WAYNE KIMMEL. *Program Analysis for State and Local Governments.* Washington, DC: Urban Institute, 1976.

ISAAC, STEPHEN, in collaboration with WILLIAM B. MICHAEL. *Handbook in Research and Evaluation.* San Diego, CA: Edits Publishers, 1971.

JONES, ANN. "Winston-Salem's Participation in the North Carolina Performance Measurement Project." *Government Finance Review,* 13, 4 (August 1997), 35–36.

KLAY, WILLIAM EARLE. "Revenue Forecasting: An Administrative Perspective." In Jack Rabin and Thomas D. Lynch (eds.), *Handbook on Public Budgeting and Financial Management.* New York: Marcel Dekker, 1983.

KLAY, WILLIAM EARLE, and GLORIA A. GRIZZLE. "Revenue Forecasting in the States: New Dimensions of Budgetary Forecasting." Paper delivered to the American Society for Public Administration at Anaheim, CA, April 14, 1986.

KRAMER, FRED A. "The Discounting to Present Value Technique as a Decision Tool." *Special Bulletin 1976E* (November 24, 1976).

LAUTH, THOMAS P. "Performance Evaluation in the Georgia Budgetary Process." *Public Budgeting and Finance,* 5, 1 (Spring 1985), 67–82.

LEE, ROBERT D., JR. "The Use of Program Analysis in State Budgeting: Changes Between 1990 and 1995." *Public Budgeting and Finance,* 17, 2 (Summer 1997), 18–36.

———. "The Use of Program Information and Analysis in State Budgeting: Trends of Two Decades." In Thomas D. Lynch and Lawrence Martin (eds.), *Handbook of Comparative Public Budgeting and Financial Management.* New York: Marcel Dekker, 1993.

MCCOLLOUGH, JANE, and HOWARD FRANK. "Incentives For Forecasting Reform Among Local Finance Officers." *Public Budgeting and Financial Management,* 4, 4 (1992), 407–429.

MOAK, LENNOX L., and KATHRYN W. KILLIAN. *Operating Budget Manual.* Chicago: Municipal Finance Officers Association, 1963.

NATIONAL CENTER FOR PRODUCTIVITY AND QUALITY OF WORK LIFE. "Improving Productivity: A Self Audit and Guide." Washington, DC: NCPQWL, 1978.

O'TOOLE, DANIEL E., JAMES MARSHALL, and TIMOTHY GREWE. "Current Local Budgeting Practices." *Government Finance Review,* 12, 6 (December 1996), 27–29.

PLOTNICK, ROBERT D., and RUSSELL M. LIDMAN. "Forecasting Welfare Caseloads: A Tool to Improve Budgeting." *Public Budgeting and Finance,* 7, 3 (Autumn 1987), 70–81.

Public Policy Institute of New York. *An Analysis of State Revenue Forecasting Systems: A Special Report.* Albany, NY: PPINYS, 1985.

ROSS, JOHN P., and JESSE BURKHEAD. *Productivity in the Local Government Sector.* Lexington, MA: D.C. Heath, 1974.

RUBIN, IRENE S. "Estimated and Actual Urban Revenues: Exploring the Gap." *Public Budgeting and Finance,* 7, 4 (Winter 1987), 83–94.

SHANAHAN, EILEEN. "Cracks in the Crystal Ball." *Governing* (December 1991), 29–32.

SHKURTI, WILLIAM J. "A User's Guide to State Revenue Forecasting." *Public Budgeting and Finance,* 10, 1 (Spring 1990), 79–94.

STEWART, J. D. "The Role of Information in Public Accountability." In Tony Hopwood and Cyril R. Tomkins (eds.), *Issues in Public Accounting.* Oxford, Great Britain: Philip Allan, 1984.

TOULMIN, LLEWELLYN M., and GLENDAL E. WRIGHT. "Expenditure Forecasting." In Jack Rabin and Thomas D. Lynch (eds.), *Handbook on Public Budgeting and Financial Management.* New York: Marcel Dekker, 1983.

URBAN INSTITUTE AND INTERNATIONAL CITY MANAGEMENT ASSOCIATION. *Measuring the Effectiveness of Basic Municipal Services.* Washington, DC: International City Management Association, February 1974.

U.S. Joint Financial Management Improvement Program. *Productivity Programs in the Federal Government.* Washington, DC: U.S. Joint Financial Management Improvement Program, July 1976.

VASCHE, JON DAVID, and BRAD WILLIAMS. "Optimal Governmental Budgeting Contingency Funds." *Public Budgeting and Finance,* 7, 1 (Spring 1987), 66–82.

WALTERS, JONATHAN. "The Benchmarking Craze." *Governing* (April 1994), 33–37.

WRIGHT, CHESTER, and MICHAEL D. TATE. *Economics and Systems Analysis: Introduction for Public Managers.* Reading, MA: Addison-Wesley, 1973.

6

ANALYTICAL PROCESSES

In public budgeting, the five analytical processes that help professionals deal more intelligently with their policy and administrative challenges are *program analysis, budget examination, process analysis, program evaluation,* and *auditing.* This chapter gives greater attention to budget examination and process analysis due to their importance as basic public budgeting techniques. Public managers should view the reports produced from each process as aids to improving their budgets. Program analysis looks *de novo* at the policy implications of major programmatic budget decisions. Budget examination is the primary analytical process that actually produces the budget. Process analysis focuses on the management process itself so that the manager can identify improvements. Program evaluation looks backward and helps the budget examiner and policy makers decide if the program was effective or sufficiently effective to justify the requested money in the BY. Auditing after implementation of the public budget is also necessarily reflective in character and helps the budget examiner focus on questions of both effectiveness and efficiency. The chapter explains the following:

- the approach essential for useful program analysis;
- how budget examiners use the various common concepts and techniques;
- a useful approach to look closely at the process and identify process improvements;
- the basics of program evaluation; and
- the essentials of auditing, especially the types of information that a program audit can bring to the policy makers and public managers.

PROGRAM ANALYSIS

Program analysis—sometimes called policy analysis—is rational thinking that focuses on properly considering new policy options that are implicit in the budget. Such analyses are often highly quantitative in character, but that need not be the situation. There are elements common to all program analyses, regardless of their character. A complaint of high-level executive officials is that they really cannot get the agencies to provide the information necessary to judge budget requests. Often this is more an admission of professional incompetence on their part than a commentary on the budget process. If a reasonable effort, as explained here, is put into budget examining by competent professionals, then the central review staff can make reasoned judgments based on agency requests and alternative policy options. Good program analysis should isolate sensitive policy questions and identify the likely implications of the various viable policy options within the limitations of the data and the analytical technique used.

Selecting Issues

Selection of potential issues can proceed systematically. What unsettled influential issues determine program direction and emphasis? What important issues do the legislature, executive, clientele, media, judiciary, and key influential stakeholders raise? What are the apparent important policy dilemmas facing the agency? The analysts can use these questions to develop a reasonable list of potential issues for analysis. Usually, program issues are abundant. The usual problem is not to find issues but to select the best issues for program review purposes in a given fiscal year and in the context of the budget process. The Urban Institute has developed the following criteria for selecting issues for analysis:

IMPORTANCE OF AN ISSUE

- What decisions should the government make?
- Can an analysis significantly assist the policy makers to consider more intelligently the various alternatives available to them?
- Do the issues involve large costs or major consequences for services?
- Is there substantial room for improving program performance?

FEASIBILITY OF ANALYSIS

- Can program analysis address the problem?
- Can analysts perform the analysis prior to when the policy makers must make the key decisions?
- Are personnel and funds available to do the analysis?
- Does sufficient data exist to undertake the analysis?
- Can analysts gather needed data within the time available?

The first consideration is the importance of the issue. As suggested by the previous criteria, the policy maker should consider the potential significance of an analysis of the issue, the consequence, and the potential for improvement of the situation in question. If no one will use an analysis of an issue, then proceeding with the analysis is certainly foolish. Given a lack of time common to the policy-making situation, analysts are wise to concentrate their time on the big issue, especially if notable improvements are possible.

The next consideration is the feasibility of analysis. Many problems do not lend themselves to program analysis, or analysts cannot conduct their necessary work in the time available in which policy makers will make their key decisions. Personnel, fund, or data limitations might exist that preclude analysis. Policy makers must assess each of those factors honestly before they begin their program analysis or their effort may be worthless. Exhibit 6–1 presents some illustrations of the issues on which a policy maker might wish to use program analysis.

EXHIBIT 6–1   Illustrative Issues for Program Analysis

Law Enforcement

- What is the most effective way of distributing limited police forces by time of day, day of week, and geographical location?
- What types of police units (for example, foot patrol, one- or two-officer police cars, special task forces, canine corps units, or others) should the policy use and in what mix?
- What types of equipment (for example, current and new technologies) should the police use for weaponry, communications, and transportation?
- How can policy makers improve the judicial process to provide more expeditious service, keep potentially dangerous persons from running loose, and at the same time protect the rights of the innocent?
- How can management improve criminal detention institutions to maximize the probability of rehabilitation, while remaining a deterrent to further crime?

Fire Protection

- Where should policy makers locate fire stations, and how many does the city need?
- How should policy makers deploy fire fighting units, and how large should those units be?
- What types of equipment should firefighters use for communications and transportation?
- Are there fire prevention activities, such as inspection of potential fire hazards or school educational programs, that the fire department can use effectively?

Health and Social Services

- What mix of treatment programs best meets the needs of the expected set of clients?
- What prevention programs are best for our clientele given the likely ailments they are likely to suffer?

Housing

- To what extent can government use housing code enforcement programs to decrease the number of families living in substandard housing? Will such programs have an adverse effect on the overall supply of low-income housing in the community?
- What is the appropriate mix of code enforcement with other housing programs to make housing in the community adequate?
- What is the best mix of housing rehabilitation, housing maintenance, and new construction to improve the quantity and quality of housing?

Employment

- What relative support should government give in terms of training and employment programs in order to serve its different client groups?
- What should be the mix among outreach programs, training programs, job-finding and matching programs, antidiscrimination programs, and postemployment follow-up programs?

Waste

- How should government collect and dispose of waste, given alternative visual, air, water, and pollution standards?
- What specific equipment and routings should government use?

Recreation and Leisure

- What type, location, and size of recreation facilities should government provide for those desiring them?
- How should government divide recreation facilities among summer and winter, daytime and nighttime, and indoor and outdoor activities?
- What and how many special summer programs should government make available for out-of-school youths?
- What charges, if any, should government impose on users, including considerations for such factors as differential usage and ability to pay?

Source: Adapted from Harry P. Hatry, Louis Blair, Donald Fisk, and Wayne Kimmel. *Program Analysis for State and Local Governments.* Washington, DC: Urban Institute, 1976, p. 11.

Issue Assessment

Once the policy maker or his or her staff defines the issues, then a policy analyst can make a preliminary assessment before he or she conducts an in-depth analysis. In most situations, an agency suggests issues and the central budget office decides which issues to investigate. Those issues selected may or may not be the ones suggested by the agency. The involvement of the central budget office is wise as it helps to ensure that the key reviewing authorities consider the eventual policy report as significant once the analyst writes it. However, regardless of the selection process of the issue, the analyst is always wise to proceed with the in-depth analysis after first conducting a preliminary assessment of the issue. In far too many analytical situations, policy makers have commissioned a report without a proper appreciation of the implications of what they requested. Sometimes due to political reasons or poor writing, the instructions requesting the study are too vague or misleading. Sometimes, further thought by the policy makers reveals that there is no real need for an analysis, thus saving thousands or even millions of dollars. Preliminary assessments are extremely useful.

The issue assessment is a written presentation that identifies and describes the major features of a significant issue facing the government. The assessment is only a few pages long, but it clearly sets out the ingredients that the analyst would consider in a major issue study. According to Harry P. Hatry of the Urban Institute, the outline or major subjects in an issue assessment are as follows:

- *The Problem.*   What is the problem and what caused the problem? Identify specific groups (for example, the poor) that the problem affects. How are they affected? Identify characteristics of the group. How large and significant is the problem now? What are the likely future dimensions of the problem?
- *Objectives and Evaluation Criteria.*   Define the fundamental purposes and benefits of the program. Identify the evaluation criteria by which an analyst can judge if the government makes progress toward achieving its program objectives.
- *Current Activities and Agencies Involved.*   Identify all relevant groups involved in attempting to deal with the problem. For each group, identify what it does in relationship to the problem, including any costs and impacts. Analysts should project any activities, costs, and benefits into the future.

- *Other Significant Factors.*   Cite the other major factors, including political realities, that affect the problem. Identify unusual resources, timing limitations, or other factors of significance.
- *Alternatives.*   Describe alternative programs designed to meet the problem and the major characteristics of each.
- *Recommendations for Follow-up.*   Making choices among alternatives is inappropriate because, by definition, this work is only an assessment. Analysts can make recommendations at the next administrative step (for example, full-scale analysis). What is the best timing for and scope of the needed follow-up analysis? Should the analysis be a quick response or an in-depth study? The analyst should cite frank descriptions of analytical difficulties. What major data problems exist? How should government deal with the data problems under the present circumstances?

The preliminary assessment serves as the basis for deciding to request a special, analytical study and for framing instructions for that study.

Commentary on Analysis

The conduct of analysis largely depends upon the subject analyzed, the context of the study, and the techniques used. Each of these subjects is outside the scope of this chapter, and the student can properly study them under the heading of microeconomics, operations research, systems analysis, and statistics. Chapter 5 discusses some elementary analytical concepts useful in budgeting, including benefit-cost analysis.

Ten Key Factors in Analysis

There are ten factors—five technical and five bureaucratic—that particularly influence the results of analysis. Those factors are the following:

- study size,
- study timing,
- methodological adequacy,
- considerations of implementation,
- nature of problem studied,
- decision maker interest,
- implementer's participation,
- single-agency issue,
- proposed changes in funding, and
- the immediate need for a decision.

From this list of important factors, the three most significant technical factors are the following:

- timing (that is, the windows of time when policy makers need the studies so that the analyst's findings are available to them at their key decision points in their decision making process);

- considerations of implementation (that is, the factors that will critically influence the study including an explicit consideration of political and administrative issues that might affect implementation of study findings); and
- nature of problem studied (that is, the study's focus, which can be on well-defined problems rather than on broad or open-ended ones).

The following two crucial "bureaucratic" factors are most significant in analysis:

- immediate decision needs (that is, can or are the policy makers likely not to address the specific issues); and
- decision maker interest (that is, on what issues have decision makers shown clear interest).

In program analysis, analysts should take care to avoid four common mistakes that occur as a result of an unrealistic desire to analyze for the sake of analysis. One mistake is "search under the lamp." A well-known story tells of the man who was searching at night for his lost watch under a streetlight. A friend comes by and offers to aid in the search. After a long common search together, the friend, in frustration, asks where the man lost the watch. The man replies that the watch was lost half a block up the street. In amazement, the friend then asks why they are searching next to the street lamp rather than half a block up the street. In obvious sincerity, the man answers that the light is much better under the streetlight than up the street. In policy analysis situations, analysts often will concentrate their investigation on where they find things easy to measure and ignore the aspects of analysis they find difficult to measure. Thus, they look under the street lamp instead of "up the street" where the watch was lost.

A second mistake is allowing technical fascination to define what an analyst examines. An intellectual challenge for an analyst is to use and develop more sophisticated analytical—often mathematical—techniques. The typical desire for an analytically proficient analyst is to select issues that require the use of more complex techniques, sometimes even when a simpler approach to analysis would be adequate. Analysts should address the analytical problems and not techniques; otherwise a "means-ends" confusion exists.

A third mistake is to permit the analyst's desire to perform the best analysis possible to delay the analyst's report beyond the essential window for policy makers to make their decision. Often, a more limited analysis is better because it is more timely than a superior analysis that is done beyond the timely point for policy makers. Interest in the analytical question itself can consume an analyst, much like crossword puzzles, mysteries, and good books consume some people. This consuming interest can overwhelm the original reason for the analysis. As was pointed out earlier, report timeliness is critical, and sometimes an analyst should sacrifice analytical purity for timeliness. The purpose of analysis is merely to help policy makers consider their possibilities; and if an analytical report is not timely, then the purpose of analysis is lost.

The fourth mistake is to overanalyze. In some situations, a good analyst quietly thinking for a few hours might produce results equal to or better than an army of survey researchers. We automatically tend to use certain well-known approaches in analysis without appreciating their limitations and the tolerance for error implicit in the issue being studied. The advantage of the issue assessment mentioned earlier is to avoid such a mistake.

A final commentary on analysis is that there may be only "poor" solutions to problems. This commentary may seem obvious, but this realization is often difficult for decision makers to accept. If an analyst conducts a program analysis and can cite only "poor" solutions, the decision maker can conclude either that solutions are indeed "poor" or that the analyst did a bad job. Thus, this situation places the analyst in an awkward position. The only professionally acceptable course of action is for the analyst to know that there are no desirable answers **and** to explain this reality to the decision maker preferably before the analyst submits his or her report.

Presentations of Results: Some Prescriptions

Providing a poor presentation of study results is a common failure of program analysis. The work may be excellent, but the presentation is inadequate. The best advice on presenting results is for the analyst to review them carefully before she or he distributes the analytical report. The pressures of meeting a deadline and the challenging work of proofing combine to discourage proper review of reports before distribution. Final checks are essential if the analyst is to avoid embarrassing mistakes or insensitive political statements.

Report findings should be in writing. Oral reports are useful, but they should supplement or summarize written reports. Written reports provide the essential records, which are often useful even years after an analyst prepares a report. Analysts must take care to prepare compact, clear summaries. The summary is typically the first important portion of the report that is read—the other material might never be read. Long, vague summaries are counterproductive, as they discourage use of the report.

Most program analyses discuss two or three alternative options. If the analyst discussed only one option, then possible critics of the report would question the report's credibility. Presentation of many options only tends to confuse matters. In most circumstances, two or three options adequately illustrate the varieties of solutions. If the range of solutions is broad, then the analyst's presentation of only two or three options illustrates the types of solutions possible for the problem under question.

Studies must set out their limitations and assumptions. Professional standards alone require such candor, and on a more practical level, frank, honest reports enhance professional reputation and the confidence level of others in the report. A decision maker might not like the qualifications, but if something goes wrong, candor protects the analyst. Also, candor apprises the decision makers of the risks inherent in their subsequent decisions. Studies should discuss potential windfalls and pitfalls related to the issue. Windfalls are collateral benefits resulting from actions and decisions. Pitfalls are collateral hazards or disadvantages. Decision makers can easily overlook both in their analyses. The potential for oversight is the reason why analysts should include this material in their report.

The studies should be clear. They should contain simple graphics where possible to communicate major findings and conclusions because most readers benefit from both written and graphic explanations. Graphics should not stand alone—analysts should make reference to them in the text. Analysts should avoid complex graphics because readers might not be able to understand them. Clarity requires avoiding jargon. If, however, jargon is well-known (for example, "piggyback containers" or "subsystem"), then it can serve clarity. Jargon is a shorthand communication for those who share a particular expertise or life experience. However, most program analysis reports are meant for managers and policy makers who commonly are not schooled in a particular jargon; thus, the jargon only makes the report more difficult for persons to read.

Analysts should write reports and studies for targeted decision makers who need the report for their purposes. Authors of reports and studies should know who the intended and likely users of their work are. What are the backgrounds, knowledge, and biases of the report and study users? If the users have extensive technical knowledge, then authors should use that fact in preparing the report. If the users have strong biases and the report finding runs counter to those biases, then the analysts should use greater care to explain and fully document their findings.

From the public budgeting perspective, one of the most obvious failures in the presentation of program analysis results is the omission of an explanation of how the manager or policy makers should translate the analyst's recommendations to operational policy or management direction. Budget analysts and other policy analysts need to translate their study findings and recommendations into operational guidance for others. For example, they can explain what ways decision makers should change the current program. They can explain specifically the present and future budget implications. Analysts should address these and similar matters in their program analysis reports and studies if their work is to be more meaningful to the budget process.

Role of the Chief Executive

The product of program analysis is meant for decision makers, especially chief executives. If there is support from the chief executive and that person uses the products of program analysis, then a reasonable chance exists that the program analysis will influence the government decision-making process. On the other hand, without top-level support and use, program analysis is worthless as an activity. Having influence does not require detailed top-level involvement, but the following types of involvement are essential. According to the Urban Institute (Hatry et al. 1976, 11), officials should do the following:

- participate actively in the selection of program and policy issues for analysis;
- assign responsibility for the analysis to a unit of the organization that can conduct the study objectively;
- ensure that participation and cooperation exist from relevant agencies;
- provide adequate staff to meet a timely reporting schedule;
- insist that the objectives, evaluation criteria, clientele group views, and program alternatives considered in the analysis include those of prime importance;
- prepare a work schedule and periodically monitor it; and
- review results, and if findings seem valid, see that they are followed.

BUDGET EXAMINATION

An important activity in the budget process is budget examination, which uses various forms of analyses to review agency budget requests and to make recommendations to legislative and executive political leaders. This section explains how budget analysts can perform sophisticated budget examination within the context of democratic government, complex technology, and current analytical techniques.

Information Sources

Reviewers of budget requests do not limit themselves to the agency budget submission in forming their analysis and conclusions. They obtain their information from the budget submissions, hearings, any available reports, other information such as newspaper stories, and answers to specific questions prior to and after budget hearings. The most important information source is usually the agency budget request because it directly addresses the information needs of the budget reviewer. Hearings are also a valuable information source as they focus upon specific inquiries. Hearings permit direct oral interchange between the agency and the reviewers. Hearings can be either informal or formal. Informal hearings between budget examiners and agency staff oftentimes allow a more frank exchange of positions and information. Formal hearings are subject to extensive public scrutiny and are often forums for public consumption lacking discussion of substantive programmatic issues. Reviewers should also make use of any available reports, such as special analytical studies and program evaluation reports. Analysts often find ad hoc or random information not organized well for budget analysis purposes, but these studies and reports do provide useful insight and suggest areas of fruitful inquiry. Budget analysts can find other information sources, such as national media reports and books, extremely helpful in framing inquiries.

Specific questions by reviewers and answers by agency officials are valuable to budget reviewers. These questions and answers can occur before and after hearings. They can be oral or written, depending upon the reviewers' request. The major limiting factor is time. Rarely do analysts ask questions prior to budget submissions because the budget submissions may contain the answers. If there is a short time interval between the submission and the hearing, then agencies might find providing written questions and answers impossible because agencies usually need at least five working days to develop answers, have top agency personnel approve them, and have them typed and transmitted. If there is an equally short time interval between the hearing and the central budget office decision on the budget, then again written questions might not be possible. Time pressures dictate that the answers must not require new analysis but use existing information.

The key to an outstanding budget review is for the reviewer to gain the necessary program information and insight. No one source of information is adequate by itself, and reviewers can tailor their inquiries for the situation. Field visits by the budget examiner allow direct observation of agency operations and the opportunity to understand program operations firsthand. The agency advocate wishes to anticipate inquiries and site visits so that she or he can build and enhance in the reviewer's mind a degree of confidence in the agency budget personnel's knowledge and management skills. Both the examiner and the analyst who prepares the submission have a set of information in common. One wishes to know the information, and the other should readily supply the information. What can a good budget examiner look for and what should a good agency budget analyst provide?

Code of Ethics

In the budget process, ethical considerations are significant, but budget reviewers and submitters tend to overlook them until a crisis occurs. Improper conduct means fraud, impotent and frustrated policy, inefficiency, counterproductive management practices, and an inability on the part of the professional to develop professionally. Thomas P. Mensor, in a survey of the entire membership of the National Association of State Budget Officers (NASBO), identified what ethical issues were most important in budgeting. Thirty-five states responded with seventeen saying impartiality—including collusion—and with fifteen saying conflict of interest were important ethical issues to them. Other issues noted less frequently were accuracy, gubernatorial loyalty, confidentiality, fairness, objectivity, honesty, compliance with codes and statutes, integrity, credibility, quality of work, and responsiveness.

The American Society for Public Administration and the Government Finance Officers Association (GFOA) have codes of ethics. Exhibit 6–2 is the GFOA code of ethics.

EXHIBIT 6–2   GFOA Code of Professional Ethics

The Government Finance Officers Association of the United States and Canada is a professional organization of public officials united to enhance and promote the professional management of governmental financial resources by identifying, developing, and advancing fiscal strategies, policies, and practices for the public benefit.

To further these objectives, all government finance officers are enjoined to adhere to legal, moral, and professional standards of conduct in the fulfillment of their professional responsibilities. Standards of professional conduct, as set forth in this code, are promulgated in order to enhance the performance of all persons engaged in public finance.

 I. Personal Standards

Governmental finance officers shall demonstrate and be dedicated to the highest ideals of honor and integrity in all public and personal relationships to merit the respect, trust, and confidence of governing officials, other public officials, employees, and of the public.
- They shall devote their time, skills, and energies to their office both independently and in cooperation with other professionals.
- They shall abide by approved professional practices and recommended standards.

 II. Responsibility as Public Officials

Government finance officers shall recognize and be accountable for their responsibilities as officials in the public sector.
- They shall be sensitive and responsive to the rights of the public and its changing needs.
- They shall strive to provide the highest quality of performance and counsel.
- They shall exercise prudence and integrity in the management of funds in their custody and in all financial transactions.
- They shall uphold both the letter and the spirit of the constitution, legislation, and regulations governing their actions and report violation of the law to the appropriate authorities.

(continued)

EXHIBIT 6–2   *(continued)*

III. Professional Development

Government finance officers shall be responsible for maintaining their own compe-tence, for enhancing the competence of their colleagues, and for providing encourage-ment to those seeking to enter the field of government finance. Finance officers shall promote excellence in the public service.

IV. Professional Integrity—Information

Government finance officers shall demonstrate professional integrity in the issuance and management of information.

- They shall not knowingly sign, subscribe to, or permit the issuance of any statement or report which contains any misstatement or which omits any material fact.
- They shall prepare and present statements and financial information pursuant of ap-plicable law and general accepted practices and guidelines.
- They shall respect and protect privileged information to which they have access by virtue of their office.
- They shall be sensitive and responsive to inquiries from the public and the media, within the framework of state or local government policy.

V. Professional Integrity—Relationships

Government finance officers shall act with honor, integrity, and virtue in all professional relationships.

- They shall exhibit loyalty and trust in the affairs and interest of the government they serve, within the confines of this Code of Ethics.
- They shall not knowingly be a party to or condone any illegal or improper activity.
- They shall respect the rights, responsibilities, and integrity of their colleagues and other public officials with whom they work and associate.
- They shall manage all matters of personnel within the scope of their authority so that fairness and impartiality govern their decisions.
- They shall promote equal employment opportunities, and in doing so, oppose any dis-crimination, harassment, or other unfair practices.

VI. Conflict of Interest

Government finance officers shall actively avoid the appearance of or the fact of con-flicting interest.

- They shall discharge their duties without favor and shall refrain from engaging in any outside matters of financial or personal interest incompatible with the impartial and ob-jective performance of their duties.
- They shall not, directly or indirectly, seek or accept personal gain, which would influ-ence, or appear to influence, the conduct of their official duties.
- They shall not use public property or resources for personal or political gain.

Source: Government Finance Officers Association. *Code of Professional Ethics.* Chicago: GFOA, 1988.

Ethical considerations are significant. Nevertheless, analysts, examiners, and policy makers *do* overlook them until a crisis occurs. The codes of ethics provide use-ful guidance in the day-to-day operations of professional conduct of budget analysts. The ethical conduct of budget examiners and analysts is critical to a successful budget process. Improper conduct can mean fraud, impotent and frustrated policy, ineffi-ciency, counterproductive management practices, and an inability on the part of the examiners to develop and grow professionally and as members of their organization.

Exhibit 6–3 is the code of ethics that was part of the handbook for budget ana-lysts in the State of Florida.

EXHIBIT 6–3   State of Florida Code of Ethics

- *No gifts or favors may be accepted by a budget analyst beyond minor social courtesies which have little or no significant value.*   This first ethical principle is obviously intended to prevent corruption and improper influence on analysis by actors in the political process. It is critical (1) if objectivity, as well as the confidence of others in that objectivity, is to be maintained; and (2) if the policy issues are to be determined through the democratic process. As stated, it does not require the analyst's total separation from influencing factors, but such a separation is not inconsistent with this principle. Some budget offices do require total separation because of the importance of the analyst's being free from the possibility of any improper influence.

- *The role of the analyst does not extend to independent action which establishes government policy.*   Analysts are expected to gather information, analyze it, and recommend policy with appropriate supporting data and documentation. Their purpose is to raise the level of debate associated with policy making, not to make policy. Budget analysts are staff functionaries whose job is to help the true policy makers—the elected officials and their appointees. They are called on to provide useful information to help the political decision makers arrive at more enlightened decisions. Often, examiners judge their success by how much they shaped policy rather than by their role in creating an environment in which more enlightened decisions are more likely to occur. As long as the budget analyst is part of a political system in which overriding policy is established by elected officials, the examiner should view his or her role as advisory. If the examiner's advice is not taken, no professional failure occurred unless his or her presentation of that information tended to inhibit enlightened decision making.

- *Examiners must maintain their objectivity, which includes presenting all aspects of issues fairly and excludes advocating an agency's position for any purpose other than to clarify the issues.*   Being emotionally committed to the agencies under review is one of the hazards of budget examination. Analysts must avoid becoming staff advocates of agency requests; instead, they must remain detached so that they can critically examine budget requests. This presents a staffing dilemma for budget offices. On the one hand, examiners must be involved with a line agency long enough to know the complexities of that agency; on the other hand, examiners must not be co-opted, which does tend to occur over time. There is no simple way to deal with this ethical principle, but it is important that the spirit of the principle be respected.

- *Every attempt must be made to ensure that managerial decisions are made by the proper line officials.*   Managers must make their own decisions, whereas analysts must be free to comment on those decisions and to facilitate a more thoughtful decision-making process.

- *Analysts must avoid acting in an arrogant manner to anyone, including other government officials.*   Analysts may have their own strong opinions, but these opinions must be kept under control. Sensitivity and respect for feelings must be shown to all individuals who are part of the budget process. Examiners are staff advisors and not managers of line government units. A professional problem stemming from the examiner's unique access to high officials and role as overseer of the budget process is a tendency to substitute his or her own decisions for those of the line manager. Sometimes the examiner will arrogantly demand information on some policy change from the line manager. Sometimes a line manager, as a ploy to escape responsibility, will ask the budget staff to make managerial decisions (for example, whether to buy or lease equipment). In either situation, the examiner must recall that his or her responsibility is primarily advisory and should maintain a cordial working relationship with the line manager.

- *In framing recommendations and in dealing with the bureaucracy, the examiner must make every effort to foster and improve the quality of government management.*   Recommendations and accompanying information should be sensitive not only to policy considerations but also to the managerial environment needed to accomplish that policy.

EXHIBIT 6–3   *(continued)*

- *The professional development and growth of the examiners is important.*   Budget analysts must continually strive to understand the substantive policy and management issues associated with the units being examined. Analysts must also strive to improve their budget examination skills and knowledge so that better work can be performed. Improved government quality does not occur automatically and improvement usually comes only after a struggle. Given other policy and management concerns, budget analysts can easily overlook or fail to emphasize the improvement of government management as a continuing priority. Ironically, examiners are in a unique position to foster and encourage those improvements. For example, funds for professional development tend to be ignored rather than treated as one of the fringe benefits associated with employment for a progressive organization. The budget analysts should ensure that such matters are not overlooked. Professional development also applies to the examiner. The tendency is to become involved in the daily tasks and neglect one's own professional development. Thus, this ethical principle calls upon analysts to recognize the importance of their own professional growth and to pursue it by means of formal education, training, and professional conferences.

Source: Thomas C. Foss and Thomas D. Suttberry (eds.). *State Budgeting in Florida: A Handbook for Budget Analysts.* Tallahassee: Florida State University, Public Managers Training and Advisory Service, 1983.

Services Performed

Results of services performed are important, as typically they are the rationale for the budget request. The budget examiner needs to know the services or types of services that agency budget advocates anticipate with their recommended budget. Sometimes, a government uses a performance budget, and the requesting agency provides the needed information. Often, the government uses a line-item budget, and the examiner must seek results of services from other sources. Agencies use historical information to illustrate the type of service they should provide with the budget as well as to establish in the minds of the reviewers that the agency can perform reliably with the requested financial support. Better budget submission indicates objectives and states them in terms of projected outputs and outcomes for the agency. The examiner looks beyond specific outputs and tries to ascertain the likely positive and negative outcomes directly and indirectly on society and individuals. Ideally, the agency budget office provides this information in the budget request with candor in order to help establish a reputation for objectivity. If not provided in the formal written budget request, the agency can provide the information in speeches or program evaluation reports.

The agency should provide an excellent explanation of its likely outputs. Any budget is a plan requiring forecasting so every budget is tentative, since there is no guarantee the events will evolve as planned. Those involved in budgeting understand this reality. The discussion of program output and outcomes (projected program benefits in society) depends upon whether the program is *demand-responsive* or *directed.* Demand-responsive programs react to individuals and groups that meet the agency's general criteria of need and seek assistance as they need it. An emergency room of a hospital is demand-responsive. In contrast, governments create directed programs to fulfill a specific need that has a planned beginning and end. Building a new highway interchange is a directed program. Demand-responsive programs are often grants-in-aid and direct benefit (for example, food stamps) programs. In demand-responsive programs, the government cannot control the rate or type of demand; thus, outside factors control these programs. In directed programs, the government has a high degree of control over exactly what it will do.

Budget examiners can probe direct programs for the management plan of the agency. The agency should have a detailed plan of how it will use its resources to achieve specific outputs and outcomes. It should have a definite fix on the likely benefits and spillover effects of the program. The examiner's role is first to make sure such a plan exists, and second to see that the plan has a reasonable chance of being successful. The plan and management should be flexible enough to meet likely contingencies.

Budget examiners handle demand-responsive programs differently, probing these programs in terms of anticipated demands and likely outputs and benefits. Agency management should have excellent forecasts of likely demand. The agency should prepare an analysis of various likely funding scenarios and estimate the likely outputs and benefits of each scenario. To the extent that the agency can control its ability to meet the program demand, the agency should explain what it can do and the significance of its action in terms of the scenarios and resulting outputs and benefits. If the agency cannot provide these explanations, then the budget examiner should strongly question the agency's ability to manage the requested funds properly.

If the budget examiner ever sees vagueness in the information provided by the agency, this should serve as a red flag for the examiner. Examiners should carefully isolate any vague subject presentation because vagueness indicates possibly serious managerial problems. If agency management does not know how to deal with a situation or there is serious internal conflict within the agency on a managerial or policy question, then the agency is likely vague about that situation in its budget request. The very nature of the unsolved uncertainty becomes apparent when the agency budget request is vague. Good agency budget officers might be able to minimize the appearance of the problem, but a good budget examiner should notice the vague answer and carefully probe the exact reason for the vagueness.

The examiner might find the vagueness was due merely to a poor presentation. However, he or she might also discover that the vagueness is due to management difficulties. If the examiner isolates the possible difficulties early enough, the budget process uses examiner questions and formal hearings to determine the exact nature of the problem. This probing process requires examination skill, but unless the agency budget officer directly lies, the budget examiner can almost always isolate the problem, given enough time. Even in the rare cases where the agency personnel lie in the budget review process, a skillful examiner can usually isolate the problem because logical consistency is difficult for liars to maintain.

Even less ethical agency personnel know that lying is foolish because catching such lies is very possible and going back year after year asking for money from those who do not trust you is a formula for failure. Nevertheless, not telling the whole and complete truth, which is a type of lying, does exist. Some agency officials realize that such quasi lying is more difficult to catch. If detected, however, agency officials can argue they were mistakes due to innocent omissions, which the examiners would tend to forgive. Such an unethical ploy is not wise and can easily create a dysfunctional relationship between the agency and its budget examiner.

Program Inputs and Outputs

The budget examiner should determine key input, process, and output measures. Chapter 5 explained those concepts in more depth. Briefly, there are measures that are more useful than other measures. They show the resources going into the program (input), what activities occur (process), and the results attributable to the program (outputs and outcomes). Analysts use those measures for comparative and trend analytical purposes. By performing elementary analysis, the budget examiner determines questionable program budget requests, poor management practices, and important changes in the program's environment that the agency did not reflect in its budget request. Exhibit 6–4 is a checklist used by the city of Los Angeles to review performance reports. As you review that exhibit, notice how the budget examiner would be sensitive to the interrelationship of input, process, and outputs. The examiner maintains and should always maintain a questioning, arm's length relationship with the agency.

The budget examiner should also check the accuracy of tables and data supplied by the agency. Exhaustive checks are not necessary, but the examiner should always check any uncommon results, important statistics, and common places where errors occur. Examiners can check tables by observing if there is proper internal consistency among tables. Often examiners can check totals of summary columns against other summary columns for internal consistency. Simple arithmetic errors do occur even in the most important budget requests. For example, commonly errors occur when agencies use incorrect pay rate scales or when agency personnel places employees into the wrong classification.

Budget examiners can carefully review the money requested and be sensitive to hidden revenue sources or "sleight-of-hand" tricks. As noted in Chapter 4, this is a conventional spender's strategy and the diligent reviewer can determine when an agency is using this strategy. The examiner who is well versed in backdoor spending techniques and budget behavior will detect their use by the agency. Additionally, the examiner can profit from the use of accounting reports such as the actual to estimated revenue statement to isolate likely errors in revenue forecasting. Useful accounting information for an examiner often includes fund transfers, lag time among administrative reservations, obligations, expenditures, and closing of accounts. Finding hidden revenue or improper expenditure estimates requires considerable knowledge of the programs, but a good examiner should detect these problems. An example of a hidden asset that careful budget examination can find is a situation where an agency can use an existing government facility rather than rent or lease new property. Another fact that an examiner can uncover is the possibility of an interagency or intergovernmental cooperative management agreement that allows an agency to save on its operating expenses as a result of using economy of scale.

EXHIBIT 6–4   Checklist for Review of Performance Reports

General

- Check total gross man [labor]-hours for department with the combined total standard hours plus paid overtime hours as shown for each pay period on the IBM Personnel Audit Reports of the Controller (on file in the City of Los Angeles Budget Administration Division).

Personnel

- Have any new activities or sub-activities been added over those shown in original work program?
- If so, how many positions are being used? Cost estimate?
- Are any previous activities or sub-activities eliminated or curtailed?
- If so, how many positions, which were included in last year's work program, have been eliminated? Cost estimate?
- Net increase or decrease in cost as result of additions and deletions?
- Are there any special projects on which work was performed on a one-time basis only?
- If so, what sub-activities were affected and how many man [labor]-hours were devoted to such special projects?
- How does the actual number of personnel utilized compare with the number of authorized positions?

Man-Hours

- Where both net man [labor]-hours and gross man [labor]-hours are reported, what is the percentage of net total to gross total? Are there any sub-activities which have lower percentages than the overall average percentage? Which are they and how much variation from average is there? What are the causes? (Vacations, sick leave, other absences?)
- How does actual work performed compare with the estimate for each sub-activity?
- Has there been an increase or decrease in the number of personnel actually utilized over last month's figures?

Man-Hours Per Unit

- How does the gross man [labor]-hours per unit for each sub-activity compare with last month's figures?
- How does the net man [labor]-hours per unit for each sub-activity compare with last month's figures?
- What is the reason for any increase or decrease?
- In sub-activities, where work performed and work units are comparable, what is the variation between gross man [labor]-hours per unit for such sub-activities?
- What is the variation between net man [labor]-hours per unit for such sub-activities?

Overall Appraisal

- Based on the above analysis, could any employees have been transferred temporarily during slack periods?
- If so, how many and in what classes of positions?
- Based on the above analysis, were any additional employees required to handle peak loads?
- If so, how many and in what classes of positions?
- Were there any backlogs of work resulting from lack of sufficient personnel?
- If so, how much?

EXHIBIT 6–4   *(continued)*

- What class of personnel and how many employees would be required to eliminate backlogs?
- Are backlogs the result of seasonal variations? Of improper scheduling of vacations? Of greater than normal absences due to sickness? Of unfilled positions? If the latter, what is the recruitment situation?
- At the end of each quarter, determine what percentage of last year's annual program has been completed for each sub-activity.
- Will the remaining portion of the annual program be completed by the end of the current fiscal year if that rate of progress is maintained?
- Will more or less personnel be required in each sub-activity to complete annual program?
- If so, how many and in what classes of positions?

Source: Los Angeles, California, City Administrator's Office.

For the budget examiner, detailed tables from agencies isolate personnel by grade, type, unit, and status (permanent, temporary, part- or full-time). A critical resource is always personnel. Does the agency have too many or too few personnel for the assigned task? Maybe the agency has enough people, but are they of the wrong grade or type? Maybe the agency distributed them poorly among the units. Two common problems occur when an agency overexpands its highest ranks and fails to reallocate its personnel once it accomplishes a major task. Examiners cannot address such questions without detailed information on personnel. Another problem is when the agency does not train the personnel properly to do upgraded and more complex work requirements. Examiners must use their judgments predicated on their knowledge of the personnel as well as of the new challenges facing the agency.

Budget examiners can often profit by comparing the agency's overhead and direct costs. A common mistake in bureaucracies is to allow *overhead* (that is, people and costs that support the organization but do not directly perform the primary objectives of the organization) to grow at the expense of *direct costs* (that is, people and costs that perform the activities directly associated with the agency's mission). Common examples of overhead are personnel, legal, housekeeping, and budget activities. The proper size of overhead and even what gets included in overhead are topics subject to debate. Ideally, overhead should be only large enough to facilitate maximum agency effectiveness and efficiency. In some situations, the agency allows the overhead activity to grow to a point where agency effectiveness and efficiency actually decrease because of the oversize of the overhead. The budget examiner needs to determine if the agency allowed its overhead functions to become excessive.

Budget examiners also need to realize that the information age allows for significant improvements in the way an organization gathers, stores, and uses information. What commonly occurs is that agencies add computers and other devices without also redesigning the organization structure and relationship with outside vendors. The trend in the information age is to redesign away from traditional structures and move toward weblike structures that transfer information in often significantly different ways. The result usually is to require higher skill levels in the organization but also to thin the ranks of middle management. Commonly, top management can significantly downsize agencies and actually improve organizational efficiency and effectiveness.

The examiner can test the reasonableness of agency expenditure forecasts. The examiner can use the data to identify relationships between program demands and workload. For example, a positive identifiable relationship can exist between the population under the age of twenty-five in a neighborhood and the number of parole officers needed. If the examiner can verify such relationships, then he or she is in a much better position to judge if the agency is asking for the correct number of police officers and the agency is using them wisely.

Trends on program inputs and outputs are valuable information for the budget examiner. For example, if the examiner determines that resources increased and outputs decreased, then she or he can raise serious questions concerning the efficiency and possibly even effectiveness of the program. For example, the examiner can ask probing questions. What are the causes underlying trends and deviations from the apparent natural trend? Does there appear to be any positive or negative relationship between and among trends? For example, is the use of salt more or less effective than sand in alleviating snow conditions? Having this information leads the examiner to suggest to the appropriations committee the use of cheaper substances that would maintain the same level of service to the public.

Comparative data on program inputs and outputs are also valuable information. Comparative data can greatly bolster budget analysis, but it is imperative that the basis of comparison be sound. The analyst should consider the characteristics of demographics, size, expenditures, and type of service delivery in developing valid comparisons between jurisdictions and their programs. The following are examples of some comparative questions that can be asked. What do comparable cities spend for the same type of services? What levels of output do they achieve? What explains the differences? Can the city achieve those positive advantages in the budget examiner's city?

Emphasis and Change

Whether the budget office requires the use of incremental or zero-base format, the budget examiner needs information on yearly budget emphases and changes in emphases from prior years. Commonly, political decision makers do not want to fight the political battles of last year. Rather, they want to know the difference between last year's budget decision and the amount being asked for this year. Examiners can best determine this by comparing the budget request with previous budget requests and actual obligation/expenditure patterns. From that difference, they can isolate the shift in policy from the last budget year. This information is particularly important for some politically sensitive programs. In addition, decision makers might wish to know how much emphasis an agency is giving to a program in terms of dollars relative to other program efforts. Often, balance among programs is a political consideration; thus, it is useful information for decision makers.

Agencies can categorize their budgets into various logical subdivisions. A single categorization is probably inadequate for the variety of analytical needs of the budget examiner. Each categorization should reflect the major agency tasks, projects, or continuing activities. Categorization might facilitate relating the inputs (for example, dollars requested) to agency goals and intended benefits. Often, a categorization can fulfill several purposes unless the agency has multiple inconsistent objectives. Usually a categorization that uses only line-item information is not particularly useful because various purposes can lie behind the use of the same items or expenditure. Thus, by knowing only about the increased money going to various items, the examiner cannot tell if a budget request advances a particular purpose or not.

Categorizations can facilitate comparative information over several fiscal years. Agencies can present dollars requested and possibly relate that information to specific inputs and outputs by prior year, current year, budget year, and possibly budget-year-plus-five. Such an array of data permits longitudinal analyses by fiscal year. Thus, an examiner can isolate program increases and decreases over time and then ask the question why the changes occur.

Complex programs, involving contracts extending beyond the budget year, can mislead an analyst in terms of increases and decreases. Agencies can make obligations for continuing, expanding, or starting programs. The decrease or increase in a given fiscal year gives useful information only on the rate of obligation and says nothing about the use of the money. The categorization used in such programs should indicate the changes in the funding level of programs divided into subcategories of continuing and expanded programs. Also, the categorization should identify any new programs as such. As noted in Chapter 4, one spender's strategy calls for the use of flexible definitions by the spender. Thus, to counter that strategy, the budget examiner should demand a consistent use of definitions and categorizations over time and across programs.

The previous categorization, plus knowing the related work associated with the programs, helps the budget examiner identify program emphases and shifts. What programs, projects, activities, or tasks receive the greatest emphasis? Analysts should judge this in the context of the available resource, the maximum effort that the agency could give, and the relative emphases among the programs. Each fact is important in judging "emphasis." What programs, projects, activities, or tasks receive increased or decreased support? In particular, the budget examiner should discover whether the agency addresses changes to existing or new programs, as this usually is politically useful information for elected decision makers. Also, the examiner should relate the change to program outputs, including anticipated benefits or harm to society and individuals. This analysis helps answer the follow-up question: is the change worth it? Budget examiners should seek *hard data* and get *written responses* to this type of inquiry in order to avoid later misunderstandings between the examiner and agency officials.

Budget procedures require program and financial plans (PFP) periodically (quarterly or semiannually). They are summary tables of the budget, categorized by major programs and activities. The PFP can include both obligations and disbursements, but information on obligations is usually sufficient for state and local government purposes. PFP information covers the past year, current year, budget, and budget-year-plus-five.

The examiner should analyze patterns reflecting policy and consistency with previously established management policy. The PFP should reflect any changes in policy, and it is particularly useful prior to the budget call to forecast possible agency requests. Examiners can make quick comparisons against past PFPs to see if the agency is evolving its policy without informing elected policy makers. If the examiners discover that no changes occurred, then the examiners should question the agency because agency policy is rarely constant and lack of change might merely reflect a neglect to update the PFP. The PFP is an advance warning, and the examiners should encourage the agency to use the PFP in that manner.

Responsiveness

A budget analyst must be sensitive to the concerns of elected political leaders and appointees and ensure that the agency programs carry out the established policy of those leaders. If not, then the budget analyst would be defeating the very concept of democracy itself. In gathering information and examining programs and their issues, budget analysts should seek useful data that reflect on the policy matters significant to the legislators. Budget examiners should identify all major policy concerns in their area that are pertinent to the budget decisions political officials wish to understand. Examiners should try to identify desired new programs and changes in existing programs. In addition, analysts should follow through on programs and projects considered legislatively important.

Even in unusual years when tax receipts are particularly high, fewer funds are available for all desired improvements in existing programs and new programs. Budget analysts must recommend "no" to some requests. Often, resources for new and improved programs are small, but that does not mean that examiners should automatically disregard new programs. In fact, the opposite is true. The case for expanded funding for improved programs are increased if

- they result in unit cost savings in those programs where growth is inevitable as reflected in unit cost analysis and marginal cost analysis;
- the improved program can be an alternative to other current programs as indicated by cost-effectiveness analysis;
- the improvements can generate benefits in the area economy over the cost of the program as implied with benefit-cost analysis; or
- the agency makes the case that intended political outcomes are significant in terms of the values of pertinent political officials.

New programs are prime candidates for funding if

- current law mandates them to begin in the BY; or
- they are a cost-effective alternative to current programs as indicated by a cost-effectiveness analysis.

If the preceding conditions exist, the budget examiner should bring them to the attention of the political appointee when she or he is considering new or improved programs. An examination should identify the likely program outcomes, the groups positively and negatively affected, and the effect on those groups. This is particularly true of new or improved programs; examiners should apprise political officials of the implications of such programs so that they can take intelligent positions on them. In addition, examiners should explain the theoretical linkages between direct budget amounts and government actions, services and products produced, and program outcomes on society and individuals. Analysts must convince policy makers that such linkages exist; and if the examiners have any doubts, they should share them with pertinent political officials. The desired agency outputs should lead to the desired agency outcomes in the BY and specified years beyond the BY. Examiners should review agency programs for timeliness, appropriateness, and necessity.

The desired agency inputs and planned management activities should lead to the desired agency outputs in the BY and beyond. This determination requires the examiners to ensure that the agency funds each program at least at the minimum level for viable operation that results in the desired outcomes. The examiner does this by determining the minimum useful output level for the agency program and determining the marginal input level (for example, salaries, expenses, and equipment) needed to produce the legislatively desired output level.

Examiners should review current programs to determine outmoded, nonproductive, duplicative, overlapping, or very low priority programs or parts of programs. When this occurs, examiners should fully document and carefully justify recommendations for the elimination of the problem because the examiners know that agency and public interest group opposition is likely. If required, the examiners should recommend statutory, ordinance, or regulation revisions as well as all costs, including staff that the examiners believe the policy makers should eliminate. To do this, examiners are likely to find cost-effectiveness analysis especially useful.

Effectiveness and Efficiency

A major concern of budget examination is program effectiveness and efficiency. The budget analyst's focus should be on the adequacy of the planned management processes to ensure that the agency manages the programs correctly. The examiner should be confident that the agency would achieve its intended outputs and outcomes. The best evidence for this is the agency's established track record of achievement. Beyond that, the budget analyst should be confident that administrative or outside factors would not prevent the intended agency outputs and outcomes from occurring. Typically, examiners acquire such confidence through site inspections and inquiries of agency officials to see if they properly anticipated the likely administrative and outside factors that could interfere with their plans.

Examiners should review programs for documented workload changes. Did unavoidable and unanticipated growth in workload exist that the agency could not reasonably absorb? Conversely, the examiner should note any workload decreases. In both situations, the examiner should consider adjustments in staffing, expenditures, and other resources. In making this determination, the examiner might find unit cost and marginal cost analyses particularly useful. Input to output ratios (productivity measures) are very useful and political officials can find them interesting, depending on the analytical abilities of the official. Marginal analysis is particularly helpful in determining the optimal input level for the most effective program operation.

Usually, examiners should recommend maximum use of nongeneral revenue sources rather than the use of the general fund to finance programs. This is important because usually there is great demand placed on the general revenue fund, and not increasing that pressure makes the decision making easier for elected officials. Budget analysts should examine user fees, grants, trust funds, and internal service funds to see if they cover the maximum amount of expenses permitted of them. Often, an examiner can find that a unit cost analysis is useful in determining proper user-fee charges. At the state and local levels, analysts usually should seek to have maximum funding of federally funded programs.

A common failure of government agencies is not to aggressively recruit and develop employees, especially professional employees. Agencies should earmark specific sums of money for agency professional development, including education, training, and professional conferences. Examiners should require agencies to document carefully not only requests for such funds but also the actual use of those funds in the current year. Although critically important, such items can also be politically sensitive, and the agency must make a written rationale for such requests and spending. The following question is a simple test on the appropriateness of the rationale: would the local newspaper's printing of the rationale or the actual spending details embarrass the government? Examiners must realize that travel and other items that can appear to benefit individual government employees or political officials are politically sensitive topics. Thus, they require a much higher level of examiner scrutiny in order to avoid unnecessary embarrassment to the government.

Interagency staff harmony and interagency and intraagency cooperation can achieve efficiencies. Examiners should determine if agencies' support processes (for example, budget, personnel, and general services) work in harmony and provide consistent management direction and control. Analysts can do this with site visits or by questioning agency personnel.

In this day of rapidly advancing technology, analysts should be certain that each agency fully uses modern technology to improve the quality of government services and to achieve the greatest efficiencies possible. Taxpayers do not appreciate ineffective and inefficient government agencies. Part of the role of an examiner is to help agencies achieve maximum program effectiveness and efficiency within the policy decisions of the elected government leadership. Should the government centralize or decentralize the information technology (IT) function to agencies? Can other agencies better share the IT function? Examiners should also determine if an agency capital purchase or leasing would improve program output and efficiency.

Exploring Private Options

If policy makers transfer a public activity to the private sector, then, *possibly,* fewer tax funds may be needed, and, *possibly,* that private company might have an extra tax burden due to its higher or increased business. Therefore, a budget examiner should explore the possibility of using private approaches for the delivery of current public services. Ultimately, using a private company might prove overly costly, but exploring the option is usually wise. In some situations, the existing policy makers might not wish to consider this alternative because of their political situation; but if they do, then the examiner should proceed and explain how the government can privatize the public activity and the likely consequences of that decision. The alternative costs are particularly important in making such decisions. The government can achieve some degree of privatization if the budget analyst and agency consider the following possibilities:

- contracting out,
- giving franchises,
- giving grants and subsidies to help someone else do the job,
- providing vouchers,
- substituting volunteers for government employees,
- encouraging self-help and do-it-yourself efforts,
- altering regulations or tax policy,
- encouraging private or even nonprofit agencies to take over a government activity,
- otherwise reducing demand for services through marketing,
- obtaining temporary help from private firms,
- adjusting user fees and charges to lower demand for government services, and
- creating joint public-private ventures.

Each of the preceding actions has consequences both for service levels and costs. For example, if the government can reduce the demand for government services, then it can cut costs and either cut taxes or add resources to other government programs. Altering regulations or tax policy as well as increasing a fee influence demand for government services. Another means to lower demand is to confront the problem directly by a variety of marketing techniques. Government can encourage people to alter their behavior in constructive ways. For example, government can use public education programs to encourage people to sort garbage, discourage unnecessary calls for ambulances, encourage water conservation, encourage the use of car pools, reduce smoking, dial "911" for emergencies, and so on.

Sometimes government can maintain public services at a lower cost by contracting out the service. For example, contracting out a service such as to a private garbage collection can sometimes reduce taxpayer cost and still maintain or even increase service levels. Labor costs are usually a large cost item in government. If volunteers will do some tasks such as picking up garbage along state roads, then government can achieve remarkable cost savings or service level improvements. Another device is to get a temporary loan of help from a private firm. Hiring a permanent expert is more expensive than getting temporary assistance for a short period of time.

Government can reduce its service costs by transferring some of its programs or part of its programs to the private sector. One way to do this is for a local government to award a franchise to a private firm to provide service within a certain geographical area. This is often done with ambulance and mass transit service. A second approach is to provide a grant or subsidy to the private sector in order to have it provide a specific service. Local governments use this approach sometimes for social welfare services such as childcare, assistance to the homeless, and so on. Another approach is to use vouchers. Government sometimes does this for medical services and education. Instead of providing a hospital for the poor, government provides vouchers to poor citizens needing hospital services. They, in turn, can select their own hospital. Another approach is to encourage self-help. The government encourages individuals or groups, such as neighborhood associations, to undertake activities for their own benefit. Examples are the programs of Alcoholics Anonymous, neighborhood crime watches, and neighborhood clean-up campaigns.

An excellent means to raise more money and take the burden off a major general fund tax source is to establish or increase user fees. If government provides the service traditionally without charge, the usual pressures of the budget process might mean the program receives minimum staff resources because of its political low priority. If government adopts a user-fee policy for a program like a zoo, some means, such as a voucher for the poor to use the zoo, needs to exist. A voucher system addresses the question of economic equity for low-income people because the voucher allows them to visit the zoo regardless of their income, and thus the user fee does not exclude them from enjoying the public services for the wrong reasons. Using vouchers in this way has the added advantage, in some circumstances, of improving the quality and responsiveness of services to the public.

If the private sector provides the service and the government supplements the service with a voucher for the poor, then a private company might have greater funding for its program and thus provide a higher-quality service to the interested public, including the recipients of the voucher. The result is less pressure on limited tax resources but higher-quality service for the public, including the poor. The problem with a voucher system is that the poor might sell their vouchers, creating an illegal secondary market (that is, a black market) in zoo vouchers. This can be a problem, but even selling vouchers means that the poor still benefit, as the money they receive would add to their income. Nevertheless, serious abuse of any voucher system can exist, and government must always be careful when it uses them.

Forecasting

Budgeting is always future oriented, and predicting the future is important in terms of both revenues and expenditures (see Chapter 5). Usually, a government has many revenue sources, of which a central authority, such as the chief state economist or county budget office, usually forecasts the largest. However, the forecasting of the smaller revenue sources typically is the concern of specific departments that forecast their receipts into the future. Examiners should always verify department forecast accuracy by comparing past forecasts and actual money received. The examiner can ask the agency to prepare and submit this analysis on a simple spreadsheet. In addition, the examiner should verify agency expenditure forecasts by checking past-year accounting reports, developing comparative cost data, and checking to avoid improper inventory buildup.

For demand-responsive programs, analysts should usually ask for marginal utility analysis, but for one-time projects, analysts should review cost estimates, especially in relationship to construction time assumptions. Careful examination of Program Evaluation and Review Technique (PERT) time and PERT cost often is particularly useful in determining the reasonableness of the expenditure forecast. PERT, which is a planning and control process, operates best when it also requires identification of program accomplishments and the time and resources to move from one accomplishment to the next.

PERT diagrams show this flow and sequence of events on projects from beginning to end. Examiners should take care to review prior-year nonrecurring expenditure summaries in order to ensure that CY projects and programs do not improperly extend into the BY. They should also identify actual and potential nonplanned cost escalations.

Some states use an interesting approach to government forecasting they call "consensus forecasting." They prepare revenue forecasts, recommend formula budgeting, and prepare expenditure-forecast models for the state. In doing this, such units use a remarkably large database, extensive computer capability, and complex economic models. They do this with economic data acquired from major national economic forecasting organizations and their own unique data collection from state sources. In addition, they gather data on state education, criminal justice, and social services. All these combine into a state database that they use with an econometric model often containing over 123 simultaneous equations. The result is a state economic forecast activity that develops forecasts for state revenues, education expenditures, criminal justice expenditures, and social service expenditures. They use the data to develop education, criminal justice, and social service formula budgets. Whenever possible, forecasters seek comparative program data. Often, they examine other public or private agencies that are doing something similar. By contrasting input, process, output, and outcome data, analysts are in a much better position to judge forecasting accuracy. If another agency in a comparable government does the same thing for less money, that fact is helpful.

Examiners make a common mistake by not demanding and receiving an accurate analysis of future-year operating expenditures of large capital and nonrecurring cost projects. Building a new facility is one consideration, but maintaining it properly is yet another matter. Budget examiners should seek such analyses, and they should carefully explain the fiscal implications to the political decision makers.

Politically Sensitive Subjects

Both political and professional officials discover that there are sensitive management practices in which error leads to serious disproportionate negative political or managerial consequences. This chapter discussed one such problem already—travel money. Examiners should identify politically sensitive subjects, check closely on the frequency of mistakes already made with those subjects, and then be sure that existing control procedures minimize the existence of these problems. Budget analysts should identify any occurrences of politically or managerially embarrassing or illegal actions. An examiner should investigate if existing procedures do address and monitor correctly those sensitive items. The goal is to isolate problems before they occur and embarrass government officials. A reality of modern public budgeting is the balancing of sophisticated analytical techniques and technical precision against the demands of a highly politicized environment that involves bargaining and game playing. The successful budgeter must excel at both.

A list of highly politically sensitive budget items includes travel (with special stress on out-of-state travel), authorized use of government positions for private use, lavish capital outlays, luxury office furniture or space, high cost levels of consulting, and mainframe computer leasing. Data processing is not only an expensive line-item category, but also one that examiners should watch carefully. Decisions on mainframe computers commit management to very expensive future hardware and software decisions, where changes in both hard- and software occur very quickly. Given the remarkable rate of technological advancement in this and related areas, examiners must take care to ensure that agency decisions are reasonable and are being reconsidered almost every year. Both budget preparation and current-year budget execution should zero base and fully document two expense items: temporary employment and consulting services. Examiners should not treat them like regular expenses, because public managers can easily abuse their use.

Detailed Budget Examination

Detailed budget examination involves looking carefully at (1) salaries, benefits, and temporary employee expenses; (2) price level increases for expenditures; and (3) operating, capital outlays, and trust fund schedules. Typically, the government's central budget office calculates across-the-board cost-of-living expenses separately. The central budget office commonly asks agencies to continue CY annual rates for authorized positions, modified for any appropriate productivity improvements. Budget analysts typically use agency information to calculate lapsed salaries rather than use an overall lapse factor. They should use care to examine vacancy rates as well as salary funds that the agency transfers or reverts to other line categories. Commonly, the budget examiner assumes any new positions at minimum current pay rates, with all necessary benefits included; benefits are calculated as percentages of the salary base. However, the examiner needs to make that assumption in the context of current labor market realities. Examiners should confirm the rates and calculations. Budget analysts might find matrix algebra extremely useful in making these adjustments.

In calculating current program expenses, examiners usually start with CY levels and adjust them for program reductions and modifications. They should take care not to drop the input to levels below those that will not produce the desired outputs. Deductions from current estimated expenditures should include nonrecurring and nonessential terms, nonessential inventory buildups, and expenses for deleted or "lapsed" (meaning "unfilled") current positions. In typical years, analysts should allow inflation increases at the wholesale price index level, but they should not be at a flat percentage because inflation does not affect programs uniformly. If one or more categories dominate the expenses, analysts should treat those price increases for those categories separately. If unusual price changes occur in significant items (for example, insurance, telephone, and travel), the analyst should calculate them separately. Analysts should also review carefully data processing expenses. Budget analysts should balance user unit costs against the data center's information. Examiners should use a general service schedule for rental space and apply the current market rate for private space. Analysts should recognize that rates could be unnecessarily high due to choice location or unnecessary co-location requests.

Budget analysts should be sure that the agency justifies each equipment item. They should use state or local contract prices, and the agency should fully document and verify additional equipment requests. The agency should use standard rules for equipment replacement unless its needs require something unusual, and in that case it needs to make its request for funding with full documentation. Examiners should be sure that the agency justifies its inventory levels and practices. Often governments use general and specific guidelines for commonly purchased items. Examiners should use those guidelines in judging agency equipment requests.

Examiners should give special attention to grant and trust programs. Usually, policy makers prefer not to replace federal cuts with their general revenue funds unless they would seriously jeopardize the basic intent of a politically necessary program. State and local governments prefer funding "in kind" rather than "cash matching." Budget analysts should ensure that jointly funded programs maximize federal and trust (for example, user fee) receipts as well as leave justifiable ending balances. Analysts should carefully examine all calculations that produce beginning and ending balances, including trust fund investments. Usually, examiners should use small working capital amounts to cover cash flow requirements.

Automation and Computerization

Governments can and should automate their budget preparation process, and most have automated at least various activities in that process and some have moved to a paperless Web site approach. For example, budget offices often automate revenue forecasting and preparation of budget allocation formulas. The former activity often involves a great deal of data, and the latter involves not only large data sets, but also "what if" types of analysis using those data sets. Some jurisdictions use computers to "roll up" the data from the lowest units to higher levels of aggregation. Some jurisdictions have a comprehensive automated budget preparation process. Typically, the weakest aspect of the system relates, not to computers, but to failure to acquire good performance (output or outcome) measures.

Regardless of the scope of automation, the keys to understanding automation are systems theory and thinking backwards from the products of the automated system. A simple input-process-output system model is central to automation. One defines the products and then designs the process and inputs to get the desired outputs (products). In budget preparation, the most important output is the appropriation act; however, the revenue estimate report can be important also. Analysts should select the hardware (that is, the computer and related equipment) and software (that is, the instructions to the computer on how to manipulate the data) in terms of desired output reports of the budget and financial management system. The input reports are the means to get the necessary data into the computer.

Automation can mean "data crunching," consideration of "what if" possibilities, preparation of complex and multiple crosswalks, and even performance of various types of analysis. The major advantages of computers are that they prepare the data and reports much more accurately and faster. They also permit much more sophisticated analysis and higher-quality budgeting. Automation also means a new set of complexities, including frustration when massive data sets are "lost" and computer breakdowns occur. Increasingly, automation becomes more important as hardware becomes less expensive and companies develop more useful software.

The personal computer (PC) microcomputer has particular relevance to the budget process, and the electronic spreadsheet is especially significant software.

Given the many tables employed in budgeting, commonly used old tools are the multiple columns and rows on light-green paper, plus the calculator. The electronic spreadsheet is the modern replacement for those tools. The grandfather of the electronic spreadsheet is the VisiCalc® program, which Daniel Bricklin and Robert Frankston conceived in 1978. The VisiCalc program produces spreadsheets of 63 columns or more by 254 rows. Modern versions of this electronic spreadsheet (for example, Quatro Pro, Lotus, or Excel) have continued to develop in both sophistication and ease of use. However, the advantages of the electronic spreadsheet go much beyond a very big sheet of data.

Analysts sometimes organize the sheet using A, B, C labels for columns and using numbers for rows. Thus, one can identify each cell of this very large matrix (for example, A24, G2, M150, AA50). One of the strengths of the electronic version is that the user can apply a formula to derive the answer for each cell, and the analyst can state the formula using other cells as variables in the formula. Thus, an analyst can calculate a cell's value by entering 7 + 13 or by telling the computer to add cell B24 (with a value of 7) to cell G177 (with a 13 value in it). A more complex cell formula is to add cell B24 from spreadsheet 2 to cell G177 from spreadsheet 3. This permits use of complex interrelations of data that we commonly need for analysis and accounting. Analytical problems, such as purchasing decisions, often use sets of data arrayed by columns and rows. Thus, they are well suited for the electronic spreadsheet. Some analytical tools, such as the crosswalk, are ideally suited.

The major frustrations with light-green ledger paper are the reality that analysts make mistakes, new ideas require major changes, and analysts often need to make "what if" analyses. The frustrations translate into many erasures and rewrites of the first spreadsheet. The power of the electronic spreadsheet is the ease of making modifications and addressing those frustrations directly. Analysts can make data changes, including adding rows and columns easily even in the middle of the spreadsheet. Computers make recalculations automatically, thus saving massive amounts of the analysts' time and eliminating many of their common entry mistakes. Thus, analysts can quickly change their data sets and even add new ideas rather easily.

The most remarkable strength is that "what if" analysis becomes dramatically easier. Instead of preparing new sheets and running the calculator on all the new numbers, the user merely finds the cells that contain the key variables and makes the changes. Automatically and within seconds, the computer makes all the recalculations. Benefit-cost analysis is no longer done with laborious hand calculations; instead, it is a matter of a few keystrokes to change either the discount rate or the time frame of useful project life. Comparing multiple capital projects using this technique is a relatively easy exercise. Most electronic spreadsheets take a set of data cells and convert them into graph, pie, and bar charts. More advanced software permits the user to link electronic spreadsheets. For example, in budgeting, let us assume we have a spreadsheet for each unit of government. In order to prepare aggregate information, the analyst needs to "roll up" some of the most important numbers to the department and government level. Analysts do this by linking spreadsheets so that the computer updates the entire set of spreadsheets when the analyst enters changes in the unit's spreadsheet.

Microcomputers (PCs) are a big hit in budgeting and financial management. Exhibit 6–5 shows their positive influence on managerial concerns. Microcomputers have increased employee satisfaction, decision making, the maintenance of schedules, and the meeting of budget limits. Exhibit 6–6 shows the remarkable effect on productivity in various tasks. Notice the improvements in budgeting, cash management, financial modeling, and forecasting. Clearly, the microcomputer radically changes the manner in which analysts do public budgeting and financial management.

Stanley B. Botner examined the extent, nature, and impact of microcomputers (PCs) in the fifty state central budget offices. Exhibit 6–7 reports his results, and it shows extensive use of microcomputers and continuing mainframe use.

Despite some evidence by Donald F. Norris and Kenneth L. Kraemer questioning the overall impact of microcomputers (PCs) in municipal governments, it is clear that their data nonetheless reveal widespread use of both PCs and mainframe computers for a variety of key functions. Exhibit 6–8 clearly depicts high utilization in the areas of budget analysis, budget development, and finance.

Moreover, although their study compared mainframe to PC environments, Exhibit 6–9 shows that municipal officials believe computers have positively impacted the work environment.

EXHIBIT 6–5   Microcomputer, the PC, and Managerial Concerns

CONCERNS	VERY POSITIVE	POSITIVE	NO CHANGE	NEGATIVE	VERY NEGATIVE
Employee Satisfaction	23.9%	56.1%	18.6%	1.1%	.3%
Worker Health	2.0	7.1	89.8	.6	.6
Employee Communications	4.5	29.4	65.0	.6	.6
Job Reductions	4.2	13.2	79.4	2.5	.6
Loss of Management Control	2.4	10.1	84.6	1.7	1.1
Security of Information	3.9	17.9	73.1	4.5	.6
Quality of Decision	17.9	59.4	22.1	.3	.3
Maintenance of Schedules	14.1	45.4	40.0	.3	.3
Meeting Budget Limits	10.2	31.8	56.8	.6	.5

Source: John W. Ostrowski, Ella P. Gardner, and Magda H. Motawi. "Microcomputers in Public Finance Organizations: A Survey of Uses and Trends." *Government Finance Review* (February 1986), p. 26. Used by permission.

EXHIBIT 6–6   Productivity and the PC Microcomputer

TASK	SUBSTANTIAL INCREASE %	MODERATE INCREASE %	NO CHANGE %	DECREASE %
Accounting	44.9	41.9	12.1	1.0
Billing	35.3	39.7	23.5	1.5
Budgeting	51.2	41.8	5.5	1.6
Cash Management	50.0	39.4	10.1	.5
Financial Modeling	51.8	39.1	9.1	0.0
Forecasting	51.0	42.5	6.5	0.0
Inventory	34.7	39.6	24.8	1.0
Payroll	34.0	35.1	27.8	3.1

Source: John W. Ostrowski, Ella P. Gardner, and Magda H. Motawi. "Microcomputers in Public Finance Organizations: A Survey of Uses and Trends." *Government Finance Review* (February 1986), p. 27. Used by permission.

EXHIBIT 6–7   Data Processing Support

FUNCTION	MICRO/PC # STATES	%	MAINFRAME # STATES	%	COMBINATION # STATES	%	NONE # STATES	%
Prep. budget worksheet	11	22.9	13	27.1	23	47.9	1	2.1
Rev. forecast.	16	33.3	5	10.4	25	52.1	2	4.2
Exp. forecast.	9	18.8	7	14.6	24	50.0	8	16.7
Dev. budget inc. budgetary alter.	9	18.8	14	29.2	22	45.8	3	6.3
Appro. bill tracking	16	33.3	19	39.6	10	20.8	3	6.3
Control of exp.	2	4.2	30	62.5	12	25.0	4	8.3
Budget reports	6	12.5	15	31.3	25	52.1	2	4.2
Special projects and studies	24	50.0	2	4.2	19	39.6	3	6.3
Program analysis prior to enact.	21	43.8	4	8.3	8	16.7	15	31.3
Program evalu.	16	33.3	5	10.4	9	18.8	18	37.5
Productivity analysis	18	37.5	2	4.2	7	14.6	21	43.8

N=48

Source: Stanely B. Botner, "Utilization and Impact of Microcomputers in State Central Budget Offices." *Public Budgeting and Finance*, 7, 3 (Autumn 1987), p. 101.

EXHIBIT 6–8   City Functions Automated

FUNCTIONS AUTOMATED (PERCENTAGE RESPONDING AFFIRMATIVELY)

FUNCTION(1)	CENTRAL SYSTEM	PC ONLY	CRAMER'S V
Word processing(2)	95.1	93.7	
Graphics	67.1	50.8	.16
Budget analysis	85.7	76.4	.12
Budget development	88.2	81.0	.10
Strategic planning	27.7	17.3	.12
Spreadsheets(3)	84.9	81.1	.05
Electronic mail	33.1	16.1	.19
Statistical analysis	39.8	26.5	.14
In-house publishing	47.9	33.7	.14
Data management	64.2	52.9	.11
Geographic information systems (GIS)	29.6	10.2	.23
Finance	92.8	83.1	.15
Utility services	76.0	60.9	.16
Personnel	75.8	54.5	.22
Administration/office support(2)	66.3	62.7	
Land record management	38.0	20.3	.19
Law enforcement	76.0	62.3	.15
Public Works	63.7	43.6	.20
Engineering	48.7	17.8	.31
Planning/community development	48.6	27.3	.21
Transportation	20.6	7.0	.18
Fire department	58.5	32.1	.26
Social services	12.7	4.7	.13
Voter registration(4)	22.7	18.0	.06
Parks and recreation	49.1	26.1	.23
Library	32.7	23.4	.10

1   Unless otherwise indicated, $p < .00$.

2   Not statistically significant.

3    $p < .02$.

4    $p < .01$.

Source: Donald F. Norris and Kenneth L. Kraemer. "Mainframe and PC Computing in American Cities: Myths and Realities." *Public Administration Review,* 56, 6 (November/December 1996), pp. 568–576.

EXHIBIT 6–9 City Improvements of PC/Mainframe Computers

COMPUTER IMPACTS[1] (NUMBER AND PERCENTAGE AGREEING WITH STATEMENT THAT "COMPUTERS . . .")

CATEGORY	CENTRAL SYSTEM		PC ONLY		PERCENTAGE	
	NUMBER	PERCENT	NUMBER	PERCENT	DIFFERENCE	DIRECTION[2]
Improve job performance	1148	96.2	1770	98.3	2.1	PC
Reduce costs	852	75.3	1323	77.6	2.3	PC
Enhance creativity	587	57.9	1646	94.2	36.3	PC
Enable in-depth analysis	856	57.9	1579	93.9	12.9	PC
Improve communication	781	75.0	1277	79.5	4.5	PC
Eliminate jobs	216	19.8	263	79.5	3.9	PC
Improve timeliness	1071	93.1	1583	91.1	1.2	PC
Improve quality	1077	94.2	1684	96.3	2.1	PC
Improve morale	679	67.0	1315	82.1	15.1	PC
Increase frustration	473	44.7	609	38.6	6.1	PC
Improve decision making	975	88.6	1527	91.2	2.6	PC

[1] The questionnaire was constructed in a manner that precluded our being able to test statistically a relationship between specific impacts (as dependent variables) and computing environment (central-system or PC-only site) as independent variables. Although one could argue that in 2 additional cases where differences were greater than 5 percent a statistically significant relationship exists, it is likely that the relationship would be quite weak.

[2] PC = PC-only site.
CS = Central-system site.

Source: Donald F. Norris and Kenneth L. Kraemer. "Mainframe and PC Computing in American Cities: Myths and Realities." *Public Administration Review,* 56, 6 (November/December 1996), pp. 568–576.

PROCESS ANALYSIS

Focus

The purpose of process analysis, in the context of public budgeting, is to help the line managers and the budget analysts understand the existing bureaucratic process between organization input and output. It is not an attempt to define the optimal process, meaning the most effective use of available resources, although a by-product might be that determination. It does seek to determine if the existing process is an effective use of resources and to identify idle or poorly used resources.

Management can overlook this subtle stress in process analysis for public budgeting. When examining a budget, the analyst seeks insight that will help higher-level decision makers and foster improved management within the organization. The budget analyst must always appreciate that he or she performs a staff function and that the line unit supervisor is responsible for conducting the primary job of the government. The analyst is only an assistant to the decision makers, such as higher-level managers and elected policy makers in the government. Thus, in the context of budget examination, finding the optimal process is not the goal of the budget analyst as that task is really the responsibility of the line manager. Instead, process analysis in budget examination is a tool used only to help others make reasonable judgments on the effectiveness of the existing process and the quality of management in that unit.

Steps

The steps in process analysis are as follows:

- define programs within the organizational divisions of the government,
- define the minimum level of service for each program, and
- develop a flow chart for the process of each program.

Define Programs Within the Organizational Divisions of the Government

Defining programs and minimum levels of service are difficult professional challenges. In order to foster greater managerial accountability, managers usually should define programs within specific lowest-level organizational units in a government. The defined programs should be the major sets of activities in an organizational unit that produces specific projects and services. If programs cut across organizational units, then both managerial and fiscal accountability are much more difficult to establish and maintain. Two major mistakes in identifying programs are using the wrong sets of activities and sometimes forcing program definitions on line managers. If those errors happen, they tend to dampen important managerial cooperation in the future. Correctly defining programs is important and managerially helpful for most administrative situations.

Define the Minimum Level of Service for Each Program

The problem of defining a program's "minimum level of service" is often a difficult challenge. "Minimum level of service," as notably used in ZBB, is the lowest amount of resources needed to conduct the program as a viable administrative undertaking. The professional challenge for the budget analyst is that line managers nearly always consider their present level as minimum, and they tend to refuse to consider the possibility of lesser amounts than what they are currently using. The best approach to take is to define with the manager the existing inputs and outputs. Then, the analyst starts posing "what if 5 percent less, 10 percent, and so on" situations to seek clarification of what would happen to the outputs. Next, the analyst should attempt to determine the impact of those smaller changed levels of outputs on the program outcomes. This might become a problem because some managers have difficulty conceptualizing their program and program outcomes. Usually, some reasonable minimum level of service becomes apparent after some discussions.

Develop a Flow Chart for the Process of Each Program

Flowcharting the process of each program involves identifying, first, what activities take place in the unit, and second, who does what aspect of each activity. The latter should include an estimate of the percentage of time in a workweek devoted to each activity by each person or class of employees in the unit. Flowcharting gets the line manager away from broad superlatives about the virtues of programs and focuses on exactly what the unit does. The document usually presents the unit's activities by stating the trigger actions within the unit (for example, a phone call from a client) and charting what follows until the unit produces a specific service or product. The chart, which the analysts can do in several ways, should show the relationship of the steps to each other. The chart shows the activities done on a day-in and day-out basis (see Exhibits 6–10 and 6–11). The second document identifies who does what activity, the payload and position description of each person, and the percent of time on each activity (see Exhibits 6–12 and 6–13).

The limitations of process analysis for the budget analyst are primarily those of time and organization size. The budget calendar forces the budget analyst to work within a finite time frame. Thus, usually the necessary time is not available to do this time-consuming analysis. The current politically hot topic or managerially sensitive subject decides the priority of the analyst's time. Depending on the nature of the political or managerial concerns and the budget office's appropriate role, those factors will determine which programs the budget analyst should or should not analyze.

Organizational size is a limitation because the technique is most effective with small units (fewer than twenty persons). For larger organizations, techniques such as regression analysis of specific inputs and outputs are effective. For example, in a large decentralized urban library system, analysts used a regression analysis (see Chapter 5) that related input (that is, full-time positions used in circulation) to output (that is, books circulated by specific branch libraries). The analysis produced a scatter diagram and drew a linear regression line. Electronic spreadsheets such as

EXHIBIT 6–10   Daily Activities

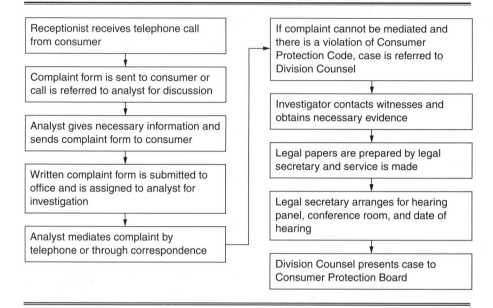

Receptionist receives telephone call from consumer	If complaint cannot be mediated and there is a violation of Consumer Protection Code, case is referred to Division Counsel
↓	↓
Complaint form is sent to consumer or call is referred to analyst for discussion	Investigator contacts witnesses and obtains necessary evidence
↓	↓
Analyst gives necessary information and sends complaint form to consumer	Legal papers are prepared by legal secretary and service is made
↓	↓
Written complaint form is submitted to office and is assigned to analyst for investigation	Legal secretary arranges for hearing panel, conference room, and date of hearing
↓	↓
Analyst mediates complaint by telephone or through correspondence	Division Counsel presents case to Consumer Protection Board

Source: Broward County, Florida, 1983.

EXHIBIT 6–11   Daily Veterans Office Activities

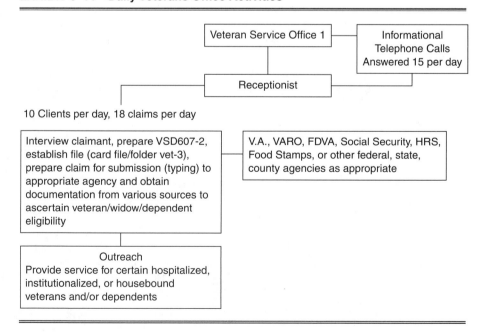

Veteran Service Office 1 — Informational Telephone Calls Answered 15 per day

Receptionist

10 Clients per day, 18 claims per day

Interview claimant, prepare VSD607-2, establish file (card file/folder vet-3), prepare claim for submission (typing) to appropriate agency and obtain documentation from various sources to ascertain veteran/widow/dependent eligibility

V.A., VARO, FDVA, Social Security, HRS, Food Stamps, or other federal, state, county agencies as appropriate

Outreach
Provide service for certain hospitalized, institutionalized, or housebound veterans and/or dependents

Source: Broward County, Florida, 1983.

EXHIBIT 6–12   Staff Analysis

Section

Supervision:	1 Assistant Director
	<u>1</u> Secretary − + I
	Total 2
North Network:	4 Family Counselor I
	2 Family Counselor II
	1 Family Counselor III
	1 Network Supervisor
	<u>1</u> Secretary − + I
Central Network:	3 Family Counselor I
	2 Family Counselor II
	1 Family Counselor III
	1 Network Supervisor
	1 Secretary − I
South Network:	3 Family Counselor I
	1 Family Counselor II
	1 Family Counselor III
	1 Network Supervisor
	<u>1</u> Secretary − + I
	Total 24 + 1 psychologist = 25 employees
Child Care Program:	1 Child Development Specialist I
	4 Child Development Specialist II
	1 Program Supervisor (C.D.S. III)
	<u>1</u> Secretary − + 1
	Total 7
Directed Job Search	1 Special Projects Coordinator
	<u>1</u> Secretary − + I
	Total 2

SECTION TOTAL: 36

Average client service per direct-service employee = 643 clients, which provides only 2.7 hours per client per employee, based on a (1) one-time service frequency. Average client is seen eight (8) sessions (8 hours of direct services, plus required indirect services).

Source: Broward County, Florida, 1983.

Excel can now make that calculation within seconds. The line represented the system's productivity for the book circulation program. Deviations from that line identified successful and unsuccessful "program management" and permitted longitudinal and comparative data analyses. Analysts should use the process analysis tool in connection with the regression analysis to determine the most and least successful units.

A patient budget office, which can plan ahead, largely mitigates the limitations of time and lack of size when conducting analyses. Time is an important constraint in budgeting, but over several years a budget office can carefully examine the key units

EXHIBIT 6–13   Performance Time Analysis

This analysis reflects performance on a monthly basis. The "available" hours are calculated by multiplying 37.5 × 4, which equals 150 available working hours.

STAFF:	Family Counselor II - 5 employees.	
Screening:	Attendance is required because of therapeutic knowledge Average screening time is 2 hours per week Average time per month:	8 hours
Counseling Services:	Individual and family counseling with a caseload of 38 cases Average time required per session:	1 hour
	Average time estimated per month (some clients require additional time if family is in critical state or has several members)	80 hours
	Average time estimated per month in recording case documentation (3 hours per week): entry in case file per session is required	
Group Counseling:	These are not youth groups as facilitated by Family Counselor I; these groups are multiproblem family groups whose children are acting out with evidenced delinquency. Average number of groups per quarter is 4	
	Average number of hours estimated per month:	32 hours
	Average recording time per month:	1 hour
Special Community Assignments:	Respond to communities who need assistance in developing youth programs and preventing local juvenile crime. Communities request speakers and parent/community groups request a one-time parenting skills or problem-solving workshop.	
	Average number of engagements, workshops; meetings attended per month is at 3 hours per session.	2
	Average number of hours per month:	6 hours
Support Services:	Attend case staffings at school, attend in-house staffings (attendance required).	
	Participate in case consultations with psychologist. (Average staffing attended = 4 per month; average length of staffing is 2 hours)	12 hours
Crisis Counseling:	Provide immediate intervention to walk-in clients. Average walk-ins for crisis counseling is 15 clients per month.	
	Average counseling session in crisis counseling is 2 hours	30 hours
	Total # of workload hours required vs.	181 hours
	Total # of work hours available	150 hours

   This difference in required hours and available hours makes it necessary for us to minimize assistance to community groups. It has further reduced the quality in case documentation and has required some clients to be placed on every-other-week and sometimes monthly service cycles. Our involvement in multiproblem family groups has already been reduced. This continued cutback will result in less effective results of diverting youth from the juvenile justice system.

Source: Broward County, Florida, 1983.

using process analysis. The budget office can use any information acquired during one fiscal year to help make its budget decisions in subsequent years. A regression analysis can help overcome the constraint of having a small budget staff because that analysis can isolate parts of line units that are particularly productive and not productive. With that insight, the budget office can target its process analysis efforts more effectively. If the necessary data is not available to do the desired regression analysis, a patient budget office can seek the development of the necessary data over several years and then use it when the budget office finally has it available. Patience can be a valuable and strategic attribute for a budget office.

Advantages

The advantages of process analysis are that it provides a useful snapshot in time that (1) helps understand the inner workings of an organization, (2) identifies ineffective use of resources, and (3) leads to management improvements. The snapshot in time is analytically important because it permits both longitudinal and comparative analyses. Line managers are often not trained in public administration. Thus, process analysis provides them and the budget analyst with a significantly heightened awareness of the activities that take place in a program and the role of each employee in those activities. Often, prior to that analysis, the line manager was not even aware of the facts and their implications on his or her role, as a manager. What is found with process analysis often surprises managers. The analysis particularly and immediately identifies weak and strong programs. Budget examiners typically find that weak managers cannot provide necessary information and that strong managers overwhelm the analyst with relevant information. Process analysis also helps mediocre programs, as it permits their managers to understand the internal processes of their organizations more logically.

Process analysis helps identify ineffective use of resources (inputs). For example, policy makers had trimmed back a government's youth services activity in a large urban county over the years, and its administrative management section with higher priced positions was quite large. A process analysis showed that the organization was top heavy with too many leaders and not enough workers. In another program in that same county, process analysis identified activities that regular personnel did but that unpaid volunteers could do just as effectively.

Process analysis significantly contributes to management improvement because it

- helps line managers understand management and the need to justify their resource requests,
- fosters a sensitivity to the importance of and the meaning of productivity,
- helps identify weak management,
- helps identify managers who need management training,
- identifies managers who have taken their organization away from policy-determined objectives, and
- trains managers in techniques that can help them manage their own programs.

Line managers usually are not educated in public administration and have no exposure to public management except for what they experience or deduce from their own values and attitudes. Budgets and the need to justify them are a new side of office life as are other day-to-day management activities. In smaller governments, central budget offices may prepare budgets for unit managers without their involvement. Process analysis treats unit managers, not as children on an allowance, but rather as professionals who must justify their resource requests and manage those resources correctly once the managers receive them.

Process analysis coupled with budget examination fosters unit management sensitivity for the meaning and importance of productivity. Managers must think in terms of input and output relationships. That type of thinking may not be present in a line manager, but process analysis requires it. Therefore, managers must learn it, or the benefits of process analysis will not accrue.

Typically, process analysis frustrates weak managers because they cannot justify or even explain what they do with their resources. Typically, budget analysts must spend a great deal more time working with weak managers. Occasionally, when confronted with the realities of weak management, a unit will withdraw its request for added resources rather than have upper levels of management realize that the program manager could not explain how the additional monies would improve the program. A useful by-product of process analysis is that specific and general managerial training needs become more apparent. If a manager has difficulty understanding "input," "output," and how to flowchart activities, then management should provide specific education or training for that person. If managers cannot understand the essential concepts, then, wherever possible, management should counsel them in their career development and encourage them to move into jobs that are more suited for their talents.

Another management plus of process analysis coupled with budget examination is the identification of organizational units that have deviated from their intended function. For example, in the 1980s, Broward County provided a mobile social service van on location in poor neighborhoods. On examination of the unit's process, the unit's two professional social workers provided assistance in voter registration and checked pulse rates of citizens. The conclusion was that the unit abandoned its stated purpose and the unit misused its professional social workers. Although the services provided were appropriate, the costs for such services were high and the budget requests did not correctly reflect what the policy makers thought were the desired use of the appropriations.

The final plus for process analysis is that the more budget examiners use it, the more unit managers will see the value of these useful managerial analytical techniques to them. For example, the earlier cited use of regression analysis in the library circulation activity impressed the urban library's management and now it uses the technique in other library programs.

Context Is Important

The previous discussion may leave the false impression that successful process analysis application is merely a central budget office decision. Top-level management should strongly support the whole concept and demand line management cooperation. Organizational resistance is difficult to overcome without that type of support. In a period of tight or declining budgets, one can often find more serious and useful cooperation and desire, especially from higher-level officials.

A possible misunderstanding for those using process analyses is that there is some cookbook approach that the analyst applies uniformly from jurisdiction to jurisdiction. Although this chapter suggests what the analyst can do, she or he must tailor the actual doing to the unique situation of each jurisdiction. She or he must adapt the concepts and techniques to new situations. Typically, the biggest practical problem inhibiting process analysis is a lack of adequate data. A proactive solution for a central budget office is to support budget requests for data collection as long as the data collected can also be useful for budget purposes.

Needed Interpersonal Skills

A working assumption of a budget analyst should be that the analyst is part of a team attempting to provide the desired levels of service at the lowest cost to government. To the extent possible, the analyst should strive to have the line managers use the same assumption. For this mind-setting process to be most effective, top-level officials must articulate this perspective and promote that attitude with their policies, decisions, and actions. The analyst should extend the mind-set so that line managers become a part of the "we" and "team."

To work properly as a "team player," the analyst should strive to appreciate and understand the manager's perspective. Both emotionally and intellectually, the *analyst* and manager must understand the difficult character of the job and the commitment to public service. Analysts should strive to appreciate how the manager feels when they must cut employees and understand the difficult challenge of supervising employees. Budget analysts must attempt to make the line manager's tasks easier whenever possible.

A proactive posture is best. The analyst and line manager should recognize that they could positively contribute to better policy making and better management of the organization. They should not be merely passive or reactive. In fact, one of the distinctive characteristics of most successful top-level line managers is being proactive, especially in the budget process. Reactive managers usually are weak managers.

Another useful working assumption is that every organization, regardless of size, can have its funds cut to some extent without loss of service. The challenge for the budget analyst is to discover how. The challenge for the line manager is to take the existing resources and maximize output levels. Thus, tension can and does exist between the two organizational actors, but that tension can be constructive. The analyst should carefully decide how to approach dealing with specific line managers in order to create in them the necessary mind-set. The line manager should decide how to respond to the data requests of the analysts so that the line manager answers the requests while also achieving effective program management at a minimum overall time and resource commitment of the line personnel.

Honesty

Budget analysts must earn their reputation for being honest and cooperative with line managers. Being doctrinaire and having a know-it-all personality can poison a useful professional relationship. Constructive cooperation is essential. Analysts must appreciate that the line manager's budget is very territorial to the manager. Managers are sensitive to any changes affecting their unit budget. Analysts must strive to achieve a trust relationship in which both parties appreciate the other's perspective. Such relationships take time to develop; thus, a wise office policy is to have budget analysts assigned to the same units for at least two years to build up the desired manager-to-analyst relationship.

The following simple practices can be very useful in establishing professional line manager/analyst relationships:

- Analysts should answer phone calls and return messages promptly.
- When possible, the analyst should strive to attend line managers' internal group meetings as well as to read their reports and studies.
- Typically, an analyst knows more about top-level developments than does the line manager. A simple sharing of information can thus be quite useful to the manager and help in establishing the desired rapport.
- An analyst should often go the extra step of initiating the news sharing rather than waiting for specific inquiries.
- The analyst should not print anything in the budget document without the line manager's knowledge. Agreement isn't always possible, but the manager should not feel that the analyst acts unilaterally.
- If there are any dollar or word changes, the analyst should notify the line manager. Again, analysts should avoid surprising managers.
- If the budget analyst does make a mistake, he or she should freely, quickly, and openly acknowledge such mistakes. To do otherwise deepens any feelings of distrust and unfortunately contributes to a conspiracy explanation of events.

Obviously, particular circumstances require exceptions to these "proverbs." However, if the analyst follows the spirit of them, then the working relationship between the analyst and the line manager should be good.

Co-optation

One concern in budget offices is that the relationship can become so strong between the analyst and the line manager that co-optation takes place. Analysts must scrutinize agency budget materials and not be overly tolerant of managerial mistakes. Analysts can avoid co-optation problems if budget office management gives the analysts new division assignments every two to three years. In fact, in order to avoid boredom, better analysts will seek rotations. One interesting phenomenon to observe is the subtle and sometimes not-so-subtle different ways that line managers treat their ex-budget analysts once the relationship changes.

PROGRAM EVALUATION

Program evaluation focuses upon program outcomes (that is, the impacts of government programs on individuals and society) and essentially focuses on program effectiveness. In program evaluation, logical positivism, or what is commonly called the scientific method, influences how analysts conduct program evaluations. Most evaluators believe that evaluation is first and foremost an application of rigorous scientific procedure to reach reliable and valid conclusions on the impact of programs. They consider program outputs as independent variables, and program outcomes as dependent variables. For example, to evaluate a new vaccine, one could use an experimental design that calls for the evaluator to take measurements before and after the doctor uses the vaccine. Two groups would be part of the experimental design, but only one would get the vaccine. The following graphically explains the research design:

experimental group O_1 X O_2
control group O_1 O_2

The evaluator wants to see if the vaccine (the X) helps the patients. By comparing first (the O_1) the "before" and "after" (O_2) observations and then the difference between the observations of the experimental and control groups, the evaluator would draw conclusions on the causal effectiveness of the vaccine. There should be significantly less disease in the group using the vaccine, which evaluators call the experimental group. One of the problems with such a research design is that the evaluator withholds treatment from the control group. If there is a reasonable hope that the vaccine can make a difference, professionals today consider such an action as unethical since the evaluator probably would not inform the patients in the control group that they received a placebo rather than the vaccine. However, without the existence of a control group, the evaluators cannot assert a definitive conclusion on the viability of the vaccine. The commonly used solution to this evaluation problem is for the evaluators to apply a quasi-experimental design, especially when they cannot use traditional research designs. The disadvantage of quasi-experimental designs is that they do not allow evaluators to reach definitive conclusions on program effectiveness, but they are better than proceeding without any evaluation or an unethical evaluation.

The typical evaluation question is this: "To what extent is the program succeeding in reaching its goals?" The steps in evaluation consist of the following:

- find out the program's goals,
- translate the goals into measurable indicators of goal achievement (desired outcomes),
- collect the data on the indicators for those who participate in the program and control group, and
- compare the data on the experimental and control groups with the desired program outcomes.

Identifying "measurable indicators of goal achievement" is difficult, and such efforts often result in anything but the desired measurement characteristics of clarity, specificity, measurability, and behaviorally oriented data. This leaves the evaluator in no position to determine if management accomplished the organization's desired program outcomes. The challenge for evaluators is to counter that natural tendency. They can do that by investigating the program, specifying reasonable goals, and seeking confirmation. Sometimes, they use elaborate, consensus-building exercises. Despite the difficulty, most approaches to program evaluation require the evaluator to develop some definition of program goals.

The next step develops the measures, including a process called *instrumentation.* Identifying attributes and describing the program outputs and outcomes, as well as interim steps between them, models the process. The Urban Institute publication *How Effective Are Your Community Services* provides a detailed list of useful attributes and measures of government services. Measures selected can deal with attitudes, work behavior, services, turnover, budgets, changes in the environment, and so on. Measures can focus on people and deal with values, attitudes, knowledge, and skills. They can focus on institutions and deal with responsiveness. Typically, evaluators attempt to conceptualize the entire chain of cause and effect from acquisition of dollars to fund the program to ultimate program outcomes. In addition, they isolate possible intervening variables. The ultimate purpose is to assert a definitive conclusion about the program's effectiveness.

The budget is a comprehensive framework to make government decisions and is a source of potentially reliable information on what government does and how well it does it. Logically, the program evaluation and the budget interrelate, but often there is little connection. Program evaluation arose in the 1960s as a broad-based institutionalized application of social and physical science research methods addressed to decision-relevant public programs and policies. Not withstanding reforms like PPB, MBO, and ZBB, policy makers made no serious attempt to relate the fruits of program evaluation with budgeting. Commonly at the federal level, policy makers decide major budget decisions not on the basis of analysis but rather on their deeply held philosophical views.

There are impediments to the use of program evaluation by budget decision makers. One is organizational separation. Budgeting and evaluation are commonly not done in the same unit. This creates communication difficulties and often-unhealthy competition and conflict. A second impediment is the conflicting perceptions of time. Decision makers make their budget decisions in a highly rigid annual cycle, whereas evaluators perform their work in terms of the research question they examine and the resources given them to address the question. Evaluators rarely can predict the time they require to complete their tasks, and often their work schedules slip months and sometimes years in order for them to achieve an acceptable evaluation product. That time orientation may be essential for evaluators, but it is not practical for time-sensitive budget decision makers. A third impediment is the conflicting intellectual frameworks of the two activities. Budgeters face many difficult decisions that often preclude consideration of long-term issues because they need to address immediate decision-making needs. Evaluators are researchers seeking answers to larger issues that often involve methodological questions that are not harmonious with either timely or pragmatic realities of the political decision-making process.

As Harry Havens argued, an integrated policy development process should include a multiyear budget and policy review effort. Such a process should involve a jointly developed system for monitoring key indicators of efficiency and effectiveness as well as discrete studies on major policy issues timed around specific public policy decision points. The one-year budget formulation process, which ignores program evaluation, tends to focus on the simple, quick fixes rather than on the carefully developed and necessarily complex long-term strategy. The marriage of evaluation and budgeting may not be compatible, but both are important in making policy decisions. Eleanor Chelimsky argued that to build the evaluators' work into the budget process, evaluators need to confront the following three problem areas:

- development of evaluation findings that decision makers can apply to specific program decisions in the budgetary process,
- development of an acceptable relationship between evaluation and budgetary time frames and schedules, and
- establishment of a dialogue between budgeters and evaluators.

AUDITING

Purpose of Auditing

Auditing is a vital activity. Its most important function is to validate the correct operation of the accounting system. This includes verifying the accuracy of inventories and existing equipment; determining that proper legal authority exists to perform current government activities; checking the adequacy of internal control practices and procedures; uncovering fraud; and isolating waste and mismanagement. Political accountability and democracy become largely meaningless unless the general public and the political leadership have a reasonably effective means to validate the correct operation of the accounting system and to establish that managers follow democratically established policy. A news story about a rash of mysterious fires in Nigeria illustrates the central importance of auditing. The fires destroyed several buildings, including a thirty-seven-story building as distinctive to the Lagos skyline as the twin World Trade Center skyscrapers were to New York. The fire also derailed an investigation into government corruption because the auditors had rented space in that landmark Lagos building. Apparently, the arsonists started the fires to cover up government embezzlement, but the reaction to the fire also provoked violent antigovernment protests by university students. Such acts of arson and shredding of documents occur around the world to cover up illegal actions.

Beyond being an essential safeguard of government accountability, auditing is also important in establishing credibility and in improving government management. It provides independent judgments of the manner in which public officials carry out their responsibilities as well as of the credibility and lawfulness of their financial statements. This is particularly important to investors when they decide to buy a government's notes and bonds. Auditing improves efficiency and economy by examining and reporting on government procedures, operations, and management policies. Auditing helps decision makers improve effectiveness by evaluating whether a manager carries his or her program forward as planned, meets his or her program objectives, and produces the desirable changes in society.

Two common forms of auditing are the pre- and post-audits. *Pre-audits* occur before managers make their obligations. In many states, the elected statewide auditor performs essentially pre-audit functions. Pre-audits focus upon determining legality and examining vouchers. The depth and detail of a pre-audit vary, but the importance of independence is always present. The disadvantages associated with pre-audits are that they

- reduce the level of responsibility,
- lead to red tape,
- foster interagency friction, and
- are costly.

The *post-audit* is the more common form of auditing. An independent group—from within the agency, from the statewide auditor's office, or from a certified public accounting firm—performs the post-audit. The post-audit usually focuses upon verifying documents, checking transactions and procedures, and examining administrative effectiveness and efficiency. Although post-auditing is not a closing of accounts, sometimes accounting offices cannot close their accounts without an audit. As mentioned, auditors can be part of units within an agency, but such auditors should be in addition to true outside independent auditors and be used to catch problems before outside auditors. If an agency uses inside auditors, the audit unit should have maximum independence and focus upon evaluating the legality of actions and effectiveness of administrative controls. Such audits commonly do the following:

- review compliance with and appraise performance under policies, plans, and procedures established by management for carrying out its responsibilities;
- examine financial transactions;
- test the reliability and usefulness of accounting and other financial and program data produced in the agency;
- check the accuracy of performance measures and the appropriateness of measures used;
- review the effectiveness with which the agency utilizes its resources; and
- examine the effectiveness of safeguards provided to prevent or minimize waste or loss of agency assets.

Internal versus External Audits

Internal audits are not *internal inspections*. The latter confirm that policy, procedures, and reporting are carried out correctly. They address employees who carry out particular operations such as meat inspection, food stamp applicant screening, and unemployment insurance interviews. Internal auditing addresses broader concerns of legality, effectiveness, and efficiency.

External audits are similar to internal audits, but independent agencies do them. A typical external audit examines accounts, checks on the accuracy of recorded transactions, confirms that inventories are correct, checks the accuracy of on-site stocks, verifies physical existence of equipment, reviews operating procedures and regulations, and confirms that performance measures are accurate and measure what managers say they measure. The congressional audit agency for the U.S. federal government is the General Accounting Office (GAO). By law, executive agencies must respond to GAO inquires, and those agencies must comment on the problems raised by GAO, including a statement of how the agencies should resolve their problems. GAO investigates fraud, waste, and mismanagement. Its audits often focus upon delegation of responsibility, policy direction (including program evaluation), budget and accounting practices, and the adequacy of internal controls, including internal auditing. At the state level, legislative audits are commonly post-audits; thus, the group appropriating the money often makes the final check on its expenditures.

Whether done internally or externally, audits should increase government accountability. The American distrust of authority influences the desire for government accountability. In 325 B.C., Aristotle said: "Some officials handle large sums of public money; it is therefore necessary to have other officials to receive and examine the accounts. These inspectors must administer no funds themselves. Different cities call them examiners, auditors, scrutinizers and public advocates" (Mosher 1979, 131). In 1777, the American Continental Congress created the inspector general of the army to find possible abuses in General Washington's army. During the Carter administration, the Congress passed the Inspector General Act of 1978; and in the Reagan administration, Congress strengthened the 1978 law to fight government fraud, waste, and abuse. This concern is a recurring theme of government reform.

Auditing Principles

The American Institute of Certified Public Accountants (AICPA), a nonprofit professional association, and the U.S. General Accounting Office (GAO) established the governmental auditing principles. In addition, the National Council of Governmental Accounting (NCGA) issued standards drawn from the AICPA auditing standards. The AICPA publications *Audits of State and Local Governmental Units* and *Standards for Audit of Governmental Organizations, Programs, Activities and Functions* contain the accepted auditing standards. Exhibit 6–14 gives the GAO audit standards that serve to guide both accountants and auditors. The standards stress assuring legal compliance and complete disclosure of government financial position and operations. Legal provisions take priority over accounting principles, and accounting systems are to provide budgetary operational control. The auditing standards do the following:

- adopt the fund accounting concepts;
- value fixed assets at their original cost;
- do not use depreciation in fund accounts;
- adopt the modified accrual method for nongeneral funds and for other funds such as enterprise and trust;
- call for revenues to be classified by fund and source, and call for expenditures to be classified by fund, function, organizational unit, character, and object class;
- assert that common terminology and classifications should be used; and
- specify that periodic and annual comprehensive financial reports be prepared, with the latter showing all government funds and financial operations.

EXHIBIT 6–14   GAO Audit Guide Outline

I. Questions on the General Standards
  1. Audit Scope
    a. Statutory Provisions
    b. Fulfillment of Responsibilities
    c. Audit Planning
  2. Staff Qualifications
    a. Education
    b. Professional Achievements
    c. Training Program
    d. Staff Appraisal System
    e. Use of Consultants
  3. Independence
    a. Head of Audit Organization
    b. Organizational Independence
    c. Audit Freedom
    d. Availability of Audit Reports
    e. Conflicts of Interest
    f. Selection of External Auditors
  4. Due Professional Care
    a. Organization and Responsibility
    b. Policies
    c. Planning System
    d. Quality Control System

II. Questions on the Examination and Evaluation Standards
  1. Audit Planning
    a. Preliminary Planning
    b. Audit Program
  2. Staff Supervision
    a. Clearly Defined Responsibilities
    b. Audit Program
  3. Compliance with Statutory and Regulatory Requirements
  4. Evidence and Auditing Procedures
  5. Evaluation of Internal Control
  6. Financial and Compliance Audits—General
  7. Audits of Economy and Efficiency Matters
  8. Audits of Program Results
  9. Workpapers
  10. Exit Conference

III. Questions on the Reporting Standards
  1. Forms and Distribution
    a. Form
    b. Distribution
  2. Timeliness
  3. Content
    a. Clarity and Conciseness
    b. Objectivity and Constructive Tone
    c. Scope
    d. Adequacy of Support and Persuasiveness
    e. Recommendations
  4. Financial Reports

The AICPA and GAO publications spell out the auditing procedures so that auditors uniformly ask specific questions, and the publications clearly define the role of the auditor. The two keys to understanding auditing are professionalism and documentation. The GAO guide stresses the importance of an independent, highly educated audit staff that systematically and carefully reviews the financial and related managerial facts in the audited unit. Audit work papers are critical. For example, they must show the following:

- that the audit staff obtained an understanding of the audited entity before determining specific audit tests and procedures;
- that the audit staff followed up on findings;
- that the auditors considered the following:
  - internal control evaluation results,
  - completion and accomplishment of audit objectives,
  - consideration of matters related to audit objectives, and
  - conformance with standards;
- that the auditors followed the program audit plan;
- that work papers show sufficient data and support findings and conclusions; and
- that the auditors budgeted and recorded their time.

The work papers serve as the basis for the audit findings and recommendations. In well-prepared work papers, the auditor completely documents all problems. The focus of the auditor's work papers is on determining the adequacy of internal control, compliance with statutory and regulatory requirements, adequacy of accounting system, existence of economy and efficient conduct, and program effectiveness. An audit includes not only a report of findings and recommendations but also an exit conference in which auditors explain their conclusions.

USE OF ANALYTICAL PROCESSES

Stanley B. Botner determined the use of analytical process patterns related to public budgeting in American cities, contrasting his findings with an earlier study of Poister and McGowan. Botner concluded there was an increase in the use of program budgeting in large cities, a decrease in the use of ZZB and MBO, a sharp increase in management information systems, and an increase in performance monitoring. Exhibit 6–15 presents Botner's findings. The high use of program budgeting, management information systems, performance monitoring, program analysis, and forward year projections and budgeting of revenues and expenditures affirms the importance of analysis in modern budgeting. Botner asked the respondents of large municipalities what the major trends in budgeting were. Eighty-one percent responded as follows:

- declining intergovernmental revenues and searches for alternative revenue sources,
- meteoric rise of computerization,
- increased emphasis on performance and productivity,
- projections of revenues and expenditures,

EXHIBIT 6–15   Large-City Use of Analytical Tools and Processes

ANALYTICAL TOOLS AND PROCESSES	NUMBER OF CITIES USING (N = 129)	PERCENT OF CITIES USING
Program Budgeting	95	74
Zero-Based Budgeting	21	16
Management By Objectives	55	43
Computerized Mgt. Inf. System	95	74
Performance Measurement	89	69
Productivity Improvement Methods		
Quality Circles	34	26
Other	22	17
Program Analysis	93	72
Program Evaluation	67	52
Projection of Revenues and Exp.	111	86
Forward-Year Budgeting of Revenues and Expenditures	58	45

Source: Stanley B. Botner. "Trends and Developments in Budgeting and Financial Management in Large Cities of the United States." *Public Budgeting and Finance,* 9, 3 (Autumn 1989), p. 38.

- program budgeting,
- strategic planning,
- concentration on efficiency, and
- increased emphasis on control and accountability.

REVIEW QUESTIONS

1. Explain how one goes about developing a useful list of major program issues and then selects from that list. Explain the usefulness of an issue assessment and what an analyst should consider in such an assessment.
2. What factors influence an analysis? Why is the chief executive particularly significant? What type of chief executive support is important?
3. Explain some of the common mistakes made in the analysis and presentation of analytical results.
4. What is the rationale behind ethical codes in general and the one described in this chapter in particular?
5. What are the differences between agency budget analysts and central budget office examiners?
6. How does a budget examiner isolate services performed? Why is this important? What key program inputs, processes, and outputs should an analyst especially examine? How does a budget examiner identify program emphasis and change?

7. From a budget examiner's perspective, how does one attempt to achieve responsiveness to duly elected political leaders? What concerns are commonly significant?

8. What does one examine in order to help establish economy and efficiency in government?

9. Explain how a budget analyst should use forecasts in his or her budget examination.

10. What types of queries are common in a detailed budget examination?

11. How does one go about automating a budget examination process?

12. Explain how to do process analysis. Why are context, interpersonal skills, and honesty important in process analysis?

13. What is the focus of program evaluation and how does research design relate to that concern? What challenges do program evaluators face?

14. What is accomplished in auditing? What are the types of audits?

15. Explain the relationship between accounting and auditing. Explain auditing procedures, especially their purpose.

REFERENCES

ADAIR, JOHN J., and REX SIMMONS. "From Voucher Auditing to Junkyard Dogs: The Evolution of Federal Inspectors General." *Public Budgeting and Finance,* 8, 2 (Summer 1988), 91–100.

BOTNER, STANLEY B. "Trends and Developments in Budgeting and Financial Management in Large Cities of the United States." *Public Budgeting and Finance,* 9, 3 (Autumn 1989), 37–42.

———. "Utilization and Impact of Microcomputers in State Central Budget Offices." *Public Budgeting and Finance,* 7, 3 (Autumn 1987), 99–108.

BRYAN, MARVIN. "Business Forecasting." *PC Magazine* (August 1986), 211–234.

CHELIMSKY, ELEANOR. *Using Evaluation in the Budget-Making Process.* Washington, DC: U.S. General Accounting Office, 1982.

FOSS, THOMAS C., and THOMAS D. SUTTBERRY (eds.). *State Budgeting in Florida: A Handbook for Budget Analysts.* Tallahassee: Florida State University, Public Managers Training and Advisory Service, 1983.

GOODNOW, FRANK J. "The Limit of Budgetary Control." In *Proceedings of the American Political Science Association,* 9, (1912), 68–77.

GOVERNMENT FINANCE OFFICERS ASSOCIATION, *Code of Professional Ethics.* Chicago: GFOA, 1988.

HATRY, HARRY P. *A Review of Private Approaches for Delivery of Public Services.* Washington, DC: Urban Institute, 1983.

HATRY, HARRY P., LOUIS BLAIR, DONALD FISK, and WAYNE KIMMEL. *Program Analysis for State and Local Governments.* Washington, DC: Urban Institute, 1976.

HAVENS, HARRY. "Integrating Evaluation and Budgeting." *Public Budgeting and Finance,* 3, 2 (Summer 1983), 102–113.

LINDBLOOM, CHARLES E. *The Policy Making Process.* 2nd ed. Englewood Cliffs, NJ: Prentice Hall, 1980.

LYNCH, THOMAS D., and SHERRY A. LYNCH. "Practical Tools for Budget Examination." Paper for the Southeastern Regional Conference of the American Society for Public Administration, Tallahassee, FL, October, 1983.

MCCAFFERY, JERRY. "MBO and the Federal Budgetary Process." *Public Administration Review,* 36, 1 (January/February 1976), 33–39.

MENSON, THOMAS P. "Ethics and State Budgeting." *Public Budgeting and Finance,* 10, 1 (Spring 1990), 95–108.

MILLER, ERNEST G. "Implementing PPBS: Problems and Prospects." *Public Administration Review,* 28, 5 (September/October 1968), 467–468.

MOAK, LENNOX L., and KATHRYN W. KILLIAN. *Operating Budget Manual.* Chicago: Municipal Finance Officers Association, 1963.

MOSHER, FREDERICK C. *The GAO: The Quest for Accountability in American Government.* Boulder, CO: Westview Press, 1979.

NORRIS, DONALD F., and KENNETH L. KRAEMER. "Mainframe and PC Computing in American Cities: Myths and Realities." *Public Administration Review,* 56, 6 (November/December 1996), 568–577.

OSTROWSKI, JOHN W., ELLA P. GARDNER, and MAGDA H. MOTAWI. "Microcomputers in Public Finance Organizations: A Survey of Uses and Trends." *Government Finance Review* (February 1986), 23–29.

ROUSMANIERE, PETER F. (ed.). *Local Government Auditing.* New York: Council on Municipal Performance, 1979.

SCHWARTZ, ELI. "The Cost of Capital and Investment Criteria in the Public Sector." *Journal of Finance,* 25 (March 1970), 135–142.

SCOTT, CLAUDIA DEVITA. *Forecasting Local Government Spending.* Washington, DC: Urban Institute, 1972.

SPENCER, BRUCE P. "Technical Issues in Allocation Formula Design." *Public Administration Review,* 42, 6 (November/December 1982), 524–529.

THAI, KHI V. "Government Financial Reporting and Auditing." In Jack Rabin and Thomas D. Lynch (eds.), *Handbook on Public Budgeting and Financial Management.* New York: Marcel Dekker, 1983.

WACHS, MARTIN. "Ethical Dilemmas in Forecasting for Public Policy." *Public Administration Review,* 42, 6 (November/December 1982), 562–567.

WEISS, CAROL H. *Evaluation Research.* Englewood Cliffs, NJ: Prentice Hall, 1972.

WEIST, JEROME D. *A Management Guide to PERT/CPM.* Englewood Cliffs, NJ: Prentice Hall, 1977.

WILDAVSKY, AARON. *The Politics of the Budgetary Process.* Boston: Little, Brown, 1964, 1984.

7

OPERATING BUDGETS AND ACCOUNTING

Once policy makers decide on budgets, then public administrators must execute the budget during the current year using the operating budget and accounting processes. The budget execution and accounting phase is not as political and behaviorally oriented as budget formulation, but those factors do exist and certainly execution is as complex as formulation. The focal point of execution is *control* as it is essential if the democratically made policy is to guide the government and the society. Policy makers want public managers *accountable* to the law; therefore, public administrators should design an execution system to achieve that *accountability*. This chapter explains the budget execution process and not-for-profit accounting, which are particularly useful to public managers. A large section describes basic accounting, which greatly aids the public management in general and budgeting in particular. Topics covered in this chapter include the following:

- achieving public management accountability by fixing responsibility;
- expenditure control concepts;
- cash management;
- basics of investing in marketable securities;
- financial management systems;
- accounting fundamentals; and
- how fundamental accounting reports are useful to public managers.

ACHIEVING CONTROL AND THUS ACCOUNTABILITY

Theory of Budget Execution

A theory often is merely a simple assertion that when a specific independent variable or variables exist then they will influence the behavior of one or more dependent variables. In budget execution theory, if a set of defined independent variables (often standard operating procedures and management practices) exists, then we assert that high-level political executives will control the actions of the bureaucracy and that organization will be accountable to the government's elected and appointed leadership. The key theory elements in this set of independent variables include the following:

- A budget that the peoples' duly elected representatives formally approve stipulates the monetary resources a bureaucracy will use in a specific fiscal year.
- The approved budget implementation should fix responsibility on who makes decisions in the implementation of the budget.
- As government employees implement the budget, they should leave a clear information or "paper or audit trail" so that subsequent auditors, inspectors, or managers can trace each financial transaction to its antecedent budget decision.
- Standard operating procedures of government should use two or more persons or groups to independently perform and verify the accuracy of financial activities where mistake, fraud, or abuse of public resources is possible.
- Standard operating procedures should minimize the temptation of employees and others who might misappropriate government resources.

Public administrators should design their budget execution and accounting systems with the preceding elements clearly in mind. As we proceed through this chapter, the reader will notice how the preceding elements continually repeat themselves in various recommended administrative and accounting practices.

Fixing Responsibility

Once the legislature passes the budget, the executive's central budget office must create a current-year operating budget that is consistent with the legislative budget enactment. In order to operationalize the yearly budget as policy determining guidance on government employees, the executive central budget office must also create specific standard operating procedures that create the necessary practices to ensure the budget execution theory is operational. In addition, legislatures also pass laws that essentially add to the body of standard operating procedures that guide government employees in their daily activities.

A key element of budget execution theory is the law or executive fixing responsibility and associating a specific program or programs with a particular government unit that clearly has one person in charge. Only the person holding that office has the power to obligate or control obligations and expenditures. Standard procedures avoid having more than one person authorizing obligations and expenditures for the program; thus, higher-level managers, auditors, and investigators can trace errors or fraud to the responsible party. When procedures split responsibility, mistakes are more difficult to detect, correct, and prosecute.

A good example of a law that creates a standard operating procedure to fix responsibility is the Federal Anti-deficiency Act. The director of the federal government's central budget office—the Office of Management and Budget (OMB)—must apportion appropriated money and other funds into specific amounts available for portions of the current fiscal year for particular legally sanctioned projects and activities. The law gives special responsibility to two agency officers. The agency head is responsible for obligations and the integrity of the budget control system. The agency budget officer is responsible for ensuring an overobligation of money does not occur. Under the law, if a person knowingly and willfully violates the apportionment, prosecutors can fine and imprison the offending party. If the person violates the apportionment without knowledge, then the mistake subjects the person to administrative discipline such as a reprimand, suspension from duty without pay, or removal from office. The Federal Anti-deficiency Act fixes responsibility quite clearly, and the law is effective.

Fixing responsibility is not sufficient, as higher executives must delegate responsibility to the correct person or persons further down the bureaucracy and follow the procedures themselves. For example, political appointees must recognize the importance of proper budget execution and actively support the budget office. No government procedure can work unless top management uses the procedures. For example, if an agency head overspends the budget or refuses to insist that lower-level employees use the required budget forms and procedures, then budget execution will be chaotic and lack control. This defeats the concept of accountability.

Ideally, the agency head should understand public budgeting sufficiently to demand proper budget execution. Certainly, the agency budget officer must understand the procedures or that person would not be sufficiently competent to hold his or her position. If an agency head supports his or her budget officer, then budget execution can work even if the agency head lacks all the desired knowledge of public budgeting. The agency should also have operating managers that support the budget system, as they must understand how the system affects them and what they must do to support it. Ideally, they should also understand the larger context of the system and public budgeting in general so that they can anticipate problems and requests. If operating managers do not support the system, then they may not fill out the needed budget and accounting reports in a timely or correct manner. Such actions cause the agency embarrassment and possibly even radical hardships, such as losing public confidence in the ability of the agency to manage its own affairs correctly.

Budget execution also depends on a qualified budget staff and a positive attitude toward the concept of public trust. If the budget staff is unaware of the needs of budget execution, then serious management problems are likely to occur. If there are insufficient people on the staff, then the work will overwhelm and force them to concentrate on current major problems, while letting routine matters become later major problems. Many public employees, especially top management and budget office employees, understand the concept of public trust and act accordingly. If they view their job as the means to further their or others' private interests, then the likelihood of corruption or distorted policy exists. Part of the public trust perspective is a desire to manage public programs with economy and efficiency. The first concern of a public manager should be to achieve program effectiveness, but once accomplished, then economy and efficiency are important because they allow the government to maximize its use of tax dollars.

Management should establish a budget execution system that gives direction to all employees and permits continuous and current review of progress to determine if organizational units meet planned objectives and milestones. To accomplish that purpose, management can link budget execution with a formalized progress setting and operating systems such as management-by-objectives (MBO). If done, the highest level of management asks lower levels to develop current-year objectives that are consistent with the legislatively approved budget and the government's top executives. Management should use a crosswalk (explained in Chapter 5) to link objectives and the current-year operating budget. Management should key the operating budget with the agency's major units so that agency unit leaders can easily understand the relationship of programs, objectives, and dollar resources to line organizational units. In addition, management must create a process to report periodical progress or lack of progress on achieving the specific unit objectives, which unit leaders articulate in nonambiguous language.

In order to work smoothly as an organization and to avoid intercommunication difficulties, management needs to establish procedures on how to change work plans, schedules, and use of funds. Management should design those procedures to ensure employees consider all factors, and management should notify key people in and outside the organization of all the important decisions in a timely manner. Circumstances do arise where agency leaders must short-circuit budget execution procedures, but if management designs them properly, then leaders will infrequently short-circuit procedures. Designing procedures is always difficult as management must take care to make them as simple and yet as effective as possible.

To fix responsibility, higher-level management must give in writing specific formal authority to each official who will order the obligation or spending of money. Higher-level management should review such authorization, ensuring each delegation of authority is permissible under the law. Management should write the authorization carefully so that any later confusion and misunderstandings about the authorization do not exist. In addition, management should coordinate all allotments and operating budgets with the formal authorizations so that officials know how much money they must deal with as well as any other guidance necessarily associated with the dollar amounts.

Management should also design accounting and related control systems to serve prescribed budgetary needs. This chapter describes accounting later in more depth. Briefly, the agency carries out the budget execution activity in a larger context than accounting, but agency employees should actually record transactions so that later accountants and other analysts can compare actual agency practice with the planned practice as defined in the budget. This ability to make this comparison is critical if management and policy makers are to know if policy is or is not carried out correctly.

In designing the budget execution system, there are three helpful operational considerations. First, if possible, management should establish performance standards—preferably in connection with strategic plans—tied to the current-year operating budget. This step is essential if the agency is to have an ongoing performance budget system and related productivity studies. Today, the use of performance measures is part of professional government management and accounting practices. Second, management should link advanced planning, performance estimates, and funding levels. Third, management should schedule in advance financial obligations and disbursements to achieve its desired rate of expenditure in order to avoid a final fiscal year deficit or surplus. City budget directors believe that this scheduling is their most important budget execution function.

Monitoring the legality, propriety, and economy of obligation decisions is another important budget execution concern. Some governments use pre-audits to monitor the legality and economy of current-year budget decisions. Management must weigh the advantage of catching errors by using an elaborate pre-audit process against the high costs and frustration of a complex process. In many grant-in-aid and highly sensitive programs, management is wise to have an elaborate system to check such matters as legality, propriety, economy, equal opportunity, environmental quality, and security.

If the program is a routine daily operation such as street maintenance, then an elaborate clearance procedure would be foolish. The complexity of the procedure requires judgment, and often the use of outside experts can help in making those decisions. Certainly, management can add special clearance procedures, but they do come at a price in terms of higher administrative costs, added frustration, and complexity.

In developing and using a budget execution system, management may find the following questions very useful. Must management prepare the operating budget under unusual legislative appropriation conditions? Is a budget revision, such as a *supplemental,* likely? Is a continuing resolution in effect? What size or structure is the organization (for example, field, regions, area offices) under question? What type of financial concepts (this and future chapters explore this later) are appropriate to use in the context of the organization? What are the sources of funds and how is that important to the budget execution system? What types of financial, work unit data, and personnel measures should management collect? How should management have the information collected? How should management enforce personnel ceilings and personnel restrictions with its budget execution system? What should be the frequency, level, and coordination means used in budget execution reporting?

Management should consider each of the questions in the context of the current and future work environment. Each answer can help budget officials better design and operate their budget execution system. Their follow-up on thinking through these questions is essential. Management needs frequent and regular reports on work progress, status of objectives yet unaccomplished, and fund status. If the reports signal problems or raise questions, then management needs prompt, regular, and careful follow-up to make sure the agency fully considers the problems and develops a clear solution. Often, the busy day-to-day activities drive out consideration of problems until a major crisis requires attention. Management needs an organized system of audits and inspections to verify and supplement budget execution reporting systems. If audits and inspections do not exist, then fraud, cheating, or merely poor operational practices become difficult to identify and resolve before they become a widespread problem.

Pitfalls to Avoid

A current-year operating budget can:

- become unmanageable to top, middle, or first-line managers unless organization designers carefully consider the impact of the budget execution process on all levels in the organization;
- be too complex and detailed for management and employees and thus become cumbersome or useless;
- be too late or too inaccurate for decision-making purposes;
- be out of synchronization with the accounting process;
- be out of touch with the rest of the budget process; and
- be ignored by top management, thus guaranteeing its ultimate failure.

Designing an operating budget system requires careful attention. For example, the budget and accounting offices involve various professionals who are trained differently. Each group views its needs separately, and often, management has the operating budget developed at a different time and by different people than those who developed the accounting system. Management must avoid this natural tendency, which leads to nonsynchronization of the two systems.

An operating budget must serve all levels of budgeting. Often, budget execution system designers demand too much of the first-line managers, making their jobs needlessly complex. Designers must take care to understand the needs and burdens that they place on each level of management. Nevertheless, ultimately the budget execution system should provide timely information to top management as well as provide essential information for all phases of the budget cycle.

If top management ignores the budget execution system, then the whole process is likely to fail. In the agency, the key person is the director, and that person has the power to make exceptions to the operating budget. This power is essential in order to provide managerial flexibility to adapt to unusual circumstances that can and do arise. If top management abuses that power by making frequent needless exceptions, then the discipline of the operating budget breaks down and the advantages of the procedures are lost. An equally serious matter is when the agency head does not even create a budget execution system or does not update the system. The agency cannot protect itself from bad management when it occurs at its highest levels.

Current-Year Adjustments

Regardless of how well policy makers and budget staff plan, they will make budget adjustments in the current year. Sometimes high-level managers merely make adjustments by transferring money from one fund or appropriation to another. Sometimes the adjustments are massive and involve new appropriations that the legislative body must pass in *supplemental appropriations*. Reasons for adjustments vary from responding to unanticipated needs (whether that be an unanticipated heavy snowfall, widespread flood, or terrorist attack), poor management, or serious policy changes. Laws vary in terms of the need for legislative passage of current-year adjustments, but regardless, a budget office is always wise to inform the legislative body and central budget office of even minor current-year adjustments, as policy makers rarely appreciate surprises from the bureaucracy. Although unwise, some governments require even the most minor changes in the current year to have legislative approval. Typically, current-year changes are small and legislatures write appropriations broadly enough so that they do not have to approve them except for serious policy shifts by an agency.

Flexibility in current-year budget execution can exist in six ways: object classification, the appropriation structure, contingency appropriations, emergency provisions, transfer authority, and reprogramming authority. Many governments permit agencies with and without central budget office approval to realign funds among object classifications. Typically, agencies do not need central budget office approval for minor realignments. Sometimes, however, tight realignment policy exists when politically sensitive subjects such as travel expenses are at issue, and when there is a lower level of trust in the management of the agency. At the federal level, sometimes flexibility extends even to when the agency spends the funds beyond the current year. Contingency appropriations (for example, disaster relief) and emergency provisions (for example, war) also provide agencies flexibility to meet unusual circumstances that a legislature cannot anticipate during the budget year. The latter provisions permit an agency to transfer large sums of money during the current year until such time as the agency receives supplemental appropriations from the legislature. Reprogramming involves fund realignment from an appropriation outside of previously approved policy. At a minimum, legislative committees anticipate giving informal approval for such reprogramming, and often laws require formal approval. When an executive transfers a function to another agency such as in a staff reorganization, the executive needs to also transfer the appropriation to the other agency. In such cases, often the sums do not change but who has control over the funds does change.

Central executive budget offices and possibly the legislative appropriation staff should rigorously review current-year adjustments, as they often are a change in policy. Generally speaking, budget adjustments should be rare or the budget year decision-making process is a fraud, as it is not deciding holistically all revenue and expenditure decisions. In addition, many current-year adjustments mean that the policy makers essentially make budget decisions twice in a highly unfair and ineffective process. Current adjustments should be unusual and limited to truly unanticipated circumstances that require flexible policy making. When agencies request budget adjustments, their requests should address the following questions:

- Was the item in the original budget request? If so, why was it not resolved at that time?
- Is the money for a recurring or nonrecurring expenditure? If recurring, why can it not wait until the regular budget process?
- What type of adjustment is the agency requesting? If it is a shift in policy, why not wait until the regular budget process?
- Does the adjustment clearly identify details such as account numbers, titles, and amount. If not, the likelihood of abuse of the system that will cause later serious problems is 100 percent.
- What is the impact on related unencumbered balance (explained later in this chapter)? When an agency requests additional money, an overobligating or spending situation can easily happen unless policy makers focus on not spending beyond any unencumbered fund balance.
- What is the reason—in writing—for the request? Policy makers must take care to limit each *supplemental request* to truly needy situations, and justifications must make the case for this unusual request.

BUDGET CONCEPTS AND REPORTS

Allotments and Other Control Concepts

After the legislature has approved the appropriations and the central budget office has apportioned the appropriations, then the agency controls the funds, using *allotments.* This agency budget control device permits the agency head and budget head to meter the apportioned funds to the agency operating units within prescribed amounts of money and within a prescribed period of time. Allotments must be consistent with all appropriations and apportionments. Agencies can combine a current-year operating budget with the allotment process because the operating budget fulfills the same purpose as allotments but usually in a more detailed manner. Agency budget offices can make allotments for organizational units, activities, geography, or object classifications, depending on policy and management needs. Usually, budget offices are wise to make allotments to the highest level possible within the agency in order to focus managerial responsibility, but sometimes those units can make their own allotments to lower-level units.

High-level agency management can use the allotments to complement the management structure and adjust them for the problems faced by the agency. Typically, allotments are quite specific on highly sensitive controllable object classifications such as travel in order to avoid agency embarrassment. Because some agencies may be in the position of having to cut current-year monies, agency budget offices often carefully parcel out controllable object classification money with allotments so that if needed they can easily divert end-of-the-fiscal-year money to unanticipated circumstances. This means if everything works as planned, agency units must spend disproportionately more allotment monies in the final quarter of the fiscal year. Agency management can call allotments or subdivisions of allotments "targets," "allowances," "work plans," "financial plans," or other terms depending on the management styles used. The terminology is not important as long as the management properly controls and delegates responsibility in a consistent and functional manner.

At the highest levels, budget terminology is fairly consistent but becomes less uniform at the lowest levels in organizations. Regardless, the concepts themselves are important and management must use them effectively. Terms such as "authorization," "appropriation," "apportionment," and "allotment" are common and remarkably uniform in their usage. Each is a hurdle an agency must meet before it can actually spend money. Other concepts that use varying names but are useful are administrative reservations, obligations, accrued expenditures, outlays, and disbursements. To this list we can add inventory and cost, even though they occur after the agency spends its money. Administrative reservations are funds set aside for specific purposes. For example, agencies use this concept to set aside grant money while the agency lawyers prepare a formal contract, thus giving the unit receiving the grant some useful assurance that the agency has grant money available for the unit's purpose while the agency is proceeding with its administrative actions. Sometimes, the lag between the reservation and formal obligation can be minutes or weeks, depending on administrative circumstances and requirements.

Expenditure Controls

Expenditure controls help ensure that an agency uses the money for the purposes established by policy makers and higher-level administrators. The two types of expenditure controls are budgetary and administrative. Agencies gear budget controls to the appropriation and apportionment, whereas agencies gear administrative controls to specific operations of the agency to ensure administrators spend monies correctly.

Policy makers intend administrative controls to minimize waste and misuse of public funds at the operational level.

The two types of current-year budget controls are allotments, which this chapter already explained, and reports, which agencies use to show administrators achieving their planned obligation and expenditure patterns during the current year. Ideally, management should merge the budget reports with the accounting process but sometimes that does not occur. Regardless of proper coordination with accounting, the agency budget office could prepare the following reports using computers: daily financial reports, monthly financial reports, quarterly financial reports, monthly performance reports, revenue generation reports, and annual reports. Commonly, daily reports show all transactions by department or agency accounts. Monthly reports cumulatively show daily information summarizing (1) personnel costs by full-time, part-time, temporary, overtime, and other, and (2) costs by major object of expenditure. Quarterly financial reports point out variances between the current and prior year's obligations and expenditures. Reports are coded, contain descriptions, identify key work units and numbers of persons engaged in those units, and offer explanations of significant variances important to management. Common data elements often include budgeted work units for the year, planned performance by month, amounts allotted compared to obligated and expended, percent already completed, and percent of variance from intended program outcomes. Analysts who design and prepare reports need to be sensitive to the management needs of all levels within the agency.

The two kinds of administrative controls are encumbrances and bid requirements. An *encumbrance* is an accounting concept explained in more detail later in this chapter, but briefly it is a legal claim on money; thus, encumbered money is not available for new obligation by anyone. The encumbrance concept and process keep officials from overspending agency funds. Encumbrance also provides officials with data on how much money they have available to them for new commitment obligations. In contrast, *bid requirements* stipulate how agency personnel can obligate money. For example, competitive bid requirements stipulate that agency personnel must solicit price quotations for goods and services from potential vendors or contractors. The commonly used expensive competitive bid requirements tend to avoid careless and possibly costly awarding of contracts, but the requirements require a much higher level of contract professionalism. The competitive bid requirement, as opposed to the negotiated bid procedure, tends to reduce the danger of awarding contracts because of illegal kickbacks or political favoritism. Other bid requirements can require contracting with vendors or contractors within the state, with veterans, or minority contractors. The latter requirement is less common today unless the government must compensate for past patterns of racial, ethnic, or gender discrimination.

Ethics versus Red Tape

Analysts preparing budget execution procedures must face the fraud/red tape dilemma. A dilemma is a choice between two or more unpleasant choices of which none is ideal. In the situation of designing budget execution procedures, the analyst knows that procedures can and do reduce the likelihood of fraud by an employee or

someone else associated with the agency. However, procedures are also costly and often significantly add to the expense of administering the agency. On the one hand, the
analyst wants to reduce the likelihood of fraud, including its indirect cost and personnel demoralization that harms an agency. On the other hand, a management analyst
wants to minimize the high cost of administrative controls, which society labels "red
tape." Often, the latter also destroys employee initiative, creativity, and needed management flexibility. Thus, a true dilemma exists because both options are bad. One
means to arrive at a solution is to weigh the cost of each bad option, and where the
cost of fraud equals the cost of red tape becomes the optimal point to minimize the
bad options. Although this analytical solution may seem best, typically the intangible
career cost of allowing fraud to exist is so negative to agency leadership that analysts
are much wiser to err on the side of having too many administrative controls. Thus,
the management analyst greatly contributes to the negative image of bureaucracy.

One way to resolve a dilemma is to "think outside the box," meaning you
should not accept the obvious conditions of the problem presented to you. In this case,
the management analyst needs to consider a third option rather than the two obvious
ones. Improving the ethics of the individuals participating in budget execution is a
third alternative. If these individuals employed higher ethical standards, then lesser
administrative controls would be necessary. Certainly, some administrative controls
would always be necessary to help isolate errors and encourage proper employee behavior. However, if ethical employees use fewer "red tape" controls, then organizations significantly lower the cost of administering their programs. Thus, in budget
execution as in all aspects of public administration, ethics is important and management should make ongoing attempts to enhance the ethical climate of an organization
by using *virtue ethics* and other forms of ethical training. At a minimum, producing
a code of ethics and setting expectations for its utilization would be appropriate. See
the NASBO Code of Ethics in Exhibit 7–1. The details of that training are beyond the
scope of this textbook, but they are critical to both public budgeting and financial
management.

CASH MANAGEMENT AND INVESTMENTS

Cash Management

Like almost all institutions, government does not collect and disburse its money so
that inflow of money exactly equals the outflow. The time lag between the in- and outflow is called *cash flow*. A *cash flow problem* is when the amount of money that government should pay exceeds its available cash. As assets can be in the form of
obligations from others or taxes owed, the government may have a cash flow problem
but still be viable financially. Another common cash flow problem is when the government does not have the needed cash but it is likely to have it within a short period
of time. The opposite of a cash flow problem is *idle cash*. This is when government
has more cash available than its immediate obligations. Often, local governments do
not have cash flow problems as they time their tax collections correctly and are not
highly dependent on slow transfer payments from other governments.

EXHIBIT 7–1 National Association of State Budget Officers (NASBO) Standards of Professional Conduct

The National Association of State Budget Officers (NASBO) has developed standards of professional conduct in order to enhance the performance of all persons engaged in public budgeting. NASBO adopted this code from materials developed by the Josephson Institute of Ethics.

HONESTY

Be scrupulously and consistently honest by being truthful, sincere, forthright, and candid where professional duties requiring confidentiality permit, so that persons are not misled or deceived.

INTEGRITY

Demonstrate integrity by (1) exhibiting conduct consistent with core beliefs and assuring that practices are congruent with principles, (2) honoring and adhering to the general principles of public service ethics, and the mission and values of the organization, and (3) expressing and fighting for your concept of what is right and upholding your convictions to the best of your ability.

COMMITMENT

Demonstrate promise-keeping by (1) fulfilling commitments by making your word your bond, (2) discharging commitments in a fair and reasonable manner, (3) exercising prudence and caution in making commitments, considering that unknown or future factors might arise which could make fulfillment of them impossible, difficult, or undesirable, and (4) assuring that commitments made are clear to all parties.

FAIRNESS

Demonstrate fairness by (1) making decisions with impartiality based on consistent and appropriate standards, (2) demonstrating a commitment to justice, the equitable treatment of individuals in all actions including recruiting, hiring, and promoting employees, (3) exercising authority with open mindedness and seeking all relevant information, including opposing perspectives, (4) voluntarily correcting personal or institutional mistakes and improprieties and refusing to take unfair advantage of mistakes or ignorance of citizens, and (5) scrupulously employing open, equitable, and impartial processes to gather and evaluate information necessary for decisions.

RESPECT FOR OTHERS

Respect others by (1) acknowledging and honoring the right of those affected by official and managerial decisions to privacy and dignity, (2) treating others with courtesy and decency, and (3) exercising authority in a way that provides others with the information they need to make informed decisions about matters within the scope of their professional duties.

PURSUIT OF EXCELLENCE

Perform your duties with excellence by (1) being diligent, reliable, careful, prepared, and informed, and (2) continuing to develop knowledge, skills, and judgment necessary for the performance of your duties.

(continued)

EXHIBIT 7–1   *(continued)*

PERSONAL ACCOUNTABILITY

Be accountable by (1) accepting personal responsibility for the foreseeable consequences of actions and inactions, (2) recognizing your special opportunities and obligations to lead by example, and (3) making decisions that take into account long-term interest and the need to exercise leadership for posterity.

LOYALTY

Demonstrate loyalty by (1) advancing and protecting the interests of those with legitimate moral claims arising from personal and institutional relationships, (2) safeguarding confidential information without violating professional duties, (3) resolving conflicting loyalties to various parties by placing obligations to the constitution, the institution of government, and fundamental principles of representative democracy above your duty to individuals, and (4) refusing to subordinate other ethical obligations in the name of loyalty such as honesty, integrity, fairness, and the obligation to make decisions on the merits, without favoritism, in the name of loyalty.

PUBLIC OFFICE AS A PUBLIC TRUST

Treat your office as a public trust by using your powers and resources to advance the public interest.

INDEPENDENT OBJECTIVE JUDGMENT

Employ independent objectives in performing your duties, deciding all matters on the merits, free from conflicts of interest and both real and apparent improper influences while discharging lawful discretionary authority to the public/taxpayers' best interest.

PUBLIC ACCOUNTABILITY

Assure the government is conducted openly, efficiently, equitably, and honorably in a manner that permits the citizenry to make informed judgments and hold government officials accountable.

DEMOCRATIC LEADERSHIP

With a positive attitude, honor and respect the principles and spirit of representative democracy and set a positive example of good citizenship by scrupulously observing the letter and spirit of laws and rules.

RESPECTABILITY AND FITNESS FOR PUBLIC OFFICE

Safeguard public confidence in the integrity of government by being honest, fair, caring, and respectful and by avoiding conduct creating the appearance of impropriety, which is unbefitting a public official.

Source: National Association of State Budget Officers at http://www.nasbo.org/TRAINING/Mod12/con02.html.

Investing idle cash to earn extra revenue for the government but also paying all obligations and debts so that government meets all its legal obligations is *cash management.* To do this, government must determine by forecasting its best *cash position* each hour of each day so that cash is available to meet obligations such as payroll but also to ensure that it invests any of its idle cash even for very short periods of time. For this to occur, analysts in large governments must forecast cash balance needs daily and maybe even hourly so that government can meet its obligations in a timely manner. Less complex governments commonly make this determination on a monthly basis.

Analysts can determine the cash position by using the minimum compensating balance, the *Economic Ordering Quality* (EOQ), and the *Miller-Orr Model.* Most governments are small and commonly use a less complex method such as merely holding a certain number of days' expenditure as a cash balance. The exact number of days depends on the judgment of the budget officer or treasurer. The EOQ is a mathematical approach cited in Exhibit 7–2 and illustrated in Exhibit 7–3. In this approach, an analyst weighs carrying costs, which foregone earned interest represents, against the total cost of the transactions. This model recognizes that the government incurs an opportunity cost for holding rather than investing the cash. And each bank transaction (for example, transferring from securities to cash) involves an administrative cost to the government. If the government is to save idle cash and earn more than its administrative costs for investing, then it must recognize that more transactions drive up the cost

EXHIBIT 7–2 Economic Ordering Quality Formula

$$P = b \left(\frac{T}{c} \right) + vT + i \left(\frac{c}{2} \right)$$

P = total cost of cash management

b = fixed cost per transaction of transferring funds from marketable securities to cash or vice versa

T = total amount of cash payments or expenditures over the period involved

c = size of transfer, which is the maximum amount of cash

v = variable cost per dollar of funds transferred

i = interest rate on marketable securities

The formula used to solve for the optimal transfer size and initial cash balance is

$$C = \sqrt{\frac{2bT}{i}}$$

The average cash balance is computed by dividing C by 2.

Source: J. Richard Aronson and Eli Schwartz. *Management Policies in Local Government Finance.* Washington, DC: International City Management Association, 1975, pp. 267–268, 271–272. Used by permission.

EXHIBIT 7–3   Illustration of the EOQ Formula

A city has total cash payments of $6 million for a six-month period. During this period, the payment (T) will be made at a steady rate, the cost per transaction (b) is $50, the interest rate (i) is 3 percent, and the cost per dollar of funds transferred (v) is 0.05 percent. Therefore:

$$c = \sqrt{\frac{2bT}{i}} = \sqrt{\frac{2(50)\,(6,000,000)}{.03}} = \$141,421$$

The optimal initial cash balance and transfer size is $141,421 and the average cash balance is $141,421 divided by 2 or $70,710. By dividing 6,000,000 by 141,421, the number of transfers (42) can be calculated. The total cost of cash management for the six-month period is:

$$= \$50\frac{(\$6,000,000)}{\$141,421} + .0005\frac{(\$6,000,000)}{1} + .03\frac{(\$141,421)}{2} = \$7,242$$

Source: J. Richard Aronson and Eli Schwartz. *Management Policies in Local Government Finance*. Washington, DC: International City Management Association, 1975, pp. 267–268, 271–272. Used by permission.

of investing. To make money on investments, more transactions require a higher cash amount to invest.

In the third approach, the Miller-Orr Model, the same basic concepts apply except the model focuses on the upper dollar limit the government needs for cash purposes. When the cash balance touches the upper boundary, then the budget person or treasurer automatically buys a predetermined amount of securities. Conversely, when the cash balance touches the lower boundary, then the same person automatically sells a predetermined amount of securities to increase the cash balance. The analyst determines the upper and lower boundaries using transaction costs and forecasted lost earned interest. The greater the likely cash fluctuations, the greater the control limits. Analysts are wiser to use the Miller-Orr Model when cash balances fluctuate randomly.

In order to maximize the investment earned on the cash balances, an analyst should develop a cash budget as part of cash management. Analysts must create a system of prioritizing urgent and important spending over less important needs. Management analysts should design administrative techniques and procedures to speed up cash management operations, minimize collection and holding costs, follow sound internal financial control policies, be attentive to good commercial relations, and make cash management more responsive to managerial decisions. Generally, analysts should establish the following as cash usage priorities:

- operation and maintenance of existing facilities and the fulfillment of legal obligations such as salaries, pensions, debt service;
- provisions of restoration of working capital;
- replacement and renewal of plant and equipment necessary to sustain operations;
- construction or acquisition of equipment and facilities to upgrade current operations and maintenance; and
- expansion of public facilities to meet additional growth.

Analysts should make cash forecasts based on the likely pattern of receipts and disbursements over a period of time. Useful information for the forecast comes from both department heads and historical records on cash receipts and disbursements. Analysts should use this forecast to build a cash budget that shows the intended daily, weekly, monthly, and yearly cash position of the government. Thus, the cash budget should have both a short- and long-term time frame. The short-term perspective helps get as much income out of idle cash as possible. The long-term perspective helps the analyst determine the higher interest rate possible for long-term investments. Analysts should use different strategies for each perspective.

Research and development on this topic is particularly useful. For example, computerized software is available to help build the cash budgets and decide the best strategies to use. Charles Coe notes that cities over 10,000 population tend to do a better job of cash management, with smaller cities and authorities (such as mental health centers, sanitary districts, and regional libraries) having a poorer record of cash management. North Carolina developed the following five criteria to evaluate its local cash management practices:

- invest at least 90 percent of the local jurisdiction funds;
- invest no more than 10 percent of the cash management portfolio in passbook savings;
- invest no more than 25 percent of the portfolio in repurchase agreements (Repos);
- invest no more than 50 percent of the portfolio in commercial paper; and
- invest no more than 75 percent of the portfolio in money market or NOW accounts.

Accelerating the receipt of revenues is one component of cash management. At the state and local levels, receipts come from tax collections, agency collections, intergovernmental transfers, and bond proceeds. In some cases, decision makers establish tax collection policy in state laws or local ordinances, but sometimes administrators make those decisions. An example of a policy that speeds up collection is when governments ask taxpayers to mail their property tax checks directly to the local government's bank for deposit. Governments can allow citizens to pay their taxes with credit cards, and they can use high late-penalty fees to encourage fast payments. The closing date of a bond is typically under the control of the government's finance director, and setting that date can help in cash management. The quickness of intergovernmental transfers varies widely but the 1992 federal Cash Management Improvement Act significantly improved former federal practices.

Some government activities are enterprise in character (such as water and sewer) and require billing much like the private sector. Thus, in such situations, governments should consider providing prompt payment discounts, hiring professional collection agencies, listing delinquents with credit reporting services, and sending monthly bills. In addition, local governments can use tax liens sent to employers and can ask state governments to subtract local tax bills from a state tax refund.

Financial Management Systems

Today, the information age influences many work activities, including public budgeting and financial management. The budgeting and financial management activity is data intensive; and, at each step in the evolution of the information age, budgeting and financial management evolved with those changes. The early and first wave, which was the "mainframe" from about 1965 to 1980, allowed governments to automate the routine accounting functions, payroll, and budgetary control mechanism. The first wave used "legacy" systems, which, although institutionalizing various technological and functional deficiencies, nevertheless increased efficiency through the reduction of clerical costs. The second "end-user computing" wave from 1980 to 1990 brought the personal computer to the forefront of government finances, especially in the application of the spreadsheet and data analysis software based on the current client-server-based systems. The third wave from 1990 to 2000 focused on the use of local networks, shared databases, and client-server technology. These systems—which enabled complete integration of the finance function including linkage to the general ledger, purchasing, and payroll—permitted greater efficiency, economy, creativity, financial control, and accessibility of information to all relevant data users. The fourth wave from 2000 focuses on advanced capabilities, including extending the network to the World Wide Web and rapid data links, and permits the new budgetary approaches discussed in Chapter 2.

Today, the financial management system (FMS) favors the *integrated system* over the older *independent stand-alone system.* That latter system focuses on single applications such as payroll and stands apart from the other activities in the budget and finance functions. In contrast, an integrated system has its own data sources, databases, software programs, hardware, and information management standards but also uses software upgrades. The integrated system has the big advantage of being modular and relatively easy to modify, as information systems always need changes. In addition, the integrated system is less expensive and poses less of an implementation risk. System designers have built the modern integrated FMS around a general ledger system, which is the heart of the accounting system.

Information technology architecture is the system of hard- and software. The clear trend in architecture is toward client-server systems and away from mainframes except in the largest governments. Today, distributive systems rely on servers commonly networked together for multiple clients. These systems place controls in the user's department, but these systems locate centrally the server to facilitate backup, security, and environments to protect the hardware. Because the platform is cooperative processing, the relationship is a shared workload between the client and the server. Typically, the system should use relational databases that organize records into a series of tables permitting linkages to tables from other databases. Almost all systems use graphic user interfaces to facilitate human-machine interaction by allowing point-and-click devices to choose among pull-down menus and options. Another feature is desktop integration that allows analysts to extract data from the FMS and manipulate it on their desktops. FMS includes data warehousing, whose costs are rapidly declining and are giving users access to more and better information. Another new feature of FMS is the Internet, which places an increasing amount of data at the disposal and use of the analyst. In some cases, electronic commerce permits exchange of data electronically such as benchmarking information or purchasing decisions data.

The major components of an integrated financial system typically are the budget development, general ledger, purchasing, human resources including payroll, accounts payable, accounts receivable and billing, fixed-asset and inventory management, project costing, and geographic information systems (GIS). The *budget development module—* which enable analysts to do "what if" scenario analysis—coordinates organizationwide operating and capital budget preparation, analysis, review, and approval. It should use decentralized real time data entry and narrative justification by departments that includes the use of performance measures and linked spreadsheets to create summary tables. The foundation of the FMS is the general ledger as it is the main accounting system for the organization. Leading edge general ledger packages should allow government to handle all the budget execution and accounting functions discussed in this chapter. Leading edge purchasing systems should streamline business processes and enable the development of procurement alternatives, contract negotiations, and the building of supplier relationships. The *human resources and payroll module* enables applicant tracking, managing employee records, administering employee benefits, and tracking position information useful for budget preparation. The *accounts payable module* records current liabilities accurately using a three-way matching, utilizes supplier discounts to reduce costs, and processes invoice payments in a timely manner. The *accounts receivable and billing module* produces bills, processes receipts, and records payments in a manner that integrates tax and fee collection permitting enterprise activities. Fixed-asset and inventory management for nonenterprise operations is essential in not-for-profit accounting as explained later in this chapter, and the FMS system designer must put this capability into the modern FMS. The *project cost module* allows managers to track project costs and commitments while leaving the appropriate audit trail and inputting data to the general ledger. Increasingly, state and local governments are using *graphic information systems* (GIS) to enhance policy analysis capabilities. Thus, an advanced FMS should have this capability. In addition, accountability and security become paramount considerations when utilizing this technology and these system configurations. This necessitates the need for encryption and multiple firewalls to preserve the integrity and confidentiality of the financial data being transmitted. Guidance and standards are promulgated by the Governance Control and Audit for Information and Related Technology or COBIT group (see http://isaca.org/cobit.htm).

Although the information age commentators widely praised integrated FMS designs, such designs remain rare as top management in government leaves each bureau to its own development agenda with little effort given to true governmentwide integration. *Business process reengineering* (BPR) is one effective method in designing and implementing an integrated FMS. BPR, which identifies processes as the fundamental units of analysis for organizational change, has the following as important principles for a successful FMS implementation:

- substituting parallel processes for sequential processes;
- bringing downstream information upstream;

- ensuring a continuous flow of the "main sequence," thus removing nonvalue-adding steps from the process;
- capturing information once at the source or point of entry; and
- organizing around outcomes rather than functions.

Cash Internal Control

In many public organizations, there is a need to deal with the day-to-day minor situations that require a simple cash or check purchase or receiving of public monies. At all levels, management needs to ensure proper cash internal control, as this is a minor but sensitive subject due to the likelihood of fraud and abuse of public monies. Management cannot prevent fraud and abuse completely, but management can discourage it to the point that it rarely occurs by using the budget execution theory described earlier in this chapter. The following twelve simple practices can make a remarkable difference in cash internal control:

Staff Should

- make all disbursements, except for petty cash, by check. Cash invites theft and fraud because it is much more difficult to trace, and auditors and managers find associating cash with specific persons difficult. Also canceled checks provide a receipt and thus an audit trail. Petty cash is an exception in that detailed controls for small items can cost more than the item purchased, thus, it does not warrant that level of control.
- never draw check to "cash." Checks should create an audited trail so that if there is fraud, investigators can isolate the illegal transaction. Staff should always associate writing a check with a specific voucher and invoice.

Standard Operating Procedures Should

- prohibit the signing of checks in advance because signed checks are similar to cash. Delaying the signing of checks just before disbursement shortens the time they are negotiable and helps ensure that the checks correspond to the purchases.
- require independent reconciliation of bank accounts in order to detect errors more easily using a second independent person. More significantly, this procedure lessens the likelihood of fraud because the crime would require the involvement of two persons instead of one.
- require staff to reconcile checks with statements using sequenced (numbered) checks. This permits tighter control of the checks and uncovers omissions much more easily. Also, if the staff uses numbered checks, investigators can more easily detect theft of checks.
- require that staff draw all checks based on written authority from a formally authorized person. Procedures should allow accountants to trace all checks to invoices, purchase orders, and encumbrances. Management should always minimize the possibility of confusion concerning the issuing of money. If the agent issuing money can prove that he or she used a written record with all his or her disbursements, then the procedure properly protects that agent.
- require strict inventory control over blank and voided checks. The absence of such controls makes fraud and theft easier, while the presence of such controls points the criminal investigator to the likely criminal.
- establish a separate bank account for each fund in order to maintain its separate identity. This procedure prevents improper mingling of money and facilitates separate accounting and auditing of funds.

- require surprise counts by management of petty cash. Elaborate controls of petty cash are not cost-effective; but management needs a less costly procedure, such as surprise counts of petty cash, to encourage honesty on the part of those responsible for the money. As a matter of management policy, no one should be above or beyond suspicion. Management should stress to employees that surprise counts are only standard operating procedure, which they should not take as a question of their personal honesty but as a means to help prove their integrity.
- require the matching of all vouchers with checks. If someone cannot trace a check to an invoice to a purchase order, then confusion can exist that leads to mistakes such as paying a bill twice, not paying some bills, and other problems.
- require staff to mark vouchers and supporting documents with the correct check number once staff issues the check. This procedure helps prevent mistakes such as the multiple use of the same document to justify disbursements.
- require staff to deposit all cash receipts and deposits at least daily and more frequently if the deposits involve large sums of money. The logging and depositing of money provide an essential audit trail that the bank received the money and when it received the money. Depositing money also protects employees against robbery and permits the investment of idle cash to earn extra income for the government.

Charles K. Coe and Curtis Ellis studied 127 cases of losses due to improper internal controls in North Carolina. The seven more common internal control failures were as follows:

- not pre-numbering receipts;
- improperly separating such accounting duties as the receipt, deposit, and reconciliation of deposits;
- not adequately securing assets such as checks, cash books, and equipment;
- not properly controlling inventories;
- insufficiently monitoring payables;
- not conducting an independent audit of a program; and
- having poor purchasing controls.

Of the 127 problems that Coe and Ellis identified, 49 (or 39 percent) resulted from separating accounting duties improperly:

- Management allowed the same person to prepare the daily cash report, to prepare the deposit slip, and to write the receipts.
- The same person wrote the checks, paid the bills, opened the mail, reconciled the bank statements, and prepared the financial reports.
- A check co-signer signed blank checks so that the other co-signer would not have to inconvenience the first co-signer.
- An account clerk wrote the check and entered the check on the accounting books without confirmation that someone made the accounting entry.

Commercial Bank Services

Which bank should a government use? Banks provide different earned interest and various types of extra bank services for large customers such as government. Thus, governments are wise to shop around for the correct bank because typically banks like government as customers. However, because government is a preferred customer, political factors, inappropriately and sometimes illegally, can enter into the choice of bank. In addition, politicians sometimes expect large political donations from bank officials. Because governments often use many accounts, there is also the possibility to spread a government's banking business among several banks.

An unusual bank service for government is the warrant discussed more in Chapter 8. A *warrant* is a conditional payment through a bank. Governments use warrants to control their disbursements. When a vendor presents a warrant for payment at a bank, the bank will not issue payment until the government approves the warrant in question. Governments use this device to regulate their cash position so that they always have adequate funds available to pay their obligations. The major disadvantages of the warrant are the high bank service charges, the high government cost to administer this method of payment, and the discouragement it gives vendors who might want to do business with government. However, when a state government is in financial crisis, this method can avoid the worst situation of not having enough funds to meet payroll.

With the greater use of computers with banking, the practice of "playing the float" is now almost obsolete. A *float* is the difference between the total amount of checks drawn on a bank account and the amount shown on the bank's books. If the government can determine the size of the float accurately, then it can have a lower bank balance and increase the idle cash invested. For the smallest of governments, the float amount is not significant, but for large governments, the amount of money can be large, and the earned interest on only a few days' investment is significant and worth the effort.

Electronic fund transfer systems make playing the float obsolete. For example the Federal Electronic Funds Transfer System links the Treasury Department with the New York Federal Reserve Bank. The system provides the capability for automatic receipt of fund transfers as well as computer-assisted generation of fund transfers among Treasury, Federal Reserve Banks, member banks, and others using the Federal Reserve Communication Systems. Thus, governments and banks process checks instantly instead of taking several days.

Governments can also use *lock box systems* and *cash concentration accounts* to reduce unwanted float. Banks sometimes use post office boxes as lock boxes in which taxpayers, user-fee payers, and others deposit payments more easily and quickly. A concentration account is a regional account that multiple funds use for initial deposits, which banks then process into separate concentration accounts for wire transfers or immediate investment.

There are common patterns in commercial bank practices. For example, most governments select their banks using a competitive bidding process with 2.3 bid average and 1 to 5 bids being the range. Cities commonly have a two-year contract with banks. In the past, banks required a minimum bank balance and did not charge for services, as they earned income from investing the government funds. Increasingly, banks charge fee services. The advantage of so-called free service is city councils need not review the details of bank arrangements. The disadvantages are the lack of linkage between the bank services provided and the lack of compensation from idle cash balances. The common practice today is for the bank to use direct fees for the various services provided. This provides a greater awareness of the bank services provided and encourages greater care in achieving cost-effectiveness.

Governments use *wire transfers* and *direct deposits*. Because some states do not wire transfer the state's tax remittance from the state to the local governments, cities sometimes maintain a *demand account* in banks the state uses to receive the monthly sales tax remittance checks. The bank can then wire transfer the funds to the respective city depository bank accounts, providing faster transfers of money and better control of the transfers themselves. The result is more income from idle cash. The other innovation is direct deposits of payroll. The city directly deposits its payroll into the bank accounts of participating employees. The advantages to the city are increased predictability of fund outflows, lower cost of payroll preparation, enhanced security by reducing the chance of misplaced or stolen checks, and increased employee goodwill. The disadvantage to government is less time to ride the float.

Using *special handling for large checks* received in the collection process and using the *paying agent services* of a bank are two particularly useful local government procedures. Because large checks are sometimes a major portion of idle cash investment yield, developing special handling for them is often wise. In such a procedure, a government opens the mail as early in the day as possible. Staff separates, bundles, and deposits large receipts before the bank's cutoff time for crediting deposits.

Often a local government can have its local bank act as its *paying agent* on the principal and interest payments of bonds. This service includes authenticating and canceling bond certificates and coupons as well as disbursing payments to investors. For small- and medium-sized city governments, banks can perform those tasks in a more cost-effective manner due to their specialization. Thus, cities can purchase these procedures from the bank at less cost than if the finance office of the city did them internally.

Controlling Payables

Paying bills can mean saving money. Given the fact that idle cash is earning interest, governments should not pay bills until they are due unless the discount for early payment is better than the earned interest. In order to maximize earned interest, governments often make grants using a *letter of credit*. This enables the government to draw interest instead of the grantee.

Management should take care to ensure that knowledgeable people pay the bills. Typically, government centralizes the management and control of payables to provide the needed expertise. In larger governments, another method used is to have field units control payables following the established spending and disbursement levels established by headquarters. The U.S. Joint Financial Improvement Committee general guidelines are useful in tailoring agency or government disbursement and collectibles policies and procedures:

- Each agency should have a carefully developed disbursement plan as a part of its forecast of outlays. The plan should be consistent with the agency's objectives, strategies, program plans, and budget.

- Management should establish a payment schedule and control system.
- Management should establish procedures for evaluating economic factors, including the time value of money, in establishing payment schedules. Unless there are significant programmatic or policy factors, accounts should make payments generally at the time they are due.
- Except for very large purchases for which management might need special analyses, cash discounts are usually desirable.
- Accounts payment personnel should review procedures to ensure that they do not delay payments to small vendors and for occasional purchases beyond the due dates.
- Management usually can make fuller use of letters of credit and other established procedures for managing the timing of payments for government programs.
- Management should establish procedures for regular comparison of actual and planned disbursements.
- Analysts should evaluate and management should adjust the disbursement plans, when necessary, for the causes and impacts of significant variance on disbursements.
- Agencies with significant amounts of receipts should have a collections plan that is a part of the overall forecasts and consistent with the agency's objectives, strategies, program plans, and budget.
- Management should establish collection schedules and control systems for billing and cash processing.
- Management analysts should consider economic factors, including the time value of money, in the development of billing cycles and collection procedures. They should recognize the importance of prompt collection and deposit of cash.
- Management should establish procedures that show regular comparisons of actual to planned collection.
- Analysts should evaluate and management should adjust plans when necessary to accommodate the causes and impacts of significant variances from planned collections.

In controlling payables, local governments have found three procedures particularly valuable: pooling cash balances into one *central concentration account,* using zero-balance accounts for disbursements, and taking timely advantage of trade discounts. The pooling of cash balances into a central concentration account gives important information to the cash manager. These concentration accounts receive all cash deposits, and cash managers make all their investments purchases from them. The aggregation is from a number of accounts in a single bank or from several banks. In addition, cash managers maintain a *zero balance* in accounts such as payroll, vendor disbursement, debt service, capital project disbursements, and others. The advantage of concentration and zero-balance accounts is that it eases the task of monitoring cash balances; cash managers need only to monitor and forecast one account.

Usually, in controlling payables, government should not pay vendors any earlier than required by the vendor agreement (for example, thirty days). The exception to this payable policy is when a vendor offers a discount for early payment. For example, an offer of "2/10 net 30" means the city may deduct 2 percent from the invoice if the vendor receives payment within ten days. If not, the vendor expects full payment within thirty days. This 2 percent discount is equivalent to a 36 percent interest rate and likely to be higher than any interest income from normal idle-cash investments. Thus, the city treasurer should meet the fast payment terms and get the discount.

Investment in Marketable Securities

Once analysts determine the cash and security position in cash management, the government is ready to invest its money for desired short periods of time. Often cash managers can invest as much as 70 percent of the total liquid assets in securities. State law often, but not always, should limit the choice of securities to "safe" investments such as U.S. Treasury securities, U.S. agency securities, obligations of other municipalities within a state, and bank certificates of deposit. In one remarkable 1990s situation (described more in Chapter 8) in Orange County, California, the state permitted the county to invest its cash assets in high risk derivatives, with the result that the county eventually filed bankruptcy. Pension fund management can take greater risks, but cash management should even avoid common stocks, which are quite acceptable and wise for pension fund purposes.

Not all securities will earn the investor the same *return on investment,* which economists call *market yield.* Analysts and the market determine it based on a combination of the following:

- length of maturity,
- default risk,
- marketability,
- call provisions, and
- tax status.

When a government decides to invest in securities, then the cash manager should watch the security market and determine what is a reasonable market yield. That determination should become the goal of the cash manager. *Long-term securities* tend to receive higher yields, but yields of fifteen to thirty years are not significantly higher. The key market influence on the yield is the expectation of what will happen to the interest rate. Generally, the market participants' expectation regarding interest rates is the key influence on the rate itself. Generally, when market participants expect the interest rate to rise, the yield also rises. In poor market conditions, persons selling securities offer investors a risk premium to induce them to invest in long-term securities. Only when market participants expect interest rates to fall significantly in the future do long-term securities—currently yielding less than short-term securities—become attractive.

Default risk is the possibility that the borrower will fail to pay the principal or interest. All other factors being constant, the greater the possibility the borrower will fail to meet the obligation, the greater the premium or market yield on the security. Of course, a very high possibility is likely to mean that no one would be willing to buy the security. The market considers U.S. Treasury and U.S. government agency issues as default-free, so they establish the lower limit for securities. The major security rating firms such as Moody's Investor's Service and Standard and Poor's judge the creditworthiness of other issues. These private firms announce their judgment on creditworthiness in publications that they sell to the public.

Marketability involves the ability of the security owners to convert the security to cash. Because governments in cash management must easily convert their securities back to cash, marketability is particularly important. Marketability concerns both the prices realized and the amount of time required selling the asset. The more marketable a security, the greater is the ability of its owner to easily execute a security transaction. Less-marketable securities require higher yields.

A *call provision* on a security allows the issuer to buy the security back at a stated price before maturity. The call provision is to the borrower's benefit because the borrower can reclaim and pay off the issues if interest rates move significantly lower. The call provision disadvantages the investor because the borrower can pay off the security in a period of low interest rates and then the investor must reinvest in securities that are likely to return a lower yield. Not surprisingly, investors commonly demand a higher yield if a call provision exists in the security. When interest rates are high, callable government securities are more popular, but they are unusual in federal government securities because they are often already low yield producing.

Tax status has two effects on market yields. First, governments—in contrast to the private sector—do not have to pay taxes on investment income, thus, this is not an expense to government. Second, state and local government securities are tax havens for many private investors; this affects the government security market by driving the yield down. Generally speaking, the fact that local governments do not pay federal income tax means that they should invest in higher-yield federal securities rather than in state and local government securities. Another difference in investment strategy involves deep discount bonds and the tax rates on ordinary and capital gains. This distinction is significant to the individual who is a taxpayer but is not significant to the investing government. Thus, a government should not take advantage of the "bargain" yields on coupon bonds selling at par or above. In general, governments should simply invest in securities showing the highest pretax return.

Cities can contract their cash management investments to private companies or other governments. However, private companies can be massive fraud schemes, and thus any city contracting with a private firm must take great care to be sure of the track record of the private firm. Cities can also contract with other governments. One such situation was the Orange County, California, example cited earlier. Not only did Orange County go bankrupt, but it caused serious financial losses to other local governments that had contracted with Orange County to invest their idle cash. Regardless of who manages cash management investments, serious problems can arise and government leaders must take great care to decide who manages the government's idle cash and pension funds.

A successful intergovernmental approach to cash management for bond proceeds is the Virginia State Non-Arbitrage Program (SNAP), which the state created as a reaction to the federal 1986 tax law. SNAP manages the cash from state and local bond proceeds, calculates the arbitrage for local bond issues, and rebates all necessary funds to the federal government to meet arbitrage requirements. This program manages over $1 billion, removes major cash management burdens from local government, has a greater chance of preventing possible arbitrage problems, and permits optimal professional cash management practices.

Revenue Collection

Generally, according to a 1997 Government Finance Officers Association and MBIA (a private company discussed in Chapter 8) survey of state and local collection practices, average collection rates are over 95 percent. Eleven percent did not respond to the questionnaire, but 28 percent said they collected 99 to 100 percent of the revenue owed them. Only 6 percent reported a tax collection rate below 90 percent. Forty-four percent had written revenue collection enforcement policies that spelled out the time periods for determining delinquency, payment arrangements for delinquencies, and write-off guidelines. Eighty-four percent imposed late fees or interest penalties on past-due balances. At least two-thirds sent collection letters, placed collection calls, and imposed tax liens. One-fourth seized property and 18 percent either garnished wages or offset tax refunds.

With the information age, governments increasingly use new approaches to boost collections including accepting electronic transfers. They also accept credit card payments, use computer programs to assist in collection through interfacing with accounting systems, use automatic generating collection notices and letters, and have online capabilities with collection agencies. Also consistent with the information age is the greater use of competition. About one-fifth of the GFOA/MBIA survey respondents reported introducing competition into the collection process by permitting public agencies and private firms to bid to private revenue collection services. Of those, 89 percent awarded the contract to private firms, usually to collect charges for services or fines. Of those using private firms, 76 percent liked the services provided.

Another innovation in collecting delinquent revenues is the sale or securitization of property tax liens or other receivables. Governments sell tax liens to investors, usually in bulk sales, but sometimes to a trust through which government securitizes the revenue stream. The government issues bonds backed by the delinquent taxes to investors, and the bond proceeds pay the government.

Types of Marketable Securities

Many state statutes limit cash management assets to the highest credit quality securities, such as U.S. Treasury obligations, federal agency securities, repurchase agreements (REPOs), bankers' acceptances, negotiable certificates of deposit (CDs), and even overnight securities. The two types of U.S. Treasury obligations are *treasury notes* and *treasury bills*. Treasury bills pay a low interest, and the federal government auctions them weekly with 91- to 182-day maturities. One-year bills are sold separately. Treasury bills carry no coupon but are sold at discount. These securities are extremely popular as short-term investments. The secondary market is excellent and transaction costs are low. Treasury notes hold one- to seven-year maturities, but investors use them in the secondary market for short-term investments. In general, these two types of securities are the safest and most marketable, but they yield the lowest return on investment.

The federal government issues other types of securities that carry the same assurances as U.S. Treasury obligations but have slightly better yields. Principal agencies issuing securities are the federal land banks, federal home-loan banks, federal intermediate credit banks, the Federal National Mortgage Association (called "Fannie Mae"), the Government National Mortgage Association ("Ginnie Mae"), and the banks for cooperatives. Maturities range from one month to fifteen years, but about two-thirds of the issues are for less than one year.

The *repurchase agreement* (REPO) is an innovation of government security dealers who recognize the selling potential of securities tailored to specific short time periods. With REPOs, dealers agree to repurchase the security at a specific future date, thus increasing the number of transactions and the resulting total fees from those transactions. Government investors benefit because they can get securities for the specific time periods they need, thus gaining the desired earned interest. There is little marketability, but that is unimportant because REPOs are usually only for a few days. There is no default risk because the securities are almost always U.S. Treasury securities.

Another commonly used short-term investment is the negotiable certificate of deposit (CD). A CD is the deposit of funds at a commercial bank for a specified period of time at a specified rate of interest. This investment device was originated in 1961, and usually it provides a yield better than treasury bills, with maturity in 30 to 360 days. A sizable secondary market exists, but marketability is usually nonexistent for small bank CDs. The possibility of bank failure, which is usually low for most banks, influences the default risk. Commonly, local governments use CDs from local banks to support their regional economy.

Portfolio

A *portfolio* is merely the collection of securities one holds. State laws, as noted before, sometimes limit local governments to a legally sanctioned list of securities. The typical most important consideration in portfolio management is to have the cash available when needed for the daily operation of the government. Default risk should be minimal and a call risk is unusual. Taxability is not a factor; therefore, analysts should find computations simplified to the return on investment. Cash managers should concentrate on maturity and marketability. For the short term, treasury bills, REPOs, and CDs satisfy most needs. Treasury bills and REPOs should meet a significant portion of any emergency liquidity needs.

Cash managers handle intermediate and long-term needs differently. They use treasury notes and bonds as well as other U.S. securities for intermediate purposes. Again, the objective for the cash manager is to ensure the government's various activities have needed cash to pay their bills including payroll when needed. Therefore, cash managers must time maturities correctly, or security marketability must be excellent if the manager's timing is not correct. U.S. agency securities provide better yields, but cash managers must weigh their marketability against their yield. In some cases, managers would use long-term investments, especially for larger potential emergencies or when they wish to accumulate funds over years for a particular purpose such as paying a sinking fund. If that is the situation, they typically use long-term treasury and agency securities. For cash managers, the most important consideration for long-term investments is the future course of interest rates. The highest yield is not as important as the date of maturity or possible marketability. Often, governments take the more conservative approach of confining their investments to short-term securities.

In summary, cash managers should invest the government's idle cash, but such investment requires an expertise with a conservative basis. This section has given the reader some of the basics of cash management, but cash managers need much more market-specific knowledge and expertise that go beyond the scope of this chapter. However, the reader will find that this chapter plus Chapter 8 will equip him or her with the essential fundamentals.

ACCOUNTING FUNDAMENTALS

Although interrelated, budgeting, accounting, and auditing focus on different time orientations. Budgeting is future oriented, but the future can be quite near in the case of current-year operating budgets. Accounting is present oriented as it consists of *recording transactions* of an agency in financial terms, including classifying, summarizing, reporting, interpreting, and analyzing those transactions for the user of the data. Auditing and evaluation are past oriented because the analysis looks at the past decisions to see what went right and wrong.

In accounting, the key words are "recording transactions." Transactions are financial decisions, such as obligating money, deciding to disburse, and setting aside funds for a purpose. Accounting includes capturing performance data on the accomplishments of programs. Various summaries and classifications of transactions permit accountants to keep track of and analyze critical information for management. Accounting provides management with a means to evaluate management performance, to plan for future operations, and to achieve desired financial control of the organization.

Accounting is very deductive in its logic and based upon principles that are deceptively simple for government accounting and reporting. Since 1984, the primary accepted rule-making body for state and local government accounting is the Governmental Accounting Standards Board (GASB), which stresses program accountability. Since 1991, the Federal Accounting Standards Advisory Board (FASAB) sets the standards for the federal government accounting and reporting. Accountability encompasses the notion that an agency must explain its actions to political leaders and justify both past actions and future requests in terms of likely consequences. GASB believes the accounting information should allow accounting users to understand if the current-year revenues are sufficient to pay the services provided that year and whether those financial decisions shift the burden of paying for services to future taxpayers. GASB, like the federal government, stresses the wisdom of identifying service efforts and accomplishments as part of government accounting. Accounting principles stress that accounting should complement legal requirements and budgets. GASB and FASAB suggest standard classifications, terminology, and reports.

Accounting principles stress the importance of disclosure and integration of accounting with other management activities such as budgeting and personnel. Full disclosure of the financial results of government is essential, or abuse can go undetected. Accounting produces financial information for management purposes that permits effective control over and ensures the accountability of all funds, property, and other assets. A reliable accounting service is the basis for preparing and supporting budget requests, for controlling the execution of the budgets, and for providing needed financial information for reviewing government performance. Government accounting, which management should integrate and make sure it is consistent with all accounting operations throughout the government, permits comparative analyses and strengthens the analytical information for management. In addition, the reporting of performance measures strengthens accountability and improves management because decision makers can see what they buy for tax money, the impacts of the programs on society, and the relative efficiency and effectiveness of the programs.

Since 1990, the federal goal is to standardize federal accounting systems and principles, integrate accounting with other financial management activities, and link accounting and budget systems. Other federal agencies concerned with financial management are the Department of the Treasury, the Office of Management and Budget (OMB), and the Joint Financial Management Improvement Program (JFMIP). The Department of the Treasury defines financial management requirements and practices because of its cash and debt-management operations. The JFMIP is a small professional staff that reports to a board composed of financial management leaders from GAO, OMB, and Treasury.

The Chief Financial Officers Act of 1990 focused concern for financial management. The act created in OMB the position of Deputy Director for Management to serve as the chief finance officer (CFO) for the federal government. In the major departments and agencies, the act created an office of federal financial management that reports to the head of the agency on all financial management matters. Its duties include (1) developing and maintaining an integrated accounting and financial management system; (2) overseeing all financial management activities relating to programs and operations of the agency; and (3) monitoring the financial execution of the budget. The act also directs the OMB to develop and update a five-year plan for improving financial management systems and to report its progress in implementing the plan to Congress.

Changes in financial reporting and accountability occur with regularity. With the drafting of Government Accounting Standards Board Statement Number 34 in June of 1999, there was a fundamental change in how government assets are to be reported. The changes require government entities to report on the value of all capital assets. Essentially, governments may account for assets by using either simple depreciation or modified accrual approaches (including maintenance expenses). This change conforms government accounting standards with those applied in the private sector. This change is indicative of the reform movement calling for better accountability of government assets and better use of tax dollars in the public sector.

Accounting Norms and Budgeting

Government accounts accept certain norms. The control accounts or fiscal accounts—which record receipts, obligations, and disbursements—must embrace the details that support the budget. If that does not occur, then analysts cannot relate budget and accounting information. Management should centralize decisions on accounting definitions and classifications, but it should decentralize the routine of accounting. In connection with accounting, management must create a system of internal inspections, evaluations, auditing, and control. Unless inspections and auditing occur to verify that employees use required accounting practices, individuals in the organization will not take the accounting requirements seriously. If that occurs, then recorded costs and performance measures are inaccurate, and analysts cannot use the data to determine management success and failures. Accounting should reflect organizational performance with an accurate reflection of both good and bad news to help managers and other decision makers understand their true situation. Management wants flexibility in accounting but only in the context of overall uniformity. Because accounting requirements sometimes inhibit the organization from responding in a timely manner to its problems or raise other managerial problems, designing accounting systems is not an easy challenge to top government accountants who must balance the need for proper accounting with the other needs of the organization.

A key step in current-year budgeting and accounting is *obligation*. For example, when an agency signs a contract or places a purchase order, it makes a formal legal commitment that it must record as an *obligation*. A purchase order is a legal offer, and the assumption is that the vendor will send the requested goods and a bill to the government at the stated price in the purchase order. In the case of personnel, a contract or a mere agreement to work for certain remuneration constitutes the obligation. Once the government places an order and the vendor accepts it, the vendor must provide the requested goods, and the government must pay the bill given that the vendor fulfills the contract. At this stage before the accountant renders payment but the government has made an obligation, the government accountant records the order as an *accounts payable* item on the accounting books. Frequently, government does not need to pay all of its obligations because some orders are deficient in some manner and those obligations are not binding.

Once the government receives and places the goods in inventory, then an accrued expenditure exists until such time as the government issues a check, which is an *expenditure*. When there are large or many purchases, the concept of accrued expenditure is useful in keeping track of cash management disbursements. In other government situations, management might find this concept not needed. This chapter does not use the concept of "accrued expenditure" because many governments find the concept unnecessary.

Expenditure is when government receives the vendor's invoice and the government issues a check or otherwise pays the obligation. Government should control expenditures closely not only for cash management purposes but also for ensuring that the goods received do fulfill the contract terms. At the federal level, expenditures are important in terms of fiscal policy, and therefore accountants must monitor and control them carefully. Once the government has the goods in hand, accountants consider them *inventory* until the agencies use them in their operations. This accounting concept is useful because management can convert inventory to cash if necessary; thus, separate treatment from used goods helps managers have a better understanding of agency convertible assets. Once the agency takes the goods from inventory and uses them, then accountants consider the goods as a *cost*. At this point, the items are no longer considered an accounting asset.

Management must key government accounting to the budget. Accounting tracks the obligations and expenditures against the budget decisions for each fiscal year. Government accounting uses the term "encumbrance" to mean a claim on budgeted money, and the concept parallels the term "obligation" used in budgeting and economics. As soon as management makes an obligation, accountants set aside the money needed to fulfill the obligation, and they make sure that the money is no longer shown as available for new commitments. In budgeting for personnel, costs are highly predictable and regular during the fiscal year. However, equipment, materials, supplies, contracts, and grants are often irregular and require a formalized encumbrance system to avoid overspending budgeted monies. The accounting system reports should provide data on encumbrances and later on expenditures.

Nonprofit accounting, including government accounting, uses the fund concept because policy makers often dedicate a specific source of revenue for specific purposes. This requires accountants to separate the flow of revenue into separately treated funds that they report on separately. *Fund accounting* controls the handling of money to ensure that government spends each dedicated set of money only for the purpose intended, such as highway construction. Although this concept reduces management flexibility and is very expense to administer, this concept is common in government.

In state and local government, a large share of resources comes from federal government grants or revenue sharing monies. Because federal law or regulations have specific requirements on each grant, commonly fund accounting is essential and required with separate records maintained on all receipts and expenditures for each grant. Usually, federal guidelines spell out in detail the permitted costs and required supporting documentation for each grant or revenue sharing program. Often, grants require a local matching amount to the federal share, but sometimes that local share can be in the form of cash gifts and the value of provided local goods and services. The GASB fund categories are general, proprietary, and fiduciary. General funds are typical government activities with subcategories of general, special revenue, capital project, and debt service. Proprietary funds reflect government activities that act like businesses. Fiduciary funds are when government acts in a trust relationship. The federal government uses general and trust funds. Exhibit 7–4 summarizes funding mechanisms used by governments.

FINANCIAL ADMINISTRATION

Good financial administration means keeping good account records. Accountants must record all financial transactions. Eventually, accounts must summarize and classify the financial data but always relate that data to the appropriate fiscal year. Although GASB prefers government eventually to use an accrual method of accounting, most governments use a *modified accrual method* rather than either a *cash* or *accrual method*. Exhibit 7–5 provides a summary of basic accounting methods used in government accounting. In the cash method, accountants record income when they receive it and record expenditures when they pay them. In other words,

EXHIBIT 7–4   Fund Accounting Summary

FUND TYPE	CATEGORY	ACCOUNTING FOCUS	ACCOUNTING BASIS
General Fund	Governmental	Spending	Modified Accrual
Special Revenue Funds	Governmental	Spending	Modified Accrual
Debt Service Funds	Governmental	Spending	Modified Accrual
Capital Project Funds	Governmental	Spending	Modified Accrual
Internal Service Funds	Proprietary	Capital	Full Accrual
Enterprise Funds	Proprietary	Capital	Full Accrual
Pension Trust Funds	Fiduciary	Capital	Full Accrual
Nonexpendable Trust Funds	Fiduciary	Spending	Modified Accrual
Expendable Trust Funds	Fiduciary	Spending	Modified Accrual
Agency Funds	Fiduciary	NA	Modified Accrual

EXHIBIT 7–5   Basic Accounting Methods

	CASH BASIS	ACCRUAL BASIS	MODIFIED ACCRUAL
When is revenue recorded?	Cash is received	Revenue is earned	Measurable and available
When are expenditures recorded?	Cash is paid	Expense is incurred	Expenditure incurred

accountants record transactions as of the date the cash changes hands. The advantages of the cash method are that it is easy to administer and the accountants can easily determine the cash balance. As private citizens, most of us use the cash method with our checkbooks. The critical disadvantage is accountability because the accountant cannot relate expenses and revenues to the budget and its proper fiscal year. In the cash method, accountants do not amortize capital items over the life of the asset, but they do record them as an expense when the accountant issues the check for the item.

In the accrual method, recording financial information is more elaborate. Accountants record revenues both when government earns money and when paying taxes becomes someone's obligation. They also record when the government actually collects the earned money and when government obligates itself to eventually spend money. Finally, accountants record when government spends money to fulfill its obligations. Although the accrual method is very helpful in terms of accountability, it also distorts the revenue and cash position. Therefore, accountants must calculate the cash position separately. GASB prefers this method, and almost all nongovernmental funds in government, such as water and sewer agencies that act as private businesses with their own revenue sources, use it. In addition, accrual accounting calls for amortizing capital items as expenses over the life of the asset.

In the popular modified accrual method that is commonly used in governmental funds, accountants record revenues when government collects the money, and the capital items are not amortized as in the cash method. In addition, accountants record expenditures when government makes its obligations as in the accrual method. By recording revenues like the cash method and not calculating amortization, governments lower their administrative expenses. Because state and local governments do not pay taxes to the federal government, deductible amortized capital expenses are not as important to them as they are to private companies. They wish to lower their tax burden by deducting their capital expenses as much as possible in each fiscal year. However, knowing the proper amortized capital expense is useful information for government when it plans replacement of capital assets.

GASB establishes the Generally Accepted Accounting Principles (GAAP) for state and local governments in the United States. GASB standards often influence state and local governments for the following reasons:

- Some states require their local governments to follow GAAP.
- The American Institute of Certified Public Accountants (AICPA) changed its guidance to auditors to recognize GASB as the primary standard setting body for state and local government.
- Bond-rating firms expect annual financial reports to comply with GASB standards.
- The federal government requires all government entities receiving federal funds to be audited in accordance with the Single Audit Act, which requires a statement as to whether the financial report complies with GASB standards.

As a means to further encourage GAAP accounting, the Government Finance Officers Association awards the Certificate of Achievement for Excellence in Financial Reporting. A government's accounting office earns the certificate after it submits a Comprehensive Annual Financial Report (CAFR) and receives a positive recommendation from an impartial peer-review committee.

The accounting profession builds accounting on three operational tools: *vouchers, journals,* and *ledgers.* A *voucher* is a document confirming that a financial transaction took place. For example, payroll checks, purchase orders, receipts for rent payment, and even appropriation laws are vouchers. The *journal* is the first record book (now sometimes a computer printout) of the transactions. It is a chronological listing of the transactions that shows the date of the transaction's occurrence, the dollars, and a brief explanation of the transaction. A *ledger* is a group of accounts that pertain to the same subject—that is, a subject matter listing of information. These tools are important because together they provide the means to record usefully, summarize, and classify the transactions.

Basic Government Accounting

Double entry bookkeeping is an important accounting convention as it makes it easier to catch entry and arithmetic mistakes and helps in assembling useful accounting information. Double entry is possible because accountants format their information based on the not-for-profit accounting equation of *Assets equal Liabilities plus Reserves plus Fund Balance.* In the private sector, accountants substitute equity (meaning stock) for fund balance. Whenever an accountant or clerk records a transaction, he or she must make entries on both sides of the accounting equation in order to key it in balance. The fundamental accounting equation is *Assets equal Equities but Equities include Liabilities, Reserves, and Fund Balance. Assets* are what the government owns and what others owe the government. *Liabilities* are claims against the government such as claims of creditors for goods and services purchased, amounts due to employees for unpaid wages, and amounts due on loans. *Reserves* are equities that are not available for potential obligations, and therefore accountants segregate them from other obligations. *Fund balance* is the residual equity in the public section.

With double entry accounting, clerks post debit and credit entries in such a way that the accounting equation always stays in balance. As a rule, accountants debit any increase in an account on the left side of the accounting equation, whereas they credit any increase in the amount on the right side. Credits are decreases in assets and increases in liability. To check for errors, accountants prepare *trial balances* of the equation, but as a practical matter finding simple entry and arithmetic errors is often time-consuming work. Fortunately, the use of the computer permits greater speeds in calculation and tends to reduce the likelihood of arithmetical error. Thus, the computer has become an essential tool for complex accounting systems.

Accounting System Design

When designing an accounting system, the generated information should be timely, accurate, and objective. Practically, accountants must trade off one desired attribute for another, especially timeliness and accuracy. All legally established minimum requirements are consistent with the system. System designers should pay particular attention to the collection and recording of information because this is where most errors occur. They must design cross- and double-checks into the system in order to isolate and correct errors easily. Another concern is classification, summarization, and storage. Proper design here rests on an excellent grasp of how managers and analysts can best use the accounting information. Thought must also go into evaluating the use of the computer to enhance organizational speed and analytical capability. Designers of accounting systems must be sensitive to potential computer-assisted fraud and the possibility of massive, extremely embarrassing mistakes.

Enhancing internal control within the organization is the final factor an accountant should weigh when designing an accounting system. For example, the accounting system should always fix responsibility on specific individuals. Designers should write policies and procedures to avoid misunderstanding among participants in the process. For example, designers should ensure that only authorized personnel performs key functions such as disbursement. Designers should create forms carefully so that the forms and the related processes themselves minimize clerical errors and fraud. Designers need to incorporate built-in cross- and double-checks of data, forms, people, and units into the computer programs. For example, designers can require the use of independent recorders to cross-check data and can require independent auditors to verify the accuracy of the books. Another key point for management is to train and to keep good people in its accounting unit. Finally, designers must realize that they must periodically reconsider all reporting systems as reports and other elements of the system become dated due to changes in the organization and computer advancements.

Accounting systems should provide a standard, systematic method of communicating relevant, complete, and accurate financial information. The following activities become particularly important:

- classifying financial transactions and economic events,
- recording the economic nature of each event,
- summarizing the economic information in a meaningful way to policy makers and managers, and
- interpreting and communicating the results to appropriate decision makers and user groups.

Not-for-profit accounting for governmental fund types use only two account groups: the general fixed asset account group (GFAAG) and the general long-term debt account group (GLTDAG). They are necessary because government funds focus on current financial resources, and they need to account for noncurrent financial resources. The GFAAG accounts for fixed assets are not available as financial resources, but decision makers use financial resources to obtain those assets. The contra-account for balancing the accounting equation is investment in fixed assets. The GLTDAG account shows the unmatured obligations of governmental funds. The GLTDAG includes the outstanding principal balances of bonds, warrants, notes, and any other long-term general obligation to which a government obligates itself. The contra-account for balancing the accounting equation is an amount government provides for the retirement of long-term debt.

Government structures can be quite complex, and the accounting profession has a standard for determining what the financial reporting entails. The *primary government* is the financially accountable organization and is inclusive of other component units whose relationship to the primary government is of such significance that their exclusion would cause the financial statements to be incomplete or misleading. A primary government must have a separately elected legal body, be legally separate with its own corporate powers, and be fiscally independent with its own determination of its budget without the approval of another government. In contrast, a component is a legally separate organization for which the elected officials of the primary government are financially accountable. Accountants can report on component units with either blending or discrete presentations. A closely related component unit has blended existence in which accountants report the component unit's transactions and balances in a manner similar to the transactions and balances of the primary unit. If the accountants present the component unit as discrete, then the accountants use separate columns in the financial statements.

COMPREHENSIVE ANNUAL FINANCIAL REPORT

If a government follows GASB, it should prepare and publish a comprehensive annual financial report (CAFR) with one component being the general-purpose financial statement (GPFS). The three CAFR sections are introductory, financial, and statistical. The introductory section includes the transmittal letter, a current Certificate of Achievement for Excellence in Financial Reporting (if applicable), listing of principal officials, and an organization chart. The statistical section contains tables and data that provide trends and other information about the entity. CAFR requires the following tables:

* General Governmental Expenditures by Function—Last Ten Fiscal Years
* General Revenues by Source—Last Ten Fiscal Years
* Property Tax Levies and Collections—Last Ten Fiscal Years
* Assessed and Estimated Actual Value of Taxable Property—Last Ten Fiscal Years
* Property Tax Rates—All Overlapping Governments—Last Ten Fiscal Years
* Special Assessment Billings and Collections—Last Ten Fiscal Years
* Ratio of Net General Bonded Debt to Assessed Value and New Bonded Debt Per Capita—Last Ten Fiscal Years
* Computation of Legal Debt Margin
* Computation of Overlapping Debt
* Ratio of Annual Debt Service for General Bonded Debt to Total General Expenditures—Last Ten Fiscal Years
* Revenue Bond Coverage—Last Ten Fiscal Years
* Demographic Statistics
* Property Value, Construction, and Bank Deposits—Last Ten Fiscal Years
* Principal Taxpayers
* Miscellaneous Statistics

Accountants segregate the financial section into subsections that use a pyramid approach to financial reporting. Each successive layer provides increasing levels of detail. The four levels are the general-purpose financial statements (GPFS), combining statements by fund type, individual fund and accounting group statements, and supporting schedules. The GPFS is the top of the reporting pyramid and accountants aggregate the statements by fund type. The GPFS provide a broad perspective of the financial position and operating results of the government and include the following statements:

* Combined Balance Sheet—All Fund Types and Account Groups
* Combined Statement and Revenues, Expenditures, and Changes in Fund Balances—All Government Fund Types and Similar Trust Funds

- Combined Statement of Revenues, Expenditures, and Changes in Fund Balances—Budget and Actual—General and Special Revenue Fund Types (and other governmental fund types that the government legally adopted as its annual budget)
- Combined Statement of Revenues, Expenses, and Changes in Retained Earnings (or Equity) and Fund Balances—All Proprietary Fund Types and Similar Trust Funds
- Statement of Cash Flows
- Notes to the Financial Statements

This chapter does not present all the complexities of not-for-profit accounting, instead, it focuses on understanding how public managers can use accounting information. To this point, this chapter has explained the essential accounting concepts that students must understand to appreciate the accounting reports and process. Now, the chapter focus turns to specific accounting reports and how managers can use them for their purposes.

Statement of Revenue

One important concern for public managers and policy makers is the accuracy of revenue forecasting. In examining the CAFR, an analyst can find a comparison between estimated and actual government revenue such as shown in Exhibit 7–6. This report essentially tells the manager and policy maker where analysts guess poorly in revenue forecasting. Accountants key this report to funds, tax sources, and fiscal year. In forecasting, analysts should make separate forecasts for each tax source. Accounting forces an examination of the forecasts by funds and fiscal years. The noted estimated amount should be the one that policy makers used in developing their annual budget. The actual revenue should be that amount the treasury actually collected.

EXHIBIT 7–6   Milesville General Fund Statement of Revenue—Estimated and Actuals, Fiscal Year Ending June 30, 2010

REVENUE SOURCE	ESTIMATED REVENUE	ACTUAL REVENUE	ACTUAL OVER- OR (UNDER) ESTIMATED
Taxes	$240,000	$290,000	$50,000
Licenses and permits	30,000	36,000	6,000
Intergovernmental revenue	120,000	90,000	(30,000)
Charges for services	40,000	45,000	5,000
Fines and forfeitures	6,000	9,000	3,000
Miscellaneous	4,000	10,000	6,000
TOTAL	$440,000	$480,000	$40,000

Source: Adapted from J. Richard Aronson and Eli Schwartz. *Management Policies in Local Government Finance.* Washington, DC: International City Management Association, 1975, pp. 267–268, 271–272. Used by permission.

Exhibit 7–6 shows where the estimation error occurs and how much the estimate was off. An analyst can easily add another column to show the percentage mistake of the revenue estimate. The most significant revenue estimating errors are those that result in significantly less revenue for the government because those errors might require current-year cutbacks in service including laying off employees. If the revenue source is small, then even large percentage errors do not require serious current-year adjustments. In contrast, if the revenue source is large, then a small percentage forecasting error can require significant mid-current-year adjustments in the budget. In the case cited, the positive and negative errors largely cancel each other, but the absolute error factor is quite significant and that fact should concern policy makers.

Some revenue-forecasting techniques employ accounting information to refine forecasts. For example, by determining the error factor of past years, an analyst can adjust the future-year forecasts using those error factors to arrive at a more accurate future-year forecast. Regardless, this exhibit does isolate where analysts make revenue-forecasting errors. Senior management and policy makers should use this information to require analysts to improve their forecasting by using other forecasting techniques or acquiring more accurate data when forecasting.

Occasionally, monitoring revenues become quite important to a government agency, especially if it is dependent on a single source of revenue. In such situations, the agency can create a system to warn of impending fiscal problems. The end-of-the-year statement of revenue is inadequate unless analysts use it to monitor the revenue flows over the entire current year. However, even this constant monitoring can be insufficient because an agency might need to forecast its likely revenue collection as the current year evolves so that the agency can adapt as early as possible to any unusual deviations from its expected revenue. Fortunately, well-developed methodologies in statistical monitoring of manufacturing processes and business plans exist, and an analyst can modify them especially to accommodate very small sample sizes. Graphical dot plots can replace traditional expected values and confidence intervals of the business methodologies. For more detail, see Ray D. Nelson and Gary C. Cornia's recommended monitoring system cited in the reference section of this chapter.

Users of accounting reports should read them holistically. Accounting reports complement each other and each tells the manager a part of a larger story. However, together they tell a reasonably comprehensive story about the government. For example, if the reading of the balance sheet (Exhibit 7–10) raises questions about encumbrances, the manager might find the ultimate answer in the appropriation and expenditure ledger account (Exhibit 7–7). The manager must read all the accounting reports and understand them as a whole including their interrelationship.

Appropriation and Expense Ledger

Exhibit 7–7 is a subsidiary or partial appropriation and expenditure ledger account. As defined, a *ledger* concerns a subject, and in this case, the subject is a specific account or fund, including information on encumbrances, expenditures, and essential voucher information. This report uses regularly and routinely collected voucher information. Managers find this report useful because it presents running totals that show how

EXHIBIT 7–7 Milesville General Fund—Supplies Account Appropriation and Expenditure Ledger Account Starting July 1, 2010

DATE	EXPLANATION	ENCUMBRANCES			EXPENDITURES		APPROPRIATIONS	
		INCREASE	DECREASE	BALANCE	AMOUNT	TOTAL	AMOUNT	UNENCUMBERED BALANCE
July 1	Budget						$125,000	$125,000
July 10	Lab. Equip. —P.O. #104	$25,000		$25,000				$100,000
Oct. 15	Autos —P.O. #410	$10,000		$35,000				$90,000
Nov. 3	Lab Equip. —P.O. #104		$25,000	$10,000	$24,500	$24,500		$90,500

Source: Adapted from J. Richard Aronson and Eli Schwartz. *Management Policies in Local Government Finance.* Washington, DC: International City Management Association, 1975, pp. 267–268, 271–272. Used by permission.

much of their section of the budget they obligated, disbursed, and still have available to them for obligation. Sometimes during the operation of the current-year operating budget, managers or policy makers need to move money from one account or fund to another. This is only possible if a more elaborate ledger such as this exhibit exists. Managers find this ledger particularly useful as the end of the fiscal year nears.

Exhibit 7–7 tells a story. On July 1, 2010, the fiscal year began with $125,000 with the city council appropriating that money to the supplies account of the general fund. This meant that the manager had $125,000 available for obligation and spending. On July 10, 2010, someone ordered laboratory equipment that cost $25,000, thus reducing the amount the manager could obligate to a total of $100,000. If the manager wanted to find out who ordered the equipment, she could look up purchase order number 104, which constituted a voucher. On October 15, 2010, someone ordered an automobile or parts for automobiles costing $10,000. This increased the encumbered balance to $35,000 and reduced the unencumbered balance to $90,000. Also of interest to the manager is that the money for the previous purchase order was not disbursed in spite of the fact that some time passed. On November 3, 2010, the ordered laboratory equipment finally arrived and the accountants paid the bill. However, either the purchasing agent found that some of the merchandise was not delivered or the vendor gave a discount to the government because the actual expenditure was $24,500. The manager can ask about purchase order 104 and find out exactly what happened if the accounting unit kept proper records. The accountants reduced the total encumbrance by $25,000 to $10,000. The difference of $500 between the encumbrance and expenditure required a $500 upward adjustment in the unencumbered balance because that money was again available for obligation.

Statement of Expenditure and Encumbrance

Just as revenue estimating is important to a public manager and policy makers, expenditure estimating is also significant. In state and local government, agency leaders must take care to control the rate of encumbrances and spending because overspending is a serious problem. Higher management can fire the responsible party and or prosecutors can put the offending person in jail. Exhibit 7–8 identifies overspending and isolates expenditure forecasting errors for managers. If there are brackets or negative numbers in the 2010 unencumbered balance or close to fund balance, there is overspending. The manager can now look up the appropriation and expenditure ledger and find out exactly how and who overspent by examining the detailed ledgers and possibly related purchase orders.

The statement of expenditure and encumbrance also informs the manager on expenditure forecasting. Typically, if a manager significantly underspends, then budget examiners assume the manager cannot forecast well and examiners tend to cut that manager's requests more significantly in subsequent years. Therefore, most managers soon learn that they need to monitor their obligations and spending to come as close as possible to their appropriation. This statement permits examiners and managers to see where expenditure forecasting was accurate or not. Once management isolates forecasting problems, it should take steps to change the forecasting technique or otherwise improve the forecast in order to avoid difficult questions from examiners. Like

EXHIBIT 7-8 Milesville General Fund Statement of Expenditures and Encumbrances Compared with Authorizations, Fiscal Year Ending June 30, 2010

	PRIOR YEAR RESERVE FOR ENCUMBRANCES	EXPENDITURES CHARGEABLE TO PRIOR YEAR RESERVE FOR ENCUMBRANCES	CLOSE TO FUND BALANCE	2010 APPROPRIATIONS	2010 EXPENDITURES	2010 ENCUMBRANCES	2010 UNENCUMBERED BALANCE
General government	$1,500	$1,500	0	$45,000	$41,000	$2,000	$2,000
Public safety	750	750	0	100,000	98,000	500	1,500
Highways and streets	450	400	50	60,000	60,000	0	0
Sanitation	250	275	(25)	40,000	39,000	0	1,000
Health	150	140	10	20,000	18,000	1,300	700
Welfare	1,000	800	200	30,000	25,000	0	5,000
Culture-recreation	400	100	300	16,000	13,200	2,000	800
Education	500	235	265	14,000	12,600	1,200	200
Transfer of funds	0	0	0	100,000	100,000	0	0
TOTAL	$5,000	$4,200	$800	$425,000	406,800	$7,000	$11,200

Note: For the sake of brevity the activities and objects were omitted.
Source: Adapted from J. Richard Aronson and Eli Schwartz. Management Policies in Local Government Finance. Washington DC: International City Management Association, 1975, pp. 267–268, 271–272. Used by permission.

revenue forecasting, the most serious problems outside overspending are when the numbers are quite large and secondarily when the percentage error is large.

Exhibit 7–8 is an elaborate summary statement of appropriations and expenditures. It is done for each separate fund and compares the appropriations with expenditures and encumbrances involving a two-year period. This statement assumes that the accounts close the fund balance at the end of two years, but often state law requires the closing of fund balances to be done at the end of the current year. A two-year closing provides sufficient time to pay obligations from the previous year. The reader should notice that the $800 "close to fund balance" and other information appear in the next exhibit, and the terms "expenditure," "encumbrances," and "unencumbered balance" appear in the previous exhibit. That fact shows the critical interconnectedness of the accounting reports. The reader should also understand that an accountant could further subdivide the information into activities and objects.

Exhibit 7–8 does help identify expenditure forecasting errors, but a serious problem exists in this example, which a reader cannot easily see. Out of $425,000 appropriated, there was left unobligated only $11,200, or about 2 percent of the total. However, most of the money was in the welfare category, and the expenditure forecast error in that category was 16 percent and certainly merits careful investigation. This error, coupled with a zero encumbrance, would raise a question for a budget analyst.

Another concern for public managers is the problem of spending recklessly at the end of the fiscal year in order to avoid criticism about leftover end of the fiscal year money. This exhibit can help managers identify such problems. Managers must examine the encumbrance column and the prior year reserve for encumbrances column. The low 2010 encumbrances total is a pleasing sign that the last-of-the-year obligation was low and the proper pacing of obligations probably took place. However, if a manager wanted to be very sure, she could examine the various appropriation and expenditure ledgers. The prior year's encumbrance total was even lower, so the manager might watch for possible laxness developing in this area, but certainly there is no cause for alarm. Large close to fund balances indicate sloppy purchasing practices, which may be due to lower-level managers making hasty end of the year obligations. Managers might be wise to check appropriation and expense ledgers near the end of the fiscal year to confirm if a problem exists and that all the last minute purchases were necessary. An examination of increases in inventory would also be wise.

An analysis of the closing entries is particularly interesting. The sanitation function had negative closing entries; more money was spent than encumbered. This is a matter of serious note as it may mean the operating budget controls were not working correctly. Other interesting occurrences were the $300 and $265 amounts in two categories. They represent 75 percent of one category and 48 percent of the other. However, even though both percentages were high, the amounts are low and that is important. Possibly, managers should further investigate it, but such an investigation is not recommended strongly. The total percentage of encumbrances to the closing entries is high at 16 percent, but the amount is low, so nothing extremely serious appears to be wrong beyond the anti-deficiency error.

To reiterate, managers need to read accounting reports holistically. By looking at the statement of expenditures and encumbrances plus the statement of revenue, a discerning reader can see if the government policy makers passed a balanced budget. In a balanced budget, the estimated revenues would equal the appropriations. In this example, the estimated revenue equals $440,000, but the appropriations equals $425,000. In other words, the city council did not pass a balanced budget because there was a $15,000 surplus.

Fund Balance Change

Managers can examine the fund balance change and get a general idea of the adequacy of revenue and expenditure forecasting and the impact of that forecasting on the financial situation of the government. The fund balance change also helps management see any unusual buildup in inventory, increases in reserves for encumbrances from the current and past year, and any unusual unspent money from the prior year. Exhibit 7–9 forces attention on available assets and the fundamental changes that occurred during a fiscal year. Accountants do a fund balances change report for each separate fund and highlight the key additions and subtractions associated with the fund change during the year. The excess of revenue over expenditure reflects weak revenue and expenditure forecasting but also a decision to have an unbalanced budget. To confirm exactly what the problem is, a manager would examine the expenditures and encumbrances ledger as well as the statement of revenue, as explained previously. The changes in fund balance deducts past-year reserves for encumbrances after deducting from it the expenditures charged to past-year funds. If any of these amounts are large, the manager should investigate as large numbers could easily mean poor accounts payable management. A large reserve for encumbrances or in-

EXHIBIT 7–9   Milesville General Fund Analysis of Changes in Fund Balance, Fiscal Year Ended June 30, 2010

Fund balance, July 1, 2009		$84,500
Add:		
Excess of revenues over expenditures, 2010		
Revenues	$480,000	
Expenditures	406,800	
		73,200
Reserve for encumbrances, June 30, 2009	$ 5,000	
Less: Expenditures charged to prior-year reserve for encumbrances	4,200	
		800
Deduct:		
Reserve for encumbrances, June 30, 2010	7,000	
Increase in reserve inventory and supplies	2,000	
		9,000
Fund balance, June 30, 2010		$149,500

Source: Adapted from J. Richard Aronson and Eli Schwartz. *Management Policies in Local Government Finance.* Washington, DC: International City Management Association, 1975, pp. 267–268, 271–272. Used by permission.

crease in reserve for inventory raises the question of excessive last of year spending. In addition, large increases in reserve for inventory might mean poor ordering practices, later possible spoilage problems, and even potentially fraud.

The fund balance change tells managers how much money they can spend without fear of overspending. It also explains the component parts of that figure. The revenue-less-expenditure figure tells us there is a 15 percent surplus, which is certainly unusual in most governments. The fund increases by $65,000, which constitutes a 77 percent yearly increase. Management and policy makers should raise questions about the size of this increase, as either policy makers could have cut taxes or increased expenditures rather than just building up idle cash. Certainly, the fund is in a healthy position to start the next fiscal year, unless policy makers anticipate an unusual expenditure increase well beyond what normal revenues would fund.

The figure of $73,200 is particularly important. It represents the sum of (1) the $40,000 revenue-forecasting errors, (2) the $11,200 plus $7,000 expenditure-forecasting errors, and (3) the $15,000 deliberate unbalanced budget. In this case, a manager can see the revenue forecasting error in Exhibit 7–6. Exhibit 7–8 shows the two elements of the expenditure-forecasting error. Reading Exhibit 7–6 with Exhibit 7–8 shows that the anticipated revenue was $440,000 but the appropriation was $425,000 or a deliberate unbalanced budget of $15,000 in surplus.

Balance Sheet

Typically, the most useful accounting report for managers is the balance sheet, and managers should examine it first because it provides an important financial overview of the government. Once a manager spots a possible problem, then the manager should look at other accounting reports and conduct other investigations to see if possible problems exist or not. Some important problems that a manager can begin to identify with the balance sheet are as follows:

- too much money in cash, indicating poor cash management;
- losses on cash management investments, indicating poor investments made in cash management;
- high amounts of property and other tax receivables, indicating possible mismanagement in the tax collection section;
- high allowances for uncollectible taxes, possibly indicating fraud in the tax collection section;
- high amounts due from other funds, possibly indicating fraud in the accounting section;
- high inventories and increases in inventory, possibly indicating fraud, waste, or abuse in inventory management;
- high accounts payable, possibly indicating poor accounts payable practices;
- high reserve for encumbrances, possibly indicating last minute purchases to use up end of the year money, and
- high increase in fund balance possibly indicating either poor forecasting or inappropriate decisions to use up idle cash.

Exhibit 7–10 is a simplified government balance sheet designed to highlight the previously mentioned problem areas. A government balance sheet is similar to a private

EXHIBIT 7–10 Milesville General Fund, Balance Sheet, Fiscal Year Ending June 30, 2010

ASSETS		2010		2009
Cash			$15,000	$8,000
Short-term investment—at cost (market value $123,000)			120,000	50,000
Property taxes receivable	$35,000			$45,000
Less: Allowances for uncollectible taxes	3,000	32,000		4,000	41,000
Due from other funds			1,500	2,200
Inventory of supplies			10,000	8,000
TOTAL ASSETS			$178,500	$109,200

LIABILITIES	2010	2009
Accounts payable	$10,000	$9,200
Payroll taxes payable	2,000	2,500
TOTAL LIABILITIES	12,000	11,700
RESERVES		
Reserve for encumbrances	7,000	5,000
Reserve for inventory of supplies	10,000	8,000
TOTAL RESERVES	17,000	13,000
FUND BALANCE	149,500	84,500
TOTAL LIABILITIES, RESERVES, AND FUND BALANCE	$178,500	$109,200

Source: Adapted from J. Richard Aronson and Eli Schwartz. *Management Policies in Local Government Finance.* Washington, DC: International City Management Association, 1975, pp. 267–268, 271–272. Used by permission.

business balance sheet, as government accountants base it on the simple accounting equation. Recall that assets are on the left side of the balance sheet. Assets include cash, short-term investments, property tax receivables, amounts due from other funds, and inventory. The right side of the balance sheet has liabilities, reserves, and fund balance. Liabilities include accounts payable and payroll taxes payable. Reserves include reserve for encumbrances and inventory of supplies. The accounting profession designed the balance sheet to emphasize available assets, especially quickly available assets. Accountants must prepare a balance sheet for each fund in each fiscal year, but they also prepare a consolidated balance sheet as explained earlier in this chapter.

The interesting features of the government balance sheet are the items not found in it. For example, with government funds, you do not see depreciation, profit, or stocks. Government funds do not yet include depreciation, but they are often found in other types of funds as explained earlier. Profit and stock simply do not make any sense given the public service orientation of government and not-for-profit corporations. Thus, fund balance replaces equity. In a private corporation, stock reflects the ownership value of the company, whereas in government, the people "own" the government and decide its policy though the political process. Governments can have a surplus, but, by definition, they cannot have "profit." If policy makers make the unusual decision to return money to the taxpayers, we call it a *rebate*. Rebates are rare because government programs should provide a service for tax money raised. Typically, if there might be a surplus in taxes or other revenues, government would rather increase service levels or lower taxes.

The balance sheet is informative, especially if the accountants present it in a format that shows more than one fiscal year. By examining Exhibit 7–10, one can see that the fund grew significantly during the year but with little growth in total liabilities. One can also quickly see that the government does not have a great deal of money in cash, and the financial manager invested the idle cash correctly in short-term investments. The investments cost the government $120,000, and the market value is $123,000. Thus, there is a small increase in the value of the investment, which is correct given the importance of investing in safe securities. The balance sheet should always use brackets in which to show the highest investment amount along with information of it being *cost* or *market value,* but the accountants should not show the highest amount in the table proper. The amount of property tax receivables and allowances for uncollectible taxes declined in this fiscal year. The inventory of supplies and its corresponding reserve did not grow radically, so unnecessary purchases probably did not take place. There was a significant increase in the fund balance, and management should investigate the reasons for this remarkable increase.

In a balance sheet, the "due from other funds" amount can be a significant item, warranting further management investigation. In this particular balance sheet (Exhibit 7–10), there is no apparent problem. But when there are many interfund transfers and the accountants have not yet transferred some money when they prepare the balance sheet, then it is possible that an abuse exists due to the hiding of the real condition of the various funds. Fraud, poor accounting, or deliberate attempts to present a better picture of financial conditions are some reasons for an abuse of transfers. Management should make an inquiry to be sure the accountants legally transferred the money and all the noted money in the accounts actually does exist instead of being lost in phantom transfers.

Computers and Accounting

This chapter discussed FMS earlier; but some additional discussion on computers, related specially to accounting, is needed here. Even small governments should computerize their accounting systems as accountants can do that on an inexpensive computer with off-the-shelf software. A fundamental ingredient of a computerized system is a codification of the accounting fields based on a state's uniform standardized chart of accounts. The use of the code does require correct coding of each accounting transaction, but an accountant—even in a small government—can make that chore easier by using an off-the-shelf data manager that uses a rational protocol. The standard code should include fields for the fund, account, object, program, and other codes as needed such as the unit responsible for managing the program or object.

The input to a computerized system should be the voucher. The data entry point varies, but often clerks responsible for the government bookkeeping perform this operation. Sometimes, they batch process the data, depending on the size of the operation. Accountants usually should consider an input edit as almost required to ensure (1) the clerks entered each transfer dually according to accepted accounting practices and each expenditure and encumbrance has the proper code, and (2) the clerks used no code number that is not on the chart of accounts. This edit catches only common mistakes and management should make sure an inspection process and an examination of accounting information exist to minimize the error factor.

As explained earlier in this chapter, integrated financial management systems, which tie together payroll, accounting, purchasing, and budgeting subsystems, use a chart of accounts and master tables as the linch pin in their computer design. The exact designs vary, but the final computer system needs to accumulate, organize, store, and make information available to all the subsystems when needed. The chart of accounts is the basic dictionary for characterizing transactions throughout the system. The standardized formats for transactions permit the system to track and monitor its own activities. The master tables permit the cross-referencing of data. The budgeting subsystem provides essential guidance to the accounting, payroll, and purchasing subsystems.

REVIEW QUESTIONS

1. Compare budget controls of apportionment, allotment, and administrative reservations with accounting concepts.
2. What are the common pitfalls one can anticipate in budget execution, and how can budget execution system design assist in minimizing these pitfalls? Compare and contrast budget and administrative controls.
3. Explain the fraud-red tape dilemma in terms of ethics.
4. Explain the importance of and how to achieve cash internal control and cash management. What are the guidelines for the various aspects of cash management?
5. Explain the fundamentals of not-for-profit accounting and contrast them to for-profit accounting. In what way does accounting support budgeting and management?

6. Review the basic accounting conventions (for example, modified accrual, accrual-based). Compare and contrast these accounting concepts.
7. Explain how one can go about making an analysis of a city's financial situation using each of the key financial reports discussed in this chapter.

REFERENCES

American Accounting Association. "Report of the Committee on Accounting for Not-for-Profit Organization." *Accounting Review,* Supplement to Vol. 46 (1971), 81–163.

APPLEBY, PAUL. "The Role of the Budget Division." *Public Administration Review,* 18, 3 (Summer 1957), 156–159.

ARONSON, J. RICHARD, and ELI SCHWARTZ (eds.). *Management Policies in Local Government Finance.* Washington, DC: International City Management Association, 1975.

BARTIZAL, JOHN R. *Budget Principle and Procedure.* Englewood Cliffs, NJ: Prentice Hall, 1942.

BATER, FRANCIS M. *The Question of Government Spending.* New York: Harper & Row, 1960.

BIERMAN, HAROLD, JR., and SEYMOUR SMIDT. *The Capital Budgeting Decision.* New York: Macmillan, 1966.

BLAND, ROBERT L., and BOBBY PRAYTOR. "Cash Management in Texas Cities." Paper presented to the American Society for Public Administration in Indianapolis, IN, March 24, 1985.

BLOCKER, JOHN GARY. *Budgeting in Relation to Distribution Cost Accounting.* Lawrence, KS: School of Business, 1937.

BUCK, ARTHUR EUGENE. *The Budget in Government of Today.* New York: Macmillan, 1934.

BURKHEAD, JESSE. *Government Budgeting.* New York: John Wiley, 1956.

COE, CHARLES K. "The Effects of Cash Management Assistance by States & Local Governments." *Public Budgeting and Finance,* 8, 2 (Summer 1988) 80–90.

COE, CHARLES K., and CURTIS ELLIS. "Internal Controls in State, Local and Non-Profit Agencies," 11, 3 (Fall 1991), 28–42.

CRECINE, JOHN P. *Government Problem Solving: A Computer Simulation of Municipal Budgeting.* Chicago: Rand McNally, 1969.

ERNEST, E. "The Accounting Preconditions of PPB(S)." *Management Account,* 53 (January 1972), 33–37.

FISHER, G. W. *Financing Local Improvement by Special Assessment.* Chicago: Municipal Finance Officers Association, 1974.

FREEMAN, ROBERT J., and EDWARD S. LYNN. *Fund Accounting.* 2nd ed. Englewood Cliffs, NJ: Prentice Hall, 1983.

HENRY, M. L. et al. "New York State's Performance Budget Experiment." *Public Administration Review* 20, 2 (Spring 1960), 69–74.

JONES, W. W. "Computerized General Ledger and Budgeting Accounting Systems." *Government Finance,* 5, 2 (May 1976), 27–32.

MOAK, LENNOX L., and KATHRYN W. KILLIAN. *Operating Budget Manual.* Chicago: Municipal Finance Officers Association, 1963.

National Committee on Government Accounting. *Government Accounting, Auditing, and Financial Reporting.* Chicago: Municipal Finance Officers Association, 1968.

NELSON, RAY D., and GARY C. CORNIA. "Monitoring Single-Source Revenue Funds throughout the Budgeting Process." *Public Budgeting and Finance,* 17, 2 (Summer 1997), 37–57.

RONDINELLI, DENNIS A. "Revenue Sharing and American Cities: Analysis of the Federal Experiment in Local Assistance." *Journal of the American Institute of Planners,* 41, 5 (September 1975), 319–333.

ROSE, PETER. "Financial Reporting." In Fred Thompson and Mark T. Green (eds.), *Handbook of Public Finance.* New York: Marcel Dekker, Inc., 1998.

STEIN, A. W. *Local Government Finance.* Lexington, MA: Lexington Books, 1975.

———. "Symposium: Performance Budgeting: Has the Theory Worked?" *Public Administration Review* 20, 2 (Spring).

THAI, KHI V. "Government Accounting." In Jack Rabin and Thomas D. Lynch (eds.), *Handbook on Public Budgeting and Financial Management.* New York: Marcel Dekker, 1983.

————. "Government Financial Reporting and Auditing." In Jack Rabin and Thomas D. Lynch (eds.), *Handbook on Public Budgeting and Financial Management*. New York: Marcel Dekker, 1983.

THIERANF, R. J., and RICHARD A. GROSSE. *Decision-Making Through Operations Research*. New York: John Wiley, 1970.

TIGUE, P., M. CORRINE LARSON, and PAUL ZORN. "GFOA/MBIA 1997 Survey on Revenue Collection in State and Local Governments." *Government Finance Review* 13, 4 (August 1997) 13–15.

TURNBULL, AUGUSTUS. *Government Budgeting and PPBS: A Programmed Introduction*. Reading, MA: Addison-Wesley, 1970.

Urban Academy. *An Introduction to IFMS*. New York: New York City Urban Academy, December 1976.

U.S. Civil Service Commission, Bureau of Training, The Management Science Training Center. *Budget Formulation*. Washington, DC: Civil Service Commission, Bureau of Training, 1976.

U.S. Joint Financial Management Improvement Program. *Money Management*. Washington, DC: U.S. Joint Financial Management Improvement Program, 1976.

————. *Operating Budgets*. Washington, DC: U.S. Joint Financial Management Improvement Program, November 1975.

8

CAPITAL BUDGETING AND DEBT ADMINISTRATION

This chapter discusses state and local debt, capital budgeting, and issuing government debt for state and local government in the American context. In addition, this chapter defines the concept of debt and explains the classifications commonly used in the marketplace. This chapter contrasts capital budgeting with operating budgeting by emphasizing capital facility planning and the capital budget cycle. This chapter also explains the practical aspects of state and local bonding, including designing an issue, the prospectus, notice of sale, debt records, reporting, and bond ratings. The chapter introduces capital budgeting and debt administration by emphasizing the specific knowledge particularly useful to a person dealing with these challenging subjects. At the completion of this chapter, the reader should understand the following:

- the commonly used definition of debt;
- why governments incur debt;
- alternatives to debt;
- types and forms of debt;
- revenue bonds;
- creative capital financing and its origin;
- nontraditional capital financing;
- commonly used tests and limits on debt;
- early warning guidelines for municipal financial operations;
- significance of the New York City, Orange County, and Washington State Public Power Supply System financial crises on debt administration;
- municipal bankruptcy, financial problems, and remedies;
- the difference between capital and operating budgets;
- capital facility planning and its significance;
- the essential decisions and expertise critical in designing a municipal bond issue;
- what is and should be in a bond prospectus and notice of sale;
- investment syndicates and their significance;
- the importance of good bond administration and data associated with debt reporting; and
- bond ratings, what influences them, and why the market finds them significant.

STATE AND LOCAL DEBT

Definitions

When persons charge items on Master Card or Visa, they incur *debt*. They receive the items and pledge that they will pay for these items within a certain time period. When they get a bank loan for a car, they incur debt. They agree to pay back the loan amount (called *principal*) plus an extra amount (called *interest*) for the privilege of borrowing the money over an extended period of time.

Governments also borrow money; thus, they incur short- and sometimes long-term obligations to pay back the principal and interest. However, some types of debt (for example, trade accounts payable and conditional repayment loans) sometimes do not involve interest payments. Debt constitutes an obligation that the government must pay under the established legal conditions. The Bureau of Census uses the following definition, which stresses interest-bearing obligation:

> All long-term credit obligations of the government and its agencies, and all interest bearing short-term (that is, repayable within one year) credit obligations. Includes judgments, mortgages, and "revenue" bonds, as well as general obligation bonds, notes, and interest bearing warrants. Excludes noninterest bearing obligations, amounts owed in a trust or agency capacity, advances and contingent loans from other governments, and rights of individuals to benefit from employee-retirement funds. (U.S. Census Bureau, 2001)

Governments incur debt for several reasons. In some cases, they need cash before they collect their revenue. They use debt to harmonize the divergent patterns of current expenditures and revenues. Often, governments wish to finance a significant capital construction project or even large equipment purchases. They cannot pay current revenues for such large purchases so they negotiate a loan. Sometimes they incur a debt in order to refinance an existing (for example, *short-term*) debt. On occasion, they incur a debt to finance operating deficits. A form of debt that often the general public does not recognize as such is a government's *pension benefit obligation*. Government rarely sells bonds for this purpose, but pensions are an increasingly significant government obligation that can place severe financial pressure on governments.

Governments do not have to incur debts, but the alternatives to debt are difficult to use effectively. The *sinking fund* is an alternative that accumulates funds over time, much like an individual's Christmas savings plan. Government invests the funds until such time as it needs the money. Another alternative is to *pay-as-you-go,* meaning the government pays for the equipment or building costs out of operating expenses. The difficulty with both alternatives is that capital facility needs of governments often do not fit the pace of financing of the funding techniques. Sometimes, a city that needs to build a water purification plant cannot wait the ten or twenty years required for a sinking fund or pay-as-you-go financing approach. Emergencies and irregular expenditure demands occur, and debt is sometimes the only practical alternative under the circumstances, especially where government experiences accelerated urban growth.

New borrowings by consumers and private businesses far exceed government debt, but in the 1980s the governmental share of the nation's total debt load rose remarkably to nearly 36 percent. In the previous decade it was 30 percent. By 2000, it was 37 percent. In one decade, all outstanding debt rose to nearly $11 trillion from the previous $4 trillion level. By 1991, the debt equaled about $43,000 per person in the United States and exceeded the nation's gross national product by 1.9 times. By the year 2000, total debt stood at $17 trillion. The total federal government debt stood at nearly $6 trillion in 2000. Driving this debt load was the large annual federal deficit of the 1980s, but by the late 1990s government policies halted that trend. Surprisingly, the annual deficit was temporarily but effectively eliminated in FY 1998 because of burgeoning revenues from a booming economy and improved financial management and oversight. In the aftermath of the 9/11 terrorist attacks on the United States, deficits are once again accumulating as the economy slows and military and emergency preparedness costs escalate as part of a beefed-up antiterrorist campaign by the United States. Deficit numbers for FY 2001 were $18.5 trillion with no end in sight given the continuing threat to national security.

Classifications of Debt

Most of the liability items in the state and local government balance sheet are debts of the government. They include bonds, certificates of indebtedness, mortgages, notes, accounts payable, warrants payable, liens, judgments, unfunded pension obligations, and selected contingent liabilities. Excluded are contingent items and reserves for encumbrances.

The largest amount of debt is in the form of bonds. They are a written promise to pay a specified sum of money (called the *face value* or *principal amount*) at a specified date or dates (called the *maturity dates*) together with periodic interest at a specific rate. Financial managers design *serial bonds,* which are the most common type of bond, so that the borrower retires a specific number of bonds each year. Financial managers also design *term bonds,* which the securities industry infrequently uses, to pay interest over time but pay the principal often at the end of the loan period. Borrowers use *sinking funds* to collect the necessary large principal payment by the end of the loan period. Before 1983, borrowers had bonds that had detachable coupons representing the interest payments to the bearer. Upon presentation of the matured coupon to the bond maker's paying agent, the borrower paid the proper interest represented on the coupon. Now, borrowers must register all bonds on the books of the issuing government or paying agent in order to provide protection to the bondholder.

The other forms of debt are typically not as significant unless they happen to involve large obligations. *Certificates of indebtedness* vary from state to state, but the securities industry uses them frequently in connection with agency resources or assets. *Mortgage bonds* use property to secure the obligation without transferring the title, but most of them still do not give the government's creditor the right to foreclose. Financial managers widely use notes to represent evidence of financial obligation, usually of a short-term nature. *Accounts payable* is a debt that includes such government liabilities as *wages earned but not yet paid* as well as the common unpaid bills. The now uncommon *warrant* is a government-issued document to the bank upon which the bank makes payment with the approval of the government. A *lien* is a claim upon property arising from failure of the owner to make timely payment of a claim. A *judgment* is a court decision that the government has a liability or debt to a person who has sought redress through the courts. Government incurs an *unfunded pension liability* when it does not set aside sufficient funds in an appropriate pension reserve fund to pay the liability of its employees' pensions. Government incurs a *contingent liability* when it agrees to take on the liability (for example, a student loan) of a third party (for example, a student) if that student defaults on the loan. Typically, government uses contingent liabilities as a matter of public policy to lower the third party's interest rate because the bank knows that the government will pay the loan, thus, that lowers radically the nonpayment risk factor.

The financial community sometimes uses the *pledge of security* to classify debts. One type is the *full-faith-and-credit* debt in which a government uses its unconditional pledge, which includes its implied power of taxation, to assure that it will pay its debt. For example, a city or state pledges that it will unconditionally pay a bond obligation, including raising taxes if necessary to meet the obligation. Another type is a debt in which the issuer or a guaranteeing government has a moral but not a legal obligation to pay. A *moral debt* is rarely of interest to the financial community unless the government takes a serious responsibility for that debt by pledging something that assures that the government will pay its debt to the investor. What commonly occurs is some government body (for example, a housing authority) pledges its user charges or some other revenue source to pay the debt, and another unit of government (for example, the state) gives its moral backing to the debt. The financial community typically requires the government to spell out a default remedy. The best pledge from the investor's point of view is a full-faith-and-credit obligation plus a specific user charge to pay the indebtedness.

Merl M. Hackbart and James Leigland (1990) devised a useful approach for understanding debt that is still relevant for use in twenty-first-century public finance. They classified long-term, tax-exempt state government debt obligations into the following four categories:

- *General obligation (GO) debt.* Government backs this debt with an unconditional pledge of any and all the government's revenue sources including its taxing power for the purposes of debt repayment.
- *Revenue debt.* This is a nonguaranteed debt, but the government dedicates one or more specific, pledged revenue sources (for example, user fees, special assessments, limited taxes) to pay the debt.
- *Special authority debt.* Government (usually a special purpose governmental unit such as a public authority, special district, board, bond bank, or corporation) issues this type of debt. The financial community does not consider it a direct obligation of the state. Specific pledged revenues of the state or governmental unit often back such debt. State governments sometimes secondarily back the local obligations.
- *Lease-backed "debt."* Financial advisors structure this debt-like instrument like a revenue bond issue using "certificates of participation" or "lease revenue bonds" secured by lease payment agreements. Although similar to revenue bonds, the financial community makes the distinction because some states do not recognize lease-backed obligations as state debt.

Like Hackbart and Leigland, M. G. Valente (1986) identified the following three broad categories of capital financing options:

- **traditional,** including current revenue, general obligation bonds, revenue bonds, special assessments, and tax increment financing;

- **public-private,** including tax exempt lease purchases, sales lease-back, exaction, and privatization; and
- **creative** bonds, including deep discount/zero coupon bonds, variable rate bonds, put option bonds, bonds with warrants, minibonds, and mininotes.

Short-Term Debt

Governments typically use short-term borrowing for the following reasons:

- The community is short of the necessary revenue to pay for services. For example, the city forecasted the revenue incorrectly, and there is not enough money to pay for planned expenditures.
- The government needs a brief loan and agrees to pay the principal back with interest as soon as it collects the taxes. Possibly the government tied its assets up in securities, but nevertheless it must pay its obligations to its employees or someone else. The government can negotiate to receive a brief loan to *bridge* (thus, it is sometimes called a *bridge loan*) this cash flow problem until it collects its money.
- The community has an emergency, and necessary funds are not available.
- The government has need for funds to start a capital improvement project, but it has not yet completed a long-term bond issue.

At one time, short-term debt vocabulary included only *tax anticipation notes* (TANs), *revenue anticipation notes* (RANs), and *bond anticipation notes* (BANs). Under Internal Revenue Service (IRS) arbitrage regulations, local governments can invest in short-term securities, yielding significant revenue, but IRS rules limit this practice significantly. Thus, there is a fifth reason for short-term borrowing: to raise revenue, as the government can borrow at a lower rate than it can earn in the security market. In addition, there are new forms of short-term borrowing, including *tax and revenue anticipation notes* (TRANs), *grant anticipation notes* (GANs), and *tax-exempt commercial paper* (TECP), which this chapter explains later. Given that they have very tight budgets and that they collect revenue primarily in the third and fourth months of a fiscal year, most large and many medium-size governments appreciate the advantages of short-term borrowing.

However, IRS arbitrage rules severely limit the revenue earning possibilities for local government. Because instruments such as TANs can actually be a money source—an added bonus—local government financial managers can distort the larger purposes of short-term borrowing and even indirectly reduce the income of the federal government. To prevent this absurdity, IRS wrote its arbitrage rules. Certainly the popularity of BANs plus their remarkably high long-term interest rates give local government finance officers huge moneymaking potential from arbitrage investments. To stop local government abuse of arbitrage, federal tax legislation in the mid-1980s changed the IRS law curtailing much of the money earning potential of short-term debt for state and local governments. Although there have been minor adjustments to the tax code relevant to state and local debt since the 1980s, this fundamental change in the treatment of debt has dramatically affected the investment decisions of local finance officers. Regardless of the government's motivation for short-term borrowing, it should carefully review IRS arbitrage rules and then properly manage its debt to maximize the benefits to the local government.

Early Developments in the Debt Concept

Starting with revenue bonds, the financial market experienced significant innovations and changes in the use of debt. The most well-known innovative debt concept is the revenue bond. In 1897 the Spokane, Washington, Water Works used revenue bonds first. However, this debt mechanism, coupled with a means to raise revenue, was not popular until after World War II. Then court decisions held that authorities (for example, the Port of New York and New Jersey and Triborough Bridge Authority) had separate legal status. People in government sought new ways to finance public facilities without increasing taxes, and revenue bonds provided an answer. Briefly, the reasons for the increased use of revenue bonds are as follows:

- Although at first revenue bonds had a higher interest cost than general obligations bonds, their cost decreased significantly, as the financial community became familiar with their use.
- There was more use of public authorities and an expansion of types of authorities (for example, airports, public parks, recreation areas and facilities, stadium and public sport facilities, power projects, housing, public markets, college dormitories, port facilities, and so on).
- Restrictions on general obligations closed that mechanism, forcing the greater use of revenue bonds.
- Governments found that obtaining revenue bond approval, especially because of the nonreferendum requirement, was relatively easy.
- Government found the public acceptable to applying user charges to pay for debt services.

A lesser used version of the revenue bond is the *lease rental bond*. Let us say a school district cannot get voter approval for a bond issue. One mechanism used is to create a nonprofit authority to build and then lease the new school to the school district. A long-term school board lease with the authority provides the authority with the necessary security to assure revenue bondholders that the money from the government's lease will pay the authority's debt service. For example, in 2001 this mechanism was used by the Greenville County School District in the State of South Carolina when it faced stiff taxpayer resistance to raising revenues to support an aging infrastructure. The school board authorized the creation of a nonprofit entity that floated bonds to pay for a major construction and rehabilitation project across the school district. Thus, the authority's revenue bond finances the building of the school and the school district gets its wanted school because of this unique financing arrangement. Because the authority is merely a financing mechanism, some financial groups treat these financial arrangements as general obligation bonds.

In order to attract private industry to a city, region, or state, state and local governments started issuing *industrial aid revenue bonds* (IDBs). The concept was simple: government paid less for interest so it would issue a bond and a new industry would pay the bond interest and use the proceeds to build a new factory that created more jobs for the economic area. Although it was a useful tool for state and local government to attract industry, the issuance of those bonds lowered federal income tax receipts because the interest on the bonds was tax exempt. The Tax Reform Act of

1986 essentially halted most of the use of that type of bond. Today, statewide caps exist on IDBs and the federal government ended the tax-exempt privilege in December 1989. However, many states now utilize the mechanism of Tax Increment Financing (TIFs) as an alternative to fund many of these same industrial and commercial projects. See the discussion of TIFs in Chapter 7.

An interesting cousin of the revenue bond is the *special obligation bond.* An issuer ties the revenue bond to the revenue-generating capacity of a government's ability to produce a service, as well as to the demand for that service. A special obligation bond ties government's revenue-generating capacity to a specific government revenue source that can be entirely outside the control of the local government and may have no logical relationship to the reason for the bond. For example, a local government can pledge its general revenue-sharing receipts from the federal government as the dedicated revenue source for a special obligation bond that the local government uses to build libraries, schools, roads, or piers.

Capital Financing in the 1980s

The early 1980s saw a remarkable change in the tax-exempt securities market. On the one hand, the need for state and local spending on public facilities became very significant (that is, $3 trillion). On the other hand, the supply of long-term investment capital decreased. This was in a period in which President Reagan's Republican administration successfully reduced federal domestic programs, many state and local areas experienced tax revolts that limited their government revenue, and the national economy experienced the worst recession since the Great Depression. This left state and local governments with debt as the only alternative in a very unstable credit market in which traditional debt instruments were inadequate.

Both the recession and legal changes instituted by the Reagan administration affected the municipal bond market. As a counter to high inflation rates prior to the recession, the Federal Reserve System imposed extremely restrictive monetary policies. That, combined with the Republican administration's massive yearly deficits, produced record high interest rates, which came down slowly when economic recovery started. Changes that the congress enacted in the Economic Recovery Tax Act of 1981 (ERTA) contributed to the higher interest rates. The act reduced the incentive for persons in higher tax brackets to use the municipal bond tax shelter and expanded other income-sheltering opportunities (for example, Individual Retirement Accounts and All Savers Certificates). In addition, ERTA permitted firms to sell tax benefits to the highest bidders, which created billions of dollars of alternative tax shelter investment opportunities and significantly lowered corporate income tax revenues. Further, the Investment Tax Credit (ITC) and Accelerated Cost Recovery Schedules (ACRS) enhanced the after-tax rate of return on private investment, thus lessening the need for tax shelters because less income was taxable. The 1982 Federal Tax Act (TEFRA) further changed the municipal security market by the partial removal of the deductibility of bank interest costs used to finance tax-exempt securities and the requirement that investors must register all of their new municipal bonds. The latter change was extremely significant, as coupon bonds were very popular among investors.

The biggest influence on the market, however, was the poor economy. This created lower business and individual profits, which had less need for municipal bonds as tax shelters. Given those environmental factors, the character of the municipal bond market changed radically. Demand for tax-exempt bonds by the two major institutional investors, namely commercial banks and casualty insurance companies, practically evaporated after 1979. The tax-exempt market reacted by stressing and more aggressively marketing bonds to individual investors. The percentage of bonds held by individual and mutual funds in the tax-exempt market shot up in 1981 and 1982. This was particularly true for short-term tax-exempt paper, which appealed to the money market mutual funds. During 1981, tax-exempt money market holdings grew by $3 billion, which represented an increase of approximately three-fourths. By the end of 1982, there were $13.2 billion in aggregate holdings.

The preceding factors, plus the extensive use of private-purpose tax-exempt borrowing, narrowed the gap between the tax-exempt and taxable markets, with the notable exception of the short-term market. Historically, tax-exempt interest rates ran from 65 to 70 percent less than comparable taxable bond yields. In 1981 and 1982, the spread shifted to 80 to 85 percent. This meant that the arbitrage advantage did not result automatically in lower bond interest charges for local and state governments. The cost of borrowing for long-term issues was about the same for government as the private sector. This radical change was partially the result of industrial revenue bonds that induced their extensive and scattered defaults (for example, Washington Public Power Supply System) and shook investor confidence in revenue bonds. The result was higher tax-exempt borrowing rates.

The Tax Reform Act of 1986 brought significant changes to municipal debt of which the most notable was the diminishing of total dollar volume of new issues from over $220 billion in 1985 to about $100 billion in 1987. Most of the decline was in nongovernmental or private activity bonds due to the legal constraints of the Tax Reform Act. But even in governmental purpose bonds, the government policy changes lowered borrowing to pre-1985 rush levels to avoid the 1986 legal changes and the stronger arbitrage earning limitations of the 1986 law that sapped demand. For those governments that did borrow after 1986, they found lower interest rates with a spread of a little over 80 percent from taxable securities. John Peterson's (1988) work offers a still timely summary of the impact of the 1986 act as follows:

- Government could finance fewer projects on a tax-exempt basis because of the restraints placed on borrowing, especially involving nongovernmental entities.
- The legal changes meant that the municipal market became fragmented and complicated by the varying tax treatments for different classes of bonds.
- Fewer opportunities then existed to earn arbitrage income by investing bond proceeds.
- Currently, there were more burdensome procedures that surrounded the issuance process.
- There was stiffer competition among underwriters and thus lower profits and fewer firms existed because there were fewer deals and constraints on flotation costs.
- The low ebb of institutional investor demand meant that the individual investor became supreme in the tax-exempt market.
- Little likelihood existed that there would be a relaxation of federal restrictions and a return to rapid tax-exempt market growth.

The Tax Reform Act of 1986 created a new security called the *taxable munici-pal bond* with the likely buyers being households influenced by the federal alterna-tive minimum income tax. Unfortunately, market buyers linked 42 percent of the early issues indirectly to the junk bond crisis associated with the then-famous secu-rities fraud of Mr. Ivan Boesky. Despite the early problems, a weak market came into existence for this new security. However, interest rates were significantly higher and even higher than corporate bonds with comparable pledges.

The Tax Reform Act of 1986 also brought other significant changes to munici-pal debt. Congress severely limited the use of tax-exempt bonds to finance "essential" or "public purpose" projects as defined in the legislation. Thus, "private purpose" projects and programs (such as loans to farms and small businesses) had to turn to the new taxable municipal bonds for funding. John E. Peterson estimated that the new market was 15 percent or higher than the dollar value of municipal securities. With the post-1986 federal caps (that is, limits) on industrial development bonds, the per-centage was sometimes higher. The likely buyers of these new taxable municipal bonds were households that the federal alternative minimum income tax influenced.

After strong initial interest in these new securities, issuers and investors balked. Investors felt the new and sometimes gimmicky nature of the early issues increased general investor concern about the subsequent demand for the taxable municipal bonds. Despite these early problems, market analysts expected the market to grow. For example, foreign investors, especially the Japanese at the time, became evident as they sought investment diversification of their holdings when their own markets became less desirable. This new set of important investors from abroad added the problem of currency exchange to the already complex municipal securities market decisions.

There is a new world for the finance officer. At the beginning of the last cen-tury, the municipal bond market was staid, straightforward, and conservative. Most financing was general obligation (GO) debt, with a gradually increasing use of rev-enue issues backed by either a user fee or a dedicated tax source. In 1960, total long-term financing was approximately $7.5 billion, of which 70 percent was general obligation. By 1975 non-GO debt accounted for 50 percent of the total new issues; and by 1981 it accounted for 70 percent, a complete reversal of the 1960 situation. During recession periods, GO debt financed only the most popular subjects (for ex-ample, building of jails) because they alone would get voter referendum approval. In November 1991, the electorate defeated more than half of the bond referendums. By 1999, non-GO debt comprised 64 percent of new issues.

One type of creative capital financing that governments have continued to use since the 1980s is the *zero coupon bonds* (ZCBs). During the Reagan administration, the Congress significantly changed the federal tax law twice. The first change prompted creative and often complex local government bonding methods. The second change essentially stopped the use of most of those same creative capital-financing methods. ZCBs are bonds without current interest coupons that governments offer at substantial discounts from par value and provide return to investors through accretion in value at maturity. Thus, for example, governments sell them for $602 when issued and investors redeem them in five years for $1,000. This approach has potential ap-peal to investors earning between $50,000 and $100,000 as they are often looking for retirement or college education financing. A package of ZCBs could provide these investors with the equivalent of a tax-free annuity stream that they would find favorably compared with taxable alternatives. Exhibit 8–1 provides an example.

EXHIBIT 8–1   Tax-Exempt ZC "Annuity" Bonds

MATURITY (IN YEARS)	AMOUNT AT MATURITY	PRICE TODAY FOR ANNUITY PAYMENT	EFFECTIVE YIELD
1	$ 1,000	$ 915.73	9.00%
2	1,000	830.58	9.50
3	1,000	746.22	10.00
4	1,000	671.70	10.20
5	1,000	602.34	10.40
6	1,000	538.10	10.60
7	1,000	478.89	10.80
8	1,000	424.58	11.00
9	1,000	375.02	11.20
10	1,000	329.99	11.40
11	1,000	289.28	11.60
12	1,000	252.64	11.80
13	1,000	219.81	12.00
14	1,000	189.28	12.25
15	1,000	164.54	12.40
16	1,000	143.71	12.50
17	1,000	125.28	12.60
18	1,000	109.01	12.70
19	1,000	95.52	12.75
20	1,000	83.62	12.80
	$20,000	$7,585.84	11.76%

EQUIVALENT TAXABLE RETURNS:

50% Tax Rate	$40,000	$7,585.84	26.11%
30% Tax Rate	28,710	7,585.84	18.16%

Source: Ronald Forbes and Edward Renshaw. "Tax-Exempt Zero Coupon Bonds." In John E. Peterson and Wesley P. Hough (eds.), *Creative Capital Financing.* Chicago: Municipal Finance Officers Association, 1982, p. 153. Used by permission.

NONTRADITIONAL

The nontraditional ways to package bond issues more attractively include external credit supports, tax-exempt commercial paper, put option securities, original issue discount bonds including ZCBs, variable rate securities, and leasing. These are means to attract new or retain old investors in the tax-exempt market. With these instruments, a negotiated sale may become superior to a competitive sale owing to the complexity of this type of sale. Regardless, technical advice is important to obtain in meeting the following purposes:

- targeting the investment vehicle toward a specific group of investors (those who have money and have a preference that they can satisfy);
- designing the instrument features, such as where to place the *put option,* what *index* to employ in a variable rate, and how to construct a *lease-purchase;*
- formalizing agreements (this chapter will explain them later);
- timing the transaction; and
- considering objectively the alternative approaches.

The forms of external credit support include a bank line of credit, municipal bond insurance, state credit assistance, and federal guarantees. A line of credit is a contingent loan arrangement with a bank in which the bank agrees to lend funds required by the government for a fixed time period. The *letter of credit* (LOC) is an unconditional pledge of the bank's credit to make principal and interest payments of a specific amount and terms on an issuer's debt. Both provide a guarantee that the backup arrangement will meet the bond issuer's future liquidity requirements. Typically, borrowers use them for smaller amounts with the size and type of issue generally unrestricted; banks usually charge an annual fee for the LOC plus normal interest charges on the principal. Especially related to LOC for American local governments starting in the mid-1980s is the increased use of Japanese and European banks instead of American banks. For example, Shelby County, Tennessee, negotiated successfully with Sanwa Bank (a Japanese bank), resulting in Shelby County annually saving $1 million on loan costs. The bond insurance premium is a one-time, up-front fee.

The LOC can lower interest cost because the LOC substitutes the creditworthiness of the bank. Also, LOC may be necessary in connection with other creative capital financing devices (for example, put options). A major private insurance group such as the Municipal Bond Insurance Association (MBIA) or the American Municipal Bond Assurance Corporation (AMBAC) can also assume the default risk of a government for a specific fee. Exhibit 8–2 presents selected features of three major private bond guarantee programs available to state and local governments.

Purchasing bond insurance should lower interest rates below the rate that a government could obtain without insurance. Thus, bond insurance makes economic sense when the local government's bond rating is low. That calculation, using a present value method, must exceed the premium cost. Typically, the insurance premium accounts for 20 to 30 basis points (100 basis points equals 1 percent in interest). Issuers can have cost savings as high as 40 to 95 basis points for new bond issues. States

EXHIBIT 8–2   Selected Features: Private Municipal Bond Guarantees

FEATURES THAT ISSUES MUST POSSESS TO BE ELIGIBLE FOR GUARANTEES

PROGRAM	TYPE OF ISSUE*	SIZE OF ISSUE (IN MILLIONS)	QUALITY LIMITATIONS	COST OF GUARANTEE (PD. AT TIME OF ISSUE)
AMBAC	GO's & Rev. Bd. of existing facilities	$0.6–$22.0 (tot. prin. & int.)	S&P BBB or better	½%–1½% of original principal *and* interest
Indemnity Corp.	GO's & Rev.'s	$0.6–$22.0 (tot. prin. & int.)	none	½%–3½% of original principal *and* interest
MBIA Rev. Bds.	GO's & Utility	$0.6–$22.0 (prin. only)	Generally, S&P BBB or better	1%–2% of original principal only

*With the exception of Indemnity Corp., all guarantees are for *new* bond issues. (Indemnity Corp. will also guarantee portfolios of outstanding bonds.)

Source: Michael O. Joehnk and David S. Kidwell. "Determining the Advantages and Disadvantages of Private Municipal Bond Guarantees." In John E. Peterson and Wesley C. Hough (eds.), *Creative Capital Financing.* Chicago: Municipal Finance Officers Association, 1983, p. 214. Used by permission.

can provide municipal credit assistance by guaranteeing local debt issues, much as a private insurance company would do. States can act as a financial intermediate via a state municipal bond bank and provide grants to subsidize local debt service requirements. Each activity can lower subjurisdiction interest and, possibly, administrative costs. The last external source of support is the federal government, which routinely provides guarantees in the areas of housing and urban renewal.

In 1971, insurance came into the municipal market and it has grown in use since then. Insured municipal bonds were about 30 percent of the $41.1 billion of long-term tax-exempt issues sold in the first four months of 1991. The percentage of insured municipal bonds broke the 50 percent level in 1997. They tend to boost bond ratings and thus lower interest rates for insuring municipal governments. The major municipal bond insurers in order are Municipal Bond Investors Assurance Indemnity Corporation (MBIA), American Municipal Bond Assurance Company (AMBAC), Financial Guaranty Insurance Company (FGIC), Bond Investors Guaranty (BIG), and Capital Guaranty Insurance Company. Each firm rates most major issues for potential investors. If the municipality has insurance on an issue, then the rating company would give the issue the highest rating possible because the risk factor of nonpayment would be low. Either a good reputation in the bond market or having bond insurance can get issuers of bonds lower interest costs because their bonds are more attractive to buyers. Interestingly, insured bonds actually trade in prices closer to double-A bonds than to uninsured triple-A bonds. In other words, insurance helps, but an earned triple-A is better than a triple-A obtained by insurance. Not all insurance companies will result in the same cost advantage. In the past, the market gave MBIA insured bonds slightly lower yields, and FGIC and AMBAC backed bonds traded 5 to 10 basis points higher. If the insurer's rating slips, so does the rating of all issues that the company insures.

An interesting creative finance development is "loan-to-lender" financing, which marries federally insured certificates of deposit to tax-exempt industrial revenue bonds. A government issues an industrial tax-exempt revenue bond, with the proceeds deposited in exchange for federally insured certificates of deposit with triple-A credit ratings. Contractual obligation dedicates the proceeds, which result from negotiation at the same rate and term as the industrial bonds, to make mortgage loans to third party developers in order to finance publicly desired projects (for example, low income housing). These increasingly popular instruments carry remarkably low interest rates.

Issuers can use *tax-exempt commercial paper* (TECP) for purposes similar to those of TANs and BANs, but a bank *line of credit,* which enhances cash liquidity, must support the paper. This new security increased in popularity when the federal government exempted the interest earned from federal taxes. The variety of maturities available and the ready liquidity make TECP an especially convenient instrument for those wishing to tailor maturities to future needs. There is a drawback: TECP has higher start-up and operating costs than traditional short-term instruments have (for example, TANs and BANs). Thus, a government should have at least $25 million of short-term borrowing a year to justify the high initial TECP costs. If the government has large short-term borrowing needs, TECP usually costs less than traditional short-term instruments. However, the issuer should retire the TECP when funds become available, and this may eliminate a government's important reinvestment earning opportunities. The latter can be an important source of local revenue.

A *put* or *tender option* in the issue often can attract long-term investors as well as take advantage of lower short-term interest rates. The *tender option* permits the investors to convert the investment to a shorter maturity, much as the call provision permits the government to do the same. The *put option* places liquidity demands on the issuer; hence, an issuer needs a letter of credit. The investor can exercise a *window put,* or *European option,* once during a defined period. In contrast, the *anniversary put,* or *American option,* allows investors to put their bonds back to the issuer periodically, generally on a given date once every year. Other things being equal, investors should value a 25-year bond with a five-year window put option higher than they would a traditional 25-year bond. The former represents a very strong protection against rising rates and falling bond prices. In high interest periods, the option saves the issuer at least 275 basis points. Beside external liquidity support, the put option requires a remarketing agreement with a bank or underwriter by which the investor exercises the option.

An *original issue discount bond* (OLD) is a long-term bond offered at a discount of the stated par value. The return occurs through gradual accretion to the bond's maturity when par is met. This is in contrast to traditional bonds, with which investors pay the par value to the municipality and receive back the principal plus the stated interest by the time of maturity. The IRS treats the difference between the par value and the purchase price as tax-exempt income. The "ultimate" original discount bond is the ZCB explained earlier. Another type of bond is the *compound interest bond* (the market also calls it the *municipal multiplier* and *capital appreciation bond*), which the issuer initially sells at par value. At maturity, investors receive payment of principal plus the amount of earned interest that the security accumulated over the life of the bond based on a semiannually compounded rate.

Variable rate securities attract investors who believe that market rates will continue to rise and wish to maintain their investment capital value. Offering securities that have floating rates accomplishes this; the security ties the yield to a formula linked to some other market factor, such as the prevailing interest rate on treasury notes. An added plus is the inclusion of a put option to increase liquidity as a trade-off for lower interest charges. The key to this type of issue is the choice of indexes by which the instrument determines the floating rates and the frequency with which the instrument readjusts the rate.

A nondebt instrument that can accomplish the same purpose as a debt is the *lease.* The various types of leases are the operating lease, the sale-leaseback, the safe-harbor lease, and the leverage lease. In the past, a lease was merely an agreement between a government unit and a private owner for the use of property or services over a period of time in exchange for rent or a fee. With creative capital financing, there are much more complex lease agreements that take advantage of federal tax incentives for private investment in capital goods. In a *true* or *operating lease,* a government unit acquires the use of an asset, with a private investor having title, a 90 percent equity investment (under IRS rules), and the use of a tax-exempt debt (for example, an industrial bond) to cover the other 80 percent. Often the lease allows the government to purchase the asset at fair market value or less when the lease expires. The result of this complex arrangement is remarkable. The private person can apply the accelerated depreciation of the asset against his or her federal income tax as an expense item and still acquire an investment tax credit advantage at a lower lease rate than the normal agreed-upon fair market value selling price.

A *sale-leaseback,* sometimes called a lease-purchase, involves the sale of government property to private investors, who receive tax advantages from the purchase while leasing back the asset to the government for its use. The local government shares the value of the tax benefit with a private party, with the "sale" proceeds used to renovate the asset used by the government. In a *safe-harbor lease,* made possible by ERTA, the government sells property (for example, mass transit vehicles) in a traditional sale-leaseback, with the advantage that the private party sells the tax write-offs to other private parties, thus reducing the federal taxes of the profit-making companies' taxes. At the end of the lease, the government can repurchase the asset for a nominal amount. In a *leverage lease,* a third party finances a large purchase. The buyer uses borrowed capital to purchase the asset leased to the local government. The local government repays the lender with a tax-exempt interest and a security interest in the property. Exhibits 8–3 and 8–4 present the government's and the investor's respective advantages from a possible sale-leaseback using the new present value concept.

Financial analysts can also use two other ideas associated with creative capital financing—warrants and small denomination bonds. The Municipal Assistance Corporation's February 1981 issue for the City of New York used the term "warrant" and gave the term an additional meaning that this book explained under cash management

EXHIBIT 8–3 Sale Leaseback from the Government Unit's Perspective

	ANNUAL	15-YEAR TOTAL	NET PRESENT VALUE @15%
Cost of Sale-Lease back Financing Alternative:			
(1) Lease Payments (net of ground lease)	$585,000	$8,775,000	$4,449,556
(2) Earnings from Escrow Account ($1 million invested at 11%)	110,000	1,650,000	836,669
(3) Repurchase of Building at End of Lease ($1.15 million less $1 million in escrow account)		150,000	35,909
(4) Net Cost of Sale-Leaseback	$475,000	$7,275,000	$3,648,796
Cost of General Obligation Bond Financing Alternative:			
(5) Debt Service if $4 Million, 15-Year Bonds at 10% were issued	$525,895	$7,888,425	$3,999,999
Savings from Sale-Leaseback:			
(GO debt service less total cost of sale-leaseback)	$50,895	$613,425	$351,203

Source: John E. Peterson and Wesley C. Hough. "Leasing." In John E. Peterson and Wesley C. Hough (eds.), *Creative Capital Financing.* Chicago: Municipal Finance Officers Association, 1983, p. 90. Used by permission.

in Chapter 7. Under this usage of the word, warrants are special certificates attached to bonds that permit investors to purchase future bonds at the same price and interest as the original issue. This is usually referred to as an *option to buy.* The market treats such certificates as bearer-redeemable securities that the investor can detach from the original bonds and sell separately.

Edward Anthony Lehan champions minimunicipal bonds, which governments sell in $100, $500, and $1,000 par amounts rather than in the traditional $5,000 par amount. He points out that they were successful when tried by local government and that they give the added advantage of permitting local citizens to invest directly in their community. Financial managers model the minibonds, in some instances, after the U.S. savings bonds, as they are essentially mini-ZCBs.

One new public finance instrument added by the 1990s was *certificates of participation* (COPs). COPs raise money without issuing debt per se as they are based on lease-backed financing, thus, they avoid the need for referendum approval. With COPs, a government agrees with another entity, such as a leasing company, to have it acquire a capital item. The government then leases the capital item and the government considers the leasing fee as an operating expense rather than debt service. This

EXHIBIT 8–4 Sale-Leaseback from the Investor's Perspective

Total Price to Investors: $5,000,000

Sources of Funds: $3,850,000 Industrial Revenue Bond
$1,150,000 Investor Equity

	YEAR 1	YEAR 2	YEARS 3–14	YEARS 15	TOTAL (000's)	NET PRESENT VALUE @ 15% (000's)
(A) Operating Expenses						
Rental Income	$585,000	$585,000	$7,020,000	$585,000	$8,775	$3,421
Sale Price at End of Lease	—	—	—	1,150,000	1,150	141
Administrative Expense	5,000	5,000	60,000	5,000	75	29
Debt Service on IDB	565,273	565,273	6,783,276	565,273	8,479	3,307
Income before Taxes	14,727	14,727	176,724	1,164,727	1,371	226
(B) Tax Advantages						
Tax Liability or Savings at 50% Bracket**	77,667	71,470	–11,535	–493,051*	–355	148
Investment Tax Credit	950,000	—	—	—	950	826
Total Return on Investment after Taxes (Income before taxes plus tax advantages)	$1,042,394	$86,197	$165,189	$671,676	$1,965	$1,200

*Includes capital gains tax.

**Tax on income after deductions for straight-line depreciation, administrative expenses, and interest paid on IRB.

Source: John E. Peterson and Wesley C. Hough. "Leasing.'" In John E. Peterson and Wesley C. Hough (eds.), *Creative Capital Financing.* Chicago: Municipal Finance Officers Association, 1983, p. 89. Used by permission.

market is primarily in California and used as a means to circumvent the California Proposition 13-type limits. The market does not tend to support COPs used for anything other than essential government purposes.

In the 1990s, a new type of financial instrument from the private sector started to appear in the public sector market because of the higher volatility of short- and longer-term rates and the desire to hedge the risk by both the issuers and investors of government bonds. The financial community calls this new instrument *derivatives* because they derive their price from other financial instruments. Derivatives have a place in the public sector financial market, but there is also the distinct possibility that improper judgment on the part of government financial managers can mean massive financial losses in the millions and billions of dollars.

Financial derivatives include *forwards, futures, options,* and *swaps.* They relate to stock, bonds, interest rates, and currencies; but in the public sector market, they are mostly associated with bonds. Forwards, futures, and swaps are a *commitment* to exchange agreed-upon cash flows at a specific future at prices or rates determined in the present. In contrast, an option provides *a right but not an obligation* to a future exchange again at a price or rate determined in the present. Thus, a financial derivative can either result in large gains or losses depending on whether the investor guesses correctly on the difference between the present and future price or rate commitment.

Financial engineering is the use of financial derivatives, typically, for risk management purposes. For example, investment experts can match the investor's requirements using derivatives to create the desired risk and provide the wanted return on investment. *Hedgers,* especially government issuers of debt, like derivatives because they use them to reduce their risk by using price or rate commitments to guard against overcommitment in the primary financial decision. Another group of derivative traders is *speculators,* who buy and sell derivatives not to reduce their risk but merely to make profit. They buy when they believe the market underpriced futures or options and sell when they believe the market overpriced futures or options. If this group of traders guesses wrong and is a significant group of speculators, this group can make or lose huge amounts of money. The third group of traders is *arbitragers,* who make profit from relative improper pricing of financials. For example, bond futures prices usually relate consistently with actual bond prices, but this need not be true. When not true, an arbitrage opportunity may arise where arbitragers buy and simultaneously sell futures when the bond futures prices are too high relative to the actual bond price.

Forwards, futures, options, and swaps have their respective advantages and disadvantages. Forwards are relatively simple to understand, and financial engineers use them for short and medium terms (up to five years). However, they have inflexible timing. Futures are more complex, and financial engineers use them for the short term (less than a year) when they do not want to constrain the timing of the cash flow. The more complex swap is a series of forward contracts that are longer term (many exceed ten years), are inflexible on timing, and are difficult to cancel or reverse. The major advantage of options is that the holder can decide not to exercise the option when the price or stipulated rate becomes unattractive.

Derivatives depend on the difference between the short- and long-term rates, the inclusion of put or call provisions in the major financial instrument, and sometimes the use of variable rate bonds. Swaps are an agreement between the issuer and a third party (the financial community calls it a *counterparty*) to exchange interest but not principal payments on an existing debt. Often they are the swap of fixed-rate payments for variable rate and thus the issuer hedges against losses when variable rates move up or "fix out," giving the issuer more peace of mind.

Floaters and *inverse floaters* are even more complex derivative innovations that isolate a portion of the interest rate payments on an otherwise plain vanilla fixed bond-rate bond. For example, the issuer strips away the interest payments and sells them separately to two sets of purchasers who take bear and bull positions, depending on how the interest rates behave. The bear receives a floating rate payment based on a market index and the bull takes the rest, creating an inverse floating security. When interest rates go up, the bear receives more interest rates at the expense of the bull, and vice versa when rates go down. In either case, the issuer continues to pay the fixed rate. Thus, the risk taker is the investor and not the issuer. Giving the investor this flexibility to buy bear or bull positions means that the investor's rewards can be greater, but of course investors can lose serious money if their judgments are poor.

As mentioned earlier, financial derivatives are sophisticated, complex, and dangerous. Thus, government financial managers must use them with utmost caution. Clearly, the use of government derivatives as an issuer is a better risk situation than when a government acts as an investor in cash management or pension fund management situations. In fact, the use of derivatives in cash management situations is rarely if ever appropriate given their need for low risk investments. In pension fund management, the manager can assume a higher risk, but even here derivatives should be a small portion of the investment portfolio. A dramatic example of the danger of derivatives is the bankruptcy of Orange County, California, in the mid-1990s. At its high point in 1991 to 1994, Orange County cash managed over $7 billion per year of its money and the money of other local governments that pooled their investments with Orange County. The county financial manager essentially bet most of the portfolio on an upward direction in interest rates, and they fell creating a $1.7 billion shortfall. He did not have sufficient liquidity or short-term credit backup to cover the losses, so the county petitioned for bankruptcy under chapter nine of the U.S. bankruptcy code.

Tests and Limits

At the local and state levels, potential investors, the investment community, and opposition political leaders raise questions when policy makers contemplate an increase in the local or state public debt. Sometimes a politician argues that no debt is best. Others argue for debt by saying that their administration would substitute capital for current expenditures such as labor costs and thus greatly increase the service to the public without increasing taxes. Others argue that capital expenditures benefit tomorrow's taxpayers and paying a debt appropriately shifts the cost of the project to future generations. Others use a more pragmatic test: if the government (1) can service the debt (that is, meet the payments as well as meet other usual expenses of government) and (2) can refinance its debt through the market, then they find a debt acceptable. Servicing a debt can be a tremendous burden on a community. A commonly used danger sign is when the debt service approaches 20 to 25 percent of the total budget. Few communities exceed this limit. Nationally, the aggregate debt figures for state and local governments are less than 10 percent of the total budgets.

The government debt situation in the United States is a mixed picture. For state and local governments, it is generally quite good except for a few odd cases like Orange County. Until the Clinton administration, there was reason for concern at the federal level as the debt service level was a significant portion of the yearly expenditure. In the George W. Bush administration, there is a yearly deficit again. The remarkable growth in the Clinton years reduced the debt service level as a percent of yearly expenditures. Having a less *net interest paid* means policy makers have more money for traditional government activities (for example, national defense and domestic programs) or lowering taxes. In addition, because most of the federal taxes are from lower-income people, payments of net interest on the debt benefit upper-income Americans and foreign investors in U.S. bonds. Thus, lowering the debt payments makes more funds available to the middle- and lower-income persons in America. The solution to a large long-term debt almost always involves cutting or limiting the yearly increases in expenditures, raising taxes, and sustaining and significantly increasing the national wealth over a long period of time. In the George W. Bush administration, the policy shifted back to lowering taxes and the yearly deficit reemerged.

Governments that have the most difficulty in financing their activities are usually those experiencing weak economic growth. If an area grows economically, then there is demand for borrowing because there is an improving tax base with which to pay that debt. If the tax base shrinks and the cost of government increases, then finance rating companies and the investors classify the government as a weak financial risk. Thus, when the city later wishes to issue a debt, it is of no interest to investors, meaning they may get no money or will pay a very high interest rate for the debt. Another common problem is a state law that easily permits local governments to issue tax-exempt bonds. For example, in the wake of Proposition 13, legal changes in California made issuing general obligation bonds difficult for communities, but vague criteria made it easy for special districts to issue bonds. This situation combined with an economic recession drives the local real estate market down and increases the likelihood that special districts will not meet their debt payments.

Governments can have trouble refinancing their short-term debt. Usually, this means that they find either retiring the short-term debt or refinancing it with another short-term debt due in the next year impossible. These situations place pressure on weaker governments when their refinancing needs are high and investor confidence from the market is low. Weaker governments find themselves unable to pay off the short-term debts, so default becomes a very real possibility in spite of the fact that typically they can meet the interest payments. In managing a debit or acquiring a loan, investors' views are significant. They are the ones who wish to buy government bonds and almost always they want to invest in safe bonds or notes that will earn them a reasonable return on their investment. Although there are no ideal indicators, investors do use the following indicators in making decisions:

- Does the ratio of debt to full value exceed 10 percent?
- What is the ratio of debt to market value of the real property? How does that compare with other governments?
- What is the debt per capita? How does this compare with other governments?
- What is the ratio of debt to personal income (per capita income)?
- What is the ratio of debt service to total budget?

Standard and Poor (a major bond rating firm) has developed a series of early warning guidelines that municipalities should consider carefully in monitoring their own financial operations. They are the following:

- current-year operating deficit;
- two consecutive years of operating fund deficit;
- current-year operating deficit that is larger than the previous year's deficit;
- a general fund deficit in the current position in the current-year balance sheet;
- a current general fund deficit (two or more years in the last five);
- short-term debt (other than BAN) greater than 5 percent of main operating fund revenues outstanding at the end of the fiscal year;
- a two-year trend of increasing short-term debt outstanding at fiscal year end;
- short-term interest and current-year debt service greater than 20 percent of total revenues;
- property taxes greater than 90 percent of the tax limit;
- debt outstanding greater than 90 percent of the tax limit;
- total property tax collections less than 90 percent of total levy;
- a trend of increasing tax collections during two consecutive years in a three-year trend;
- declining market valuations during two consecutive years in a three-year trend;
- overall net debt ratio to percent higher than previous year; and
- overall net debt ratio 50 percent higher than four years ago.

The International City County Management Association has developed an analytical tool called the *Financial Trend Monitoring System* (FTMS). It does not provide concrete answers as to whether a particular financial trend indicates a fiscal problem, but it does help decision makers more objectively consider a local government's financial condition. As the reader can see from the Standard and Poor list of indicators, evaluating a jurisdiction's financial condition is difficult and no single indicator tells the whole story, especially if the jurisdiction invests in derivatives. Some indicators are more important than others, but the analysts cannot be sure which are more important until they assemble all the key indicators. The FTMS has twelve factors with indicators for each factor. The six financial factors are revenues, expenditures, operating position, debt structure, unfunded liabilities, and condition of the capital plant. The five environmental factors are community needs and resources, external economic conditions, intergovernmental constraints, natural disasters and emergencies, and political culture. The twelfth factor is legislative policies and management practices. The FTMS groups the indicators by factors, using historical profiles for each indicator.

Exhibit 8–5 illustrates that state constitutions and laws do establish artificial debt limits. They vary greatly from state to state as well as by type of local government. Typically, they express the limit as a percent of the property tax base. Often state laws add provisions so those jurisdictions that tax the same citizens have lower limits. This avoids greater taxpayer liabilities for citizens from two or more overlapping jurisdictions. Also state laws sometimes establish artificial limits based on the tax imposed for servicing the debt. Another common state limitation is the procedural requirement calling for a referendum on long-term indebtedness bond issues.

Investors treat revenue bonds much like private corporation bonds. State law often does not prescribe limits and the market establishes the limits. Investors examine forecasts of income to ensure local governments will meet their debt services and the investors' investments are safe.

LOOKING BACK FOR FUTURE LESSONS: SOME IMPORTANT CASES

New York City Financial Crisis

In April 1975, New York City hovered on the brink of default on its obligations. With help from New York State, the federal government, and others, it averted default, but two significant consequences emerged after the crisis. The first was that state and local governments now paid higher interest rates. The second was the financial community now required more elaborate financial disclosures.

The nation felt the effects of the New York crisis, and North Carolina is one example. In *Southern City* Kenneth Murray (1976, 6) reported that a study by the Municipal Finance Officers Association (MFOA) showed "that the New York City financial crisis already cost local governments in North Carolina $424,000 in first-year added interest costs on bonded indebtedness and $5.1 million total in interest over the life of municipal bonds issued in 1975."

Exhibit 8–6 shows the credit rating change for New York City. Notice from 1965 to 1975 the remarkable drop to a low of Caa. Also note that since 1977 the rating has improved. In the precrisis era, state and local governments sold their bonds without revealing much about their financial situation. Since the crisis, investors have demanded greater disclosure of facts about the community and bonds.

Washington State Public Power Supply System (WPPSS)

In 1983, the WPPSS defaulted on its revenue bonds because the revenue from the nuclear power electric generation did not meet debt service requirements. WPPSS defaulted on payments of $2.3 billion in bonds issued to finance two nuclear power plants in the state of Washington. Epple and Spatt argued that the default of the WPPSS raised that state's general obligation borrowing costs. Because the market held the jurisdiction responsible for repayment of principal and interest of this revenue bond default, potential GO bondholders viewed the revenue bond default as

EXHIBIT 8–5   State Debt Limitations of the 50 States

STATE	AMOUNT OF GO DEBT LIMIT	CONSTITUTIONAL OR STATUTORY	OVERRIDE PROVISIONS	AMOUNT OF SHORT-TERM DEBT LIMIT	CONSTITUTIONAL OR STATUTORY	OVERRIDE PROVISIONS
Alabama	U	C	—	$300,000	C	—
Alaska	U	—	—	U	C	—
Arizona	$350,000	C	—	—	—	—
Arkansas	$1,350,000,000	C	—	N	—	—
California	U	—	—	—	—	—
Colorado	U	C	—	N	S	X
Connecticut	1.6 × Rev.	S	—	—	S	—
Delaware	—	S	—	—	—	—
Florida	—	C	—	N	—	—
Georgia	10% Rev.	C	—	—	—	—
Hawaii	—	C	—	—	—	—
Idaho	$2,000,000	C	X	$2,000,000	C	X
Illinois	—	C,S	X	15% total app.	C,S	—
Indiana	N	C	—	N	C	—
Iowa	$250,000	C	—	U	S	—
Kansas	$1,000,000	C	X	U	U	—
Kentucky	$500,000	C	—	U	U	—
Louisiana	—	C,S	X	—	—	0
Maine	U	—	—	5% of G.F.	S	—
Maryland	—	—	—	$100,000,000	S	0
Massachusetts	—	S	—	—	—	—
Michigan	—	C,S	—	—	C	—
Minnesota	3% non—ded. Rev.	—	—	—	S	—
Mississippi	1.5 × Rev.	C	—	5% of G.F.	S	—
Missouri	1,000,000	C	C	N	C	X

Montana	U	—	—	U	—	—
Nebraska	N	2% of assessed val	—	N	C	—
Nevada	C	10% Rev.	—	—	—	—
New Hampshire	S	1% of G.F.	Referendum	$125,000,000	—	—
New Jersey	C	—	—	N	—	—
New Mexico	C	—	—	$200,000	C	—
New York*	C/S	U	Popular Vote	$1,000,000,000	S	X
North Carolina	C	U	X	50% yr. total	C	X
North Dakota	C	$10,000,000	—	N	—	—
Ohio	C	—	—	—	C,S	—
Oklahoma	U	—	Const. Amendment	U	—	—
Oregon	C	—	—	—	—	—
Pennsylvania	C	—	Referendum	20% of rev.	S	—
Rhode Island	C	$50,000	Referendum	$150,000,000	C,S	—
South Carolina	C	—	—	N	—	X
South Dakota	N	—	X	$100,000	C	—
Tennessee	S	—	X	N	—	—
Texas	C,S	5% of GR	X	—	—	X
Utah	C,S	20% of state appr. limit	C	—	—	—
Vermont	S	U	—	—	S	—
Virginia	C	9,425,434,000	—	3,310,975,000	C	—
Washington	C,S	7 or 9% of general Rev.	—	—	—	—
West Virginia	C	per amendment	—	per statute	S	—
Wisconsin	C	formula	X	10% of G.F.	S	S
Wyoming	C	1% assessed value	—	N	—	—
Puerto Rico	C	Annual pmt. < – 15%	—	—	S	—

Codes:

C ... Constitutional   U ... Unlimited
S ... Statutory   N ... No debt allowed

Source: As adapted from National Association of State Budget Officers. *Budget Processes in States*, Washington, DC: NASBO, 2002.

EXHIBIT 8–6   Moody's Rating for New York City

DATES	RATINGS
07/65	Baa
05/68	Baa1
12/72	A
10/75	Ba
10/75	Caa
05/77	B
11/81	Ba1
11/83	Baa
07/85	Baa1
08/88	A
07/93	Baa1
02/98	A3

Source: *Moody's Municipal Credit Report.* Used by permission. City of New York, Bureau of Debt Management, 2002.

evidence that the jurisdiction managed itself poorly. Epple and Spatt posited that reputation costs affect borrowing across all jurisdictions within a state when a local bond default occurs. Moreover, following years of contentious bankruptcy proceedings, the jurisdiction did make some $500 million in payments to bondholders.

Orange County, California

The more significant local government financial crisis was the Orange County situation discussed earlier in this chapter. Orange County, one of the wealthiest local governments in the world, defaulted on general obligation bonds. Prior to that time, American local government, with very few exceptions, considered GO debt "sacred," with governments going to great lengths to protect their GO bond rating. Overnight, Orange County changed the rules and traditional financial emergency signals, which this chapter explains later, were inadequate in dealing with poor financial management using derivatives.

What are the consequences of Orange County? Fortunately, investors did not abandon the municipal market, which investors had considered about the safest place to invest. Interest rates did not spike up, except for California issuers. Most of Orange County bond investors were money market fund managers, and they reacted by either buying at par or by acquiring letters of credit or portfolio insurance with the permission of the U.S. Security Exchange Commission. Fortunately, the bond fund managers sold off their shares to investors because they realized that the Orange County median family income was a full 20 percent higher than that of the state as a whole. Unfortunately, the county's voters rejected a half-cent increase in the county sales tax to address the debt problem, but the county did divert other revenues to debt service, did radically cut services (41 percent), and selectively did refinance portions of the debt. Unlike when other cities fell into fiscal disgrace, California State government did nothing due to its own weak fiscal situation and the antigovernment citizen attitude in the state. One clear consequence is that Orange County and California taxpayers in general shall pay many millions more for debt service for many years in the future.

Government Financial Emergencies

There are rather clear warning signs for a municipality that is in financial trouble:

- an operating fund revenue/expenditure imbalance in which current expenditures significantly exceed current revenues in one fiscal period (a well-managed government, under some conditions such as an excessively large fund balance, could properly have this type of imbalance);
- a consistent pattern of current expenditures exceeding current revenues by small amounts for several years;
- an excess of current operating liabilities over current assets (a fund deficit);
- short-term operating loans outstanding at the conclusion of a fiscal year, the borrowing of cash from restricted funds, or an increase in unpaid bills in lieu of short-term operating loans;
- a high and rising rate of property tax delinquency;
- a sudden substantial decrease in assessed values for unexpected reasons;
- an unfunded or underfunded pension liability, unless done over a long period of time such as 40 years; and
- poor budgeting, accounting, and reporting.

Once the government recognizes that it has financial problems, it and the financial community can consider financial management improvements. Typically, the first major hurdle is the government's self-recognition that a problem exists. Acquiring the courage to communicate that problem to the public including the financial community is the second hurdle. The most common remedy is to eliminate the imbalance between revenues and expenditures. Often, an appropriate remedy is to develop safeguards against misuse of short-term operating funds. Another common remedy could be to fund the retirement system adequately. Governments in trouble must make significant improvements in their municipal accounting and reporting systems as they commonly do not have financial reporting systems that communicate bad news to the key decision makers in a timely manner.

If self-remedies are ineffective, then governments in trouble and others can take more significant steps. For example, some states create administrative bodies to assist troubled local governments. If that is inadequate, the courts can demand that local governments in trouble hire consultants such as Morgan Guarantee Trust and, if necessary, they can arrange for direct agreements with creditors. This is usually adequate for temporary or technical financial emergencies. If the problem continues, states sometimes have the power to force special remedies on a local government. Agreements usually undergo state review, approval, and supervision. The federal role is to provide a means to devise financial adjustments, which a majority of the creditors approve.

Under chapter 9 of the federal bankruptcy law, the government facing bankruptcy must develop a plan of composition or financial adjustments. First, the eligible local government unit must file a voluntary petition for bankruptcy and a plan of composition with the petition. Those holding 51 percent of the securities affected by the plan must accept it. Upon filing, judges enter an order either approving or dismissing the plan. If approved, the resources of the debtor come within the jurisdiction of the court and the court fixes a time and place for a hearing. The court gives notice to the creditors, creditors and others can file answers, and the court holds the hearing. After the hearing, the court may confirm a plan of composition that the creditors involved in two-thirds of the aggregate amount accepted. The court may but seldom does continue jurisdiction after the confirmation of the plan.

CAPITAL BUDGETING

Operating versus Capital Budgeting

Most local and state governments have two types of budgets: operating and capital. The operating budget deals with everyday types of activities. The capital budget deals with large expenditures for capital items. They differ in the nature of items that they purchase, the methods of financing, and even the accompanying decision-making process. In most instances, government depletes operating expenses in a single year. Typically, capital items have long-range returns and useful life spans, are relatively expensive, and have physical presence, such as a building, road, water supply system, or sewage system. Fifty-six percent of American cities have a separate capital budget, and 73 percent of cities over 100,000 have them. Over forty states have capital budgets. Interestingly, the U.S. federal government does not have a capital budget, but the U.S. General Accounting Office champions this reform strongly.

The most significant difference between operating and capital budgeting is the method of financing. Governments finance capital budget items through borrowing, but they can also fund them by saving money over a period of years for the capital item or by using grants, special assessment, and the general revenue fund. Because government debts are often complex and can create financial hardships if local governments manage them incorrectly, state laws, not surprisingly, do establish debt limits (usually associated with the assessed value of property). Also, states often require equalization rates to ensure consistent treatment throughout each state. The debt limits vary from state to state, and there are exceptions to the limit and application of equalization rates.

Some local governments shift as many expenses as possible from operating to capital budgets. For example, in both West Point, Mississippi, and New York City, the local governments called band uniforms capital budget items. This tendency can lead to corruption of the concept of a capital item to such an extent that the government has two operating budgets, with one financed through borrowing. That situation in turn leads to overuse of bonding, greater government resources used for debt retirement, and proportionately less money used to meet operating budget demands. Eventually, the debt can become large enough that a government cannot meet its payments, and the community must face the possibility of management bankruptcy. Traditionally, government uses debt to finance items with a life expectancy that lasts as long as the debt payments. The effect of this practice is to limit the overuse of debt financing and to make the debt more politically defensible as the future taxpayers identify how they benefit from the decision to finance the item by borrowing money.

In capital budgeting, planning and careful, deliberate actions are essential. Government needs planning to integrate the capital items with the remainder of the physical structure in the community. Capital improvement plans are essential to coordinate the work by time, funding possibilities, and physical plans. If capital budgeting involves a building, then the process of executing decisions involves study of the possibilities, site selection and acquisition, and planning and design as well as construction financing. Delays translate to higher construction costs due to inflation, especially rising labor costs; thus, government must avoid delays. Also, the increased operating and maintenance expense incurred on account of the new facility is an important factor, which government should consider in the planning phase. Communities have built facilities they cannot afford to operate or maintain (for example, stadiums).

Capital Facilities Planning

Governments can make decisions to add a public facility or make extensive repairs on the basis of understanding the needs of the community and the resources available. The best approach to identifying the resources is to inventory the existing public facilities. The next step is to catalog the proposed public facilities. The key facts in the catalog include the location of the proposed facility, the year of construction, cost priority, project description, financing schedule, prior or sunk costs, projection of future related fund requests, operating costs, and savings in operating and maintenance costs. Public managers can update their inventory and file of proposed projects at least once a year to ensure that policy makers base their decisions on the correct facts.

Making decisions on proposed projects is not easy, and managers can aid policy makers greatly if there are clear, detailed answers to the following questions:

- What is the relationship of the proposed project to the overall development of the city?
- The project will help how many citizens and it will harm or inconvenience how many citizens if the government does not construct the project? Which citizens will benefit or hurt from the project?
- Will the proposed project replace a present worn-out service or structure or is it an additional responsibility of government?
- Will the project add to the property value of the area, thus increasing the value of city property and receipts from property tax? How much will the city realize from the increase?
- Will the construction of the improvement add to the city's operation and maintenance budget? How much?
- Will the project increase the efficiency of performance? How much and where? What cost savings will result? Will the project reduce the cost of performance for a particular service? How much and where?
- Will the project provide a service required for economic growth and development of the municipality?
- Is the estimated cost of the improvement within the city's ability to pay?

Ultimately, policy makers must decide and make their priorities. Sometimes decision makers find analytical techniques such as cost-benefit analysis useful, but regardless of the techniques that policy makers employ, they cannot avoid making judgments. Some communities use a point system to establish priorities. One scale used is as follows:

- urgent (highest priority),
- essential,
- necessary,
- desirable,
- acceptable, and
- deferrable (lowest priority).

Capital Budget Cycle

The budget cycle for capital budgeting is similar to the operating budget cycle. The phases are identical. Government needs a capital budget call and calendar just as in an operating budget. Government must collect detailed information such as the illustrations developed by Girard Miller for the Government Finance Officers Association noted in this chapter's references.

Many governments prepare a multiyear capital improvement program each year. This helps those relying on capital decisions to understand the likely physical facilities in the near future. Governments usually fund capital projects through borrowing, grants, and sometimes the operating budget. The government formally approves the capital improvement plan and passes an ordinance or law that clearly explains what the government approved and the method of financing the program or project.

Policy makers and staff carefully review capital budgets. Both budget analysts and planners review the plans for possible errors and potential problems. Governments hold public hearings commonly, especially if the government uses revenue-sharing money to fund the capital budget. Careful consideration goes into deciding the best financing plan. Ultimately, the official government policy-making unit, such as the city council (and possibly even the electorate, if the law requires electoral approval of the bond issue) approves the capital budget.

Realities of Capital Budgeting

John P. Forrester empirically examined municipal capital budgeting in the United States. Although most students of budgeting associate capital budgeting with economic rational decision making as described earlier, political and managerial concerns lace the actual process, as they do in operational budgeting. The Forrester survey did link the CIP with capital budgeting, but some respondents said the linkage did not exist in their city. Some said they used economic criteria, such as benefit-cost analysis, to make their capital budget decisions, but others identified less rational managerial and political factors. Also the respondents tended to separate capital and operational budgeting, but when they made actual capital decisions they said their short-term orientation and being identical budget actors with the operational budget were the deciding factors. Although planning for such reasons as growth and change does influence the capital budget decision makers, more traditional and human budget policy criteria are more significant, with short-term considerations being the most significant.

BONDING

Designing an Issue

Once a government decides to borrow money, it must go to the financial market with a bond offering. The government must follow the bond disclosure rules of the Securities and Exchange Commission (SEC), which apply only to bond issues over $1 million. Two approaches to bonding are possible: use competitive bidding or arrange a negotiated sale to a specific underwriter. Often, governments use competitive bidding to seek the lowest bidder, especially in general obligation bonds; but revenue bonds and very small general obligation bonds more frequently employ negotiated sales. Underwriters affect issuers' costs due to their differing profit spread and their ability and willingness to locate investors to repurchase the bonds.

Competitiveness tends to encourage underwriters to lower their profit spread and try harder to locate investors. With negotiated sales, financial managers can tailor issues to meet the unique needs designed for the specific interests or preferences of a particular underwriter. This might mean that the particular underwriter might be in a better position to offer a lower bid for the bonds. The following are six common reasons for choosing a negotiated sale:

- A new credit instrument may need such a sale to get customer interest.
- Sometimes, issues are too large for only one syndicate to buy through competition.
- Sometimes, a government has a low credit rating and they have no other choice.
- The issues are very small, and there is no interest in submitting a competitive bid.
- The securities market is very volatile, and the government will receive few competitive bids.
- The issue is complex, and a negotiated bid can better deal with the complexity.

In public finance, one of the most enduring debates involves whether competitive or negotiated sales best services the issuer's interest because each method has its strengths and weaknesses. The major advantage to competitive sales is that it keeps the effective cost as low as possible, as history indicates especially in general obligation and revenue bond issues. The second advantage is that the process is open and fair, thus precluding favoritism and lessening the chances of corruption. The major disadvantage to competitive sales is its creation of a risk premium in the underwriter's bid to compensate for uncertainty about market demand. Another disadvantage is the process makes last minute timing and structural changes difficult. In addition, there is minimal control over the underwriter selection and bond distribution. The major advantage of negotiated sales is that the underwriter assists the issuer in preparing the issue for the sale. More extensive presale marketing is possible, thus better gauging the market demand for the bonds. Unlike competitive sales, negotiated sales are more flexible and give the issuer greater potential influence over the underwriter selection and bond distribution. Under negotiated sales, pricing is less subject to the rigors of competition, thus requiring more issuer vigilance in terms of pricing, favoritism, and corruption.

If there is a choice, the issuer should systematically evaluate the following:

- If the issuer is less familiar with the market, the presale marketing associated with negotiated sales becomes significant.
- The higher the quality of the credit, the less need there is for a negotiated sale.
- If issuers' control over underwriter selection or bond distribution is important, then a negotiated sale is best. However, the possibility of favoritism and corruption is stronger in these circumstances.
- If the debt instrument is new and unfamiliar to the market, then a negotiated sale is wiser.
- If the issue size is unusually small or large, then a negotiated sale is wiser.
- If unusual events or conditions surround the sale, the presale marketing of a negotiated sale is important.

If neither competitive nor negotiated sales seem best, then there are alternatives. The issuer can use the legal framework of a negotiated sale combined with pricing the issue through the solicitation of bonds from all interested underwriters. This approach provides the flexibility offered by the negotiated sale with the competition of pricing offered by the competitive sale. Another alternative is to infuse competition in the negotiated sales by using the *request for qualification* process or *request for proposal* process in the selection of the underwriter. Hiring a financial advisor or investment banker for only portions of the sale is a third alternative.

Regardless of the choice made, issuers must take responsibility for the issue as the government is responsibile for the public's interest. The issuer must understand the likely demand level of the bond and focus on the total financing cost. If in-house expertise is not adequate, then the issuer should hire a financial advisor. The issuer should not place blind faith in any sale method, but rather evaluate each sale method for each separate circumstance.

Issuers who must make the negotiated or competitive sales decision need to reflect carefully on the principal-agent ethical problem. The agent must reveal any benefit he or she gets as a result of the principal-agent relationship to the principal. If not, one type of principal-agent ethical problem exists. The agent owes the principal due care, obedience, and loyalty or the agent has a conflict of interest. The underwriter in a negotiated sale is an agent of the issuer, who must act solely for the public interest rather than for personal or political self-interest or for the interest of any elected or appointed officials.

Unfortunately, in some negotiated sales situations the fiduciary interest of the public is of less importance than the relationship between the issuer and the underwriter. For example, not withstanding the reality that competitive sales usually result in better interest rates for the issuer than negotiated sales, Oregon moved to 82 percent negotiated sales for general obligation bonds sales within one year after the legislature no longer required competitive bidding. The principal-agent problem arises for several reasons. Sometimes a local government official's concerns for his or her campaign fund contribution overrides the concern for achieving the lowest interest rate on bond sales for his or her community. Underwriters are major contributors to local and state government campaign funds. Sometimes the issuer to underwriter working relationship is more important than low interest rates, possibly because underwriters enhance that relationship with minor or major favors for the issuers.

Deciding Issue Details

Prior to publishing the invitation to bid, financial managers must make decisions on the maturity, the size of the issue, the call terms, the principal and interest return structure, the interest cost limit, and the option to reject the bids, plus a wide variety of financing considerations such as a put option and ZCBs. Commonly, a financial advisor helps government's financial managers make these decisions. Maturities vary in length and size. Sometimes they are thirty years, but more commonly they are twenty years or less. Traditionally, the length of the maturity of the issue is no longer than the useful life of the capital facility that is the reason for the issue. Issuers can divide serial bonds on an approximately equal basis, but it is also possible to negotiate a deferral of payments during the first two to five years, resulting in a large final payment (called a *balloon*). If the issue is simple, it is called *plain vanilla* bonds; the financial community calls unusual or complicated bonds that require more effort to sell *story bonds*.

If the issue appeals to the larger banking and security community, it should not be less than $1 million; $4.2 million is a usual size, but issues of more than $100 million do exist. The changing federal tax laws have shifted the makeup of the bond market. For example, the alternative minimum tax has caused many banks to leave the bond market. If the insurance companies follow the banks, the market will consist only of private households, which tend to be the most volatile group.

Large issues require buyers to form *syndicates,* which are temporary financial partnerships to buy and sell securities. The primary buyer is called an *underwriter,* which can be a syndicate. Eventually, these buyers sell the securities to groups and even to other syndicates. The use of syndicates is commonplace. Interestingly, underwriters sometimes make their complex million-dollar agreements by phone in a remarkably informal manner. If the issuer plans a negotiated sale, he or she must focus on the following:

- defining coupon interest rates so that an issue's yield curve will conform to the market yield curve for the appropriate grade of security,
- ensuring the underwriter involved will properly promote and place the bonds so as to get the best possible price, and
- selecting an acceptable level of underwriting compensation.

Underwriters should know several weeks in advance that they will have a specific product to sell. Thus, they can test the market and even change such things as a bond's size to improve the bonds' marketability. The provisions in the bond offering are important. Together with the credit standing, they largely determine the marketability of the issue. If many seek to invest in the security, then the government can get a lower interest rate. The variety of ways to structure the issue is remarkably complex. The key to the decision is to structure the issue to achieve the lowest price and other benefits for the government. The real cost of interest payments depends on the time value of money. The future dollar is worth less to the investor than near-term dollar. To accommodate the common preference for shorter-term maturity bonds, the issuer can design "front-loaded" bonds that give high coupon rates on short-maturity bonds. Another consideration is that buyers seek specific maturities that are similar to what the market finds attractive. Thus, coupon rates should enable the market to sell bonds at or near their par value. If this occurs, the financial community calls them *efficient.* If they are not efficient, then underwriters would have to resell bonds at prices that are substantially above or below their par value. Such a requirement typically makes such sales difficult and sometimes costly to the underwriter. Thus, in designing an issue an issuer wants an "efficient" coupon rate.

For most bidders, the fact that there is a tax advantage for municipal bonds is significant, but taxable government bonds do exist. Exhibit 8–7 illustrates the importance of municipal bonds across tax brackets. In nontaxable bonds, the interest income is exempt from federal income taxation and is often exempt from the income

EXHIBIT 8–7   Advantage of Municipal Bonds Across Tax Brackets

2001 FEDERAL INCOME TAX RATES

Tax Bracket	28%	31%	36%	39.6%
Single	$27,050–65,550	$65,551–136,750	$136,751–297,350	$297,351 and up
Joint	$45,200–109,250	$109,251–166,500	$166,501–297,350	$297,351 and up
Tax-Exempt Yield%		TAXABLE EQUIVALENT YIELD (%)		
4.00	5.55	5.80	6.25	6.62
4.50	6.25	6.52	7.03	7.45
5.00	6.94	7.25	7.81	8.28
5.50	7.64	7.97	8.59	9.11
6.00	8.33	8.70	9.38	9.93
6.50	9.02	9.42	10.16	10.76

- Find the appropriate return (single or joint).
- Determine your income tax bracket by finding your taxable income category.
- In your tax-bracket column, identify the taxable equivalent yield for each of the tax-exempt yields in the far left column.

For example, an investor in the 28 percent federal tax bracket would have to earn a 6.94 percent yield from a taxable bond to match a 5.00 percent yield from a tax-exempt bond. For residents of those states with state income taxes, the advantage of investing in municipals may be even further enhanced.

Source: Morgan and Stanley at http://www.morganstanleyindividual.com/markets/bondcenter/school/insured/pdf, 2002. Used by permission.

tax in the state of issue. In *South Carolina v. Baker,* the Supreme Court ruled that the doctrine of reciprocal tax immunity does not apply, but the Congress did not repeal federal laws revoking tax immunity. However, if a state or local government improperly places the loaned proceeds in revenue-generating investments (for example, only for reinvestment purposes), then the Internal Revenue Service would call the bonds arbitrage and tax the interest income from the bond. Without such a rule, local governments would take advantage of their unique lower interest rates to invest in higher interest bearing bonds and make a profit from the difference in interest rates.

Bond-issuing governments use three basic methods for awarding bond issues to competing bidders. They are the *unrestricted net interest cost* (NIC) method, the *net interest cost with constraints* (NIC-C) method, and the *true interest cost* (TIC) method. Of the three, the newer TIC tends to minimize interest costs the best. The NIC method looks at the total coupon interest payments over the life of the issue. It takes special account for the time value of money. Thus, this method encourages bidders to front-load their bids and produce inefficient bids that result in penalty yields. NIC-C imposes constraints on the bidding process to overcome the shortcomings of the NIC method. For example, the coupon rate on any particular bond, which must be at least as high as the rate on bonds having the shortest maturity, establishes a constraint. This constraint helps in terms of front-loading and penalty yields, but it can still result in bond issues awarded to bidders who do not bid the lowest true interest cost among the bids submitted. In the TIC method, government evaluates the bond bids on the interest payments required in terms of their present value or present worth. Many states have laws that do not permit the use of the TIC method yet.

The government can also consider other factors before it offers a bond. The government may wish to establish an interest cost limit to protect itself from bids that are, as a group, unreasonable. In some circumstances, such ceilings can raise costs, especially when tax-exempt yields are very high for a prolonged period of time. Such ceilings force postponement of projects and thus possibly raise project costs even higher. States are wiser to remove statutory interest rate ceilings or have them indexed. Governments sometimes add a stipulation that they can reject all bids to further protect themselves. In designing a bond issue, other decisions include the bond date, the place and time of sale, payment dates for principal and interest, who will receive and read the bids, who will print the bonds to avoid counterfeiting and theft, and what to do if the government receives no bids.

Many local governments do not have the necessary expertise to handle bonding or special types of bonding. Thus, getting outside assistance is common, especially for complex issues. Some states provide financial advisory assistance, but typically governments use private advisory services. The amount and degree of assistance vary with the amount and kind of funding contemplated. In moderate-sized, full-faith-and-credit transactions, groups such as local commercial banks, investment bankers, bond counsels, and state agencies may provide the services at no direct or minimum charge on negotiated sales. However, such services would be minimal, and there might be the expectation that the private party would develop or protect an advantageous relationship. Often, the underwriter or potential underwriter can be helpful in suggesting approaches with a stronger market appeal.

Services of financial advisors include developing a sale schedule, sizing and structuring the issue, preparing the sale document, arranging for the rating, coordinating sale advertising, verifying bids/interest rates, and assisting with closing. Commonly, government pays financial advisors on a flat fee for services basis, but government can pay them based on the amount of the debt issued depending on state laws and industry practices. If done on the basis of the debt issue, the agreement with the advisor states that payment is in terms of a dollar amount per note or bond issues (for example, $.75 per $1,000 of the principal amount of the issue).

Some states permit pooling of debt issues of more than one local government to reduce costs and enhance marketability of the bonds. A state bond bank assists local governments to sell their debts. Since 1970, states like Vermont have created a state authority to pool the debt of small communities into a single larger authority issue. This permits the state to use its stronger credit to provide small communities access to national credit markets at reduced borrowing costs. Given the large need for government investments in infrastructure, state efforts to create infrastructure banks give local jurisdictions a sustained and predictable bond proceed revenue for capital improvements without burdening a state's own general obligation borrowing capacity. Some states permit umbrella bond insurance programs, thus reducing the bond risk and lowering borrowing costs.

Purchasers of bonds want assurance that the bond itself is legal, and they prefer not to check the public record themselves. Therefore, they want a bond counsel to certify the following:

- the legal existence of the government offering the bond,
- the propriety of authorization of the bond,
- the correctness of the procedures that the government followed in the conduct of the sale,
- the absence of litigation with respect to the validity of the bond issue, and
- the correctness of the signatures on the bond.

This assurance carries more weight if the bond counsel commands wide respect among investment bankers and investors.

Bond Prospectus, Notice of Sale, and Sale

Since the mid-1970s, investors require a more elaborate bond prospectus (see Exhibit 8–8). The prospectus is merely the information needed by investors to decide whether or not they wish to invest in the bonds. Key information in the prospectus often includes the following:

- description of the bonds,
- security for the bonds,
- description of the government,
- financial procedures pertinent to the issue,
- fund revenues and disbursements,
- explanation of the fund's budget,
- local economic factors,

EXHIBIT 8–8   Sample Bond Prospectus

PRELIMINARY OFFICIAL STATEMENT DATED APRIL 1, 2002

Moody's: Aa3
S&P: A+

NEW ISSUE — BOOK-ENTRY ONLY   Ratings: See "Ratings" herein

In the opinion of Orrick, Herrington & Sutcliffe LLP, Bond Counsel, based upon an analysis of existing laws, regulations, rulings and court decisions, and assuming, among other matters, the accuracy of certain representations and compliance with certain covenants, interest on the Series 2002A Bonds is excluded from gross income for federal income tax purposes under Section 103 of the Internal Revenue Code of 1986, and is exempt from State of California personal income taxes. In the further opinion of Bond Counsel, interest on the Series 2002A Bonds is not a specific preference item for purposes of the federal individual or corporate alternative minimum taxes, although Bond Counsel observes that such interest is included in adjusted current earnings when calculating corporate alternative minimum taxable income. Bond Counsel expresses no opinion regarding any other tax consequences related to the ownership or disposition of, or the accrual or receipt of interest on, the Series 2002A Bonds. See "TAX MATTERS" herein.

$174,820,000*
TRUSTEES OF THE CALIFORNIA STATE UNIVERSITY SYSTEMWIDE REVENUE BONDS SERIES 2002A

Dated: April 1, 2002   **Due: November 1, as shown on inside cover**

The Trustees of the California State University Systemwide Revenue Bonds Series 2002A (the "Series 2002A Bonds") are being issued by the Trustees of the California State University (the "Board") pursuant to an Indenture dated as of April 1, 2002 (the "Indenture") between the Board and the Treasurer of the State of California, as trustee (the "State Treasurer") which constitutes the Fifty-Second Supplemental Bond Resolution under the 1968 Bond Resolution (as defined herein). The Series 2002A Bonds are being issued (i) to finance and refinance the acquisition, construction, renovation and improvement of certain facilities of the California State University, including, but not limited to student housing, parking, student union, and student centers facilities, and (ii) to refund certain outstanding indebtedness of the Board. See "REFUNDING PLAN," "THE PROJECTS" and Appendix H — "PROJECTS FINANCED AND BONDS REFUNDED WITH SERIES 2002A BONDS."

The Series 2002A Bonds are being issued on a parity with other bonds issued by the Board pursuant to the 1968 Bond Resolution. Upon purchasing the Series 2002A Bonds, the Underwriters, as initial purchasers, will consent to certain amendments to the 1968 Bond Resolution prior to delivering the Series 2002A Bonds to individual purchasers. See "SECURITY FOR THE SERIES 2002A BONDS — Amendments to 1968 Bond Resolution."

The Series 2002A Bonds will be issued in fully registered form in denominations of $5,000 each or any integral multiple thereof, and following their purchase by the Underwriters will be registered in the name of Cede & Co., as nominee of The Depository Trust Company ("DTC"), New York, New York. DTC will act as securities depository of the Series 2002A Bonds. Individual purchases will be made in book-entry form only, in principal amounts of $5,000 and integral multiples thereof. Purchasers will not receive certificates representing their interests in the Series 2002A Bonds purchased. See "THE BONDS — Book Entry Only System."

Interest on the Series 2002A Bonds is payable on November 1, 2002, and semiannually thereafter on May 1 and November 1 of each year, and principal of and interest on the Series 2002A Bonds are payable by the State Treasurer, as trustee, to DTC. DTC is required to remit such principal and interest to its Participants for subsequent disbursement to the Beneficial Owners of the Series 2002A Bonds, as described herein. See Appendix G — "BOOK-ENTRY ONLY SYSTEM."

The Series 2002A Bonds are subject to redemption prior to their stated maturities, as described herein. See "THE BONDS — Redemption."

MATURITIES, AMOUNTS, INTEREST RATES, AND PRICES OR YIELDS SEE INSIDE COVER

THE SERIES 2002A BONDS ARE LIMITED OBLIGATIONS OF THE BOARD, PAYABLE UNTIL THE TRANSITION DATE (AS HEREINAFTER DEFINED) FROM NET REVENUES AND OTHER FUNDS PLEDGED UNDER THE 1968 BOND RESOLUTION AND, AFTER THE TRANSITION DATE FROM GROSS REVENUES AND OTHER AMOUNTS PLEDGED UNDER THE INDENTURE. NEITHER THE PAYMENT OF THE PRINCIPAL OF THE SERIES 2002A BONDS NOR ANY PART THEREOF, NOR ANY INTEREST THEREON, CONSTITUTES A DEBT, LIABILITY OR OBLIGATION OF THE STATE OF CALIFORNIA. THE SERIES 2002A BONDS ARE NOT SECURED BY A LEGAL OR EQUITABLE PLEDGE OF, OR CHARGE, LIEN OR OTHER ENCUMBRANCE UPON, ANY OF THE PROPERTY OF THE STATE OF CALIFORNIA OR OF THE BOARD, EXCEPT TO THE EXTENT OF THE AFOREMENTIONED PLEDGES. THE OWNERS OF THE SERIES 2002A BONDS HAVE NO RIGHT TO COMPEL THE EXERCISE OF ANY TAXING POWER OF THE STATE OF CALIFORNIA. THE BOARD HAS NO TAXING POWER.

The pledge and lien on certain Net Revenues under the 1968 Bond Resolution and Gross Revenues under the Indenture is subordinate to the pledge and lien of certain other indebtedness of the Board and on a parity with certain other indebtedness of the Board. See "SECURITY FOR THE SERIES 2002A BONDS," "—Senior Lien Indebtedness" and "—Parity Lien Indebtedness."

This cover page contains information for quick reference only. It is not a summary of this issue. Potential investors must read the entire Official Statement to obtain information essential to making an informed investment decision.

The Series 2002A Bonds are offered when, as and if issued, subject to the approval of certain legal matters by Orrick, Herrington & Sutcliffe LLP, San Francisco, California, Bond Counsel. Certain legal matters will be passed upon for the Board by its General Counsel and for the Underwriters by Stradling Yocca Carlson & Rauth, a Professional Corporation, Newport Beach, California. It is anticipated that the Series 2002A Bonds will be available for delivery to DTC in New York, New York, on or about April 30, 2002.

Lehman Brothers

Banc of America Securities LLC	**Siebert Brandford Shank & Co., LLC**
E.J. De La Rosa	**Great Pacific Securities**
Jackson Securities Inc.	**Loop Capital Markets, LLC**
RBC Dain Rauscher	**Salomon Smith Barney**
The Chapman Company	**UBS PaineWebber**

Dated: April   , 2002

* Preliminary, subject to change.

- debt administration applicable to the issue,
- description of the capital improvement program,
- any contingent liabilities,
- tax exemptions,
- ratings,
- certificates from necessary officials,
- assessed valuation and tax rate,
- tax levies and collections,
- fund revenues and expenditures, and
- comparative statement of financial conditions.

The GFOA "Disclosure Guidelines for Offerings of Securities by State and Local Governments" is the best guide to preparing a prospectus. It provides essential guidance, and the financial community recognizes it as the authoritative source. The Oregon Bond Disclosure Guidelines is an excellent practical digest.

The government or its agent prints and distributes the prospectus with the *notice of sale*. It is sent to investment bankers, a list of large investors, financial newspapers, and ratings and information agencies. The *notice of sale* includes the following:

- the correct legal name of the issuing bond as well as the special law under which the government organized and granted the authority to issue the bonds;
- the type of bonds issued, the amount and purpose of the issue, the maturity schedule, and the call feature;
- the date, time, and place of sale and the manner in which the government will receive the bid;
- limitations as to interest rate, payment dates of interest, and when and where the investor will pay the principal;
- denomination and registration privileges;
- basis for bidding;
- amount of good faith check required;
- bid form and basis for award;
- name of approving attorney and statement on legality;
- provisions made for payment of principal and interest;
- total tax rate in the government unit and legal limits;
- methods and place for settlement and delivery of the bonds; and
- the right to reject any or all bids.

The bond market accepts some practices fairly well. For example, governments date bonds as near as possible to the delivery date to avoid improper interest charges. Government typically issues bonds in $5,000 denominations except for odd amounts that governments should retire the first year. Government pays interest semiannually, and bond owners often have the option of registering principal only or principal and interest. If the government sells the issue on a wide market, then the government makes payments at large financial centers for the convenience of the bondholders. Government must make prompt payments or default occurs.

Highly competitive investment *syndicates* that underwriters organize just for the purpose of buying the issue often buy large issues. The practice of these limited partnerships is to resell the issues as soon as possible to other investors. The syndicate members make their profit on the slight difference (called the *spread*) of what they bought and sold for each issue. Thus, factors (such as maturity, coupon structure, points, rate limits) under the control of the issuer permit easy syndicate reselling of municipalities and thus make syndicates more interested in bond offerings. If syndicates can easily resell bonds, then the municipality should get a lower interest rate on its bonds.

Most of the information in this section assumes that governments will use open competitive bidding rather than direct negotiations. Generally speaking, one is wiser to use open competitive bidding, but experienced governmental negotiators can often secure the lowest interest rates as well as better terms through negotiations. Robert L. Bland noted a positive correlation between experienced negotiators and lower interest costs, but there was a limit to the advantage of having more experience. Using experienced negotiators for sale of securities might be advisable, but government should not use them for first-time or very infrequent issuers.

For larger issues, a government might decide to contract with a fiscal or paying agent. Paying agents typically are in large financial centers, and they make the necessary principal and interest payments on bonds. Fiscal agents have broader powers, including replacing lost or destroyed original bonds, exchanging coupons for registered bonds, canceling paid bonds and coupons, cremating canceled bonds and coupons, answering routine correspondence, and signing bonds. The advantage of having an agent at a financial center is the saving of time in the movement of credit, coupons, bonds, and checks. This translates to the government saving money.

Debt Records and Reporting

Reputation is important. The local government must develop among investors a reputation for accuracy and integrity so that investors can place full trust in the local government debt records, reports, and payment calendar. Governments should avoid surprising the investment community. Thus, government should apply scrupulous attention to each detail of its issue. If it does not pay such attention to detail, the market automatically discounts its credit and the government must pay higher interest on later issues. Government bond dealers, bond-rating agencies, and, of course, the investors require reports.

Essentially, the investor wants to know primarily about the government's ability to make timely payments of principal and interest. The investor makes this judgment call on the basis of accounting data and reports. The National Committee on Government Accounting, in *Governmental Accounting, Auditing, and Financial Reporting,* has established basic standards for reporting on debt, and Chapter 7 discusses the necessary information. The issuer cannot segregate this information from the other financial reports of a government because of the interrelationship of the data and the potential significance of other financial data in understanding the government's debt and financial condition. Briefly, the investor wants to see the balance sheet, the amount of debt outstanding, the status of the debt reserves, the record and the ability of the government to meet the payments, willingness of officials to use their power to service debt, and the record of the community in debt and other financial management. Also the investor wants to know the assessments, the area's economic condition, the market value of its property, the tax habits of its citizens, and any overlapping of debt with other local governments.

Timely information is important to investors. Therefore, the issuer should make every reasonable effort to provide reports promptly and frequently.

Bond Ratings

Private firms (such as Standard and Poor) rate state and local government bonds when they issue new bonds, and those ratings reflect the likely interest rate that the government will get on its new issues in the marketplace. The fact that a government spends less per capita and thus has lower budgets does not necessarily mean better bond ratings. There is wisdom in the adage: "Reduce your debt and increase the value of taxable property." Investors do look at such ratios, and both factors may be within the control of the government. The use of budget controls or a certificate from the Government Finance Officers Association will not lower rates. However, as noted by Earl R. Wilson, the use of budgets to plan and manage government does often result in lower interest rates.

The Standard and Poor's municipal bond rating process involves four broad factors: *economic, debt, administrative,* and *fiscal. Economic factors* include the economic diversity of the tax base as well as the diversity and growth of area economic opportunities. *Debt factors* include debt burden, debt history, trend, and type of security. *Administrative factors* include tax rate, levy limitations, debt limits, and other information indicating the likely ability to meet debt payments. *Fiscal factors* include the assets and liabilities in the balance sheet as well as trends in assets and liabilities, especially pension liabilities and the use of derivatives in their investment portfolio. In the fiscal factors, rating companies and investors make comparisons between assets and liabilities to see if assets exceed expenditures in the present and the foreseeable future. The bond rating process does not proceed without the necessary information. Since the 1970s, rating companies require more meetings on the issues, more extensive field trips, and more extensive analyses of state or municipal government bonds. Rating companies base their rating decisions, in varying degrees, on the following:

- the likelihood of default, which is a rating company's determination of the capacity and willingness of the obligator to observe the timely payment of interest and repayment of principal in accordance with the terms of the obligation;
- the nature of provisions in the obligation; and
- the protection afforded by and the relative position of the obligation in the event of bankruptcy, reorganization, or other arrangement under the laws of bankruptcy and other laws affecting creditors' rights.

Moody's Investors Services, which is another major rating company, considers factors similar to but not the same as those considered by Standard and Poor. Moody focuses on debt, economic, administration, and financial factors. The two most frequently used statistical ratios are *debt burden* and *net debt per capita*. The former is a ratio of the government's net debt (gross debt less bonds fully supported by enterprise revenues, and short-term debt plus overlapping debt) to the estimated full value of taxable property. Those ratios are helpful in understanding the total tax-supported debt. The rating company compares both indicators to national medians for governments of similar size. With inflation of property values, another supplemental indicator is *debt service as a percent of local expenditures.* A high or rapidly rising figure is often a significant warning. For revenue bonds, a commonly used measure is *debt service coverage* (defined as net revenue) divided by principal plus interest requirements for the year. Another measure is the *safety margin* (that is, the net revenue less debt service requirements for the year divided by gross revenue and income). Clearly, today the use of derivatives is another important factor. Moody also looks at the government's fund balance and, generally, considers a fund balance of 5 percent of the budget as prudent and indicative of the capability to meet the debt obligation in a full and timely manner. See Exhibit 8–9 for the information required by Moody's to rate a debt issue.

A common Moody national distribution of general obligation bond ratings by category is: Aaa - 1%; Aa1 - 2%; Aa - 9%; A1 - 19%; A - 37%; Baa1 - 16%; Baa - 15%; and Ba1 and below - 1%.

Ratings provide the investor and others with an informed opinion of the creditworthiness of a particular issue. Ratings do not establish interest rates, but higher ratings usually translate into lower interest cost to the issuer. Larger investors conduct their own analyses of issues, but Moody's and Standard and Poor's rating services provide additional guidance on creditworthiness, and rating services influence small investors in particular.

REVIEW QUESTIONS

1. What is a government debt? What are the various types and forms of debt? Why do they exist? What are the alternatives to debt and why are municipalities likely to incur debt?
2. Compare and contrast revenue bonds, general obligation bonds, short-term borrowing, and creative financing.
3. What criteria can you use to judge the correct level of state and local debt? Justify the criteria cited.
4. Explain the significance of the New York City and Orange County financial crises for (a) each government, (b) other local governments, and (c) the bond market, including prospectus requirements (GFOA, federal, others).
5. Why is the term "bankruptcy" inaccurate and somewhat misleading for municipal governments? What can a local government do to anticipate and remedy its own financial crisis?
6. Explain the advantages and disadvantages of the various debt instruments.

EXHIBIT 8–9   Information Requirements for Debt Ratings

DOCUMENTS	TAX-SUPPORTED BONDS	REVENUE BONDS	BOND ANTICIPATION NOTES	REVENUE BOND ANTICIPATION NOTES	TAX AND/OR REVENUE ANTICIPATION NOTES	LETTER OF CREDIT
PRIMARY:						
Official statement or prospectus	X	X	X	X	X	X
Notice of sale (if public)	X	X	X	X	X	
Annual reports or audits (last 3 years)[1]	X	X	X	X	X	
Most recent budget for operations	X	X	X	X	X	
Capital budget or planning document	X	X				
Legal opinion	X	X	X	X	X	X
Law(s) under which notes are to be issued[2]	X	X		X	X	
Note resolution or ordinance			X	X	X	
Bond resolution or ordinance, trust indenture, and any other legal documents relevant to the bonds and notes		X	X	X		X
Engineer's report (if available)		X	X	X		
Bond purchase commitment letter, if sale of the bonds has been prearranged (i.e., to an agency of the United States Government)			X	X		
Copy of local charter or document which describes governmental structure	X					
For school districts; ten-year enrollment trend and projection; school plant description, including facilities and capacity	X					

330

(continued)

Item	Col 1	Col 2	Col 3	Col 4
Cash flow statements[3]	X			
Financial feasibility study including projections (if available)			X	
Rate study (if available)			X	
SUPPORT: (for information not contained in any of the above documents)				
Maturity schedule for bond anticipation notes, including final statutory maturity date for this and outstanding notes		X	X	
Interest rate computation, 360 or 365 day basis		X	X	
Complete debt statement of issuer, including debt-incurring capacity		X	X	X
Interest rate limitations on bonds and notes		X	X	X
List of last five bond issues of type that will fund notes, including amount, sale date, number of bids received (if public sale), and net interest cost		X		X
Enterprise system description[4]		X	X	
Descriptions of rate setting process; record of revisions for past five years		X	X	
Investment policy; formal document or brief description of practices	X		X	
Public employees: number employed and trend, status of contracts, unions, pension funds, latest actuarial study (if available)	X		X	X
Tax assessment and collection procedures, including due dates and penalty rates	X			X
Tax and levy limitations	X			X
List of ten largest taxpayers, their assessed valuation, and type of business	X			X

(continued)

331

EXHIBIT 8–9 Information Requirements for Debt Ratings, *(continued)*

DOCUMENTS	TAX-SUPPORTED BONDS	REVENUE BONDS	BOND ANTICIPATION NOTES	REVENUE BOND ANTICIPATION NOTES	TAX AND/OR REVENUE ANTICIPATION NOTES	LETTER OF CREDIT
Economic data for service area	X	X				
List of operating loan borrowings[5]					X	
Assumptions used in preparing cash flows					X	
Assessed valuation for last five years	X				X	
Equalization ratios for last five years	X				X	
Current population and latest census estimates	X				X	
Statement of direct debt and debt of overlapping debt issuers, including allocable share	X				X	
Future borrowing plans	X	X	X	X	X	X
Number of building permits—last five years, plus the dollar amount	X				X	
Local and area unemployment rates	X	X				
List of ten major employers, number of employees, and type of business	X	X				
Area of the issuer (in square miles) and percentage of land that is developed	X	X				
Current number of government employees; whether unionized and contract status	X	X			X	
Debt (outstanding and new); segregate by security; actual principal maturities and interest requirements for each year, pro-forma debt service schedule for new debt including interest rate assumptions	X					

(continued)

Letter of credit and reimbursement agreement	X
Loan or lease agreement	X
Bank counsel enforceability opinions (domestic and foreign)	X
Preference (bankruptcy) opinion	X
Remarketing agent agreement	X
Tender agent agreement	X
Pledge and security agreement	X
Standby bond purchase agreement	X
Mortgage and/or other collateral documents	X
Other documents as applicable	X

[1] For revenue bonds, include interim financial results for recently concluded but unaudited period of year-to-date results and comparable period in prior year.

[2] This requirement is waived if the law(s) have been previously submitted and have not been subsequently amended.

[3] Include at least one full fiscal year actual; current fiscal year actual/estimate; and projections for the next fiscal year through note maturity. *Note:* These are strictly cash basis and should not include or show negative receipts or disbursements or negative balances.

[4] For revenue bonds, include system capacity and trend of usage, particularly customers and consumption (output) by year for past five years, percent of service purchased by each major user.

[5] Over last five fiscal years, including type and amount issued in fiscal year, amount outstanding at year end, and interest rates on the notes.

Source: Moody's Municipal Issues, 4, 1 (February 1987). Used by permission.

7. Explain why deciding on using competitive versus negotiated sale is often a difficult decision.
8. How does the decision-making process differ in capital versus operating budgeting?
9. Why is judgment central to any capital budget decision? What analytical questions are especially useful and why?
10. What takes place in designing an issue? What is particularly important and why? Why are syndicates significant? Why is a prospectus important?
11. What can a government do if it gets low bond ratings?

REFERENCES

Advisory Commission on Intergovernmental Relations. *City Financial Emergencies: The Intergovernmental Dimension.* Washington, DC: Government Printing Office, July 1973.

———. *Significant Features of Fiscal Federalism.* Vols. 1 and 2. Washington, DC: Government Printing Office, June 1976 and March 1977.

———. *Significant Features of Fiscal Federalism.* Vol. 2, *Revenues and Expenditures, 1991.* Washington, DC: Government Printing Office, October 1991.

———. *Understanding the Market for State and Local Debt.* Washington, DC: Government Printing Office, May 1976.

ARONSON, J. RICHARD, and ELI SCHWARTZ (eds.). *Management Policies in Local Government Finance.* Washington, DC: International City Management Association, Municipal Finance Officers Association, 1975.

BAKER, KEVIN. "Financing Government." *Governing* (April 1990), 5A–22A.

BALDASSARE, MARK. *When Government Fails: The Orange County Bankruptcy.* Berkeley, CA: University of California Press, 1998.

BLAND, ROBERT L. "The Interest Cost Savings From Experience in the Municipal Bond Market." *Public Administration Review,* 45, 1 (January/February 1985), 233–237.

BLAND, ROBERT L., and LI-KHAN CHEN. "Taxable Municipal Bonds: State and Local Governments Confront the Tax-Exempt Limitation Movement." *Public Administration Review,* 50, 1 (January/February 1990), 42–48.

CHOATE, PAT. "Case for a National Capital Budget." *Public Budgeting and Finance,* 1, 4 (Winter 1981), 21–26.

COE, CHARLES K. "Competitive V. Negotiated Sale of General Obligation Bonds: A State-Based Comparison." Paper presented at the SECOPA conference at Charlotte, North Carolina, September 1991.

DOSS, BRADLEY C. "Capital Budgeting Practices." In Thomas D. Lynch and Lawrence Martin (eds.), *Handbook of Comparative Public Budgeting and Financial Management.* New York: Marcel Dekker, 1993.

DOSS, BRADLEY C., JR. "The Use of Capital Budgeting Procedures in U.S. Cities." *Public Budgeting and Finance,* 7, 2 (Autumn 1987), 57–69.

DOTSON, BETSY, CATHERINE SPAIN, and BARBARA WEISS. "Financial Derivatives: Governments as End Users." *Government Finance Review,* 10, 4 (August 1994), 14–17.

EPPLE, DENNIS, and CHESTER SPATT. "State Restrictions on Local Debt." *Journal of Public Economics,* 29 (1986), 199–221.

FORRESTER, JOHN P. "Municipal Capital Budgeting." *Public Budgeting and Finance,* 13, 2 (Summer 1993), 85–103.

GROVES, SANFORD M., W. MAUREEN GODSEY, and MARTHA A. SHULMAN. "Financial Indicators for Local Government." *Public Budgeting and Finance,* 1, 2 (Summer 1981), 5–19.

HACKBART, MERL M., and JAMES LEIGLAND. "State Debt Management Policy: A National Survey." *Public Budgeting and Finance,* 10, 1 (Spring 1990), 37–54.

HUMPHREY, NANCY P., and DIANE RAUSA MAURICE. "Infrastructure Bond Bank Initiatives: Policy Implications and Credit Concerns." *Public Budgeting and Finance,* 6, 3 (Autumn 1986), 38–56.

HUSH, LAWRENCE W., and KATHLEEN PEROFF. "The Variety of State Capital Budgets: A Survey." *Public Budgeting and Finance,* 8, 2 (Summer 1988), 67–79.

International City/County Management Association. *Evaluating Financial Condition: A Handbook & Local Government,* 4th Edition. Washington, DC: ICMA, 2001.

JUAREZ, STEVE, and CHARMETTE BONPUA. "Passion in Public Finance: The Debate Over Competitive vs. Negotiated Underwriting." *Government Finance Review,* 10, 6 (December 1994), 11–15.

JOHNSON, CRAIG, and MARILY MARKS RUBIN. "The Municipal Bond Market: Structure and Changes." In Fred Thompson and Mark T. Green (eds.), *Handbook of Public Finance.* New York: Marcel Dekker, 1998.

LEHAN, EDWARD A. *Simplified Government Budgeting.* Chicago: Municipal Finance Offices Association, 1981.

LEMOV, PENELOPE. "The Brave New World of Public Finance." *Governing* (February 1992), 27–28.

———. "Deriving Forces." *Governing* (September 1993), 69–74.

———. "For Municipal Bonds, Its Not A Plain Vanilla World Anymore." *Governing* (June 1990), 52–58.

LEVITAN, DONALD, and MICHAEL J. BYRNE. "Capital Improvement Programming." In Jack Rabin and Thomas D. Lynch (eds.), *Handbook on Public Budgeting and Financial Management.* New York: Marcel Dekker, 1983.

MILLER, GIRARD (compiler). *Capital Budgeting: Blueprint for Change.* Chicago: Government Finance Officers Association, 1984.

MOAK, LENNOX L. *Administration of Local Government Debt.* Chicago: Municipal Finance Officers Association, 1970.

Moody's Investor Services. *Moody's Municipal Issues,* 2, 2 (May 1985).

Moody's Investor Services. *Moody's Municipal Issues,* 4, 1 (February 1987).

Municipal Finance Officers Association. "Disclosure Guidelines for Offerings of Securities by State and Local Governments." Chicago: MFOA, 1983.

MURRAY, KENNETH. "New York Crisis—Its Effect on North Carolina." *Southern City.* Raleigh, NC: North Carolina League of Municipalities (January 1976), p. 6.

National Committee on Government Accounting. *Governmental Accounting, Auditing, and Financial Reporting.* Chicago: Government Finance Officers Association, 1983.

PETERSON, JOHN E. "The Municipal Bond Market in a Changing Economy." *Public Budgeting and Finance,* 8, 4 (Winter 1988), 22–34.

———. "Municipal Bond Market: Post–Orange County Era." *Governing* (November 1999), 77–115.

PETERSON, JOHN E., and PAT WATT. *The Price of Advice.* Washington, DC: The Government Finance Research Center of the Government Finance Officers Association, 1986.

PETERSON, JOHN E., and WESLEY C. HOUGH. *Creative Capital Financing for State and Local Governments.* Chicago: Municipal Finance Officers Association, 1983.

REDHEAD, KEITH. *Financial Derivatives.* Hemel Hempstead, England: Prentice Hall Eurpose, 1997.

SIMONSEN, BILL, and LARRY HILL. "Municipal Bond Issuance: Is there Evidence of a Principal-Agent Problem?" *Public Budgeting and Finance,* 18, 4 (Winter 1998). 71–100.

STANFIELD, ROCHELLE L. "It's a Tougher World for City Bonds." *National Journal,* 9, 34 (20 August 1977), 1300–1303.

State of Oregon. *Bond Disclosure Guidelines.* 1983.

STEISS, ALAN WALTER. *Local Government Finance.* Lexington, MA: D.C. Heath, 1975.

United States Census Bureau. *Federal State and Local Governments. Government Finance and Employment Classification Manual.* Washington, DC: U.S. Census Bureau, Grants Division, 2001.

VALENTE, MAUREEN G. "Local Government Capital Financing: Options and Decisions." *Municipal Year Book.* Washington DC: International City Management Association, 1986.

VASCHE, JOHN DAVID. "State and Local Government Options for Reducing Borrowing Costs." *Public Budgeting and Finance,* 3, 4 (Winter 1983), 42–56.

WILSON, EARL R. "Fiscal Performance and Municipal Bond Borrowing Costs." *Public Budgeting and Finance,* 3, 4 (Winter 1983), 28–41.

9

REVENUE SYSTEMS

There are two sides to every budget. One is expenditure and the other is revenue. This chapter discusses intergovernmental revenue systems, property tax, and other revenue sources. It explains the revenue side of budgeting in an intergovernmental context involving the growth of government and the current patterns in government revenue. The most controversial yet most important local tax is the property tax. This chapter explains the tax, the controversy, and the administration of the tax. The same is done for income and sales taxes. At the completion of this chapter, the reader should know the following:

- the latest trend in fiscal federalism;
- the relative tax burden in the United States;
- a definition of property tax and the major criticisms of the tax;
- the major suggested property tax reforms, including the *Serrano v. Priest* decision and its implication;
- how government assesses property as well as means to test assessment practices;
- the assessment cycle, application of tax rates, and foreclosures; and
- the definition, significance, issues, and administration of both income and sales taxes.

INTERGOVERNMENTAL REVENUE SYSTEMS

Historical Background

American government is a complexity of intergovernmental financed programs, with the current pattern explainable by means of American political history. At the republic's beginning, state governments dominated the form of government. But the federal government took on a more significant role by assuming the states' Revolutionary War debt; financially assisting large transportation projects like canals, harbor improvement, and railroad expansion; plus supporting education through land grants. The federal government even used land grants for social purposes such as homestead programs. In the 1930s, the federal government involved itself extensively with social programs, but this time the government financed the programs with dollars. In the 1950s, the federal government designed new large grant programs, which it channeled through state governments, to help air and highway transportation. In the 1960s and 1970s, the federal government greatly expanded the number, variety, and type of grants. In the 1970s, grant consolidation was the theme; in the 1980s, fiscal constraint was the theme. The 1990s' theme was one of selective devolution of federal grant programs.

In 1989, John Shannon and James Edwin Kee argued that a fundamental shift in American public finance took place, which decidedly veered the intergovernmental system away from centralized federalism. This was due to five factors. The first was the disappearance of the federal government's fiscal advantage due to individual income tax reform, including using indexation for inflation. The second was the important legacy of President Reagan, who accelerated the popular swing away from federal power toward increased state responsibility. The third was the resiliency of the state-local system, which was able to rebound from the taxpayer revolts (for example, Proposition 13 in California), the early 1980s recession, and reductions in federal aid. The fourth was the emergence of relatively strong state-local revenue systems, which became more balanced and broad-based with a proportional tax structure. The last factor was state and local government institutional reforms, which federal actions such as *Baker v. Carr* ("one person, one vote") and civil rights laws sometimes induced.

The early 1990s created extreme budget pressures on many state governments due to the recession; increased the demand for services, especially for Medicaid and prison construction; and resulted in less transfer payments from the federal government. For example, in fiscal year 1992, ten states were not able to start their fiscal years with a budget—highly unusual at the state level. In that year, states increased their revenues by $15 billion, which topped the $10 billion increase in fiscal year 1991. During that same period, spending growth was cut $10.2 billion, with increasing demands for more services and lower taxes.

The late 1990s witnessed a reversal of fortunes in the states. Primarily the result of a booming economy, in 1998 only two states had to exact budget cuts, in 1999 three states instituted cuts, and by FY 2000 only one state needed to implement budget cuts. Similarly, state revenues witnessed a reversal of trends. From 1992 to 2001, states were not feeling the same pressures to increase revenues and cut spending. Revenues actually decreased an average of $2.6 billion per year during this period. In addition, many states finished their fiscal years with significant year-end balances during this time frame. As the George W. Bush administration unfolded, the economy slowed and state revenues again were inadequate for traditional services of state government.

The tax burden is not constant from region to region or from state to state. According to the U.S. Advisory Commission on Intergovernmental Relations, New England, the Midwest, and the Far West collected more state and local taxes per person, and the Southeast and Southwest collected fewer taxes. The state that collects the highest amount of taxes per citizen is Alaska because of its unusual oil tax revenue at $3,922, but the next highest amount is $3,714 in the District of Columbia. The lowest tax collected per person was Mississippi at $1,184. The national average was $1,888. Some states have a relatively larger tax capacity, with Alaska, Connecticut, and Massachusetts having the highest capacity. The lowest was Mississippi. The states with the highest capacity are not always equally high in tax effort. The states with the highest tax effort were the District of Columbia and New York. The lowest effort was New Hampshire. The state with the biggest positive spread between tax capacity and tax effort was Nevada, and the biggest negative spread was New York.

American federal, state, and local taxes have increased in dollars but are about the same as a percentage of the gross national product since 1976. After World War II to 1972, there was a slight increase, and the early 1980s saw a slight decrease. The federal, state, and local tax revenue is about 20.9 percent of the gross national product. What is more interesting is the distribution change. State and local tax revenue grew from 5.1 percent in 1948 to 9.0 percent in 1989. In contrast, the federal tax revenue shrank from 14.5 percent to 11.8 percent in that same period. Property tax remains the important tax source for local government, whereas individual income tax and sales tax are about equally important to state government.

American federal, state, and local taxes have increased in dollars but declined slightly as a percentage of the gross national product since 1970. After World War II to 1970, there was a steady increase in the public sector, but it has steadily declined from a 24.3 percent peak to a 20 percent level in 1986. The income tax is important to both state and federal governments, with the latter very dependent on that tax source. This trend continued through the late 1990s. In 1998, the individual income tax accounted for some 26 percent of state-owned revenues. By 2002, the federal individual income tax accounted for some 47 percent of the budget. Property tax to local governments and sales tax to state governments are extremely important taxes. Property taxes accounted for 47 percent of local government revenues while the sales tax generated some 37 percent of state-owned revenues (U.S. Census Bureau 2001).

A Significant Trend

The Advisory Commission on Intergovernmental Relations uses the three Rs—the revolt of the taxpayers, reduced federal aid, and recessionary pressures with no federal bailout—to describe the reasons behind the trend in fiscal federalism. These three jolts came in rapid succession and created a new fiscal conservative perspective, especially for American state and local governments. Although California's Proposition 13, which rolled back property tax to 1 percent of market value, was not the first conservative tax reform, it was the most dramatic and served as the model for other states. Government growth shifted from a hefty 4.4 percent average annual increase in adjusted per capita expenditure to a revised 0.5 percent increase. The major state tax increases in the post–Proposition 13 era were due, not to "big spenders," but rather to severe fiscal crisis. The second R—reduced federal aid—began to occur in the second half of the Carter administration; the Reagan administration accelerated it, and it was started again in the George W. Bush administration. The third R—recession with no federal bailout—was the big jolt because painfully large government shortfalls severely hurt state and local government programs. Traditional federal actions in a recession, such as a national economic stimulus program, would have bailed out state and local governments, but they were not forthcoming, especially during the Reagan administration. The effect was painful belt tightening and politically unpleasant state and local tax increases.

Since the tax revolt, state governments have followed a predictable series of actions. When unanticipated revenue shortfalls occur, government typically follows a three-step pattern. First, it tightens its belt; then, the government adds to the user charges, including the semi-user-fee gas tax. The government's third step is to increase *sin taxes* (for example, cigarette taxes), and finally, government increases the general sales or individual income tax. Government takes the latter step when political actors see a severe revenue shortfall. Interestingly, these major state tax increases are sometimes scheduled to self-destruct in a fixed time, such as six months to a year. The three Rs have had their impact on state legislative behavior. A review of state fiscal actions in the recessionary period of the early 2000s reveals the same "tried and true" three-step approach for dealing with budget shortfalls.

PROPERTY TAX AND CONTROVERSY

A Simple Idea

Property tax is a simple revenue-generating idea. First, government assesses the property locally in order to determine the property value of each piece of property in the jurisdiction of the government. Second, the tax assessor and political leadership determine a tax rate and apply the rate to each property based on its value. If the property owner fails to pay the taxes, then the government can fine the owner, and, as a last resort, the government can take the property in order to pay the taxes owed on the property.

This form of taxation is still one of the most significant revenue sources for most state and local governments. At one time, property reflected wealth; thus, a real estate property tax could have been a progressive tax. Today, wealth is not reflected in real property; therefore, this form of taxation cannot be used to tax wealth uniformly and progressively. The relative significance of property tax as a revenue generator has declined because it has not provided sufficient revenue by itself. Property tax is less significant today, but it is still highly important as a revenue generator.

Government places property tax on personal and real property. Tangible personal property includes machinery, equipment, and motor vehicles. Intangible personal property includes stocks, bonds, mortgages, and money. Real property includes land as well as improvements to the land such as buildings. Typically, the local government administers the property taxes locally. Not all property is taxed at a universal rate. In some cases, the tax is regressive, but a government can add special features to minimize regressive burdens. Another interesting fact is that government can hold one person responsible for taxes on both personal and real property. Also a citizen might live in overlapping local governments, and thus a taxpayer can pay local taxes on the same property to two jurisdictions. Double taxation has become an important fiscal issue in many local areas.

Criticisms

According to the Advisory Commission on Intergovernmental Relations, the property tax is the least fair tax and federal income tax is the second. Thirty percent of the nation's citizens regard property tax as the worst or least fair tax. In contrast, 26 percent think the federal income tax is the worst tax. Taxes are never popular, but property tax beat the others in nonpopularity. Why?

- This form of taxation bears down harshly on low-income households. Lower-income families must pay a higher percentage of their incomes for real estate taxes.
- Property tax is an antihousing levy. It discourages homeownership and does provide preferential treatment for shelter cost as commonly found in income and sales taxes. Also, as taxes increase, many view property tax as a threat to their continued home-ownership. As property values go up, property taxes increase, but the owner does not see a benefit from the "paper profit" until it is converted to a profit on the sale of the house, but that might be years later. This means that the government increases the property taxes, but the property remains the same.
- The administration of property tax is difficult and often poorly done. At best, the assessment is an informed estimate, that is, a subjective judgment of market value. At worst, the government can use the assessment for political or economic advantage.
- The infrequent mass reappraisals in periods of inflation result in severe taxpayer shock and hardship. Taxes go up radically, and taxpayers might not be in economic positions to absorb sometimes doubling and tripling of tax bills. No other tax has such severe hikes.
- Property owners can find property taxes painful to pay. Often, government collects the property taxes with the homeowner's monthly mortgage payment charge. Such a "pay-as-you-go" technique is less painful for most taxpayers. Often, however, local government does not permit such practices, and homeowners must make payments on a yearly basis, thus causing hardships.
- Property tax does contribute to urban blight. If government must foreclose some houses due to nonpayment of taxes, such houses are likely to be in marginal neighborhoods. The long foreclosure process will probably stimulate extreme negligence to the house, thus harming an already weak housing market. Values will drop, and the neighborhood will deteriorate.

One very complex problem is the perennial conflict between state valuation and local assessment practices. The property tax laws of most states require that the government assess all classes of property at the same percentage of current market value. This sounds reasonable, but most state tax administrators are unable to hold county assessment at any uniform percentage of current market value. The most frequent beneficiaries—not victims—of the extralegal assessment practices are farmers and homeowners. Governments tend to assess farmland at a lower percentage of market value than residential property, whereas they assess income-producing property such as a factory site at a higher rate. A company that is the dominant employer in a community might get a low tax bill, but this is an uncommon practice.

There is a natural reluctance on the part of state officials to raise the assessments of all classes of property to the state valuation standard. Such reforms are politically grim to those officials. Local rate makers should cut back tax rates if the state hikes local assessment; thus, each taxpayer would pay about the same tax amount. However, negative economic conditions can press local governments for added revenue, so by not lowering the tax rate, local governments can generate more income while placing the tax hike blame on the state. The creation of a uniform tax policy is another problem for states because uniformity means that the state will repeal the popular "little assessment break" given farmers and homeowners. Such repeals are major headaches and political liabilities for state officials, and they rarely want the public to associate them with such a policy. Tax reform designed to bring the law and practice into reasonable alignment does require heroic action. Thus, such reforms—when they do occur—take place typically because of court rather than legislative or administrative action.

Property Tax Reforms

Given the number of criticisms of property taxes, not surprisingly there is, or has been, an active reform movement addressed to reforming property tax. Few reformers argue that the legislature or the people by referendum should eliminate the tax because it does generate large quantities of tax revenue. Given the number of criticisms of the property tax, there have been active reform movements calling for drastic changes in the property tax. However, few reformers argue that legislative or other political leaders should eliminate the tax. Most reformers have proposed less radical, and politically expedient, changes that seek to lower property taxes.

Some obvious less radical improvements are to have better assessors and to use better assessment techniques. Better pay would attract more qualified people. Governments should give added training to persons hired as property assessors. Also, government should select assessors on the basis of professional merit, not as a result of a local election. Governments can improve assessment by using cadastral maps and parcel information files. The work of assessment lends itself to data processing; thus, computers can and should do much of the routine work. Another technique is to use building permit data to alert assessors to important changes. Another useful device is to enact a real property transfer tax act, which includes a provision requiring that the recorder of deeds automatically notify the assessor about any changes in market value. Assessors can use statistical techniques like multiple regression analysis to identify market data that best indicate rapid changes in market value. Other reforms are to use professional consulting firms, especially for major reassessments.

Another reform involves government reorganization. Governments can often consolidate assessment districts because this reform sometimes leads to economies of scale. Such a reform also permits more specialization, better job development for assessors, and the use of sophisticated equipment, which an assessor could not justify in a small operation.

A reform addressed to correcting the regressive character of property tax is called a *circuit breaker*. It is typically designed to aid families with the lowest incomes or the elderly. The details of circuit breakers vary from state to state, with Louisiana having the largest at $75,000 deduction on each home. A typical circuit breaker can be only for the elderly, can aid renters as well as homeowners, may limit benefits to households with incomes below some amount such as $5,000 with no asset test, and grant a maximum total relief of $500 or less. In Louisiana, each property owner has a $75,000 deduction so that the assessor taxes a $100,000 home at the assessment level of $25,000.

Political advocates sometimes argue for more radical reforms. One is the *site value approach,* which exempts reproducible capital from the property tax base. Proponents argue that there would be no tax loss but government would tax in a different way. They say taxing the building as improved property tends to slow down renewal, whereas taxing only land does the opposite. Thus, they argue this approach to taxation would improve urban areas. These debates will continue as long as there are legitimate criticisms of the property tax.

Proposition 13 and Property Taxes

The most notable property tax reform was California Proposition 13, in 1978, which Idaho, Nevada, Massachusetts, and other states copied. This reform radically cut California's property tax back to 1 percent of the market value and moved property assessment back to the 1975–76 rolls. In addition, it provided for a 2 percent growth rate annually. California's property tax rate moved from a 2.21 percent average effective tax rate to a 0.98 percent rate with that single reform. The average effective property tax rate in the United States average is 1.21 percent, with eight states near the 1 percent rate, five states at over 2 percent, and twelve at less than 0.9 percent. Reducing property tax receipts does not mean a uniform decrease in state and local government services because some services rely more heavily on property tax than others do. Changes to property tax do not affect state government directly, but because school districts and townships rely heavily on property tax, the major tax cutbacks hurt them the most, and they tend to ask state governments for relief for the hardship that impacts them.

Serrano v. Priest

A particularly significant reform has shifted the property tax to the state from the local school district level. Reformers point out that this reform solves many of the problems of rich versus poor school districts. In 1971, the State of California Supreme Court ruled in *Serrano v. Priest* that the state government must break the relationship between a district's property tax wealth per pupil and its educational expenditure. In other words, local government may administer the property tax, but the funds must go into a statewide pool. The level of spending for a child's education may not be a function of wealth, other than the wealth of the state as a whole.

This decision has remarkable property tax implications. At least in education, there is no longer such a thing as a rich or poor district as the states pool the property tax money at the state level and then send it back to the districts on some sort of formula basis. The *Serrano* decision, strictly applied, would invalidate many existing patterns of real property school financing. The decision does not void real estate but does require a major design constraint on the tax.

In 1973, the U.S. Supreme Court in *San Antonio Independent School District v. Rodriguez* did not extend the Serrano decision to the national level. In a five-to-four opinion, the Court ruled that education is not one of the fundamental rights; thus, it is not covered under the equal protection clause of the Constitution. Interestingly, the lawyers for Rodriguez did not base their argument on discrimination and equal opportunity; if they had, then the Court might have decided otherwise. However, the Court ruling meant that the *Serrano* decision did not apply on a national level.

On a state-by-state basis, most state courts and some legislatures follow the California reasoning. Some call this a Robin Hood approach as the state serves to equalize the tax among the local districts. Colin Campbell and William Fischel point out that the *San Antonio v. Rodriguez* decision shifted the arguments from one equal opportunity to state constitutional grounds (1996). Since many states include education in their constitutions, judges used these provisions to hold locally funded school systems unconstitutional. In essence, the courts were trying to redress spending variability and tax base variability between districts. As a result of these decisions, state governments typically ended up paying more of the costs of education. The *Serrano* decision was influential, and many states revised property tax laws due to that decision.

ASSESSMENT AND TAXATION

Taxable Property and Assessment

States typically define *real property* to include the land, structures, and fixtures. The key test is "Is the item fixed?" (For example, the law considers an item nailed to the wall as "fixed.") If the answer to the test is "yes," the state and local taxing district consider the fixed item part of the real property for tax purposes. Tax laws do not consider repairs as adding per se to the property value, but improvements do change property value. Here the test is "Is the change an addition or alteration, as opposed to restoration to a previous condition?" Both tests are difficult to apply and controversy can arise out of using them. For example, one common problem is how to handle mobile homes because, as the name implies, they are not fixed to the property. Most states supplement the test of being fixed by using the length of time the mobile home is on the property or other actions taken to indicate fixture, such as removing wheels.

The assessment process is complex. It must be accurate and uniform or taxpayers can raise charges of unfairness, resulting in possible court action. The first step in property taxation is to determine the tax base. The taxing authority must take an inventory of the property in the district. This is usually done using owner declarations, surveys, and building permits. Tax assessors must take care to record properly all relevant details, especially improvements to the property.

Typically, the assessor bases his or her assessment on a uniform fraction of market value or on *full market value* of each property. Governments tax classes of property (for example, farms, vacant land, one-family residences, and multiple residences) at different rates. Sometimes tax exemptions exist, such as homestead, elderly, sovereignty (for example, an Indian tribe and a foreign embassy), or meritorious service (for example religious, charitable, educational, and veterans).

Assessors usually make their assessment on market price value of the property under question. Whenever possible, they use the market price for the property because that price meets the definition of market price. That definition is the price at which a willing seller will sell and a willing buyer will buy and where the seller is not forced to sell and the buyer is not forced to buy. If the assessor discovers that the owner recently sold the property, then that actual selling price would constitute the fair market value in almost all circumstances. Because properties are not selling every year, assessors look for comparable property values to determine market value of the property under question.

Often, the assessor cannot determine property values by the typical market value approach. For example, possibly the property being assessed has no comparable property like it in existence and it was not recently sold or not sold under market conditions. Under conditions where the assessor cannot determine comparability easily, the assessor might use sales information as a means to make a reasoned judgment on the worth of the property. An assessor would develop a sales ratio, that is, the ratio between price and assessed value, based on sales reports. The assessor would merely multiply the ratio to the sales information and make his or her determination on the value of the property in question.

Assessors apply statistical measures, such as central tendency and dispersion, to the sales ratios. This helps the assessor isolate current assessed value inaccuracies as well as determine the quality of assessment. The assessor can then use these ratios to develop a percentage factor to adjust improper assessments. A more sophisticated approach is multiple regression analysis, which identifies variables reflecting market value. Assessors can use this approach to find property value indicators and use them to update assessments. Another approach is to analyze market data to select independent variables that help to predict or estimate sales prices accurately, or identify comparable properties to determine property value.

In some situations, assessors must use other market approaches in making their assessment. One is the *cost* or *replacement cost approach.* This approach is a particularly useful means of determining the value of large numbers of buildings. This approach stresses how much it would cost to replace the building at the time of assessment. The assessor gathers data from builders and others to determine the reproduction cost of the building. Then he or she determines the age and condition of the building to calculate the depreciation factor. Next, the assessor estimates the land. Finally, he or she compares the replacement cost minus depreciation against the recent sale price of similar property.

A third approach is the *income approach,* but an assessor seldom uses it as the sole basis for assessment. It is particularly useful where the market for the property is imperfect (for example, no willing buyer). The assessor first calculates the net income for the property and then divides it by the current discount rate to arrive at an estimated property value. The assessor should validate this value using the income approach on similar property in which the assessor used the market approach. The results should be comparable.

Assessors should do their assessments frequently enough so that each assessment is closely comparable with the market price of the property. In many assessing jurisdictions—which are sometimes not the same as taxing jurisdictions—the practice is to have extremely infrequent reassessments. This leads to the "welcome stranger distortion." The property appraiser automatically assesses new people who move into an area based on the price they paid for their house because that ideally fits the definition of market value. In contrast, the property appraiser assesses long-time residents who did not buy their homes recently at lower assessments because determining their market value is difficult, and typically the assessor gives them the benefit of the doubt. Thus, newcomers tend to pay higher property taxes for their property than comparable property not sold recently. In states that adopted Proposition 13 reforms, their revised constitution essentially institutionalized the welcome stranger distortion. This raises the question that the Proposition 13 reform might be violating the "equal protection" clause of the federal Constitution. In a 1992 ruling, the U.S. Supreme Court in an eight-to-one ruling upheld California's Proposition 13 cap in spite of the equal protection argument made by new property owners in the state.

A hardship that a reassessment sometimes causes involves circuit breakers. As inflation occurs and drives up the cost of a property, an owner can find his or her property taxes move from nearly zero to significantly higher amounts because the property value moves beyond the limits set by the circuit breaker. However, a remedy is to have the circuit breaker carefully worded to provide a gradual increase in property taxes rather than the harsher drastic increase.

So-called tax havens do exist, and some property owners pay little or no property tax because of them. Let us say a family owns an expensive, even highly assessed home. Typically, this would mean high property taxes. But if that home is in a tax district that has a great deal of industry, then the tax on residential property is likely to be low because the industrial property tax owners generate enough revenue at their tax rates to cover the needs of the local government. This situation is a *tax haven* for the residential property owners. Taxes are a function of both the assessment and the tax rate of all the classes of property in the tax district.

A state requires a *uniform property tax assessment* throughout the state, but the practical problem is that there are many local assessing jurisdictions. One means to achieve the desired objective is for a state board of equalization to convert each local assessment into a uniform statewide assessment. Assessors can make this adjustment by multiplying the local assessment by a ratio or rate much like the one used in the sales ratio assessment approach. The *state equalization rate* is the ratio of assessed value of real property to market value. Exhibit 9–1 explains how a state determines the equalization rate. The equalization rate serves as a measure of assessment quality. If the market value of a house is $140,000 and the equalization rate is 50 percent, then the assessment should be about $70,000. If it is not, then the house is either under- or overassessed.

Testing Assessments

The assessment process is often highly controversial. People do not want to pay any more taxes than necessary, especially when a local government increases the tax as a result of a recent tax reassessment that applies to a large set of properties.

When many property owners protest increased reassessments, the local government has a "taxpayer rebellion." If there is no Proposition 13 constitutional reform in place, rebellions happen typically when property values go up radically, yearly reassessments do not keep up with the rapid prices increases, and a massive

EXHIBIT 9–1   State Equalization Rate Determination

Step 1.   The assessor establishes the assessed value of the property by using the local government assessment rolls.

Step 2.   He or she establishes the market value of all property. The assessor does this by examining sales information and bases the estimate for all the property on sales information.

Step 3.   The assessor determines ratios for all classes of property based on the assessed and market values.

Step 4.   For each class of property, the assessor determines the total number of taxed properties and market to assessed value rate for each county. The computation appears as follows for one class of property.

TAXING DISTRICT	MARKET VALUE	ASSESSED VALUATION	RATIO	NUMBER OF TAXED PROPERTIES	PRODUCTS
A	A_m	A_r	Ar:Am	A_p	$(A_r{:}A_m)A_p$
B	B_m	B_r	Br:Bm	B_p	$(B_r{:}B_m)B_p$
C	C_m	C_r	Cr:Cm	C_p	$(C_r{:}C_m)C_p$
N	etc.	etc.	etc.	etc.	
				T_p	P

$P \div T_p$ = state equalized ratio

Step 5.   The state assessor informs each taxing district of the state equalization ratio for each class of property. The state assessor requires each district to apply (multiply) this ratio to the determined full market value based on the state uniform percent of full market value applicable to the taxing district.

Source: As adapted from Thomas A. Dorsey. *Understanding the Real Property Tax.* Syracuse, NY: Syracuse Governmental Research Bureau, 1974.

reassessment occurs in a later year that affects many homeowners at the same time. Property assessment is often subjective and is an activity where assessors can easily make mistakes causing significant differences in the taxes due. Individual taxpayer complaints and appeals are common. This section discusses several tests that a person wishing to improve property tax assessment can apply.[1] There are three key questions:

- Has the assessor apportioned the property tax burden among owners on the basis of the value of their property?
- Does the assessor tend to favor or to discriminate against certain types of property?
- Are the higher-priced properties underassessed?

---

[1] This section draws heavily from Arnold H. Raphaelson, "Property Assessment and Tax Administration." In J. Richard Aronson and Eli Schwartz (eds.), *Management Policies in Local Government Finance.* Washington, DC: International City Management Association, 1975.

The test for apportioning the tax burden on the basis of value is the *coefficient of dispersion* for the district. The coefficient reflects how closely the assessment values are to each other relative to market value. The steps for calculation are as follows:

- Determine the assessment ratio for each of a sample of properties sold. Let us say there are three parcels. Each is sold for $100,000 and assessed separately at $50,000, $60,000, and $70,000. The separate assessment ratios:

50% 60% 70%

- Determine the average of these assessment ratios for the sample of transactions. Average (or median) assessment ratio:

60%

- Compute the average deviation of the separate assessment ratios from the average or median assessment ratio. Average deviation:

$$(10\% + 0\% + 10\%) \div 3 = 6.6\%$$

- Relate the average deviation to the median or average assessment ratio. Coefficient of dispersion:

$$6.6\% \div 60\% = 0.11 \text{ or } 11\%$$

Note: Margin of 10% expected given imperfection in data.

In the preceding explanation, the test tells us the assessor did *not* apportion the property tax burden among the owners on the basis of their properties' value. The coefficient of dispersion was 11 percent, which is 1 percent over the excusable margin. The problem is probably not significant, but a problem does exist.

By substituting for each preceding category the average assessment ratio for each coefficient of dispersion category assessment ratio, an analyst can determine if the assessor is discriminating against some types of property. This analysis relates the average category assessment ratio to the overall ratio, thus relating the shares of the property tax burden of the different categories. The calculations are similar to the ones cited previously. For example:

1. The assessment ratios for each category:

40% 60% 80%

2. Average of median assessment ratio:

60%

3. Average deviation:

$$(20\% + 0\% + 20\%) \div 3 = 13.3\%$$

4. Coefficient of dispersion:

$$13.3\% \div 60\% = 0.22 \text{ or } 22\%$$

The *coefficient of dispersion* indicates definite discrimination.

By calculating the price-related differential, the analyst can determine if the higher-priced properties are underassessed. This analysis is a measure of the relative accuracy of higher- and lower-priced property assessments. The steps for calculation are as follows:

- Calculate the aggregate assessment-sales ratio, which the analyst weights using the values of the parcels in the sample. Let us say the following example exists:

SALE PRICE	ASSESSED VALUE	ASSESSMENT RATIO
$100,000	$20,000	20%
10,000	4,000	40%
10,000	4,000	40%
10,000	4,000	40%
$130,000	$32,000	140%

- The aggregate assessment-sales ratio:

$$(\$32,000 \div \$130,000) = 0.246 \text{ or } 24.6\%$$

- Calculate the average of the assessment ratios of the separate parcels. The average assessment ratio of properties:

$$1.40 \div 4 = 0.350 \text{ or } 35\%$$

- Divide the mean of the assessment ratios by the aggregate assessment-sales ratio and then determine the price-related differential. The price-related differential:

$$35.0 \div 24.6 = 1.42 \text{ or } 142\%$$

The deviation from 100 percent is the key concern in this analysis. If the calculations result in about 100 percent, then there is no under- or overassessment. If the calculations result in more than 100 percent, then there is underassessment of higher-priced properties. If the calculations result in less than 100 percent, then there is underassessment of lower-priced properties. In the preceding example, 142 percent is significantly more than 100 percent; therefore, there is underassessment of the $100,000 property.

There are three types of improper assessment situations: *illegal assessment, inequitable assessment,* and *overvaluation. Illegal assessment* is when the assessor violates some specific legal rule or law in the assessment process. *Inequity* is when assessed value exceeds the uniform percentage for the class of property. *Overvaluation* is when assessment exceeds the actual market value. The following illustrates the concepts:

	HOUSE A	HOUSE B	HOUSE C
Current market value	$20,000	$20,000	$20,000
Equalization rate	.50	.50	.50
Calculated assessed value	10,000	10,000	10,000
Actual assessed value	25,000	10,000	15,000
	overvaluation	equitable assessment	inequitable assessment

The assessor can expect complaints from the owners of both houses A and C.

Assessment Cycle, Taxation, and Foreclosure

The assessment cycle builds upon an assessment calendar much like the budget calendar. By the taxable-status day, the assessor must determine the value of the property. By the tentative completion date, the assessor should consider the assessment role complete and he or she should file legal copies. By the grievance day, unhappy taxpayers should file formal petitions for change of assessment to the review board. The final completion day is the beginning of court reviews of review board decisions. Eventually, the state or local legislative body must certify the assessment. The final step is when the assessment roll becomes the tax roll. All this must be done each year.

The state or local government now must calculate how much revenue it needs and the tax rate needed to generate that amount of revenue. The government computes estimated expenditures and subtracts other revenue. The so-called *tax of last resort*—the property tax—must generate the remainder of the money needed to run the government. The analyst divides the needed revenue by the assessed valuation, which he or she converts into a rate per thousand assessed value. The tax rate is a function of the tax base and the amount of money needed to run the government.

The process does have its constraints. Often a law establishes a maximum tax rate. Certainly, there are economic constraints because high rates discourage commerce and discourage people from living in an area. There are also political constraints because high tax rates can lead to taxpayer rebellions, which can force some officials out of office.

The yield from property tax is due both to the tax rate and to the assessed value. The tax yield can increase if the assessed value goes up or the policy makers increase the tax rate. If the local government is at the maximum tax rate, then pressures increase for reassessment, which many assessors often neglect. If a community has a growing tax base, then it has the advantage of getting a greater yield without necessarily increasing the tax rate or reassessing the established property. However, if a community has a shrinking tax base, then it has the unfortunate prospect of reaching its tax rate limit and reassessing its property as much as possible. This tends to discourage commerce and to encourage greater flight from the community.

Governments collect taxes in a variety of ways. Some demand a yearly or possibly a quarterly payment directly to them. Most people must borrow money from a bank to buy a home, and they have monthly mortgage payments to make to the bank. Often, the bank will also collect the property taxes as a part of the monthly payment. The tax amount goes into an escrow account until payment is due to the government. If the government does not receive payment, there is an extra interest charge or penalty amount added on to the already delinquent tax obligation.

If the owner or mortgage banker makes no payment for the owner, then a long, complex foreclosure begins. The process varies from state to state, but the following illustrates a typical situation. First, the government imposes a tax lien, which includes all interests and penalties. Tax liens are in the form of tax certificates. They are negotiable securities that government can sell because they represent a debt that the homeowner must liquidate before he or she can convey clear title. The property itself serves as the security for the debt.

Legislatures design the whole process to give the taxpayers a fair opportunity to retain their property. Government must give public notice on major foreclosure actions on the property in question, but sometimes the law does not require notice directly to the homeowner. At the sale, the government gives a certificate for the title, and the owner has one year to redeem or to lose the property. If the former owner does not redeem the certificate, then the government conveys the title of the property to the owner of the tax certificate unless there is actual occupancy of the property or the property is also subject to a mortgage. If those conditions exist, the tax certificate owner can foreclose on the property. This process takes years. Often, whoever occupies or technically owns the certificate or property in question neglects the property during this period. Its value goes down, and it becomes an eyesore to the neighborhood.

Property tax delinquency is not a big problem in most places and most property owners pay delinquent taxes eventually. The Great Depression saw severe property tax delinquency, with an average state and local delinquency rate of 20.5 percent. Larry DeBoer compiled the data cited in Exhibit 9–2. It shows the comparative property tax delinquency rates for forty-eight major American cities. Most cities had very low rates, but some such as Houston, Newark, Portland (Oregon), and St. Louis had higher delinquency rates.

OTHER REVENUE SOURCES

Income Tax

Income tax is thought of as a federal tax, but it is also a revenue source for state and local government. For example, in 1998, the United States collected $879,480 million in income taxes, of which $189,309 million was state and local income tax revenue. About $16,555 million was local income tax revenue. At the federal level, government collects income tax from both corporations and individuals, with the latter being much more significant. The federal government collects taxes on all types

EXHIBIT 9–2 Property Tax Delinquency Rates in 48 Major U.S. Cities, 1933, 1950–74, and Recent Year

CITY	1933	DELINQUENCY RATES AVERAGES, 1950–74	RECENT (YEAR)
Atlanta, GA	3.3	3.2	5.6 (84)
Baltimore, MD	14.9	2.9	0 (86)
Birmingham, AL	17.7	0.2	0.9 (87)
Boston, MA	8.4	9.2	0.7 (84)
Bridgeport, CT	14.1	2.1	7.2 (87)
Cedar Rapids, IA	n/a	0.4	4.3 (86)
Charleston, SC	n/a	6.7	10.0 (82)
Chicago, IL	40.6*	10.9	5.3 (84)
Cincinnati, OH	n/a	2.1	4.1 (86)
Cleveland, OH	n/a	2.5	7.5 (86)
Dallas, TX	13.2	1.4	2.9 (86)
Denver, CO	10.6	0.7	0.8 (84)
Des Moines, IA	15.5	0.5	1.3 (86)
Detroit, MI	35.1	2.2	8.5 (86)
Fargo, ND	n/a	4.2	9.5 (86)
Ft. Wayne, IN	n/a	3.0	2.6 (85)
Hartford, CT	21.4	1.6	3.7 (86)
Houston, TX	22.3	11.0	29.7 (85)
Indianapolis, IN	n/a	2.1	2.6 (86)
Kansas City, MO	n/a	2.7	4.4 (87)
Little Rock, AR	n/a	3.0	4.6 (86)
Los Angeles, CA	10.1	2.0	7.8 (83)
Louisville, KY	6.6	5.5	6.6 (87)
Memphis, TN	23.6	3.0	3.7 (86)
Miami, FL	27.8	1.5	4.1 (86)
Milwaukee, WI	37.6	0.7	2.0 (86)
New Orleans, LA	15.4	1.9	7.1 (86)
New York, NY	10.4	5.1	5.2 (87)
Newark, NJ	19.4	9.2	17.1 (84)
Norfolk, VA	26.1	5.4	6.7 (87)
Oakland, CA	8.7	2.1	3.2 (82)
Oklahoma City, OK	22.3	2.5	7.8 (86)
Philadelphia, PA	15.5	3.1	9.9 (86)
Phoenix, AZ	n/a	2.1	7.0 (87)
Pittsburgh, PA	25.2	6.1	6.5 (86)
Portland, OR	24.6	7.5	10.3 (86)
Richmond, VA	5.1	3.7	2.0 (86)
St. Louis, MO	24.3	5.8	11.8 (87)
Salt Lake City, UT	n/a	3.8	6.2 (86)
San Francisco, CA	5.4	1.3	3.1 (87)
Seattle, WA	51.2	3.0	3.3 (87)
Spokane, WA	21.4	3.6	6.5 (86)
Toledo, OH	n/a	2.8	4.1 (86)
Topeka, KS	n/a	1.3	3.9 (86)
Tucson, AZ	n/a	3.0	8.4 (86)
Wheeling, WV	n/a	3.8	6.6 (85)
Youngstown, OH	n/a	4.6	1.2 (85)

*1932

n/a = not available

Source: Table prepared by Larry DeBoer and reported in "Property Tax Delinquency and Tax Sales: A Review of the Literature." Public Budgeting and Financial Management, 2, 2 (1990), p. 315.

of income, but there are many complex exceptions that are beyond the scope of this text. The state income taxes usually are related closely to the federal tax, with some specific changes mandated by each state's legislature. Local income taxes are typically flat-rate taxes on wages and salaries.

Like the property tax, the income tax has its share of issues. The complexity of the federal tax and the related "tax loopholes" are typical issues in elections. At the state and local level, taxation of nonresidents and taxation of nonlabor income are frequent subjects of controversy. Most agree that taxation should be a means to redistribute revenue among classes and among localities, but disagreement exists on how much government should redistribute wealth and on which localities should receive the benefit. One particular concern to state and local governments is that a perceived burdensome tax can produce an out-migration of individuals and businesses to areas where taxes are lower.

Tax loopholes, which economists call "tax expenditures," are a legal reduction in effective tax rates for certain classes of taxpayers, resulting in lower taxes due from nominal tax burdens. The technical term emphasizes the granting of government largess upon tax expenditure beneficiaries who gain just as much as those people who receive regularly budgeted expenditures such as veterans or those on welfare. The public usually does not think of the IRS deduction for home mortgages and related taxes as similar to welfare or veterans' benefits, but policy makers design each loophole to benefit a certain targeted class or set of people. More affluent income classes and corporations tend to be the beneficiaries of tax expenditures for the following reasons:

- Low-income groups often do not pay taxes and therefore do not benefit from tax expenditures.
- High-income groups often are in higher tax brackets and thus benefit more from tax expenditure policy.
- Politically sophisticated groups realize that tax expenditures are less visible governmental benefits to them.
- Tax expenditure benefits continue indefinitely once enacted as contrasted to budget benefits.
- Tax expenditures tend to be held to a lower standard of performance than budget benefits.
- Tax expenditures reduce overall government revenue and thus correspond more easily to the conservative feelings of many high-income people.

The details of income taxation administration vary, but the major features are rates, base, withholding, administrative staff and equipment, revenue potential, and implementation. Federal income rates provide the *progressive* feature of the tax because government taxes higher income at a higher rate. Federal and state income taxes have progressive rates, but most local governments use an income tax with a *flat* or nonprogressive rate. The taxpayer multiplies the *tax rate* and the *base* to arrive at his or her tax. At the local level, the taxpayer determines his or her tax base by simply combining the wages and salaries. At the federal level, the base is difficult to calculate, but it is the *net taxable income* after the taxpayer makes various IRS *allowable adjustments*. Employers often collect *withholding taxes* by pay periods. That requirement of employers is a key administrative feature of this tax because it makes tax payment less painful to the average taxpayer. Thus, the government has set aside an amount that should pay the yearly taxes for the individual taxpayer.

The income tax is difficult to administer and the government needs a qualified staff plus sophisticated equipment, such as very large computers to administer this tax. The revenue potential is quite good for this tax, and sophisticated revenue estimating procedures are often important, as explained in an earlier chapter. Tax administration involves maintaining a bookkeeping and audit staff and reporting forms, the continuing surveillance of tax collections, and prosecution of tax evasion and fraud cases.

A popular tax alternative to the income tax is a flat tax, which is a much simpler tax that applies a flat rate to a much simplified tax base calculation. The policy debate on this alternative centers on its advocates stressing its noncomplexity and its opponents stressing that the tax significantly benefits the wealthy as opposed to the middle and lower classes.

Sales Tax

The *sales tax* is primarily a state tax, but some local governments use it. Out of $346,532 million in taxes collected in 1998 from sales, gross receipts, and customs, $239,367 million went to the state level, $51,626 million to the local level, and $55,540 million to the federal level. A sales tax applies to goods and services usually levied at the retail stores and expressed in percentage terms. Sales tax can be *general* (that is, broadly applicable) or *selective* (that is, limited to a few items). The use of this tax increased as a result of the need for greater revenue than the income or property tax alone could provide. The sales tax is a highly successful tax in terms of revenue generation, but in periods of recession, revenue generation drops off significantly.

The policy issues related to sales tax include jurisdictional liability, loss of business, and compliance. Should government establish sales tax liability for a particular transaction at the *place of delivery* or at the *location of the vendor?* The *place of delivery* answer would result in added tax revenue but also add administrative headaches. One way to deal with the problem is the *use tax.* It is a tax levied in lieu of the sales tax on an item purchased outside the sales tax jurisdiction but still used and enjoyed in that jurisdiction. In practice, governments poorly enforce use taxes and the *location of the vendor* is the most practical jurisdictional liability test to apply. A community does lose retail business if its sales tax is higher than that of adjacent areas. The best policy is to have sales tax uniformity throughout a county or metropolitan area. Compliance problems always exist with contractors, itinerant sellers, installation workers, and multiple operations having locations in different cities.

Four other policy issues are regressivity, overlapping governments, allocation, and expansion of tax to cover services. Sales tax applies mostly to the consumers, and thus with sales tax, the poor must pay considerably more taxes in terms of a percentage of their resources. Therefore, economists label the sales tax as *regressive.* One policy that lessens *regressivity* of the sales tax is to exempt food and similar vital items from it. Often, more than one government unit covers an area and each imposes sales tax. Thus, often there is an *overlapping* of local sales taxes, creating a potential sales tax policy conflict and certainly confusion for the retailers collecting the tax.

Another issue is allocation of the revenue from this tax source. If the state collects the tax, the problem tends not to exist, but if a city determines and collects the sales tax, then allocation can be a serious problem. At the local level, there is a poor correlation between where the sales tax is collected and revenue needs of a community. Areas with concentrations of retail stores, such as shopping centers, benefit greatly from the tax and often provide remarkable tax havens for the lucky property owners who live near the shopping area. However, the poorer neighborhoods have greater needs for tax resources, but they have fewer stores to generate sales taxes. If the policy makers consider the sales tax as a statewide tax and place the money in a general fund, then allocation is not a significant problem. However, there are many local governments that collect sales taxes themselves, and matching revenue generation with revenue needs is politically difficult.

Another major policy issue is the government expanding the coverage of the sales tax from traditional retail sales to include sales in the service industries such as hairdressers, lawyers, and advertising. This expansion is a natural development given that that economy of the nation is more service oriented. But the service industry—especially the legal profession and the media, which relies on advertising—significantly resists this change. In particular, the latter group is politically powerful, and expansion of the sales tax to their activities is unlikely.

There are four steps in administration of the sales tax. First, the government must prepare or update a list of vendors or those that should collect this tax as they perform their business. Second, vendors must prepare and return forms explaining the tax they collected. Third, vendors must mail the forms and collections, with government stressing the importance of speed in transferring the forms and money to the government. The government must compare the return lists with the vendor list so that the government isolates delinquent vendors. Sometimes court action is necessary to get the returns. The fourth step is to have trained auditors examine a sample of vendor accounts and records. This is essential to maintain successful retail sales administration. Each step requires expertise and careful attention to detail.

User Charges

Another important revenue source for government is the *user fee, toll, license fee,* and *impact fee.* In many cases due to the general public value of a government service, the government can and does charge a *user fee* for services rendered. Sometimes the fee income covers the cost of the service, but sometimes user-fee incomes do not completely cover the cost of the government service. In such cases, other revenue sources subsidize the government service. Policy makers should know how to price a government service and realize when they have to decide to subsidize a service from another revenue source. Accurate user-fee pricing assists the public in understanding the economic worth of a government service. Accurate pricing avoids subsidies of a particular group (for example, golfers or boat owners at a marina) by the entire community or creating a reverse subsidy of a particular group to the general public.

Cost-volume-profit (CVP), or break-even analysis, often provides a means to determine user-fee charges more accurately. The focus of the analysis is on the inter-action of the price, volume, variable, and fixed cost. It produces a break-even point in volume or dollar value where total revenue and total costs are equal. A detailed ex-planation of this type of analysis is beyond the scope of the text, but the following case illustrates the usefulness of this type of analysis.

Stephen V. Senge (1986) discusses the proper charge for cars at a local govern-ment recreation area that caters to family groups who arrive by car. There are 7,500 carloads of people projected to use the park next year, and an analyst projects the traceable fixed costs (for example, permanent salaries, insurance, equipment mainte-nance, and utilities) at $40,000 and the allocated fixed costs (for example, park over-head and general government overhead) at $8,000. The analyst projects the variable cost (for example, clean-up, supplies, part-time workers) at $2 per car. A city coun-cil budgets a general fund subsidy of $18,000 for this activity.

The equation used is as follows:

$$P = \frac{VC + [(TFC + AFC) - S]}{Q}$$

Where P is the correct user-fee charge per car.
VC is the variable cost per car.
TFC is the traceable fixed costs.
AFC is the allocated fixed costs.
S is the subsidy.
Q is the total number of carloads of people.

Substituting values into the formula gives the following:

$$P = \frac{2 + [(40,000 + 8,000) - 18,000]}{7,500}$$

$$P = 2 + \frac{30,000}{7,500}$$

P = 2 + 4
P = 6 or $6 per car is the correct user fee

Another important tax source, especially in high-growth areas, is the *impact fee*. New development can have a significant impact on both infrastructure and community resources. Local governments intend impact fees to make the develop-ers pay a part of those high-growth costs rather than letting the entire burden fall on existing or future residents. New development typically means added waste-water treatment, sewers, schools, local traffic, park usage, libraries, and so on. Commonly, developers pass on impact fees to the new homebuyer, thus forcing up the price of new homes. However, communities see impact fees as a means to raise needed revenue without raising taxes. Courts require a rational relationship between the fee and the improvements acquired from the fee. The five major communities with a history of broad impact fee use are San Francisco, California; Palm Beach County, Florida; Montgomery County, Maryland; Boston, Massachusetts; and Minneapolis, Minnesota.

Other Taxes

Various other taxes and charges exist, for example, transfer taxes and charges for legal transactions, utility and inventory taxes, and special assessments. The other major industrial countries of the world use a value-added tax (VAT) as a national tax, but the U.S. government has not adopted this tax. If the federal government decides to change its tax structure to have less reliance on the income tax, the VAT is a policy option, especially if it is directed toward most businesses except retail business and the politically powerful media.

REVIEW QUESTIONS

1. What are the major trends in intergovernmental revenue systems? Explain the implications of those trends.
2. Why is the property tax considered an onerous tax? Explain why achieving a uniform, full-market-value property tax is extremely difficult.
3. What are the most easily adopted property tax reforms, and why is it difficult to achieve those reforms? Why is *Serrano v. Priest* an important case?
4. Explain why judgment is important in applying the key tests associated with property tax. Explain the various approaches to assessment and why it is a difficult judgment to make.
5. What are equalization rates in real property tax? How are they applied? What aspects should an analyst test in the assessment process, and should this be done? How should an analyst determine the tax rate?
6. How are property taxes collected, and what happens if taxes are not paid?
7. Compare and contrast the issues surrounding the imposition of the income and sales taxes. How would these issues impact on the administration of taxes?
8. How would you "package" a series of tax or other revenue measures to address your state's financial crisis? Explain the thought process behind your approach. Why would you adopt certain taxes and measures and not others?

REFERENCES

Advisory Commission on Intergovernmental Relations. *Changing Public Attitudes on Government and Taxes.* Washington, DC: Government Printing Office, 1982.

————. *Significant Features of Fiscal Federalism, 1981–82.* Washington, DC: Government Printing Office, April 1983.

ANGELL, CYNTHIA, and CHARLES A. SHORTER. "Impact Fees: Private-Sector Participation in Infrastructure Financing." *Government Finance Review,* 4, 5 (October 1988), 19–21.

ARONSON, J. RICHARD, and ELI SCHWARTZ (eds.). *Management Policies in Local Government Finance.* Washington, DC: International City Management Association, Municipal Finance Officers Association, 1975.

ARRON, HENRY J. *Who Pays the Property Tax?* Washington, DC: Brookings Institution, 1975.

BLECHMON, BARRY E., EDWARD M. GRAMLICK, and ROBERT W. HARTMAN. *Setting National Priorities: The 1976 Budget.* Washington, DC: Brookings Institution, 1976.

BLINDER, ALAN S., et al. *The Economics of Public Finance.* Washington, DC: Brookings Institution, 1974.

BREAK, GEORGE F. *Agenda for Local Tax Reform.* Berkeley: University of California, Institute of Governmental Studies, 1970.

CAMPBELL, COLIN D., and WILLIAM A. FISCHEL. "Preferences for School Finance Systems: Voters versus Judges." *National Tax Journal,* 49, 1 (March 1996), 1–15.

DeBOER, LARRY. "Property Tax Delinquency and Tax Sales: A Review of the Literature." *Public Budgeting and Financial Management,* 2, 2 (1990), 311–349.

DORSEY, THOMAS A. *Understanding the Real Property Tax.* Syracuse, NY: Syracuse Governmental Research Bureau, 1974.

DUNCOMBE, SYDNEY, and THOMAS D. LYNCH. "Taxpayer Revolt." In Thomas D. Lynch (ed.), *Contemporary Public Budgeting.* New Brunswick, NJ: Transaction Books, 1981.

Ecker-Racz, L. L. *The Politics and Economics of State-Local Finance.* Englewood Cliffs, NJ: Prentice Hall, 1970.

GALAMBOS, EVA C., and ARTHUR F. SCHREIBER. "The Analysis of Double Taxation." *Public Budgeting and Finance,* 1, 2 (Summer 1981), 31–40.

MAXWELL, JAMES, and J. RICHARD ARONSON. *Financing State and Local Governments.* Washington, DC: Brookings Institution, 1977.

MIKESELL, JOHN L., and KENNETH OLDFIELD (eds.). "Special Issue on Property Taxes: A Symposium of Its History and Prospects for Improved Administration, Relief and Reform." *Public Budgeting and Financial Management,* 2 (1990), 145–406.

National Association of State Budget Officers. *The Fiscal Survey of States.* Washington, DC: NASBO, 2002.

——. *Quick Rebound? State Fiscal Recovery Could Be Gradual, Lag National Economy 12–18 Months.* Washington, DC: NASBO, 2002.

PETERSON, GEORGE E. (ed.). *Property Tax Reform.* Washington, DC: Urban Institute, 1973.

RAPHAELSON, ARNOLD H. "Property Assessment and Tax Administration." *Management Policies in Local Government Finance.* In J. Richard Aronson and Eli Schwartz (eds.). Washington, DC: International City Managers Association, 1975.

SENGE, STEPHEN V. "Local Government User Charges and Cost-Volume-Profit Analysis." *Public Budgeting and Finance,* 6, 3 (Autumn 1986), 92–105.

SHANNON, JOHN, and JAMES EDWIN KEE. "The Rise of Competitive Federalism." *Public Budgeting and Finance,* 9, 4 (Winter 1989), 5–20.

U.S. Census Bureau. *Government Finances 1998–99.* Washington, DC: Government Printing Office, 2001.

——. "Federal Government Finances and Employment." *Statistical Abstract of the United States.* Washington, DC: Government Printing Office, 2001.

WHICKER, MARCIA LYNN. "Evaluating State and Local Tax Expenditures." Paper presented to the Southeastern Conference on Public Administration, New Orleans, LA, October, 1987.

10

INTERNAL SERVICE

FUNCTIONS

This chapter covers three important financial management topics: (1) property management, (2) risk management, and (3) pension funds. These public financial management subjects are important and useful for a person working in budgeting. At the conclusion of this chapter, the reader should know the following:

- the steps in a systematic preliminary review of property management;
- what purchasing is and why a specialist in purchasing is useful to a government;
- what competitive bidding is and its disadvantages;
- the importance of standardization and specifications;
- the usefulness of preventative group replacement, computing maintenance and equipment cost in purchasing decisions, and cooperative intergovernmental arrangements;
- the usefulness of central stores and the challenge of inventory management;
- the significance of property control;
- the potential applications of bar-code technology;
- what risk management is and why it is an important concern;
- what exposure identification is and how one goes about risk evaluation;
- what risk control is and its significance;
- what self-insurance is and when it is appropriate;
- what insurance is, how a risk manager selects it, and some general standards applicable to it;
- the elements of administration related to proper risk management;
- the significance of retirement plans to public budgeting;
- the significance of pensions to budgets; and
- the policy issues relevant to public pension funds.

PROPERTY MANAGEMENT

Preliminary Review

A government may own extensive and valuable property that administrators can neglect and not properly manage. The first fundamental responsibility for property management is to know exactly what property the government owns and the condition of that property. In systematic property management, the first step is to inventory or update the inventory of the government property. For each property, that means describing its location, identifying its use, recording its value, and identifying the person or persons responsible for the property. The second step is to determine if up-to-date and comprehensive regulations and procedures exist for the government's property. This step includes reviewing the property accounting system and adequacy, including the frequency and scope of internal audits addressed to government property. Auditing should complement property management by discerning whether audits cover property management practices and whether decision makers seriously consider audit findings. In addition, employees using the system are often the best source of ideas for improvement, and a third step should be checking whether decision makers sought and used employee opinions on government property. One last step is reviewing the risk associated with the property. This chapter covers that subject later.

A sound property management system ensures that no one individual or small group controls all aspects of property management transactions. Managers should divide certain specific duties, such as purchasing, receiving, accounting for, paying for, and disposing of property, among different people to minimize the possibility of pilferage or misuse of property. Managers should identify and document duties and responsibilities so that each employee clearly knows his or her role. If separation of key functions is impossible, then management reviews and internal controls should be more frequent. In addition, personnel need adequate training in their responsibilities, including care and protection of property, proper and safe practices, and the ethical implications of their jobs.

The following is a more detailed list of the duties that should be separated whenever possible:

- requesting purchases;
- authorizing purchases;
- purchasing;
- receiving and inspecting property;
- maintaining physical custody of property or inventories;
- maintaining property ledgers or detailed inventory records;
- maintaining financial accounting records for property or inventories;
- conducting physical inventories;
- reconciling physical inventory counts with property book balances;
- performing surveys for shortages, losses, thefts, or damage;
- authorizing transfers or disposition of property;
- reconciling property records with accounting records;
- making payments for purchases; and
- performing reviews and audits.

Purchasing

In an organization, management must acquire goods and services. This activity, which mangers call *purchasing,* involves procuring materials, supplies, and equipment. Purchasers need to find goods or services that public managers ideally need to do their jobs, including ordering the correct quantity as needed for the units in a timely manner. The proper timing of orders should include anticipating potential emergency shortage situations. Management should purchase the goods, services (including technical services), or equipment at the lowest possible price but also at the desired level of quality needed to get the job done correctly. And once the government no longer needs the property, then property managers should dispose of it appropriately.

A central purchasing agent should be in charge of the government's or department's procurement activity, but unit program managers can perform many smaller and less complex purchasing responsibilities directly as long as they follow guidelines established by the purchasing agent. Often, more complex purchasing requires knowledge of supply sources, pricing, business practices, market conditions, and appropriate laws, ordinances, and regulations. Thus, under many conditions, the unit program manager needs to work closely with and even delegate some purchasing decisions to the central purchasing agent. Management should devise its procurement system to ensure that procurement takes discounts, tests the quality of goods purchased, receives and stores items properly, and ensures prompt deliveries. The procurement function needs expertise in dealing with salespersons, contractors, and people in the government seeking goods and services to get their jobs done. In other words, procurement in many circumstances is a separate administrative specialty and central purchasing agents can do the best job.

Current research on how local governments handle the purchasing function reflects a mix of centralized and decentralized approaches. Many local governments give decentralized elements of the purchasing responsibilities to individual agencies or officers. This provides managers with direct input in determining the resources and supplies they need to do their jobs. However, most local governments still retain a centralized function with many offices moving, or desiring to move, to a hybrid type of arrangement where both centralized and decentralized purchasing occur (McCue 2002).

In spite of the obvious advantages, there are serious problems in properly conducting purchasing operations. As a result of political pressure and problems of ethics, management sometimes, unfortunately, awards a contract to favorite persons or groups that provide poor services, engage in payoffs, or supply kickbacks. Because of the enormous amounts of money involved, corruption is always a threat that management must address carefully. Another problem is that procurement approaches (discussed later) do not lend themselves to undisputedly proper purchases of services, especially if procurement needs require high levels of talent. Also, the complex process can make quick or simple purchases impossible, thus causing undue hardship on the performance of work done by government and driving up the cost of the purchase. In other words, procurement is not an easy administrative undertaking.

Procurement

Purchasing challenges and requirements in government often justify the hiring of a specialist or specialists in purchasing to whom management assigns the role of *central purchasing agent*. A specialist can take the time to better monitor delivery services, develop a list of qualified vendors, improve purchased items through standardization, use standard specifications more easily, perform better inspections, and conduct tests on purchased goods. In addition, management can more easily fix the responsibility for procurement if there is a purchasing agent. Also, central purchasing agents provide management greater and often better fiscal control over expenditures involving materials, supplies, and equipment. These benefits do not come automatically as they require high levels of professionalism, especially the cooperative capabilities of the government's management team. Often, having a central purchasing agent means friction between the ordering department and the purchasing department as well as other problems if the purchasing department is inefficient, corrupt, or lacks sufficient budget authority. If the central purchasing office is the least bit incompetent and higher-level management requires unit managers to work through the central purchasing agent, then central purchasing becomes a remarkable bottleneck that greatly lowers the productivity of government. Competency of the central purchasing agent is important.

In most governments, the law requires management to make most, and sometimes all but the smallest, purchases with competitive bidding in order to minimize cost and avoid corruption. At the same time, it is important to recognize the role for flexibility of purchases delegated to frontline managers when shortfalls or timing of stock replenishment is an issue. In many states and localities, managers are allowed to make purchases under $5,000 without the need for a competitive bidding process. However, even in these jurisdictions there is usually a preselected/approved suppliers list or clearinghouse from which managers are allowed to make these types of purchases. Procurement should advertise for almost all bids and maintain up-to-date lists of competent suppliers to keep within the spirit of the law. The government should retain the opportunity to reject bids unilaterally in most circumstances. The invitation or *request for bids* should set out what the government wishes to purchase using detailed specifications and any specific conditions such as the date of delivery. Procurement personnel should publicly open the sealed bids, and they must clearly explain—in the terms of their previously stated contract award criteria—why they awarded the contract to other than the lowest bidder. They must make their awards in accordance with their stated specifications; and government must encourage competent vendors to participate in the bidding process but also prevent any illegal or unethical collusion between the vendor and the purchasing agent or any other government employee.

Sometimes procurement uses qualifiers to constrain or filter out who will receive a contract. Such constraints on competitive bidding can achieve socially important goals such as improving the procurement process, but if improperly stated, these constraints can lead to lower-quality work by the contractor or can make finding good contractors difficult or impossible. An often-positive tool is the procurement qualifier of "lowest responsible bidder," which disqualifies vendors with a negative performance history. An often-dysfunctional tool is the qualifier that requires procurement to award the contract only to a contractor from a specific geographic area such as within the state. Often such procurement qualifiers increase the price of the contract and lower the quality of the work performed. Another means to limit competition is a purchasing procedure that does not allow procurement to select professional service contracts competitively. Although competition for professional service contracts is often best, the nature of the requested work or the difficulty in getting highly skilled professionals to bid for a competitive contract might mean a negotiated bid is the wiser policy for a professional service contract. Procurement must avoid "backdoor selling," which means gaining vendor favor by means of gifts, kickbacks, paid trips, and friendships. One last category of competition constraint is bidder anticompetition practices such as rotating the lowest bid among bidders and allocation of business based on a geographic location. Although often illegal, such bidder practices are hard to detect.

Because of affirmative action regulations, which policy makers use to stimulate business for women or minorities, a procurement contract qualifier can stipulate that a person from a minority group or a woman must own the enterprise that does business with government. Occasionally policy makers frame these constraints in terms of specific percentages of contracts awarded, such as management awarding no less than 20 percent of the contracts to minority contractors. This policy is under question by both courts and Congress. The Clinton administration proposed that procurement contract officers use affirmative action qualifiers only where there was a clear pattern of discrimination in the industry. Otherwise, government would not use this qualifier.

The disadvantages of competitive bidding are that it is inflexible; takes a long time to process; and does not lend itself to small purchases, emergency buying, or contracts for professional services. If procurement receives only one or even a few bids, then the government must have the option to refuse the bid; otherwise, the process might result in higher rather than lower prices. In such circumstances, procurement might find negotiated bidding to be a better practice.

Standardization and *specification* are important procurement activities. *Standardization* of purchased items can lead to reducing the number and kinds of items purchased, thus reducing cost through quantity buying. Exceptions to standardization exist, especially with highly specialized and technical goods. However, procurement usually finds standardization desirable because it should lead to price savings, quality improvements, and lower administrative costs. A *specification* is a product or material description upon which procurement solicits bids. An adequate specification is accurate and complete, but not overspecific. Good specification should place all bidders on an equal basis, minimize disputes, and avoid expensive brand-name buying. Preparing and using standardization and specification requires enormous work and a highly qualified staff. If specifications serve no practical purpose in a given context, procurement should avoid them as they increase, not lower, efficiency. A specification must do the following:

- describe the methods of inspection and testing;
- state special requirements such as packing;
- conform, if possible, to national standards; and
- be internally consistent and simply stated.

Procurement should inspect and test the received goods as well as dispose of property. Were the goods delivered on time and in good condition? Were the goods received those that were ordered? Are the goods of the quality ordered? Inspection and testing should always answer these vital questions. However, procurement need not inspect all items, as a random sample might be adequate.

The purchasing department also disposes of government property. If possible, management should reassign items to other parts of the government, however, the time comes when the purchasing department should trade, sell at auction, or sell items as surplus. The management objective is to save the government money by using items as much as possible and then by recovering any value of the goods after they have ceased being useful to the government.

The field of purchasing has made advances. Formal organizations like the National Association of State Purchasing Officers (NASPO) have been created to promulgate guidelines and fund studies aimed at improving the professionalization of the field and promoting the use of technological advances in purchasing systems (see www.naspo.org). The American Bar Association published the *Model Procurement Code,* which has stimulated public awareness and interest in improving government purchasing. It recommends that management separate purchasing policy and operations. A chief procurement officer with at least eight years' purchasing experience should direct day-to-day purchasing. Procurement specialists have an increased ethical awareness because of the federal 1986 Anti-Kickback Act and the 1988 book *Ethics and Quality Purchasing* by Stanley D. Zemansky. According to Charles Coe (1993), there is an increased use of purchasing techniques such as the following:

- *value engineering* (analyzing a product or service so that management can perform its function at the lowest possible overall cost without sacrificing quality);
- *computerization;*
- *total-cost purchasing* (looking at other factors such as cost of supplies, energy, parts, warranties, maintenance);
- *faxing* and *e-mail;*
- *commodity coding* (a standard classification system developed by the National Institute of Government Purchasing); and
- *life-cycle costing* (considers the total cost of ownership of a commodity or building).

Selected Purchasing Challenges

Sometimes management can save money by replacing a whole group of items at once rather than by replacing many items separately because of the higher maintenance costs of making the ad hoc changes. For example, a preventative maintenance program can make overall savings by replacing all items in a given category (for example, light bulbs) at one time rather than individually because group replacement is sometimes cheaper owing to efficiency in scheduling labor and to quantity price discounts. If this is the management policy, then management should establish a replacement cycle so that it can buy goods and schedule labor in a coordinated manner. Also, management needs to do some research in order to decide the expected life of the item and the best replacement time.

Procurement should understand *total purchasing cost,* which procurement can compute by adding maintenance cost to the purchasing cost of the equipment. The supplier or the operators of the equipment can estimate maintenance cost. In fact, the

EXHIBIT 10–1   Total-Cost Purchasing or Least-Cost Purchasing

Three suppliers bid as follows on heavy equipment:

SUPPLIER	PURCHASE PRICE	TOTAL FIVE-YEAR GUARANTEED MAINTENANCE COST	REPURCHASE PRICE
A	$23,000	$11,000	$2,000
B	30,000	5,000	15,000
C	26,000	12,000	10,000

Supplier C has specified a five-year guarantee of $800 times the age of the machine each year. Suppliers A and B have agreed to apportion their guarantees evenly over the five years (i.e., $2,200 per annum for A and $1,000 per annum for B).
    The formula to calculate total cost is as follows:

$$K = P + B \sum_{i=1}^{5} R_i \cdot \frac{1}{1.2} \le R - T \cdot \frac{1}{1.2}^{5} \le$$

where

K = net present value R_i = maintenance cost in year 1
P = purchase price   T = repurchase price

Using a 20 percent discount, the formula results in the following:

SUPPLIER	PURCHASE PRICE	+	PRESENT VALUE OF MAINTENANCE COST	−	PRESENT VALUE OF REPURCHASED PRICE	=	NET PRESENT VALUE
A	$23,000		$6,579		$ 804		$28,775
B	30,000		2,991		6,029		26,962
C	26,000		6,318		4,019		28,299

Source: Wayne A. Corcoran. "Financial Management." in J. Richard Aronson and Eli Schwartz (eds.) *Management Policies in Local Government Finance,* Washington, DC: International City, Managers Association, 1975, pp. 263–282.

contract with the supplier can include a proviso declaring the maximum maintenance cost and guaranteeing that the seller will reimburse any excessive maintenance cost. Corcoran provides an illustration of total cost purchasing in Exhibit 10–1.

    Maintaining cooperative intergovernmental arrangements can mean cost savings, but decision makers should undertake them with a clear understanding of all the factors involved. For example, decision makers should negotiate a basis for cost sharing. The level of service should be the same as existing service; or, if reduced, then policy makers must accept this. Labor disputes can sometimes arise when management eliminates jobs. Also, the parties must understand and accept who controls the planning, specifications, and service availability. Although very useful, cooperative arrangements are often difficult to apply because of disagreements over uniform items, the need for detailed records, and the allocation of shared costs. Besides cost-savings advantages, cooperative programs lead to a better sharing of ideas and greater personnel growth opportunities. Some important services that decision makers can contract or share include street lighting, garbage disposal, sanitation services, health services, tax assessment and collection, water supply, law enforcement, and street and highway maintenance.

Central Stores and Inventory

Proper central warehousing, including tanks and storage yards, can foster significant savings since it makes possible quantity buying at the right time and price. Although just-in-time delivery using computer reordering makes central stores less desirable, they do permit better use of lead time to stock for emergencies and allow the management of uneven requirements for some types of goods. The disadvantage of central stores is the administrative cost of operation. Thus, management should minimize the use of warehousing and avoid the following problems:

1. overstocking, especially if the goods can become obsolete;
2. a nonrestrictive inventory, not limited to substantial demand items;
3. failure to balance stocking cost against value of having the item in stock when units of government need it; and
4. failure to consider the final range of cost elements.

The critical challenge of inventory is to calculate and achieve the optimum amount of commodities so those necessary goods are available while minimizing storage costs. If supplies were available instantly and if purchase unit price did not vary by such factors as size of purchase, there would be no need for inventory. However, management requires inventory to reduce the likelihood of being out of needed goods and to obtain lower prices through bulk purchase and by taking advantage of fluctuations in market price. Management must balance those "savings" against storage costs. This calculation is much like the decisions to invest idle cash discussed in an earlier chapter.

Managers must determine the correct levels of *safety stock*. There are various ways to determine that level of stock, but they all should recognize the various inventory costs:

- *ordering cost*—preparing specifications, obtaining competitive bids, negotiating, receiving items;
- *incremental cost*—unique extra costs due to specific orders;
- *carrying cost*—deterioration, obsolescence, storing, issuing, theft, handling, interest, and insurance; and
- *shortage cost*—associated with disappointing a client, legal settlements, lost labor costs, other costs due to delay or failure to provide service.

The solution for optimal safety stock is to keep the total costs and expected shortage costs minimal. These calculations assume sound estimates, but once an analyst determines those costs, the actual calculation for optimal safety stock is relatively simple, especially with a computer. Analysts can develop rules of thumb in terms of days of typical use. Ideally, analysts should check these rules of thumb against the more sophisticated calculations.

Another calculation involves ordering cost. For this, analysts use the *economic ordering quantity* (EOQ) model. The analyst weighs the ordering costs against the holding costs that arise on account of the size of the order. The calculation is similar to the optimal safety stock determination. When the total of the two types of costs are at a minimum, the analysts find the optimum ordering quantity. Exhibit 10–2 presents an example of the EOQ model.

Again, most analysts develop simpler rules of thumb. However, they should test their rule of thumb against the more sophisticated approach discussed here. Analysts can calculate *total desirable inventory* by adding the EOQ and safety stock solution. A more accurate solution would use a simultaneous solution, but practical requirements do not usually warrant that higher degree of accuracy. The preceding calculations use quantifiable costs, but often analysts cannot reduce important government or social costs to numbers. Managers and analysts should understand this when applying the techniques.

Property Control

Management needs a *property control* officer to ensure its employees efficiently manage government property, including its equipment. No operational control is necessary, but management should devise some minimum procedures and monitor practices to ensure efficient management. Management should apply more detailed control only in cases where the poor use of items can easily mean a safety problem, inefficiency, corruption, or other serious problems if employees lack proper conduct. *Records control* fixes actual responsibility for the care of an item. Management needs

EXHIBIT 10–2   Copy of EOQ Model

$$Q = 2 \overline{2C_oD} , C_H$$

where
Q = the optimum (that is, most economic) quantity to order
C_O = the cost of ordering per order
C_H = the cost of holding per unit per time period
D = the quantity of units used or demanded in each time period

An example is as follows:

D = 110 cubic yards of gravel used per day
C_o = \$20.00 per order (ordering costs)
C_H = \$0.02 per yard per day (holding costs)
Q = 2 $\overline{2(20)110}$, .02 = 469 yards

periodic reports on the condition of the item. Records help with insurance loss claims, preventative maintenance decisions, and reordering. Records should use identifying numbers, acquisition purchase orders, transfers, and repair and disposal orders. An option to owning goods is leasing. This is an alternative that may be the best economic investment. The calculations to determine this are similar to the ones involving present value discussed in an earlier chapter.

Bar-Code Technology

In the early 1960s, supermarkets and their suppliers began using bar codes to identify items for automatically checking out items and other inventory control purposes. Since then, managers have used bar codes and other machine-readable symbols (see Exhibit 10–3) on material components, finished goods, shipping containers, warehouse bins, bills of lading, and other distribution documentation. Optical scanners are increasingly common in factories, private warehouses, and government agencies. Scanners convert the symbols into acceptable computer input. The hardware consists of the optical code reader and bar-coded labels. The reader is a minicomputer that records, stores, and transmits coded data to the main computer. The scanner projects a special light beam on the bar-coded surfaces to sense reflections. The reader may also have a computerized display that shows the data being scanned as it updates the record on the item. It may be online—interfaced directly with a large computer—or off-line, with interface devices used on occasion to transmit stored data. For inventory and property control, employees more widely use the portable, hand-held models. Analysts must read bar-code labels easily, the machines themselves must be durable, and the labeled items must hold the labels easily.

Due to information technology, great productivity gains in property management can result from bar-code technology. When the workplace finds faster and more accurate data entry is important, then this technology leads to increased operational effectiveness. The following are some of the more common bar-code applications:

- forms management;
- document sorting;
- tracking and locating work in progress;
- production control;
- order processing and automatic billing;
- quality control inspection;
- distribution or warehouse control;
- mail operations, including sorting and tracking;
- motor vehicle accountability and maintenance;
- productivity measurement;
- "job shops" for billing purposes;
- libraries/central files;
- security in controlling access to restricted areas; and
- shipping and receiving control.

EXHIBIT 10–3 Examples of Bar Codes and Machine-Readable Symbols

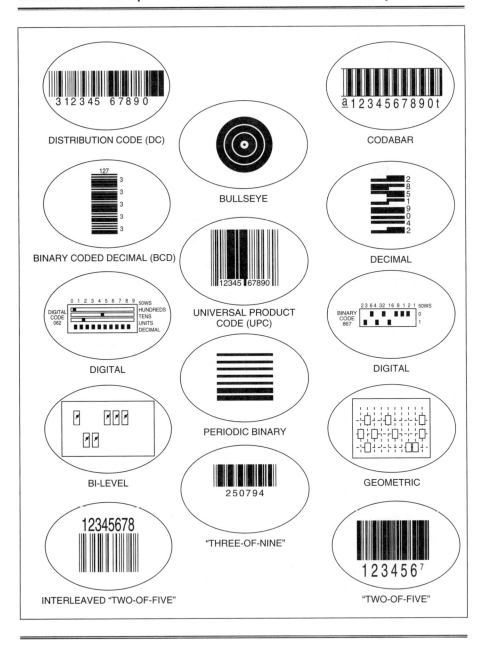

PROPERTY MAINTENANCE

Property maintenance, whether preventive or corrective, is an important activity of government. Upkeep and repair of equipment and facilities can result in significant savings, and both are necessary if the government is to work effectively and efficiently. The following factors make maintenance even more important today:

- changing from slow- to high-speed process and production equipment;
- changing from manual to automatically controlled equipment that requires a higher-grade engineering talent for maintenance;
- increasing cost-per-hour of productive labor and thus a higher cost of equipment downtime;
- increasing cost of production, with greater management pressure to better utilize equipment; and
- increasing ratio of maintenance employees to production employees, with fewer people actually using the equipment and more assigned to keeping the equipment and facilities ready to operate.

A well-run maintenance department should have a systematic work-order system, employ material and personnel controls, maintain histories of equipment repair and repair cost, use cost-accounting procedures, employ work-sampling and work-performance measures, review costs through materials studies, and employ training to update old and create new employee skills. Because of the computer, much more effective use of information is possible. In particular, the following data are useful:

- trend studies in the cost of maintenance per unit of product or service;
- recorded histories of equipment use;
- status reports of backlogged work orders; and
- surveys of plant operating and housekeeping conditions.

Preventive maintenance, corrective maintenance, and *maintenance prevention* are the most significant recent advances in maintenance management. *Preventive maintenance* involves (1) periodic inspections to discover conditions that lead to breakdowns or harmful wear, and (2) upkeep designed to rectify those negative conditions while they are still insignificant. *Corrective maintenance* focuses on high-repair-cost items. Once management identifies these items, then it can focus its effort on either reducing or eliminating the conditions that cause high-cost repair problems or eliminating the aspect of the problem that makes it expensive. *Maintenance prevention* is minimizing maintenance itself by means of good equipment and facility design.

RISK MANAGEMENT

A Practical Necessity

Both public and private concerns are subject to significant risks, which could be costly. Managers use risk management to decide how best to deal with the risks and to manage the problem accordingly. Insurance is one tool in dealing with risk, but the cost of insurance is often high, and sometimes insurance is not even possible to acquire. Government risks or liabilities include civil damages, breach of contract, dishonesty protection, workers' compensation, activity interruption, and even health protection. What losses can take place? Thieves, sometimes including government employees, can steal government property. People can get sick. Each represents a loss that can cost a government significant sums of money.

The most serious loss exposure concerns third-party liabilities. If a public employee has an accident, the government pollutes the environment, or a public employee causes other serious harm to someone, then liability damage occurs and courts grant awards to third parties. For example, a tired drunk driver successfully sued the City of Tamarac after he hit a 560-pound decorative limestone boulder placed in the road's median. Damages included $4.7 million paid by the city and $1.15 million paid by the county that placed the boulder on the median. The New York State Thruway Authority faced lawsuits in the millions of dollars in the 1980s when a rock face collapsed on motorists along a congested section of highway in the New York City metropolitan region and when a bridge collapsed in upstate New York. These examples from New York were natural disasters, yet present liabilities for government because of the question about whether the government did all it could to maintain this infrastructure and anticipate these events. An environmental example is the town of Hopewell, Virginia. Citizens along the James River successfully sued government for either actively or passively condoning the contamination of the James River by a small firm connected with Allied Chemical Company. Today, lawyers continue to identify new loss exposures for their clients and successfully bring legal claims of damages to the courts. For example, jail inmates sued Dutchess County, New York, for providing inadequate medical treatment. Because aircraft noise reduced the property value for owners near the city airport, they sued the City of Los Angeles. The potential cost to state and local governments of these suits is remarkably high.

Exposure Identification and Risk Evaluation

The first step in risk management is the identification of government resources and the losses that are possible. What kind of damages to people and property could take place? What type of damage can result if government does not meet its responsibility? What happens if someone is in an accident, is sick, or is dishonest? This step requires an inventory of the government's resources and a careful evaluation of responsibilities and potential damages. Knowledge of the types of risks permits the analysts to identify the government's liabilities and the types of claims currently found in the courts associated with those liabilities. A risk manager must do this step on a continuing basis by using checklists, questionnaires and interviews with employees, physical inspections, and a careful monitoring of the contemporary risk management literature.

Part of exposure identification must be a full understanding of the *tort doctrine of government immunity*. This doctrine gave government immunity from many civil tort actions, such as negligence. However, the courts and legislatures have reconsidered this doctrine since the 1940s, and governments are increasingly vulnerable in lawsuits. This means, for example, that a lawyer can sue governments for not maintaining property that results in injuries to his or her clients. Decision makers must take particular care in the analysis of risks for which government was formally not liable as sometimes judgments can be remarkably high against government. In order to understand the status of the doctrine of government immunity in each particular state, risk managers need an awareness of state law.

Information is the key to exposure identification. Analysts need accurate and timely data on costs so that they can associate those costs with specific departments and activities. Financial statements, especially involving capital projects, help identify property exposures and areas of new activity not analyzed for risks. Another useful source of data is analyses of operations. By following through the process, the risk manager can identify disreputable services, potential hazards in procedures, health dangers, and equipment safety concerns. In looking over such data, the manager is concerned, in particular, with the likely frequency and severity of the exposure potential. Other concerns include neat storage of goods and equipment, proximity of storage to fire sources, freedom of movement so that people can escape from dangerous situations and proper officials can have easy access to them, and special handling of flammable liquids. Exhibit 10–4 is a useful risk and insurance checklist. This checklist can aid in a systematic review of the exposures facing a government unit.

Risk managers cannot easily accomplish the measurement of potential losses. They need a complete inventory of property, including (1) distance from building location to hazards; (2) proximity to highway, air, or rail traffic; (3) available fire protection, including quality indicators such as water pressure; and (4) a description of the surrounding property. The inventory should also include the construction details, specifics of safety protections used, and building and equipment replacement costs. In measuring liability exposure, an evaluation of the laws covering government immunity, a review of the current history of local claim awards, and a review of all contract terms are essential. In measuring fidelity exposure, analysts must carefully examine cash receipts, opportunities to convert assets to cash, and potential for dealings between high officials and vendors or grantees. Periodic outside audits are essential. Risk managers must review (1) the audits, (2) accounting reports that show balances, (3) purchasing procedures, (4) electronic data processing concerning money, (5) the location and volume of cash, and (6) cash internal control procedures. Analysts must weigh losses in terms of exposure and severity.

Given the difficulty of gathering information and other aspects of risk management, previous government practice, not surprisingly, was to buy insurance and transfer the risk. This permitted the government officials to forget about the risk and pay attention to other, more pressing problems. Today, government cannot afford to handle risk in that manner for the following reasons:

- Premiums are expensive and are increasing in price.
- Some forms of coverage do not exist.
- Government immunity is shrinking.
- Damage awards are radically increasing beyond maximum insurance award limits.
- Preventative and safety programs can dramatically reduce exposure risks.
- Self-insurance is often a cheaper alternative than insurance.
- Knowledge of insurance and exposure risks can translate into better insurance coverage at less cost.

EXHIBIT 10–4   Risk and Insurance Checklist

1. Real Property
   a. Buildings owned
      (1) Nature, use, and location
      (2) Value replacement and actual cash value
      (3) Rental value of space used
      (4) Income from space rented to others
      (5) Laws and ordinances for demolition and for replacement standards
   b. Buildings rented from others
      (1) Nature, use, and location
      (2) Value of improvements and betterments made by tenant
      (3) Total rent paid by tenant
      (4) Rental income derived from subletting space to others
      (5) Value of the lease (is the lease favorable?)
      (6) Type of insurance clauses and hold-harmless agreements in the lease
   c. All buildings and other real property (includes a and b above)
      (1) Alterations and additions in progress or contemplated
      (2) Boilers and pressure vessels in operation
      (3) Power machinery in operation (switchboards, motors, engines, generators, etc.)
      (4) Cold storage vaults and other special provisions for maintaining controlled temperature or humidity
      (5) Electric or neon signs
      (6) Plate or ornamental glass
      (7) Elevators and escalators
      (8) Possible fire department service charges
      (9) Fire and other protection (sprinklers, alarms, watchmen)
2. Personal Property
   a. Stock, including packaging materials (each location)
      (1) Peak value and low values (month by month)
      (2) Susceptibility to crime loss
      (3) Values dependent on parts difficult to replace
      (4) Values susceptible to damage by lack of heat or cold.
   b. Furniture and fixtures attached to the building
      (1) Those permanently attached to the building
      (2) Unattached furniture, fixtures, machinery, office equipment
      (3) Supplies and prepaid expense items
   c. Personal property belonging to others
   d. Personal property in the custody of others
   e. Coins and currency (maximum amounts)
      (1) Payroll cash (when)
      (2) Other cash
      (3) Cash in custody of each bank messenger
      (4) Cash in custody of each truck driver or collector
      (5) Cash kept in safes overnight
      (6) Liability limit or armored car carrier
   f. Incoming checks (maximum amounts)
      (1) On premises
      (2) In safes overnight
      (3) In custody of each bank messenger
      (4) In custody of each truck driver or collector
   g. Bank accounts (locations, amounts, uses)
   h. Securities (maximum amounts)
      (1) In safes
      (2) In custody of each bank messenger
      (3) In safe deposit vaults
      (4) At other locations (specify)

EXHIBIT 10–4 *(continued)*

    i. Especially valuable property (maximum amounts) (e.g., precious stones, fine arts, antiques, rare metals, isotopes, radium)
      (1) In safes
      (2) Elsewhere on premises
      (3) In custody of each truck driver
      (4) In safe deposit vault
      (5) At other locations or in transit (specify)
    j. Valuable papers, documents, records
      (1) Kind
      (2) Where kept
      (3) Value
      (4) Protection afforded
    k. Accounts receivable
      (1) Maximum and minimum values
      (2) Where account records are kept
      (3) How protected
    l. Automobiles, airplanes, boats, trains, buses (owned or used)
      (1) Ownership
        (a) Owned
        (b) Nonowned
      (2) Value and extent of concentration in one place at one time
3. Operations
    a. Central operations: principal services
      (1) Nature of all services regularly provided
      (2) Sources of materials and supplies used
      (3) Flow of goods, steps or processes in provision of services: any bottlenecks
      (4) Extent, nature, and location of goods on installment or similar credit arrangements
      (5) Installation, demonstration, or servicing away from premises
      (6) Quality control
    b. Service for employees
      (1) Operation of a hospital, infirmary, or first-aid station
      (2) Operation of a restaurant for employees
      (3) Sponsorship of employee athletic teams
    c. Operation of a medical facility or other service in which a malpractice hazard exists
    d. Operation of a restaurant for the general public
    e. Work let out under contract
    f. Advertising signs, vending machines, booths, etc., owned or operated away from the premises
    g. Sponsorship of outside athletic team
    h. Liability assumed under contract
      (1) Sidetrack agreements
      (2) Leases
      (3) Hold-harmless agreements
      (4) Purchase orders
      (5) Elevator or escalator maintenance agreements
      (6) Easements
      (7) Service agreements (for or by the entity)
      (8) Other contracts
      (9) Warranties
    i. Shipments (values shipped annually and the maximum value of any one shipment, both incoming and outgoing)
      (1) Own trucks
      (2) Truckmen

(continued)

EXHIBIT 10–4   *(continued)*

      (3) Rail
      (4) Railway express
      (5) Air
      (6) Parcel post prepaid and C.O.D.
      (7) Registered mail
      (8) Inland or coastal water
      (9) Foreign
    (10) Marine cargo
  j. "Time element" exposures
      (1) Payroll: key persons; "ordinary" payroll
      (2) Cost of merchandise
      (3) Cost of heat, light, and power
      (4) Trend of revenue for current year; estimate for next year
      (5) Maximum time required to replace facilities subject to damage
      (6) Percentage of revenue that would be affected by a business-interruption loss
      (7) The availability and probable cost of substitute facilities to reduce loss of revenue in case of damage to present facilities
      (8) Extra expense to maintain operations following loss
      (9) If plans are interdependent, the percentage of revenue affected by a stoppage at each such plant or location, assuming damage at only one location
    (10) Extent to which operations are dependent on outside sources of heat, light, or power
4. Personnel
  a. Home-state employees
      (1) Duties
      (2) Use of automobiles
      (3) Estimated annual payroll
  b. Employees in other states
      (1) Residence state and states traveled
      (2) Duties
      (3) Use of automobiles
      (4) Estimated annual payroll
  c. Employees' annual payroll
  d. Employees required to use or travel in aircraft
  e. Classification of employees according to duties
  f. Key individuals (individuals whose loss might seriously affect operations)
5. Principal Property Hazards (Probable Maximum Loss)
  a. Fire
  b. Earthquake
  c. Flood
  d. Other
6. Data Processing Machines
  a. Owned or leased
  b. Protection
  c. Lease to others?
  d. Disaster plan
  e. Analysis of extra expense costs

Source: Gerald M. Surfus. "Identifying and Evaluating Potential Risk." *Government Finances,* 6, 28 (May 1977), 28–29.

EXHIBIT 10–5   Occupational Safety Risk

Incidence Rates per 100 Full-Time Employees, 1999

INDUSTRY	LOST WORKDAY CASES	CASES INVOLVING DAYS AWAY FROM WORK AND DEATHS	NONFATAL CASES WITHOUT LOST WORK	LOST WORKDAYS	DAYS AWAY FROM WORK
All Industries	3.37	1.11	4.62	84	25
Agriculture, etc.	1.20	0.85	2.55	27	22
Mining	1.43	0.46	2.58	40	18
Construction	1.24	0.51	1.76	32	14
Manufacturing	4.07	1.19	5.99	102	27
Transportation, etc.	2.20	1.11	1.96	51	22
Sales	4.49	1.79	3.65	100	45
Services	1.11	0.59	1.12	28	10
Government	2.44	1.49	2.92	52	29

Source: National Safety Council. *Injury Facts 2000 Edition.*

Risk Control

Risk control is the reduction of risk or loss through careful procedures and practices in security, personnel safety, fire prevention, auto safety, product safety, environmental protection, and emergency planning. For the most part, state and local governments do not perform adequate risk control. The National Safety Council uses lost workday cases, cases involving days away from work and deaths, nonfatal cases with lost workdays, lost workdays, and days away from work as indicators of industrial safety problems. Exhibit 10–5 presents the industrial averages for the major industrial groups including government. Each indicator shows that the safety record for government is the worst— and often significantly worse than industries traditionally considered dangerous such as agriculture, mining, and construction. This is a record of inaction and inadequate attention to safety. If elected policy makers more often adopted the following sound risk control programs, the safety record for government would significantly improve:

- *security*—preventative techniques and procedures to combat theft, burglary, and vandalism;
- *personnel safety*—meeting occupational safety and health standards, setting work safety standards, monitoring work environment and record keeping on accidents, maintaining safety training and safety committees;
- *fleet safety*—systematic review of driving records and implementation of stringent defensive driving courses;
- *property conservation*—regular inspection by fire, electrical, police, and other officials to identify and to correct hazards to physical property;

- *environmental protection*—procedures to dispose of solid, liquid, and gaseous wastes in accordance with state and federal standards;
- *emergency preparedness*—plans for and practice in dealing with a wide variety of emergencies, such as bomb threats, national disasters including fires and floods, and nuclear war; and
- *contract liability*—procedures to review likely contracts so that the government will not assume liability for others, as well as care to get contractors for public authorities who show evidence of adequate insurance to sign stiff hold-harmless agreements.

Over the years, risk managers have found the following safety beliefs helpful: (1) unsafe acts and conditions lead to accidents and injuries; (2) reducing the frequency of injury will also lessen the severity of injury; and (3) safety means education, engineering, and enforcement. The key person for safety is the first-line supervisor. Postinjury investigations are essential to identify and remove unsafe acts and conditions. Safety programs translate to caring actively about safety and implementing the proper remedies. Safety plans should reflect those beliefs in most instances.

Risk control costs money, as does insurance. A public authority can approach decisions on risk control and insurance on the basis of lowest cost to the government. Exhibit 10–6 illustrates how risk managers can chart the cost. Analysts calculate the cost of risk control and contrast it to the likely cost of insurance and self-insurance.

EXHIBIT 10–6   Risk Control Plus Insurance

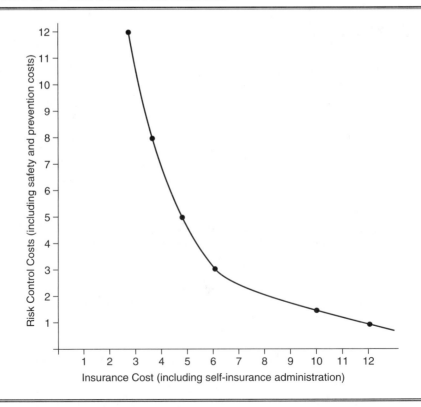

The best solution is the lowest joint risk control and insurance cost. Obviously, human compassion dictates that organizations should spend higher sums of money for risk control than a simple economic analysis suggests. Nevertheless, the chart does help us see the relationship between safety and insurance costs.

Risk Funding and Self-Insurance

Risk funding means providing sufficient funds to meet possible loss situations. One option for a public body is to retain the risk and pay losses through extraordinary means or the regular budget. Another option is to transfer the risk through a *pooling of insurance*. The *self-insurance* or *partial self-insurance* option is often desirable because it is the most economical approach for a public body. Even the insurance industry encourages the use of high deductibles—that is partial self-insurance—today.

Insurance is merely the pooling of risks plus adding charges for administering that pooling. Insurance companies will generally collect from $1.50 to $2.00 in premiums for every dollar spent in claims. Some governments are larger than insurance companies and are in a better position to fund the potential losses than are the companies. A government body should be willing to accept up to one-tenth of 1 percent of its operating budget in uninsured losses arising out of a single occurrence, or up to 1 percent of the operating budget as the aggregate of all such self-insured losses in a single fiscal year.

The following corollary objectives exist in risk funding:

- Decision makers should provide sufficient funds to meet the worst possible loss event. Some use a "maximum foreseeable loss" criterion, and others also use a "maximum probable loss" to make that determination.
- The management of risk funding should include proper use of idle cash reserves.
- Decision makers should maintain the maximum stability of risk funding over time.
- Administration should be both as efficient and as effective as possible.

Governments are in a much better position to absorb losses than are most private concerns because of the following special factors:

- using federal disaster assistance (Public law 93–288);
- money reserves set aside or an insurance policy created to address this type of problem;
- the ability to spread the payment of any adverse judgments against government over, say, a ten-year period;
- using bond issues to pay for any damage;
- the ability to create special tax levies to raise needed money; and
- seeing and getting citizen or group donations to raise needed funds.

Another type of self-insurance option is pooling on a local, regional, or state basis. For example, the cities in Contra Costa County, California, have pooled together their liability and property risks. Pools for workers' compensation claims have been set up in Alabama, Texas, and Maine. Judy Greenwald describes how the National Public Entity Excess Program (NAPEX) offers broad liability coverage with significant savings for its 450 public agency participants. This risk pool program provides participants with $21 million in coverage limits, with an optional $10 million in excess coverage available. She reports that participants have saved more than $600,000 per year, saving 28 percent over similar purchases for excess liability coverage. This alternative does work well; and as the liability insurance marketplace deteriorates, this joint action may become the only practical alternative. The biggest problem with pooling is the challenge of reaching administrative consensus on such matters as the cost allocation system. As self-insurance and intergovernmental risk pools have grown over the past twenty years, one problem has been the loss of data compiled by the insurance industry for covered public entities. Analysis of insurance claims, and the related data, has been an important tool to manage risk control costs for government. As risk pools replace traditional insurance coverage, this data is no longer available. Catherine Spain reports that in 1995 a nonprofit entity was created for the purpose of generating a database of information ranging from loss frequency, loss severity, trends, and other factors associated with the cost of risk. The Public Risk Database Project (PRDP) was actually created as a result of an antitrust lawsuit between the insurance industry and a number of states. The database can be accessed to retrieve liability loss and exposure data, as well as workers' compensation and other data sets that state and local governments can use to better manage risk. The accompanying Exhibit 10–7 is a useful guideline on risk retention.

Risk managers can practice *partial self-insurance* by selecting high deductibles and special insurance plans that permit a sharing of risk with the insurance company. The decision makers on this subject should weigh premium credits and administrative savings. They should not risk a lot for a little. A deductible should result in savings commensurate with the risk that the government retains. However, the government should set the deductible at the level it can afford based on its own financial ability and not on the savings generated in any one year. Analysts should use the annual aggregate deductible rather than a single occurrence deductible because this provides

EXHIBIT 10–7   Risk Retention

TYPE OF RISK	RETENTION POLICY
Low frequency and low severity	Government should retain this risk due to the low exposure.
High frequency and low severity	Usually, government should retain this risk as self-insurance.
High frequency and high severity	Handling this risk depends on the size of the government and insurance marketplace. Workers' compensation is a typical exposure of this type.
Low frequency and high severity	Government usually cannot absorb this risk; risk transfer by means of insurance is wise. An alternative is partial self-insurance. This can reduce insurance and total risk costs. Property and liability exposures are prime examples of this type.

greater budgeting certitude. The following list addresses common practices by type of insurance:

- *fire insurance*—governments often use high deductibles here. Typically, the deductible should be on a "per occurrence" basis and not on a "per loss" basis because a single windstorm represents one occurrence but many losses. Also, government should use an aggregate deductible.
- *workers' compensation*—most private bodies—and increasingly, public bodies—use self-insurance for catastrophic loss.
- *public liability*—the use of insurance above set limits is critical, but often such insurance is difficult to obtain.

However, as governments continue to face fiscal pressures and escalating insurance costs, the self-insurance route represents a viable alternative. Rodd Zolkos reports that in 1996–1997 alone the average cost of insurance for government rose 8.1 percent from 1994–1995. For the same period, risk costs were broken down as follows: worker's compensation (56 percent), property (13 percent), and liability (31 percent). The planning process for self-insurance takes about six months. The first month is spent gathering data, especially on premiums and losses, as discussed earlier. In the second month, the government analyst should determine the maximum amount that the government can retain. In the third month, the insurance bidding process should begin. In the fourth month, the risk manager should review the bids or negotiated costs. In the fifth month, the decision makers should award the contracts.

A true self-insurance program means that the government performs all the various functions that an insurance carrier would handle. These functions include accounting for premiums, a safety and loss control service, adjusting services, legal services, and funding for losses. Decision makers must establish a fund from which the risk manager will pay loss up to the retained limit. Governments accumulate such funds on a gradual basis, and during the accumulation process, the cash manager invests the idle funds. Also, the accounting unit should charge back a predetermined amount of each loss to the department incurring the loss. This serves to encourage department heads to be sensitive to their risks and the importance of risk control.

Insurance

Many public authorities require bidding for insurance. There is some controversy associated with bidding. Advocates point out that *open competitive bidding* gives every company a fair opportunity to receive the contract, and the process leads to the best price for the government. Those against the process point to several problems. Yearly bidding discourages long-term company-to-client relationships, thus negating a potential advantage and adding to the cost of overhead in the insurance industry. Increasingly, fewer companies want to bid; thus, artificially high bids do exist. If individual negotiations occur instead, they might result in lower bids. An alternative approach is *limited competitive bidding,* in which the technique places stress on selecting qualified agents or brokers. Risk managers select two or three and ask them to submit firm quotations. The government awards the contract on the basis of those bids. The forms of insurance include *property insurance, crime coverage, liability coverage,* and *employee benefits. Property insurance* includes fire and "all risk" contracts on buildings, contents, property, and other coverage. *Crime coverage* includes employee dishonesty, faithful performance bonds, and protection against burglary, robbery, and theft. *Liability coverage* includes all forms of public liability insurance, automobile insurance, and workers' compensation. Umbrella protection is essential and should include the governing body, all boards, commissions, elected officials, employees, and even volunteers. Employee benefits are often subject to labor-management negotiations, but they can include health insurance, major medical insurance, long-term disability income insurance, accident insurance, group life insurance, and pension plans. In any event, Exhibit 10–8 shows that insurance represents an ever-increasing cost for state and local governments.

A few general standards apply to all insurance contracts. The risk manager should have the named insured group on all policies and should update actual cash or replacement value on all property limits. The risk manager should have a 60-day written notice of cancellation, nonrenewal, or material reduction on all insurance contracts. The risk manager should carefully spell out in the contract all retention and participation in risk. Proper notification of loss should begin after the risk manager becomes aware of the loss, and all payments on losses should be to the governmental body. Typically, all the contracts, or as many as possible, should expire at the end of the fiscal year. Risk managers should make any cash flow arrangements to the advantage of the government's idle cash management program.

There are some general suggestions on content. Coverage should be very broad because of the variety of risk exposures found in government. Risk managers should use large maximum limits. Umbrella coverage is sometimes difficult to obtain, so risk managers must insure separately some risks, such as airport, aircraft, and bus line liability.

EXHIBIT 10–8   Insurance Rates for Health Services

	1987	1993	1994	1995	1996	1997	1998	1999	2000
State and Local Government Spending for Health Services	71.1	13.2	146.9	153.8	159.3	168.7	180.3	196.5	212.1
Employer Contribution for Private Health Insurance Premiums	16.4	36.3	39	39.8	41.8	44.1	45.2	52	56.9
Perfect Growth from Previous Year Shown	NA	14.2	7.6	2.1	4.9	5.5	2.5	15	9.6

Source: Cathy A. Cowar, Patricia A. McDonnell, Katherine R. Levit, and Mark A. Zezza. "Burden of Health Care Costs." *Health Care Financing Review,* 23, 3 (Spring 2002), 131–160.

Administration

A risk management program requires continuous direction and careful attention. For larger governments, a full-time risk manager is essential, and an additional safety staff would be wise. For smaller governments, this activity can be part of the budget office responsibilities. For both large and small governments, outside assistance can be quite valuable at times, owing to the complex and technical nature of this subject.

A government should develop a formal risk management policy that has active top legislative and executive support. The policy should establish the goals of the program, define authority and responsibility in this area, and spell out the necessary types of interdepartmental coordination. The policy should state risk retention guidelines in the context of the risk management philosophy of loss reduction and prevention. The risk managers should centralize insurance purchasing. Exhibit 10–9 is a model policy statement.

Two keys to risk management are communication and cooperation. Risk identification depends on getting the necessary information for the governing body, the legal staff, the program units, the personnel department, purchasing, and others. A government has an outstanding in-house expertise that the risk manager should tap. The expertise includes the fire department, police, inspection units, attorney's office, finance, personnel, and others. Each can be quite helpful. For example, the fire department can help devise loss prevention effort, and the finance office can help devise the best means to deal with idle cash resulting from the risk management program.

The risk managers should report annually on their program to top management. The report should point out major changes in the program, the outline of new program departures in the future, and comparisons to programs with similar government units. The risk manager should present the loss prevention program and state the total cost savings. The report should also contain an analysis of claims paid, the status on any reserves, and administrative and legal costs.

EXHIBIT 10–9   Risk Management Policy

1. The function of risk management has as its purpose:
   a. Protecting the municipality from catastrophic losses
   b. Minimizing the total cost of accidental loss to the municipality
2. Risk management is to place the greatest emphasis on reduction rather than reimbursement of loss, through professional attention to loss control techniques, motivational incentives, prompt claims payments, and other loss-prevention measures.
3. The city risk-management department shall purchase all insurance.
4. Subject to the risk manager's discretion, the amount of insurance purchased shall provide protection whenever a single accidental loss would result in property loss in excess of $50,000 per incident or liability judgment that would potentially exceed $50,000 per incident. Lesser amounts may be retained if financially feasible.

Source: Adapted from Lennox I. Moak and Albert M. Hillhouse. "Risk Management in Local Government." *Government Finances,* 6, 2 (May 1977), 40.

In conclusion, the risk manager should have responsibility for the following:

- aiding units in analyzing risks, including accidental losses;
- advising and adjusting major losses for all units on loss prevention, safety, and self-insurance levels;
- allocating insurance and risk costs to the units;
- maintaining records of losses, loss costs, premiums, and related costs;
- reviewing all new contracts for hold-harmless requirements;
- purchasing insurance; and
- coordinating all activities involving risk.

PENSION FUNDS

Budget Concerns

Pensions are budget concerns. Salaries and wages constitute a significant portion of government expenses—especially for local governments—and half of the related fringe benefits are pensions and social security payments. Such costs vary, but some governments pay 42 percent or much more of salaries and wages for fringe benefits. In the court-determined contractual relationship between governments and their employees, such expenses represent a mandatory liability and an appropriation due to former employees. Pensions thus have first or near-first demand on government revenue. Typically, governments establish special pension funds to which both the employer and the employee make payments in each pay period. Pension fund liability is usually covered wholly or partially from the pension fund, which receives its revenue from employer and employee payments plus investment income. There are approximately 6,600 public pension plans in the United States, with 90 percent of all employees belonging to the 100 largest plans. Pension assets are in the hundreds of billions of dollars and often have a rapid growth rate of over 12 percent a year. Exhibit 10–10 ranks the top twenty-five public pension plans by value of assets.

Like risk management, the key to pension funds is to spread liability among many people. With pension funds, the liability is the future pension benefits that each former employee will receive from retirement until death. Thus, the future costs of the pension benefit payments and associated administrative expenses must equal the combined employee and employer fringe-benefit payments, investment income from the fund, and any general fund subsidy. Many systems do have a partial or full subsidy. If the existing members finance the pension payments, a "pay-as-you-go" system exists. If an analyst calculates the pension fund income to cover future likely pension outlays without present or future general fund subsidy, then the system is *actuarially sound*. The latter type of system is not always present, even though the municipal finance investment community, in judging creditworthiness, prefers and sometimes demands that governments completely fund pension plans. However, fully funded pension funds are more costly in the budget year, whereas a pay-as-you-go strategy will meet immediate pension expenses and be less expensive in the BY. There is a strong temptation to use the less expensive approach and let future legis-

EXHIBIT 10–10   Top Twenty-Five Public Pension Funds (in millions)

1	California Public Employees	$143,887
2	New York State Common	106,091
3	California State Teachers	95,553
4	Federal Retirement Thrift	93,328
5	Florida State Board	88,514
6	Texas Teachers	75,109
7	New York State Teachers	74,915
8	New Jersey	66,691
9	Wisconsin Investment Board	55,473
10	New York City Retirement	54,412
11	North Carolina	52,573
12	Ohio Public Employees	50,459
13	Michigan Retirement	49,266
14	Pennsylvania School Employees	48,000
15	Ohio State Teachers	47,336
16	Washington State Board	41,916
17	New York City Teachers	41,802
18	Minnesota State Board	39,538
19	Georgia Teachers	39,230
20	Oregon Employees	35,051
21	Virginia Retirement	34,744
22	Alabama Retirement	27,295
23	Colorado Employees	26,928
24	Massachusetts PRIM	26,802
25	Maryland State Retirement	26,608

Source: Pensions & Investments. January 21, 2002.

latures or city councils find the money to meet the future expenses. In summary, the case for a fully funded pension plan is as follows:

- Good fiscal management means knowing what programs cost.
- It adds security to the pension obligation.
- It protects employers from overgenerous benefit arguments in labor-management negotiations because the future pension burden on the budget is more easily understood.
- The financial community, in determining government creditworthiness, increasingly demands fully funded pension plans.

Both private and public pensions are so common today that most people are surprised by their recent origin. In 1857, the New York City police force started the first public pension program. However, it was not until the twentieth century that pension systems became widely adopted in either public or the private sector. Today, local policy makers commonly fragment pension plans, with a city sometimes maintaining separate plans for police, fire, sanitation, general administration, and other employee groups. Because the Tenth Amendment to the Constitution addresses the rights of states, there is little federal regulatory oversight; but at the state level one finds increasing state oversight concern, even to the extent of having a state-administered pension fund in which both state and local employees participate.

Pension policy is often a concern of labor-management negotiations. Union negotiators often use a tactic called *leapfrogging,* which means establishing higher benefits for one union and then demanding comparable features for another union. For example, the firefighters' union would argue for added benefits, and it might win added benefits. Then, in its negotiations with the city, the police union would note the firefighters' negotiation success and use that to argue for added benefits for the police union. In the public sector, unlike the private sector, legislative policy makers usually set pension policy. Thus, unions can and do lobby legislators for pension policy changes. Rarely are pension policies major political issues because they require specialized skills and knowledge, have long-term implications, and have low visibility. In addition, pension systems have no general authoritative standards and system growth has been haphazard. These conditions are ideal for negotiated settlements, which can have expensive, hidden long-term budget implications.

The Investment Process

According to Girard Miller, the general investment process conceptual framework should consist of the following five parts:

- Identify and establish specific, explicit written policies on the investor's opportunities, constraints, preferences, and capabilities.
- Identify investment opportunities.
- Formulate and implement investment strategies on the purchase of financial securities and related instruments in the marketplace.
- Monitor, document, and report on the investor's circumstances, market conditions, and related security values.
- Respond to new objectives and changing circumstances by making portfolio adjustments.

Miller suggests the following cookbook approach to implementing the conceptual framework:

- Identify the entity's objectives, constraints, preferences, and capabilities.
- Develop investment policies.
- Develop administrative systems and internal controls.
- Prepare cash forecast.
- Determine the investment horizon.
- Establish an investment outlook and strategy.
- Analyze the yield curve.
- Select optimizing instruments.

- Monitor the markets and investment results.
- Report results.
- Adjust and rebalance the portfolio accordingly.

Policy Issues

Managers can view pension fund policy in terms of benefits, investments, and administration. Benefit policy involves questions of how much money employees can collect and of when they can collect it. Investment policy concerns questions of who controls the investments, limitations on investment, and investment performance.

Since the first public employee pension plan in 1857, the number of plans has grown to over 6,600 in the United States, with 90 percent of state and municipal workers in the 350 systems with over 1,000 or more members. The largest plan is the California Public Employees Retirement System (CALPERS), which invests in the hundreds of billions. In contrast, the AT&T pension fund is less than half the CALPERS amount. The consolidation of smaller systems into larger systems usually results in significant economic gains. Sometimes, policy makers direct pension funds to promote local economic development or social goals. For example, at one time the $1.4 billion Wyoming Retirement System invested $10 million in Dow's Wyoming operation. Sometimes, such investments lose money, such as the 1980s Alaska public employee and teachers' retirement funds loan for $165 million for multifamily houses, in which 40 percent went delinquent or resulted in foreclosures. The Alaska $4 billion pension fund was able to manage the loss.

With large funds comes economic power in which a public pension fund manager can rebuke a major firm such as Salomon Brothers for cornering the market on U.S. Treasuries. For example, CALPERS owns 1 percent of practically all the major traded companies and thus can demand action with some success from the largest corporations. In New York State, the governor's business-labor task force recommended curbing the power of New York State's public pension fund. The task force felt that the fund managers should not oppose company management in takeover fights and proxy votes. The task force also opposed financing hostile leverage buyouts or backing buyout firms that do not promise to avoid them. During the early years of the twenty-first century, large pension funds now own a major portion of the corporate world, and therefore the mushrooming economic power of pension funds is an important public policy issue. Policy makers might wisely require pension fund managers to focus on the long-term health of corporations and the economy as a whole. Such a policy would significantly encourage American private companies to avoid focusing on short-term profits and instead focus on gaining market shares, conducting more research and development, training employees, initiating, and other long-term oriented policies.

Until the 1990s, public pension funds were fairly successful at fending off attempts to transfer their money to other funds. However, in tighter economic times, raiding pension funds becomes an issue. Two common methods to raid pension funds are to (1) simply commandeer them and (2) cut back on the annual contribution to the funds. The first method is politically difficult and can lead to lawsuits. Raiders typically use the second method, which has two versions: (1) changing the actuarial and investment income assumptions, thus lowering the government contribution to the pension fund and (2) simply deferring the payments. The latter method is especially expensive, as the state must pay not only the contribution but also the equivalent interest earned. A dramatic raid occurred in 1991 when then Governor Pete Wilson of California transferred $1.6 billion from the state's pension fund to the general fund in order to balance the state's 1991 budget.

The major concern of those who deal with pension funds is the benefit package. The four major benefit policy issues are *wage replacement,* who pays *contributions* to the fund, *indexing,* and *double coverage.* Not surprisingly, employees would like retirement benefits to replace their wages, but that is costly. Exhibit 10–11 is an illustration of one common method of calculating retirement benefits. Typically, analysts use an average of the last three or five years to calculate retirement benefits. One government used the last day of regular employment and found that this produced an artificially high amount because this method allowed the employee to add overtime to the already high last salary day.

The second concern of those who deal with pension funds is who contributes—employees prefer that the employers pay all costs. The third concern is inflation, which can particularly hurt retired employees living on a fixed pension. The solution is to link the benefits to a cost-of-living index such as the Consumer Price Index. Not surprisingly, indexing is popular with employees, but it becomes very expensive in subsequent years. The fourth concern is double coverage, which typically results from an overlap with social security benefits—an employer option for state and local governments.

Three other pension issues not illustrated by Exhibit 10-11 are *vesting, portable systems,* and *disability/survivor protection.* What if you are fired just before retirement? Will you collect any retirement benefits? The answer depends on whether or not your employer vested (that is, whether you worked the number of years required before an employee can collect any money at retirement) you in the retirement system. Vesting varies from system to system. Typically, the policy is three to five years, but some systems use ten years. What if your employer vested you in one government pension plan, but you took a new job with another government? Can your new government contribute to your old pension plan? Usually, the answer is no, but some states have combined state and local systems that do permit some *portability.*

What if you become disabled? Do you receive retirement benefits (or does your spouse, in the event of your death)? Again, provisions vary. For example, if you incurred your disability while you were at work, analysts compute your benefits in the manner described in Exhibit 10-11. If you incurred your disability outside the workplace, you may still be eligible but you must meet other requirements, such as ten years of service. Survivor benefits are also common. For example, under one plan, if an employee dies in the line of duty, his or her spouse receives a monthly benefit of half the regular monthly salary until the spouse's remarriage or death. If an employee dies elsewhere, the spouse receives benefits calculated under the policy in force at the time of death.

Investment policy debates center on who controls the investments, on what investment limitations should exist, and finally on the adequacy of the investment

EXHIBIT 10–11 Sample Calculations of Retirement Benefits

Step 1. *Creditable Service and Percentage Value*

	% VALUE PER YEAR OF SERVICE	TOTAL YEARS OF SERVICE	TOTAL % VALUE PER PLAN
Retirement up to Age 62 or 30 Years	1.60%	×_____	= _____
Retirement at Age 63 or 31 Years	1.63%	× 25	= 40.75
Retirement at Age 64 or 32 Years	1.65%	×_____	= _____
Retirement at Age 65 or 33 Years or More	1.68%	×_____	= _____
Total Years		25	

Step 2. *Average Final Compensation (AFC)*

Mr. Smith worked 25 years under the system and retired at age 63. In this step we list his five highest fiscal year salaries and divide their total by five.	11,257.00
	12,851.00
	13,201.00
	13,706.00
	13,904.00
	Total $64,919.00

$64,919.00 ÷ 5 = $12,983.80 = Average Final Compensation (AFC)

Step 3. *Monthly Benefit Calculation*

Average final compensation (step 2) $12,983.80
Total % value per plan (step 1) × .4075
$ 5,290.90 Annual benefit
$ 5,290.90 ÷ 12 = $440.91 Monthly benefit

---

performance. Unions rarely control government pensions, as sometimes occurs in the private sector. The dispute over control centers on the issue of decentralized versus centralized state systems. The advantages of a centralized state system include uniform benefits, greater decision-making expertise, greater cost-effectiveness, and potentially higher yields, given the advantage of size. Nevertheless, many local governments prefer to retain control over pension investments. This is especially true if making investments that will benefit the local community is a concern of the portfolio managers. Advocates of this policy stress that such investments achieve both important public policy goals and employees' economic security. One example is the use of pension funds for local mortgage projects. In the case of New York City, unions used pension funds that they controlled to buy city bonds when the city could find no other investors. However, there are often times great risks associated with aggressive investment strategies that seek to maximize earnings and avoid tax increases in other areas of the jurisdiction's budget. A good case in point is the overaggressive investment strategy employed by Orange County, California, in the early 1900s where a policy of investments in risky financial derivatives (with promises of quick returns on investments) led to massive financial problems for the county and bailout assistance from state government (Baldassare 1998).

State governments place some restrictions and limitations upon pension fund investments. The *major* types of investment restrictions are as follows:

- maximum percentage of fund assets that a pension fund manager can invest in *common stock;*
- maximum percentage of fund assets that a pension fund manager can invest in the securities of any *one company;*
- maximum use of derivatives;
- maximum percentage of funds that a pension fund manager can invest in securities of any *one industry;*
- maximum percentage of fund assets that a pension fund manager can invest in *real estate mortgages;*
- maximum percentage of funds that a pension fund manager can invest in *real estate equities;*
- maximum percentage of assets that a pension fund manager can hold in *cash reserves;*
- minimum *size* of company in which pension fund manager can invest;
- minimum total *rate of return* for income that a pension fund manager can earn on investments;
- minimum *quality of bonds* in which a pension fund manager can invest the funds;
- maximum *price/earning ratio* on common stocks in which a pension fund manager can invest the fund; and
- minimum number of consecutive years of *dividends paid* on common stock (dividend-payment record).

The adequacy of investment performance is an important matter to budget officials because a stronger performance means a decrease in employer and employee contributions. In general, managers of public pension plans are cautious investors who prefer fixed income obligations rather than equity securities (for example, common stock). In a survey conducted by the Government Finance Officers Association, public pensions did better than private pensions, but the commentator attributed that fact to the relatively greater use of equity securities by the private pension funds during a period of declining stock prices. One interesting finding was that public pensions outperformed private pensions in the rate of return of equities. Private pensions, however, outperformed public pensions on bond portfolios. Probably, public and private pension plans perform at about the same level.

Administrative policy disputes center on the largely unregulated and unknown status of pension funds. Controversy about disclosure practices has arisen because there is disagreement over what information pension fund managers should make known, in what form they should give the information, who should make it known, and who should receive it. Pension information can be expensive to prepare, but the pension fund manager must balance those expenses against the importance of acquiring good forecasts, especially those that are actuarially sound. The frequency and quality of the latter are critical to the accuracy and value of pension plan financial disclosures. They inform employees and government policy makers of the relative soundness of the pension funds.

When recessionary pressures on state and local governments grow, concerns increase that (1) governments might not meet future pension liabilities, (2) governments might divert pension funds to other areas such as the general operating fund, and (3) pension fund managers might not invest properly. Unfortunately, the typical shortage of adequate data only increases fears. Not surprisingly, some argue for federal regulations, but the former U.S. Advisory Commission on Intergovernmental Relations (ACIR) has taken a position against federal regulation of public pension systems. Exhibit 10–12 presents the ACIR argument.

The Government Accounting Standards Board (GASB) believes that pension fund managers should disclose more pension data. Such a ruling is politically significant to local governments because following the rule can make a local government appear to be over- or underfunded in its pension liability. The GASB rule requires that state and local governments disclose their own unfunded pension liability using a GASB prescribed actuarial technique. Retirement systems can continue to use a different method to determine how much money to actually contribute to the pension plan. The GASB approach permits financial analysts who consider investing in government securities to compare pension systems more easily.

Public pensions are significant activities, and they significantly affect government budgets.

**EXHIBIT 10–12   Advisory Commission on Intergovernmental Relations:
Reasons for the Commission's Recommendation Against
Federal Regulation**

In recommending against federal regulation of state and local pension systems, the Commission rested its case upon five major arguments.

- Our federal system with its emphasis on state sovereignty requires that states have full responsibility for determining all basic components of their public employees' compensation, and that of the local employees within the states.
- The unique and diverse nature of state and local retirement systems requires the kind of adaptation and fine-tuning that only state and local government control and regulation can provide.
- State and local governments have made significant progress during the past few years in putting their own retirement systems in order.
- There is no convincing evidence that the federal government has any compelling "national interest" in regulating state and local public pension systems.
- Even mild or limited forms of federal regulations are undesirable, given the tendency for federal regulatory agencies and the courts to take a friendly piece of legislation and turn it into an unfriendly set of regulations.

Source: ACIR. *State and Local Pension Systems.* Washington, DC: ACIR, December 1980, p. 54.

REVIEW QUESTIONS

1. Explain what should take place in a review of property management. Explain also the challenge of procurement, including the difficulty of using a competitive bidding process.
2. Explain the administrative implications of bar-code technology on government property management.
3. Explain the relationship between risk control and insurance. Explain what factors analysts should weigh in deciding how much risk government should retain.
4. What type of knowledge and skill do analysts need for exposure identification and risk evaluation? What types of continuous direction and careful attention connote excellent risk management?
5. The proper funding of public pensions has budgetary implications. What are the concepts behind pension funds, the policy issues related to pensions, and the budgetary implications of pension funds?

REFERENCES

Advisory Commission on Intergovernmental Relations. *State and Local Pension Systems.* Washington, DC: Advisory Commission on Intergovernmental Relations, December 1980.

BALDASSARE, MARK. *When Government Fails: The Orange County Bankruptcy.* Berkeley, CA: University of California Press, 1998.

COE, CHARLES K. "Government Purchasing: The State of the Practice." In Thomas D. Lynch and Lawrence Martin (eds.), *Handbook of Comparative Public Budgeting and Financial Management.* New York: Marcel Dekker, 1993.

CORCORAN, A. WAYNE. "Financial Management." In J. Richard Aronson and Eli Schwartz (eds.), *Management Policies in Local Government Finance.* Washington, DC: International City Management Association, 1975.

COWAR, CATHY A., PATRICIA A. MCDONNELL, KATHERINE R. LEVITT, and MARK A. ZEZZA. "Burden of Health Care Costs." *Health Care Financing Review,* 23, 3 (Spring 2002), 131–160.

Government Finance Officers Association. *Guidelines for the Preparation of a Public Employee Retirement System Comprehensive Annual Financial Report.* Chicago: Government Finance Officers Association, May 1980.

———. "Pension Training Seminar." *Resources in Review,* 2, 1 (September/October 1979), 6–7.

———. "Public Employee Retirement." Number 3 in *Elements of Financial Management.* Washington, DC: Government Finance Officers Association, Government Finance Research Center, 1981.

GREENWALD, JUDY. "Public Entities Hope for Group Savings." *Business Insurance,* 31 (3 February 1997), 1–2.

HILDRETH, W. BARTLEY, and GERALD J. MILLER. "Risk Management and Pension Systems." In Jack Rabin and Thomas D. Lynch (eds.), *Handbook on Public Budgeting and Financial Management.* New York: Marcel Dekker, 1983.

International City Management Association. *Municipal Finance Administration.* 6th ed. Chicago: International City Management Association, 1962.

MCCUE, CLIFFORD, P. "Decentralized Purchasing: Implications for Control and Accountability of the Finance Function." Nonpublished paper presented at the Annual Conference of the Association for Budgeting and Financial Management held in Washington, DC, January 19, 2002.

MILLER, GIRARD. "The Investment of Public Funds: A Research Agenda." *Public Budgeting and Finance,* 7, 3 (Autumn 1987), 47–56.

MOAK, LENNOX L., and ALBERT M. HILLHOUSE. *Local Government Finance.* Chicago: Municipal Finance Officers Association, 1975.

———. "Risk Management in Local Government." *Government Finances,* 6, 2 (May 1977). 30–45.

PETERSON, JOHN E. *A Summary of State and Local Government Public Employee Retirement System Investment Practices and Policies.* Washington, DC: Government Finance Officers Association, Government Finance Research Center, December 1980.

———. *State and Local Pension Fund Investment Performance.* Washington, DC: Government Finance Officers Association, Government Finance Research Center, December 1980.

POPE, RALPH A. "Economies of Scale in Large State and Municipal Retirement Systems." *Public Budgeting and Finance,* 6, 3 (Autumn 1986), 70–80.

ROSS, NESTOR R., and JOSEPH S. GERBER. *Governmental Risk Management Manual.* Tucson, AZ: Risk Management Publishing Company, 1977.

ROTHMAN, MATT. "CALPERS Director Is Financial Force to Be Reckoned With." *San Francisco Examiner,* 23 February 1992, E-1.

SPAIN, CATHERINE L. "Controlling the Cost of Risk in State and Local Governments." *Government Finance Review,* 16, 5 (October 2000), 48–55.

SURFUS, GERALD M. "Identifying and Evaluating Potential Risk." *Government Finances,* 6, 28 (May 1977), 28–29.

U.S. Joint Financial Management Improvement Program. *Bar Code Technology: A Means to Improve Operational Efficiency and Internal Control.* Washington, DC: U.S. Joint Financial Management Improvement Program, May 1982.

———. *Property Management Evaluation Guide for Federal Agencies.* Washington, DC: U.S. Joint Financial Management Improvement Program, March 1982.

WHITE, JAMES A. "Panel Urges Curb On Pension Funds' Power." *Wall Street Journal,* 22 June 1989, C–1.

———. "Pension Fund Investments Get Strange." *Wall Street Journal,* 17 November 1989, C–1.

ZOLKOS, RODD. "Public Entities Cost of Risk Up 8 Percent." *Business Insurance,* 32, 25 (22 June 1998), 12–13.

GLOSSARY

Ability to Pay   The principle that the tax burden should be distributed proportionally among taxpayers, according to the size of their income. It is based on the assumption that as a person's income increases, the person can and should contribute a larger percentage of his or her income to support government activities.

Accounting System   The total structure of records and procedures that record, classify, and report information on the financial position and operations of a government unit or any of its funds, balanced account groups, and organizational components.

Accounts Payable   Amounts owed to others for goods and services received and assets acquired.

Accounts Receivable   Amounts due from others for goods furnished and services rendered. Such amounts include reimbursements earned and refunds receivable. (*See also* Accounts Payable.)

Accrual Basis of Accounting   The basis of accounting under which revenues are recorded when earned and expenditures are recorded when goods are received and services performed, even though receipt of the revenue or payment of the expenditure may take place, in whole or part, in another accounting period.

Accrued Expenditures   Liabilities incurred during a given period that reflect the need to pay for (a) services performed by employees, contractors, other government accounts, vendors, carriers, grantees, lessors, and other payees; (b) goods and other tangible property received; and (c) amounts owed under programs for which no current service or performance is required (such as annuities, insurance claims, other benefit payments, and some cash grants, but excluding the repayment of debt, which is considered neither an obligation nor an expenditure). Expenditures accrue regardless of when cash payments are made, whether invoices have been rendered, or, in some cases, whether goods or other tangible property have been physically delivered.

Agency   Generally, any department, independent commission, board, bureau, office, or other establishment of the government, including independent regulatory commissions and boards.

Allocations   The amount of obligational authority from one agency, bureau, or account that is set aside in a transfer appropriation account to carry out the purposes of the parent appropriation or fund.

Allotment   An authorization by the head (or other authorized employee) of an agency to his or her subordinates to incur obligations within a specified amount.

Annual Budget   Revenues and expenditures for one fiscal year period.

Anti-Deficiency Act of 1906   Legislation enacted by Congress (a) to prevent the incurring of obligations or the making of expenditures (outlays) in excess of amounts available in appropriations or funds; (b) to fix responsibility within an agency for the creation of any obligation or the making of any expenditure in excess of an apportionment or reapportionment or in excess of other subdivisions established pursuant to 31 U.S.C. 665(g); and (c) to assist in bringing about the most effective and economical use of appropriations and funds.

Apportionment   The distribution by the Central Budget Office of amounts available for obligation, including budgetary reserves established pursuant to law, in appropriations or fund accounts. In an apportionment, amounts available for obligation are divided among specific time periods (usually quarters), activities, projects, objects, or a combination thereof. The amounts so apportioned limit the amount of obligations that may be incurred.

Appropriation   A legislative authorization that permits government agencies to incur obligations and to make payments out of the treasury for specified purposes. An appropriation usually follows enactment of authorizing legislation. An appropriation act is the most common means of providing budget authority, but in some cases the authorizing legislation itself provides the budget authority. (*See also* Backdoor Authority.) Appropriations do not represent cash actually set aside in the treasury for purposes specified in the appropriation act; they represent limitations of amounts that agencies may obligate during the period of time specified in the relevant appropriation act. Several types of appropriations are not counted as budget authority, since they do not provide authority to incur additional obligations. Examples of these include (a) appropriations to liquidate contract authority—congressional action to provide funds to pay obligations incurred against contract authority; (b) appropriations to reduce outstanding debt—congressional action to provide funds for debt retirement; and (c) appropriations for refunds of receipts.

Appropriation Act   A statute that generally provides authorization for agencies to incur obligations and to make payments out of the treasury for specified purposes. An appropriation act, the most common means of providing budget authority, generally follows enactment of authorizing legislation unless the authorizing legislation itself provides the budget authority.

Appropriation Limitation   A statutory restriction in appropriation acts that establishes the maximum or minimum amount that may be obligated or expended for specified purposes.

Arbitrage Bonds   The exemption from income tax of government bonds as long as state and local governments do not use the funds from the bonds for investment rather than for the prescribed public purpose.

Asset   Any item of economic value owned by a government unit. The item may be tangible (that is, physical and actual) or intangible (that is, a right to ownership, expressed in terms of cost or some other value).

Audit   An investigation of the accuracy and correct operation of an agency's accounting system, including validation of inventories and existing equipment, documentation of proper legal authority to carry out agency activities, adequacy of controls on fraud, waste, and mismanagement, and the effectiveness of the agency's programs.

Authorizing Committee   A standing legislative committee with jurisdiction over the subject matter of those laws, or parts of laws, that set up or continue the legal operation of programs or agencies. An authorizing committee also has jurisdiction in those instances in which backdoor authority is provided through substantive legislation.

Authorizing Legislation   Substantive legislation that sets up or continues the legal operation of a program or agency, either indefinitely or for a specific period of time, or that sanctions a particular type of obligation or expenditure within a program. Authorizing legislation is typically a prerequisite for an appropriation. It may place a limit on the amount of budget authority to be included in appropriation acts or it may authorize the appropriation of "such sums as may be necessary." In some instances, authorizing legislation may provide authority to incur debts or to mandate payment to particular persons or political subdivisions of the country.

Automatic Stabilizer   A mechanism having a countercyclical effect that automatically moderates changes in incomes and outputs in the economy without specific decisions to change government policy. Unemployment insurance and the income tax are among the most important of the automatic stabilizers used in the United States. Also known as a built-in stabilizer.

Backdoor Authority   Budget authority provided in legislation outside the normal appropriations process (that is, through appropriations committees). The most common forms of backdoor authority are authority to borrow (also called borrowing authority or authority to spend debt receipts) and contract authority. In other cases (for example, interest on the public debt), a permanent appropriation is provided that becomes available without any current action by Congress. Section 401 of the Congressional Budget and Impoundment Control Act of 1974 (31 U.S.C. 1351) specifies certain limits on the use of backdoor authority.

Balance of Payments   A statistical record of economic transactions between one country—for example, the United States—and the rest of the world. Balance of payments accounts typically distinguish among transactions involving goods, services, short-term capital, and long-term capital.

Balance Sheet   An accounting statement designed to balance total assets, total liabilities, and fund balance.

Balanced Budget   A budget in which receipts are equal to outlays.

Benefit-Cost Analysis   *See* Cost-Benefit Analysis.

Block Grant   *See* Grant.

Bond   A written promise to pay a specified sum of money (called the face value or principal amount) at a specified date or dates (called the maturity dates) together with periodic interest at a specified rate.

Bond Maturity   A set period of time at the end of which the principal on a bond is completely paid. The length of the maturity typically is not longer than the useful life of the facility that is being financed.

Bond Prospectus   The formal statement of information used by bond sellers to help investors decide whether or not they wish to invest in the bonds.

Borrowing Authority   Authority to spend debt receipts; statutory authority that permits an agency to incur obligations and to make payments for specified purposes out of borrowed monies. (*See also* Debt.)

Box-Jenkins   One of a class of models called ARIMA, for Autoregressive Integrated Moving Average. Identifies possible useful models and checks each in turn against the time series until it finds the point that fits.

Budget   A plan for the accomplishment, within a definite time period, of programs related to established objectives and goals, setting forth estimates of the resources required and the resources available (usually in comparison with one or more past periods) and showing future requirements. Also, a request for funds to run the government.

Budget and Accounting Act of 1921   Federal legislation that provided for an executive budget for the national government and for an independent audit of government accounts.

Budget and Accounting and Procedures Act of 1950   Federal legislation that gave the president authority to prescribe the contents and arrangement of the budget, to simplify its presentation, to broaden appropriations, and to mandate progress toward performance budgeting.

Budget Authority   Authority provided by law to enter into obligations that will result in immediate or future outlays of government funds; it does not include authority to ensure or guarantee the repayment of indebtedness incurred by another person or government. The basic forms of budget authority are appropriations, borrowing authority, and contract authority. Budget authority may be classified by the period of availability (one-year, multiple-year, no-year), by the timing of legislative action (current or permanent), or by the manner of determining the amount available (definite or indefinite).

Budget Call An announcement distributed by the budget office to all government departments and agencies, instructing them to prepare the budget and providing guidance on proper procedures to use. Much of the guidance is standardized and published in official bulletins and circulars.

Budget Execution System A set of procedures that gives direction to ongoing agency activities and allows for continuous and current reviews to determine if planned objectives are being met. One approach is to link an operating budget with management-by-objectives.

Budget-Wise Model An approach to budgeting in which all government decisions are perceived to be politically motivated, to the exclusion of all other factors. A person following this model stresses the futility of trying to make decisions on the basis of anything but political expediency and insists that a budget staff can do nothing but react to political events as they unfold.

Budget Year (BY) The fiscal year for which the budget is being considered; the fiscal year following the current year.

Built-in Stabilizer *See* Automatic Stabilizer.

Business Cycles The recurrent phases of expansion and contraction in overall business activity, evidenced by fluctuations in measures of aggregate economic activity, notably real gross national product. Both the duration and the magnitude of individual cycles vary greatly.

Call Provision The right of the borrower to buy back bonds at set prices regardless of the current market rate.

Capital In economic theory, one of the three major factors of production (the others being land and labor). Capital can refer either to physical capital, such as plant and equipment, or to the financial resources required to purchase physical capital.

Capital Budget A budget that deals with large expenditures for capital items typically financed by borrowing. Usually, capital items have long-range returns and useful life spans, are relatively expensive, and have a physical presence (for example, buildings, roads, and sewage systems).

Case *See* Observation.

Cash Basis of Accounting The basis of accounting whereby revenues are recorded when received and expenditures (outlays) are recorded when paid, without regard to the accounting period in which the transactions occurred.

Categorical Grant *See* Grant.

Circuit Breaker A reform recommendation for property taxation that would reduce the regressive nature of the tax. Circuit breakers often provide for tax exemptions to families at the lowest income level or to elderly people on fixed incomes to relieve them of paying some of their property taxes.

Clientele Group The people who are perceived to be affected by an agency's programs and who take an active interest in its policies and actions.

Comprehensive Budget All revenues and expenditures included in the budget.

Confidence Interval A group of values used to estimate a statistical parameter. The confidence interval tends to include the true value of the parameter at a predetermined proportion of the time (for instance; 90 percent). The process of finding the group of values is repeated a number of times.

Congressional Budget and Impoundment Control Act of 1974 Federal legislation that was one of several reforms directed toward strengthening the legislative branch. It created the new Senate and House Budget Committees and the new Congressional Budget Office, required a current services budget, and required various reforms in the presidential budget and in presidential impoundment powers. It created a unified congressional budget approach. (*See also* First Concurrent Resolution of the Budget *and* Second Concurrent Resolution of the Budget.)

Congressional Budget Office (CBO) Federal office responsible for presenting the Congress with reasonable and viable forecasts of aggregate levels of spending and revenue. The office also makes cost estimates for proposed legislation reported to the floor and provides cost projections for all existing legislation.

Consolidated Decision Package Package prepared at high organizational and program levels that summarizes and supplements information contained in decision packages received from subordinate units in an agency using zero-base budgeting.

Constant Dollar A dollar value adjusted for changes in prices. Constant dollars are derived by dividing current dollar amounts by an appropriate price index, a process generally known as deflating. The result is a constant dollar series as it would presumably exist if prices and transactions were the same in all subsequent years as in the base year. Any changes in such a series would reflect only changes in the real volume of goods and services. Constant dollar figures are commonly used for computing the gross national product and its components and for estimating total budget outlays.

Consumer Price Index (CPI) Either of two measures of change in the price of a fixed "market basket" of goods and services customarily purchased by urban consumers. CPI-U is based on a market basket determined by expenditure patterns of *all urban households,* while the market basket for CPI-W is determined by expenditure patterns of *urban-wage-earner and clerical-worker families.* The level of CPI shows the relative cost of purchasing the specified market basket compared to the cost in a designated base year, while the current rate of change in the CPI measures how fast prices are currently rising or falling. Current rates of change can be expressed as either monthly or annual rates. Although the consumer price index is often called the "cost-of-living index," it measures only price changes, which constitute just one of several important factors affecting living costs. Both CPI-U and CPI-W are published monthly by the U.S. Bureau of Labor Statistics.

Contingent Liability   An existing condition, situation, or set of circumstances involving uncertainty about a possible loss to an agency that will ultimately be resolved when one or more events either occur or fail to occur. Contingent liabilities include such items as loan guarantees and bank deposit insurance.

Continuing Resolution   If a decision has not been reached on appropriations prior to the beginning of the new current year, then Congress can pass a resolution that says that the government can continue to obligate and spend at last year's budget levels or the lowest level passed by a chamber of Congress. The wording is usually framed to permit spending at the lowest amount the legislature is likely to pass.

Contract Authority   Statutory authority that permits obligations to be incurred in advance of appropriations or in anticipation of receipts to be credited to a revolving fund or other account. Contract authority is unfunded and must subsequently be funded by an appropriation to liquidate obligations incurred under the contract authority or by the collection and use of receipts.

Cost Accounting Standard   A statement promulgated by the Cost Accounting Standards Board that becomes effective unless disapproved by Congress. These statements are intended to achieve uniform and consistent standards in the cost accounting practices followed by defense contractors.

Cost-Based Budgeting   An approach to budgeting that is based on the costs to be incurred—that is, on the resources that will be consumed in carrying out a program, regardless of when the funds to acquire the resources were obligated or paid, and regardless of the source of funds (that is, the appropriation). For example, inventory items become costs when they are withdrawn from inventory, and the cost of buildings is distributed over time, through periodic depreciation charges, rather than in a lump sum when the buildings are acquired.

Cost-Benefit Analysis   An analytical technique that compares the economic and social costs and benefits of proposed programs or policy actions. All losses and gains experienced by society are included and measured in dollar terms. The net benefits created by an action are calculated by subtracting the losses incurred by some sectors of society from the gains that accrue to others. Alternative actions are compared to determine which ones yield the greatest net benefits, or ratio of benefits to costs.

Cost-Effectiveness Analysis   An analytical technique used to choose the most efficient method for achieving a program or policy goal. The costs of alternatives are measured by their requisite estimated dollar expenditures. Effectiveness is defined by the degree of goal attainment and may also (but not necessarily) be measured in dollars. A comparison is made between either the net effectiveness (effectiveness minus costs) or the cost-effectiveness ratios of the various alternatives. The most cost-effective method may involve one or more alternatives.

Countercyclical Action   Action aimed at smoothing out swings in economic activity. Countercyclical actions may take the form of monetary and fiscal policy (such as countercyclical revenue sharing or jobs programs). Automatic (built-in) stabilizers have a countercyclical effect without necessitating changes in government policy.

Crosswalk   Any procedure for expressing the relationship between different classifications of budgetary data, such as between appropriation accounts and government programs.

Current Dollar   The dollar value of a good or service in terms of prices current at the time the good or service was sold. This is in contrast to the value of the good or service in constant dollars.

Current Services Budget   An executive budget projection that alerts the Congress—especially the Congressional Budget Office, the budget committees, and the appropriation committees—to anticipate specific revenue, expenditure, and debt levels, assuming that current policy is unchanged. It also provides a baseline of comparison to the presidential budget.

Current Year   The fiscal year in progress.

Data Points   The number of values a statistical software package can process in a procedure at one time. Often the allowable number of data points is equal to the number of variables allowed multiplied by the number of observations allowed.

Debt   A government credit obligation.

Decision Package   In zero-base budgeting, a brief justification document containing the information managers need in order to judge program or activity levels and resource requirements. Each decision package presents a level of request for a decision unit, stating the costs and performance associated with that level. Separate decision packages are prepared for incremental spending levels.

    1. *Minimum Level.*   Associated with performance below which it is not feasible for the decision unit to continue because no constructive contribution could be made toward fulfilling the unit's objectives.

    2. *Intermediate Level.*   Performance between the minimum and current levels. There may be more than one intermediate level.

3. *Current Level.*   Performance that would be reflected if activities for the budget year were carried on at current year service or output levels without major policy changes. This level permits internal realignments of activities within existing statutory authorizations.

4. *Enhancement Level.*   Level at which increased output or service is consistent with major objectives and at which sufficient benefits are expected to warrant the serious review of higher authorities. A series of decision packages is prepared for each decision unit. Cumulatively, the packages represent the total budget request for that unit.

Decision Package Set   A set of documents used in zero-base budgeting, consisting of the decision unit overview and the decision packages for the decision unit.

Decision Unit   In zero-base budgeting, that part or component of the basic program or organizational entity for which budget requests are prepared and for which managers make significant decisions on the amount of spending and the scope or quality of work to be performed.

Decision Unit Overview   In zero-base budgeting, that part of the decision package set that provides information necessary to evaluate and make budget decisions on each of the decision packages; eliminates repetition of the same information in each package.

Default Risk   The possibility that a borrower will fail to pay the principal or interest on a loan. All other factors being constant, the greater the possibility that the borrower will fail to meet the obligation, the greater the premium or market yield on the security.

Deferral of Budget Authority   Any action or inaction by an officer or employee of the government that temporarily withholds, delays, or effectively precludes the obligation or expenditure of budget authority, including authority to obligate by contract in advance of appropriations as specifically authorized by law.

Deficiency Apportionment   A distribution by the U.S. Office of Management and Budget of available budgetary resources for the fiscal year that anticipates the need for supplemental budget authority. Such apportionments may only be made under certain specified conditions provided for under the Anti-Deficiency Act, 31 U.S.C. 665(e).

Deficiency Appropriation   An appropriation made to an expired account to cover obligations that have been incurred in excess of available funds.

Deficit Financing   A situation in which the federal government's excess of outlays over receipts for a given period is financed primarily by borrowing from the public.

Definite Authority   Authority that is stated as covering a specific sum at the time the authority is granted. This includes authority stated as "not to exceed" a specified amount.

Deflation   A decrease in the general price level, usually accompanied by declining levels of output, increasing unemployment, and a contraction of the supply of money and credit.

Deobligation   A downward adjustment of previously recorded obligations. This may be attributable to the cancellation of a project or contract, to price revisions, or to corrections of estimates previously recorded as obligations.

Depreciation   The systematic and rational allocation of the costs of equipment and buildings (having a life of more than one year) over their useful lives. To match costs with related revenues in measuring income or determining the costs of carrying out program activities, depreciation reflects the use of the asset(s) during specific operating periods.

Deseasonalization   A method of removing any seasonal fluctuations that may distort the meaning of the data.

Devaluation   In a system of fixed exchange rates, the lowering of the value of a nation's currency in relation to gold, or to the currency of other countries, when this value is set by government intervention in the exchange market. (In a system of flexible exchange rates, if the value of the currency falls, it is referred to as depreciation; if the value of the currency rises, it is referred to as appreciation.)

Differencing   A method of taking out seasonality by subtracting the second data point from the first, the third from the second, and so on.

Direct Loan   A disbursement of funds (not in exchange for goods or services) that is contracted to be repaid with or without interest.

Discount Rate   The interest rate that a commercial bank pays when it borrows from a Federal Reserve bank. The discount rate is one of the three tools of monetary policy used by the Federal Reserve System. The Federal Reserve customarily raises or lowers the discount rate to restrain or ease its money and credit policies.

Discounting to Present Value   A method of adjusting dollar values in order to compare dollars expected to be received or spent in the future with dollars received or spent today.

Disposable Personal Income   Personal income less personal taxes and nontax payments to the federal government. It is the income available to persons for consumption or saving.

Durbin-Watson Figure   A model that determines if the variable in the equation is serially correlated, a condition that casts doubt on the reliability of the forecast.

Earmarked Revenue   Funds from a specific course to be spent only for a designated activity (for example, gasoline taxes that can be spent only for highway construction and maintenance).

Econometrics   The application of statistical methods to the study of economic data.

Economic Growth   An increase in a nation's productive capacity leading to an increase in the production of goods and services. Economic growth is usually measured by the annual rate of increase in real gross national product (as measured in constant dollars).

Economic Indicator   Statistics that have a systematic relationship to the business cycle. Each indicator is classified as leading, coincident, or lagging, depending on whether the indicator generally changes direction in advance of, at the same time as, or subsequent to changes in the overall economy. Although no one indicator or set of indicators is a wholly satisfactory predictor of the business cycle, taken as a whole they are valuable tools for identifying and analyzing changes in business cycles.

Economic Ordering Quantity   A means to determine total desirable inventory. The cost of ordering must be weighed against the cost of holding a sizable quantity of goods.

Eigenvalue   A scalar associated with a given linear transformation of a vector space.

Electronic Funds Transfer System   A communication system that provides the capability for automatic receipt of funds, as well as for computer assisted generation of fund transfers among the treasury, the Federal Reserve banks, member banks, and other institutions. Processing of checks takes an instant rather than several days, thus virtually eliminating the float.

Employment Act of 1946   Federal legislation that called for economic planning and for a budget policy directed toward achieving maximum national employment and production.

Employment Rate   In economic statistics, the total number of people who, during a specific week, did any work for pay or profit, or who worked for 15 hours or more without pay on a farm or in a business operated by a member of the person's family. Also included are those who neither worked nor looked for work but who had a job or business from which they were temporarily absent during the week.

Entitlement   Benefits mandated by law to be paid to any person or unit of government that meets the eligibility requirements established by such law. Authorizations for entitlements constitute a binding obligation on the part of the government, and eligible recipients have legal recourse if the obligation is not fulfilled. Budget authority for such payments is not necessarily provided in advance; thus, entitlement legislation requires the subsequent enactment of appropriations unless the existing appropriation is permanent. Examples of entitlement programs are social security benefits and veterans' compensation or pensions.

Expenditure   Payment of an obligation.

Exponential Smoothing   A method of transforming time series data for a better fit by creating a weighted average.

External Audit   An investigation carried out by separate independent agencies that examine accounts, check on the accuracy of recorded transactions and inventories, make on-site reviews of stocks, verify physical existence of equipment, and review operating procedures and regulations.

Federal Reserve System (Fed)   The central banking system of the United States, which operates to control the economy's supply of money and credit.

First Concurrent Resolution on the Budget   The annual resolution, containing governmentwide budget targets of receipts, budget authority, and outlays, that guides Congress in its subsequent consideration of appropriations and revenue measures. It is required to be adopted by both houses of Congress no later than May 15, pursuant to the Congressional Budget and Impoundment Control Act of 1974 (P.L. 93–344, 31 U.S.C. 1324).

Fiscal Policy   Collectively, all federal government policies on taxes, spending, and debt management; intended to promote the nation's macroeconomic goals, particularly with respect to employment, gross national product, price-level stability, and equilibrium in balance of payments. The budget process is a major vehicle for determining and implementing federal fiscal policy. The other major component of federal macroeconomic policy is monetary policy.

Fiscal Year (FY)   Any yearly accounting period, without regard to its relationship to the calendar year. The fiscal year of the federal government begins on October 1 and ends on September 30. (Prior to fiscal year 1977, the Federal fiscal year began on July 1 and ended on June 30.) The fiscal year is designated by the calendar year in which it ends; for example, fiscal year 1980 for the federal government is the year beginning October 1, 1979, and ending September 30, 1980. (*See also* Budget Year; Current Year; Prior Year.)

Fixed Costs   Those costs in any project or program that remain constant, regardless of the increase or decrease in units produced.

Float   The difference between the total amount of checks drawn on a bank account by the government and the amount shown for that account on the bank's books.

Formula Grant   *See* Grant.

Fourier Analysis   *See* Spectral Analysis.

Full Employment Budget   The estimated receipts, outlays, and surplus or deficit that would occur if the U.S. economy were continually operating at full capacity.

Full-Faith-and-Credit Debt   A long-term debt in which the credit (including the implied power of taxation) is unconditionally pledged by the government.

Full Funding   Provision of budgetary resources to cover the total cost of a program or project at the time it is undertaken. (The alternative is incremental funding, in which budget authority is provided or recorded for only a portion of total estimated obligations expected to be incurred during a single fiscal year.) Full funding is generally discussed in terms of multiyear programs, whether or not obligations for the entire program are made in the first year.

Functional Classification A system of classifying budget resources by function so that budget authority and outlays of budget and off-budget entities, loan guarantees, and tax expenditures can be related in terms of the needs being addressed. Budget accounts are generally placed in the single budget function that best reflects its major end purpose (for example, national defense or health), regardless of the agency administering the program. A function may be divided into two or more subfunctions, depending upon the complexity of the need addressed by that function.

Fund Accounting The legal requirement for agencies to establish separate accounts for separate programs—that is, to segregate revenues and other resources, together with all related liabilities, obligations, and reserves, for the purpose of carrying on specific activities or attaining certain objectives in accordance with special regulations, restrictions, or limitations. The aim is to control the handling of money to ensure that it will be spent only for the purpose intended. Fund accounting, in a broad sense, is required by the government to demonstrate agency compliance with requirements of existing legislation for which funds have been appropriated or otherwise authorized.

General Accounting Office (GAO) The congressional audit agency for the federal government. This agency reports directly to Congress. GAO investigates fraud, waste, and mismanagement. Its audits focus upon delegation of responsibility, policy direction and program evaluation, budget and accounting practices, and the adequacy of internal controls, including internal auditing.

GNP Gap The difference between the economy's output of goods and services and its potential output at full employment—that is, the difference between actual GNP (gross national product) and potential GNP.

Government Corporation Act of 1945 Federal legislation that directed the General Accounting Office to audit public corporations in terms of their performance rather than merely in terms of the legality and propriety of their expenditures.

Grant A transfer of funds from the federal government to another unit of government. The two major forms of federal grants are block and categorical.

1. *Block grants.* These are given primarily to general-purpose government units in accordance with a statutory formula. Such grants can be used for a variety of activities within a broad functional area. Examples of federal block grant programs are the Omnibus Crime Control and Safe Streets Act of 1968, the Comprehensive Employment and Training Act of 1973, the Housing and Community Development Act of 1974, and the 1974 amendments to the Social Security Act of 1935 (Title XX).

2. *Categorical grants.* These can be used only for specific programs and are usually limited to narrowly defined activities. Categorical grants consist of formula, project, and formula-project grants. Formula grants allocate federal funds to states or their subdivisions in accordance with a distribution formula prescribed by law or administrative regulation. Project grants provide federal funding for fixed or known periods for specific projects or for the delivery of specific services or products.

Grant-in-Aid For budget purposes, a grant-in-aid consists of a budget outlay by the federal government to support state or local programs of government service to the public. Grants-in-aid do not include purchases from state or local governments or assistance awards to other classes of recipients (for example, outlays for research or support of federal prisoners).

Gross National Product (GNP) The gross national product is the total productive activity in a country during a certain period of time. It is the sum of personal consumption plus gross private domestic investment plus government purchases of goods and services plus net exports of goods and services.

Identification Code An eleven-digit code assigned to each appropriation or fund account in the Budget of the United States Government that identifies (a) the agency; (b) the account; (c) the timing of the transmittal to Congress; (d) the type of fund; and (e) the account's functional classification. Such codes are common in budget systems.

Impoundment Any action or inaction by an officer or employee of the U.S. government that precludes the obligation or expenditure of budget authority provided by Congress.

Impoundment Resolution A resolution by either the House of Representatives or the Senate that expresses disapproval of the president's proposed deferral of budget authority as set forth in a special message transmitted by the president, as required under Sec. 1013(a) of the Impoundment Control Act of 1974, P.L. 93–344, 31 U.S.C. 1403.

Income Tax Revenue source used at all levels of government, but principally at the federal level. The tax is levied on the income of both corporations and individuals. It can be graduated or a flat percentage.

Incremental Budgeting An approach to budgeting that focuses on the budget request, with emphasis on increases from the current year. Analysts of such a budget usually want information on all activities being planned in the budget year, but most of their attention will be on the program changes from the current year.

Incremental Funding The provision or recording of budgetary resources for a program or project based on obligations estimated to be incurred within a fiscal year when such budgetary resources will cover only a portion of the obligations to be incurred in completing the program or project as planned. (The alternative is full funding, in which budgetary resources are provided or recorded for the total estimated obligations of a program or project in the initial year of funding.)

Indefinite Authority   Budget authority for which a specific sum is not stated but which is determined by other factors, such as the receipts from a certain source or obligations incurred. Borrowing authority that is limited to a specified amount that may become outstanding at any time (that is, revolving debt authority) is considered to be indefinite budget authority.

Indirect Cost   Any cost incurred for common objectives that therefore cannot be charged directly to any single cost objective. Indirect costs are allocated to the various classes of work in proportion to the benefit to each class. Indirect cost is also referred to as overhead or burden cost.

Inflation   A persistent rise in the general price level that results in a decline in the purchasing power of money.

Input   In a systems model, the resources used by a system to accomplish its work.

Internal Audit   An investigation of legality, effectiveness, and efficiency within the agency.

Internal Control   The plan of organization and all of the coordinating methods and measures adopted within a federal agency to safeguard the agency's assets, check the accuracy and reliability of its accounting data, promote operational efficiency, and encourage adherence to prescribed managerial policies.

Issue Assessment   A written presentation that identifies and describes the major features of a significant issue facing the government. The assessment is only a few pages long, but it clearly sets forth the ingredients that would be considered in preparing a study of a major issue.

Iterative   Refers to mathematical procedures that find an optimum figure by performing repeated calculations dealing with the same data.

Journal   A chronological listing of transactions, setting forth the date and dollar amount of each transaction and a brief explanation.

Lag   In regression calculations, observations for one of the variables may be "lagged" or shifted by one or more time periods to achieve a more realistic comparison between the variables. For instance, an advertising expenditure this month may affect sales for next month.

Least Squares   A basic method of fitting a regression line mathematically so that the sum of the squared errors is smaller than any other straight-line model.

Legal Reserve Requirement   One of the three tools used by the Federal Reserve to promote economic stabilization. The FED can tighten the money supply by requiring a greater reserve to be maintained, thus shrinking the amount available for loans. The converse usually increases the money supply.

Liability   Amount owed for items received, services rendered, expenses incurred, assets acquired, or construction performed (regardless of whether invoices have been received); also, amounts received but as yet unearned.

Lien   A claim on property arising from failure of the owner to make timely payment of a previous claim.

Line-Item Budget   A budget format that presents the exact amount planned to be spent for every separate good or service to be purchased.

Macroeconomics   The branch of economics concerned with aggregate economic analysis. Macroeconomics includes the study of the general price level, national output and income, and national employment.

Management-by-Objectives (MBO)   A technique for establishing specific objectives for agencies; it requires regular periodic reports on the agency's progress toward achieving those objectives.

Method of Averages   A technique of forecasting revenue by averaging the revenue generated over the last three to five years. It assumes the existence of a growth trend in the tax receipts and the economy.

Microeconomics   The branch of economics concerned with the analysis of individual economic units, markets, or industries. Microeconomics includes the study of the prices of individual commodities, individual incomes, and the employment practices of individual firms. (*See also* Macroeconomics.)

Miller-Orr Model   A method of determining a government's proposed fund cash balance that focuses on the upper dollar limit needed for cash purposes. When the cash balance touches the upper boundary, a predetermined amount of securities are automatically purchased. When the cash balance touches zero or an amount slightly above zero, then a predetermined amount of securities are sold, thus increasing the cash balance.

Monetary Policy   Collectively, those policies affecting the money supply, interest rates, and credit availability that are intended to promote national macroeconomic goals, particularly with respect to employment, gross national product, price level stability, and equilibrium in balance of payments. Monetary policy is directed primarily by the Board of Governors of the Federal Reserve System and by the Federal Open Market Committee. Monetary policy works by influencing the cost and availability of bank reserves. This is accomplished through (a) open-market operations (the purchase and sale of securities, primarily government securities); (b) changes in the ratio of reserves to deposits that commercial banks are required to maintain; and (c) changes in the discount rate.

Money Supply   The amount of money in the economy. The supply is divided into categories. M1-A consists of currency (coin and paper notes) plus demand deposits at commercial banks, foreign banks, official institutions, and the U.S. government. M1-B consists of M1-A plus other verifiable deposits, including negotiable orders of withdrawal and automatic transfers from savings accounts at commercial banks and thrift institutions, credit unions' shared draft accounts, and demand deposits at mutual savings banks. M-2 consists of M1-B plus savings and small denomination time deposits at all depository institutions, overnight repurchase agreements at commercial banks, Eurodollars held overnight by U.S. residents other than Caribbean branches of member banks, and money market mutual fund shares. M-3 consists of M-2 plus large denomination time deposits at all depository institutions and term repurchase agreements at commercial banks and savings and loan associations.

Monthly Treasury Statement (MTS)   A summary statement prepared from agency accounting reports and issued by the Treasury Department. The MTS presents the receipts, outlays, and resulting budget surplus or deficit for the month and the fiscal year to date.

Mortgage Bond   A type of bond that uses property to secure the debt obligation without transferring the title.

Moving Average   A method for using the average of past forecasting errors to calculate new forecasts.

Muckrakers   Journalists and book writers who document abuses and advocate reform; in the United States, their heyday was in the early twentieth century. As a result of their efforts, many government budgeting reforms were enacted successfully, especially at the municipal level.

Multiyear Authority   Budget authority that is available for a specified period of time in excess of one fiscal year. This authority generally takes the form of two-year, three-year, or some other yearly period of availability, but may cover periods that do not coincide with the start or end of a fiscal year. For example, the authority may be available from July 1 of one year through September 30 of the following fiscal year (15 months). This type of multiyear authority is sometimes referred to as forward funding.

Multiyear Budget Planning   A budget-planning process designed to make sure that the long-range consequences of budget decisions are identified and reflected in the budget totals.

National Income Accounts   Accounts prepared and published quarterly and annually by the U.S. Department of Commerce, providing a detailed statistical description of aggregate economic activity within the American economy. These accounts depict in dollar terms the composition and use of the nation's output and the distribution of national income to different recipients. The accounts make it possible to trace trends and fluctuations in economic activity.

Net National Product (NNP)   The net market value of finished goods and services produced by labor and property supplied by the residents of the United States. Net national product equals gross national product less capital consumption allowances, which are estimates of the value of the capital goods "used up" in producing the gross national product.

Nonguaranteed Debt   A long-term debt payable from earnings of revenue-producing activities, from special assessments, or from specific nonproperty taxes. The government does not guarantee its assets and earnings in support of the debt. Also known as moral debt.

No-Year Authority   Budget authority that remains available for obligation for an indefinite period of time, usually until the objectives for which the authority was made available are attained.

Object Classification   A uniform classification identifying the transactions of the government by the nature of the goods or services purchased (such as personnel compensation, supplies and materials, and equipment), without regard to the agency involved or the purpose of the programs for which they are used. Data category titles arranged by object classification are provided in an object classification schedule.

Obligational Authority   The sum of (a) budget authority provided for a given fiscal year, (b) balances of amounts brought forward from prior years that remain available for obligation, and (c) amounts authorized to be credited to a specific fund or account during that year, including transfers between funds or accounts.

Obligations Incurred   Amounts of orders placed, contracts awarded, services received, and similar transactions during a given period that will require payments during the same or a future period. Such amounts will include outlays for which obligations had not been previously recorded and will reflect adjustments for differences between obligations previously recorded and actual outlays to liquidate those obligations.

Observation   An individual value recorded for a variable. For example, in a list showing monthly telephone expenses for a year, the amount of the bill for any one month would constitute an observation.

Off-Budget Federal Entities   Certain federally owned and controlled entities whose transactions (for example, budget authority or outlays) have been excluded from budget totals by law. The fiscal activities of these entities are therefore not reflected in either budget authority or budget outlay totals. However, the outlays of off-budget federal entities are added to the budget deficit to derive the total government deficit that has to be financed by borrowing from the public or by other means.

Off-Budget Outlays   Outlays of off-budget federal entities whose transactions have been excluded from the budget totals by law, even though these outlays are part of total government spending.

One-Year Authority   Budget authority that is available for obligation only during a specified fiscal year and that expires at the end of that time. Also known as annual authority.

Open-Ended Expenditure Forecasting   An approach to estimating future expenditures, based either on detailed work plans that often take months to prepare or on quick judgments involving a few minutes' preparation.

Open-Market Operations   The purchase and sale in the open market of various securities, chiefly marketable federal government securities, by the Federal Reserve System for the purpose of implementing Federal Reserve monetary policy. Open-market operations, one of the most flexible instruments of monetary policy, affects the reserves of member banks and thus the supply of money and the availability and cost of credit.

Operating Budget   The current year budget that guides agencies' everyday activities.

Outcome   In the systems model used in this book, a benefit to individuals and society resulting from an agency program.

Outlay   The liquidation of an obligation, usually by the issuance of a check or the disbursement of cash, but also by the maturing of interest coupons (in the case of some bonds), by the issuance of bonds or notes, or by increases in the redemption value of bonds outstanding. Outlays during a fiscal year may be for payment of obligations incurred in a prior year (prior year outlays) or in the same year. Outlays therefore derive partly from unexpended balances of prior year budget authority and partly from budget authority provided for the year in which the money is spent.

Output   In the systems model used in this book, the specific products and services produced by a government unit.

Overhead Cost   *See* Indirect Cost.

Oversight Committee   The legislative committee charged with general oversight of the operation of an agency or program. In most cases, but not all, the oversight committee for an agency is also the authorizing committee for that agency's programs.

Performance Budgeting   A budget format that presents government program input and output, thus allowing easy verification of the program's economy and efficiency.

Personal Income   In the national income accounts, income received by persons (that is, individuals, nonprofit institutions, private uninsured welfare funds, and private trust funds) from all sources. These sources include production transfer payments from government and business and government interest, which is treated as a transfer payment. Personal income is the sum of wage and salary disbursements, other income from labor, proprietary income, rental income, dividends, personal interest income, and transfer payments, less personal contributions for social insurance.

Planning-Programming-Budgeting (PPB)   An attempt in the federal government and some state and local governments to bring more analysis into the budgeting process. It is not itself an analytical technique, but it stresses the use of analytical tools in deciding budget issues related to specific government programs.

Policy Letter   Document used in government to convey executive guidance and budget ceilings to the lower levels of the executive branch.

Potential Gross National Product   An estimate of how much the economy could produce with full utilization of its productive resources and existing technology.

Prime Rate   The rate of interest charged by commercial banks for short-term loans to their most creditworthy customers.

Prior Year   The fiscal year immediately preceding the current year.

Process Analysis   An analytical approach that seeks to determine if an agency's existing process makes effective use of resources and to identify idle or partly used resources.

Producer Price Index   A set of indicators that measures average changes in the prices received in all stages of processing by producers of commodities in the manufacturing, agriculture, forestry, fishing, mining, gas and electricity, and public utilities industries. Producer price indexes can be organized either by commodity or by stage of processing (finished goods, intermediate materials, or crude materials). Stage-of-processing indexes are more useful for analyzing general price trends. Formerly known as wholesale price index.

Productivity   A measure of efficiency, usually expressed as the ratio of the quantity of output to the quantity of input used in the production of that output. Usually, it focuses on output per work-hour of change or on changes in cost per unit of output.

Program and Financial Plan (PFP)   A set of summary budget tables, categorized by major programs and activities. In the federal government, the PFP includes both obligations and disbursements. For some state and local governments, obligations alone or expenditures alone are sufficient. The information in a PFP covers the prior year, current year, budget year, and budget-year-plus-five additional years. The PFP should reflect any policy changes; it is particularly useful prior to a budget call to forecast possible agency requests.

Program Budget   A budget format in which the budget material is arranged in such a way as to aid the executive and legislature to understand the broader policy implications of their decisions.

Project Grant   *See* Grant.

Property Tax   A revenue source for local and some state governments. Property (such as real estate) is typically assessed by the local government; then a tax rate is determined and applied on the basis of property value.

Quality Indicator   A measurement of characteristics, duration, content, extent, or degree used in evaluating outputs and outcomes.

Ratio Indicator   A measurement of the quantity of government service or product in relation to some larger entity such as population or area size.

Rational Decision-Making Model   An approach to budgeting that emphasizes (a) setting goals and objectives; (b) defining the alternatives; (c) analyzing the alternatives in terms of the established goals and objectives; and (d) selecting the best option.

Reactive Budget Decision Model   An approach to budgeting that is based on a stimulus-response pattern. Those who take this approach consider budgeting merely as a task to be done as defined in the job description. They act in response to the requirements of the budget calendar and the request, but give little thought to shaping events or making a difference.

Recession   A decline in overall business activity that is pervasive, substantial, and of at least several months' duration. Historically, recessions have been identified by a decline in gross national product for at least two consecutive quarters.

Registered Bonds   Type of bond that provides more protection to the bond holder because its ownership is registered on the books of the issuing government or its paying agent.

Regression   An analysis that expresses a dependent variable as the result of a formula approximation involving one or more independent variables.

Reimbursement   A repayment for commodities sold or services furnished, either to the public or to another government account, that is authorized by law to be credited directly to specific appropriation and fund accounts. These amounts are deducted from the total obligations incurred (and outlays) in determining net obligations (and outlays) for such accounts.

Reprogramming   Utilization of funds in an appropriation account for purposes other than those contemplated at the time of appropriation.

Repurchase Agreement   An innovation of government security dealers who recognize the selling potential of securities tailored to specific short time periods. Dealers agree to repurchase a security at a specific future date, thus increasing the number of transactions and the resulting total fees from those transactions.

Rescission   The consequence of executive and legislative action that cancels budget authority previously provided by Congress before the time when the authority would otherwise have lapsed (that is, when appropriated funds would have ceased to be available for obligation). The Congressional Budget and Impoundment Control Act of 1974 (P.L. 93–344; 31 U.S.C. 1402) specifies that whenever the president determines that all or part of any budget authority will not be needed to carry out the full objectives or scope of programs for which the authority was provided, the president will propose to Congress that the funds be rescinded. Likewise, if all or part of any budget authority limited to a fiscal year—that is, annual appropriations, or budget authority of a multiyear appropriation in the last year of availability—is to be reserved from obligation for the entire fiscal year, a rescission will be proposed. Budget authority may also be proposed for rescission for reasons of fiscal policy or other reasons. Generally, an amount proposed for rescission is withheld for up to 45 legislative days while the proposal is considered by Congress. All funds for rescission, including those withheld, must be reported to Congress in a special message. If both houses have not completed action on the rescission proposed by the president within 45 calendar days of continuous session, any funds withheld must be made available for obligation.

Rescission Bill   A bill or joint resolution that cancels, in whole or in part, budget authority previously granted by Congress. Rescissions proposed by the president must be transmitted in a special message to Congress. Under Sec. 1012 of the Congressional Budget and Impoundment Control Act of 1974 (P.L. 93–344), unless both houses of Congress complete action on a rescission bill within 45 days of continuous session after receipt of the proposal, the budget authority must be restored. (*See also* Rescission.)

Research and Development   Research is systematic, intensive study directed toward fuller scientific knowledge or understanding of the subject studied. Development is the systematic use of the knowledge and understanding gained from research, directed toward the production of useful products or services.

Reserve Requirement   The percentage of deposit liabilities that U.S. commercial banks are required to hold as a reserve either at their Federal Reserve bank, as cash in their vaults, or as directed by state banking authorities. The reserve requirement is one of the three tools of monetary policy. Federal Reserve authorities can control the lending capacity of the banks (thus influencing the money supply) by varying the ratio of reserves to deposits that commercial banks are required to maintain.

Residuals   The difference obtained when you subtract the forecast or "fitted" values from the actual values.

Revenue Forecasting   Any of several systematic approaches used by governments to estimate the levels of revenue they can anticipate in future years.

Revenue Shaping   The distribution, by formula, of federal funds to state and local governments, with few or no limits on the purposes for which the funds may be used and few restrictions on the procedures that must be followed in spending the funds.

Risk Control   The reduction of risk or loss through careful procedures and practices in security, personnel safety, fire prevention, auto safety, product safety, environmental protection, and emergency resources.

Risk Funding   The provision of sufficient funds to meet loss situations, if they occur, through the most effective use of internal and external financial resources.

Rule of Penultimate Year   A technique for forecasting that calls for the forecaster to use the last completed year as a basis for estimating future revenue. This technique assumes growth in the economy and in related revenue sources.

Safety Stock   The level of inventory that should be maintained for effective operations.

Scorekeeping   A procedure for tracking the status of congressional budgetary actions. Examples of scorekeeping documents are up-to-date tabulations and reports on congressional actions affecting budget authority, receipts, outlays, surplus or deficit, and the public debt limit, as well as outlay and receipt estimates and reestimates. Scorekeeping data published by the Congressional Budget Office include, but are not limited to, status reports on the effects of congressional actions (and, in the case of scorekeeping reports prepared for the Senate Budget Committee, the budget effects of potential congressional actions), and comparisons of these actions to targets and ceilings set by Congress in the budget resolutions.

Second Concurrent Resolution on the Budget   The annual resolution adopted by Congress that contains budget ceilings classified by function for budget authority and outlay and a floor for budget receipts. This resolution may retain or revise the levels set earlier in the year in the first concurrent resolution, and may include directives to the appropriations committees and to other committees with jurisdiction over budget authority or entitlement authority. The second resolution may also direct the appropriations committees to recommend changes in budget receipts or in the statutory limit on public debt. Changes recommended by various committees pursuant to the second budget resolution are reported in a reconciliation bill (or resolution, in some cases) on which Congress must complete action by September 25, a few days before the next fiscal year commences on October 1.

Serial Bond   The most common type of bond. It matures periodically (typically, every year).

Spectral Analysis   Decomposing the data into a sum of trigonometric components to create a waveform that is most appropriate for analyzing data with a pattern of repeating cycles.

Spending Authority   The collective designation for appropriations, borrowing authority, contract authority, and entitlement authority for which the budget authority is not provided in advance by appropriation acts. The latter three authorities are also commonly referred to as backdoor authority.

Stagflation   The simultaneous existence of high unemployment and high inflation.

State Space   A forecasting technique that exploits the relationship of time series techniques to an advanced procedure called canonical correlation analysis.

Substantive Law   Statutory public law other than appropriation law; sometimes referred to as basic law. Substantive law usually authorizes, in broad general terms, the executive branch to carry out a program of work. Annual determination of the amount of work to be done is usually thereafter embodied in appropriation law.

Supplemental Appropriations   An act appropriating funds in addition to those in an annual appropriation act. Supplemental appropriations provide additional budget authority beyond the original estimates for programs or activities (including new programs authorized after the date of the original appropriation act) in cases where the need for funds is too urgent to be postponed until enactment of the next regular appropriation bill. Supplemental appropriations sometimes include items not appropriated in the regular bills for lack of timely authorizations.

Sunset Legislation   Laws requiring the automatic expiration of government programs unless positive action is taken to renew them every few years by the legislature. In many cases, the sunset provisions permit the program to remain on the law books after the legal authorization for funds expires.

Tax Anticipation Note   Borrowing by a local government against future anticipated tax revenue.

Tax Certificate   A form of tax lien on property owned by a delinquent taxpayer. Tax certificates are negotiable securities and can be sold, as they represent a debt which must be liquidated before a clear title to the property can be given. At the sale of the property, certificates on the title are presented and the owner typically has one year to redeem them. If they are not redeemed, the property goes to the holder of the certificates.

Tax Credit   Any special provision of law that results in a dollar-for-dollar reduction in tax liabilities that would otherwise be due. In some cases, tax credits may be carried forward or backward from one tax year to another; other tax credits lapse if not used in the year earned. Tax credits may result in a reduction of tax collections or an increase in the value of tax refunds.

Term Bond   A bond that matures at one time. A sinking fund is typically used to accumulate the necessary funds over time.

Time Series   The type of regression analysis employed in forecasting. It assumes that the data used was gathered at evenly spaced intervals in time. Box-Jenkins is an advanced form of time series analysis.

Transaction   A financial decision, such as obligating money, deciding on disbursement, or setting aside funds for a purpose.

Transfer Payments   Money moved from one government to another or to private persons. They often serve as automatic stabilizers built into the economy. These payments usually rise substantially during periods of recession and fall during periods of prosperity. For example, the unemployed receive unemployment compensation; in recessionary times, they may eventually receive welfare and food stamps as well.

Transformation   A mathematical adjustment made to a set of figures to improve the fit of the regression line.

Treasury Bills   The shortest-term federal security. The maturity dates of treasury bills typically vary from three to twelve months. They are sold at a discount face value, instead of carrying a specific rate of interest.

Trend-Line Approach   A forecasting technique that develops and extends an agency's trend line of expenditures or revenue from the past into the desired forecast period.

Unemployment Rate   In economic statistics, the total number of people who, during a specific week, had no employment but were available for work and who sought employment within the past four weeks, were laid off from their jobs, or were waiting to report to a new job within thirty days; expressed as a percentage of the civilian labor force. (*See also* Employment Rate.)

Unemployment Rate, Insured   The number of insured unemployed (that is, those persons who are eligible to receive unemployment compensation benefits) expressed as a percentage of covered employment.

Value   The quantity of money, goods, or services that an article is likely to command in the long run as distinct from its price in an individual instance.

Variable   An observable characteristic of an object or event that can be described according to some well-defined classification or measurement scheme.

Volume Indicators   The quantity of a government unit's service or products, such as the number of graduates from a university.

Voucher   A document that confirms the fact that a financial transaction has taken place.

Wages and Salaries   Monetary remuneration of employees, including the compensation, commissions, tips, bonuses, and receipts in kind that represent income to the recipients.

Warrant   A banking service in which a draft is paid through a bank with the express permission of the government. It is used to slow and control disbursements. When a warrant is presented for payment, the bank will not pay until the warrant is accepted by the government.

Wholesale Price Index   *See* Producer Price Index.

Wise Budget Model   An approach to budgeting whose proponents recognize that politics is extremely important and sometimes of overriding importance. They also believe that, while analysis has its limitations, it can often help greatly in decision-making situations.

Zero-Base Budgeting (ZBB)   An approach to public budgeting in which each budget year's activities are judged anew, with no reference to the policy precedents or dollar amounts of past years.

INDEX